AUTOMOTIVE ELECTRICITY AND ELECTRONICS

THIRD EDITION

James D. Halderman

Prentice Hall
Boston   Columbus   Indianapolis   New York   San Francisco   Upper Saddle River
Amsterdam   Cape Town   Dubai   London   Madrid   Milan   Munich   Paris   Montreal
Toronto   Delhi   Mexico City   Sao Paulo   Sydney   Hong Kong   Seoul   Singapore   Taipei   Tokyo

Editor in Chief: Vernon Anthony
Acquisitions Editor: Wyatt Morris
Editorial Assistant: Tanika Henderson
Director of Marketing: David Gesell
Marketing Manager: Kara Clark
Senior Marketing Coordinator: Alicia Wozniak
Marketing Assistant: Les Roberts
Senior Managing Editor: JoEllen Gohr
Project Manager: Jessica H. Sykes
Senior Operations Supervisor: Pat Tonneman

Operations Specialist: Laura Weaver
Senior Art Director: Diane Ernsberger
Text and Cover Designer: Anne DeMarinis
Cover Art: Shutterstock
Media Editor: Michelle Churma
Lead Media Project Manager: Karen Bretz
Full-Service Project Management: Kelli Jauron
Composition: S4Carlisle Publishing Services
Printer/Binder: R.R. Donnelley/Willard
Cover Printer: Lehigh-Phoenix Color/Hagerstown
Text Font: Helvetica Neue

10 9 8 7 6 5 4 3 2 1

Prentice Hall
is an imprint of

www.pearsonhighered.com

ISBN 10:   0-13-512406-9
ISBN 13: 978-0-13-512406-2

PREFACE

PROFESSIONAL TECHNICIAN SERIES Part of Pearson Automotive's Professional Technician Series, the third edition of *Automotive Electricity and Electronics* represents the future of automotive textbooks. The series is a full-color, media-integrated solution for today's students and instructors. The series includes textbooks that cover all 8 areas of ASE certification, plus additional titles covering common courses.

Current revisions are written by a team of very experienced writers and instructors. The series is also peer reviewed for technical accuracy.

UPDATES TO THE THIRD EDITION

- All content is correlated to the latest NATEF and ASE tasks.

- A dramatic, new full-color design enhances the subject material.

- Exactly 100 new color photos and line drawings have been added to this edition.

- Content has been streamlined for easier reading and comprehension.

- This text is fully integrated with MyAutomotiveKit, an online supplement for homework, quizzing, testing, multimedia activities, and videos.

- Unlike other textbooks, this book is written so that the theory, construction, diagnosis, and service of a particular component or system is presented in one location. There is no need to search through the entire book for other references to the same topic.

NATEF CORRELATED NATEF certified programs need to demonstrate that they use course material that covers NATEF tasks. All Professional Technician textbooks have been correlated to the appropriate NATEF task lists. These correlations can be found in two locations:

- As an appendix to each book.
- At the beginning of each chapter in the Annotated Instructor's Guide.

A COMPLETE INSTRUCTOR AND STUDENT SUPPLEMENTS PACKAGE All Professional Technician textbooks are accompanied by a full set of instructor and student supplements. Please see page vi for a detailed list of supplements.

A FOCUS ON DIAGNOSIS AND PROBLEM SOLVING The Professional Technician Series has been developed to satisfy the need for a greater emphasis on problem diagnosis. Automotive instructors and service managers agree that students and beginning technicians need more training in diagnostic procedures and skill development. To meet this need and demonstrate how real-world problems are solved, "Real World Fix" features are included throughout and highlight how real-life problems are diagnosed and repaired.

The following pages highlight the unique core features that set the Professional Technician Series book apart from other automotive textbooks.

chapter 1

SERVICE INFORMATION, TOOLS, AND SAFETY

OBJECTIVES

After studying Chapter 1, the reader will be able to:

1. Understand the ASE knowledge content for vehicle identification and the proper use of tools and shop equipment.
2. Retrieve vehicle service information.
3. Identify the strength ratings of threaded fasteners.
4. Describe how to safely hoist a vehicle.
5. Discuss how to safely use hand tools.
6. Identify the personal protective equipment (PPE) that all service technicians should wear.
7. Describe what tool is the best to use for each job.
8. Discuss how to safely use hand tools.
9. Explain the difference between the brand name (trade name) and the proper name for tools.
10. Explain how to maintain hand tools.
11. Discuss how to safely use power tools.
12. Identify the precautions that should be followed when working on hybrid electric vehicles.

KEY TERMS

Adjustable wrench 9	Metric bolts 6
Bench grinders 25	Nuts 8
Bolts 5	Open-end wrench 9
Box-end wrench 9	PPE 25
Breaker bar 11	Pinch weld seam 29
Bump cap 25	Pitch 5
Calibration codes 3	Pliers 15
Campaign 4	Punches 18
Casting number 3	Ratchet 11
Cheater bar 13	Recall 4
Chisels 19	Screwdrivers 13
Drive sizes 11	Snips 18
Extensions 11	Socket 10
Eye wash station 34	Socket adapter 13
Files 17	Spontaneous
Fire blanket 33	combustion 27
Fire extinguisher	SST 22
classes 33	Stud 5
GAWR 3	Tensile strength 7
Grade 6	Trouble light 22
GVWR 3	TSB 4
Hacksaws 19	UNC 5
Hammers 14	UNF 5
Hybrid electric vehicles	Universal joint 11
(HEVs) 35	VECI 3
Light-emitting diode	VIN 2
(LED) 23	Washers 8
Line wrench 9	Wrenches 9

1

OBJECTIVES AND KEY TERMS appear at the beginning of each chapter to help students and instructors focus on the most important material in each chapter. The chapter objectives are based on specific ASE and NATEF tasks.

TECH TIP

It Just Takes a Second

Whenever removing any automotive component, it is wise to screw the bolts back into the holes a couple of threads by hand. This ensures that the right bolt will be used in its original location when the component or part is put back on the vehicle.

TECH TIPS feature real-world advice and "tricks of the trade" from ASE-certified master technicians.

SAFETY TIP

Shop Cloth Disposal

Always dispose of oily shop cloths in an enclosed container to prevent a fire. ● **SEE FIGURE 1–69.** Whenever oily cloths are thrown together on the floor or workbench, a chemical reaction can occur, which can ignite the cloth even without an open flame. This process of ignition without an open flame is called **spontaneous combustion.**

SAFETY TIPS alert students to possible hazards on the job and how to avoid them.

REAL WORLD FIX

The Electric Mirror Fault Story

Often, a customer will notice just one fault even though other lights or systems may not be working correctly. For example, a customer noticed that the electric mirrors stopped working. The service technician checked all electrical components in the vehicle and discovered that the interior lights were also not working.

The interior lights were not mentioned by the customer as being a problem most likely because the driver only used the vehicle in daylight hours.

REAL WORLD FIXES present students with actual automotive scenarios and shows how these common (and sometimes uncommon) problems were diagnosed and repaired.

FREQUENTLY ASKED QUESTION

How Many Types of Screw Heads Are Used in Automotive Applications?

There are many, including Torx, hex (also called Allen), plus many others used in custom vans and motor homes. ● **SEE FIGURE 1–9.**

FREQUENTLY ASKED QUESTIONS are based on the author's own experience and provide answers to many of the most common questions asked by students and beginning service technicians.

NOTE: Claw hammer has a claw used to remove nails; therefore, it is not for automotive service.

NOTES provide students with additional technical information to give them a greater understanding of a specific task or procedure.

CAUTION: Do not use a screwdriver as a pry tool or chisel. Screwdrivers use hardened steel only at the tip and are not designed to be pounded on or used for prying because they could bend easily. Always use the proper tool for each application.

CAUTIONS alert students about potential damage to the vehicle that can occur during a specific task or service procedure.

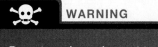

WARNING

Do not use incandescent trouble lights around gasoline or other flammable liquids. The liquids can cause the bulb to break and the hot filament can ignite the flammable liquid, which can cause personal injury or even death.

WARNINGS alert students to potential dangers to themselves during a specific task or service procedure.

SUMMARY

1. Bolts, studs, and nuts are commonly used as fasteners in the chassis. The sizes for fractional and metric threads are different and are not interchangeable. The grade is the rating of the strength of a fastener.
2. Whenever a vehicle is raised above the ground, it must be supported at a substantial section of the body or frame.
3. Wrenches are available in open end, box end, and combination open and box end.
4. An adjustable wrench should only be used where the proper size is not available.
5. Line wrenches are also called flare-nut wrenches, fitting wrenches, or tube-nut wrenches and are used to remove fuel or refrigerant lines.
6. Sockets are rotated by a ratchet or breaker bar, also called a flex handle.
7. Torque wrenches measure the amount of torque applied to a fastener.
8. Screwdriver types include straight blade (flat tip), Phillips, and Torx.
9. Hammers and mallets come in a variety of sizes and weights.
10. Pliers are a useful tool and are available in many different types, including slip-joint, multigroove, linesman's, diagonal, needle-nose, and locking pliers.
11. Other common hand tools include snap-ring pliers, files, cutters, punches, chisels, and hacksaws.
12. Hybrid electric vehicles should be de-powered if any of the high-voltage components are going to be serviced.

REVIEW QUESTIONS

1. List three precautions that must be taken whenever hoisting (lifting) a vehicle.
2. Describe how to determine the grade of a fastener, including how the markings differ between fractional and metric bolts.
3. List four items that are personal protective equipment (PPE).
4. List the types of fire extinguishers and their usage.
5. Why are wrenches offset 15 degrees?
6. What are the other names for a line wrench?
7. What are the standard automotive drive sizes for sockets?
8. Which type of screwdriver requires the use of a hammer or mallet?
9. What is inside a dead-blow hammer?
10. What type of cutter is available in left and right cutters?

CHAPTER QUIZ

1. The correct location for the pads when hoisting or jacking the vehicle can often be found in the _____.
   a. Service manual   c. Owner's manual
   b. Shop manual   d. All of the above
2. For the best working position, the work should be _____.
   a. At neck or head level   c. Overhead by about 1 foot
   b. At knee or ankle level d. At chest or elbow level
3. A high-strength bolt is identified by _____.
   a. A UNC symbol   c. Strength letter codes
   b. Lines on the head   d. The coarse threads
4. A fastener that uses threads on both ends is called a _____.
   a. Cap screw   c. Machine screw
   b. Stud   d. Crest fastener
5. When working with hand tools, always _____.
   a. Push the wrench—don't pull it toward you
   b. Pull a wrench—don't push it away from you
6. The proper term for Channel Locks is _____.
   a. Vise-Grip
   b. Crescent wrench
   c. Locking pliers
   d. Multigroove adjustable pliers
7. The proper term for Vise-Grip is _____.
   a. Locking pliers   c. Side cuts
   b. Slip-joint pliers   d. Multigroove adjustable pliers
8. Two technicians are discussing torque wrenches. Technician A says that a torque wrench is capable of tightening a fastener with more torque than a conventional breaker bar or ratchet. Technician B says that a torque wrench should be calibrated regularly for the most accurate results. Which technician is correct?
   a. Technician A only
   b. Technician B only
   c. Both Technicians A and B
   d. Neither Technician A nor B
9. What type of screwdriver should be used if there is very limited space above the head of the fastener?
   a. Offset screwdriver   c. Impact screwdriver
   b. Stubby screwdriver   d. Robertson screwdriver
10. What type of hammer is plastic coated, has a metal casing inside, and is filled with small lead balls?
    a. Dead-blow hammer
    b. Soft-blow hammer
    c. Sledge hammer
    d. Plastic hammer

SERVICE INFORMATION, TOOLS, AND SAFETY   39

THE SUMMARY, REVIEW QUESTIONS, AND CHAPTER QUIZ at the end of each chapter help students review the material presented in the chapter and test themselves to see how much they've learned.

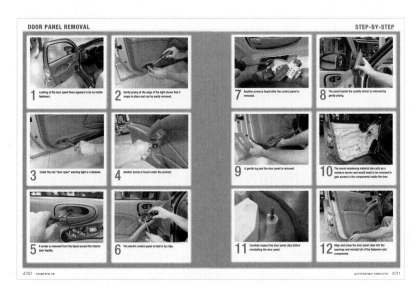

DOOR PANEL REMOVAL   **STEP-BY-STEP**

1 Looking at the door panel there appears to be no visible fasteners.
2 Gently prying at the edge of the light shows that it snaps in place and can be easily removed.
7 Another screw is found after the control panel is removed.
8 The panel beside the outside mirror is removed by gently prying.
3 Under the red "door open" warning light is a fastener.
4 Another screw is found under the armrest.
9 A gentle tug and the door panel is removed.
10 The sound-deadening material also acts as a moisture barrier and would need to be removed to gain access to the components inside the door.
5 A screw is removed from the bezel around the interior door handle.
6 The electric control panel is held in by clips.
11 Carefully inspect the door panel clips before reinstalling the door panel.
12 Align and press the door panel clips into the openings and reinstall all of the fasteners and components.

430 CHAPTER 26   ACCESSORY CIRCUITS 431

STEP-BY-STEP photo sequences show in detail the steps involved in performing a specific task or service procedure.

SUPPLEMENTS

INSTRUCTOR SUPPLEMENTS The instructor supplement package has been completely revamped to reflect the needs of today's instructors. The all new **Annotated Instructor's Guide (ISBN 0-13-705215-4)** is the cornerstone of the package and includes:

- Chapter openers that list
  - NATEF/ASE tasks covered in the chapter
  - all key terms
  - all Chapter Objectives
- The entire text (matching page numbers with student edition) with margin notes. These notes include:
  - Tips for in-class demonstrations
  - Suggested hands-on activities
  - Cross-curricular activities
  - Internet search tips
  - Assessments
  - Safety tips
  - Classroom discussion questions
- A guide to using MyAutomotiveKit in the course

Also, in every Professional Technician Series Annotated Instructor's Guide there is an **Instructor's CD** that contains:

- PowerPoint presentations*
- Image Library containing every image in the book for use in class or customized PowerPoints*
- Test Generator software and test bank*
- Chapter Quizzes
- Chapter Review Questions
- English and Spanish Glossary*
- NATEF Correlated task Sheets* (also available as a printed supplement [ISBN: 0-13-705263-4])
- NATEF/ASE Correlation Charts

* All of these are available for download from www.pearson-highered.com

To access supplementary materials online, instructors need to request an instructor access code. Go to www.pearsonhighered.com/irc to register for an instructor access code. Within 48 hours of registering, you will receive a confirming e-mail including an instructor access code. Once you have received your code, locate your text in the online catalog and click on the Instructor Resources button on the left side of the catalog product page. Select a supplement, and a login page will appear. Once you have logged in, you can access instructor material for all Prentice Hall textbooks. If you have any difficulties accessing the site or downloading a supplement, please contact Customer Service at http://247.prenhall.com.

MYAUTOMOTIVEKIT An offshoot of the extremely popular MyAutomotiveLab, these online kits can be used with all Professional Technician Series textbooks for quizzing, testing, homework, and multimedia activities. All assignments are automatically graded and entered into a gradebook for the course. In addition to assessment materials, MyAutomotiveKit includes:

- **Interactive Animations**
- Two- to five-minute **video clips** showing procedures
- A **3D virtual garage** that simulates the shop experience in the real world by focusing on customer complaints, conducting tests to determine the problem with the vehicle, and submitting a written work order to the instructor.
- All materials are broken down by chapter for easy navigation and use.

To get instructor access to MyAutomotiveKit, please visit

www.myautomotivekit.com

STUDENT SUPPLEMENTS NO MORE CDs!!
As a result of extensive student input, Pearson is no longer binding CDs into automotive students' textbooks. Today's student has more access to the Internet than ever, so all supplemental materials are downloadable at the following site for no additional charge:

www.pearsoned.com/autostudent

On the site, students will find:

- PowerPoint presentations
- Chapter review questions and quizzes
- English and Spanish Glossary
- A full Spanish translation of the text
- Links to MyAutomotiveKit

MYAUTOMOTIVEKIT FOR THE STUDENT For the student, **MyAutomotiveKit** is a one-stop shop for homework, quizzes, tests, and a new way of learning. Key concepts are reinforced through media. Students will find part identification activities, word search games, interactive animations, and a 3D virtual garage for help with diagnosis.

ACKNOWLEDGMENTS

A large number of people and organizations have cooperated in providing the reference material and technical information used in this text. The author wishes to express sincere thanks to the following organizations for their special contributions:

ASE
Automotion, Inc.
Automotive Parts Rebuilders Association (APRA)
Society of Automotive Engineers (SAE)
Toyota Motor Sales, USA, Inc.
Wurth USA, Inc.

TECHNICAL AND CONTENT REVIEWERS The following people reviewed the manuscript before production and checked it for technical accuracy and clarity of presentation. Their suggestions and recommendations were included in the final draft of the manuscript. Their input helped make this textbook clear and technically accurate while maintaining the easy-to-read style that has made other books from the same author so popular.

Jim Anderson
Greenville High School

Victor Bridges
Umpqua Community College

Dr. Roger Donovan
Illinois Central College

A. C. Durdin
Moraine Park Technical College

Herbert Ellinger
Western Michigan University

Al Engledahl
College of Dupage

Larry Hagelberger
Upper Valley Joint Vocational School

Oldrick Hajzler
Red River College

Betsy Hoffman
Vermont Technical College

Richard Krieger
Michigan Institute of Technology

Steven T. Lee
Lincoln Technical Institute

Carlton H. Mabe, Sr.
Virginia Western Community College

Roy Marks
Owens Community College

Tony Martin
University of Alaska Southeast

Kerry Meier
San Juan College

Fritz Peacock
Indiana Vocational Technical College

Dennis Peter
NAIT (Canada)

Kenneth Redick
Hudson Valley Community College

Mitchell Walker
St. Louis Community College at Forest Park

Jennifer Wise
Sinclair Community College

Special thanks to instructional designer **Alexis I. Skriloff James.**

PHOTO SEQUENCES The author wishes to thank Blaine Heeter, Mike Garblik, and Chuck Taylor of Sinclair Community College in Dayton, Ohio, and James (Mike) Watson, who helped with many of the photos. A special thanks to Dick Krieger for his detailed and thorough reviews of the manuscript before publication.

Most of all, I wish to thank Michelle Halderman for her assistance in all phases of manuscript preparation.

—James D. Halderman

ABOUT THE AUTHOR

JIM HALDERMAN brings a world of experience, knowledge, and talent to his work. His automotive service experience includes working as a flat-rate technician, a business owner, and a professor of automotive technology at a leading U.S. community college for more than 20 years.

He has a Bachelor of Science Degree from Ohio Northern University and a Masters Degree in Education from Miami University in Oxford, Ohio. Jim also holds a U.S. Patent for an electronic transmission control device. He is an ASE certified Master Automotive Technician and Advanced Engine Performance (L1) ASE certified.

Jim is the author of many automotive textbooks all published by Prentice Hall.

Jim has presented numerous technical seminars to national audiences including the California Automotive Teachers (CAT) and the Illinois College Automotive Instructor Association (ICAIA). He is also a member and presenter at the North American Council of Automotive Teachers (NACAT). Jim was also named Regional Teacher of the Year by General Motors Corporation and an outstanding alumnus of Ohio Northern University.

Jim and his wife, Michelle, live in Dayton, Ohio. They have two children. You can reach Jim at

jim@jameshalderman.com

BRIEF CONTENTS

CONTENTS

chapter 24
DRIVER INFORMATION AND NAVIGATION SYSTEMS 353

chapter 25
HORN, WIPER, AND BLOWER MOTOR CIRCUITS 382

chapter 26
ACCESSORY CIRCUITS 397

SERVICE INFORMATION, TOOLS, AND SAFETY

OBJECTIVES

After studying Chapter 1, the reader will be able to:

1. Understand the ASE knowledge content for vehicle identification and the proper use of tools and shop equipment.
2. Retrieve vehicle service information.
3. Identify the strength ratings of threaded fasteners.
4. Describe how to safely hoist a vehicle.
5. Discuss how to safely use hand tools.
6. Identify the personal protective equipment (PPE) that all service technicians should wear.
7. Describe what tool is the best to use for each job.
8. Discuss how to safely use hand tools.
9. Explain the difference between the brand name (trade name) and the proper name for tools.
10. Explain how to maintain hand tools.
11. Discuss how to safely use power tools.
12. Identify the precautions that should be followed when working on hybrid electric vehicles.

KEY TERMS

FIGURE 1–1 Typical vehicle identification number (VIN) as viewed through the windshield.

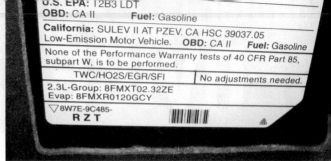

FIGURE 1–2 The vehicle emissions control information (VECI) sticker is placed under the hood.

VEHICLE IDENTIFICATION

MAKE, MODEL, AND YEAR All service work requires that the vehicle and its components be properly identified. The most common identification is the make, model, and year of the vehicle.

Make: e.g., Chevrolet

Model: e.g., Impala

Year: e.g., 2008

VEHICLE IDENTIFICATION NUMBER The year of the vehicle is often difficult to determine exactly. A model may be introduced as the next year's model as soon as January of the previous year. Typically, a new model year starts in September or October of the year prior to the actual new year, but not always. This is why the **vehicle identification number,** usually abbreviated **VIN,** is so important. ● **SEE FIGURE 1–1.**

Since 1981, all vehicle manufacturers have used a VIN that is 17 characters long. Although every vehicle manufacturer assigns various letters or numbers within these 17 characters, there are some constants, including:

- The first number or letter designates the country of origin. ● **SEE CHART 1–1.**
- The fourth and fifth character is the vehicle line/series.
- The sixth character is the body style.
- The seventh character is the restraint system.
- The eighth character is often the engine code. (Some engines cannot be determined by the VIN.)
- The tenth character represents the year on all vehicles. ● **SEE CHART 1–2.**

1 = United States	J = Japan	W = Germany
2 = Canada	K = Korea	X = Russia
3 = Mexico	L = China	Y = Sweden
4 = United States	R = Taiwan	Z = Italy
5 = United States	S = England	
6 = Australia	T = Czechoslovakia	
8 = Argentina	U = Romania	
9 = Brazil	V = France	

CHART 1–1

The first letter in the VIN identifies the country where the vehicle was made.

A = 1980/2010	L = 1990/2020	Y = 2000/2030
B = 1981/2011	M = 1991/2021	1 = 2001/2031
C = 1982/2012	N = 1992/2022	2 = 2002/2032
D = 1983/2013	P = 1993/2023	3 = 2003/2033
E = 1984/2014	R = 1994/2024	4 = 2004/2034
F = 1985/2015	S = 1995/2025	5 = 2005/2035
G = 1986/2016	T = 1996/2026	6 = 2006/2036
H = 1987/2017	V = 1997/2027	7 = 2007/2037
J = 1988/2018	W = 1998/2028	8 = 2008/2038
K = 1989/2019	X = 1999/2029	9 = 2009/2039

CHART 1–2

The pattern repeats every 30 years for the year of manufacture.

FIGURE 1–3 A typical calibration code sticker on the case of a controller. The information on the sticker is often needed when ordering parts or a replacement controller.

FIGURE 1–4 Casting numbers on major components can be either cast or stamped.

VEHICLE SAFETY CERTIFICATION LABEL A vehicle safety certification label is attached to the left side pillar post on the rearward-facing section of the left front door. This label indicates the month and year of manufacture as well as the **gross vehicle weight rating (GVWR),** the **gross axle weight rating (GAWR),** and the VIN.

VECI LABEL The **vehicle emissions control information (VECI)** label under the hood of the vehicle shows informative settings and emission hose routing information. ● **SEE FIGURE 1–2.**

The VECI label (sticker) can be located on the bottom side of the hood, the radiator fan shroud, the radiator core support, or on the strut towers. The VECI label usually includes the following information.

- Engine identification
- Emissions standard that the vehicle meets
- Vacuum hose routing diagram
- Base ignition timing (if adjustable)
- Spark plug type and gap
- Valve lash
- Emission calibration code

CALIBRATION CODES **Calibration codes** are usually located on powertrain control modules (PCMs) or other controllers. Whenever diagnosing an engine operating fault, it is often

necessary to use the calibration code to be sure that the vehicle is the subject of a technical service bulletin or other service procedure. ● **SEE FIGURE 1–3.**

CASTING NUMBERS When an engine part such as a block is cast, a number is put into the mold to identify the casting. ● **SEE FIGURE 1–4.** These **casting numbers** can be used to identify the part and to check dimensions, such as the cubic inch displacement, and other information, such as the year of manufacture. Sometimes changes are made to the mold, yet the casting number is not changed. Most often the casting number is the best piece of identifying information that the service technician can use for identifying an engine.

SERVICE INFORMATION

SERVICE MANUALS Service information is used by the service technician to determine specifications and service procedures, and any needed special tools.

Factory and aftermarket service manuals contain specifications and service procedures. While factory service manuals cover just one year and one or more models of the same vehicle, most aftermarket service manufacturers cover multiple years and/or models in one manual.

FIGURE 1–5 Electronic service information is available from aftermarket sources such as All-Data and Mitchell-on-Demand, as well as on websites hosted by vehicle manufacturers.

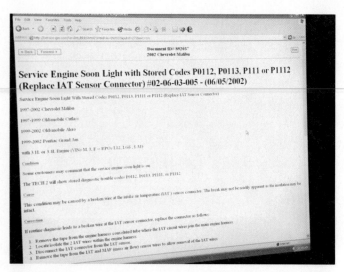

FIGURE 1–6 Technical service bulletins (TSBs) are issued by vehicle manufacturers when a fault occurs that affects many vehicles with the same problem. The TSB then provides the fix for the problem including any parts needed and detailed instructions.

SERVICE INFORMATION (CONTINUED)

Included in most service manuals are the following:

- Capacities and recommended specifications for all fluids
- Specifications including engine and routine maintenance items
- Testing procedures
- Service procedures including the use of special tools when needed

ELECTRONIC SERVICE INFORMATION Electronic service information is available mostly by subscription and provides access to an Internet site where service manual–type information is available. ● **SEE FIGURE 1–5.** Most vehicle manufacturers also offer electronic service information to their dealers and to most schools and colleges that offer corporate training programs.

TECHNICAL SERVICE BULLETINS **Technical service bulletins,** often abbreviated **TSBs,** sometimes called *technical service information bulletins (TSIBs)* are issued by the vehicle manufacturer to notify service technicians of a problem and include the necessary corrective action. Technical service bulletins are designed for dealership technicians but are republished

by aftermarket companies and made available along with other service information to shops and vehicle repair facilities. ● **SEE FIGURE 1–6.**

INTERNET The Internet has opened the field for information exchange and access to technical advice. One of the most useful websites is the International Automotive Technician's Network at **www.iatn.net.** This is a free site but service technicians must register to join. For a small monthly sponsor fee, the shop or service technician can gain access to the archives, which include thousands of successful repairs in the searchable database.

RECALLS AND CAMPAIGNS A **recall** or **campaign** is issued by a vehicle manufacturer and a notice is sent to all owners in the event of a safety-related fault or concern. Although these faults may be repaired by shops, it is generally handled by a local dealer. Items that have created recalls in the past include potential fuel system leakage problems, exhaust leakage, or electrical malfunctions that could cause a possible fire or the engine to stall. Unlike technical service bulletins whose cost is only covered when the vehicle is within the warranty period, a recall or campaign is always done at no cost to the vehicle owner.

FREQUENTLY ASKED QUESTION

What Should Be Included on a Work Order?

A work order is a legal document that should include the following information.

1. Customer information
2. Identification of the vehicle including the VIN
3. Related service history information
4. The "three Cs":
   - Customer concern (complaint)
   - Cause of the concern
   - Correction or repairs that the vehicle required to return it to proper operation

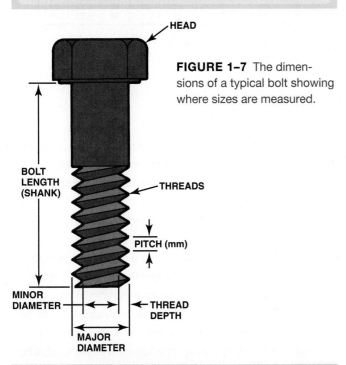

FIGURE 1–7 The dimensions of a typical bolt showing where sizes are measured.

FIGURE 1–8 Thread pitch gauge used to measure the pitch of the thread. This bolt has 13 threads to the inch.

THREADED FASTENERS

BOLTS AND THREADS Most of the threaded fasteners used on vehicles are **bolts.** Bolts are called *cap screws* when they are threaded into a casting. Automotive service technicians usually refer to these fasteners as bolts, regardless of how they are used. In this chapter, they are called bolts. Sometimes, studs are used for threaded fasteners. A **stud** is a short rod with threads on both ends. Often, a stud will have coarse threads on one end and fine threads on the other end. The end of the stud with coarse threads is screwed into the casting. A nut is used on the opposite end to hold the parts together.

The fastener threads *must* match the threads in the casting or nut. The threads may be measured either in fractions of an inch (called fractional) or in metric units. The size is measured across the outside of the threads, called the major diameter or the *crest* of the thread. ● **SEE FIGURE 1–7.**

FRACTIONAL BOLTS Fractional threads are either coarse or fine. The coarse threads are called **Unified National Coarse (UNC),** and the fine threads are called **Unified National Fine (UNF).** Standard combinations of sizes and number of threads per inch (called **pitch**) are used. Pitch can be measured with a thread pitch gauge as shown in ● **FIGURE 1–8.** Bolts are identified by their diameter and length as measured from below the head, not by the size of the head or the size of the wrench used to remove or install the bolt.

Fractional thread sizes are specified by the diameter in fractions of an inch and the number of threads per inch. Typical

FREQUENTLY ASKED QUESTION

How Many Types of Screw Heads Are Used in Automotive Applications?

There are many, including Torx, hex (also called Allen), plus many others used in custom vans and motor homes. ● **SEE FIGURE 1–9.**

ROUND HEAD SCREW · FLATHEAD SCREW · CAPSCREW · HEX-HEAD BOLT · TORX® BOLT · ALLEN BOLT · CHEESE HEAD SCREW · PAN HEAD SCREW

FIGURE 1–9 Bolts and screws have many different heads. The head determines what tool is needed.

| SIZE | THREADS PER INCH | | OUTSIDE DIAMETER INCHES |
	NC UNC	NF UNF	
0	..	80	0.0600
1	64	..	0.0730
1	..	72	0.0730
2	56	..	0.0860
2	..	64	0.0860
3	48	..	0.0990
3	..	56	0.0990
4	40	..	0.1120
4	..	48	0.1120
5	40	..	0.1250
5	..	44	0.1250
6	32	..	0.1380
6	..	40	0.1380
8	32	..	0.1640
8	..	36	0.1640
10	24	..	0.1900
10	..	32	0.1900
12	24	..	0.2160
12	..	28	0.2160
1/4	20	..	0.2500
1/4	..	28	0.2500
5/16	18	..	0.3125
5/16	..	24	0.3125
3/8	16	..	0.3750
3/8	..	24	0.3750
7/16	14	..	0.4375
7/16	..	20	0.4375
1/2	13	..	0.5000
1/2	..	20	0.5000
9/16	12	..	0.5625
9/16	..	18	0.5625
5/8	11	..	0.6250
5/8	..	18	0.6250
3/4	10	..	0.7500
3/4	..	16	0.7500
7/8	9	..	0.8750
7/8	..	14	0.8750
1	8	..	1.0000
1	..	12	1.0000

CHART 1–3

American Standard is one method of sizing fasteners.

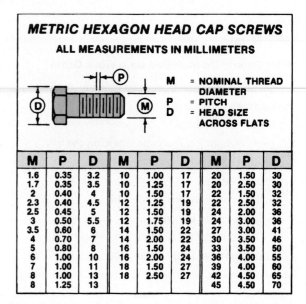

METRIC HEXAGON HEAD CAP SCREWS
ALL MEASUREMENTS IN MILLIMETERS

M = NOMINAL THREAD DIAMETER
P = PITCH
D = HEAD SIZE ACROSS FLATS

M	P	D	M	P	D	M	P	D
1.6	0.35	3.2	10	1.00	17	20	1.50	30
1.7	0.35	3.5	10	1.25	17	20	2.50	30
2	0.40	4	10	1.50	17	22	1.50	32
2.3	0.40	4.5	12	1.25	19	22	2.50	32
2.5	0.45	5	12	1.50	19	24	2.00	36
3	0.50	5.5	12	1.75	19	24	3.00	36
3.5	0.60	6	14	1.50	22	27	3.00	41
4	0.70	7	14	2.00	22	30	3.50	46
5	0.80	8	16	1.50	24	33	3.50	50
6	1.00	10	16	2.00	24	36	4.00	55
7	1.00	11	18	1.50	27	39	4.00	60
8	1.00	13	18	2.50	27	42	4.50	65
8	1.25	13				45	4.50	70

FIGURE 1–10 The metric system specifies fasteners by diameter, length, and pitch.

THREADED FASTENERS (CONTINUED)

M8 and M12. Fine metric threads are specified by the thread diameter followed by X and the distance between the threads measured in millimeters (M8 X 1.5). ● **SEE FIGURE 1–10.**

GRADES OF BOLTS
Bolts are made from many different types of steel, and for this reason some are stronger than others. The strength or classification of a bolt is called the **grade.** The bolt heads are marked to indicate their grade strength.

The actual grade of bolts is two more than the number of lines on the bolt head. Metric bolts have a decimal number to indicate the grade. More lines or a higher grade number indicate a stronger bolt. Higher grade bolts usually have threads that are rolled rather than cut, which also makes them stronger. ● **SEE FIGURE 1–11.** In some cases, nuts and machine screws have similar grade markings.

CAUTION: *Never* use hardware store (nongraded) bolts, studs, or nuts on any vehicle steering, suspension, or brake component. Always use the exact size and grade of hardware that is specified and used by the vehicle manufacturer.

TENSILE STRENGTH OF FASTENERS
Graded fasteners have a higher tensile strength than nongraded fasteners. **Tensile strength** is the maximum stress used under tension (lengthwise force) without causing failure of the fastener. Tensile strength is specified in pounds per square inch (psi).

UNC thread sizes would be 5/16-18 and 1/2-13. Similar UNF thread sizes would be 5/16-24 and 1/2-20. ● **SEE CHART 1–3.**

METRIC BOLTS
The size of a **metric bolt** is specified by the letter *M* followed by the diameter in millimeters (mm) across the outside (crest) of the threads. Typical metric sizes would be

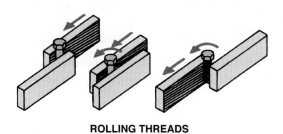

FIGURE 1–11 Stronger threads are created by cold-rolling a heat-treated bolt blank instead of cutting the threads, using a die.

4.6	8.8	9.8	10.9	METRIC CLASS
60,000	120,000	130,000	150,000	APPROXIMATE MAXIMUM POUND FORCE PER SQUARE INCH

FIGURE 1–12 Metric bolt (cap screw) grade markings and approximate tensile strength.

SAE BOLT DESIGNATIONS

SAE GRADE NO.	SIZE RANGE	TENSILE STRENGTH, PSI	MATERIAL	HEAD MARKING
1	1/4 through 1 1/2	60,000	Low or medium carbon steel	
2	1/4 through 3/4	74,000		
	7/8 through 1 1/2	60,000		
5	1/4 through 1	120,000	Medium carbon steel, quenched and tempered	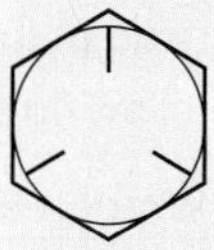
	1 1/8 through 1 1/2	105,000		
5.2	1/4 through 1	120,000	Low carbon martensite steel,* quenched and tempered	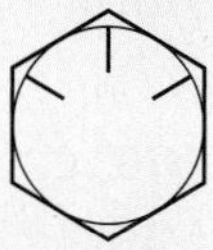
7	1/4 through 1 1/2	133,000	Medium carbon alloy steel, quenched and tempered	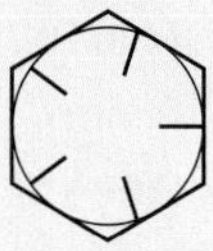
8	1/4 through 1 1/2	150,000	Medium carbon alloy steel, quenched and tempered	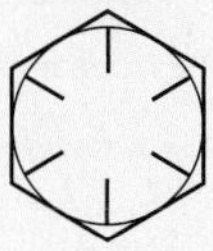
8.2	1/4 through 1	150,000	Low carbon martensite steel,* quenched and tempered	

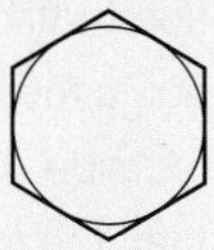

CHART 1–4

The tensile strength rating system as specified by the Society of Automotive Engineers (SAE).
*Martensite steel is steel that has been cooled rapidly, thereby increasing its hardness. It is named after a German metallurgist, Adolf Martens.

The strength and type of steel used in a bolt is supposed to be indicated by a raised mark on the head of the bolt. The type of mark depends on the standard to which the bolt was manufactured. Most often, bolts used in machinery are made to SAE standard J429. ● **CHART 1–4** shows the grade and specified tensile strength.

Metric bolt tensile strength property class is shown on the head of the bolt as a number, such as 4.6, 8.8, 9.8, and 10.9; the higher the number, the stronger the bolt. ● **SEE FIGURE 1–12.**

| HEX NUT | JAM NUT | NYLON LOCK NUT | CASTLE NUT | ACORN NUT |

| FLAT WASHER | LOCK WASHER | STAR WASHER | STAR WASHER |

FIGURE 1-13 Nuts come in a variety of styles, including locking (prevailing torque) types, such as the distorted thread and nylon insert type.

FIGURE 1-14 Washers come in a variety of styles, including flat and star (serrated), used to help prevent a fastener from loosening.

THREADED FASTENERS (CONTINUED)

TECH TIP

A 1/2 Inch Wrench Does Not Fit a 1/2 Inch Bolt

A common mistake made by persons new to the automotive field is to think that the size of a bolt or nut is the size of the head. The size of the bolt or nut (outside diameter of the threads) is usually smaller than the size of the wrench or socket that fits the head of the bolt or nut. Examples are given in the following table.

Wrench Size	Thread Size
7/16 in.	1/4 in.
1/2 in.	5/16 in.
9/16 in.	3/8 in.
5/8 in.	7/16 in.
3/4 in.	1/2 in.
10 mm	6 mm
12 mm or 13 mm*	8 mm
14 mm or 17 mm*	10 mm

* European (Systeme International d'Unites, or SI) metric

TECH TIP

It Just Takes a Second

Whenever removing any automotive component, it is wise to screw the bolts back into the holes a couple of threads by hand. This ensures that the right bolt will be used in its original location when the component or part is put back on the vehicle. Often, the same diameter of fastener is used on a component, but the length of the bolt may vary. Spending just a couple of seconds to put the bolts and nuts back where they belong when the part is removed can save a lot of time when the part is being reinstalled. Besides making certain that the right fastener is being installed in the right place, this method helps prevent bolts and nuts from getting lost or kicked away. How much time have you wasted looking for that lost bolt or nut?

NUTS Nuts are the female part of a threaded fastener. Most nuts used on cap screws have the same hex size as the cap screw head. Some inexpensive nuts use a hex size larger than the cap screw head. Metric nuts are often marked with dimples to show their strength. More dimples indicate stronger nuts. Some nuts and cap screws use interference fit threads to keep them from accidentally loosening. This means that the shape of the nut is slightly distorted or that a section of the threads is deformed. Nuts can also be kept from loosening with a nylon washer fastened in the nut or with a nylon patch or strip on the threads. ● SEE FIGURE 1-13.

NOTE: Most of these "locking nuts" are grouped together and are commonly referred to as *prevailing torque nuts*. This means that the nut will hold its tightness or torque and not loosen with movement or vibration. Most prevailing torque nuts should be replaced whenever removed to ensure that the nut will not loosen during service. Always follow the manufacturer's recommendations. Anaerobic sealers, such as Loctite, are used on the threads where the nut or cap screw must be both locked and sealed.

WASHERS Washers are often used under cap screw heads and under nuts. ● SEE FIGURE 1-14. Plain flat washers are used to provide an even clamping load around the fastener. Lock washers are added to prevent accidental loosening. In some accessories, the washers are locked onto the nut to provide easy assembly.

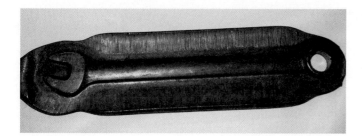

FIGURE 1–15 A forged wrench after it has been forged but before the flashing (extra material around the wrench) has been removed.

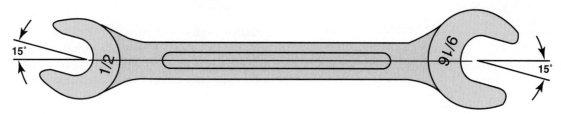

FIGURE 1–16 A typical open-end wrench. Note the size difference on each end and that the head is angled 15 degrees at the end.

HAND TOOLS

WRENCHES Wrenches are the most used hand tool by service technicians. **Wrenches** are used to grasp and rotate threaded fasteners. Most wrenches are constructed of forged alloy steel, usually chrome-vanadium steel. ● **SEE FIGURE 1–15.**

After the wrench is formed, it is hardened, and then tempered to reduce brittleness, and then chrome plated. There are several types of wrenches.

- An **open-end wrench** is often used to loosen or tighten bolts or nuts that do not require a lot of torque. Because of the *open* end, this type of wrench can be easily placed on a bolt or nut with an angle of 15 degrees, which allows the wrench to be flipped over and used again to continue to rotate the fastener. The major disadvantage of an open-end wrench is the lack of torque that can be applied due to the fact that the open jaws of the wrench only contact two flat surfaces of the fastener. An open-end wrench has two different sizes, one at each end. ● **SEE FIGURE 1–16.**

- A **box-end wrench,** also called a *closed-end wrench,* is placed over the top of the fastener and grips the points of the fastener. A box-end wrench is angled 15 degrees to allow it to clear nearby objects.

Therefore, a box-end wrench should be used to loosen or to tighten fasteners because it grasps around the entire head of the fastener. A box-end wrench has two different sizes, one at each end. ● **SEE FIGURE 1–17.**

Most service technicians purchase *combination wrenches,* which have the open end at one end and the same size box end on the other end. ● **SEE FIGURE 1–18.**

A combination wrench allows the technician to loosen or tighten a fastener using the box end of the wrench, turn it around, and use the open end to increase the speed of rotating the fastener.

- An **adjustable wrench** is often used where the exact size wrench is not available or when a large nut, such as a wheel spindle nut, needs to be rotated but not tightened. An adjustable wrench should not be used to loosen or tighten fasteners because the torque applied to the wrench can cause the movable jaws to loosen their grip on the fastener, causing it to become rounded. ● **SEE FIGURE 1–19.**

- **Line wrenches,** also called *flare-nut wrenches, fitting wrenches,* or *tube-nut wrenches,* are designed to grip almost all the way around a nut used to retain a fuel, brake or refrigerant line, and yet be able to be installed over the line. ● **SEE FIGURE 1–20.**

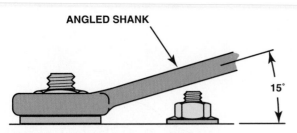

FIGURE 1–17 The end of a box-end wrench is angled 15 degrees to allow clearance for nearby objects or other fasteners.

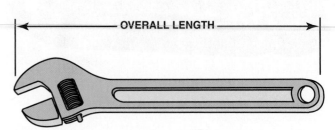

FIGURE 1–19 An adjustable wrench. Adjustable wrenches are sized by the overall length of the wrench, not by how far the jaws open. Common sizes of adjustable wrenches include 8 in., 10 in., and 12 in.

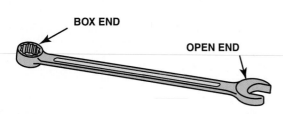

FIGURE 1–18 A combination wrench has an open end at one end and a box end at the other end.

FIGURE 1–20 The end of a typical line wrench, which shows that it is capable of grasping most of the head of the fitting.

HAND TOOLS (CONTINUED)

TECH TIP

Hide Those from the Boss

An apprentice technician started working for a dealership and put his top tool box on a workbench. Another technician observed that, along with a complete set of good-quality tools, the box contained several adjustable wrenches. The more experienced technician said, "Hide those from the boss." The boss does not want any service technician to use adjustable wrenches. If any adjustable wrench is used on a bolt or nut, the movable jaw often moves or loosens and starts to round the head of the fastener. If the head of the bolt or nut becomes rounded, it becomes that much more difficult to remove.

SAFE USE OF WRENCHES Wrenches should be inspected before use to be sure they are not cracked, bent, or damaged. All wrenches should be cleaned after use before being returned to the tool box. Always use the correct size of wrench for the fastener being loosened or tightened to help prevent the rounding of the flats of the fastener. When attempting to loosen a fastener, pull a wrench—do not push it. If you push a wrench, your knuckles may be hurt when forced into another object if the fastener breaks loose or if the wrench slips. Always keep wrenches and all hand tools clean to help prevent rust and to allow for a better, firmer grip. Never expose any tool to excessive heat. High temperatures can reduce the strength ("draw the temper") of metal tools.

Never use a hammer on any wrench unless you are using a special *staking face wrench* designed to be used with a hammer. Replace any tools that are damaged or worn.

RATCHETS, SOCKETS, AND EXTENSIONS A **socket** fits over the fastener and grips the points and/or flats of the bolt or nut. The socket is rotated (driven) using either a long bar called

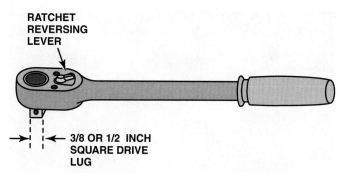

FIGURE 1–21 A typical ratchet used to rotate a socket. A ratchet makes a ratcheting noise when it is being rotated in the opposite direction from loosening or tightening. A knob or lever on the ratchet allows the technician to switch directions.

FIGURE 1–22 A typical flex handle used to rotate a socket; also called a breaker bar, because it usually has a longer handle than a ratchet and, therefore, can be used to apply more torque to a fastener than a ratchet.

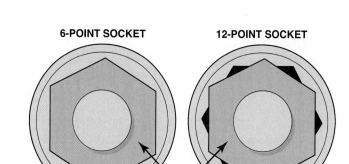

FIGURE 1–23 The most commonly used socket drive sizes include 1/4 in., 3/8 in., and 1/2 in. drive.

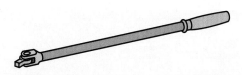

FIGURE 1–24 A 6-point socket fits the head of a bolt or nut on all sides. A 12-point socket can round off the head of a bolt or nut if great force is applied.

a **breaker bar** (flex handle) or a ratchet. ● **SEE FIGURES 1–21 AND 1–22.**

A **ratchet** is a tool that turns the socket in only one direction and allows the rotating of the ratchet handle back and forth in a narrow space. Socket **extensions** and **universal joints** are also used with sockets to allow access to fasteners in restricted locations.

DRIVE SIZE. Sockets are available in various **drive sizes,** including 1/4 in., 3/8 in., and 1/2 in. sizes for most automotive use. ● **SEE FIGURES 1–23 AND 1–24.**

TECH TIP

Right to Tighten

It is sometimes confusing which way to rotate a wrench or screwdriver, especially when the head of the fastener is pointing away from you. To help visualize while looking at the fastener, say "righty tighty, lefty loosey."

Many heavy-duty truck and/or industrial applications use 3/4 in. and 1 in. sizes. The drive size is the distance of each side of the square drive. Sockets and ratchets of the same size are designed to work together.

Regular and deep well sockets are available in regular length for use in most applications or in a deep well design that allows for access to a fastener that uses a long stud or other similar conditions. ● **SEE FIGURE 1–25.**

TORQUE WRENCHES Torque wrenches are socket turning handles designed to apply a known amount of force to the fastener. The two basic types of torque wrenches include:

1. **Clicker type.** This type of torque wrench is first set to the specified torque and then it "clicks" when the set torque value has been reached. When force is removed from the torque wrench handle, another click is heard. The setting on a clicker-type torque wrench should be set back to zero after use and checked for proper calibration regularly. ● **SEE FIGURE 1–26.**

2. **Beam or dial type.** This type of torque wrench is used to measure torque, but instead of presenting the value, the actual torque is displayed on the dial of the wrench as the

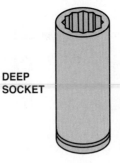

FIGURE 1–25 Allows access to the nut that has a stud plus other locations needing great depth, such as spark plugs.

DEEP SOCKET

REGULAR SOCKET

FIGURE 1–26 Using a torque wrench to tighten connecting rod nuts on an engine.

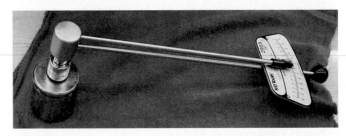

FIGURE 1–27 A beam-type torque wrench that displays the torque reading on the face of the dial. The beam display is read as the beam deflects, which is in proportion to the amount of torque applied to the fastener.

HAND TOOLS (CONTINUED)

fastener is being tightened. Beam or dial-type torque wrenches are available in 1/4 in., 3/8 in., and 1/2 in. drives and both English (standard) and metric units. ● **SEE FIGURE 1–27.**

SAFE USE OF SOCKETS AND RATCHETS
Always use the proper size socket that correctly fits the bolt or nut. All sockets and ratchets should be cleaned after use before being placed back into the tool box. Sockets are available in short and deep well designs. Never expose any tool to excessive heat. High temperatures can reduce the strength ("draw the temper") of metal tools.

Never use a hammer on a socket handle unless you are using a special *staking face wrench* designed to be used with a hammer. Replace any tools that are damaged or worn.

Also select the appropriate drive size. For example, for small work, such as on the dash, select a 1/4 in. drive. For most general service work, use a 3/8 in. drive and for suspension and steering and other large fasteners, select a 1/2 in. drive. When loosening a fastener, always pull the ratchet toward you rather than push it outward.

 **TECH TIP**

Check Torque Wrench Calibration Regularly

Torque wrenches should be checked regularly. For example, Honda has a torque wrench calibration set-up at each training center. It is expected that a torque wrench be checked for accuracy before every use. Most experts recommend that torque wrenches be checked and adjusted as needed at least every year and more often if possible. ● **SEE FIGURE 1–28.**

FIGURE 1–28 Torque wrench calibration checker.

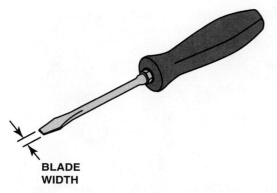

**BLADE
WIDTH**

FIGURE 1–29 A flat-tip (straight-blade) screwdriver. The width of the blade should match the width of the slot in the fastener being loosened or tightened.

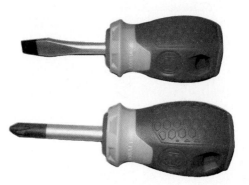

FIGURE 1–30 Two stubby screwdrivers used to access screws that have limited space above. A straight blade is on top and a #2 Phillips screwdriver is on the bottom.

TECH TIP

Use Socket Adapters with Caution

A **socket adapter** allows the use of one size of socket and another drive size ratchet or breaker bar. Socket adapters are available and can be used for different drive size sockets on a ratchet. Combinations include:

1/4 in. drive – 3/8 in. sockets
3/8 in. drive – 1/4 in. sockets
3/8 in. drive – 1/2 in. sockets
1/2 in. drive – 3/8 in. sockets

Using a larger drive ratchet or breaker bar on a smaller size socket can cause the application of too much force to the socket, which could crack or shatter. Using a smaller size drive tool on a larger socket will usually not cause any harm, but would greatly reduce the amount of torque that can be applied to the bolt or nut.

SCREWDRIVERS

- **Straight-blade screwdriver.** Many smaller fasteners are removed and installed using a **screwdriver.** Screwdrivers are available in many sizes and tip shapes. The most commonly used screwdriver is called a *straight blade* or *flat tip.* Flat-tip screwdrivers are sized by the width of the blade, and this width should match the width of the slot in the screw. ● **SEE FIGURE 1–29.**

CAUTION: Do not use a screwdriver as a pry tool or chisel. Screwdrivers use hardened steel only at the tip and are not designed to be pounded on or used for prying because they could bend easily. Always use the proper tool for each application.

TECH TIP

Avoid Using "Cheater Bars"

Whenever a fastener is difficult to remove, some technicians will insert the handle of a ratchet or a breaker bar into a length of steel pipe sometimes called a **cheater bar.** The extra length of the pipe allows the technician to exert more torque than can be applied using the drive handle alone. However, the extra torque can easily overload the socket and ratchet, causing them to break or shatter, which could cause personal injury.

- **Phillips screwdriver.** Another type of commonly used screwdriver is the Phillips screwdriver, named for Henry F. Phillips, who invented the crosshead screw in 1934. Due to the shape of the crosshead screw and screwdriver, a Phillips screw can be driven with more torque than can be achieved with a slotted screw.

  A Phillips head screwdriver is specified by the length of the handle and the size of the point at the tip. A #1 tip has a sharp point, a #2 tip is the most commonly used, and a #3 tip is blunt and is only used for larger sizes of Phillips head fasteners. For example, a #2 × 3 in. Phillips screwdriver would typically measure 6 in. from the tip of the blade to the end of the handle (3 in. long handle and 3 in. long blade) with a #2 tip.

  Both straight-blade and Phillips screwdrivers are available with a short blade and handle for access to fasteners with limited room. ● **SEE FIGURE 1–30.**

FIGURE 1–31 An offset screwdriver is used to install or remove fasteners that do not have enough space above to use a conventional screwdriver.

FIGURE 1–32 An impact screwdriver used to remove slotted or Phillips head fasteners that cannot be broken loose using a standard screwdriver.

HAND TOOLS (CONTINUED)

- **Offset screwdriver.** Offset screwdrivers are used in places where a conventional screwdriver cannot fit. An offset screwdriver is bent at the ends and is used similar to a wrench. Most offset screwdrivers have a straight blade at one end and a Phillips head at the opposite end. ● **SEE FIGURE 1–31.**

- **Impact screwdriver.** An *impact screwdriver* is used to break loose or tighten a screw. A hammer is used to strike the end after the screwdriver holder is placed in the head of the screw and rotated in the desired direction. The force from the hammer blow does two things: It applies a force downward holding the tip of the screwdriver in the slot and then applies a twisting force to loosen (or tighten) the screw. ● **SEE FIGURE 1–32.**

SAFE USE OF SCREWDRIVERS Always use the proper type and size screwdriver that matches the fastener. Try to avoid pressing down on a screwdriver because if it slips, the screwdriver tip could penetrate your hand, causing serious personal injury. All screwdrivers should be cleaned after use. Do not use a screwdriver as a pry bar; always use the correct tool for the job.

HAMMERS AND MALLETS Hammers and mallets are used to force objects together or apart. The shape of the back part of the hammer head (called the *peen*) usually determines the name. For example, a ball-peen hammer has a rounded end like a ball and is used to straighten oil pans and valve covers, using the hammer head, and to shape metal, using the ball peen. ● **SEE FIGURE 1–33.**

> **?** **FREQUENTLY ASKED QUESTION**
>
> **What Is a Torx and a Robertson Screwdriver?**
> **TORX**-A Torx is a six-pointed star shaped tip that was developed by Camcar (formerly Textron) to offer higher loosening and tightening torque than is possible with a straight (flat tip) or Phillips. Torx is very commonly used in the automotive field for many components.
> **Robertson**-P. L. Robertson invented the Robertson screw and screwdriver in 1908, which uses a square-shaped tip with a slight taper. The Robertson screwdriver uses color-coded handles because different size screws require different tip sizes. Robertson screws are commonly used in Canada and in the recreational vehicle (RV) industry in the United States.

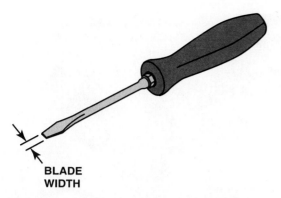

BLADE WIDTH

FIGURE 1–29 A flat-tip (straight-blade) screwdriver. The width of the blade should match the width of the slot in the fastener being loosened or tightened.

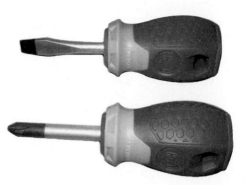

FIGURE 1–30 Two stubby screwdrivers used to access screws that have limited space above. A straight blade is on top and a #2 Phillips screwdriver is on the bottom.

TECH TIP

Use Socket Adapters with Caution

A **socket adapter** allows the use of one size of socket and another drive size ratchet or breaker bar. Socket adapters are available and can be used for different drive size sockets on a ratchet. Combinations include:

1/4 in. drive – 3/8 in. sockets
3/8 in. drive – 1/4 in. sockets
3/8 in. drive – 1/2 in. sockets
1/2 in. drive – 3/8 in. sockets

Using a larger drive ratchet or breaker bar on a smaller size socket can cause the application of too much force to the socket, which could crack or shatter. Using a smaller size drive tool on a larger socket will usually not cause any harm, but would greatly reduce the amount of torque that can be applied to the bolt or nut.

SCREWDRIVERS

- **Straight-blade screwdriver.** Many smaller fasteners are removed and installed using a **screwdriver.** Screwdrivers are available in many sizes and tip shapes. The most commonly used screwdriver is called a *straight blade* or *flat tip*.

  Flat-tip screwdrivers are sized by the width of the blade, and this width should match the width of the slot in the screw. ● **SEE FIGURE 1–29.**

CAUTION: Do not use a screwdriver as a pry tool or chisel. Screwdrivers use hardened steel only at the tip and are not designed to be pounded on or used for prying because they could bend easily. Always use the proper tool for each application.

TECH TIP

Avoid Using "Cheater Bars"

Whenever a fastener is difficult to remove, some technicians will insert the handle of a ratchet or a breaker bar into a length of steel pipe sometimes called a **cheater bar**. The extra length of the pipe allows the technician to exert more torque than can be applied using the drive handle alone. However, the extra torque can easily overload the socket and ratchet, causing them to break or shatter, which could cause personal injury.

- **Phillips screwdriver.** Another type of commonly used screwdriver is the Phillips screwdriver, named for Henry F. Phillips, who invented the crosshead screw in 1934. Due to the shape of the crosshead screw and screwdriver, a Phillips screw can be driven with more torque than can be achieved with a slotted screw.

  A Phillips head screwdriver is specified by the length of the handle and the size of the point at the tip. A #1 tip has a sharp point, a #2 tip is the most commonly used, and a #3 tip is blunt and is only used for larger sizes of Phillips head fasteners. For example, a #2 × 3 in. Phillips screwdriver would typically measure 6 in. from the tip of the blade to the end of the handle (3 in. long handle and 3 in. long blade) with a #2 tip.

  Both straight-blade and Phillips screwdrivers are available with a short blade and handle for access to fasteners with limited room. ● **SEE FIGURE 1–30.**

FIGURE 1–31 An offset screwdriver is used to install or remove fasteners that do not have enough space above to use a conventional screwdriver.

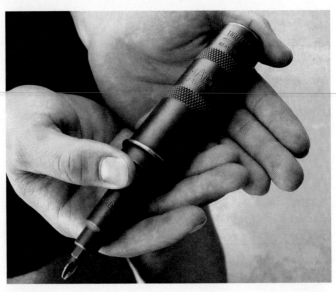

FIGURE 1–32 An impact screwdriver used to remove slotted or Phillips head fasteners that cannot be broken loose using a standard screwdriver.

HAND TOOLS (CONTINUED)

- **Offset screwdriver.** Offset screwdrivers are used in places where a conventional screwdriver cannot fit. An offset screwdriver is bent at the ends and is used similar to a wrench. Most offset screwdrivers have a straight blade at one end and a Phillips head at the opposite end. ● **SEE FIGURE 1–31.**

- **Impact screwdriver.** An *impact screwdriver* is used to break loose or tighten a screw. A hammer is used to strike the end after the screwdriver holder is placed in the head of the screw and rotated in the desired direction. The force from the hammer blow does two things: It applies a force downward holding the tip of the screwdriver in the slot and then applies a twisting force to loosen (or tighten) the screw. ● **SEE FIGURE 1–32.**

SAFE USE OF SCREWDRIVERS Always use the proper type and size screwdriver that matches the fastener. Try to avoid pressing down on a screwdriver because if it slips, the screwdriver tip could penetrate your hand, causing serious personal injury. All screwdrivers should be cleaned after use. Do not use a screwdriver as a pry bar; always use the correct tool for the job.

HAMMERS AND MALLETS **Hammers** and mallets are used to force objects together or apart. The shape of the back part of the hammer head (called the *peen*) usually determines the name. For example, a ball-peen hammer has a rounded end like a ball and is used to straighten oil pans and valve covers, using the hammer head, and to shape metal, using the ball peen. ● **SEE FIGURE 1–33.**

> **?** **FREQUENTLY ASKED QUESTION**
>
> **What Is a Torx and a Robertson Screwdriver?**
>
> **TORX**-A Torx is a six-pointed star shaped tip that was developed by Camcar (formerly Textron) to offer higher loosening and tightening torque than is possible with a straight (flat tip) or Phillips. Torx is very commonly used in the automotive field for many components.
>
> **Robertson**-P. L. Robertson invented the Robertson screw and screwdriver in 1908, which uses a square-shaped tip with a slight taper. The Robertson screwdriver uses color-coded handles because different size screws require different tip sizes. Robertson screws are commonly used in Canada and in the recreational vehicle (RV) industry in the United States.

FIGURE 1–33 A typical ball-peen hammer.

FIGURE 1–34 A rubber mallet used to deliver a force to an object without harming the surface.

FIGURE 1–35 A dead-blow hammer that was left outside in freezing weather. The plastic covering was damaged, which destroyed this hammer. The lead shot is encased in the metal housing and then covered.

NOTE: A claw hammer has a claw used to remove nails; therefore, it is not for automotive service.

A hammer is usually sized by the weight of the hammer's head and the length of the handle. For example, a commonly used ball-peen hammer has an 8 oz head and 11 in. handle.

- **Mallets.** *Mallets* are a type of hammer with a large striking surface, which allows the technician to exert force over a larger area than a hammer, so as not to harm the part or component. Mallets are made from a variety of materials including rubber, plastic, or wood. ● **SEE FIGURE 1–34.**

- **Dead-blow hammer.** A shot-filled plastic hammer is called a *dead-blow hammer*. The small lead balls (shot) inside a plastic head prevent the hammer from bouncing off of the object when struck. ● **SEE FIGURE 1–35.**

SAFE USE OF HAMMERS AND MALLETS
All mallets and hammers should be cleaned after use and not exposed to extreme temperatures. Never use a hammer or mallet that is damaged in any way and always use caution to avoid doing damage to the components and the surrounding area. Always follow the hammer manufacturer's recommended procedures and practices.

PLIERS

- **Slip-joint pliers.** Pliers are capable of holding, twisting, bending, and cutting objects and are an extremely useful classification of tools. The common household type of pliers is called the *slip-joint pliers.* There are two different positions where the junction of the handles meets to achieve a wide range of sizes of objects that can be gripped. ● **SEE FIGURE 1–36.**

TECH TIP

Pound with Something Softer

If you must pound on something, be sure to use a tool that is softer than what you are about to pound on to avoid damage. Examples are given in the following table.

The Material Being Pounded	What to Pound With
Steel or cast iron	Brass or aluminum hammer or punch
Aluminum	Plastic or rawhide mallet or plastic-covered dead-blow hammer
Plastic	Rawhide mallet or plastic dead-blow hammer

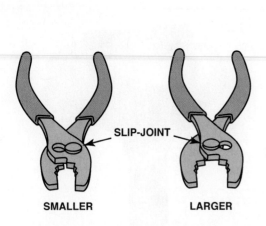

FIGURE 1–36 Typical slip-joint pliers are common household pliers. The slip joint allows the jaws to be opened to two different settings.

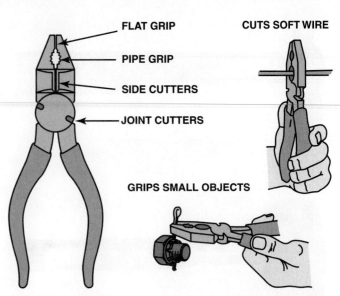

FIGURE 1–38 Linesman's pliers are very useful because they can help perform many automotive service jobs.

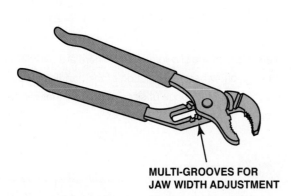

FIGURE 1–37 Multigroove adjustable pliers are known by many names, including the trade name Channel Locks.

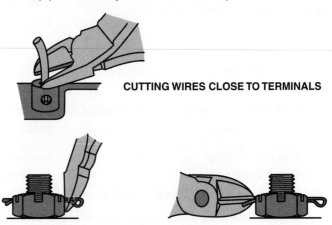

FIGURE 1–39 The diagonal-cut pliers is another common tool that has many names.

HAND TOOLS (CONTINUED)

- **Multigroove adjustable pliers.** For gripping larger objects, a set of *multigroove adjustable pliers* is a commonly used tool of choice by many service technicians. Originally designed to remove the various size nuts holding rope seals used in water pumps, the name *water pump pliers* is also used. ● SEE FIGURE 1–37.

- **Linesman's pliers.** *Linesman's pliers* are specifically designed for cutting, bending, and twisting wire. While commonly used by construction workers and electricians, linesman's pliers are a very useful tool for the service technician who deals with wiring. The center parts of the jaws are designed to grasp round objects such as pipe or tubing with slipping. ● SEE FIGURE 1–38.

- **Diagonal pliers.** *Diagonal pliers* are designed to cut only. The cutting jaws are set at an angle to make it easier to cut wires. Diagonal pliers are also called *side cuts* or *dikes*. These pliers are constructed of hardened steel and they are used mostly for cutting wire. ● SEE FIGURE 1–39.

- **Needle-nose pliers.** *Needle-nose pliers* are designed to grip small objects or objects in tight locations. Needle-nose pliers have long, pointed jaws to allow the tips to reach into narrow openings or groups of small objects. ● SEE FIGURE 1–40.

Most needle-nose pliers have a wire cutter located at the base of the jaws near the pivot. There are several variations of needle-nose pliers, including right angle jaws or slightly angled jaws to allow access to certain cramped areas.

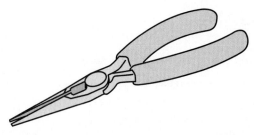

FIGURE 1–40 Needle-nose pliers are used where there is limited access to a wire or pin that needs to be installed or removed.

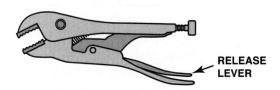

RELEASE LEVER

FIGURE 1–41 Locking pliers are best known by the trade name Vise-Grip®.

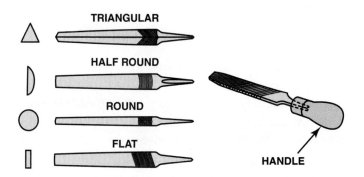

TRIANGULAR

HALF ROUND

ROUND

FLAT

HANDLE

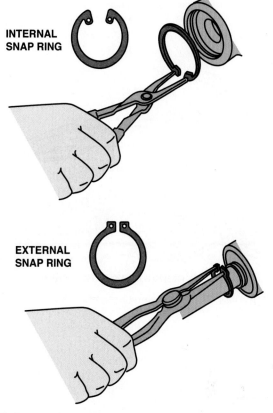

INTERNAL SNAP RING

EXTERNAL SNAP RING

FIGURE 1–42 Snap-ring pliers are also called lock-ring pliers, and most are designed to remove internal and external snap rings (lock rings).

FIGURE 1–43 Files come in many different shapes and sizes. Never use a file without a handle.

- **Locking pliers.** *Locking pliers* are adjustable pliers that can be locked to hold objects from moving. Most locking pliers also have wire cutters built into the jaws near the pivot point. Locking pliers come in a variety of styles and sizes and are commonly referred to by the trade name Vise-Grip®. The size is the length of the pliers, not how far the jaws open. ● **SEE FIGURE 1–41.**

- **Snap-ring pliers.** *Snap-ring pliers* are used to remove and install snap rings. Many snap-ring pliers are designed to be able to remove and install both inward and outward expanding snap rings. Snap-ring pliers can be equipped with serrated-tipped jaws for grasping the opening in the snap ring, while others are equipped with

points, which are inserted into the holes in the snap ring. ● **SEE FIGURE 1–42.**

SAFE USE OF PLIERS Pliers should not be used to remove any bolt or other fastener. Pliers should only be used when specified for use by the vehicle manufacturer.

FILES Files are used to smooth metal and are constructed of hardened steel with diagonal rows of teeth. Files are available with a single row of teeth called a *single cut file,* as well as two rows of teeth cut at an opposite angle called a *double cut file.* Files are available in a variety of shapes and sizes including small flat files, half-round files, and triangular files. ● **SEE FIGURE 1–43.**

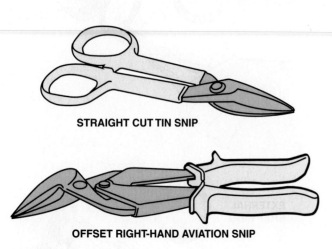

STRAIGHT CUT TIN SNIP

OFFSET RIGHT-HAND AVIATION SNIP

FIGURE 1–44 Tin snips are used to cut thin sheets of metal or carpet.

🔧 **TECH TIP**

Brand Name versus Proper Term

Technicians often use slang or brand names of tools rather than the proper term. This results in confusion for new technicians. Some examples are given in the following table.

Brand Name	Proper Term	Slang Name
Crescent wrench	Adjustable wrench	Monkey wrench
Vise-Grip®	Locking pliers	Pump pliers
Channel Locks	Water pump pliers or multigroove adjustable pliers	
	Diagonal cutting pliers	Dikes or side cuts

HAND TOOLS (CONTINUED)

SAFE USE OF FILES Always use a file with a handle. Because files only cut when moved forward, a handle must be attached to prevent possible personal injury. After making a forward strike, lift the file and return the file to the starting position; avoid dragging the file backward.

SNIPS Service technicians are often asked to fabricate sheet metal brackets or heat shields and need to use one or more types of cutters available called **snips.** The simplest cutter is called a *tin snips,* designed to make straight cuts in a variety of materials such as sheet steel, aluminum, or even fabric. A variation of the tin snips is called the *aviation tin snips.* There are three designs of aviation snips including one designed to cut straight (called a *straight cut aviation snip*), one designed to cut left (called an *offset left aviation snip*), and one designed to cut right (called an *offset right aviation snip*). The handles are color coded for easy identification. These include yellow for straight, red for left, and green for right. ● **SEE FIGURE 1–44.**

UTILITY KNIFE A *utility knife* uses a replaceable blade and can cut a variety of materials such as carpet, plastic, wood, and paper products such as cardboard. ● **SEE FIGURE 1–45.**

SAFE USE OF CUTTERS Whenever using cutters, always wear eye protection or a face shield to guard against the possibility of metal pieces being ejected during the cut. Always follow recommended procedures.

PUNCHES A **punch** is a small diameter steel rod that has a smaller diameter ground at one end. A punch is used to drive a pin out that is used to retain two components. Punches come in a variety of sizes, which are measured across the diameter of the machined end. Sizes include 1/16 in., 1/8 in., 3/16 in., and 1/4 in. ● **SEE FIGURE 1–46.**

CHISELS A **chisel** has a straight, sharp cutting end that is used for cutting off rivets or to separate two pieces of an assembly. The most common design of chisel used for automotive service work is called a *cold chisel.*

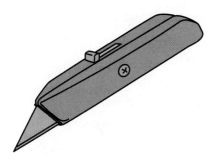

FIGURE 1–45 A utility knife uses replaceable blades and can cut carpet and other materials.

PIN

FIGURE 1–46 A punch used to drive pins from assembled components. This type of punch is also called a pin punch.

FIGURE 1–47 Warning stamped in the side of a punch that goggles should be worn when using this tool. Always follow safety warnings.

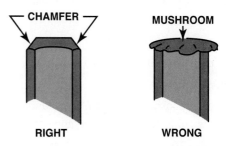

CHAMFER   MUSHROOM

RIGHT   WRONG

FIGURE 1–48 Use a grinder or a file to remove the mushroom material on the end of a punch or chisel.

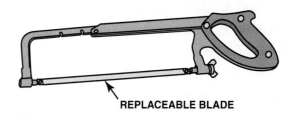

REPLACEABLE BLADE

FIGURE 1–49 A typical hacksaw that is used to cut metal. If cutting sheet metal or thin objects, then use a blade with more teeth.

SAFE USE OF PUNCHES AND CHISELS Always wear eye protection when using a punch or a chisel because the harden steel is brittle and parts of the punch could fly off and cause serious personal injury. See the warning stamped on the side of the automotive punch in ● **FIGURE 1–47.**

The tops of punches and chisels that become rounded off from use are referred to as being "mushroomed." This material must be ground off to help prevent the overhanging material from becoming loosened and airborne during use. ● **SEE FIGURE 1–48.**

HACKSAWS A **hacksaw** is used to cut metals such as steel, aluminum, brass, or copper. The cutting blade of a hacksaw is replaceable and the sharpness and number of

teeth can be varied to meet the needs of the job. Use 14 or 18 teeth per inch (TPI) for cutting plaster or soft metals such as aluminum and copper. Use 24 or 32 TPI for steel or pipe. Hacksaw blades should be installed with the teeth pointing away from the handle. This means that a hacksaw only cuts while the blade is pushed in the forward direction. ● **SEE FIGURE 1–49.**

SAFE USE OF HACKSAWS Check that the hacksaw is equipped with the correct blade for the job and that the teeth are pointed away from the handle. When using a hacksaw, move the hacksaw slowly away from you, then lift slightly and return for another cut.

BASIC HAND TOOL LIST

The following is a list of hand tools every automotive technician should possess. Specialty tools are not included.

Safety glasses

Tool chest

1/4 in. drive socket set (1/4 to 9/16 in. standard and deep sockets; 6 to 15 mm standard and deep sockets)

1/4 in. drive ratchet

1/4 in. drive, 2 in. extension

1/4 in. drive, 6 in. extension

1/4 in. drive handle

3/8 in. drive socket set (3/8 to 7/8 in. standard and deep sockets; 10 to 19 mm standard and deep sockets)

3/8 in. drive Torx set (T40, T45, T50, and T55)

3/8 in. drive, 13/16 in. plug socket

3/8 in. drive, 5/8 in. plug socket

3/8 in. drive ratchet

3/8 in. drive, 1 1/2 in. extension

3/8 in. drive, 3 in. extension

3/8 in. drive, 6 in. extension

3/8 in. drive, 18 in. extension

3/8 in. drive universal

1/2 in. drive socket set (1/2 to 1 in. standard and deep sockets)

1/2 in. drive ratchet

1/2 in. drive breaker bar

1/2 in. drive, 5 in. extension

1/2 in. drive, 10 in. extension

3/8 to 1/4 in. adapter

1/2 to 3/8 in. adapter

3/8 to 1/2 in. adapter

Crowfoot set (fractional inches)

Crowfoot set (metric)

3/8 to 1 in. combination wrench set

10 to 19 mm combination wrench set

1/16 to 1/4 in. hex wrench set

2 to 12 mm hex wrench set

3/8 in. hex socket

13 to 14 mm flare nut wrench

15 to 17 mm flare nut wrench

5/16 to 3/8 in. flare nut wrench

7/16 to 1/2 in. flare nut wrench

1/2 to 9/16 in. flare nut wrench

Diagonal pliers

Needle pliers

Adjustable-jaw pliers

Locking pliers

Snap-ring pliers

Stripping or crimping pliers

Ball-peen hammer

Rubber hammer

Dead-blow hammer

Five-piece standard screwdriver set

Four-piece Phillips screwdriver set

#15 Torx screwdriver

#20 Torx screwdriver

Awl

Mill file

Center punch

Pin punches (assorted sizes)

Chisel

Utility knife

Valve core tool

Filter wrench (large filters)

Filter wrench (smaller filters)

Test light

Feeler gauge

Scraper

Pinch bar

Magnet

FIGURE 1–50 A typical beginning technician tool set that includes the basic tools to get started.

FIGURE 1–51 A typical large tool box, showing just one of many drawers.

TOOL SETS AND ACCESSORIES

A beginning service technician may wish to start with a small set of tools before purchasing an expensive tool set. ● **SEE FIGURES 1–50 AND 1–51.**

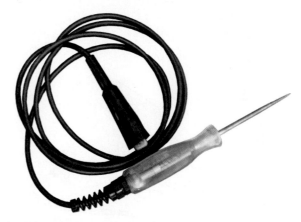

FIGURE 1–52 A typical 12 volt test light.

 **TECH TIP**

Need to Borrow a Tool More Than Twice? Buy It!

Most service technicians agree that it is okay for a beginning technician to borrow a tool occasionally. However, if a tool has to be borrowed more than twice, then be sure to purchase it as soon as possible. Also, whenever you borrow a tool, be sure that you clean the tool and let the technician you borrowed the tool from know that you are returning it. These actions will help in any future dealings with other technicians.

ELECTRICAL WORK HAND TOOLS

TEST LIGHT A test light is used to test for electricity. A typical automotive test light consists of a clear plastic screwdriver-like handle that contains a light bulb. A wire is attached to one terminal of the bulb, which the technician connects to a clean metal part of the vehicle. The other end of the bulb is attached to a point that can be used to test for electricity at a connector or wire. When there is power at the point and a good connection at the other end, the light bulb lights. ● **SEE FIGURE 1–52.**

ELECTRIC SOLDERING GUNS This type of soldering gun is usually powered by 110 volt AC and often has two power settings expressed in watts. A typical electric soldering gun will produce from 85 to 300 watts of heat at the tip, which is more than adequate for soldering.

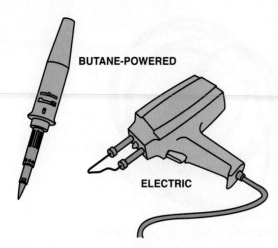

BUTANE-POWERED

ELECTRIC

FIGURE 1–53 Electric and butane-powered soldering guns used to make electrical repairs. Soldering guns are sold by the wattage rating: The higher the wattage, the greater the amount of heat created. Most solder guns used for automotive electrical work usually fall within the 60 to 160 watt range.

ELECTRICAL WORK HAND TOOLS (CONTINUED)

- **Electric soldering pencil.** This type of soldering iron is less expensive and creates less heat than an electric soldering gun. A typical electric soldering pencil (iron) creates 30 to 60 watts of heat and is suitable for soldering smaller wires and connections.

- **Butane-powered soldering iron.** A butane-powered soldering iron is portable and very useful for automotive service work because an electrical cord is not needed. Most butane-powered soldering irons produce about 60 watts of heat, which is enough for most automotive soldering. ● **SEE FIGURE 1–53.**

ELECTRICAL WORK HAND TOOLS
In addition to a soldering iron, most service technicians who do electrical-related work should have the following:

- Wire cutters
- Wire strippers
- Wire crimpers
- Heat gun for heat shrink tubing

DIGITAL METER
A digital meter is a necessary tool for electrical diagnosis and troubleshooting. A digital multimeter, abbreviated DMM, is usually capable of measuring the following units of electricity.

- DC volts
- AC volts
- Ohms
- Amperes

HAND TOOL MAINTENANCE

Most hand tools are constructed of rust-resistant metals but they can still rust or corrode if not properly maintained. For best results and long tool life, the following steps should be taken.

- Clean each tool before placing it back into the tool box.
- Keep tools separated. Moisture on metal tools will start to rust more readily if the tools are in contact with another metal tool.
- Line the drawers of the tool box with a material that will prevent the tools from moving as the drawers are opened and closed. This helps to quickly locate the proper tool and size.
- Release the tension on all clicker-type torque wrenches.
- Keep the tool box secure.

TROUBLE LIGHTS

INCANDESCENT *Incandescent lights* use a filament that produces light when electric current flows through the bulb. This was the standard **trouble light,** also called a *work light,* for many years until safety issues caused most shops to switch to safer fluorescent or LED lights. If incandescent light bulbs are used, try to locate bulbs that are rated "rough service," which is designed to withstand shock and vibration more than conventional light bulbs.

FLUORESCENT A trouble light is an essential piece of shop equipment, and for safety, should be fluorescent rather than incandescent. Incandescent light bulbs can scatter or break if

FIGURE 1–55 A typical 1/2 in. drive air impact wrench. The direction of rotation can be changed to loosen or tighten a fastener.

FIGURE 1–54 A fluorescent trouble light operates cooler and is safer to use in the shop because it is protected against accidental breakage where gasoline or other flammable liquids would happen to come in contact with the light.

FIGURE 1–56 A typical battery-powered 3/8 in. drive impact wrench.

gasoline were to be splashed onto the bulb, creating a serious fire hazard. Fluorescent light tubes are not as likely to be broken and are usually protected by a clear plastic enclosure. Trouble lights are usually attached to a retractor, which can hold 20 to 50 feet of electrical cord. ● **SEE FIGURE 1–54.**

LED TROUBLE LIGHT Light-emitting diode (LED) trouble lights are excellent to use because they are shock resistant, long lasting, and do not represent a fire hazard. Some trouble lights are battery powered and therefore can be used in places where an attached electrical cord could present problems.

AIR AND ELECTRICALLY OPERATED TOOLS

IMPACT WRENCH An impact wrench, either air or electrically powered, is used to remove and install fasteners. The air-operated 1/2 in. drive impact wrench is the most commonly used unit. ● **SEE FIGURE 1–55.**

Electrically powered impact wrenches commonly include:

■ Battery-powered units. ● **SEE FIGURE 1–56.**

■ 110 volt AC-powered units. This type of impact is very useful, especially if compressed air is not readily available.

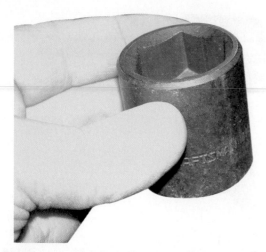

FIGURE 1–57 A black impact socket. Always use an impact-type socket whenever using an impact wrench to avoid the possibility of shattering the socket, which could cause personal injury.

AIR AND ELECTRICALLY OPERATED TOOLS
(CONTINUED)

FIGURE 1–58 An air ratchet is a very useful tool that allows fast removal and installation of fasteners, especially in areas that are difficult to reach or do not have room enough to move a hand ratchet or wrench.

> ☠ **WARNING**
>
> Always use impact sockets with impact wrenches, and always wear eye protection in case the socket or fastener shatters. Input sockets are thicker walled and constructed with premium alloy steel. They are hardened with a black oxide finish to help prevent corrosion and distinguish them from regular sockets. ● SEE FIGURE 1–57.

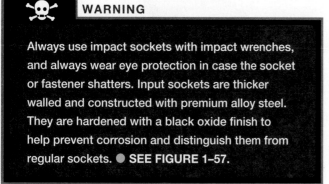

FIGURE 1–59 This typical die grinder surface preparation kit includes the air-operated die grinder and a variety of sanding disks for smoothing surfaces or removing rust.

AIR RATCHET An air ratchet is used to remove and install fasteners that would normally be removed or installed using a ratchet and a socket. ● SEE FIGURE 1–58.

DIE GRINDER A die grinder is a commonly used air-powered tool which can also be used to sand or remove gaskets and rust. ● SEE FIGURE 1–59.

BENCH-MOUNTED OR PEDESTAL-MOUNTED GRINDER

These high-powered grinders can be equipped with a wire brush wheel and/or a stone wheel.

- **Wire brush wheel.** This type is used to clean threads of bolts and to remove gaskets from sheet metal engine parts.
- **Stone wheel.** This type is used to grind metal and to remove the mushroom from the top of punches or chisels. ● SEE FIGURE 1–60.

FIGURE 1–60 A typical pedestal grinder with a wire wheel on the left side and a stone wheel on the right side. Even though this machine is equipped with guards, safety glasses or a face shield should always be worn whenever using a grinder or wire wheel.

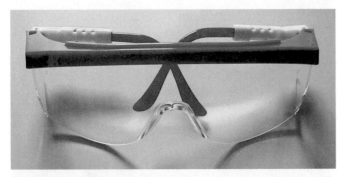

FIGURE 1–61 Safety glasses should be worn at all times when working on or around any vehicle or servicing any components.

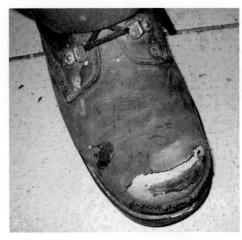

FIGURE 1–62 Steel-toed shoes are a worthwhile investment to help prevent foot injury due to falling objects. Even these well-worn shoes can protect the feet of this service technician.

> ☠ **WARNING**
>
> Always wear a face shield when using a wire wheel or a grinder.

Most **bench grinders** are equipped with a grinder wheel (stone) on one end or the other of a wire brush. A bench grinder is a useful piece of shop equipment, and the wire wheel end can be used for the following:

- Cleaning threads of bolts
- Cleaning gaskets from sheet metal parts, such as steel valve covers

CAUTION: Only use a steel wire brush on steel or iron components. If a steel wire brush is used on aluminum or copper-based metal parts, it can remove metal from the part.

The grinding stone end of the bench grinder can be used for the following:

- Sharpening blades and drill bits
- Grinding off the heads of rivets or parts
- Sharpening sheet metal parts for custom fitting

PERSONAL PROTECTIVE EQUIPMENT

Service technicians should wear protective devices to prevent personal injury. The personal protective devices include the following equipment.

SAFETY GLASSES Be sure that safety glasses meet standard ANSI Z87.1. They should be worn at all times while servicing any vehicle. ● **SEE FIGURE 1–61.**

STEEL-TOED SAFETY SHOES Steel-toed safety shoes help prevent foot injury due to falling objects. ● **SEE FIGURE 1–62.** If safety shoes are not available, then leather-topped shoes offer more protection than canvas or cloth.

BUMP CAP Service technicians working under a vehicle should wear a **bump cap** to protect the head against under-vehicle objects and pads of the lift. ● **SEE FIGURE 1–63.**

HEARING PROTECTION Hearing protection should be worn if the sound around you requires that you raise your voice (sound level higher than 90 dB). For example, a typical lawnmower produces noise at a level of about 110 dB. This means that everyone who uses a lawnmower or other lawn or garden equipment should wear ear protection.

GLOVES Many technicians wear gloves not only to help keep their hands clean but also to help protect their skin from the effects of dirty engine oil and other possibly hazardous materials.

FIGURE 1–63 One version of a bump cap is a molded plastic insert worn inside a regular cloth cap.

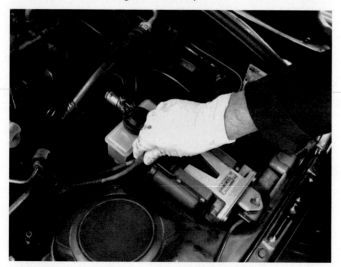

FIGURE 1–64 Protective gloves are available in several sizes and materials.

PERSONAL PROTECTIVE EQUIPMENT (CONTINUED)

Several types of gloves and their characteristics are as follows:

- **Latex surgical gloves.** These gloves are relatively inexpensive, but tend to stretch, swell, and weaken when exposed to gas, oil, or solvents.
- **Vinyl gloves.** These gloves are also inexpensive and are not affected by gas, oil, or solvents.
- **Polyurethane gloves.** These gloves are more expensive, yet strong. Even though these gloves are also not affected by gas, oil, or solvents, they tend to be slippery.
- **Nitrile gloves.** These gloves are exactly like latex gloves, but are not affected by gas, oil, or solvents, yet they tend to be expensive.
- **Mechanic's gloves.** These gloves are usually made of synthetic leather and spandex and provide thermo protection, as well as protection from dirt and grime.

● **SEE FIGURE 1–64.**

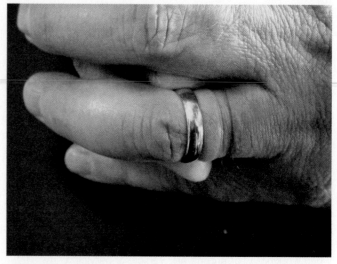

FIGURE 1–65 Remove all jewelry before performing service work on any vehicle.

SAFETY PRECAUTIONS

Besides wearing personal safety equipment, the following actions should be performed to keep safe in the shop.

- Remove jewelry that may get caught on something or act as a conductor to an exposed electrical circuit. ● **SEE FIGURE 1–65.**
- Take care of your hands. Keep your hands clean by washing with soap and hot water that is at least 110°F (43°C).
- Tie back long hair to keep from getting it caught in moving components.
- Avoid loose or dangling clothing.
- When lifting any object, get a secure grip with solid footing. Keep the load close to your body to minimize the strain. Lift with your legs and arms, not your back.
- Do not twist your body when carrying a load. Instead, pivot your feet to help prevent strain on the spine.
- Ask for help when moving or lifting heavy objects.
- Push a heavy object rather than pull it. (This is opposite to the way you should work with tools—never push a wrench! If you do and a bolt or nut loosens, your entire weight is used to propel your hand(s) forward. This usually results in cuts, bruises, or other painful injury.)
- Always connect an exhaust hose to the tailpipe of any running vehicle to help prevent the buildup of carbon monoxide inside a closed garage space. ● **SEE FIGURE 1–66.**
- When standing, keep your objects, parts, and tools between chest height and waist height. If seated, work at tasks that are at elbow height.
- Always be sure the hood is securely held open.

FIGURE 1–66 Always connect an exhaust hose to the tailpipe of a vehicle to be run inside a building.

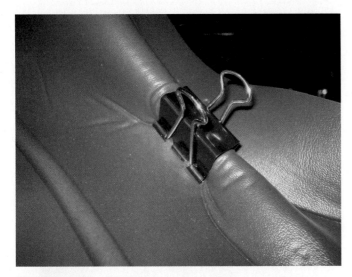

FIGURE 1–67 A binder clip keeps a fender cover from falling off.

FIGURE 1–68 Covering the interior as soon as the vehicle comes in for service helps improve customer satisfaction.

VEHICLE PROTECTION

FENDER COVERS Whenever working under the hood of any vehicle be sure to use fender covers. They not only help protect the vehicle from possible damage but also provide a clean surface to place parts and tools. The major problem with using fender covers is that they tend to move and often fall off the vehicle. To help prevent the fender covers from falling off, secure them to a lip of the fender using a *binder clip* available at most office supply stores. ● **SEE FIGURE 1–67.**

INTERIOR PROTECTION Always protect the interior of the vehicle from accidental damage or dirt and grease by covering the seat, steering wheel, and floor with a protective covering. ● **SEE FIGURE 1–68.**

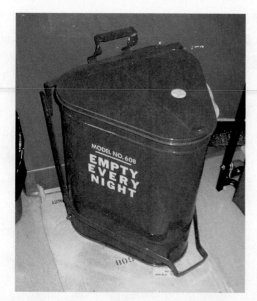

FIGURE 1–69 All oily shop cloths should be stored in a metal container equipped with a lid to help prevent spontaneous combustion.

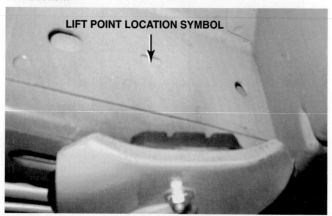

LIFT POINT LOCATION SYMBOL

FIGURE 1–70 Most newer vehicles have a triangle symbol indicating the recommended hoisting lift location.

SAFETY IN LIFTING (HOISTING) A VEHICLE

Many chassis and underbody service procedures require that the vehicle be hoisted or lifted off the ground. The simplest methods involve the use of drive-on ramps or a floor jack and safety (jack) stands, whereas in-ground or surface-mounted lifts provide greater access.

Setting the pads is a critical part of this hoisting procedure. Owner's, shop and service manuals include recommended locations to be used when hoisting (lifting) a vehicle. Newer vehicles have a triangle decal on the driver's door indicating the recommended lift points. The recommended standards for the lift points and lifting procedures are found in SAE standard JRP- 2184. ● **SEE FIGURE 1–70.**

(a)

(b)

FIGURE 1–71 (a) Tall safety stands can be used to provide additional support for the vehicle while on the hoist.
(b) A block of wood should be used to avoid the possibility of doing damage to components supported by the stand.

These recommendations typically include the following points.

1. The vehicle should be centered on the lift or hoist so as not to overload one side or put too much force either forward or rearward. ● **SEE FIGURE 1–71.**

2. The pads of the lift should be spread as far apart as possible to provide a stable platform.

FIGURE 1–72 This training vehicle fell from the hoist because the pads were not set correctly. No one was hurt, but the vehicle was damaged.

(a)

(b)

FIGURE 1–73 (a) An assortment of hoist pad adaptors that are often needed to safely hoist many pickup trucks, vans, and sport utility vehicles (SUVs). (b) A view from underneath a Chevrolet pickup truck showing how the pad extensions are used to attach the hoist lifting pad to contact the frame.

3. Each pad should be placed under a portion of the vehicle that is strong and capable of supporting the weight of the vehicle.
   a. Pinch welds at the bottom edge of the body are generally considered to be strong.

CAUTION: Even though pinch weld seams are the recommended location for hoisting many vehicles with unitized bodies (unit-body), care should be taken not to place the pad(s) too far forward or rearward. Incorrect placement of the vehicle on the lift could cause the vehicle to be imbalanced, and the vehicle could fall. This is exactly what happened to the vehicle in ● FIGURE 1–72.

   b. Boxed areas of the body are the best places to position the pads on a vehicle without a frame. Be careful to note whether the arms of the lift might come into contact with other parts of the vehicle before the pad touches the intended location. Commonly damaged areas include the following:

   (1) Rocker panel moldings
   (2) Exhaust system (including catalytic converter)
   (3) Tires or body panels (● **SEE FIGURES 1–73 AND 1–74.**)

(a)

(b)

FIGURE 1–74 (a) The pad arm is just contacting the rocker panel of the vehicle. (b) The pad arm has dented the rocker panel on this vehicle because the pad was set too far inward underneath the vehicle.

**SAFETY IN LIFTING
(HOISTING) A VEHICLE (CONTINUED)**

4. The vehicle should be raised about 1 foot (30 centimeters [cm]) off the floor, then stopped and shaken to check for stability. If the vehicle seems to be stable when checked at a short distance from the floor, continue raising the vehicle and continue to view the vehicle until it has reached the desired height. The hoist should be lowered onto the mechanical locks, and then raised off of the locks before lowering.

   CAUTION: Do not look away from the vehicle while it is being raised (or lowered) on a hoist. Often one side or one end of the hoist can stop or fail, resulting in the vehicle being slanted enough to slip or fall, creating physical damage not only to the vehicle and/or hoist but also to the technician or others who may be nearby.

   HINT: Most hoists can be safely placed at any desired height. For ease while working, the area where you are working should be at chest level. When working on brakes or suspension components, it is not necessary to work on them down near the floor or over your head. Raise the hoist so that the components are at chest level.

5. Before lowering the hoist, you must release the safety latch(es) and reverse the direction of the controls. The speed downward is often adjusted to be as slow as possible for additional safety.

FLOOR JACKS

DESCRIPTION Floor jacks are used to lift one side or end of a vehicle. They are portable and relatively inexpensive and must be used with safety (jack) stands.

OPERATING PRINCIPLES A floor jack uses an hydraulic cylinder to raise a vehicle. ● **SEE FIGURE 1–75.**

A jack operates as follows:

- When the jack handle is twisted clockwise, the release valve is closed.
- When the jack handle is moved upward, hydraulic oil is drawn from the reservoir into the pump assembly.
- When the jack handle is moved downward, the oil is forced into the hydraulic cylinder, which forces the ram out and the lifting pad upward.
- When the cylinder ram reaches its maximum height, a bypass valve opens, which directs the oil back into the reservoir.
- When the jack handle is twisted counterclockwise, the release valve opens and allows the oil to flow back into the reservoir.

CAUTION: The valve must be closed to allow the jack handle to remain in the upright position. If the release valve is opened, the jack handle will drop toward the floor.

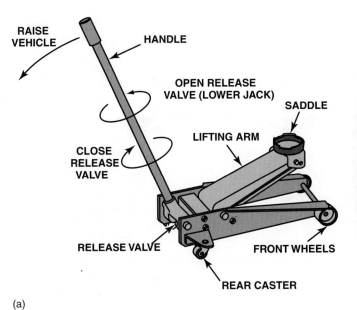

(a)　　　　　　　　　　　　　　　　　　　　　　　　(b)

FIGURE 1–75 (a) A typical 3 ton (6,000 lb) capacity hydraulic jack. (b) Whenever a vehicle is raised off the ground, a safety stand should be placed under the frame, axle, or body to support the weight of the vehicle.

SAFE USE OF A FLOOR JACK

To safely use a floor jack, perform the following steps.

STEP 1 Read, understand, and follow all operating and safety items listed in the instructions.

STEP 2 Be sure the vehicle is on a flat, level, and hard surface.

STEP 3 Chock (block) the wheels of the vehicle to prevent it from moving during the lifting operation.

STEP 4 Check vehicle service information to determine the specified lifting point under the vehicle.

STEP 5 Place the lifting pad of the jack under the specified lifting point.

STEP 6 Close the release valve of the jack by rotating the jack handle clockwise. Move the jack handle downward until the lifting pad contacts the vehicle lifting point. Double check that the jack is located in the specified location.

STEP 7 Continue to move the jack handle downward, and then up and down again until the vehicle has been raised to the desired height.

STEP 8 Place safety (jack) stand(s) under the vehicle.

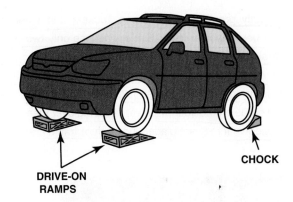

FIGURE 1–76 Drive-on ramps are dangerous to use. The wheels on the ground level must be chocked (blocked) to prevent accidental movement down the ramp.

STEP 9 To lower the vehicle, raise the vehicle just enough to remove the safety stands, and then rotate the jack handle *slowly* counterclockwise.

DRIVE-ON RAMPS Ramps are an inexpensive way to raise the front or rear of a vehicle. ● **SEE FIGURE 1–76.** Ramps are easy to store, but may be dangerous because they can "kick out" when driving the vehicle onto the ramps.

CAUTION: Professional repair shops do not use ramps because they are dangerous. Use only with extreme care.

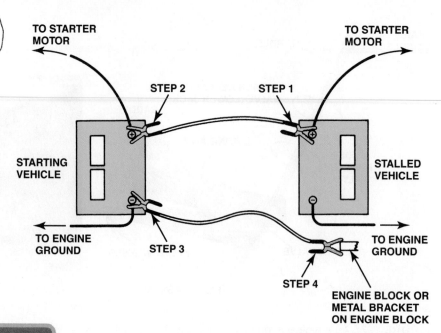

FIGURE 1–77 Jumper cable usage guide. Follow the same connections if using a portable jump box.

TO STARTER MOTOR

TO STARTER MOTOR

STEP 2

STEP 1

STARTING VEHICLE

STALLED VEHICLE

TO ENGINE GROUND

TO ENGINE GROUND

STEP 3

STEP 4

ENGINE BLOCK OR METAL BRACKET ON ENGINE BLOCK

ELECTRICAL CORD SAFETY

Use correctly grounded three-prong sockets and extension cords to operate power tools. Some tools use only two-prong plugs. Make sure these are double insulated and repair or replace any electrical cords that are cut or damaged to prevent the possibility of an electrical shock. When not in use, keep electrical cords off the floor to prevent tripping over them. Tape the cords down if they are placed in high foot traffic areas.

JUMP STARTING AND BATTERY SAFETY

To jump start another vehicle with a dead battery, connect either good quality copper jumper cables as indicated in ● **FIGURE 1–77** or a jump box. The last connection made should always be on the engine block or an engine bracket on the dead vehicle as far from the battery as possible. It is normal for a spark to be created when the jumper cables finally complete the jumping circuit, and this spark could cause an explosion of the gases around the battery. Many newer vehicles have special ground connections built away from the battery just for the purpose of jump starting. Check the owner's manual or service information for the exact location.

Batteries contain acid and should be handled with care to avoid tipping them greater than a 45-degree angle. Always remove jewelry when working around a battery to avoid the possibility of electrical shock or burns, which can occur when the metal comes in contact with a 12 volt circuit and ground, such as the body of the vehicle.

FIGURE 1–78 The air pressure going to the nozzle should be reduced to 30 psi or less to help prevent personal injury.

 SAFETY TIP

Air Hose Safety

Improper use of an air nozzle can cause blindness or deafness. Compressed air must be reduced to less than 30 psi (206 kPa). ● **SEE FIGURE 1–78.** If an air nozzle is used to dry and clean parts, make sure the air stream is directed away from anyone else in the immediate area. Always use an OSHA-approved nozzle with side slits that limit the maximum pressure at the nozzle to 30 PSI. Coil and store air hoses when they are not in use.

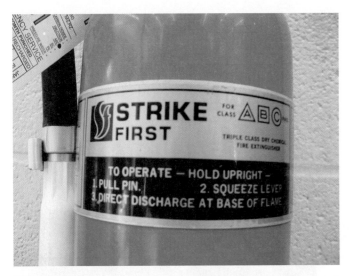

FIGURE 1–79 A typical fire extinguisher designed to be used on type A, B, or C fires.

FIGURE 1–80 A CO_2 fire extinguisher being used on a fire set in an open drum during a demonstration at a fire training center.

FIRE EXTINGUISHERS

There are four **fire extinguisher classes.** Each class should be used on specific fires only, as follows:

- **Class A** is designed for use on general combustibles, such as cloth, paper, and wood.
- **Class B** is designed for use on flammable liquids and greases, including gasoline, oil, thinners, and solvents.
- **Class C** is used only on electrical fires.
- **Class D** is effective only on combustible metals such as powdered aluminum, sodium, or magnesium.

The class rating is clearly marked on the side of every fire extinguisher. Many extinguishers are good for multiple types of fires. ● **SEE FIGURE 1–79.**

When using a fire extinguisher, remember the word "PASS."

P = Pull the safety pin.

A = Aim the nozzle of the extinguisher at the base of the fire.

S = Squeeze the lever to actuate the extinguisher.

S = Sweep the nozzle from side to side.

● **SEE FIGURE 1–80.**

TYPES OF FIRE EXTINGUISHERS Types of fire extinguishers include the following:

- **Water.** A water fire extinguisher, usually in a pressurized container, is good to use on Class A fires by reducing the temperature to the point where a fire cannot be sustained.
- **Carbon dioxide (CO_2).** A carbon dioxide fire extinguisher is good for almost any type of fire, especially Class B or Class C materials. A CO_2 fire extinguisher works by

FIGURE 1–81 A treated wool blanket is kept in an easy-to-open, wall-mounted holder and should be placed in a central location in the shop.

removing the oxygen from the fire and the cold CO_2 also helps reduce the temperature of the fire.

- **Dry chemical (yellow).** A dry chemical fire extinguisher is good for Class A, B, or C fires by coating the flammable materials, which eliminates the oxygen from the fire. A dry chemical fire extinguisher tends to be very corrosive and will cause damage to electronic devices.

FIRE BLANKETS

Fire blankets are required to be available in the shop areas. If a person is on fire, a fire blanket should be removed from its storage bag and thrown over and around the victim to smother the fire. ● **SEE FIGURE 1–81** showing a typical fire blanket.

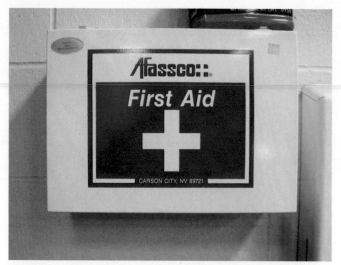

FIGURE 1–82 A first aid box should be centrally located in the shop and kept stocked with the recommended supplies.

FIRST AID AND EYE WASH STATIONS

All shop areas must be equipped with a first aid kit and an eye wash station that are centrally located and kept stocked with emergency supplies. ● **SEE FIGURE 1–82.**

FIRST AID KIT A first aid kit should include:

- Bandages (variety)
- Gauze pads
- Roll gauze
- Iodine swab sticks
- Antibiotic ointment
- Hydrocortisone cream
- Burn gel packets
- Eye wash solution
- Scissors
- Tweezers
- Gloves
- First aid guide

Every shop should have a person trained in first aid. If there is an accident, call for help immediately.

EYE WASH STATION An **eye wash station** should be centrally located and used whenever any liquid or chemical gets into the eyes. If such an emergency does occur, keep eyes in a constant stream of water and call for professional assistance. ● **SEE FIGURE 1–83.**

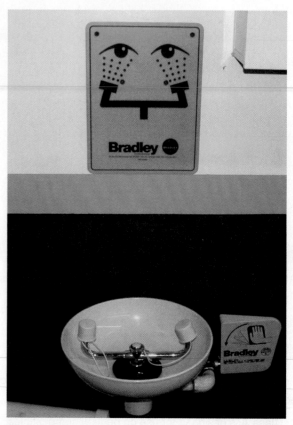

FIGURE 1–83 A typical eye wash station. Often a thorough flushing of the eyes with water is the first and often the best treatment in the event of eye contamination.

+ SAFETY TIP

Infection Control Precautions

Working on a vehicle can result in personal injury including the possibility of being cut or hurt enough to cause bleeding. Some infections such as hepatitis B, HIV (which can cause acquired immunodeficiency syndrome, or AIDS), hepatitis C virus, and others are transmitted in the blood. These infections are commonly called blood-borne pathogens. Report any injury that involves blood to your supervisor and take the necessary precautions to avoid coming in contact with blood from another person.

FIGURE 1–84 A warning label on a Honda hybrid warns that a person can be killed due to the high-voltage circuits under the cover.

FIGURE 1–85 The high-voltage disconnect switch is in the trunk area on a Toyota Prius. High-voltage lineman's gloves should be worn when removing this plug. (Courtesy of Tony Martin)

HYBRID ELECTRIC VEHICLE SAFETY ISSUES

Hybrid electric vehicles (HEVs) use a high-voltage (HV) battery pack and electric motor(s) to help propel the vehicle. ● **SEE FIGURE 1–84** for an example of a typical warning label on a hybrid electric vehicle. The gasoline or diesel engine also is equipped with a generator or a combination starter and an integrated starter generator (ISG) or integrated starter alternator (ISA). To safely work around a hybrid electric vehicle, the high-voltage battery and circuits should be shut off following these steps:

STEP 1 Turn off the ignition key (if equipped) and remove the key from the ignition switch. (This will shut off all high-voltage circuits if the relay[s] is[are] working correctly.)

STEP 2 Disconnect the high-voltage circuits.

 WARNING

Some vehicle manufacturers specify that rubber-insulated *lineman's gloves* be used whenever working around the high-voltage circuits to prevent the danger of electrical shock.

TOYOTA PRIUS The cutoff switch is located in the trunk on the Toyota Prius. To gain access, remove three clips holding the upper left portion of the trunk side cover. To disconnect the high-voltage system, pull the orange handled plug while wearing insulated rubber lineman's gloves. ● **SEE FIGURE 1–85.**

FORD ESCAPE AND MERCURY MARINER Ford and Mercury specify that the following steps should be included when working with the high-voltage (HV) systems of a hybrid vehicle.

- Four orange cones are to be placed at the four corners of the vehicle to create a buffer zone.

- High-voltage insulated gloves are to be worn with an outer leather glove to protect the inner rubber glove from possible damage.

- The service technician should also wear a face shield, and a fiberglass hook should be in the area and used to move a technician in the event of electrocution.

The high-voltage shut-off switch is located in the rear of the vehicle under the right side carpet. ● **SEE FIGURE 1–86.** Rotate the handle to the "service shipping" position, lift it out

FIGURE 1–86 The high-voltage shut-off switch on a Ford Escape hybrid. The switch is located under the carpet at the rear of the vehicle.

FIGURE 1–87 The shut-off switch on a GM parallel hybrid truck is green because this system uses 42 volts instead of higher, and possible fatal, voltages used in other hybrid vehicles.

HYBRID ELECTRIC VEHICLE SAFETY ISSUES (CONTINUED)

to disable the high-voltage circuit, and wait five minutes before removing high-voltage cables.

HONDA CIVIC To totally disable the high-voltage system on a Honda Civic, remove the main fuse (labeled number 1) from the driver's side underhood fuse panel. This should be all that is necessary to shut off the high-voltage circuit. If this is not possible, then remove the rear seat cushion and seat back. Remove the metal switch cover labeled "up" and remove the red locking cover. Move the "battery module switch" down to disable the high-voltage system.

CHEVROLET SILVERADO AND GMC SIERRA PICKUP TRUCK The high-voltage shut-off switch is located under the rear passenger seat on these Chevrolet and GMC vehicles. Remove the cover marked "energy storage box" and turn the green service disconnect switch to the horizontal position to turn off the high-voltage circuits. ● **SEE FIGURE 1–87.**

☠ **WARNING**

Do not touch any orange wiring or component without following the vehicle manufacturer's procedures and wearing the specified personal protective equipment.

1 The first step in hoisting a vehicle is to properly align the vehicle in the center of the stall.

2 Most vehicles will be correctly positioned when the left front tire is centered on the tire pad.

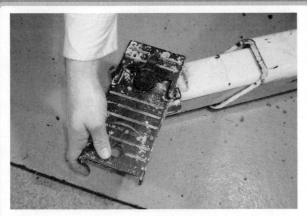

3 The arms can be moved in and out and most pads can be rotated to allow for many different types of vehicle construction.

4 Most lifts are equipped with short pad extensions that are often necessary to use to allow the pad to contact the frame of a vehicle without causing the arm of the lift to hit and damage parts of the body.

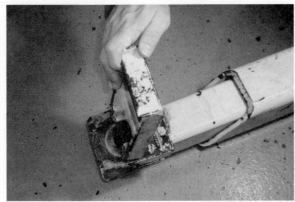

5 Tall pad extensions can also be used to gain access to the frame of a vehicle. This position is needed to safely hoist many pickup trucks, vans, and sport utility vehicles.

6 An additional extension may be necessary to hoist a truck or van equipped with running boards to give the necessary clearance.

CONTINUED ▶

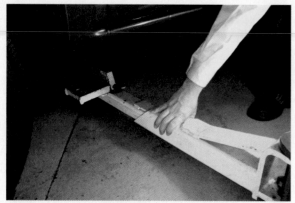

7 Position the pads under the vehicle at the recommended locations.

8 After being sure all pads are correctly positioned, use the electromechanical controls to raise the vehicle.

9 With the vehicle raised one foot (30 cm) off the ground, push down on the vehicle to check to see if it is stable on the pads. If the vehicle rocks, lower the vehicle and reset the pads. The vehicle can be raised to any desired working level. Be sure the safety is engaged before working on or under the vehicle.

10 If raising a vehicle without a frame, place the flat pads under the pinch weld seam to spread the load. If additional clearance is necessary, the pads can be raised as shown.

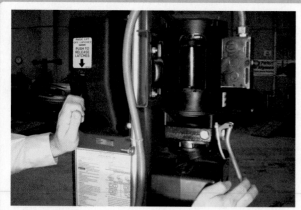

11 When the service work is completed, the hoist should be raised slightly and the safety released before using the hydraulic lever to lower the vehicle.

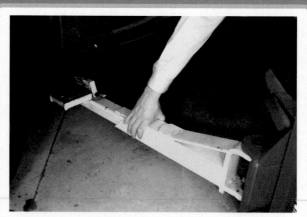

12 After lowering the vehicle, be sure all arms of the lift are moved out of the way before driving the vehicle out of the work stall.

SUMMARY

1. Bolts, studs, and nuts are commonly used as fasteners in the chassis. The sizes for fractional and metric threads are different and are not interchangeable. The grade is the rating of the strength of a fastener.

2. Whenever a vehicle is raised above the ground, it must be supported at a substantial section of the body or frame.

3. Wrenches are available in open end, box end, and combination open and box end.

4. An adjustable wrench should only be used where the proper size is not available.

5. Line wrenches are also called flare-nut wrenches, fitting wrenches, or tube-nut wrenches and are used to remove fuel or refrigerant lines.

6. Sockets are rotated by a ratchet or breaker bar, also called a flex handle.

7. Torque wrenches measure the amount of torque applied to a fastener.

8. Screwdriver types include straight blade (flat tip), Phillips, and Torx.

9. Hammers and mallets come in a variety of sizes and weights.

10. Pliers are a useful tool and are available in many different types, including slip-joint, multigroove, linesman's, diagonal, needle-nose, and locking pliers.

11. Other common hand tools include snap-ring pliers, files, cutters, punches, chisels, and hacksaws.

12. Hybrid electric vehicles should be de-powered if any of the high-voltage components are going to be serviced.

REVIEW QUESTIONS

1. List three precautions that must be taken whenever hoisting (lifting) a vehicle.

2. Describe how to determine the grade of a fastener, including how the markings differ between fractional and metric bolts.

3. List four items that are personal protective equipment (PPE).

4. List the types of fire extinguishers and their usage.

5. Why are wrenches offset 15 degrees?

6. What are the other names for a line wrench?

7. What are the standard automotive drive sizes for sockets?

8. Which type of screwdriver requires the use of a hammer or mallet?

9. What is inside a dead-blow hammer?

10. What type of cutter is available in left and right cutters?

CHAPTER QUIZ

1. The correct location for the pads when hoisting or jacking the vehicle can often be found in the _____.
   a. Service manual
   b. Shop manual
   c. Owner's manual
   d. All of the above

2. For the best working position, the work should be _____.
   a. At neck or head level
   b. At knee or ankle level
   c. Overhead by about 1 foot
   d. At chest or elbow level

3. A high-strength bolt is identified by _____.
   a. A UNC symbol
   b. Lines on the head
   c. Strength letter codes
   d. The coarse threads

4. A fastener that uses threads on both ends is called a _____.
   a. Cap screw
   b. Stud
   c. Machine screw
   d. Crest fastener

5. When working with hand tools, always _____.
   a. Push the wrench—don't pull it toward you
   b. Pull a wrench—don't push it away from you

6. The proper term for Channel Locks is _____.
   a. Vise-Grip
   b. Crescent wrench
   c. Locking pliers
   d. Multigroove adjustable pliers

7. The proper term for Vise-Grip is _____.
   a. Locking pliers
   b. Slip-joint pliers
   c. Side cuts
   d. Multigroove adjustable pliers

8. Two technicians are discussing torque wrenches. Technician A says that a torque wrench is capable of tightening a fastener with more torque than a conventional breaker bar or ratchet. Technician B says that a torque wrench should be calibrated regularly for the most accurate results. Which technician is correct?
   a. Technician A only
   b. Technician B only
   c. Both Technicians A and B
   d. Neither Technician A nor B

9. What type of screwdriver should be used if there is very limited space above the head of the fastener?
   a. Offset screwdriver
   b. Stubby screwdriver
   c. Impact screwdriver
   d. Robertson screwdriver

10. What type of hammer is plastic coated, has a metal casing inside, and is filled with small lead balls?
   a. Dead-blow hammer
   b. Soft-blow hammer
   c. Sledge hammer
   d. Plastic hammer

chapter 2

ENVIRONMENTAL AND HAZARDOUS MATERIALS

OBJECTIVES

After studying Chapter 2, the reader will be able to:

1. Prepare for the ASE assumed knowledge content required by all service technicians to adhere to environmentally appropriate actions and behavior.

2. Define the Occupational Safety and Health Act (OSHA).

3. Explain the term material safety data sheet (MSDS).

4. Identify hazardous waste materials in accordance with state and federal regulations and follow proper safety precautions while handling and disposing of hazardous waste materials.

5. Define the steps required to safely handle and store automotive chemicals and waste.

KEY TERMS

Aboveground storage tank (AGST) 45
Asbestosis 43
BCI 47
CAA 42
CFR 41
EPA 41
Hazardous waste materials 41
HEPA vacuum 43

Mercury 49
MSDS 42
OSHA 41
RCRA 42
Right-to-know laws 41
Solvent 43
Used oil 44
UST 45
WHMIS 42

HAZARDOUS WASTE

When handling hazardous waste material, one must always wear the proper protective clothing and equipment detailed in the right-to-know laws. This includes respirator equipment. All recommended procedures must be followed accurately. Personal injury may result from improper clothing, equipment, and procedures when handling hazardous materials.

Hazardous waste materials are chemicals, or components, that the shop no longer needs that pose a danger to the environment and people if they are disposed of in ordinary garbage cans or sewers. However, no material is considered hazardous waste until the shop has finished using it and is ready to dispose of it.

FEDERAL AND STATE LAWS

OCCUPATIONAL SAFETY AND HEALTH ACT The United States Congress passed the **Occupational Safety and Health Act (OSHA)** in 1970. This legislation was designed to assist and encourage the citizens of the United States in their efforts to ensure the following:

- Safe and healthful working conditions, by providing research, information, education, and training in the field of occupational safety and health
- Safe and healthful working conditions for working men and women, by authorizing enforcement of the standards developed under the act

Because about 25% of workers are exposed to health and safety hazards on the job, the OSHA standards are necessary to monitor, control, and educate workers regarding health and safety in the workplace.

EPA The **Environmental Protection Agency (EPA)** publishes a list of hazardous materials that is included in the **Code of Federal Regulations (CFR)**. The EPA considers waste hazardous if it is included on their list of hazardous materials, or it has one or more of the following characteristics.

- **Reactive.** Any material that reacts violently with water or other chemicals is considered hazardous.
- **Corrosive.** If a material burns the skin, or dissolves metals and other materials, a technician should consider it hazardous. A pH scale is used, with the number 7 indicating neutral. Pure water has a pH of 7. Lower numbers indicate an acidic solution and higher numbers indicate a caustic solution. If a material releases cyanide gas, hydrogen sulfide gas, or similar gases when exposed to low pH acid solutions, it is considered hazardous.

- **Toxic.** Materials are hazardous if they leak one or more of eight different heavy metals in concentrations greater than 100 times the primary drinking water standard.
- **Ignitable.** A liquid is hazardous if it has a flash point below 140°F (60°C), and a solid is hazardous if it ignites spontaneously.
- **Radioactive.** Any substance that emits measurable levels of radiation is radioactive. When individuals bring containers of a highly radioactive substance into the shop environment, qualified personnel with the appropriate equipment must test them.

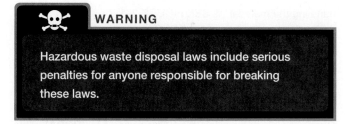

WARNING

Hazardous waste disposal laws include serious penalties for anyone responsible for breaking these laws.

RIGHT-TO-KNOW LAWS The **right-to-know laws** state that employees have a right to know when the materials they use at work are hazardous. The right-to-know laws started with the Hazard Communication Standard published by the Occupational Safety and Health Administration (OSHA) in 1983. Originally, this document was intended for chemical companies and manufacturers that required employees to handle hazardous materials in their work situation, but the federal courts have decided to apply these laws to all companies, including automotive service shops. Under the right-to-know laws, the employer has responsibilities regarding the handling of hazardous materials by their employees. All employees must be trained about the types of hazardous materials they will encounter in the workplace. The employees must be informed about their rights under legislation regarding the handling of hazardous materials.

MATERIAL SAFETY DATA SHEETS All hazardous materials must be properly labeled, and information about each hazardous material must be posted on **material safety data sheets (MSDS)** available from the manufacturer. In Canada, MSDS are called **workplace hazardous materials information systems (WHMIS)**.

The employer has a responsibility to place MSDS where they are easily accessible by all employees. These sheets provide the following information about the hazardous material: chemical name, physical characteristics, protective handling equipment, explosion/fire hazards, incompatible materials, health hazards, medical conditions aggravated by exposure, emergency and first aid procedures, safe handling, and spill/leak procedures.

The employer also has a responsibility to ensure that all hazardous materials are properly labeled. The label information must include health, fire, and reactivity hazards posed by the material, as well as the protective equipment necessary to handle the material. The manufacturer must supply all warning and precautionary information about hazardous materials. This information must be read and understood by the employee before handling the material. ● **SEE FIGURE 2–1.**

RESOURCE CONSERVATION AND RECOVERY ACT

Federal and state laws control the disposal of hazardous waste materials and every shop employee must be familiar with these laws. Hazardous waste disposal laws include the **Resource Conservation and Recovery Act (RCRA)**. This law states that hazardous material users are responsible for hazardous materials from the time they become a waste until the proper waste disposal is completed. Many shops hire an independent hazardous waste hauler to dispose of hazardous waste material. The shop owner, or manager, should have a written contract with the hazardous waste hauler. Rather than have hazardous waste material hauled to an approved hazardous waste disposal site, a shop may choose to recycle the

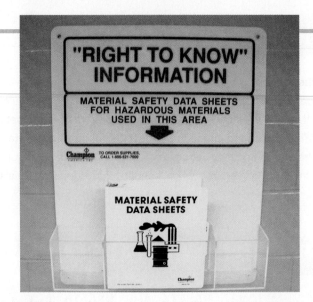

FIGURE 2–1 Material safety data sheets (MSDS) should be readily available for use by anyone in the area who may come into contact with hazardous materials.

material in the shop. Therefore, the user must store hazardous waste material properly and safely, and be responsible for the transportation of this material until it arrives at an approved hazardous waste disposal site, where it can be processed according to the law. The RCRA controls the following types of automotive waste.

- Paint and body repair products waste
- Solvents for parts and equipment cleaning
- Batteries and battery acid
- Mild acids used for metal cleaning and preparation
- Waste oil, and engine coolants or antifreeze
- Air-conditioning refrigerants and oils
- Engine oil filters

CLEAN AIR ACT Air-conditioning (A/C) systems and refrigerant are regulated by the **Clean Air Act (CAA)**, Title VI, Section 609. Technician certification and service equipment is also regulated. Any technician working on automotive A/C systems must be certified. A/C refrigerants must not be released or vented into the atmosphere, and used refrigerants must be recovered.

Friction materials such as brake and clutch linings often contain asbestos. While asbestos has been eliminated from most original equipment friction materials, the automotive service technician cannot know whether the vehicle being serviced is or is not equipped with friction materials containing asbestos. It is important that all friction materials be handled as if they contain asbestos.

Asbestos exposure can cause scar tissue to form in the lungs. This condition is called **asbestosis**. It gradually causes increasing shortness of breath, and the scarring to the lungs is permanent.

Even low exposures to asbestos can cause *mesothelioma*, a type of fatal cancer of the lining of the chest or abdominal cavity. Asbestos exposure can also increase the risk of *lung cancer* as well as cancer of the voice box, stomach, and large intestine. It usually takes 15 to 30 years or more for cancer or asbestos lung scarring to show up after exposure. (Scientists call this the *latency period*.)

Government agencies recommend that asbestos exposure be eliminated or controlled to the lowest level possible. These agencies have developed recommendations and standards that the automotive service technician and equipment manufacturer should follow. These U.S. federal agencies include the National Institute for Occupational Safety and Health (NIOSH), Occupational Safety and Health Administration (OSHA), and Environmental Protection Agency (EPA).

ASBESTOS OSHA STANDARDS
The Occupational Safety and Health Administration (OSHA) has established three levels of asbestos exposure. Any vehicle service establishment that does either brake or clutch work must limit employee exposure to asbestos to less than 0.2 fibers per cubic centimeter (cc) as determined by an air sample.

If the level of exposure to employees is greater than specified, corrective measures must be performed and a large fine may be imposed.

NOTE: Research has found that worn asbestos fibers such as those from automotive brakes or clutches may not be as hazardous as first believed. Worn asbestos fibers do not have sharp flared ends that can latch on to tissue, but rather are worn down to a dust form that resembles talc. Grinding or sawing operations on unworn brake shoes or clutch discs *will* contain *harmful* asbestos fibers. To limit health damage, always use proper handling procedures while working around any component that may contain asbestos.

ASBESTOS EPA REGULATIONS
The federal Environmental Protection Agency (EPA) has established procedures for the removal and disposal of asbestos. The EPA procedures require that products containing asbestos be "wetted" to prevent the asbestos fibers from becoming airborne. According to the EPA, asbestos-containing materials can be disposed of as regular waste. Only when asbestos becomes airborne is it considered to be hazardous.

ASBESTOS HANDLING GUIDELINES
The air in the shop area can be tested by a testing laboratory, but this can be expensive. Tests have determined that asbestos levels can easily be kept below the recommended levels by using a liquid, like water, or a special vacuum.

NOTE: Even though asbestos is being removed from brake and clutch lining materials, the service technician cannot tell whether the old brake pads, shoes, or clutch discs contain asbestos. Therefore, to be safe, the technician should assume that all brake pads, shoes, or clutch discs contain asbestos.

- **HEPA vacuum.** A special **high-efficiency particulate air (HEPA) vacuum** system has been proven to be effective in keeping asbestos exposure levels below 0.1 fibers per cubic centimeter.
- **Solvent spray.** Many technicians use an aerosol can of brake cleaning solvent to wet the brake dust and prevent it from becoming airborne. A **solvent** is a liquid used to dissolve dirt, grime, or solid particles. Commercial brake cleaners are available that use a concentrated cleaner mixed with water. ● SEE FIGURE 2–2.

The waste liquid is filtered, and when dry, the filter can be disposed of as solid waste.

CAUTION: Never use compressed air to blow brake dust. The fine, talclike brake dust can create a health hazard even if asbestos is not present or is present in dust rather than fiber form.

- **Disposal of brake dust and brake shoes.** The hazard of asbestos occurs when asbestos fibers are airborne. Once the asbestos has been wetted down, it is then considered to be solid waste, rather than hazardous waste. Old brake shoes and pads should be enclosed, preferably in a plastic bag, to help prevent any of the brake material from becoming airborne. *Always follow current federal and local laws concerning disposal of all waste.*

USED OIL

Used oil is any petroleum-based or synthetic oil that has been used. During normal use, impurities such as dirt, metal scrapings, water, or chemicals can get mixed in with the oil. Eventually, this used oil must be replaced with virgin or re-refined oil. The EPA's used oil management standards include a three-pronged approach to determine if a substance meets the definition of *used oil*. To meet the EPA's definition of used oil, a substance must meet each of the following three criteria.

- **Origin.** The first criterion for identifying used oil is based on the oil's origin. Used oil must have been refined from crude oil or made from synthetic materials. Animal and vegetable oils are excluded from the EPA's definition of used oil.

- **Use.** The second criterion is based on whether and how the oil is used. Oils used as lubricants, hydraulic fluids, heat transfer fluids, and for other similar purposes are considered used oil. Unused oil, such as bottom clean-out waste from virgin fuel oil storage tanks or virgin fuel oil recovered from a spill, does not meet the EPA's definition of used oil because these oils have never been "used." The EPA's definition also excludes products used as cleaning agents, as well as certain petroleum-derived products like antifreeze and kerosene.

- **Contaminants.** The third criterion is based on whether or not the oil is contaminated with either physical or chemical impurities. In other words, to meet the EPA's definition, used oil must become contaminated as a result of being used. This aspect of the EPA's definition includes residues and contaminants generated from handling, storing, and processing used oil.

NOTE: The release of only 1 gallon of used oil (a typical oil change) can make 1 million gallons of fresh water undrinkable.

If used oil is dumped down the drain and enters a sewage treatment plant, concentrations as small as 50 to 100 parts per million (PPM) in the waste water can foul sewage treatment processes. Never mix a listed hazardous waste, gasoline, waste water, halogenated solvent, antifreeze, or an unknown waste material with used oil. Adding any of these substances will cause the used oil to become contaminated, which classifies it as hazardous waste.

FIGURE 2–2 All brakes should be moistened with water or solvent to help prevent brake dust from becoming airborne.

USED BRAKE FLUID

Most brake fluid is made from polyglycol, is water soluble, and can be considered hazardous if it has absorbed metals from the brake system.

STORAGE AND DISPOSAL OF BRAKE FLUID

- Collect brake fluid in containers clearly marked to indicate that it is dedicated for that purpose.
- If your waste brake fluid is hazardous, manage it appropriately and use only an authorized waste receiver for its disposal.
- If your waste brake fluid is nonhazardous (such as old, but unused), determine from your local solid waste collection provider what should be done for its proper disposal.
- Do not mix brake fluid with used engine oil.
- Do not pour brake fluid down drains or onto the ground.
- Recycle brake fluid through a registered recycler.

STORAGE AND DISPOSAL OF USED OIL Once oil has been used, it can be collected, recycled, and used over and over again. An estimated 380 million gallons of used oil are recycled each year. Recycled used oil can sometimes be used again for the same job or can take on a completely different task. For example, used engine oil can be re-refined and sold at the store as engine oil or processed for furnace fuel oil. After collecting used oil in an appropriate container, such as a 55 gallon steel drum, the material must be disposed of in one of two ways:

1. Shipped offsite for recycling

2. Burned in an onsite or offsite EPA-approved heater for energy recovery

Used oil must be stored in compliance with an existing **underground storage tank (UST)** or an **aboveground storage tank (AGST)** standard, or kept in separate containers. ● **SEE FIGURE 2–3.** Containers are portable receptacles, such as a 55 gallon steel drum.

- **Keep used oil storage drums in good condition.** This means that they should be covered, secured from vandals, properly labeled, and maintained in compliance with local fire codes. Frequent inspections for leaks, corrosion, and spillage are an essential part of container maintenance.

- **Never store used oil in anything other than tanks and storage containers.** Used oil may also be stored in units that are permitted to store regulated hazardous waste.

- **Follow used oil filter disposal regulations.** Used oil filters contain used engine oil that may be hazardous. Before an oil filter is placed into the trash or sent to be recycled, it must be drained using one of the following hot draining methods approved by the EPA.

  - Puncture the filter antidrain back valve or filter dome end and hot drain for at least 12 hours

  - Hot drain and crush

  - Dismantle and hot drain

  - Use another hot draining method to remove all used oil from the filter

After the oil has been drained from the oil filter, the filter housing can be disposed of in any of the following ways.

- Sent for recycling

- Picked up by a service contract company

- Disposed of in regular trash

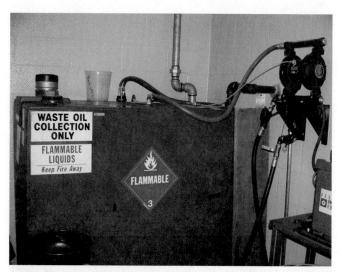

FIGURE 2–3 A typical aboveground oil storage tank.

SOLVENTS

The major sources of chemical danger are liquid and aerosol brake cleaning fluids that contain chlorinated hydrocarbon solvents. Several other chemicals that do not deplete the ozone, such as heptane, hexane, and xylene, are now being used in nonchlorinated brake cleaning solvents. Some manufacturers are also producing solvents they describe as environmentally responsible, which are biodegradable and noncarcinogenic (not cancer causing).

There is no specific standard for physical contact with chlorinated hydrocarbon solvents or the chemicals replacing them. All contact should be avoided whenever possible. The law requires an employer to provide appropriate protective equipment and ensure proper work practices by an employee handling these chemicals.

EFFECTS OF CHEMICAL POISONING The effects of exposure to chlorinated hydrocarbon and other types of solvents can take many forms. Short-term exposure at low levels can cause one or more of the following symptoms.

- Headache

- Nausea

- Drowsiness

- Dizziness

- Lack of coordination

- Unconsciousness

It may also cause irritation of the eyes, nose, and throat, and flushing of the face and neck. Short-term exposure to higher concentrations can cause liver damage with symptoms such as yellow jaundice or dark urine. Liver damage may not become evident until several weeks after the exposure.

FIGURE 2–4 Washing hands and removing jewelry are two important safety habits all service technicians should practice.

FIGURE 2–5 Typical fireproof flammable storage cabinet.

SOLVENTS (CONTINUED)

 SAFETY TIP

Hand Safety

Service technicians should wash their hands with soap and water after handling engine oil or differential or transmission fluids, or wear protective rubber gloves. Another safety hint is that the service technician should not wear watches, rings, or other jewelry that could come in contact with electrical or moving parts of a vehicle. ● **SEE FIGURE 2–4.**

SOLVENT HAZARDOUS AND REGULATORY STATUS

Most solvents are classified as hazardous wastes. Other characteristics of solvents include the following:

- Solvents with flash points below 140°F (25°C) are considered flammable and, like gasoline, are federally regulated by the Department of Transportation (DOT).

- Solvents and oils with flash points above 140°F (25°C) are considered combustible and, like engine oil, are also regulated by the DOT. All flammable items must be stored in a fireproof container. ● **SEE FIGURE 2–5.**

It is the responsibility of the repair shop to determine if its spent solvent is hazardous waste. Waste solvents that are considered hazardous waste have a flash point below 140°F (60°C). Hot water or aqueous parts cleaners may be used to avoid disposing of spent solvent as hazardous waste. Solvent-type parts cleaners with filters are available to greatly extend solvent life and reduce spent solvent disposal costs. Solvent reclaimers are available that clean and restore the solvent so it lasts indefinitely.

USED SOLVENTS Used or spent solvents are liquid materials that have been generated as waste and may contain xylene, methanol, ethyl ether, and methyl isobutyl ketone (MIBK). These materials must be stored in OSHA-approved safety containers with the lids or caps closed tightly. These storage receptacles must show no signs of leaks or significant damage due to dents or rust. In addition, the containers must be stored in a protected area equipped with secondary containment or a spill protector, such as a spill pallet. Additional requirements include the following:

- Containers should be clearly labeled "Hazardous Waste" and the date the material was first placed into the storage receptacle should be noted.

- Labeling is not required for solvents being used in a parts washer.

- Used solvents will not be counted toward a facility's monthly output of hazardous waste if the vendor under contract removes the material.

FIGURE 2–6 Using a water-based cleaning system helps reduce the hazards from using strong chemicals.

FIGURE 2–7 Used antifreeze coolant should be kept separate and stored in a leakproof container until it can be recycled or disposed of according to federal, state, and local laws. Note that the storage barrel is placed inside another container to catch any coolant that may spill out of the inside barrel.

- Used solvents may be disposed of by recycling with a local vendor, such as SafetyKleen®, to have the used solvent removed according to specific terms in the vendor agreement. ● **SEE FIGURE 2–6.**

- Use aqueous-based (nonsolvent) cleaning systems to help avoid the problems associated with chemical solvents.

COOLANT DISPOSAL

Coolant is a mixture of antifreeze and water. New antifreeze is not considered to be hazardous even though it can cause death if ingested. Used antifreeze may be hazardous due to dissolved metals from the engine and other components of the cooling system. These metals can include iron, steel, aluminum, copper, brass, and lead (from older radiators and heater cores).

- Coolant should be recycled either onsite or offsite.

- Used coolant should be stored in a sealed and labeled container. ● **SEE FIGURE 2–7.**

- Used coolant can often be disposed of into municipal sewers with a permit. Check with local authorities and obtain a permit before discharging used coolant into sanitary sewers.

LEAD-ACID BATTERY WASTE

About 70 million spent lead-acid batteries are generated each year in the United States alone. Lead is classified as a toxic metal and the acid used in lead-acid batteries is highly corrosive. The vast majority (95% to 98%) of these batteries are recycled through lead reclamation operations and secondary lead smelters for use in the manufacture of new batteries.

BATTERY DISPOSAL Used lead-acid batteries must be reclaimed or recycled in order to be exempt from hazardous waste regulations. Leaking batteries must be stored and transported as hazardous waste. Some states have more strict regulations, which require special handling procedures and transportation. According to the **Battery Council International (BCI),** battery laws usually include the following rules.

1. Lead-acid battery disposal is prohibited in landfills or incinerators. Batteries are required to be delivered to a battery retailer, wholesaler, recycling center, or lead smelter.

2. All retailers of automotive batteries are required to post a sign that displays the universal recycling symbol and indicates the retailer's specific requirements for accepting used batteries.

3. Battery electrolyte contains sulfuric acid, which is a very corrosive substance capable of causing serious personal injury, such as skin burns and eye damage. In addition, the battery plates contain lead, which is highly poisonous. For this reason, disposing of batteries improperly can cause environmental contamination and lead to severe health problems.

BATTERY HANDLING AND STORAGE

Batteries, whether new or used, should be kept indoors if possible. The storage location should be an area specifically designated for battery storage and must be well ventilated (to the outside). If outdoor storage is the only alternative, a sheltered and secured area with acid-resistant secondary containment is strongly recommended. It is also advisable that acid-resistant secondary containment be used for indoor storage. In addition, batteries should be placed on acid-resistant pallets and never stacked!

FUEL SAFETY AND STORAGE

Gasoline is a very explosive liquid. The expanding vapors that come from gasoline are extremely dangerous. These vapors are present even in cold temperatures. Vapors formed in gasoline tanks on many vehicles are controlled, but vapors from gasoline storage may escape from the can, resulting in a hazardous situation. Therefore, place gasoline storage containers in a well-ventilated space. Although diesel fuel is not as volatile as gasoline, the same basic rules apply to diesel fuel and gasoline storage. These rules include the following:

1. Use storage cans that have a flash arresting screen at the outlet. These screens prevent external ignition sources from igniting the gasoline within the can when someone pours the gasoline or diesel fuel.

2. Use only a red approved gasoline container to allow for proper hazardous substance identification. ● SEE FIGURE 2–8.

3. Do not fill gasoline containers completely full. Always leave the level of gasoline at least 1 inch from the top of the container. This action allows expansion of the gasoline at higher temperatures. If gasoline containers are completely full, the gasoline will expand when the temperature increases. This expansion forces gasoline from the can and creates a dangerous spill. If gasoline or diesel fuel containers must be stored, place them in a designated storage locker or facility.

4. Never leave gasoline containers open, except while filling or pouring gasoline from the container.

5. Never use gasoline as a cleaning agent.

6. Always connect a ground strap to containers when filling or transferring fuel or other flammable products from one container to another to prevent static electricity that could result in explosion and fire. These ground wires prevent the buildup of a static electric charge, which could result in a spark and disastrous explosion.

FIGURE 2–8 This red gasoline container holds about 30 gallons of gasoline and is used to fill vehicles used for training.

AIRBAG DISPOSAL

Airbag modules are pyrotechnic devices that can be ignited if exposed to an electrical charge or if the body of the vehicle is subjected to a shock. Airbag safety should include the following precautions.

1. Disarm the airbag(s) if you will be working in the area where a discharged bag could make contact with any part of your body. Consult service information for the exact procedure to follow for the vehicle being serviced. The usual procedure is to deploy the airbag using a 12 volt power supply, such as a jump start box, using long wires to connect to the module to ensure a safe deployment.

2. Do not expose an airbag to extreme heat or fire.

3. Always carry an airbag pointing away from your body.

4. Place an airbag module facing upward.

5. Always follow the manufacturer's recommended procedure for airbag disposal or recycling, including the proper packaging to use during shipment.

6. Wear protective gloves if handling a deployed airbag.

7. Always wash your hands or body well if exposed to a deployed airbag. The chemicals involved can cause skin irritation and possible rash development.

USED TIRE DISPOSAL

Used tires are an environmental concern because of several reasons, including the following:

1. In a landfill, they tend to "float" up through the other trash and rise to the surface.

2. The inside area traps and holds rainwater, which is a breeding ground for mosquitoes. Mosquito-borne diseases include encephalitis and dengue fever.

3. Used tires present a fire hazard and, when burned, create a large amount of black smoke that contaminates the air.

Used tires should be disposed of in one of the following ways.

1. Used tires can be reused until the end of their useful life.

2. Tires can be retreaded.

3. Tires can be recycled or shredded for use in asphalt.

4. Derimmed tires can be sent to a landfill. (Most landfill operators will shred the tires because it is illegal in many states to landfill whole tires.)

5. Tires can be burned in cement kilns or other power plants where the smoke can be controlled.

6. A registered scrap tire handler should be used to transport tires for disposal or recycling.

AIR-CONDITIONING REFRIGERANT OIL DISPOSAL

Air-conditioning refrigerant oil contains dissolved refrigerant and is therefore considered to be hazardous waste. This oil must be kept separated from other waste oil or the entire amount of oil must be treated as hazardous. Used refrigerant oil must be sent to a licensed hazardous waste disposal company for recycling or disposal. ● **SEE FIGURE 2–9.**

WASTE CHART All automotive service facilities create some waste, and while most of it is handled properly, it is important that all hazardous and nonhazardous waste be accounted for and properly disposed. ● **SEE CHART 2–1** for a list of typical wastes generated at automotive shops, plus a checklist for keeping track of how these wastes are handled.

FIGURE 2–9 Air-conditioning refrigerant oil must be kept separated from other oils because it contains traces of refrigerant and must be treated as hazardous waste.

FIGURE 2–10 Placard near driver's door, including what devices in the vehicle contain mercury.

 TECH TIP

Remove Components That Contain Mercury

Some vehicles have a placard near the driver's side door that lists the components that contain the heavy metal, mercury. **Mercury** can be absorbed through the skin and is a heavy metal that once absorbed by the body does not leave. ● **SEE FIGURE 2–10.**

These components should be removed from the vehicle before the rest of the body is sent to be recycled to help prevent releasing mercury into the environment.

WASTE STREAM	TYPICAL WASTES		
	TYPICAL CATEGORY IF NOT MIXED WITH OTHER HAZARDOUS WASTE	IF DISPOSED IN LANDFILL AND NOT MIXED WITH A HAZARDOUS WASTE	IF RECYCLED
Used oil	Used oil	Hazardous waste	Used oil
Used oil filters	Nonhazardous solid waste, if completely drained	Nonhazardous solid waste, if completely drained	Used oil, if not drained
Used transmission fluid	Used oil	Hazardous waste	Used oil
Used brake fluid	Used oil	Hazardous waste	Used oil
Used antifreeze	Depends on characterization	Depends on characterization	Depends on characterization
Used solvents	Hazardous waste	Hazardous waste	Hazardous waste
Used citric solvents	Nonhazardous solid waste	Nonhazardous solid waste	Hazardous waste
Lead-acid automotive batteries	Not a solid waste if returned to supplier	Hazardous waste	Hazardous waste
Shop rags used for oil	Used oil	Depends on used oil characterization	Used oil
Shop rags used for solvent or gasoline spills	Hazardous waste	Hazardous waste	Hazardous waste
Oil spill absorbent material	Used oil	Depends on used oil characterization	Used oil
Spill material for solvent and gasoline	Hazardous waste	Hazardous waste	Hazardous waste
Catalytic converter	Not a solid waste if returned to supplier	Nonhazardous solid waste	Nonhazardous solid waste
Spilled or unused fuels	Hazardous waste	Hazardous waste	Hazardous waste
Spilled or unusable paints and thinners	Hazardous waste	Hazardous waste	Hazardous waste
Used tires	Nonhazardous solid waste	Nonhazardous solid waste	Nonhazardous solid waste

CHART 2–1

Typical wastes generated at auto repair shops and typical category (hazardous or nonhazardous) by disposal method.

 **TECH TIP**

What Every Technician Should Know

The Hazardous Materials Identification Guide (HMIG) is the standard labeling for all materials. The service technician should be aware of the meaning of the label. ● **SEE FIGURE 2–11.**

Hazardous Materials Identification Guide (HMIG)

TYPE HAZARD		DEGREE	
○ HEALTH		4 - Extreme	
○ FLAMMABILITY		3 - Serious	
○ REACTIVITY		2 - Moderate	
○ PROTECTIVE EQUIPMENT		1 - Slight	
		0 - Minimal	

HAZARD RATING AND PROTECTIVE EQUIPMENT

Health	Flammable	Reactive
Type of Possible Injury	Susceptibility of materials to burn	Susceptibility of materials to release energy
4 Highly Toxic. May be fatal on short-term exposure. Special protective equipment required.	4 Extremely flammable gas or liquid. Flash Point below 73°F.	4 Extreme. Explosive at room temperature.
3 Toxic. Avoid inhalation or skin contact.	3 Flammable. Flash Point 73°F to 100°F.	3 Serious. May explode if shocked, heated under confinement or mixed w/ water.
2 Moderately Toxic. May be harmful if inhaled or absorbed.	2 Combustible. Requires moderate heating to ignite. Flash Point 100°F to 200°F.	2 Moderate. Unstable, may react with water.
1 Slightly Toxic. May cause slight irritation.	1 Slightly Combustible. Requires strong heating to ignite.	1 Slight. May react if heated or mixed with water.
0 Minimal. All chemicals have a slight degree of toxicity.	0 Minimal. Will not burn under normal conditions.	0 Minimal. Normally stable, does not react with water.

Protective Equipment

A	Safety Glasses	E	Safety Glasses + Gloves + Dust Respirator	I	Safety Glasses + Gloves + Combination Dust & Vapor Respirator
B	Safety Glasses + Gloves	F	Safety Glasses + Gloves + Apron + Dust Respirator	J	Chemical Goggles + Gloves + Apron + Combination Dust & Vapor Respirator
C	Safety Glasses + Gloves + Apron	G	Safety Glasses + Gloves + Vapor Respirator	K	Apron + Gloves + Full Protection Suit + Boots
D	Faceshield + Gloves + Apron	H	Chemical Goggles + Gloves + Apron + Vapor Respirator	X	Ask your supervisor for guidance.

FIGURE 2–11 The Environmental Protection Agency (EPA) Hazardous Materials Identification Guide is a standardized listing of the hazards and the protective equipment needed.

1. Hazardous materials include common automotive chemicals, liquids, and lubricants, especially those whose ingredients contain *chlor* or *fluor* in their name.
2. Right-to-know laws require that all workers have access to material safety data sheets (MSDS).
3. Asbestos fibers should be avoided and removed according to current laws and regulations.
4. Used engine oil contains metals worn from parts and should be handled and disposed of properly.
5. Solvents represent a serious health risk and should be avoided as much as possible.
6. Coolant should be disposed of properly or recycled.
7. Batteries are considered to be hazardous waste and should be discarded to a recycling facility.

REVIEW QUESTIONS

1. List five common automotive chemicals or products that may be considered hazardous materials.
2. List five precautions to which every technician should adhere when working with automotive products and chemicals.

CHAPTER QUIZ

1. Hazardous materials include all of the following *except* _____.
   a. Engine oil
   b. Asbestos
   c. Water
   d. Brake cleaner

2. To determine if a product or substance being used is hazardous, consult _____.
   a. A dictionary
   b. An MSDS
   c. SAE standards
   d. EPA guidelines

3. Exposure to asbestos dust can cause what condition?
   a. Asbestosis
   b. Mesothelioma
   c. Lung cancer
   d. All of the above are possible

4. Wetted asbestos dust is considered to be _____.
   a. Solid waste
   b. Hazardous waste
   c. Toxic
   d. Poisonous

5. An oil filter should be hot drained for how long before disposing of the filter?
   a. 30 to 60 minutes
   b. 4 hours
   c. 8 hours
   d. 12 hours

6. Used engine oil should be disposed of by all *except* one of the following methods.
   a. Disposed of in regular trash
   b. Shipped offsite for recycling
   c. Burned onsite in a waste oil-approved heater
   d. Burned offsite in a waste oil-approved heater

7. All of the following are the proper ways to dispose of a drained oil filter *except* _____.
   a. Sent for recycling
   b. Picked up by a service contract company
   c. Disposed of in regular trash
   d. Considered to be hazardous waste and disposed of accordingly

8. Which act or organization regulates air-conditioning refrigerant?
   a. Clean Air Act (CAA)
   b. MSDS
   c. WHMIS
   d. Code of Federal Regulations (CFR)

9. Gasoline should be stored in approved containers that include what color(s)?
   a. Red container with yellow lettering
   b. Red container
   c. Yellow container
   d. Yellow container with red lettering

10. What automotive devices may contain mercury?
    a. Rear seat video displays
    b. Navigation displays
    c. HID headlights
    d. All of the above

chapter 3
ELECTRICAL FUNDAMENTALS

OBJECTIVES

After studying Chapter 3, the reader will be able to:

1. Prepare for ASE Electrical/Electronic Systems (A6) certification test content area "A" (General Electrical/Electronic System Diagnosis).
2. Define electricity.
3. Explain the units of electrical measurement.
4. Discuss the relationship among volts, amperes, and ohms.
5. Explain how magnetism is used in automotive applications.

KEY TERMS

Ammeter 58
Ampere 58
Atom 54
Bound electrons 56
Conductors 56
Conventional theory 57
Coulomb 58
Electrical potential 58
Electricity 54
Electrochemistry 60
Electromotive force (EMF) 59
Electron theory 57
Free electrons 56
Insulators 56
Ion 55
Neutral charge 54
Ohmmeter 59

Ohms 59
Peltier effect 60
Photoelectricity 60
Piezoelectricity 60
Positive temperature coefficient (PTC) 61
Potentiometer 62
Resistance 59
Rheostat 62
Semiconductor 57
Static electricity 60
Thermocouple 60
Thermoelectricity 60
Valence ring 55
Volt 58
Voltmeter 59
Watt 59

INTRODUCTION

The electrical system is one of the most important systems in a vehicle today. Every year more and more components and systems use electricity. Those technicians who really know and understand automotive electrical and electronic systems will be in great demand.

Electricity may be difficult for some people to learn for the following reasons.

- It cannot be seen.
- Only the results of electricity can be seen.
- It has to be detected and measured.
- The test results have to be interpreted.

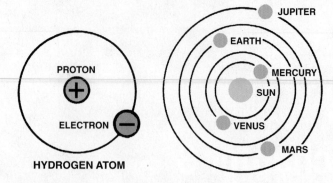

FIGURE 3–1 In an atom (left), electrons orbit protons in the nucleus just as planets orbit the sun in our solar system (right).

ELECTRICITY

BACKGROUND Our universe is composed of matter, which is *anything* that has mass and occupies space. All matter is made from slightly over 100 individual components called *elements*. The smallest particle that an element can be broken into and still retain the properties of that element is known as an **atom.** ● SEE FIGURE 3–1.

DEFINITION **Electricity** is the movement of electrons from one atom to another. The dense center of each atom is called the nucleus. The nucleus contains:

- *Protons*, which have a positive charge
- *Neutrons*, which are electrically neutral (have no charge)

Electrons surround the nucleus in orbits. Each atom contains an equal number of electrons and protons. The physical aspect of all protons, electrons, and neutrons are the same for all atoms. It is the *number* of electrons and protons in the atom that determines the material and how electricity is conducted. Because the number of negative-charged electrons is balanced with the same number of positive-charged protons, an atom has a **neutral charge** (no charge).

NOTE: As an example of the relative sizes of the parts of an atom, consider that if an atom were magnified so that the nucleus were the size of the period at the end of this sentence, the whole atom would be bigger than a house.

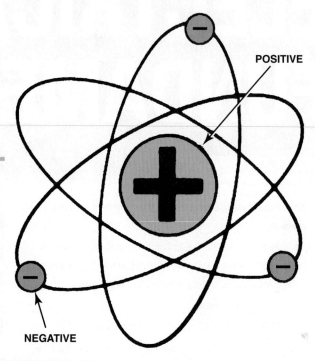

FIGURE 3–2 The nucleus of an atom has a positive (+) charge and the surrounding electrons have a negative (−) charge.

POSITIVE AND NEGATIVE CHARGES The parts of the atom have different charges. The orbiting electrons are negatively charged, while the protons are positively charged. Positive charges are indicated by the "plus" sign (+), and negative charges by the "minus" sign (−), as shown in ● **FIGURE 3–2.**

These same + and − signs are used to identify parts of an electrical circuit. Neutrons have no charge at all. They are neutral. In a normal, or balanced, atom, the number of negative particles equals the number of positive particles. That is, there are as many electrons as there are protons. ● SEE FIGURE 3–3.

MAGNETS AND ELECTRICAL CHARGES An ordinary magnet has two ends, or poles. One end is called the south pole, and the other is called the north pole. If two magnets are brought

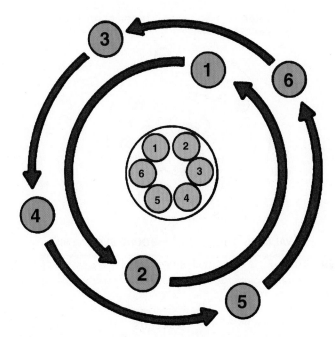

FIGURE 3–3 This figure shows a balanced atom. The number of electrons is the same as the number of protons in the nucleus.

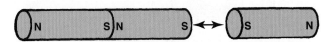

FIGURE 3–4 Unlike charges attract and like charges repel.

close to each other with like poles together (south to south or north to north), the magnets will push each other apart, because like poles repel each other. If the opposite poles of the magnets are brought close to each other, south to north, the magnets will snap together, because unlike poles attract each other.

The positive and negative charges within an atom are like the north and south poles of a magnet. Charges that are alike will repel each other, similar to the poles of a magnet. ● **SEE FIGURE 3–4.**

That is why the negative electrons continue to orbit around the positive protons. They are attracted and held by the opposite charge of the protons. The electrons keep moving in orbit because they repel each other.

IONS   When an atom loses any electrons, it becomes unbalanced. It will have more protons than electrons, and therefore will have a positive charge. If it gains more electrons than protons, the atom will be negatively charged. When an atom is not balanced, it becomes a charged particle called an **ion**. Ions try to regain their balance of equal protons and electrons by exchanging electrons with neighboring atoms. The flow of electrons during the "equalization" process is defined as the flow of electricity. ● **SEE FIGURE 3–5.**

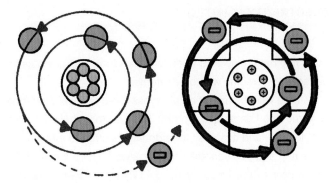

FIGURE 3–5 An unbalanced, positively charged atom (ion) will attract electrons from neighboring atoms.

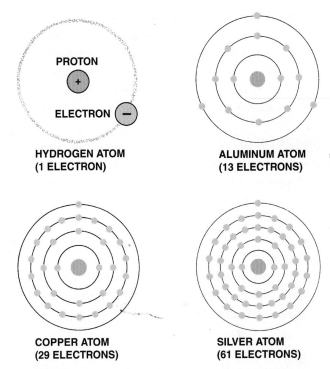

HYDROGEN ATOM (1 ELECTRON)   **ALUMINUM ATOM (13 ELECTRONS)**

COPPER ATOM (29 ELECTRONS)   **SILVER ATOM (61 ELECTRONS)**

FIGURE 3–6 The hydrogen atom is the simplest atom, with only one proton, one neutron, and one electron. More complex elements contain higher numbers of protons, neutrons, and electrons.

ELECTRON SHELLS   Electrons orbit around the nucleus in definite paths. These paths form shells, like concentric rings, around the nucleus. Only a specific number of electrons can orbit within each shell. If there are too many electrons for the first and closest shell to the nucleus, the others will orbit in additional shells until all electrons have an orbit within a shell. There can be as many as seven shells around a single nucleus. ● **SEE FIGURE 3–6.**

FREE AND BOUND ELECTRONS   The outermost electron shell or ring, called the **valence ring**, is the most important part of understanding electricity. The number of electrons in this outer ring determines the valence of the atom, and indicates its capacity to combine with other atoms.

If the valence ring of an atom has three or fewer electrons in it, the ring has room for more. The electrons there are held very loosely, and it is easy for a drifting electron to join the valence ring and push another electron away. These loosely held electrons are called **free electrons.** When the valence ring has five or more electrons in it, it is fairly full. The electrons are held tightly, and it is hard for a drifting electron to push its way into the valence ring. These tightly held electrons are called **bound electrons.** ● **SEE FIGURES 3–7 AND 3–8.**

The movement of these drifting electrons is called current. Current can be small, with only a few electrons moving, or it can be large, with a tremendous number of electrons moving. Electric current is the controlled, directed movement of electrons from atom to atom within a conductor.

CONDUCTORS

Conductors are materials with fewer than four electrons in their atom's outer orbit. ● **SEE FIGURE 3–9.**

Copper is an excellent conductor because it has only one electron in its outer orbit. This orbit is far enough away from the nucleus of the copper atom that the pull or force holding the outermost electron in orbit is relatively weak. ● **SEE FIGURE 3–10.**

Copper is the conductor most used in vehicles because the price of copper is reasonable compared to the relative cost of other conductors with similar properties. Examples of other commonly used conductors include:

- Gold
- Silver
- Aluminum
- Steel
- Cast iron

? FREQUENTLY ASKED QUESTION

Is Water a Conductor?

Pure water is an insulator; however, if anything is in the water, such as salt or dirt, then the water becomes conductive. Because it is difficult to keep it from becoming contaminated, water is usually thought of as being capable of conducting electricity, especially high-voltage household 110 or 220 volt outlets.

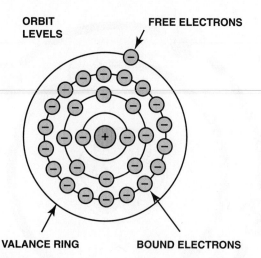

FIGURE 3–7 As the number of electrons increases, they occupy increasing energy levels that are farther from the center of the atom.

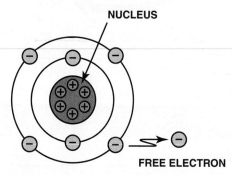

FIGURE 3–8 Electrons in the outer orbit, or shell, can often be drawn away from the atom and become free electrons.

INSULATORS

Some materials hold their electrons very tightly; therefore, electrons do not move through them very well. These materials are called insulators. **Insulators** are materials with more than four electrons in their atom's outer orbit. Because they have more than four electrons in their outer orbit, it becomes easier for these materials to acquire (gain) electrons than to release electrons. ● **SEE FIGURE 3–11.**

Examples of insulators include:

- Rubber
- Plastic
- Nylon
- Porcelain
- Ceramic
- Fiberglass

Examples of insulators include plastics, wood, glass, rubber, ceramics (spark plugs), and varnish for covering (insulating) copper wires in alternators and starters.

SEMICONDUCTORS

Materials with exactly four electrons in their outer orbit are neither conductors nor insulators, but

CONDUCTORS

FIGURE 3–9 A conductor is any element that has one to three electrons in its outer orbit.

COPPER

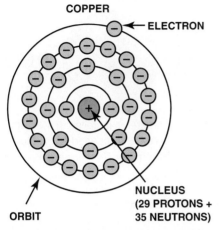

← **ELECTRON**

ORBIT

NUCLEUS (29 PROTONS + 35 NEUTRONS)

FIGURE 3–10 Copper is an excellent conductor of electricity because it has just one electron in its outer orbit, making it easy to be knocked out of its orbit and flow to other nearby atoms. This causes electron flow, which is the definition of electricity.

INSULATORS

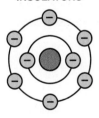

FIGURE 3–11 Insulators are elements with five to eight electrons in the outer orbit.

are called **semiconductors.** Semiconductors can be either an insulator or a conductor in different design applications. ● **SEE FIGURE 3–12.**

Examples of semiconductors include:

■ Silicon

■ Germanium

■ Carbon

Semiconductors are used mostly in transistors, computers, and other electronic devices.

SEMICONDUCTORS

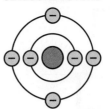

FIGURE 3–12 Semiconductor elements contain exactly four electrons in the outer orbit.

COPPER WIRE

POSITIVE (+) CHARGE

NEGATIVE (-) CHARGE

FIGURE 3–13 Current electricity is the movement of electrons through a conductor.

HOW ELECTRONS MOVE THROUGH A CONDUCTOR

CURRENT FLOW The following events occur if a source of power, such as a battery, is connected to the ends of a conductor—a positive charge (lack of electrons) is placed on one end of the conductor and a negative charge is placed on the opposite end of the conductor. For current to flow, there *must* be an imbalance of excess electrons at one end of the circuit and a deficiency of electrons at the opposite end of the circuit.

■ The negative charge will repel the free electrons from the atoms of the conductor, whereas the positive charge on the opposite end of the conductor will attract electrons.

■ As a result of this attraction of opposite charges and repulsion of like charges, electrons will flow through the conductor. ● **SEE FIGURE 3–13.**

CONVENTIONAL THEORY VERSUS ELECTRON THEORY

■ **Conventional theory.** It was once thought that electricity had only one charge and moved from positive to negative. This theory of the flow of electricity through a conductor is called the **conventional theory** of current flow. ● **SEE FIGURE 3–14.**

■ **Electron theory.** The discovery of the electron and its negative charge led to the **electron theory,** which states that there is electron flow from negative to positive. Most automotive applications use the conventional theory. This book will use the conventional theory (positive to negative) unless stated otherwise.

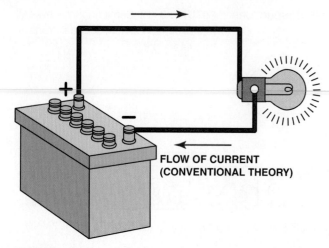

FIGURE 3–14 Conventional theory states that current flows through a circuit from positive (+) to negative (−). Automotive electricity uses the conventional theory in all electrical diagrams and schematics.

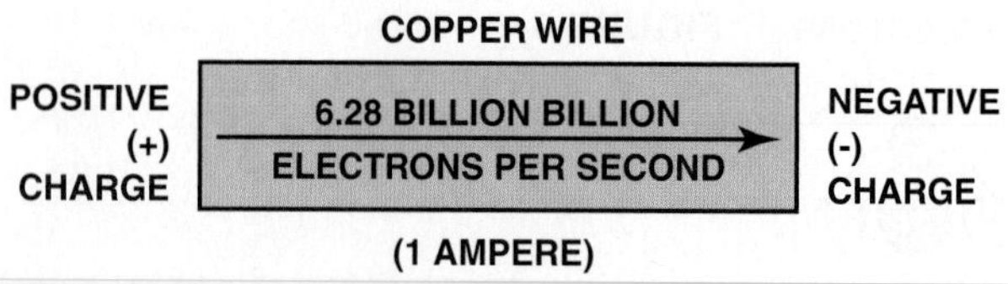

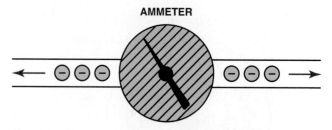

FIGURE 3–15 One ampere is the movement of 1 coulomb (6.28 billion billion electrons) past a point in 1 second.

FIGURE 3–16 An ammeter is installed in the path of the electrons similar to a water meter used to measure the flow of water in gallons per minute. The ammeter displays current flow in amperes.

UNITS OF ELECTRICITY

Electricity is measured using meters or other test equipment. The three fundamentals of electricity-related units include the ampere, volt, and ohm.

AMPERES The **ampere** is the unit used throughout the world to measure current flow. When 6.28 billion billion electrons (the name for this large number of electrons is a **coulomb**) move past a certain point in 1 second, this represents 1 ampere of current. ● **SEE FIGURE 3–15.**

The ampere is the electrical unit for the amount of electron flow, just as "gallons per minute" is the unit that can be used to measure the quantity of water flow. It is named for the French electrician, Andrè Marie Ampére (1775–1836). The conventional abbreviations and measurement for amperes are as follows:

1. The ampere is the unit of measurement for the amount of current flow.

2. *A* and *amps* are acceptable abbreviations for *amperes*.

3. The capital letter *I*, for *intensity*, is used in mathematical calculations to represent amperes.

4. Amperes do the actual work in the circuit. It is the actual movement of the electrons through a light bulb or motor that actually makes the electrical device work. Without amperage through a device it will not work at all.

5. Amperes are measured by an **ammeter** (not ampmeter). ● **SEE FIGURE 3–16.**

VOLTS The **volt** is the unit of measurement for electrical pressure. It is named for an Italian physicist, Alessandro Volta

(1745–1827). The comparable unit using water pressure as an example would be pounds per square inch (psi). It is possible to have very high pressures (volts) and low water flow (amperes). It is also possible to have high water flow (amperes) and low pressures (volts). Voltage is also called **electrical potential**, because if there is voltage present in a conductor, there is a potential (possibility) for current flow. This electrical pressure is a result of the following:

- Excess electrons remain at one end of the wire or circuit.

- There is a lack of electrons at the other end of the wire or circuit.

- The natural effect is to equalize this imbalance, creating a pressure to allow the movement of electrons through a conductor.

- It is possible to have pressure (volts) without any flow (amperes). For example, a fully charged 12 volt battery sitting on a workbench has 12 volts of pressure potential, but because there is not a conductor (circuit) connected between the positive and negative posts of the battery, there is no flow (amperes). Current will only flow when there is pressure and a circuit for the electrons to flow in order to "equalize" to a balanced state.

Voltage does *not* flow through conductors, but voltage does cause current (in amperes) to flow through conductors. ● **SEE FIGURE 3–17.**

The conventional abbreviations and measurement for voltage are as follows:

1. The volt is the unit of measurement for the amount of electrical pressure.

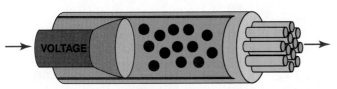

VOLTAGE IS PRESSURE

FIGURE 3–17 Voltage is the electrical pressure that causes the electrons to flow through a conductor.

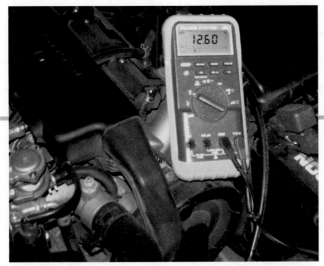

FIGURE 3–18 This digital multimeter set to read DC volts is being used to test the voltage of a vehicle battery. Most multimeters can also measure resistance (ohms) and current flow (amperes).

2. **Electromotive force**, abbreviated **EMF,** is another way of indicating voltage.

3. *V* is the generally accepted abbreviation for *volts*.

4. The symbol used in calculations is *E*, for *electromotive force*.

5. Volts are measured by a **voltmeter.** ● **SEE FIGURE 3–18.**

OHMS **Resistance** to the flow of current through a conductor is measured in units called **ohms,** named after the German physicist, George Simon Ohm (1787–1854). The resistance to the flow of free electrons through a conductor results from the countless collisions the electrons cause within the atoms of the conductor. ● **SEE FIGURE 3–19.**

The conventional abbreviations and measurement for resistance are as follows:

1. The ohm is the unit of measurement for electrical resistance.

2. The symbol for ohms is Ω (Greek capital letter omega), the last letter of the Greek alphabet.

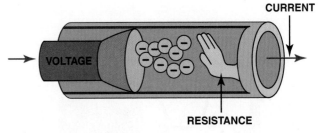

RESISTANCE

FIGURE 3–19 Resistance to the flow of electrons through a conductor is measured in ohms.

FIGURE 3–20 A display at the Henry Ford Museum in Dearborn, Michigan, which includes a hand-cranked generator and a series of light bulbs. This figure shows a young man attempting to light as many bulbs as possible. The crank gets harder to turn as more bulbs light because it requires more power to produce the necessary watts of electricity.

3. The symbol used in calculations is *R*, for *resistance*.

4. Ohms are measured by an **ohmmeter**.

5. Resistance to electron flow depends on the material used as a conductor.

WATTS A **watt** is the electrical unit for *power,* the capacity to do work. It is named after a Scottish inventor, James Watt (1736–1819). The symbol for power is *P*. Electrical power is calculated as amperes times volts:

P (power) = I (amperes) × E (volts)

The formula can also be used to calculate the amperage if the wattage and the voltage are known. For example, a 100 watt light bulb powered by 120 volts AC in the shop requires how many amperes?

A (amperes) = P (watts) divided by E (volts)

A = 0.83 amperes

● **SEE FIGURE 3–20.**

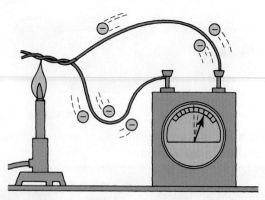

FIGURE 3–21 Electron flow is produced by heating the connection of two different metals.

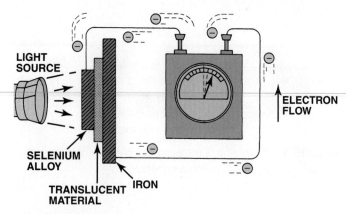

FIGURE 3–22 Electron flow is produced by light striking a light-sensitive material.

SOURCES OF ELECTRICITY

FRICTION   When certain different materials are rubbed together, the friction causes electrons to be transformed from one to the other. Both materials become electrically charged. These charges are not in motion, but stay on the surface where they were deposited. Because the charges are stationary, or static, this type of voltage is called **static electricity.** Walking across a carpeted floor creates a buildup of a static charge in your body which is an insulator and then the charge is discharged when you touch a metal conductor. Vehicle tires rolling on pavement often create static electricity that interferes with radio reception.

HEAT   When pieces of two different metals are joined together at both ends and one junction is heated, current passes through the metals. The current is very small, only millionths of an ampere, but this is enough to use in a temperature-measuring device called a **thermocouple.** ● **SEE FIGURE 3–21.**

Some engine temperature sensors operate in this manner. This form of voltage is called **thermoelectricity**.

Thermoelectricity was discovered and has been known for over a century. In 1823, a German physicist, Thomas Johann Seebeck, discovered that a voltage was developed in a loop containing two dissimilar metals, provided the two junctions were maintained at different temperatures. A decade later, a French scientist, Jean Charles Athanase Peltier, found that electrons moving through a solid can carry heat from one side of the material to the other side. This effect is called the **Peltier effect**. A Peltier effect device is often used in portable coolers to keep food items cool if the current flows in one direction and keep items warm if the current flows in reverse.

LIGHT   In 1839, Edmond Becquerel noticed that by shining a beam of sunlight over two different liquids, he could develop an electric current. When certain metals are exposed to light, some of the light energy is transferred to the free electrons of the metal. This excess energy breaks the electrons loose from the surface of the metal. They can then be collected and made to flow in a conductor. ● **SEE FIGURE 3–22.**

This **photoelectricity** is widely used in light-measuring devices such as photographic exposure meters and automatic headlamp dimmers.

PRESSURE   The first experimental demonstration of a connection between the generation of a voltage due to pressure applied to a crystal was published in 1880 by Pierre and Jacques Curie. Their experiment consisted of voltage being produced when prepared crystals, such as quartz, topaz, and Rochelle salt, had a force applied. ● **SEE FIGURE 3–23.**

This current is used in crystal microphones, underwater hydrophones, and certain stethoscopes. The voltage created is called **piezoelectricity**. A gas grille igniter uses the principle of piezoelectricity to produce a spark, and knock sensor (KS) use piezoelectricity to create a voltage signal for use as an input as an engine computer input signal.

CHEMICAL   Two different materials (usually metals) placed in a conducting and reactive chemical solution create a difference in potential, or voltage, between them. This principle is called **electrochemistry** and is the basis of the automotive battery.

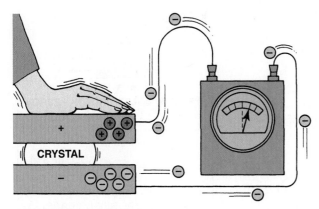

FIGURE 3–23 Electron flow is produced by pressure on certain crystals.

1	Silver
2	Copper
3	Gold
4	Aluminum
5	Tungsten
6	Zinc
7	Brass (copper and zinc)
8	Platinum
9	Iron
10	Nickel
11	Tin
12	Steel
13	Lead

CHART 3–1

Conductor ratings (starting with the best).

MAGNETISM Electricity can be produced if a conductor is moved through a magnetic field or a moving magnetic field is moved near a conductor. This is the principle of how many automotive devices work, including:

- Starter motor
- Alternator
- Ignition coils
- Solenoids and relays

 FREQUENTLY ASKED QUESTION

Why Is Gold Used if Copper Has Lower Resistance?

Copper is used for most automotive electrical components and wiring because it has low resistance and is reasonably priced. Gold is used in airbag connections and sensors because it does not corrode. Gold can be buried for hundreds of years and when dug up it is just as shiny as ever.

CONDUCTORS AND RESISTANCE

All conductors have some resistance to current flow. The following are principles of conductors and their resistance.

- **If the conductor length is doubled, its resistance doubles.** This is the reason why battery cables are designed to be as short as possible.

- **If the conductor diameter is increased, its resistance is reduced.** This is the reason starter motor cables are larger in diameter than other wiring in the vehicle.

- **As the temperature increases, the resistance of the conductor also increases.** This is the reason for installing heat shields on some starter motors. The heat shield helps to protect the conductors (copper wiring inside the starter) from excessive engine heat and so reduces the resistance of starter circuits. Because a conductor increases in resistance with increased temperature, the conductor is called a **positive temperature coefficient (PTC)** resistor.

- **Materials used in the conductor have an impact on its resistance.** Silver has the lowest resistance of any conductor, but is expensive. Copper is the next lowest in resistance and is reasonably priced. ● **SEE CHART 3–1** for a comparison of materials.

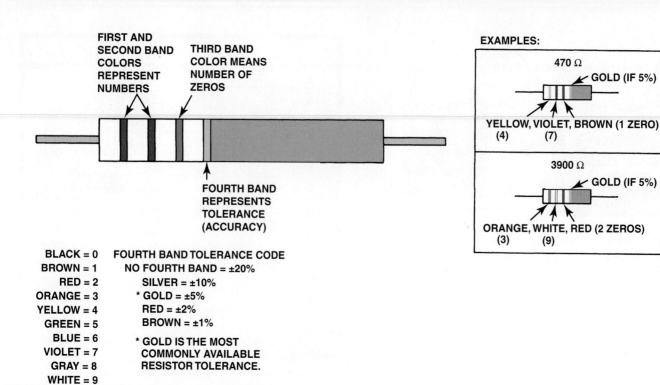

FIRST AND SECOND BAND COLORS REPRESENT NUMBERS

THIRD BAND COLOR MEANS NUMBER OF ZEROS

FOURTH BAND REPRESENTS TOLERANCE (ACCURACY)

EXAMPLES:

470 Ω

GOLD (IF 5%)

YELLOW, VIOLET, BROWN (1 ZERO)
(4)   (7)

3900 Ω

GOLD (IF 5%)

ORANGE, WHITE, RED (2 ZEROS)
(3)   (9)

BLACK = 0
BROWN = 1
RED = 2
ORANGE = 3
YELLOW = 4
GREEN = 5
BLUE = 6
VIOLET = 7
GRAY = 8
WHITE = 9

FOURTH BAND TOLERANCE CODE
NO FOURTH BAND = ±20%
SILVER = ±10%
* GOLD = ±5%
RED = ±2%
BROWN = ±1%

* GOLD IS THE MOST COMMONLY AVAILABLE RESISTOR TOLERANCE.

FIGURE 3–24 This figure shows a resistor color-code interpretation.

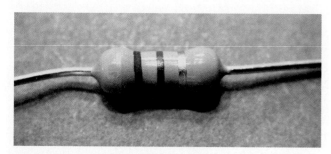

FIGURE 3–25 A typical carbon resistor.

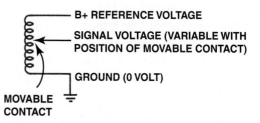

B+ REFERENCE VOLTAGE

SIGNAL VOLTAGE (VARIABLE WITH POSITION OF MOVABLE CONTACT)

GROUND (0 VOLT)

MOVABLE CONTACT

FIGURE 3–26 A three-wire variable resistor is called a potentiometer.

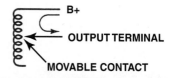

B+

OUTPUT TERMINAL

MOVABLE CONTACT

FIGURE 3–27 A two-wire variable resistor is called a rheostat.

RESISTORS

FIXED RESISTORS Resistance is the opposition to current flow. Resistors represent an electrical load, or resistance, to current flow. Most electrical and electronic devices use resistors of specific values to limit and control the flow of current. Resistors can be made from carbon or from other materials that restrict the flow of electricity and are available in various sizes and resistance values. Most resistors have a series of painted color bands around them. These color bands are coded to indicate the degree of resistance. ● **SEE FIGURES 3–24 AND 3–25.**

VARIABLE RESISTORS Two basic types of mechanically operated variable resistors are used in automotive applications.

■ A **potentiometer** is a three-terminal variable resistor where a wiper contact provides a variable voltage output. ● **SEE FIGURE 3–26.** Potentiometers are most commonly used as throttle position (TP) sensors on computer-equipped engines. A potentiometer is also used to control audio volume, bass, treble, balance, and fade.

■ Another type of mechanically operated variable resistor is the **rheostat.** A rheostat is a *two*-terminal unit in which all of the current flows through the movable arm. ● **SEE FIGURE 3–27.** A rheostat is commonly used for a dash light dimmer control.

1. Electricity is the movement of electrons from one atom to another.

2. In order for current to flow in a circuit or wire, there must be an excess of electrons at one end and a deficiency of electrons at the other end.

3. Automotive electricity uses the conventional theory that electricity flows from positive to negative.

4. The ampere is the measure of the amount of current flow.

5. Voltage is the unit of electrical pressure.

6. The ohm is the unit of electrical resistance.

7. Sources of electricity include friction, heat, light, pressure, and chemical.

REVIEW QUESTIONS

1. What is electricity?

2. What are the ampere, volt, and ohm?

3. What are three examples of conductors and three examples of insulators?

4. What are the four sources of electricity?

CHAPTER QUIZ

1. An electrical conductor is an element with _____ electrons in its outer orbit.
   a. Less than 2
   b. Less than 4
   c. Exactly 4
   d. More than 4

2. Like charges _____.
   a. Attract
   b. Repel
   c. Neutralize each other
   d. Add

3. Carbon and silicon are examples of _____.
   a. Semiconductors
   b. Insulators
   c. Conductors
   d. Photoelectric materials

4. Which unit of electricity does the work in a circuit?
   a. Volt
   b. Ampere
   c. Ohm
   d. Coulomb

5. As temperature increases, _____.
   a. The resistance of a conductor decreases
   b. The resistance of a conductor increases
   c. The resistance of a conductor remains the same
   d. The voltage of the conductor decreases

6. The _____ is a unit of electrical pressure.
   a. Coulomb
   b. Volt
   c. Ampere
   d. Ohm

7. Technician A says that a two-wire variable resistor is called a rheostat. Technician B says that a three-wire variable resistor is called a potentiometer. Which technician is correct?
   a. Technician A only
   b. Technician B only
   c. Both Technicians A and B
   d. Neither Technician A nor B

8. Creating electricity by exerting a force on a crystal is called _____.
   a. Electrochemistry
   b. Piezoelectricity
   c. Thermoelectricity
   d. Photoelectricity

9. The fact that a voltage can be created by exerting force on a crystal is used in which type of sensor?
   a. Throttle position (TP)
   b. Manifold absolute pressure (MAP)
   c. Barometric pressure (BARO)
   d. Knock sensor (KS)

10. A potentiometer, a three-wire variable resistance, is used in which type of sensor?
    a. Throttle position (TP)
    b. Manifold absolute pressure (MAP)
    c. Barometric pressure (BARO)
    d. Knock sensor (KS)

ELECTRICAL CIRCUITS AND OHM'S LAW

OBJECTIVES

After studying Chapter 4, the reader will be able to:

1. Prepare for ASE Electrical/Electronic Systems (A6) certification test content area "A" (General Electrical/Electronic Systems Diagnosis).
2. Explain Ohm's law.
3. Identify the parts of a complete circuit.
4. Explain Watt's law.
5. Describe the characteristics of an open, a short-to-ground, and a short-to-voltage.

KEY TERMS

Circuit 65
Complete circuit 65
Continuity 65
Electrical load 65
Grounded 67
High resistance 67
Load 65
Ohm's law 68
Open circuit 65

Power path 65
Power source 65
Protection 65
Return path (ground) 65
Shorted 66
Short-to-ground 66
Short-to-voltage 66
Watt 69
Watt's law 69

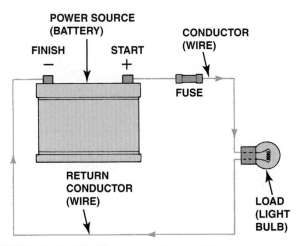

FIGURE 4–1 All complete circuits must have a power source, a power path, protection (fuse), an electrical load (light bulb in this case), and a return path back to the power source.

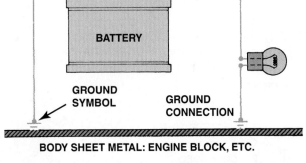

FIGURE 4–2 The return path back to the battery can be any electrical conductor, such as a copper wire or the metal frame or body of the vehicle.

CIRCUITS

DEFINITION A **circuit** is a complete path that electrons travel from a power source (such as a battery) through a **load** such as a light bulb and back to the power source. It is called a *circuit* because the current must start and finish at the same place (power source).

For *any* electrical circuit to work at all, it must be continuous from the battery (power), through all the wires and components, and back to the battery (ground). A circuit that is continuous throughout is said to have **continuity.**

PARTS OF A COMPLETE CIRCUIT Every **complete circuit** contains the following parts. ● **SEE FIGURE 4–1.**

1. A **power source,** such as a vehicle's battery

2. **Protection** from harmful overloads (excessive current flow) (Fuses, circuit breakers, and fusible links are examples of electrical circuit protection devices.)

3. The **power path** for the current to flow through from the power source to the resistance (This path from a power source to the load—a light bulb in this example—is usually an insulated copper wire.)

4. The **electrical load** or resistance which converts electrical energy into heat, light, or motion

5. A **return path (ground)** for the electrical current from the load back to the power source so that there is a *complete* circuit (This return, or ground, path is usually the metal body, frame, ground wires, and engine block of the vehicle. ● **SEE FIGURE 4–2.)**

6. Switches and controls that turn the circuit on and off (● **SEE FIGURE 4–3.)**

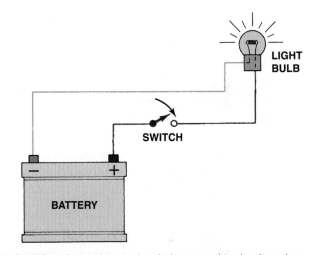

FIGURE 4–3 An electrical switch opens the circuit and no current flows. The switch could also be on the return (ground) path wire.

CIRCUIT FAULT TYPES

OPEN CIRCUITS An **open circuit** is any circuit that is *not* complete, or that lacks continuity, such as a broken wire. ● **SEE FIGURE 4–4.**

Open circuits have the following features.

1. *No current at all* will flow through an open circuit.

2. An open circuit may be created by a break in the circuit or by a switch that opens (turns off) the circuit and prevents the flow of current.

3. In any circuit containing a power load and ground, an opening anywhere in the circuit will cause the circuit not to work.

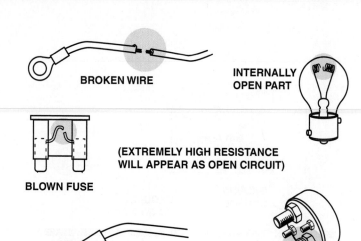

FIGURE 4–4 Examples of common causes of open circuits. Some of these causes are often difficult to find.

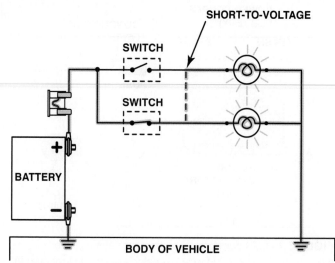

FIGURE 4–5 A short circuit permits electrical current to bypass some or all of the resistance in the circuit.

CIRCUIT FAULT TYPES (CONTINUED)

4. A light switch in a home and the headlight switch in a vehicle are examples of devices that open a circuit to control its operation.

5. A blown (open) fuse occurs (caused by another fault in the circuit), but the fuse stopped (opened the circuit) to prevent any harm to the component or the wiring as a result of the fault.

SHORT-TO-VOLTAGE *If a wire (conductor) or component is shorted to voltage, it is commonly referred to as being* **shorted**. A **short-to-voltage** occurs when the power side of one circuit is electrically connected to the power side of another circuit. ● **SEE FIGURE 4–5.**

A short circuit has the following features.

1. It is a complete circuit in which the current usually bypasses *some* or *all* of the resistance in the circuit.

2. It involves the power side of the circuit.

3. It involves a copper-to-copper connection (two power-side wires touching together).

4. It is also called a *short-to-voltage.*

5. It usually affects more than one circuit. In this case if one circuit is electrically connected to another circuit,

---

TECH TIP

"Open" Is a Four-Letter Word

An open in a circuit breaks the path of current flow. The open can be any break in the power side, load, or ground side of a circuit. A switch is often used to close and open a circuit to turn it on and off. Just remember,

Open = no current flow

Closed = current flow

Trying to locate an open circuit in a vehicle is often difficult and may cause the technician to use other four-letter words, such as "HELP"!

---

one of the circuits may operate when it is not supposed to because it is being supplied power from another circuit.

6. It *may* or *may not* blow a fuse. ● **SEE FIGURE 4–6.**

SHORT-TO-GROUND A **short-to-ground** is a type of short circuit that occurs when the current bypasses part of the normal circuit and flows directly to ground. A short-to-ground has the following features.

1. Because the ground return circuit is metal (vehicle frame, engine, or body), it is often identified as having current flowing from copper to steel.

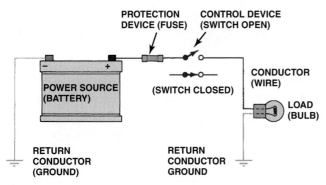

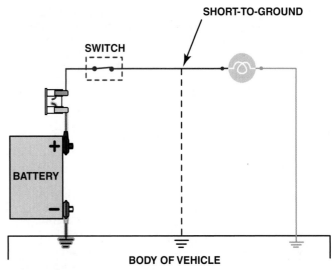

FIGURE 4–6 A fuse or circuit breaker opens the circuit to prevent possible overheating damage in the event of a short circuit.

REAL WORLD FIX

The Short-to-Voltage Story

A technician was working on a Chevrolet pickup truck with the following unusual electrical problems.

1. When the brake pedal was depressed, the dash light and the side marker lights would light.
2. The turn signals caused all lights to blink and the fuel gauge needle to bounce up and down.
3. When the brake lights were on, the front parking lights also came on.

   The technician tested all fuses using a conventional test light and found them to be okay. All body-to-engine block ground wires were clean and tight. All bulbs were of the correct trade number as specified in the owner's manual.

NOTE: Using a single-filament bulb (such as a #1156) in the place of a dual-filament bulb (such as a #1157) could also cause many of these same problems.

Because most of the trouble occurred when the brake pedal was depressed, the technician decided to trace all the wires in the brake light circuit. The technician discovered the problem near the exhaust system. A small hole in the tailpipe (after the muffler) directed hot exhaust gases to the wiring harness containing all of the wires for circuits at the rear of the truck. The heat had melted the insulation and caused most of the wires to touch. Whenever one circuit was activated (such as when the brake pedal was applied), the current had a complete path to several other circuits. A fuse did not blow because there was enough resistance in the circuits being energized, so the current (in amperes) was too low to blow any fuses.

FIGURE 4–7 A short-to-ground affects the power side of the circuit. Current flows directly to the ground return, bypassing some or all of the electrical loads in the circuit. There is no current in the circuit past the short.

2. It occurs any place where a power path wire accidentally touches a return path wire or conductor. ● **SEE FIGURE 4–7.**
3. A defective component or circuit that is shorted to ground is commonly called **grounded.**
4. A short-to-ground almost always results in a blown fuse, damaged connectors, or melted wires.

HIGH RESISTANCE **High resistance** can be caused by any of the following:

- Corroded connections or sockets
- Loose terminals in a connector
- Loose ground connections

If there is high resistance anywhere in a circuit, it may cause the following problems.

1. Slow operation of a motor-driven unit, such as the windshield wipers or blower motor
2. Dim lights
3. "Clicking" of relays or solenoids
4. No operation of a circuit or electrical component

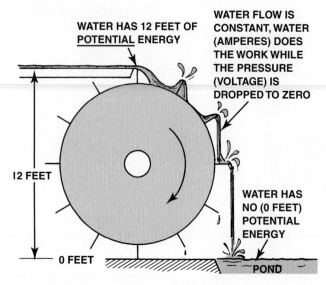

WATER HAS 12 FEET OF POTENTIAL ENERGY

WATER FLOW IS CONSTANT, WATER (AMPERES) DOES THE WORK WHILE THE PRESSURE (VOLTAGE) IS DROPPED TO ZERO

12 FEET

WATER HAS NO (0 FEET) POTENTIAL ENERGY

0 FEET

POND

FIGURE 4–8 Electrical flow through a circuit is similar to water flowing over a waterwheel. The more the water (amperes in electricity), the greater the amount of work (waterwheel). The amount of water remains constant, yet the pressure (voltage in electricity) drops as the current flows through the circuit.

 **TECH TIP**

Think of a Waterwheel

A beginner technician cleaned the positive terminal of the battery when the starter was cranking the engine slowly. When questioned by the shop foreman as to why only the positive post had been cleaned, the technician responded that the negative terminal was "only a ground." The foreman reminded the technician that the current, in amperes, is constant throughout a series circuit (such as the cranking motor circuit). If 200 amperes leave the positive post of the battery, then 200 amperes must return to the battery through the negative post.

The technician could not understand how electricity can do work (crank an engine), yet return the same amount of current, in amperes, as left the battery. The shop foreman explained that even though the current is constant throughout the circuit, the voltage (electrical pressure or potential) drops to zero in the circuit. To explain further, the shop foreman drew a waterwheel. ● **SEE FIGURE 4–8.**

As water drops from a higher level to a lower level, high potential energy (or voltage) is used to turn the waterwheel and results in low potential energy (or lower voltage). The same amount of water (or amperes) reaches the pond under the waterwheel as started the fall above the waterwheel. As current (amperes) flows through a conductor, it performs work in the circuit (turns the waterwheel) while its voltage (potential) drops.

OHM'S LAW

DEFINITION The German physicist, George Simon Ohm, established that electric pressure (EMF) in volts, electrical resistance in ohms, and the amount of current in amperes flowing through any circuit are all related. **Ohm's law** states:

It requires 1 volt to push 1 ampere through 1 ohm of resistance.

This means that if the voltage is doubled, then the number of amperes of current flowing through a circuit will also double if the resistance of the circuit remains the same.

FORMULAS Ohm's law can also be stated as a simple formula used to calculate one value of an electrical circuit if the other two are known. ● **SEE FIGURE 4–9.**

$$I = \frac{E}{R}$$

where

I = Current in amperes (A)

E = Electromotive force (EMF) in volts (V)

R = Resistance in ohms (Ω)

1. Ohm's law can determine the resistance if the volts and amperes are known: $R = \frac{E}{I}$

2. Ohm's law can determine the *voltage* if the resistance (ohms) and amperes are known: $E = I \times R$

3. Ohm's law can determine the amperes if the resistance and voltage are known: $I = \frac{E}{R}$

NOTE: Before applying Ohm's law, be sure that each unit of electricity is converted into base units. For example, 10 KΩ should be converted to 10,000 ohms and 10 mA should be converted into 0.010 A.

● **SEE CHART 4–1.**

OHM'S LAW APPLIED TO SIMPLE CIRCUITS If a battery with 12 volts is connected to a resistor of 4 ohms, as shown in ● **FIGURE 4–10,** how many amperes will flow through the circuit?

Using Ohm's law, we can calculate the number of amperes that will flow through the wires and the resistor. Remember, if two factors are known (volts and ohms in this

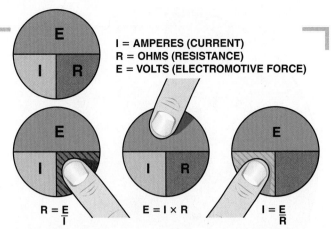

I = AMPERES (CURRENT)
R = OHMS (RESISTANCE)
E = VOLTS (ELECTROMOTIVE FORCE)

$$R = \frac{E}{I}$$

$$E = I \times R$$

$$I = \frac{E}{R}$$

FIGURE 4–9 To calculate one unit of electricity when the other two are known, simply use your finger and cover the unit you do not know. For example, if both voltage (E) and resistance (R) are known, cover the letter *I* (amperes). Notice that the letter *E* is above the letter *R,* so divide the resistor's value into the voltage to determine the current in the circuit.

VOLTAGE	RESISTANCE	AMPERAGE
Up	Down	Up
Up	Same	Up
Up	Up	Same
Same	Down	Up
Same	Same	Same
Same	Up	Down
Down	Up	Down
Down	Same	Down

CHART 4–1

Ohm's law relationship with the three units of electricity.

example), the remaining factor (amperes) can be calculated using Ohm's law.

$$I = \frac{E}{R} = \frac{12\,V}{4}\,A$$

The values for the voltage (12) and the resistance (4) were substituted for the variables E and R, and I is thus 3 amperes

$$\left(\frac{12}{4} = 3\right)$$

If we want to connect a resistor to a 12 volt battery, we now know that this simple circuit requires 3 amperes to operate. This may help us for two reasons.

1. We can now determine the wire diameter that we will need based on the number of amperes flowing through the circuit.

2. The correct fuse rating can be selected to protect the circuit.

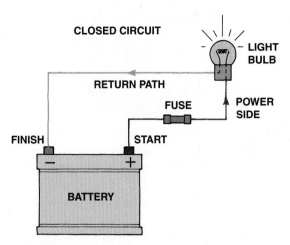

FIGURE 4–10 This closed circuit includes a power source, power-side wire, circuit protection (fuse), resistance (bulb), and return path wire. In this circuit, if the battery has 12 volts and the electrical load has 4 ohms, then the current through the circuit is 4 amperes.

WATT'S LAW

BACKGROUND James Watt (1736–1819), a Scottish inventor, first determined the power of a typical horse while measuring the amount of coal being lifted out of a mine. The power of one horse was determined to be 33,000 foot-pounds per minute. Electricity can also be expressed in a unit of power called a watt and the relationship is known as **Watt's law,** which states:

A watt is a unit of electrical power represented by a current of 1 ampere through a circuit with a potential difference of 1 volt.

FORMULAS A **watt** is a unit of electrical power represented by a current of 1 ampere through a circuit with a potential difference of 1 volt.

The symbol for a watt is the capital letter *W*. The formula for watts is:

$$W = I \times E$$

Another way to express this formula is to use the letter *P* to represent the unit of power. The formula then becomes:

$$P = I \times E$$

HINT: An easy way to remember this equation is that it spells "pie."

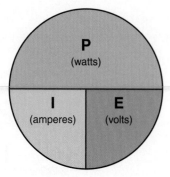

FIGURE 4–11 To calculate one unit when the other two are known, simply cover the unknown unit to see what unit needs to be divided or multiplied to arrive at the solution.

WATT'S LAW (CONTINUED)

Engine power is commonly rated in watts or kilowatts (1,000 watts equal 1 kilowatt), because 1 horsepower is equal to 746 watts. For example, a 200 horsepower engine can be rated as having the power equal to 149,200 watts or 149.2 kilowatts (kW).

To calculate watts, both the current in amperes and the voltage in the circuit must be known. If any two of these factors are known, then the other remaining factor can be determined by the following equations:

$$P = I \times E \text{ (watts equal amperes times voltage)}$$

$$I = \frac{P}{E} \text{ (amperes equal watts divided by voltage)}$$

$$E = \frac{P}{I} \text{ (voltage equals watts divided by amperes)}$$

A Watt's circle can be drawn and used like the Ohm's law circle diagram. ● **SEE FIGURE 4–11,**

MAGIC CIRCLE The formulas for calculating any combination of electrical units are shown in ● **FIGURE 4–12.**

It is almost impossible to remember all of these formulas, so this one circle showing all of the formulas is nice to have available if needed.

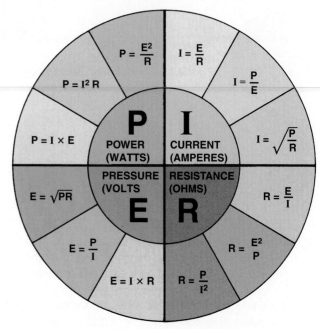

FIGURE 4–12 "Magic circle" of most formulas for problems involving Ohm's law. Each quarter of the "pie" has formulas used to solve for a particular unknown value: current (amperes), in the upper right segment; resistance (ohms), in the lower right; voltage (E), in the lower left; and power (watts), in the upper left.

> ### TECH TIP
>
> #### Wattage Increases by the Square of the Voltage
>
> The brightness of a light bulb, such as an automotive headlight or courtesy light, depends on the number of watts available. The watt is the unit by which electrical power is measured. If the battery voltage drops, even slightly, the light becomes noticeably dimmer. The formula for calculating power (P) in watts is $P = I \times E$. This can also be expressed as Watts = Amps × Volts.
>
> According to Ohm's law, $I = \frac{E}{R}$. Therefore, $\frac{E}{R}$ can be substituted for I in the previous formula resulting in $P = \frac{E}{R} \times E$ or $P = \frac{E^2}{R}$.
>
> E^2 means E multiplied by itself. A small change in the voltage (E) has a big effect on the total brightness of the bulb. (Remember, household light bulbs are sold according to their wattage.) Therefore, if the voltage to an automotive bulb is reduced, such as by a poor electrical connection, the brightness of the bulb is *greatly* affected. A poor electrical ground causes a voltage drop. The voltage at the bulb is reduced and the bulb's brightness is reduced.

1. All complete electrical circuits have a power source (such as a battery), a circuit protection device (such as a fuse), a power-side wire or path, an electrical load, a ground return path, and a switch or a control device.

2. A short-to-voltage involves a copper-to-copper connection and usually affects more than one circuit.

3. A short-to-ground usually involves a power path conductor coming in contact with a return (ground) path conductor and usually causes the fuse to blow.

4. An open is a break in the circuit resulting in absolutely no current flow through the circuit.

REVIEW QUESTIONS

1. What is included in a complete electrical circuit?

2. What is the difference between a short-to-voltage and a short-to-ground?

3. What is the difference between an electrical open and a short?

4. What is Ohm's law?

5. What occurs to current flow (amperes) and wattage if the resistance of a circuit is increased because of a corroded connection?

CHAPTER QUIZ

1. If an insulated wire rubbed through a part of the insulation and the wire conductor touched the steel body of a vehicle, the type of failure would be called a(n) _____.
   a. Short-to-voltage
   b. Short-to-ground
   c. Open
   d. Chassis ground

2. If two insulated wires were to melt together where the copper conductors touched each other, the type of failure would be called a(n) _____.
   a. Short-to-voltage
   b. Short-to-ground
   c. Open
   d. Floating ground

3. If 12 volts are being applied to a resistance of 3 ohms, _____ amperes will flow.
   a. 12
   b. 3
   c. 4
   d. 36

4. How many watts are consumed by a light bulb if 1.2 amperes are measured when 12 volts are applied?
   a. 14.4 watts
   b. 144 watts
   c. 10 watts
   d. 0.10 watt

5. How many watts are consumed by a starter motor if it draws 150 amperes at 10 volts?
   a. 15 watts
   b. 150 watts
   c. 1,500 watts
   d. 15,000 watts

6. High resistance in an electrical circuit can cause _____.
   a. Dim lights
   b. Slow motor operation
   c. Clicking of relays or solenoids
   d. All of the above

7. If the voltage increases in a circuit, what happens to the current (amperes) if the resistance remains the same?
   a. Increases
   b. Decreases
   c. Remains the same
   d. Cannot be determined

8. If 200 amperes flow from the positive terminal of a battery and operate the starter motor, how many amperes will flow back to the negative terminal of the battery?
   a. Cannot be determined
   b. Zero
   c. One half (about 100 amperes)
   d. 200 amperes

9. What is the symbol for voltage used in calculations?
   a. R
   b. E
   c. EMF
   d. I

10. Which circuit failure is most likely to cause the fuse to blow?
    a. Open
    b. Short-to-ground
    c. Short-to-voltage
    d. High resistance

chapter 5
SERIES CIRCUITS

OBJECTIVES

After studying Chapter 5, the reader will be able to:

1. Prepare for ASE Electrical/Electronic Systems (A6) certification test content area "A" (General Electrical/Electronic System Diagnosis).
2. Identify a series circuit.
3. Explain Kirchhoff's voltage law.
4. Calculate voltage drops in a series circuit.
5. Explain series circuit laws.

KEY TERMS

SERIES CIRCUITS

DEFINITION A **series circuit** is a complete circuit that has only one path for current to flow through all of the electrical loads. Electrical components such as fuses and switches are generally not considered to be included in the determination of a series circuit.

CONTINUITY The circuit must be continuous without any breaks. This is called **continuity.** Every circuit must have continuity in order for current to flow through the circuit. Because there is only one path for current to flow, the current is the same everywhere in a complete series circuit.

NOTE: Because an electrical load needs both a power and a ground to operate, a break (open) anywhere in a series circuit will cause the current in the circuit to stop.

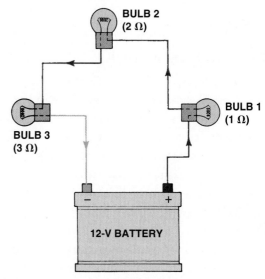

FIGURE 5–1 A series circuit with three bulbs. All current flows through all resistances (bulbs). The total resistance of the circuit is the sum of the individual resistances of each bulb, and the bulbs will light dimly because of the increased resistance and the reduction of current flow (amperes) through the circuit.

OHM'S LAW AND SERIES CIRCUITS

SERIES CIRCUIT TOTAL RESISTANCE A series circuit is a circuit containing more than one resistance in which all current must flow through all resistances in the circuit. Ohm's law can be used to calculate the value of one unknown (voltage, resistance, or amperes) if the other two values are known.

Because *all* current flows through all resistances, the total resistance is the sum (addition) of all resistances. ● **SEE FIGURE 5–1.**

The total resistance of the circuit shown here is 6 ohms (1 Ω + 2 Ω + 3 Ω). The formula for total resistance (R_T) for a series circuit is:

$$R_T = R_1 + R_2 + R_3 + \ldots$$

Using Ohm's law to find the current flow, we have:

$$I = \frac{E}{R} = \frac{12 \text{ V}}{6 \text{ }\Omega} = 2 \text{ A}$$

Therefore, with a total resistance of 6 ohms using a 12 volt battery in the series circuit shown, 2 amperes of current will flow through the entire circuit. If the amount of resistance in a series circuit is reduced, more current will flow.

For example, in ● **FIGURE 5–2,** one resistance (3 ohm bulb) has been eliminated compared to Figure 5–1, and now the total resistance is 3 ohms (1 Ω + 2 Ω).

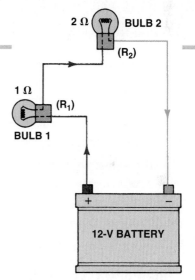

FIGURE 5–2 A series circuit with two bulbs.

Using Ohm's law to calculate current flow yields 4 amperes.

$$I = \frac{E}{R} = \frac{12 \text{ V}}{3 \text{ }\Omega} = 4 \text{ A}$$

Notice that the current flow was doubled (4 amperes instead of 2 amperes) when the resistance was cut in half (from 6 ohms to 3 ohms). The current flow would also double if the applied voltage was doubled.

Farsighted Quality of Electricity

Electricity almost seems to act as if it knows what resistances are ahead on the long trip through a circuit. If the trip through the circuit has many high-resistance components, very few electrons (amperes) will choose to attempt to make the trip. If a circuit has little or no resistance (for example, a short circuit), then as many electrons (amperes) as possible attempt to flow through the complete circuit. If another load, such as a light bulb, were added in series, the current flow would decrease and the bulbs would be dimmer than before the other bulb was added. If the flow exceeds the capacity of the fuse or the circuit breaker, then the circuit is opened and all current flow stops.

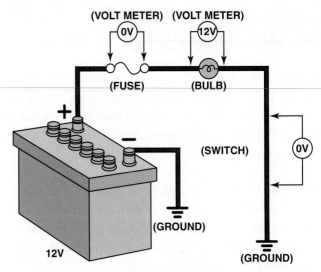

FIGURE 5–3 As current flows through a circuit, the voltage drops in proportion to the amount of resistance in the circuit. Most, if not all, of the resistance should occur across the load such as the bulb in this circuit. All of the other components and wiring should produce little, if any, voltage drop. If a wire or connection did cause a voltage drop, less voltage would be available to light the bulb and the bulb would be dimmer than normal.

KIRCHHOFF'S VOLTAGE LAW

DEFINITION A German physicist, Gustav Robert Kirchhoff (1824–1887), developed laws about electrical circuits. His second law, **Kirchhoff's voltage law,** concerns voltage drops. It states:

> The voltage around any closed circuit is equal to the sum (total) of the voltage drops across the resistances.

For example, the voltage that flows through a series circuit drops with each resistor in a manner similar to that in which the strength of an athlete drops each time a strenuous physical feat is performed. The greater the resistance is, the greater the drop in voltage.

APPLYING KIRCHHOFF'S VOLTAGE LAW Kirchhoff states in his second law that the voltage will drop in proportion to the resistance and that the total of all voltage drops will equal the applied voltage. ● **SEE FIGURE 5–3.**

Using ● **FIGURE 5–4,** the total resistance of the circuit can be determined by adding the individual resistances ($2\,\Omega + 4\,\Omega + 6\,\Omega = 12\,\Omega$).

The current through the circuit is determined by using Ohm's law, $I = \dfrac{E}{R} = \dfrac{12\text{ V}}{12\,\Omega} = 1$ A.

Therefore, in the circuit shown, the following values are known.

Resistance = $12\,\Omega$

Voltage = 12 V

Current = 1 A

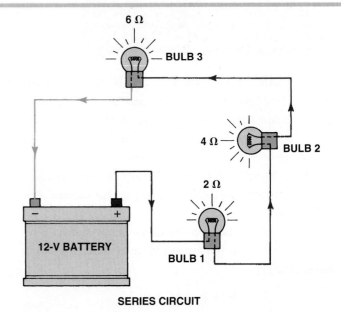

SERIES CIRCUIT

FIGURE 5–4 In a series circuit, the voltage is dropped or lowered by each resistance in the circuit. The higher the resistance is, the greater the drop in voltage.

Everything is known *except* the voltage drop caused by each resistance. A **voltage drop** is the drop in voltage across a resistance when current flows through a complete circuit. In other words, a voltage drop is the amount of voltage (electrical pressure) required to push electrons through a resistance. The voltage drop can be determined by using Ohm's law and calculating for voltage (E) using the value of each resistance individually, as follows:

$$E = I \times R$$

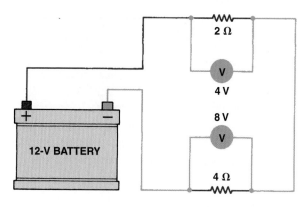

A. I = E/R (TOTAL "R" = 6 Ω)
   = 12/6 = 2A

B. E = I/R (VOLTAGE DROP)
   AT 2 Ω RESISTANCE =
   E = 2 x 2 = 4 V
   AT 4 Ω RESISTANCE =
   E = 2 x 4 = 8 V

C. 4 + 8 = 12 V
   SUM OF VOLTAGE DROP
   EQUALS APPLIED VOLTAGE

FIGURE 5–5 A voltmeter reads the differences of voltage between the test leads. The voltage read across a resistance is the voltage drop that occurs when current flows through a resistance. A voltage drop is also called an "IR" drop because it is calculated by multiplying the current (I) through the resistance (electrical load) by the value of the resistance (R).

where

E = Voltage

I = Current in the circuit (Remember, the current is constant in a series circuit; only the voltage varies.)

R = Resistance of only one of the resistances

The voltage drops are as follows:

Voltage drop for bulb 1: $E = I \times R = 1 A \times 2 \Omega = 2 V$

Voltage drop for bulb 2: $E = I \times R = 1 A \times 4 \Omega = 4 V$

Voltage drop for bulb 3: $E = I \times R = 1 A \times 6 \Omega = 6 V$

NOTE: Notice that the voltage drop is proportional to the resistance. In other words, the higher the resistance is, the greater the voltage drop. A 6 ohm resistance dropped the voltage three times as much as the voltage drop created by the 2 ohm resistance.

According to Kirchhoff, the sum (addition) of the voltage drops should equal the applied voltage (battery voltage).

Total of voltage drops = 2 V + 4 V
+ 6 V = 12 V = Battery voltage

This proves Kirchhoff's second (voltage) law. Another example is illustrated in ● **FIGURE 5–5.**

VOLTAGE DROPS

VOLTAGE DROPS USED IN CIRCUITS A voltage drop indicates resistance in the circuit. Often a voltage drop is not wanted in a circuit because it causes the electrical load to not operate correctly. Some automotive electrical systems use voltage drops in cases such as the following:

1. **Dash lights.** Most vehicles are equipped with a method of dimming the brightness of the dash lights by turning a variable resistor. This type of resistor can be adjusted and therefore varies the voltage to the dash light bulbs. A high voltage to the bulbs causes them to be bright, and a low voltage results in a dim light.

2. **Blower motor** (heater or air-conditioning fan). Speeds can be controlled by a fan switch sending current through high-, medium-, or low-resistance wire resistors. The highest resistance will drop the voltage the most, causing the motor to run at the lowest speed. The highest speed of the motor will occur when *no* resistance is in the circuit and full battery voltage is switched to the blower motor.

VOLTAGE DROPS AS A TESTING METHOD Any resistance in a circuit causes the voltage to drop in proportion to the amount of the resistance. Because a high resistance will drop the voltage more than a lower resistance, a voltmeter, as well as an ohmmeter, can be used to measure resistance. In fact, measuring the voltage drop is the preferred method recommended by most vehicle manufacturers to locate or test a circuit for excessive resistance. The formula for voltage drop is $E = I \times R$, where E is the voltage drop and I is the current in the circuit. Notice that as the value of the resistance (R) increases, the voltage drop increases.

SERIES CIRCUIT LAWS

Electrical loads or resistance connected in series behave following **series circuit laws**.

LAW 1 The total resistance in a series circuit is the sum total of the individual resistances. The resistance values of each electrical load are simply added together.

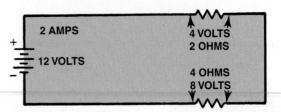

FIGURE 5–6 In this series circuit with a 2 ohm resistor and a 4 ohm resistor, current (2 amperes) is the same throughout, even though the voltage drops across each resistor are different.

FREQUENTLY ASKED QUESTION

Why Check the Voltage Drop Instead of Measuring the Resistance?

Imagine a wire with all strands cut except for one. An ohmmeter can be used to check the resistance of this wire and the resistance would be low, indicating that the wire was okay, but this one small strand cannot properly carry the current (amperes) in the circuit. A voltage drop test is therefore a better test to determine the resistance in components for two reasons:

- An ohmmeter can only test a wire or component that has been disconnected from the circuit and is not carrying current. The resistance can, and does, change when current flows.
- A voltage drop test is a dynamic test because as the current flows through a component, the conductor increases in temperature, which in turn increases resistance. This means that a voltage drop test is testing the circuit during normal operation and is therefore the most accurate way of determining circuit conditions.

A voltage drop test is also easier to perform because the resistance does not have to be known, only that the loss of voltage in a circuit should be less than 3%, or less than about 0.36 volt for any 12 volt circuit.

TECH TIP

Light Bulbs and Ohm's Law

If the resistance of a typical automotive light bulb is measured at room temperature, the resistance will often be around 1 ohm. If 12 volts were to be applied to this bulb, a calculated current of 12 amperes would be expected ($I = \dfrac{E}{R} = 12 \div 1 = 12$ A). However, as current flows through the filament of the bulb, it increases in temperature and becomes incandescent, thereby giving off light. When the bulb is first connected to a power sourceand current starts to flow, a high amount of current, called surge current, flows through the filament. Then within a few thousandths of a second, the current flow is reduced to about 10% of the surge current due to the increasing resistance of the filament, resulting in an actual current flow of about 1.2 A or about 100 ohms of resistance when the bulb is working.

As a result, using Ohm's law to calculate current flow does not take into account the differences in temperature of the components during actual operation.

SERIES CIRCUIT LAWS (CONTINUED)

LAW 2 The current is the same throughout the entire circuit.
● **SEE FIGURE 5–6.**

If 2 amperes of current leave the battery, 2 amperes of current return to the battery.

LAW 3 Although the current (in amperes) is constant, the voltage drops across each resistance in the circuit can vary at each resistor. The voltage drop across each load is proportional to the value of the resistance compared to the total resistance. For example, if the resistance of each resistor in a two-resistor circuit is half of the total resistance, the voltage drop across that resistance will be half of the applied voltage. The sum total of all individual voltage drops equals the applied source voltage.

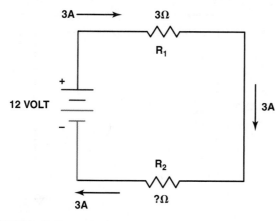

FIGURE 5–7 Example 1.

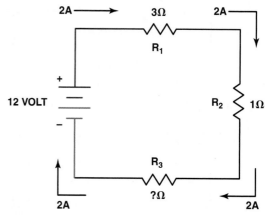

FIGURE 5–8 Example 2.

SERIES CIRCUIT EXAMPLES

Each of the four examples includes solving for the following:

- Total resistance in the circuit
- Current flow (amperes) through the circuit
- Voltage drop across each resistance

Example 1:

(● SEE FIGURE 5–7.)

The unknown in this problem is the value of R_2. Because the source voltage and the circuit current are known, the total circuit resistance, can be calculated using Ohm's law.

$$R_{Total} = \frac{E}{I} = 12 \text{ volts} \div 3 \text{ A} = 4 \text{ }\Omega$$

Because R_1 is 3 ohms and the total resistance is 4 ohms, therefore the value of R_2 is 1 ohm.

Example 2:

(● SEE FIGURE 5–8.)

The unknown in this problem is the value of R_3. The total resistance, however, can be calculated using Ohm's law.

$$R_{Total} = \frac{E}{I} = 12 \text{ volts} \div 2 \text{ A} = 6 \text{ }\Omega$$

The total resistance of R_1 (3 ohms) and R_2 (1 ohm) equals 4 ohms, so that the value of R_3 is the difference between the total resistance (6 ohms) and the value of the known resistance (4 ohms).

$$6 = 4 = 2 \text{ ohms} = R_3$$

Example 3:

(● SEE FIGURE 5–9.)

The unknown value in this problem is the voltage of the battery. To solve for voltage, use Ohm's law ($E - I \times R$). The R in this problem refers to the total resistance (R_T). The total resistance of a series circuit is determined by adding the values of the individual resistors.

$$R_T = 1 \text{ }\Omega + 1 \text{ }\Omega + 1 \text{ }\Omega$$

$$R_T = 3 \text{ }\Omega$$

Placing the value for the total resistance (3 Ω) into the equation results in a battery voltage of 12 volts.

$$E = 4 \text{ A} \times 3\Omega$$

$$E = 12 \text{ volts}$$

Example 4:

(● SEE FIGURE 5–10.)

The unknown in this example is the current (amperes) in the circuit. To solve for current, use Ohm's law.

$$I = \frac{E}{R} = 12 \text{ volts} \div 6 \text{ ohms} = 2 \text{ A}$$

Notice that the total resistance in the circuit (6 ohms) was used in this example, which is the total of the three individual resistors (2 Ω + 2 Ω + 2 Ω = 6 Ω). The current through the circuit is 2 amperes.

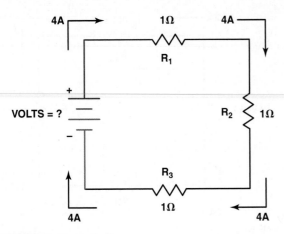

FIGURE 5–9 Example 3.

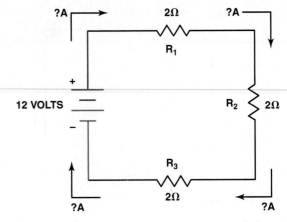

FIGURE 5–10 Example 4.

SUMMARY

1. In a simple series circuit, the current remains constant throughout, but the voltage drops as current flows through each of the resistances of the circuit.

2. The voltage drop across each resistance or load is directly proportional to the value of the resistance compared to the total resistance in the circuit.

3. The sum (total) of the voltage drops equals the applied voltage (Kirchhoff's voltage law).

4. An open or a break anywhere in a series circuit stops all current from flowing.

REVIEW QUESTIONS

1. What is Kirchhoff's voltage law?

2. What would current (amperes) do if the voltage were doubled in a circuit?

3. What would current (amperes) do if the resistance in the circuit were doubled?

4. What is the formula for voltage drop?

CHAPTER QUIZ

1. The amperage in a series circuit is _____.
   a. The same anywhere in the circuit
   b. Variable in the circuit due to the different resistances
   c. High at the beginning of the circuit and decreases as the current flows through the resistance
   d. Always less returning to the battery than leaving the battery

2. The sum of the voltage drops in a series circuit equals the _____.

   a. Amperage
   b. Resistance
   c. Source voltage
   d. Wattage

3. If the resistance and the voltage are known, what is the formula for finding the current (amperes)?
   a. $E = I \times R$
   b. $I = E \times R$
   c. $R = E \times I$
   d. $I = \dfrac{E}{R}$

4. A series circuit has three resistors of 6 ohms each. The voltage drop across each resistor is 4 volts. Technician A says that the source voltage is 12 volts. Technician B says that the total resistance is 18 ohms. Which technician is correct?
   a. Technician A only
   b. Technician B only
   c. Both Technicians A and B
   d. Neither Technician A nor B

5. If a 12 volt battery is connected to a series circuit with three resistors of 2 ohms, 4 ohms, and 6 ohms, how much current will flow through the circuit?
   a. 1 ampere
   b. 2 amperes
   c. 3 amperes
   d. 4 amperes

6. A series circuit has two 10 ohm bulbs. A third 10 ohm bulb is added in series. Technician A says that the three bulbs will be dimmer than when only two bulbs were in the circuit. Technician B says that the current in the circuit will increase. Which technician is correct?
   - **a.** Technician A only
   - **b.** Technician B only
   - **c.** Both Technicians A and B
   - **d.** Neither Technician A nor B

7. Technician A says that the sum of the voltage drops in a series circuit should equal the source voltage. Technician B says that the current (amperes) varies depending on the value of the resistance in a series circuit. Which technician is correct?
   - **a.** Technician A only
   - **b.** Technician B only
   - **c.** Both Technicians A and B
   - **d.** Neither Technician A nor B

8. Two light bulbs are wired in series and one bulb burns out (opens). Technician A says that the other bulb will work. Technician B says that the current will increase in the circuit because one electrical load (resistance) is no longer operating. Which technician is correct?
   - **a.** Technician A only
   - **b.** Technician B only
   - **c.** Both Technicians A and B
   - **d.** Neither Technician A nor B

9. Four resistors are connected to a 12 volt battery in series. The values of the resistors are 10 ohms, 100 ohms, 330 ohms, and 470 ohms. Technician A says that the greatest voltage drop will occur across the 10 ohm resistor. Technician B says that the greatest voltage drop will occur across the 470 ohm resistor. Which technician is correct?
   - **a.** Technician A only
   - **b.** Technician B only
   - **c.** Both Technicians A and B
   - **d.** Neither Technician A nor B

10. Three light bulbs are wired in series. A fourth bulb is connected to the circuit in series. Technician A says that the total voltage drop will increase. Technician B says that the current (amperes) will decrease. Which technician is correct?
   - **a.** Technician A only
   - **b.** Technician B only
   - **c.** Both Technicians A and B
   - **d.** Neither Technician A nor B

chapter 6
PARALLEL CIRCUITS

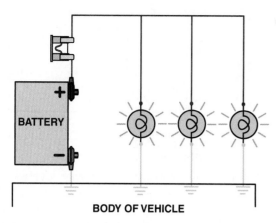

FIGURE 6–1 A typical parallel circuit used in vehicles includes many of the interior and exterior lights.

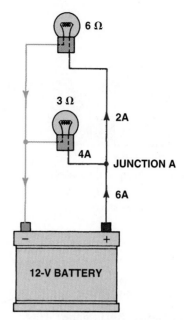

FIGURE 6–2 The amount of current flowing into junction point A equals the total amount of current flowing out of the junction.

PARALLEL CIRCUITS

DEFINITION A **parallel circuit** is a complete circuit that has more than one path for the current to flow. The separate paths that split and meet at junction points are called **branches, legs,** or **shunts.** The current flow through each branch or leg varies depending on the resistance in that branch. A break or open in one leg or section of a parallel circuit does not stop the current flow through the remaining legs of the parallel circuit. Most circuits in vehicles are parallel circuits and each branch is connected to the 12 volt power supply. ● **SEE FIGURE 6–1.**

KIRCHHOFF'S CURRENT LAW

DEFINITION **Kirchhoff's current law** (his first law) states: The current flowing into any junction of an electrical circuit is equal to the current flowing out of that junction.

Kirchhoff's law states that the amount of current flowing into junction A will equal the current flowing out of junction A.

Example:

Because the 6 ohm leg requires 2 amperes and the 3 ohm resistance leg requires 4 amperes, it is necessary that the wire from the battery to junction A be capable of handling 6 amperes. Also notice that the sum of the current flowing *out* of a junction (2 + 4 = 6 A) is equal to the current flowing *into* the junction (6 A), proving Kirchhoff's current law. ● **SEE FIGURE 6–2.**

Why Are Parallel Circuits Used Instead of Series Circuits?

Parallel circuits are used for most automotive circuits for the following reasons.

1. In a series circuit, any circuit fault such as an open would stop the flow of electricity to all of the electrical components in the circuit.
2. In a parallel circuit if one device fails, the other units will continue to work because each device has its own power supply wire.

PARALLEL CIRCUIT LAWS

LAW 1 The total resistance of a parallel circuit is always less than that of the smallest-resistance leg. This occurs because not all of the current flows through each leg or branch. With many branches, more current can flow from the battery just as more vehicles can travel on a road with five lanes compared to only one or two lanes.

LAW 2 The voltage is the same for each leg of a parallel circuit.

LAW 3 The sum of the individual currents in each leg will equal the total current. The amount of current flow through

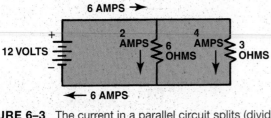

FIGURE 6–3 The current in a parallel circuit splits (divides) according to the resistance in each branch. Each branch has 12 volts applied to the resistors.

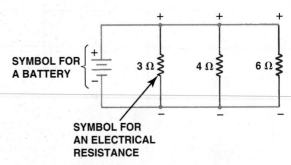

FIGURE 6–4 In a typical parallel circuit, each resistance has power and ground and each leg operates independently of the other legs of the circuit.

TECH TIP

The Path of Least Resistance

There is an old saying that electricity will always take the path of least resistance. This is true, especially if there is a fault such as in the secondary (high-voltage) section of the ignition system. If there is a path to ground that is lower resistance than the path to the spark plug, the high-voltage spark will take the path of least resistance. In a parallel circuit where there is more than one path for the current to flow, most of the current will flow through the branch with the lower resistance. This does not mean that all of the current will flow through the lowest resistance, because the other path provides a path to ground and the amount of current flow through the other branches is determined by the resistance and the applied voltage according to Ohm's law.

Therefore, the only place where electricity takes the path of least resistance is in a series circuit where there are not other paths for the current to flow.

PARALLEL CIRCUIT LAWS (CONTINUED)

a parallel circuit may vary for each leg depending on the resistance of that leg. The current flowing through each leg results in the same voltage drop (from the power side to the ground side) as for every other leg of the circuit. ● SEE FIGURE 6–3.

NOTE: A parallel circuit drops the voltage from source voltage to zero (ground) across the resistance in each leg of the circuit.

DETERMINING TOTAL RESISTANCE IN A PARALLEL CIRCUIT

There are five methods commonly used to determine total resistance in a parallel circuit.

NOTE: Determining the total *resistance* of a parallel circuit is very important in automotive service. Electronic fuel injector and diesel engine glow plug circuits are two of the most commonly tested circuits where parallel circuit knowledge is required. Also, when installing extra lighting, the technician must determine the proper gauge wire and protection device.

METHOD 1 The total *current* (in amperes) can be calculated first by treating each leg of the parallel circuit as a simple circuit. ● SEE FIGURE 6–4.

Each leg has its own power (+) and ground (−) and, therefore, the current through each leg is independent of the current through any other leg.

Current through the 3 Ω resistance =

$$I = \frac{E}{R} = \frac{12V}{3\Omega} = 4\,A$$

Current through the 4 Ω resistance =

$$I = \frac{E}{R} = \frac{12V}{4\Omega} = 3\,A$$

Current through the 4 Ω resistance =

$$I = \frac{E}{R} = \frac{12V}{6\Omega} = 2\,A$$

The total current flowing from the battery is the sum total of the individual currents for each leg. Total current from the battery is, therefore, 9 amperes (4 A + 3 A + 2 A = 9 A).

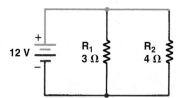

FIGURE 6–5 A schematic showing two resistors in parallel connected to a 12 volt battery.

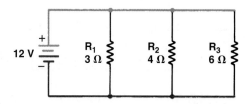

FIGURE 6–6 A parallel circuit with three resistors connected to a 12 volt battery.

If **total circuit resistance** (R_T) is needed, Ohm's law can be used to calculate it because voltage (E) and current (I) are now known.

$$R_T = \frac{E}{I} = \frac{12\,V}{9\,A} = 1.33\,\Omega$$

Note that the total resistance (1.33 Ω) is smaller than that of the smallest-resistance leg of the parallel circuit. This characteristic of a parallel circuit holds true because not all of the total current flows through all resistances as in a series circuit.

Because the current has alternative paths to ground through the various legs of a parallel circuit, as additional resistances (legs) are added to a parallel circuit, the total current from the battery (power source) *increases*.

Additional current can flow when resistances are added in parallel, because each leg of a parallel circuit has its own power and ground and the current flowing through each leg is strictly dependent on the resistance of *that* leg.

METHOD 2 If only two resistors are connected in parallel, the total resistance (R_T) can be found using the formula $R_T = \left(\dfrac{R_1 \times R_2}{R_1 + R_2}\right)$. For example, using the circuit in

● **FIGURE 6–5** and substituting 3 ohms for R_1 and 4 ohms for R_2, $R_T = \dfrac{(3 \times 4)}{(3 + 4)} = \dfrac{12}{7} = 1.7\,\Omega$.

Note that the total resistance (1.7 Ω) is smaller than that of the smallest-resistance leg of the circuit.

NOTE: Which resistor is R_1 and which is R_2 is not important. The position in the formula makes no difference in the multiplication and addition of the resistor values.

This formula can be used for more than two resistances in parallel, but only two resistances can be calculated at a time. After solving for R_T for two resistors, use the value of R_T as R_1 and the additional resistance in parallel as R_2. Then solve for another R_T. Continue the process for all resistance legs of the parallel circuit. However, note that it might be easier to solve for R_T when there are more than two resistances in parallel by using either method 3 or method 4.

METHOD 3 A formula that can be used to find the total resistance for any number of resistances in parallel is $\dfrac{1}{R_T} = \dfrac{1}{R_1} + \dfrac{1}{R_2} + \dfrac{1}{R_3} + \ldots$

To solve for R_T for the three resistance legs in ● **FIGURE 6–6,** substitute the values of the resistances for R_1, R_2, and R_3: $\dfrac{1}{R_T} = \dfrac{1}{3} + \dfrac{1}{4} + \dfrac{1}{6}$.

The fractions cannot be added together unless they all have the same denominator. The lowest common denominator in this example is 12. Therefore, $\dfrac{1}{3}$ becomes $\dfrac{4}{12}$, $\dfrac{1}{4}$ becomes $\dfrac{3}{12}$, and $\dfrac{1}{6}$ becomes $\dfrac{2}{12}$.

$\dfrac{1}{R_T} = \dfrac{4}{12} + \dfrac{3}{12} + \dfrac{2}{12}$ or $\dfrac{9}{12}$. Cross multiplying

$R_T = \dfrac{12}{9} = 1.33\,\Omega$.

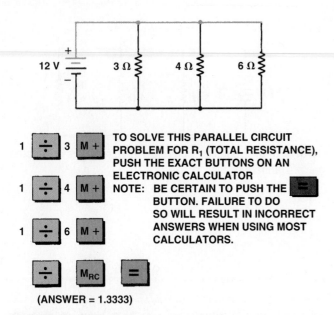

TO SOLVE THIS PARALLEL CIRCUIT PROBLEM FOR R_1 (TOTAL RESISTANCE), PUSH THE EXACT BUTTONS ON AN ELECTRONIC CALCULATOR

NOTE: BE CERTAIN TO PUSH THE = BUTTON. FAILURE TO DO SO WILL RESULT IN INCORRECT ANSWERS WHEN USING MOST CALCULATORS.

(ANSWER = 1.3333)

FIGURE 6–7 Using an electronic calculator to determine the total resistance of a parallel circuit.

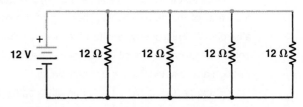

USE AN ELECTRONIC CALCULATOR TO SOLVE:

$R_T = 1$ ÷ 20 M+

1 ÷ 1000 M+

1 ÷ 45 M+

1 ÷ M_{RC} =

NOTE:

THE TOTAL RESISTANCE (R_T) MUST BE LESS THAN THE SMALLEST RESISTANCE (LESS THAN 20 Ω IN THIS EXAMPLE).

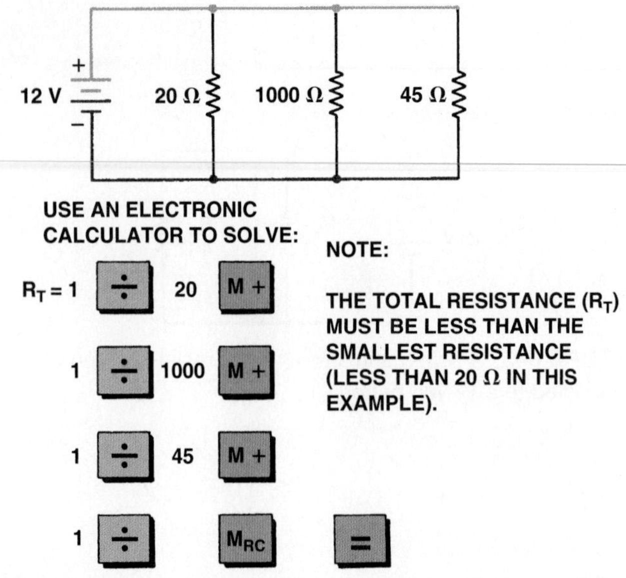

FIGURE 6–8 Another example of how to use an electronic calculator to determine the total resistance of a parallel circuit. The answer is 13.45 ohms. Notice that the effective resistance of this circuit is less than the resistance of the lowest branch (20 ohms).

DETERMINING TOTAL RESISTANCE IN A PARALLEL CIRCUIT (CONTINUED)

Note that the result (1.33 Ω) is the same regardless of the method used (see method 1). The most difficult part of using this method (besides using fractions) is determining the lowest common denominator, especially for circuits containing a wide range of ohmic values for the various legs. For an easier method using a calculator, see method 4.

METHOD 4 This method uses an electronic calculator, commonly available at very low cost. Instead of determining the lowest common denominator as in method 3, one can use the electronic calculator to convert the fractions to decimal equivalents. The memory buttons on most calculators can be used to keep a running total of the fractional values. Using ● **FIGURE 6–7,** calculate the total resistance (R_T) by pushing the indicated buttons on the calculator.

● Also **SEE FIGURE 6–8.**

FIGURE 6–9 A parallel circuit containing four 12 ohm resistors. When a circuit has more than one resistor of equal value, the total resistance can be determined by simply dividing the value of the resistance (12 ohms in this example) by the number of equal-value resistors (4 in this example) to get 3 ohms.

NOTE: This method can be used to find the total resistance of any number of resistances in parallel.

The memory recall (MRC) and equals (=) buttons invert the answer to give the correct value for total resistance (1.33 Ω). The inverse $\left(\frac{1}{X} \text{ or } X^{-1}\right)$ button can be used with the sum (SUM) button on scientific calculators without using the memory button.

METHOD 5 This method can be easily used when two or more resistances connected in parallel are of the same value. ● **SEE FIGURE 6–9.**

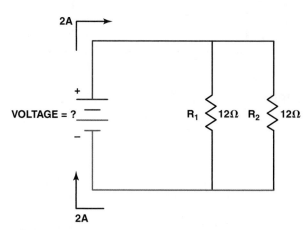

FIGURE 6–10 Example 1.

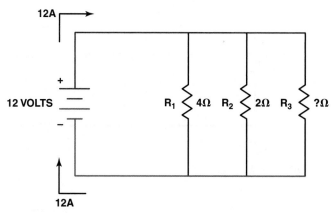

FIGURE 6–11 Example 2.

To calculate the total resistance (R_T) of equal-value resistors, divide the number of equal resistors into the value of the resistance: R_T Value of equal resistance/Number of equal resistances

$$= \frac{12\,\Omega}{4} = 3\,\Omega.$$

NOTE: Because most automotive and light-truck electrical circuits involve multiple use of the same resistance, this method is the most useful. For example, if six additional 12 ohm lights were added to a vehicle, the additional lights would represent just 2 ohms of resistance $\left(\frac{12\,\Omega}{6}\ \text{lights} = 2\right)$. Therefore, 6 amperes of additional current would be drawn by the additional lights $\left(I = \frac{E}{R} = \frac{12\,V}{2\,\Omega} = 6\,A\right)$.

PARALLEL CIRCUIT CALCULATION EXAMPLES

Each of the four examples includes solving for the following:

- Total resistance
- Current flow (amperes) through each branch as well as total current flow
- Voltage drop across each resistance

Example 1:

(● **SEE FIGURE 6–10.**)

In this example, the voltage of the battery is unknown and the equation to be used is $E = I \times R$, where R represents the total resistance of the circuit. Using the equation for two resistors in parallel, the total resistance is 6 ohms.

$$R_T = \frac{R_1 \times R_2}{R_1 + R_2} = \frac{12 \times 12}{12 + 12} = \frac{144}{24} = 6\,\Omega$$

Placing the value of the total resistors into the equation results in a value for the battery voltage of 12 volts.

$$E = I \times R$$

$$E = 2\,A \times 6\,\Omega$$

$$E = 12\,\text{volts}$$

Example 2:

(● **SEE FIGURE 6–11.**)

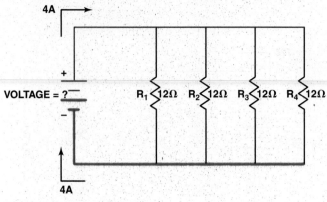

FIGURE 6–12 Example 3.

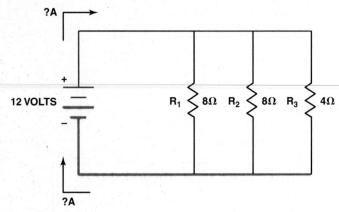

FIGURE 6–13 Example 4.

PARALLEL CIRCUIT CALCULATION EXAMPLES (CONTINUED)

In this example, the value of R_3 is unknown. Because the voltage (12 volts) and the current (12 A) are known, it is easier to solve for the unknown resistance by treating each branch or leg as a separate circuit. Using Kirchhoff's law, the total current equals the total current flow through each branch. The current flow through R_1 is 3 A $\left(I = \dfrac{E}{R} = \dfrac{12V}{4\,\Omega} = 3A \right)$ and the current flow through R_2 is 6 A $\left(I = \dfrac{E}{R} = \dfrac{12V}{2\,\Omega} = 6A \right)$. Therefore, the total current through the two known branches equals 9 A (3 A + 6 A = 9 A). Because there are 12 A leaving and returning to the battery, the current flow through R_3 must be 3 A (12 A − 9 A = 3 A). The resistance must therefore be 4 Ω $\left(I = \dfrac{E}{R} = \dfrac{12V}{4\,\Omega} = 3A \right)$.

Example 3:

(● SEE FIGURE 6–12.)

In this example, the voltage of the battery is unknown. The equation to solve for voltage according to Ohm's law is:

$$E = I \times R$$

The R in this equation refers to the total resistance. Because there are four resistors of equal value, the total can be determined by the following equation.

$$R_{Total} = \frac{\text{Value of resistors}}{\text{Number of equal resistors}} = \frac{12\,\Omega}{4} = 3\,\Omega$$

Inserting the value of the total resistors of the parallel circuit (3 Ω) into Ohm's law results in a battery voltage of 12 V.

$$E = 4\,A \times 3\,\Omega$$

$$E = 12\,V$$

Example 4:

(● SEE FIGURE 6–13.)

The unknown is the amount of current in the circuit. The Ohm's law equation for determining current is:

$$I = \frac{E}{R}$$

The R represents the total resistance. Because there are two equal resistances (8 Ω), these two can be replaced by one resistance of 4 Ω $\left(R_{Total} = \dfrac{\text{Value}}{\text{Number}} = \dfrac{8\,\Omega}{2} = 4\,\Omega \right)$.

The total resistance of this parallel circuit containing two 8 ohm resistors and one 4 ohm resistor is 2 ohms. The current flow from the battery is then calculated to be 6 A.

$$I = \frac{E}{R} = \frac{12\,V}{2\,\Omega} = 6\,A$$

SUMMARY

1. Parallel circuits are used in most automotive applications.

2. The total resistance of a parallel circuit is always lower than the smallest resistance in the leg of the circuit.

3. The separate paths which split and meet at junction points are called branches, legs, or shunts.

4. Kirchhoff's current law states: The current flowing into any junction of an electrical circuit is equal to the current flowing out of that junction.

5. There are five basic methods that can be used to calculate the total resistance in a parallel circuit.

REVIEW QUESTIONS

1. Why is the total resistance of a parallel circuit less than the smallest resistance?

2. Why are parallel circuits (instead of series circuits) used in most automotive applications?

3. What does Kirchhoff's current law state?

4. What are three of the five ways to calculate the total resistance of a parallel circuit?

CHAPTER QUIZ

1. Two bulbs are connected in parallel to a 12 volt battery. One bulb has a resistance of 6 ohms and the other bulb has a resistance of 2 ohms. Technician A says that only the 2 ohm bulb will light because all of the current will flow through the path with the least resistance and no current will flow through the 6 ohm bulb. Technician B says that the 6 ohm bulb will be dimmer than the 2 ohm bulb. Which technician is correct?
   a. Technician A only
   b. Technician B only
   c. Both Technicians A and B
   d. Neither Technician A nor B

2. Calculate the total resistance and current in a parallel circuit with three resistors of 4 Ω, 8 Ω, and 16 Ω, using any one of the five methods (calculator suggested). What are the values?
   a. 27 ohms (0.4 ampere)
   b. 14 ohms (0.8 ampere)
   c. 4 ohms (3 amperes)
   d. 2.3 ohms (5.3 amperes)

3. If an accessory such as an additional light is spliced into an existing circuit in parallel, what happens?
   a. The current increases in the circuit.
   b. The current decreases in the circuit.
   c. The voltage drops in the circuit.
   d. The resistance of the circuit increases.

4. A 6-cylinder engine uses six fuel injectors connected electrically in two groups of three injectors in parallel. What would be the resistance if the three 12 ohm injectors were connected in parallel?
   a. 36 ohms
   b. 12 ohms
   c. 4 ohms
   d. 3 ohms

5. A vehicle has four taillight bulbs all connected in parallel. If one bulb burns out (opens), the total current flow in the circuit _____.
   a. Increases and the other bulbs get brighter
   b. Decreases because only three bulbs are operating
   c. Remains the same because all the bulbs are wired in parallel
   d. Drops to zero and the other three bulbs go out

6. Two identical bulbs are connected to a 12 volt battery in parallel. The voltage drop across the first bulb is 12 volts as measured with a voltmeter. What is the voltage drop across the other bulb?
   a. 0 volt
   b. 1 volt
   c. 6 volts
   d. 12 volts

7. Three resistors are connected to a 12 volt battery in parallel. The current flow through each resistor is 4 amperes. What is the value of the resistors?
   a. 1 ohm
   b. 2 ohms
   c. 3 ohms
   d. 4 ohms

8. Two bulbs are connected to a 12 volt battery in parallel. Another bulb is added in parallel. Technician A says that the third bulb will be dimmer than the other two bulbs due to reduced current flow through the filament of the bulb. Technician B says that the amount of current flowing from the battery will decrease due to the extra load. Which technician is correct?
   a. Technician A only
   b. Technician B only
   c. Both Technicians A and B
   d. Neither Technician A nor B

9. A vehicle has four parking lights all connected in parallel and one of the bulbs burns out. Technician A says that this could cause the parking light circuit fuse to blow (open). Technician B says that it would decrease the total current in the circuit. Which technician is correct?
   a. Technician A only
   b. Technician B only
   c. Both Technicians A and B
   d. Neither Technician A nor B

10. Three resistors are connected in parallel to a 12 volt battery. The total current flow from the battery is 12 amperes. The first resistor is 3 ohms and the second resistor is 6 ohms. What is the value of the third resistor?
    a. 1 Ω
    b. 2 Ω
    c. 3 Ω
    d. 4 Ω

chapter 7
SERIES-PARALLEL CIRCUITS

OBJECTIVES

After studying Chapter 7, the reader will be able to:

1. Prepare for ASE Electrical/Electronic Systems (A6) certification test content area "A" (General Electrical/Electronic System Diagnosis).

2. Identify a series-parallel circuit.

3. Calculate current flow and voltage drops in a series-parallel circuit.

4. Identify where faults in a series-parallel circuit can be detected or determined.

KEY TERMS

Combination circuit 90
Compound circuit 90
Series-parallel circuits 90

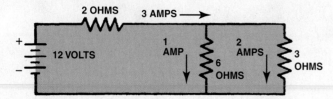

FIGURE 7–1 A series-parallel circuit.

SERIES-PARALLEL CIRCUITS

DEFINITION **Series-parallel circuits** are a combination of series and parallel segments in one complex circuit. A series-parallel circuit is also called a **compound** or **combination circuit.** Many automotive circuits include sections that are in parallel and in series.

TYPES OF SERIES-PARALLEL CIRCUITS A series-parallel circuit includes both parallel loads or resistances, plus additional loads or resistances that are electrically connected in series. There are two basic types of series-parallel circuits.

- A circuit where the load is in series with other loads is parallel. ● **SEE FIGURE 7–1.**

  An example of this type of series-parallel circuit is a dash light dimming circuit. The variable resistor is used to limit current flow to the dash light bulbs, which are wired in parallel.

- A circuit where either a parallel circuit contains resistors or loads are in series in one or more branches. A headlight and starter circuit is an example of this type of series-parallel circuit. A headlight switch is usually connected in series with a dimmer switch and in parallel with the dash light dimmer resistors. The headlights are also connected in parallel along with the taillights and side marker lights. ● **SEE FIGURE 7–2.**

SERIES-PARALLEL CIRCUIT FAULTS If a conventional parallel circuit, such as a taillight circuit, had an electrical fault that increased the resistance in one branch of the circuit, then the amount of current flow through that one branch will be reduced. The added resistance, due to corrosion or other similar cause, would create a voltage drop. As a result of this drop in voltage, a lower voltage would be applied and the bulb in the taillight would be dimmer than normal because the brightness of the bulb depends on the voltage and current applied. If, however, the added resistance occurred in a part of the circuit that fed both taillights, then both taillights would be dimmer than normal. In this case, the added resistance created a series-parallel circuit that was originally just a simple parallel circuit.

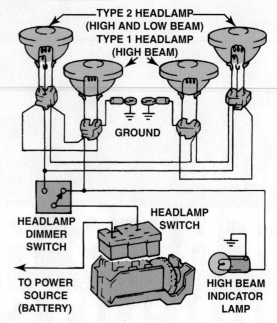

FIGURE 7–2 This complete headlight circuit with all bulbs and switches is a series-parallel circuit.

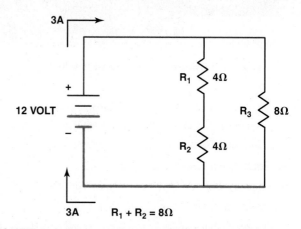

FIGURE 7–3 Solving a series-parallel circuit problem.

SOLVING SERIES-PARALLEL CIRCUIT CALCULATION PROBLEMS

The key to solving series-parallel circuit problems is to combine or simplify as much as possible. For example, if there are two loads or resistances in series within a parallel branch or leg, then the circuit can be made simpler if the two are first added together before attempting to solve the parallel section. ● **SEE FIGURE 7–3.**

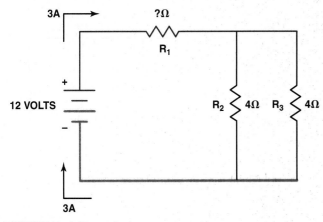

FIGURE 7–4 Example 1.

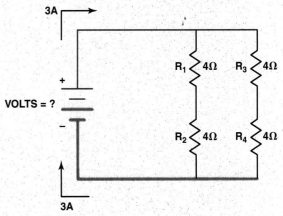

FIGURE 7–5 Example 2.

SERIES-PARALLEL CIRCUIT CALCULATION EXAMPLES

Each of the four examples includes solving for the following:

- Total resistance
- Current flow (amperes) through each branch, as well as total current flow
- Voltage drop across each resistance

Example 1

(● SEE FIGURE 7–4.)

The unknown resistor is in series with the other two resistances, which are connected in parallel. The Ohm's law equation to determine resistance is:

$$R = \frac{E}{I} = \frac{12\,V}{3} = 4\,\Omega$$

The total resistance of the circuit is therefore 4 ohms and the value of the unknown can be determined by subtracting the value of the two resistors that are connected in parallel. The parallel branch resistance is 2 ohms.

$$R_T = \frac{4 \times 4}{4 + 4} = \frac{16}{8} = 2\,\Omega$$

The value of the unknown resistance is therefore 2 Ω. Total R = 4 Ω − 2 Ω = 2 Ω.

Example 2

(● SEE FIGURE 7–5.)

The unknown unit in this circuit is the voltage of the battery. The Ohm's law equation is:

$$E = I \times R$$

Before solving the problem, the total resistance must be determined. Because each branch contains two 4 ohm resistors in series, the value in each branch can be added to help simplify the circuit. By adding the resistors in each branch together, the parallel circuit now consists of two 8 ohm resistors.

$$R_T = \frac{R_1 \times R_2}{R_1 + R_2} = \frac{8 \times 8}{8 + 8} = \frac{64}{16} = 4\,\Omega$$

Inserting the value for the total resistance into the Ohm's law equation results in a value of 12 volts for the battery voltage.

$$E = I \times R$$

$$E = 3\,A \times 4\,\Omega$$

$$E = 12\ volts$$

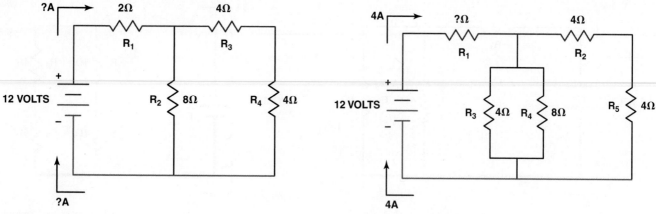

FIGURE 7–6 Example 3.

FIGURE 7–7 Example 4.

SERIES-PARALLEL CIRCUIT CALCULATION EXAMPLES (CONTINUED)

Example 3

(● **SEE FIGURE 7–6.**)

In this example, the total current through the circuit is unknown. The Ohm's law equation to solve for is:

$$I = \frac{E}{R}$$

The total resistance of the parallel circuit must be determined before the equation can be used to solve for current (amperes). To solve for total resistance, the circuit can first be simplified by adding R_3 and R_4 together, because these two resistors are in series in the same branch of the parallel circuit. To simplify even more, the resulting parallel section of the circuit, now containing two 8 ohm resistors in parallel, can be replaced with one 4 ohm resistor.

$$R_T = \frac{R_1 \times R_2}{R_1 + R_2} = \frac{8 \times 8}{8 + 8} = \frac{64}{16} = 4 \ \Omega$$

With the parallel branches now reduced to just one 4 ohm resistor, this can be added to the 2 ohm (R_1) resistor because it is in series, creating a total circuit resistance of 6 ohms. Now the current flow can be determined from Ohm's law.

$$I = \frac{E}{R} = 12 \div 6 = 2 \ A$$

Example 4

(● **SEE FIGURE 7–7.**)

In this example, the value of resistor R_1 is unknown. Using Ohm's law, the total resistance of the circuit is 3 ohms.

$$R = \frac{E}{I} = \frac{12 \ V}{4A} = 3 \ \Omega$$

However, knowing the total resistance is not enough to determine the value of R_1. To simplify the circuit, R_2 and R_5 can combine to create a parallel branch resistance value of 8 ohms because they are in series. To simplify even further, the two 8 ohm branches can be reduced to one branch of 4 ohms.

$$R_T = \frac{R_1 \times R_2}{R_1 + R_2} = \frac{8 \times 8}{8 + 8} = \frac{64}{16} = 4 \ \Omega$$

Now the circuit has been simplified to one resistor in series (R_1) with two branches with 4 ohms in each branch. These two branches can be reduced to equal one 2 ohm resistor.

$$R_T = \frac{R_1 \times R_2}{R_1 + R_2} = \frac{4 \times 4}{4 + 4} = \frac{16}{8} = 2 \ \Omega$$

Now the circuit includes just one 2 ohm resistor plus the unknown R_1. Because the total resistance is 3 ohms, the value of R_1 must be 1 ohm.

$$3 \ \Omega - 2 \ \Omega = 1 \ \Omega$$

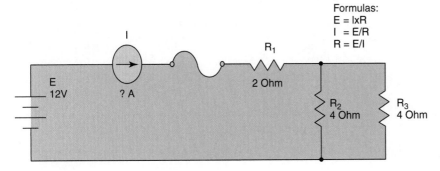

FIGURE 7–8 Chapter Quiz question 3.

Formulas:
$E = I \times R$
$I = E/R$
$R = E/I$

R_1

2 Ohm

I

E
12V

? A

R_2
4 Ohm

R_3
4 Ohm

E = 12V
R_1 = 2 Ohm
R_2 = 4 Ohm
R_3 = 4 Ohm
R_t = 4 Ohm
I =

SUMMARY

1. A series-parallel circuit is called a compound circuit or a combination circuit.

2. A series-parallel circuit is a combination of a series and a parallel circuit.

3. A fault in a series portion of a series-parallel circuit would affect the entire circuit operation if the series part was in the power or the ground side of the parallel portion of the circuit.

4. A fault in one leg of a series-parallel circuit will affect just the component(s) in that one leg.

REVIEW QUESTIONS

1. Explain why an increase in resistance in the series part of a series-parallel circuit will affect the current (amperes) through the parallel legs (branches).

2. What would be the effect of an open circuit in one leg of a parallel portion of a series-parallel circuit?

3. What would be the effect of an open circuit in a series portion of a series-parallel circuit?

CHAPTER QUIZ

1. Half of the dash is dark. Technician A says that a defective dash light dimmer can be the cause because it is in series with the bulbs that are in parallel. Technician B says that one or more bulbs could be defective. Which technician is correct?
   a. Technician A only
   b. Technician B only
   c. Both Technicians A and B
   d. Neither Technician A nor B

2. All brake lights are dimmer than normal. Technician A says that bad bulbs could be the cause. Technician B says that high resistance in the brake switch could be the cause. Which technician is correct?
   a. Technician A only
   b. Technician B only
   c. Both Technicians A and B
   d. Neither Technician A nor B

3. See ● **FIGURE 7–8** to solve for total resistance (R_T) *and* total current (I_T).
   a. 10 ohms and 1.2 A   c. 6 ohms and 2 A
   b. 4 ohms and 3 A   d. 2 ohms and 6 A

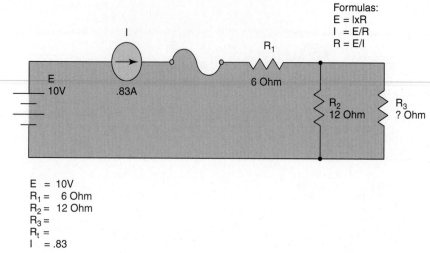

FIGURE 7–9 Chapter Quiz question 4.

Formulas:
E = IxR
I = E/R
R = E/I

I

E
10V

.83A

R₁
6 Ohm

R₂
12 Ohm

R₃
? Ohm

E = 10V
R₁ =   6 Ohm
R₂ = 12 Ohm
R₃ =
Rₜ =
I   = .83

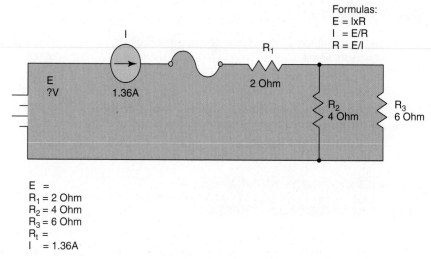

FIGURE 7–10 Chapter Quiz question 5.

Formulas:
E = IxR
I = E/R
R = E/I

I

E
?V

1.36A

R₁
2 Ohm

R₂
4 Ohm

R₃
6 Ohm

E =
R₁ = 2 Ohm
R₂ = 4 Ohm
R₃ = 6 Ohm
Rₜ =
I   = 1.36A

4. See ● **FIGURE 7–9** to solve for the value of R₃ *and* total resistance (Rₜ).
    a. 12 ohms and 12 ohms
    b. 1 ohm and 7 ohms
    c. 2 ohms and 8 ohms
    d. 6 ohms and 6 ohms

5. See ● **FIGURE 7–10** to solve for voltage (E) *and* total resistance (Rₜ).
    a. 16.3 volts and 12 ohms
    b. 3.3 volts and 2.4 ohms
    c. 1.36 volts and 1 ohm
    d. 6 volts and 4.4 ohms

6. See ● **FIGURE 7–11** to solve for R₁ *and* total resistance (Rₜ).
    a. 3 ohms and 15 ohms   **c.** 2 ohms and 5 ohms
    b. 1 ohm and 15 ohms   **d.** 5 ohms and 5 ohms

7. See ● **FIGURE 7–12** to solve for total resistance (Rₜ) *and* total current (I).
    a. 3.1 ohms and 7.7 amperes
    b. 5.1 ohms and 4.7 amperes
    c. 20 ohms and 1.2 amperes
    d. 6 ohms and 4 amperes

8. See ● **FIGURE 7–13** to solve for the value of E *and* total resistance (Rₜ).
    a. 13.2 volts and 40 ohms
    b. 11.2 volts and 34 ohms
    c. 8 volts and 24.2 ohms
    d. 8.6 volts and 26 ohms

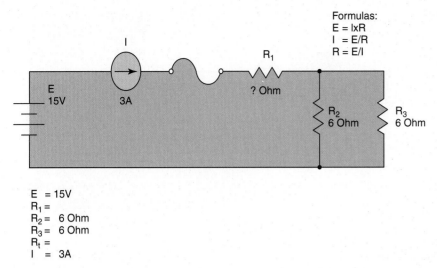

FIGURE 7–11 Chapter Quiz question 6.

Formulas:
E = IxR
I = E/R
R = E/I

E = 15V
R₁ =
R₂ = 6 Ohm
R₃ = 6 Ohm
Rₜ =
I = 3A

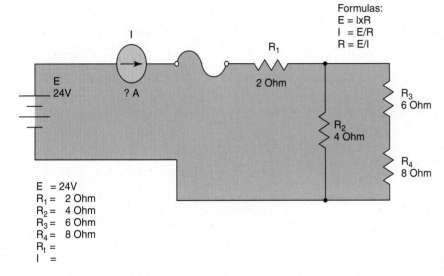

FIGURE 7–12 Chapter Quiz question 7.

Formulas:
E = IxR
I = E/R
R = E/I

E = 24V
R₁ = 2 Ohm
R₂ = 4 Ohm
R₃ = 6 Ohm
R₄ = 8 Ohm
Rₜ =
I =

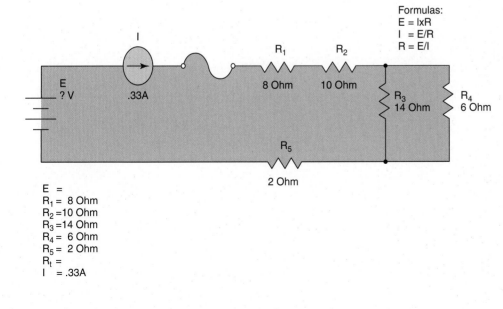

FIGURE 7–13 Chapter Quiz question 8.

Formulas:
E = IxR
I = E/R
R = E/I

E =
R₁ = 8 Ohm
R₂ =10 Ohm
R₃ =14 Ohm
R₄ = 6 Ohm
R₅ = 2 Ohm
Rₜ =
I = .33A

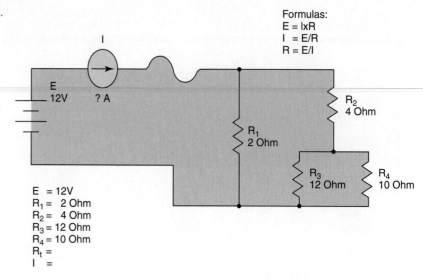

FIGURE 7-14 Chapter Quiz question 9.

Formulas:
E = IxR
I = E/R
R = E/I

E
12V

I
? A

R₂
4 Ohm

R₁
2 Ohm

R₃
12 Ohm

R₄
10 Ohm

E = 12V
R₁ =   2 Ohm
R₂ =   4 Ohm
R₃ = 12 Ohm
R₄ = 10 Ohm
Rₜ =
I   =

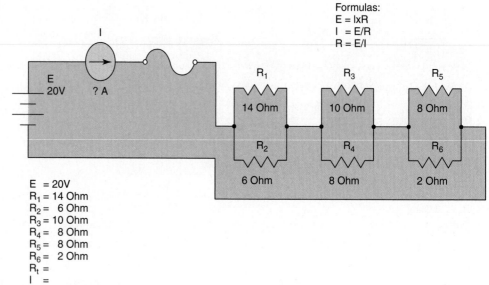

FIGURE 7-15 Chapter Quiz question 10.

Formulas:
E = IxR
I = E/R
R = E/I

E
20V

I
? A

R₁
14 Ohm

R₃
10 Ohm

R₅
8 Ohm

R₂
6 Ohm

R₄
8 Ohm

R₆
2 Ohm

E = 20V
R₁ = 14 Ohm
R₂ =   6 Ohm
R₃ = 10 Ohm
R₄ =   8 Ohm
R₅ =   8 Ohm
R₆ =   2 Ohm
Rₜ =
I   =

9. See ● **FIGURE 7-14** to solve for total resistance (R_T) *and* total current (I).
   a. 1.5 ohms and 8 amperes
   b. 18 ohms and 0.66 ampere
   c. 6 ohms and 2 amperes
   d. 5.5 ohms and 2.2 amperes

10. See ● **FIGURE 7-15** to solve for total resistance (R_T) *and* total current (I).
   a. 48 ohms and 0.42 ampere
   b. 20 ohms and 1 ampere
   c. 30 ohms and 0.66 ampere
   d. 10.2 ohms and 1.96 amperes

chapter 8

CIRCUIT TESTERS AND DIGITAL METERS

OBJECTIVES

After studying Chapter 8, the reader will be able to:

1. Prepare for ASE Electrical/Electronic Systems (A6) certification test content area "A" (General Electrical/Electronic System Diagnosis).

2. Discuss how to safely use a fused jumper wire, a test light, and a logic probe.

3. Explain how to set up and use a digital meter to read voltage, resistance, and current.

4. Explain meter terms and readings.

5. Interpret meter readings and compare to factory specifications.

6. Discuss how to properly and safely use meters.

KEY TERMS

FUSED JUMPER WIRE

DEFINITION A fused jumper wire is used to check a circuit by bypassing the switch or to provide a power or ground to a component. A fused jumper wire, also called a lead, can be purchased or made by the service technician. ● **SEE FIGURE 8–1.**

It should include the following features.

- **Fused.** A typical fused jumper wire has a blade-type fuse that can be easily replaced. A 10 ampere fuse (red color) is often the value used.

- **Alligator clip ends.** Alligator clips on the ends allow the fused jumper wire to be clipped to a ground or power source while the other end is attached to the power side or ground side of the unit being tested.

- **Good-quality insulated wire.** Most purchased jumper wire is about 14 gauge stranded copper wire with a flexible rubberized insulation to allow it to move easily even in cold weather.

USES OF A FUSED JUMPER WIRE

A fused jumper wire can be used to help diagnose a component or circuit by performing the following procedures.

- **Supply power or ground.** If a component, such as a horn, does not work, a fused jumper wire can be used to supply a temporary power and/or ground. Start by unplugging the electrical connector from the device and connect a fused jumper lead to the power terminal. Another fused jumper wire may be needed to provide the ground. If the unit works, the problem is in the power side or ground side circuit.

CAUTION: Never use a fused jumper wire to bypass any resistance or load in the circuit. The increased current flow could damage the wiring and could blow the fuse on the jumper lead.

FIGURE 8–1 A technician-made fused jumper lead, which is equipped with a red 10 ampere fuse. This fused jumper wire uses terminals for testing circuits at a connector instead of alligator clips.

TEST LIGHTS

NONPOWERED TEST LIGHT A 12 volt test light is one of the simplest testers that can be used to detect electricity. A **test light** is simply a light bulb with a probe and a ground wire attached. ● **SEE FIGURE 8–2.**

It is used to detect battery voltage potential at various test points. Battery voltage cannot be seen or felt, and can be detected only with test equipment.

The ground clip is connected to a clean ground on either the negative terminal of the battery or a clean metal part of the body and the probe touched to terminals or components. If the test light comes on, this indicates that voltage is available. ● **SEE FIGURE 8–3.**

A purchased test light could be labeled a "12 volt test light." Do not purchase a test light designed for household current (110 or 220 volts), as it will not light with 12 to 14 volts.

USES OF A 12 VOLT TEST LIGHT

A 12 volt test light can be used to check the following:

- **Electrical power.** If the test light lights, then there is power available. It will not, however, indicate the voltage level or if there is enough current available to operate an electrical load. This indicates only that there is enough voltage and current to light the test light (about 0.25A).

- **Grounds.** A test light can be used to check for grounds by attaching the clip of the test light to the positive terminal of the battery or any 12 volt electrical terminal. The tip of the test light can then be used to touch the ground wire. If there is a ground connection, the test light will light.

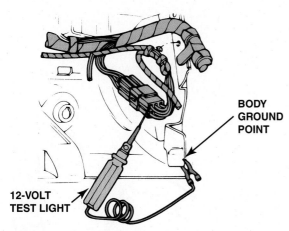

FIGURE 8–2 A 12 volt test light is attached to a good ground while probing for power.

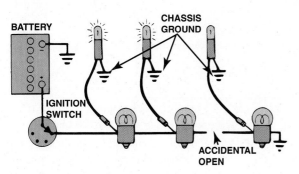

FIGURE 8–3 A test light can be used to locate an open in a circuit. Note that the test light is grounded at a different location than the circuit itself.

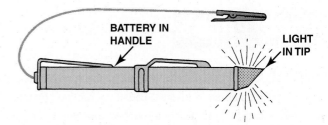

FIGURE 8–4 A continuity light should not be used on computer circuits because the applied voltage can damage delicate electronic components or circuits.

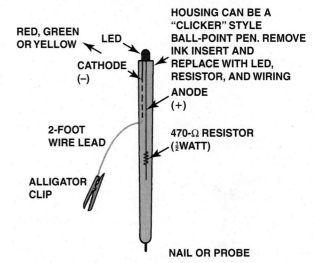

FIGURE 8–5 An LED test light can be easily made using low cost components and an old ink pen. With the 470 ohm resistor in series with the LED, this tester only draws 0.025 ampere (25 milliamperes) from the circuit being tested. This low current draw helps assure the technician that the circuit or component being tested will not be damaged by excessive current flow.

CONTINUITY TEST LIGHTS A **continuity light** is similar to a test light but includes a battery for self-power. A continuity light illuminates whenever it is connected to both ends of a wire that has continuity or is not broken. ● **SEE FIGURE 8–4.**

CAUTION: The use of a self-powered (continuity) test light is not recommended on any electronic circuit, because a continuity light contains a battery and applies voltage; therefore, it may harm delicate electronic components.

HIGH-IMPEDANCE TEST LIGHT A high-impedance test light has a high internal resistance and therefore draws very low current in order to light. High-impedance test lights are safe to use on computer circuits because they will not affect the circuit current in the same way as conventional 12 volt test lights when connected to a circuit. There are two types of high-impedance test lights.

- Some test lights use an electronic circuit to limit the current flow, to avoid causing damage to electronic devices.

- An **LED test light** uses a light-emitting diode (LED) instead of a standard automotive bulb for a visual indication of voltage. An LED test light requires only about 25 milliamperes (0.025 ampere) to light; therefore, it can be used on electronic circuits as well as on standard circuits.

● **SEE FIGURE 8–5** for construction details for a homemade LED test light.

PURPOSE AND FUNCTION A **logic probe** is an electronic device that lights up a red (usually) LED if the probe is touched to battery voltage. If the probe is touched to ground, a green (usually) LED lights. ● **SEE FIGURE 8–6.**

A logic probe can "sense" the difference between high- and low-voltage levels, which explains the name *logic*.

- A typical logic probe can also light another light (often amber color) when a change in voltage levels occurs.
- Some logic probes will flash the red light when a pulsing voltage signal is detected.
- Some will flash the green light when a pulsing ground signal is detected.

This feature is helpful when checking for a variable voltage output from a computer or ignition sensor.

USING A LOGIC PROBE A logic probe must first be connected to a power and ground source such as the vehicle battery. This connection powers the probe and gives it a reference low (ground).

Most logic probes also make a distinctive sound for each high- and low-voltage level. This makes troubleshooting easier when probing connectors or component terminals. A sound (usually a beep) is heard when the probe tip is touched to a changing voltage source. The changing voltage also usually lights the pulse light on the logic probe. Therefore, the probe can be used to check components such as:

- Pickup coils
- Hall-effect sensors
- Magnetic sensors

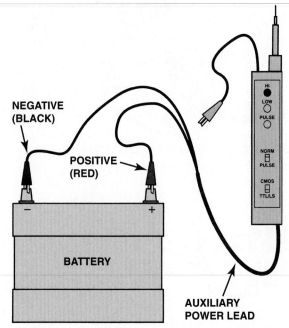

FIGURE 8–6 A logic probe connected to the vehicle battery. When the tip probe is connected to a circuit, it can check for power, ground, or a pulse.

DIGITAL MULTIMETERS

TERMINOLOGY **Digital multimeter (DMM)** and **digital volt-ohm-milliammeter (DVOM)** are terms commonly used for electronic **high-impedance test meters.** *High impedance* means that the electronic internal resistance of the meter is high enough to prevent excessive current draw from any circuit being tested. Most meters today have a minimum of 10 million ohms (10 megohms) of resistance. This high internal resistance between the meter leads is present only when measuring volts. The high resistance in the meter itself reduces the amount of current flowing through the meter when it is being used to measure voltage, leading to more accurate test results because the meter does not change the load on the circuit. High-impedance meters are required for measuring computer circuits.

CAUTION: Analog (needle-type) meters are almost always lower than 10 megohms and should not be used to measure any computer or electronic circuit. Connecting an analog meter to a computer circuit could damage the computer or other electronic modules.

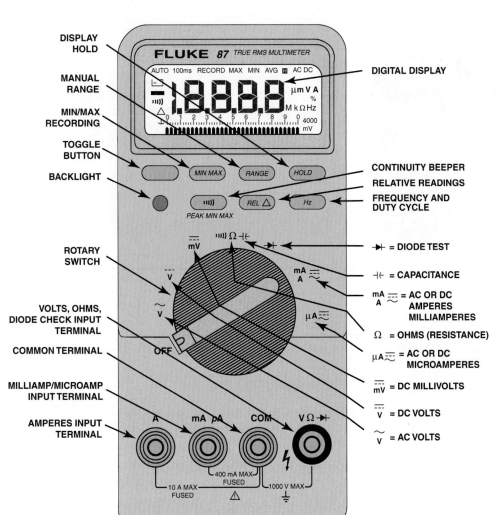

FIGURE 8–7 Typical digital multimeter. The black meter lead always is placed in the COM terminal. The red meter test lead should be in the volt-ohm terminal except when measuring current in amperes.

SYMBOL	MEANING
AC	Alternating current or voltage
DC	Direct current or voltage
V	Volts
mV	Millivolts (1/1,000 volts)
A	Ampere (amps), current
mA	Milliampere (1/1,000 amps)
%	Percent (for duty cycle readings only)
Ω	Ohms, resistance
kΩ	Kilohm (1,000 ohms), resistance
MΩ	Megohm (1,000,000 ohms), resistance
Hz	Hertz (cycles per second), frequency
kHz	Kilohertz (1,000 cycles/sec.), frequency
Ms	Milliseconds (1/1,000 sec.) for pulse width measurements

CHART 8–1

Common symbols and abbreviations used on digital meters.

A high-impedance meter can be used to measure any automotive circuit within the ranges of the meter. ● **SEE FIGURE 8–7.**

The common abbreviations for the units that many meters can measure are often confusing. ● **SEE CHART 8–1** for the most commonly used symbols and their meanings.

MEASURING VOLTAGE A voltmeter measures the *pressure* or potential of electricity in units of volts. A voltmeter is connected to a circuit in parallel. Voltage can be measured by selecting either AC or DC volts.

- **DC volts (DCV).** This setting is the most common for automotive use. Use this setting to measure battery voltage and voltage to all lighting and accessory circuits.

- **AC volts (ACV).** This setting is used to check for unwanted AC voltage from alternators and some sensors.

- **Range.** The range is automatically set for most meters but can be manually ranged if needed.

● **SEE FIGURES 8–8 AND 8–9.**

FIGURE 8–8 Typical digital multimeter (DMM) set to read DC volts.

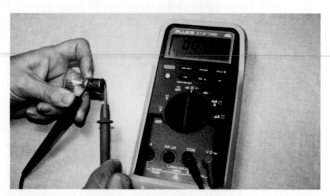

FIGURE 8–10 Using a digital multimeter set to read ohms (Ω) to test this light bulb. The meter reads the resistance of the filament.

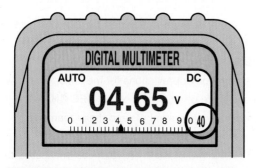

BECAUSE THE SIGNAL READING IS BELOW 4 VOLTS, THE METER AUTORANGES TO THE 4-VOLT SCALE. IN THE 4-VOLT SCALE, THIS METER PROVIDES THREE DECIMAL PLACES.

(A)

WHEN THE VOLTAGE EXCEEDED 4 VOLTS, THE METER AUTORANGES INTO THE 40-VOLT SCALE. THE DECIMAL POINT MOVES ONE PLACE TO THE RIGHT LEAVING ONLY TWO DECIMAL PLACES.

(B)

FIGURE 8–9 A typical autoranging digital multimeter automatically selects the proper scale to read the voltage being tested. The scale selected is usually displayed on the meter face. (a) Note that the display indicates "4," meaning that this range can read up to 4 volts. (b) The range is now set to the 40 volt scale, meaning that the meter can read up to 40 volts on the scale. Any reading above this level will cause the meter to reset to a higher scale. If not set on autoranging, the meter display would indicate OL if a reading exceeds the limit of the scale selected. (*Courtesy of Fluke Corporation*)

DIGITAL MULTIMETERS (CONTINUED)

MEASURING RESISTANCE An ohmmeter measures the resistance in ohms of a component or circuit section when no current is flowing through the circuit. An ohmmeter contains a battery (or other power source) and is connected in series with the component or wire being measured. When the leads are connected to a component, current flows through the test leads and the difference in voltage (voltage drop) between the leads is measured as resistance. Note the following facts about using an ohmmeter.

- Zero ohms on the scale means that there is no resistance between the test leads, thus indicating continuity or a continuous path for the current to flow in a closed circuit.
- Infinity means no connection, as in an open circuit.
- Ohmmeters have no required polarity even though red and black test leads are used for resistance measurement.

CAUTION: The circuit must be electrically open with no current flowing when using an ohmmeter. If current is flowing when an ohmmeter is connected, the reading will be incorrect and the meter can be destroyed.

Different meters have different ways of indicating infinity resistance, or a reading higher than the scale allows. Examples of an over limit display include:

- **OL,** meaning **over limit** or overload
- Flashing or solid number 1
- Flashing or solid number 3 on the left side of the display

Check the meter instructions for the exact display used to indicate an open circuit or over range reading. ● **SEE FIGURES 8–10 AND 8–11.**

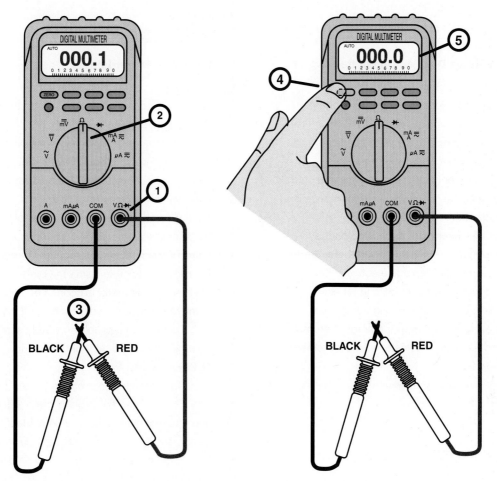

FIGURE 8–11 Many digital multimeters can have the display indicate zero to compensate for test lead resistance. (1) Connect leads in the V Ω and COM meter terminals. (2) Select the Ω scale. (3) Touch the two meter leads together. (4) Push the "zero" or "relative" button on the meter. (5) The meter display will now indicate zero ohms of resistance.

To summarize, open and zero readings are as follows:

0.00 Ω = Zero resistance (component or circuit has continuity)

OL = An open circuit or reading is higher than the scale selected (no current flows)

MEASURING AMPERES An ammeter measures the flow of *current* through a complete circuit in units of amperes. The ammeter has to be installed in the circuit (in series) so that it can measure all the current flow in that circuit, just as a water flow meter would measure the amount of water flow (cubic feet per minute, for example). ● **SEE FIGURE 8–12.**

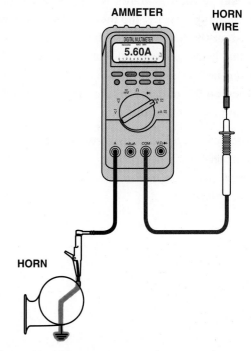

FIGURE 8–12 Measuring the current flow required by a horn requires that the ammeter be connected to the circuit in series and the horn button be depressed by an assistant.

How Much Voltage Does an Ohmmeter Apply?

Most digital meters that are set to measure ohms (resistance) apply 0.3 to 1 volt to the component being measured. The voltage comes from the meter itself to measure the resistance. Two things are important to remember about an ohmmeter.

1. The component or circuit must be disconnected from any electrical circuit while the resistance is being measured.

2. Because the meter itself applies a voltage (even though it is relatively low), a meter set to measure ohms can damage electronic circuits. Computer or electronic chips can be easily damaged if subjected to only a few milliamperes of current, similar to the amount an ohmmeter applies when a resistance measurement is being performed.

DIGITAL MULTIMETERS (CONTINUED)

CAUTION: An ammeter must be installed in series with the circuit to measure the current flow in the circuit. If a meter set to read amperes is connected in parallel, such as across a battery, the meter or the leads may be destroyed, or the fuse will blow, by the current available across the battery. Some digital multimeters (DMMs) beep if the unit selection does not match the test lead connection on the meter. However, in a noisy shop, this beep sound may be inaudible.

Digital meters require that the meter leads be moved to the ammeter terminals. Most digital meters have an ampere scale that can accommodate a maximum of 10 amperes. See the Tech Tip, "Fuse Your Meter Leads!"

TECH TIP

Fuse Your Meter Leads!

Most digital meters include an ammeter capability. When reading amperes, the leads of the meter must be changed from volts or ohms (V or Ω) to amperes (A), milliamperes (mA), or microamperes (μA).

A common problem may then occur the next time voltage is measured. Although the technician may switch the selector to read volts, often the leads are not switched back to the volt or ohm position. Because the ammeter lead position results in zero ohms of resistance to current flow through the meter, the meter or the fuse inside the meter will be destroyed if the meter is connected to a battery. Many meter fuses are expensive and difficult to find.

To avoid this problem, simply solder an inline 10 ampere blade-fuse holder into one meter lead. **SEE FIGURE 8–13.**

Do not think that this technique is for beginners only. Experienced technicians often get in a hurry and forget to switch the lead. A blade fuse is faster, easier, and less expensive to replace than a meter fuse or the meter itself. Also, if the soldering is done properly, the addition of an inline fuse holder and fuse does not increase the resistance of the meter leads. All meter leads have some resistance. If the meter is measuring very low resistance, touch the two leads together and read the resistance (usually no more than 0.2 ohm). Simply subtract the resistance of the leads from the resistance of the component being measured.

? FREQUENTLY ASKED QUESTION

What Does "CE" Mean on Many Meters?

The "CE" means that the meter meets the newest European Standards and the letters CE stands for a French term for "Conformite' Europeenne" meaning European Conformity in French.

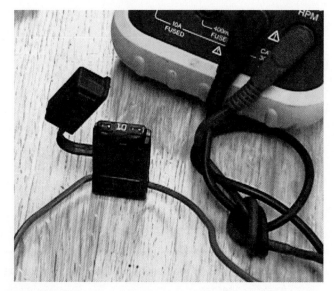

FIGURE 8–13 Note the blade-type fuse holder soldered in series with one of the meter leads. A 10 ampere fuse helps protect the internal meter fuse (if equipped) and the meter itself from damage that may result from excessive current flow if accidentally used incorrectly.

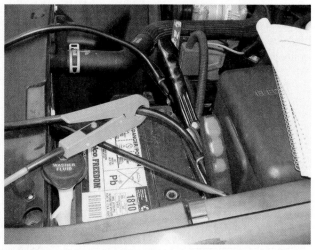

FIGURE 8–14 An inductive ammeter clamp is used with all starting and charging testers to measure the current flow through the battery cables.

INDUCTIVE AMMETERS

OPERATION **Inductive ammeters** do not make physical contact with the circuit. They measure the strength of the magnetic field surrounding the wire carrying the current, and use a Hall-effect sensor to measure current. The Hall-effect sensor detects the strength of the magnetic field that surrounds the wire carrying an electrical current. ● **SEE FIGURE 8–14.**

This means that the meter probe surrounds the wire(s) carrying the current and measures the strength of the magnetic field that surrounds any conductor carrying a current.

AC/DC CLAMP-ON DIGITAL MULTIMETERS An **AC/DC clamp-on digital multimeter (DMM)** is a useful meter for automotive diagnostic work. ● **SEE FIGURE 8–15.**

The major advantage of the clamp-on-type meter is that there is no need to break the circuit to measure current (amperes). Simply clamp the jaws of the meter around the power lead(s) or ground lead(s) of the component being measured and read the display. Most clamp-on meters can also measure alternating current, which is helpful in the diagnosis of

FIGURE 8–15 A typical mini clamp-on-type digital multimeter. This meter is capable of measuring alternating current (AC) and direct current (DC) without requiring that the circuit be disconnected to install the meter in series. The jaws are simply placed over the wire and current flow through the circuit is displayed.

an alternator problem. Volts, ohms, frequency, and temperature can also be measured with the typical clamp-on DMM, but use conventional meter leads. The inductive clamp is only used to measure amperes.

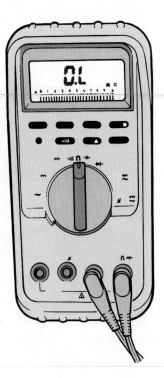

FIGURE 8-16 Typical digital multimeter showing OL (over limit) on the readout with the ohms (Ω) unit selected. This usually means that the unit being measured is open (infinity resistance) and has no continuity.

DIODE CHECK, PULSE WIDTH, AND FREQUENCY

DIODE CHECK Diode check is a meter function that can be used to check diodes including light-emitting diodes (LEDs).

The meter is able to text diodes by way of the following:

- The meter applies roughly a 3 volt DC signal to the text leads.

- The voltage is high enough to cause a diode to work and the meter will display:
  1. 0.4 to 0.7 volt when testing silicon diodes such as found in alternators
  2. 1.5 to 2.3 volts when testing LEDs such as found in some lighting applications

TECH TIP

Over Limit Display Does Not Mean the Meter Is Reading "Nothing"

The meaning of the over limit display on a digital meter often confuses beginning technicians. When asked what the meter is reading when an over limit (OL) is displayed on the meter face, the response is often, "Nothing." Many meters indicate *over limit* or *over load,* which simply means that the reading is over the maximum that can be displayed for the selected range. For example, the meter will display OL if 12 volts are being measured but the meter has been set to read a maximum of 4 volts.

Autoranging meters adjust the range to match what is being measured. Here OL means a value higher than the meter can read (unlikely on the voltage scale for automobile usage), or infinity when measuring resistance (ohms). Therefore, OL means infinity when measuring resistance or an open circuit is being indicated. The meter will read 00.0 if the resistance is zero, so "nothing" in this case indicates continuity (zero resistance), whereas OL indicates infinity resistance. Therefore, when talking with another technician about a meter reading, make sure you know exactly what the reading on the face of the meter means. Also be sure that you are connecting the meter leads correctly. ● **SEE FIGURE 8-16.**

PULSE WIDTH Pulse width is the amount of time in a percentage that a signal is on compared to being off.

- 100% pulse width indicates that a device is being commanded on all of the time.

- 50% pulse width indicates that a device is being commanded on half of the time.

- 25% pulse width indicates that a device is being commanded on just 25% of the time.

Pulse width is used to measure the on time for fuel injectors and other computer-controlled solenoid and devices.

FREQUENCY Frequency is a measure of how many times per second a signal changes. Frequency is measured in a unit called hertz, formerly termed "cycles per second."

Frequency measurements are used when checking the following:

- Mass airflow (MAF) sensors for proper operation

- Ignition primary pulse signals when diagnosing a no-start condition

- Checking a wheel speed sensor

ELECTRICAL UNIT PREFIXES

DEFINITIONS Electrical units are measured in numbers such as 12 volts, 150 amperes, and 470 ohms. Large units over 1,000 may be expressed in kilo units. **Kilo (k)** means 1,000.
● **SEE FIGURE 8–17.**

4,700 ohms = 4.7 kilohms (kΩ)

If the value is over 1 million (1,000,000), then the prefix **mega (M)** is often used. For example:

1,100,000 volts = 1.1 megavolts (MV)

4,700,000 ohms = 4.7 megohms (MΩ)

Sometimes a circuit conducts so little current that a smaller unit of measure is required. Small units of measure expressed in 1/1,000 are prefixed by **milli (m).** To summarize:

mega (M) = 1,000,000 (decimal point six places to the right = 1,000,000)

kilo (k) = 1,000 (decimal point three places to the right = 1,000)

milli (m) = 1/1,000 (decimal point three places to the left = 0.001)

HINT: Lowercase *m* equals a small unit (milli), whereas a capital *M* represents a large unit (mega).

● **SEE CHART 8–2.**

THE SYMBOL ON THE RIGHT SIDE OF THE DISPLAY INDICATES WHAT RANGE THE METER HAS BEEN SET TO READ.

Ω = OHMS

IF THE ONLY SYMBOL ON THE DISPLAY IS THE OHMS SYMBOL, THE READING ON THE DISPLAY IS EXACTLY THE RESISTANCE IN OHMS.

KΩ = KILOHMS = OHMS TIMES 1000

A "K" IN FRONT OF THE OHMS SYMBOL MEANS "KILOHMS"; THE READING ON THE DISPLAY IS IN KILOHMS. YOU HAVE TO MULTIPLY THE READING ON THE DISPLAY BY 1000 TO GET THE RESISTANCE IN OHMS.

MΩ = MEGOHMS = OHMS TIMES 1,000,000

A "M" IN FRONT OF THE OHMS SYMBOL MEANS "MEGOHMS"; THE READING ON THE DISPLAY IS IN MEGOHMS. YOU HAVE TO MULTIPLY THE READING ON THE DISPLAY BY 1,000,000 TO GET THE RESISTANCE IN OHMS.

FIGURE 8–17 Always look at the meter display when a measurement is being made, especially if using an autoranging meter.

TO/ FROM	MEGA	KILO	BASE	MILLI
Mega	0 places	3 places to the right	6 places to the right	9 places to the right
Kilo	3 places to the left	0 places	3 places to the right	6 places to the right
Base	6 places to the left	3 places to the left	0 places	3 places to the right
Milli	9 places to the left	6 places to the left	3 places to the left	0 places

CHART 8–2

A conversion chart showing the decimal point location for the various prefixes.

USE OF PREFIXES The prefixes can be confusing because most digital meters can express values in more than one unit, especially if the meter is autoranging. For example, an ammeter reading may show 36.7 mA on autoranging. When the scale is changed to amperes ("A" in the window of the display), the number displayed will be 0.037 A. Note that the resolution of the value is reduced.

HINT: Always check the face of the meter display for the unit being measured. To best understand what is being displayed on the face of a digital meter, select a manual scale and move the selector until *whole units appear,* such as "A" for amperes instead of "mA" for milliamperes.

Think of Money

Digital meter displays can often be confusing. The display for a battery measured as 12 1/2 volts would be 12.50 V, just as $12.50 is 12 dollars and 50 cents. A 1/2 volt reading on a digital meter will be displayed as 0.50 V, just as $0.50 is half of a dollar.

It is more confusing when low values are displayed. For example, if a voltage reading is 0.063 volt, an autoranging meter will display 63 millivolts (63 mV), or 63/1,000 of a volt, or $63 of $1,000. (It takes 1,000 mV to equal 1 volt.) Think of millivolts as one-tenth of a cent, with 1 volt being $1.00. Therefore, 630 millivolts are equal to $0.63 of $1.00 (630 tenths of a cent, or 63 cents).

To avoid confusion, try to manually range the meter to read base units (whole volts). If the meter is ranged to base unit volts, 63 millivolts would be displayed as 0.063 or maybe just 0.06, depending on the display capabilities of the meter.

HOW TO READ DIGITAL METERS

STEPS TO FOLLOW Getting to know and use a digital meter takes time and practice. The first step is to read, understand, and follow all safety and operational instructions that come with the meter. Use of the meter usually involves the following steps.

STEP 1 **Select the proper unit of electricity for what is being measured.** This unit could be volts, ohms (resistance), or amperes (amount of current flow). If the meter is not autoranging, select the proper scale for the anticipated reading. For example, if a 12 volt battery is being measured, select a meter reading range that is higher than the voltage but not too high. A 20 or 30 volt range will accurately show the voltage of a 12 volt battery. If a 1,000 volt scale is selected, a 12 volt reading may not be accurate.

STEP 2 **Place the meter leads into the proper input terminals.**

- The black lead is inserted into the common (COM) terminal. This meter lead usually stays in this location for all meter functions.
- The red lead is inserted into the volt, ohm, or diode check terminal usually labeled "VΩ" when voltage, resistance, or diodes are being measured.
- When current flow in amperes is being measured, most digital meters require that the red test lead be inserted in the ammeter terminal, usually labeled "A" or "mA."

CAUTION: If the meter leads are inserted into ammeter terminals, even though the selector is set to volts, the meter may be damaged or an internal fuse may blow if the test leads touch both terminals of a battery.

STEP 3 **Measure the component being tested.** Carefully note the decimal point and the unit on the face of the meter.

- **Meter lead connections.** If the meter leads are connected to a battery backwards (red to the battery negative, for example), the display will still show the correct reading, but a negative sign (−) will be displayed in front of the number. The correct polarity is not important when measuring resistance (ohms) except where indicated, such as measuring a diode.
- **Autorange.** Many meters automatically default to the autorange position and the meter will display the value in the most readable scale. The meter can be manually ranged to select other levels or to lock in a scale for a value that is constantly changing.

  If a 12 volt battery is measured with an autoranging meter, the correct reading of 12.0 is given. "AUTO" and "V" should show on the face of the meter. For example, if a meter is manually set to the

VOLTAGE BEING MEASURED

Scale Selected	0.01 V (10 MV)	0.150 V (150 MV)	1.5 V	10.0 V	12.0 V	120 V
	Voltmeter will display:					
200 mV	10.0	150.0	OL	OL	OL	OL
2 V	0.100	0.150	1.500	OL	OL	OL
20 V	0.1	1.50	1.50	10.00	12.00	OL
200 V	00.0	01.5	01.5	10.0	12.0	120.0
2 kV	00.00	00.00	000.1	00.10	00.12	0.120
Autorange	10.0 mV	15.0 mV	1.50	10.0	12.0	120.0

RESISTANCE BEING MEASURED

Scale Selected	10 OHMS	100 OHMS	470 OHMS	1 KILOHM	220 KILOHMS	1 MEGOHM
	Ohmmeter will display:					
400 ohms	10.0	100.0	OL	OL	OL	OL
4 kilohms	010	100	0.470 k	1000	OL	OL
40 kilohms	00.0	0.10 k	0.47 k	1.00 k	OL	OL
400 kilohms	000.0	00.1 k	00.5 k	0.10 k	220.0 k	OL
4 megohms	00.00	0.01 M	0.05 M	00.1 M	0.22 M	1.0 M
Autorange	10.0	100.0	470.0	1.00 k	220 k	1.00 M

CURRENT BEING MEASURED

Scale Selected	50 MA	150 MA	1.0 A	7.5 A	15.0 A	25.0 A
	Ammeter will display:					
40 mA	OL	OL	OL	OL	OL	OL
400 mA	50.0	150	OL	OL	OL	OL
4 A	0.05	0.00	1.00	OL	OL	OL
40 A	0.00	0.000	01.0	7.5	15.0	25.0
Autorange	50.0 mA	150.0 mA	1.00	7.5	15.0	25.0

CHART 8–3

Sample meter readings using manually set and autoranging selection on the digital meter control.

2 kilohm scale, the highest that the meter will read is 2,000 ohms. If the reading is over 2,000 ohms, the meter will display OL. ● **SEE CHART 8–3.**

STEP 4 **Interpret the reading.** This is especially difficult on autoranging meters, where the meter itself selects the proper scale. The following are two examples of different readings.

Example 1: A voltage drop is being measured. The specifications indicate a maximum voltage drop of 0.2 volt. The meter reads "AUTO" and "43.6 mV." This reading means that the voltage drop is 0.0436 volt, or 43.6 mV, which is far lower than the 0.2 volt (200 millivolts). Because the number showing on the meter face is much larger than the specifications, many beginner technicians are led to believe that the voltage drop is excessive.

NOTE: Pay attention to the units displayed on the meter face and convert to whole units.

Example 2: A spark plug wire is being measured. The reading should be less than 10,000 ohms for each foot in length if the wire is okay. The wire being tested is 3 ft long (maximum allowable resistance is 30,000 ohms). The meter reads "AUTO" and "14.85 kΩ." This reading is equivalent to 14,850 ohms.

NOTE: When converting from kilohms to ohms, make the decimal point a comma.

Because this reading is well below the specified maximum allowable, the spark plug wire is okay.

RMS VERSUS AVERAGE Alternating current voltage waveforms can be true sinusoidal or nonsinusoidal. A true

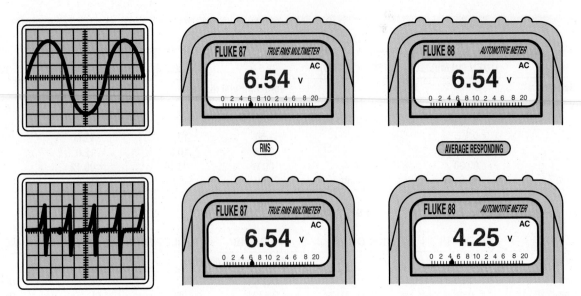

FIGURE 8-18 When reading AC voltage signals, a true RMS meter (such as a Fluke 87) provides a different reading than an average responding meter (such as a Fluke 88). The only place this difference is important is when a reading is to be compared with a specification.

HOW TO READ DIGITAL METERS (CONTINUED)

 **TECH TIP**

Purchase a Digital Meter That Will Work for Automotive Use

Try to purchase a digital meter that is capable of reading the following:

- DC volts
- AC volts
- DC amperes (up to 10 A or more is helpful)
- Ohms (Ω) up to 40 MΩ (40 million ohms)
- Diode check

Additional features for advanced automotive diagnosis include:

- Frequency (hertz, abbreviated Hz)
- Temperature probe (°F and/or °C)
- Pulse width (millisecond, abbreviated ms)
- Duty cycle (%)

sine wave pattern measurement will be the same for both **root-mean-square (RMS)** and average reading meters. RMS and averaging are two methods used to measure the true effective rating of a signal that is constantly changing. ● **SEE FIGURE 8-18.**

Only true RMS meters are accurate when measuring non-sinusoidal AC waveforms, which are seldom used in automotive applications.

RESOLUTION, DIGITS, AND COUNTS   Meter resolution refers to how small or fine a measurement the meter can make. By knowing the resolution of a DMM you can determine whether the meter could measure down to only 1 volt or down to 1 millivolt (1/1,000 of a volt).

You would not buy a ruler marked in 1 in. segments (or centimeters) if you had to measure down to 1/4 in. (or 1 mm). A thermometer that only measured in whole degrees is not of much use when your normal temperature is 98.6°F. You need a thermometer with 0.1° *resolution.*

The terms *digits* and *counts* are used to describe a meter's resolution. DMMs are grouped by the number of counts or digits they display.

■ A 3 1/2-digit meter can display three full digits ranging from 0 to 9, and one "half" digit that displays only a 1 or is left blank. A 3 1/2-digit meter will display up to 1,999 counts of resolution.

FIGURE 8–19 This meter display shows 052.2 AC volts. Notice that the zero beside the 5 indicates that the meter can read over 100 volts AC with a resolution of 0.1 volt.

- A 4 1/2-digit meter can display up to 19,000 counts of resolution. It is more precise to describe a meter by counts of resolution than by 3 1/2 or 4 1/2 digits. Some 3 1/2-digit meters have enhanced resolution of up to 3,200 or 4,000 counts.

Meters with more counts offer better resolution for certain measurements. For example, a 1,999 count meter will not be able to measure down to a tenth of a volt when measuring 200 volts or more. ● **SEE FIGURE 8–19.**

However, a 3,200 count meter will display a tenth of a volt up to 320 volts. Digits displayed to the far right of the display may at times flicker or constantly change. This is called *digit rattle* and represents a changing voltage being measured on the ground (COM terminal of the meter lead). High-quality meters are designed to reject this unwanted voltage.

ACCURACY **Meter accuracy** is the largest allowable error that will occur under specific operating conditions. In other words, it is an indication of how close the DMM's displayed measurement is to the actual value of the signal being measured.

Accuracy for a DMM is usually expressed as a percent of reading. An accuracy of ±1% of reading means that for a displayed reading of 100.0 V, the actual value of the voltage could be anywhere between 99.0 V and 101.0 V. Thus, the lower the percent of accuracy is, the better.

- Unacceptable = 1.00%
- Okay = 0.50% (1/2%)
- Good = 0.25% (1/4%)
- Excellent = 0.10% (1/10%)

For example, if a battery had 12.6 volts, a meter could read between the following, based on its accuracy.

± 0.1%	high = 12.61	
	low = 12.59	
± 0.25%	high = 12.63	
	low = 12.57	
± 0.50%	high = 12.66	
	low = 12.54	
± 1.00%	high = 12.73	
	low = 12.47	

Before you purchase a meter, check the accuracy. Accuracy is usually indicated on the specifications sheet for the meter.

Meter Usage on Hybrid Electric Vehicles

Many hybrid electric vehicles use system voltage as high as 650 volts DC. Be sure to follow all vehicle manufacturer's testing procedures; and if a voltage measurement is needed, be sure to use a meter and test leads that are designed to insulate against high voltages. The **International Electrotechnical Commission (IEC)** has several categories of voltage standards for meter and meter leads. These categories are ratings for overvoltage protection and are rated CAT I, CAT II, CAT III, and CAT IV. The higher the category, the greater the protection against voltage spikes caused by high-energy circuits. Under each category there are various energy and voltage ratings.

CAT I Typically a CAT I meter is used for low-energy voltage measurements such as at wall outlets in the home. Meters with a CAT I rating are usually rated at 300 to 800 volts.

CAT II This higher rated meter would be typically used for checking higher energy level voltages at the fuse panel in the home. Meters with a CAT II rating are usually rated at 300 to 600 volts.

CAT III This minimum rated meter should be used for hybrid vehicles. The CAT III category is designed for high-energy levels and voltage measurements at the service pole at the transformer. Meters with this rating are usually rated at 600 to 1,000 volts.

CAT IV CAT IV meters are for clamp-on meters only. If a clamp-on meter also has meter leads for voltage measurements, that part of the meter will be rated as CAT III.

NOTE: Always use the highest CAT rating meter, especially when working with hybrid vehicles. A CAT III, 600 volt meter is safer than a CAT II, 1,000 volt meter because of the energy level of the CAT ratings.

Therefore, for best personal protection, use only meters and meter leads that are CAT III or CAT IV rated when measuring voltage on a hybrid vehicle. ● **SEE FIGURES 8–20 AND 8–21.**

FIGURE 8–20 Be sure to only use a meter that is CAT III rated when taking electrical voltage measurements on a hybrid vehicle.

FIGURE 8–21 Always use meter leads that are CAT III rated on a meter that is also CAT III rated, to maintain the protection needed when working on hybrid vehicles.

1 For most electrical measurements, the black meter lead is inserted in the terminal labeled COM and the red meter lead is inserted into the terminal labeled V.

2 To use a digital meter, turn the power switch and select the unit of electricity to be measured. In this case, the rotary switch is turned to select DC volts.

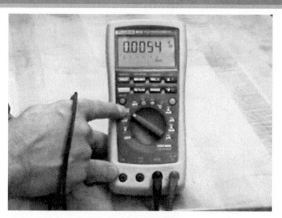

3 For most automotive electrical use such as for measuring battery voltage, select DC volts.

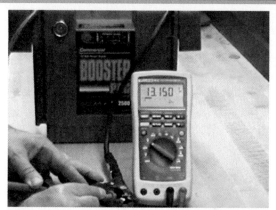

4 Connect the red meter lead to the positive (+) terminal of a battery and the black meter lead to the negative (−) terminal of a battery. The meter reads the voltage difference between the leads.

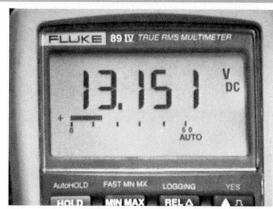

5 This jump start battery unit measures 13.151 volts with the meter set on autoranging on the DC voltage scale.

6 Another meter (Fluke 87 III) displays four digits when measuring the voltage of the battery jump start unit.

CONTINUED ▶

STEP-BY-STEP (CONTINUED)

7 To measure resistance turn the rotary dial to the ohm (Ω) symbol. With the meter leads separated, the meter display reads OL (over limit).

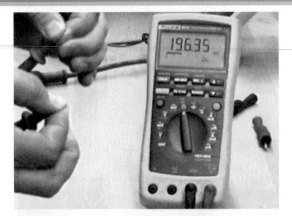

8 The meter can read your own body resistance if you grasp the meter lead terminals with your fingers. The reading on the display indicates 196.35 kΩ.

9 When measuring anything; be sure to read the meter face. In this case, the meter is reading 291.10 kΩ.

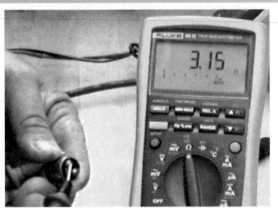

10 A meter set on ohms can be used to check the resistance of a light bulb filament. In this case, the meter reads 3.15 ohms. If the bulb were bad (filament open), the meter would display OL.

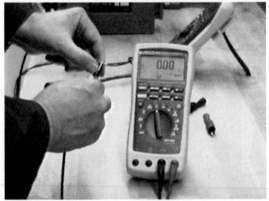

11 A digital meter set to read ohms should measure 0.00 as shown when the meter leads are touched together.

12 The large letter V means volts and the wavy symbol over the V means that the meter measures alternating current (AC) voltage if this position is selected.

13 The next symbol is a V with a dotted and a straight line overhead. This symbol stands for direct current (DC) volts. This position is most used for automotive service.

14 The symbol mV indicates millivolts or 1/1000 of a volt (0.001). The solid and dashed line above the mV means DC mV.

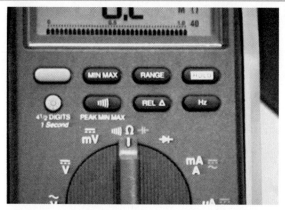

15 The rotary switch is turned to Ω (ohms) unit of resistance measure. The symbol to the left of the Ω symbol is the beeper or continuity indicator.

16 Notice that auto is in the upper left and the MΩ is in the lower right. This MΩ means megaohms or that the meter is set to read in millions of ohms.

17 The symbol shown is the symbol of a diode. In this position, the meter applies a voltage to a diode and the meter reads the voltage drop across the junction of a diode.

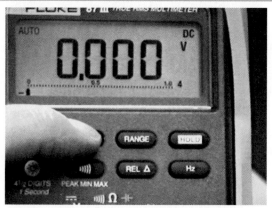

18 One of the most useful features of this meter is the MIN/MAX feature. By pushing the MIN/MAX button, the meter will be able to display the highest (MAX) and the lowest (MIN) reading.

CONTINUED ▶

19 Pushing the MIN/MAX button puts the meter into record mode. Note the 100 mS and "rec" on the display. In this position, the meter is capturing any voltage change that lasts 100 mS (0.1 sec) or longer.

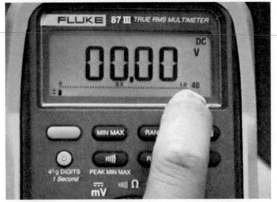

20 To increase the range of the meter touch the range button. Now the meter is set to read voltage up to 40 volts DC.

21 Pushing the range button one more time changes the meter scale to the 400-voltage range. Notice that the decimal point has moved to the right.

22 Pushing the range button again changes the meter to the 4000-volt range. This range is not suitable to use in automotive applications.

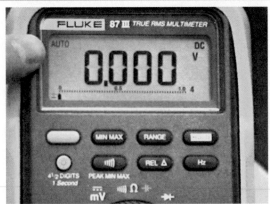

23 By pushing and holding the range button, the meter will reset to autorange. Autorange is the preferred setting for most automotive measurements except when using MIN/MAX record mode.

SUMMARY

1. Digital multimeter (DMM) and digital volt-ohm-milliammeter (DVOM) are terms commonly used for electronic high-impedance test meters.

2. Use of a high-impedance digital meter is required on any computer-related circuit or component.

3. Ammeters measure current and must be connected in series in the circuit.

4. Voltmeters measure voltage and are connected in parallel.

5. Ohmmeters measure resistance of a component and must be connected in parallel, with the circuit or component disconnected from power.

6. Logic probes can indicate the presence of power, ground, or pulsed signals.

REVIEW QUESTIONS

1. Why should high-impedance meters be used when measuring voltage on computer-controlled circuits?

2. How is an ammeter connected to an electrical circuit?

3. Why must an ohmmeter be connected to a disconnected circuit or component?

CHAPTER QUIZ

1. Inductive ammeters work because of what principle?
   a. Magic
   b. Electrostatic electricity
   c. A magnetic field surrounds any wire carrying a current
   d. Voltage drop as it flows through a conductor

2. A meter used to measure amperes is called a(n) _____.
   a. Amp meter
   b. Ampmeter
   c. Ammeter
   d. Coulomb meter

3. A voltmeter should be connected to the circuit being tested _____.
   a. In series
   b. In parallel
   c. Only when no power is flowing
   d. Both a and c

4. An ohmmeter should be connected to the circuit or component being tested _____.
   a. With current flowing in the circuit or through the component
   b. When connected to the battery of the vehicle to power the meter
   c. Only when no power is flowing (electrically open circuit)
   d. Both b and c

5. A high-impedance meter _____.
   a. Measures a high amount of current flow
   b. Measures a high amount of resistance
   c. Can measure a high voltage
   d. Has a high internal resistance

6. A meter is set to read DC volts on the 4 volt scale. The meter leads are connected at a 12 volt battery. The display will read _____.
   a. 0.00
   b. OL
   c. 12 V
   d. 0.012 V

7. What could happen if the meter leads were connected to the positive and negative terminals of the battery while the meter and leads were set to read amperes?
   a. Could blow an internal fuse or damage the meter
   b. Would read volts instead of amperes
   c. Would display OL
   d. Would display 0.00

8. The highest amount of resistance that can be read by the meter set to the 2 kΩ scale is _____.
   a. 2,000 ohms
   b. 200 ohms
   c. 200 kΩ (200,000 ohms)
   d. 20,000,000 ohms

9. If a digital meter face shows 0.93 when set to read kΩ, the reading means _____.
   a. 93 ohms
   b. 930 ohms
   c. 9,300 ohms
   d. 93,000 ohms

10. A reading of 432 shows on the face of the meter set to the millivolt scale. The reading means _____.
    a. 0.432 volt
    b. 4.32 volts
    c. 43.2 volts
    d. 4,320 volts

OSCILLOSCOPES AND GRAPHING MULTIMETERS

OBJECTIVES

After studying Chapter 9, the reader will be able to:

1. Prepare for ASE Electrical/Electronic Systems (A6) certification test content area "A" (General Electrical/Electronic System Diagnosis).

2. Use a digital storage oscilloscope to measure voltage signals.

3. Interpret meter and scope readings and determine if the values are within factory specifications.

4. Explain time base and volts per division settings.

KEY TERMS

AC coupling 121
BNC connector 124
Cathode ray tube (CRT) 119
Channel 122
DC coupling 121
Digital storage oscilloscope (DSO) 119
Division 119
Duty cycle 121
External trigger 124

Frequency 121
GMM 124
Graticule 119
Hertz 121
Oscilloscope (scope) 119
Pulse train 121
Pulse width 121
PWM 121
Time base 119
Trigger level 124
Trigger slope 124

TYPES OF OSCILLOSCOPES

TERMINOLOGY An **oscilloscope** (usually called a **scope**) is a visual voltmeter with a timer that shows when a voltage changes. Following are several types of oscilloscopes.

- An *analog scope* uses a **cathode ray tube (CRT)** similar to a television screen to display voltage patterns. The scope screen displays the electrical signal constantly.

- A *digital scope* commonly uses a liquid crystal display (LCD), but a CRT may also be used on some digital scopes. A digital scope takes samples of the signals that can be stopped or stored and is therefore called a **digital storage oscilloscope, or DSO.**

- A digital scope does not capture each change in voltage but instead captures voltage levels over time and stores them as dots. Each dot is a voltage level. Then the scope displays the waveforms using the thousands of dots (each representing a voltage level) and then electrically connects the dots to create a waveform.

- A DSO can be connected to a sensor output signal wire and can record over a long period of time the voltage signals. Then it can be replayed and a technician can see if any faults were detected. This feature makes a DSO the perfect tool to help diagnose intermittent problems.

- A digital storage scope, however, can sometimes miss faults called *glitches* that may occur between samples captured by the scope. This is why a DSO with a high "sampling rate" is preferred. Sampling rate means that a scope is cable of capturing voltage changes that occur over a very short period of time. Some digital storage scopes have a capture rate of 25 million (25,000,000) samples per second. This means that the scope can capture a glitch (fault) that lasts just 40 nano (0.00000040) seconds long.

- A scope has been called "a voltmeter with a clock."
  - The voltmeter part means that a scope can capture and display changing voltage levels.
  - The clock part means that the scope can display these changes in voltage levels within a specific time period; and with a DSO it can be replayed so that any faults can be seen and studied.

OSCILLOSCOPE DISPLAY GRID A typical scope face usually has eight or ten grids vertically (up and down) and ten grids horizontally (left to right). The transparent scale (grid),

used for reference measurements, is called a **graticule**. This arrangement is commonly 8 × 10 or 10 × 10 divisions. ● **SEE FIGURE 9–1.**

NOTE: These numbers originally referred to the metric dimensions of the graticule in centimeters. Therefore, an 8 × 10 display would be 8 cm (80 mm or 3.14 in.) high and 10 cm (100 mm or 3.90 in.) wide.

- Voltage is displayed on a scope starting with zero volts at the bottom and higher voltage being displayed vertically.

- The scope illustrates time left to right. The pattern starts on the left and sweeps across the screen from left to right.

SCOPE SETUP AND ADJUSTMENTS

SETTING THE TIME BASE Most scopes use 10 graticules from left to right on the display. Setting the **time base** means setting how much time will be displayed in each block called a **division**. For example, if the scope is set to read 2 seconds per division (referred to as *s/div*), then the total displayed would be 20 seconds (2 × 10 divisions = 20 sec.). The time base should be set to an amount of time that allows two to four events to be displayed. Milliseconds (0.001 sec.) are commonly used in scopes when adjusting the time base. Sample time is milliseconds per division (indicated as *ms/div*) and total time. ● **SEE CHART 9–1.**

MILLISECONDS PER DIVISION (MS/DIV)	TOTAL TIME DISPLAYED
1 ms	10 ms (0.010 sec.)
10 ms	100 ms (0.100 sec.)
50 ms	500 ms (0.500 sec.)
100 ms	1 sec. (1.000 sec.)
500 ms	5 sec. (5.0 sec.)
1,000 ms	10 sec. (10.0 sec.)

CHART 9–1

The time base is milliseconds (ms) and total time of an event that can be displayed.

FIGURE 9–1 A scope display allows technicians to take measurements of voltage patterns. In this example, each vertical division is 1 volt and each horizontal division is set to represent 50 milliseconds.

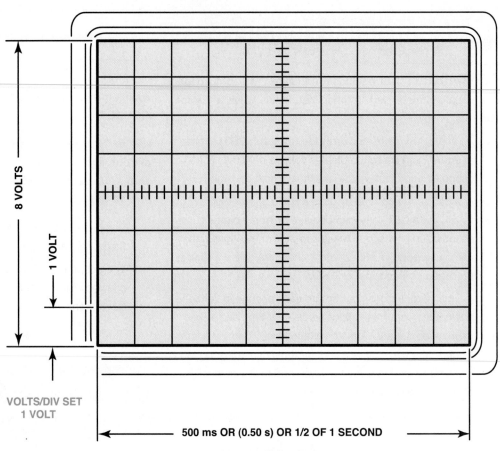

8 VOLTS

1 VOLT

VOLTS/DIV SET
1 VOLT

500 ms OR (0.50 s) OR 1/2 OF 1 SECOND

TIME BASE SET TO "50 ms"

SCOPE SETUP AND ADJUSTMENTS (CONTINUED)

NOTE: Increasing the time base reduces the number of samples per second.

The horizontal scale is divided into 10 divisions (sometimes called *grats*). If each division represents 1 second of time, then the total time period displayed on the screen will be 10 seconds. The time per division is selected so that several events of the waveform are displayed. Time per division settings can vary greatly in automotive use, including:

- MAP/MAF sensors: 2 ms/div (20 ms total)
- Network (CAN) communications network: 2 ms/div (20 ms total)
- Throttle position (TP) sensor: 100 ms per division (1 sec. total)
- Fuel injector: 2 ms/div (20 ms total)
- Oxygen sensor: 1 sec. per division (10 sec. total)
- Primary ignition: 10 ms/div (100 ms total)
- Secondary ignition: 10 ms/div (100 ms total)
- Voltage measurements: 5 ms/div (50 ms total)

The total time displayed on the screen allows comparisons to see if the waveform is consistent or is changing. Multiple waveforms shown on the display at the same time also allow for measurements to be seen more easily. ● **SEE FIGURE 9–2** for an example of a throttle position sensor waveform created by measuring the voltage output as the throttle was depressed and then released.

VOLTS PER DIVISION The volts per division, abbreviated *V/div*, should be set so that the entire anticipated waveform can be viewed. Examples include:

Throttle position (TP) sensor: 1 V/div (8 V total)

Battery, starting and charging: 2 V/div (16 V total)

Oxygen sensor: 200 mV/div (1.6 V total)

Notice from the examples that the total voltage to be displayed exceeds the voltage range of the component being tested. This ensures that all the waveform will be displayed. It also allows for some unexpected voltage readings. For example, an oxygen sensor should read between 0 V and 1 V (1,000 mV). By setting the V/div to 200 mV, up to 1.6 V (1,600 mV) will be displayed.

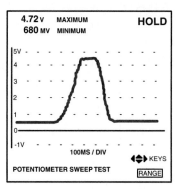

FIGURE 9–2 The display on a digital storage oscilloscope (DSO) displays the entire waveform from idle to wide-open throttle and then returns to idle. The display also indicates the maximum reading (4.72 V) and the minimum (680 mV or 0.68 V). The display does not show anything until the throttle is opened, because the scope has been set up to only start displaying a waveform after a certain voltage level has been reached. This voltage is called the trigger or trigger point.

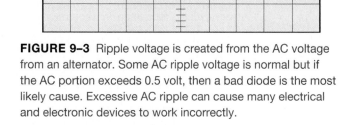

FIGURE 9–3 Ripple voltage is created from the AC voltage from an alternator. Some AC ripple voltage is normal but if the AC portion exceeds 0.5 volt, then a bad diode is the most likely cause. Excessive AC ripple can cause many electrical and electronic devices to work incorrectly.

DC AND AC COUPLING

DC COUPLING **DC coupling** is the most used position on a scope because it allows the scope to display both alternating current (AC) voltage signals and direct current (DC) voltage signals present in the circuit. The AC part of the signal will ride on top of the DC component. For example, if the engine is running and the charging voltage is 14.4 volts DC, this will be displayed as a horizontal line on the screen. Any AC ripple voltage leaking past the alternator diodes will be displayed as an AC signal on top of the horizontal DC voltage line. Therefore, both components of the signal can be observed at the same time. ● **SEE FIGURE 9–3.**

AC COUPLING When the **AC coupling** position is selected, a capacitor is placed into the meter lead circuit, which effectively blocks all DC voltage signals but allows the AC portion of the signal to pass and be displayed. AC coupling can be used to show output signal waveforms from sensors such as:

- Distributor pickup coils
- Magnetic wheel speed sensors
- Magnetic crankshaft position sensors
- Magnetic camshaft position sensors
- Magnetic vehicle speed sensors

NOTE: Check the instructions from the scope manufacturer for the recommended settings to use. Sometimes it is necessary to switch from DC coupling to AC coupling or from AC coupling to DC coupling to properly see some waveforms.

PULSE TRAINS

DEFINITION Scopes can show all voltage signals. Among the most commonly found in automotive applications is a DC voltage that varies up and down and does not go below zero like an AC voltage. A DC voltage that turns on and off in a series of pulses is called a **pulse train**. Pulse trains differ from an AC signal in that they do not go below zero. An alternating voltage goes above and below zero voltage. Pulse train signals can vary in several ways. ● **SEE FIGURE 9–4.**

FREQUENCY **Frequency** is the number of cycles per second measured in **hertz.** The engine revolutions per minute (RPM) signal is an example of a signal that can occur at various frequencies. At low engine speed, the ignition pulses occur fewer times per second (lower frequency) than when the engine is operated at higher engine speeds (RPM).

DUTY CYCLE **Duty cycle** refers to the percentage of on-time of the signal during one complete cycle. As on-time increases, the amount of time the signal is off decreases and is usually measured in percentage. Duty cycle is also called **pulse-width modulation (PWM)** and can be measured in degrees. ● **SEE FIGURE 9–5.**

PULSE WIDTH The **pulse width** is a measure of the actual on-time measured in milliseconds. Fuel injectors are usually controlled by varying the pulse width. ● **SEE FIGURE 9–6.**

1. FREQUENCY - FREQUENCY IS THE NUMBER OF CYCLES THAT TAKE PLACE PER SECOND. THE MORE CYCLES THAT TAKE PLACE IN ONE SECOND, THE HIGHER THE FREQUENCY READING. FREQUENCIES ARE MEASURED IN HERTZ, WHICH IS THE NUMBER OF CYCLES PER SECOND. AN EIGHT HERTZ SIGNAL CYCLES EIGHT TIMES PER SECOND.

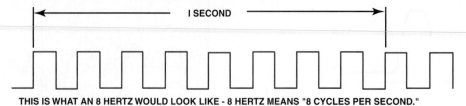

THIS IS WHAT AN 8 HERTZ WOULD LOOK LIKE - 8 HERTZ MEANS "8 CYCLES PER SECOND."

2. DUTY CYCLE - DUTY CYCLE IS A MEASUREMENT COMPARING THE SIGNAL ON-TIME TO THE LENGTH OF ONE COMPLETE CYCLE. AS ON-TIME INCREASES, OFF-TIME DECREASES. DUTY CYCLE IS MEASURED IN PERCENTAGE OF ON-TIME. A 60% DUTY CYCLE IS SIGNAL A THAT'S ON 60% OF THE TIME, AND OFF 40% OF THE TIME. ANOTHER WAY TO MEASURE DUTY CYCLE IS DWELL, WHICH IS MEASURED IN DEGREES INSTEAD OF PERCENT.

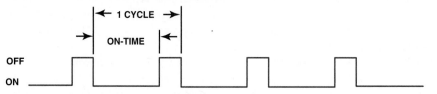

DUTY CYCLE IS THE RELATIONSHIP BETWEEN ONE COMPLETE CYCLE, AND THE SIGNAL'S ON-TIME. A SIGNAL CAN VARY IN DUTY CYCLE WITHOUT AFFECTING THE FREQUENCY.

3. PULSE WIDTH - PULSE WIDTH IS THE ACTUAL ON-TIME OF A SIGNAL, MEASURED IN MILLISECONDS. WITH PULSE WIDTH MEASUREMENTS, OFF-TIME DOESN'T REALLY MATTER - THE ONLY REAL CONCERN IS HOW LONG THE SIGNAL'S ON. THIS IS A USEFUL TEST FOR MEASURING CONVENTIONAL INJECTOR ON-TIME, TO SEE THAT THE SIGNAL VARIES WITH LOAD CHANGE.

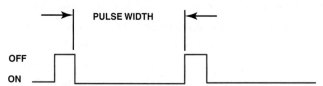

PULSE WIDTH IS THE ACTUAL TIME A SIGNAL'S ON, MEASURED IN MILLISECONDS. THE ONLY THING BEING MEASURED IS HOW LONG THE SIGNAL IS ON.

FIGURE 9–4 A pulse train is any electrical signal that turns on and off, or goes high and low in a series of pulses. Ignition module and fuel-injector pulses are examples of a pulse train signal.

NUMBER OF CHANNELS

DEFINITION Scopes are available that allow the viewing of more than one sensor or event at the same time on the display. The number of events, which require leads for each, is called a **channel**. A channel is an input to a scope. Commonly available scopes include:

- **Single channel.** A single channel scope is capable of displaying only one sensor signal waveform at a time.

- **Two channel.** A two-channel scope can display the waveform from two separate sensors or components at the same time. This feature is very helpful when testing the camshaft and crankshaft position sensors on an engine to see if they are properly timed. ● **SEE FIGURE 9–7.**

- **Four channel.** A four-channel scope allows the technician to view up to four different sensors or actuators on one display.

NOTE: Often the capture speed of the signals is slowed when using more than one channel.

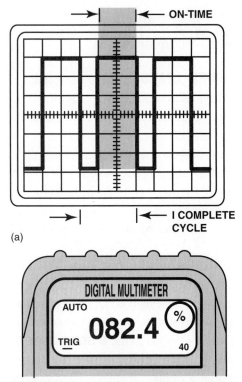

(a)

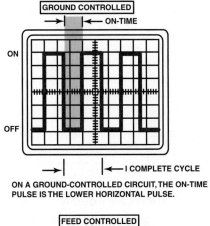

ON A GROUND-CONTROLLED CIRCUIT, THE ON-TIME
PULSE IS THE LOWER HORIZONTAL PULSE.

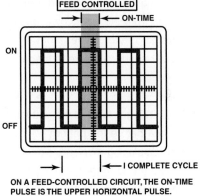

ON A FEED-CONTROLLED CIRCUIT, THE ON-TIME
PULSE IS THE UPPER HORIZONTAL PULSE.

THE % SIGN IN THE UPPER RIGHT CORNER
OF THE DISPLAY INDICATES THAT THE METER
IS READING A DUTY CYCLE SIGNAL.

(b)

FIGURE 9–5 (a) A scope representation of a complete cycle showing both on-time and off-time. (b) A meter display indicating the on-time duty cycle in a percentage (%). Note the trigger and negative (−) symbol. This indicates that the meter started to record the percentage of on-time when the voltage dropped (start of on-time).

FIGURE 9–6 Most automotive computer systems control the device by opening and closing the ground to the component.

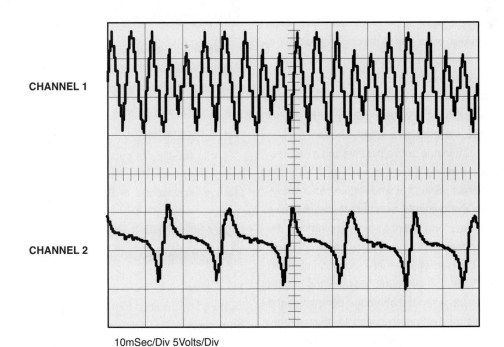

10mSec/Div 5Volts/Div

FIGURE 9–7 A two-channel scope being used to compare two signals on the same vehicle.

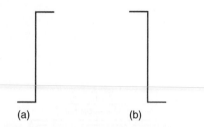

FIGURE 9–8 (a) A symbol for a positive trigger—a trigger occurs at a rising (positive) edge of the signal (waveform). (b) A symbol for a negative trigger—a trigger occurs at a falling (negative) edge of the signal (waveform).

TRIGGERS

EXTERNAL TRIGGER An **external trigger** is when the waveform starts when a signal is received from another external source rather than from the signal pickup lead. A common example of an external trigger comes from the probe clamp around the cylinder #1 spark plug wire to trigger the start of an ignition pattern.

TRIGGER LEVEL **Trigger level** is the voltage that must be detected by the scope before the pattern will be displayed. A scope will only start displaying a voltage signal when it is triggered or is told to start. The trigger level must be set to start the display. If the pattern starts at 1 volt, then the trace will begin displaying on the left side of the screen *after* the trace has reached 1 volt.

TRIGGER SLOPE The **trigger slope** is the voltage direction that a waveform must have in order to start the display. Most often, the trigger to start a waveform display is taken from the signal itself. Besides trigger voltage level, most scopes can be adjusted to trigger only when the voltage rises past the trigger-level voltage. This is called a *positive slope*. When the voltage falling past the higher level activates the trigger, this is called a *negative slope*.

The scope display indicates both a positive and a negative slope symbol. For example, if a waveform such as a magnetic sensor used for crankshaft position or wheel speed starts moving upward, a positive slope should be selected. If a negative slope is selected, the waveform will not start showing until the voltage reaches the trigger level in a downward direction. A negative slope should be used when a fuel-injector circuit is being analyzed. In this circuit, the computer provides the ground and the voltage level drops when the computer commands the injector on. Sometimes the technician needs to change from negative to positive or positive to negative trigger if a waveform is not being shown correctly. ● **SEE FIGURE 9–8.**

USING A SCOPE

USING SCOPE LEADS Most scopes, both analog and digital, normally use the same test leads. These leads usually attach to the scope through a **BNC connector**, a miniature standard coaxial cable connector. BNC is an international standard that is used in the electronics industry. If using a BNC connector, be sure to connect one lead to a good clean, metal engine ground. The probe of the scope lead attaches to the circuit or component being tested. Many scopes use one ground lead and then each channel has it own signal pickup lead.

MEASURING BATTERY VOLTAGE WITH A SCOPE One of the easiest things to measure and observe on a scope is battery voltage. A lower voltage can be observed on the scope display as the engine is started and a higher voltage should be displayed after the engine starts. ● **SEE FIGURE 9–9.**

An analog scope displays rapidly and cannot be set to show or freeze a display. Therefore, even though an analog scope shows all voltage signals, it is easy to miss a momentary glitch on an analog scope.

CAUTION: Check the instructions for the scope being used before attempting to scope household AC circuits. Some scopes, such as the Snap-On MODIS, are not designed to measure high-voltage AC circuits.

GRAPHING MULTIMETER

A **graphing multimeter**, abbreviated **GMM**, is a cross between a digital meter and a digital storage oscilloscope. A graphing multimeter displays the voltage levels at two places:

- On a display screen
- In a digital readout

It is usually not capable of capturing very short duration faults or glitches that would likely be captured with a digital storage oscilloscope. ● **SEE FIGURE 9–10.**

GRAPHING SCAN TOOLS

Many scan tools are capable of displaying the voltage levels captured by the scan tool through the data link connector (DLC) on a screen. This feature is helpful where seeing changes in voltage levels is difficult to detect by looking at numbers that are constantly changing. Read and follow the instructions for the scan tool being used.

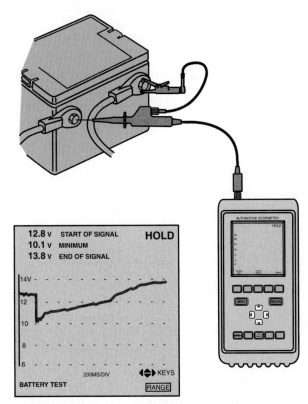

FIGURE 9–9 Battery voltage is represented by a flat horizontal line. In this example, the engine was started and the battery voltage dropped to about 10 V as shown on the left side of the scope display. When the engine started, the alternator started to charge the battery and the voltage is shown as climbing.

FIGURE 9–10 A typical graphing multimeter that can be used as a digital meter, plus it can display the voltage levels on the display screen.

SUMMARY

1. Analog oscilloscopes use a cathode ray tube to display voltage patterns.

2. The waveforms shown on an analog oscilloscope cannot be stored for later viewing.

3. A digital storage oscilloscope (DSO) creates an image or waveform on the display by connecting thousands of dots captured by the scope leads.

4. An oscilloscope display grid is called a graticule. Each of the 8 × 10 or 10 × 10 dividing boxes is called a division.

5. Setting the time base means establishing the amount of time each division represents.

6. Setting the volts per division allows the technician to view either the entire waveform or just part of it.

7. DC coupling and AC coupling are two selections that can be made to observe different types of waveforms.

8. A graphing multimeter is not capable of capturing short duration faults but can display usable waveforms.

9. Oscilloscopes display voltage over time. A DSO can capture and store a waveform for viewing later.

REVIEW QUESTIONS

1. What are the differences between an analog and a digital oscilloscope?

2. What is the difference between DC coupling and AC coupling?

3. Why are DC signals that change called pulse trains?

4. What is the difference between an oscilloscope and a graphing multimeter?

1. Technician A says an analog scope can store the waveform for viewing later. Technician B says that the trigger level has to be set on most scopes to be able to view a changing waveform. Which technician is correct?
   a. Technician A only
   b. Technician B only
   c. Both Technicians A and B
   d. Neither Technician A nor B

2. An oscilloscope display is called a _____.
   a. Grid
   b. Graticule
   c. Division
   d. Box

3. A signal showing the voltage of a battery displayed on a digital storage oscilloscope (DSO) is being discussed. Technician A says that the display will show one horizontal line above the zero line. Technician B says that the display will show a line sloping upward from zero to the battery voltage level. Which technician is correct?
   a. Technician A only
   b. Technician B only
   c. Both Technicians A and B
   d. Neither Technician A nor B

4. Setting the time base to 50 ms per division will allow the technician to view a waveform how long in duration?
   a. 50 ms
   b. 200 ms
   c. 400 ms
   d. 500 ms

5. A throttle position sensor waveform is going to be observed. At what setting should the volts per division be set to see the entire waveform from 0 to 5 volts?
   a. 0.5 V/division
   b. 1.0 V/division
   c. 2.0 V/division
   d. 5.0 V/division

6. Two technicians are discussing the DC coupling setting on a DSO. Technician A says that the position allows both the DC and AC signals of the waveform to be displayed. Technician B says that this setting allows just the DC part of the waveform to be displayed. Which technician is correct?
   a. Technician A only
   b. Technician B only
   c. Both Technicians A and B
   d. Neither Technician A nor B

7. Voltage signals (waveforms) that do not go below zero are called _____.
   a. AC signals
   b. Pulse trains
   c. Pulse width
   d. DC coupled signals

8. Cycles per second are expressed in _____.
   a. Hertz
   b. Duty cycle
   c. Pulse width
   d. Slope

9. Oscilloscopes use what type of lead connector?
   a. Banana plugs
   b. Double banana plugs
   c. Single conductor plugs
   d. BNC

10. A digital meter that can show waveforms is called a _____.
    a. DVOM
    b. DMM
    c. GMM
    d. DSO

chapter 10

AUTOMOTIVE WIRING AND WIRE REPAIR

OBJECTIVES

After studying Chapter 10, the reader will be able to:

1. Prepare for ASE Electrical/Electronic Systems (A6) certification test content area "A" (General Electrical/Electronic Systems Diagnosis).

2. Explain the wire gauge number system.

3. Describe how fusible links and fuses protect circuits and wiring.

4. List the steps for performing a proper wire repair.

KEY TERMS

Adhesive-lined heat shrink tubing 139
American wire gauge (AWG) 128
Auto link 133
Battery cables 130
Braided ground straps 129
Circuit breakers 133
Cold solder joint 138
Connector 136
CPA 136
Crimp-and-seal connectors 139
Fuse link 133

Fuses 131
Fusible link 135
Heat shrink tubing 139
Jumper cables 130
Lock tang 136
Metric wire gauge 128
Pacific fuse element 133
Primary wire 129
PTC circuit protection 134
Rosin-core solder 138
Skin effect 130
Terminal 136
Twisted pair 130

AUTOMOTIVE WIRING

DEFINITION AND TERMINOLOGY Most automotive wire is made from strands of copper covered by insulating plastic. Copper is an excellent conductor of electricity that is reasonably priced and very flexible. However, copper can break when moved repeatedly; therefore, most copper wiring is constructed of multiple small strands that allow for repeated bending and moving without breaking. Solid copper wire is generally used for components such as starter armature and alternator stator windings that do not bend or move during normal operation. Copper is the best electrical conductor besides silver, which is a great deal more expensive. The conductivity of various metals is rated. ● **SEE CHART 10–1.**

AMERICAN WIRE GAUGE Wiring is sized and purchased according to gauge size as assigned by the **American wire gauge (AWG)** system. AWG numbers can be confusing because as the gauge number *increases,* the size of the conductor wire *decreases.* Therefore, a 14 gauge wire is smaller than a 10 gauge wire. The *greater* the amount of current (in amperes) that is flowing through a wire, the *larger the diameter (smaller gauge number)* that will be required. ● **SEE CHART 10–2,** which compares the AWG number to the actual wire diameter in inches. The diameter refers to the diameter of the metal conductor and does not include the insulation.

Following are general applications for the most commonly used wire gauge sizes. Always check the installation instructions or the manufacturer's specifications for wire gauge size before replacing any automotive wiring.

- 20 to 22 gauge: radio speaker wires
- 18 gauge: small bulbs and short leads
- 16 gauge: taillights, gas gauge, turn signals, windshield wipers
- 14 gauge: horn, radio power lead, headlights, cigarette lighter, brake lights
- 12 gauge: headlight switch-to-fuse box, rear window defogger, power windows and locks
- 10 gauge: alternator-to-battery
- 4, 2, or 0 (1/0) gauge: battery cables

METRIC WIRE GAUGE Most manufacturers indicate on the wiring diagrams the **metric wire gauge** sizes measured in square millimeters (mm^2) of cross-sectional area. The following

1.	Silver
2.	Copper
3.	Gold
4.	Aluminum
5.	Tungsten
6.	Zinc
7.	Brass (copper and zinc)
8.	Platinum
9.	Iron
10.	Nickel
11.	Tin
12.	Steel
13.	Lead

CHART 10–1

The list of relative conductivity of metals, showing silver to be the best.

WIRE GAUGE DIAMETER TABLE	
AMERICAN WIRE GAUGE (AWG)	**WIRE DIAMETER IN INCHES**
20	0.03196118
18	0.040303
16	0.0508214
14	0.064084
12	0.08080810
10	0.10189
8	0.128496
6	0.16202
5	0.18194
4	0.20431
3	0.22942
2	0.25763
1	0.2893
0	0.32486
00	0.3648

CHART 10–2

American wire gauge (AWG) number and the actual conductor diameter in inches.

Do They Make 13 Gauge Wire?

Yes. AWG sizing of wire includes all gauge numbers, including 13, even though the most commonly used sizes are even numbered, such as 12, 14, or 16.

Because the sizes are so close, wire in every size is not commonly stocked, but can be ordered for a higher price. Therefore, if a larger wire size is needed, it is common practice to select the next lower, even-numbered gauge.

METRIC SIZE (MM²)	AWG SIZE
0.5	20
0.8	18
1.0	16
2.0	14
3.0	12
5.0	10
8.0	8
13.0	6
19.0	4
32.0	2
52.0	0

CHART 10–3

Metric wire size in squared millimeters (mm²) conversion chart to American wire gauge (AWG).

chart gives conversions or comparisons between metric gauge and AWG sizes. Notice that the metric wire size increases with size (area), whereas the AWG size gets smaller with larger size wire. ● **SEE CHART 10–3.**

The AWG number should be decreased (wire size increased) with increased lengths of wire. ● **SEE CHART 10–4.**

For example, a trailer may require 14 gauge wire to light all the trailer lights, but if the wire required is over 25 ft long, 12 gauge wire should be used. Most automotive wire, except for spark plug wire, is often called **primary wire** (named for the voltage range used in the primary ignition circuit) because it is designed to operate at or near battery voltage.

12 V	RECOMMENDED WIRE GAUGE (AWG) (FOR LENGTH IN FEET)*						
AMPS	3'	5'	7'	10'	15'	20'	25'
5	18	18	18	18	18	18	18
7	18	18	18	18	18	18	16
10	18	18	18	18	16	16	16
12	18	18	18	18	16	16	14
15	18	18	18	18	14	14	12
18	18	18	16	16	14	14	12
20	18	18	16	16	14	12	10
22	18	18	16	16	12	12	10
24	18	18	16	16	12	12	10
30	18	16	16	14	10	10	10
40	18	16	14	12	10	10	8
50	16	14	12	12	10	10	8
100	12	12	10	10	6	6	4
150	10	10	8	8	4	4	2
200	10	8	8	6	4	4	2

* When mechanical strength is a factor, use the next larger wire gauge.

CHART 10–4

Recommended AWG wire size increases as the length increases because all wire has internal resistance. The longer the wire is, the greater the resistance. The larger the diameter is, the lower the resistance.

GROUND WIRES

PURPOSE AND FUNCTION All vehicles use ground wires between the engine and body and/or between the body and the negative terminal of the battery. The two types of ground wires are:

- Insulated copper wire
- Braided ground straps

Braided grounds straps are uninsulated. It is not necessary to insulate a ground strap because it does not matter if it touches metal, as it already attaches to ground. Braided ground straps are more flexible than stranded wire. Because the engine will move slightly on its mounts, the braided ground strap must be able to flex without breaking. ● **SEE FIGURE 10–1.**

FIGURE 10–1 All lights and accessories ground to the body of the vehicle. Body ground wires such as this one are needed to conduct all of the current from these components back to the negative terminal of the battery. The body ground wire connects the body to the engine. Most battery negative cables attach to the engine.

FIGURE 10–2 Battery cables are designed to carry heavy starter current and are therefore usually 4 gauge or larger wire. Note that this battery has a thermal blanket covering to help protect the battery from high underhood temperatures. The wiring is also covered with plastic conduit called split-loom tubing.

GROUND WIRES (CONTINUED)

SKIN EFFECT The braided strap also dampens out some radio-frequency interference that otherwise might be transmitted through standard stranded wiring due to the skin effect.

The **skin effect** is the term used to describe how high-frequency AC electricity flows through a conductor. Direct current flows through a conductor, but alternating current tends to travel through the outside (skin) of the conductor. Because of the skin effect, most audio (speaker) cable is constructed of many small-diameter copper wires instead of fewer larger strands, because the smaller wire has a greater surface area and therefore results in less resistance to the flow of AC voltage.

NOTE: Body ground wires are necessary to provide a circuit path for the lights and accessories that ground to the body and flow to the negative battery terminal.

FREQUENTLY ASKED QUESTION

What Is a Twisted Pair?

A **twisted pair** is used to transmit low-voltage signals using two wires that are twisted together. Electromagnetic interference can create a voltage in a wire and twisting the two signal wires cancels out the induced voltage. A twisted pair means that the two wires have at least nine turns per foot (turns per meter). A rule of thumb is a twisted pair should have one twist per inch of length.

BATTERY CABLES

Battery cables are the largest wires used in the automotive electrical system. The cables are usually 4 gauge, 2 gauge, or 1 gauge wires (19 mm² or larger). ● **SEE FIGURE 10–2**.

Wires larger than 1 gauge are called 0 gauge (pronounced "ought"). Larger cables are labeled 2/0 or 00 (2 ought) and 3/0 or 000 (3 ought). Electrical systems that are 6 volts require battery cables two sizes larger than those used for 12 volt electrical systems, because the lower voltage used in antique vehicles resulted in twice the amount of current (amperes) to supply the same electrical power.

JUMPER CABLES

Jumper cables are 4 to 2/0 gauge electrical cables with large clamps attached and are used to connect a vehicle that has a discharged battery to a vehicle that has a good battery. Good-quality jumper cables are necessary to prevent excessive voltage drops caused by cable resistance. Aluminum wire jumper cables should not be used, because even though aluminum is a good electrical conductor (although not as good as copper), it is less flexible and can crack and break when bent or moved repeatedly. The size should be 6 gauge or larger.

Ought gauge welding cable can be used to construct an excellent set of jumper cables using welding clamps on both

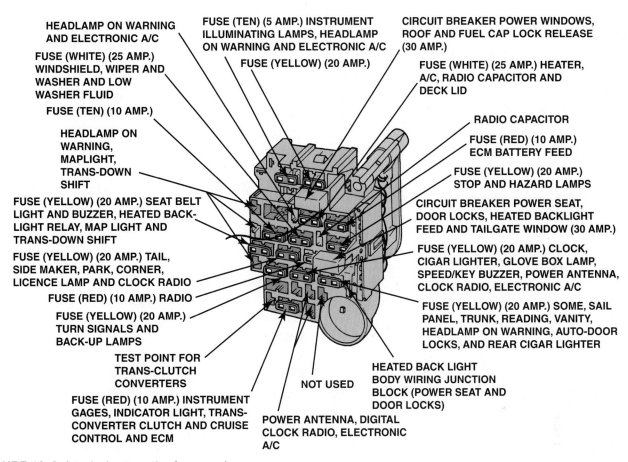

HEADLAMP ON WARNING AND ELECTRONIC A/C

FUSE (WHITE) (25 AMP.) WINDSHIELD, WIPER AND WASHER AND LOW WASHER FLUID

FUSE (TEN) (10 AMP.)

HEADLAMP ON WARNING, MAPLIGHT, TRANS-DOWN SHIFT

FUSE (YELLOW) (20 AMP.) SEAT BELT LIGHT AND BUZZER, HEATED BACK-LIGHT RELAY, MAP LIGHT AND TRANS-DOWN SHIFT

FUSE (YELLOW) (20 AMP.) TAIL, SIDE MAKER, PARK, CORNER, LICENCE LAMP AND CLOCK RADIO

FUSE (RED) (10 AMP.) RADIO

FUSE (YELLOW) (20 AMP.) TURN SIGNALS AND BACK-UP LAMPS

TEST POINT FOR TRANS-CLUTCH CONVERTERS

FUSE (RED) (10 AMP.) INSTRUMENT GAGES, INDICATOR LIGHT, TRANS-CONVERTER CLUTCH AND CRUISE CONTROL AND ECM

FUSE (TEN) (5 AMP.) INSTRUMENT ILLUMINATING LAMPS, HEADLAMP ON WARNING AND ELECTRONIC A/C

FUSE (YELLOW) (20 AMP.)

NOT USED

POWER ANTENNA, DIGITAL CLOCK RADIO, ELECTRONIC A/C

CIRCUIT BREAKER POWER WINDOWS, ROOF AND FUEL CAP LOCK RELEASE (30 AMP.)

FUSE (WHITE) (25 AMP.) HEATER, A/C, RADIO CAPACITOR AND DECK LID

RADIO CAPACITOR

FUSE (RED) (10 AMP.) ECM BATTERY FEED

FUSE (YELLOW) (20 AMP.) STOP AND HAZARD LAMPS

CIRCUIT BREAKER POWER SEAT, DOOR LOCKS, HEATED BACKLIGHT FEED AND TAILGATE WINDOW (30 AMP.)

FUSE (YELLOW) (20 AMP.) CLOCK, CIGAR LIGHTER, GLOVE BOX LAMP, SPEED/KEY BUZZER, POWER ANTENNA, CLOCK RADIO, ELECTRONIC A/C

FUSE (YELLOW) (20 AMP.) SOME, SAIL PANEL, TRUNK, READING, VANITY, HEADLAMP ON WARNING, AUTO-DOOR LOCKS, AND REAR CIGAR LIGHTER

HEATED BACK LIGHT BODY WIRING JUNCTION BLOCK (POWER SEAT AND DOOR LOCKS)

FIGURE 10–3 A typical automotive fuse panel.

ends. Welding cable is usually constructed of many very fine strands of wire, which allow for easier bending of the cable as the strands of fine wire slide against each other inside the cable.

NOTE: Always check the wire gauge of any battery cables or jumper cables and do not rely on the outside diameter of the wire. Many lower cost jumper cables use smaller gauge wire, but may use thick insulation to make the cable look as if it is the correct size wire.

FUSES AND CIRCUIT PROTECTION DEVICES

CONSTRUCTION **Fuses** should be used in every circuit to protect the wiring from overheating and damage caused by excessive current flow as a result of a short circuit or other malfunction. The symbol for a fuse is a wavy line between two points: •~•

A fuse is constructed of a fine tin conductor inside a glass, plastic, or ceramic housing. The tin is designed to melt and open the circuit if excessive current flows through the fuse. Each fuse is rated according to its maximum current-carrying capacity.

Many fuses are used to protect more than one circuit of the automobile. ● **SEE FIGURE 10–3.**

A typical example is the fuse for the cigarette lighter that also protects many other circuits, such as those for the courtesy lights, clock, and other circuits. A fault in one of these circuits can cause this fuse to melt, which will prevent the operation of all other circuits that are protected by the fuse.

NOTE: The SAE term for a cigarette lighter is *cigar lighter* because the diameter of the heating element is large enough for a cigar. The term *cigarette lighter* will be used throughout this book because it is the most common usage.

FUSE RATINGS Fuses are used to protect the wiring and components in the circuit from damage if an excessive amount of

NORMAL CURRENT IN THE CIRCUIT (AMPERES)	FUSE RATING
7.5 A	10 A
16 A	20 A
24 A	30 A

CHART 10–5

The fuse rating should be 20% higher than the maximum current in the circuit to provide the best protection for the wiring and the component being protected.

AMPERAGE RATING	COLOR
1	Dark green
2	Gray
2.5	Purple
3	Violet
4	Pink
5	Tan
6	Gold
7.5	Brown
9	Orange
10	Red
14	Black
15	Blue
20	Yellow
25	White
30	Green

CHART 10–6

The amperage rating and the color of the blade fuse are standardized.

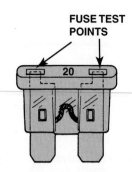

FIGURE 10–4 Blade-type fuses can be tested through openings in the plastic at the top of the fuse.

current flows. The fuse rating is normally about 20% higher than the normal current in the circuit. See ● **CHART 10–5** for a typical fuse rating based on the normal current in the circuit. In other words, the normal current flow should be about 80% of the fuse rating.

BLADE FUSES Colored blade-type fuses are also referred to as ATO fuses and have been used since 1977. The color of the plastic of blade fuses indicates the maximum current flow, measured in amperes.

See ● **CHART 10–6** for the color and the amperage rating of blade fuses.

Each fuse has an opening in the top of its plastic portion to allow access to its metal contacts for testing purposes. ● **SEE FIGURE 10–4.**

MINI FUSES To save space, many vehicles use mini (small) blade fuses. Not only do they save space but they also allow the vehicle design engineer to fuse individual circuits instead of grouping many different components on one fuse. This improves customer satisfaction because if one component fails, it only affects that one circuit without stopping electrical power to several other circuits as well. This makes troubleshooting a lot easier too, because each circuit is separate. ● **SEE CHART 10–7** for the amperage rating and corresponding fuse color for mini fuses.

AMPERAGE RATING	COLOR
5	Tan
7.5	Brown
10	Red
15	Blue
20	Yellow
25	Natural
30	Green

CHART 10–7

Mini fuse amperage rating and colors.

AMPERAGE RATING	COLOR
20	Yellow
30	Green
40	Amber
50	Red
60	Blue
70	Brown
80	Natural

CHART 10–8

Maxi fuse amperage rating and colors.

MAXI FUSES
Maxi fuses are a large version of blade fuses and are used to replace fusible links in many vehicles. Maxi fuses are rated up to 80 amperes or more. ● **SEE CHART 10–8** for the amperage rating and corresponding color for maxi fuses.

● **SEE FIGURE 10–5** for a comparison of the various sizes of blade-type fuses.

PACIFIC FUSE ELEMENT
First used in the late 1980s, **Pacific fuse elements** (also called a **fuse link** or **auto link**) are used to protect wiring from a direct short-to-ground. The housing contains a short link of wire sized for the rated current load. The transparent top allows inspection of the link inside. ● **SEE FIGURE 10–6.**

TESTING FUSES
It is important to test the condition of a fuse if the circuit being protected by the fuse does not operate. Most blown fuses can be detected quickly because the center conductor is melted. Fuses can also fail and open the circuit because of a poor connection in the fuse itself or in the fuse holder. Therefore, just because a fuse "looks okay" does not mean that it *is* okay. All fuses should be tested with a test light. The test light should be connected to first one side of the fuse and then the other. A test light should light on both sides. If the test light only lights on one side, the fuse is blown or open. If the test light does not light on either side of the fuse, then that circuit is not being supplied power. ● **SEE FIGURE 10–7.** An ohmmeter can be used to test fuses.

CIRCUIT BREAKERS
Circuit breakers are used to prevent harmful overload (excessive current flow) in a circuit by opening the circuit and stopping the current flow to prevent overheating and possible fire caused by hot wires or electrical components. **Circuit breakers** are mechanical units made of two different

FIGURE 10–5 Three sizes of blade-type fuses: mini on the left, standard or ATO type in the center, and maxi on the right.

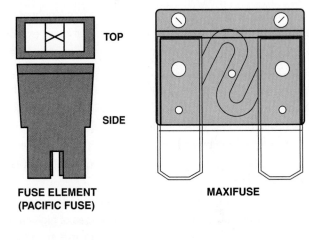

FUSE ELEMENT (PACIFIC FUSE)   MAXIFUSE

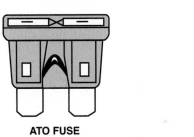
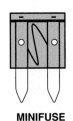

ATO FUSE   MINIFUSE

FIGURE 10–6 A comparison of the various types of protective devices used in most vehicles.

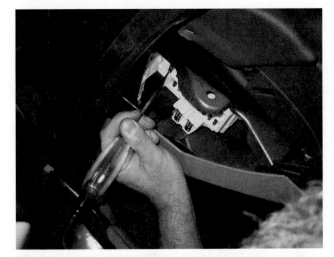

FIGURE 10–7 To test a fuse, use a test light to check for power at the power side of the fuse. The ignition switch and lights may have to be on before some fuses receive power. If the fuse is good, the test light should light on both sides (power side and load side) of the fuse.

FUSES AND CIRCUIT PROTECTION
DEVICES (CONTINUED)

metals (bimetallic) that deform when heated and open a set of contact points that work in the same manner as an "off" switch. ● **SEE FIGURE 10–8.**

Cycling-type circuit breakers, therefore, are reset when the current stops flowing, which causes the bimetallic strip to cool and the circuit to close again. A circuit breaker is used in circuits that could affect the safety of passengers if a conventional non-resetting fuse were used. The headlight circuit is an excellent example of the use of a circuit breaker rather than a fuse. A short or grounded circuit anywhere in the headlight circuit could cause excessive current flow and, therefore, the opening of the circuit. Obviously, a sudden loss of headlights at night could have disastrous results. A circuit breaker opens and closes the circuit rapidly, thereby protecting the circuit from overheating and also providing sufficient current flow to maintain at least partial headlight operation.

Circuit breakers are also used in other circuits where conventional fuses could not provide for the surges of high current commonly found in those circuits. See ● **FIGURE 10–9** for the electrical symbols used to represent a circuit breaker.

Examples are the circuits for the following accessories.

1. Power seats
2. Power door locks
3. Power windows

PTC CIRCUIT PROTECTORS **Positive temperature coefficient (PTC) circuit protectors** are solid state (without moving parts). Like all other circuit protection devices, PTCs are installed in series in the circuit being protected. If excessive current flows, the temperature and resistance of the PTC increase.

This increased resistance reduces current flow (amperes) in the circuit and may cause the electrical component in the circuit not to function correctly. For example, when a PTC circuit protector is used in a power window circuit, the increased resistance causes the operation of the power window to be much slower than normal.

Unlike circuit breakers or fuses, PTC circuit protection devices do *not* open the circuit, but rather provide a very high resistance between the protector and the component. ● **SEE FIGURE 10–10.**

In other words, voltage will be available to the component. This fact has led to a lot of misunderstanding about how these circuit protection devices actually work. It is even more confusing when the circuit is opened and the PTC circuit protector cools down. When the circuit is turned back on, the component

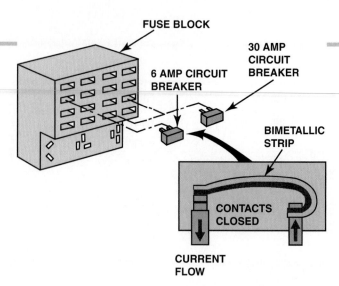

FIGURE 10–8 Typical blade circuit breaker fits into the same space as a blade fuse. If excessive current flows through the bimetallic strip, the strip bends and opens the contacts and stops current flow. When the circuit breaker cools, the contacts close again, completing the electrical circuit.

FIGURE 10–9 Electrical symbols used to represent circuit breakers.

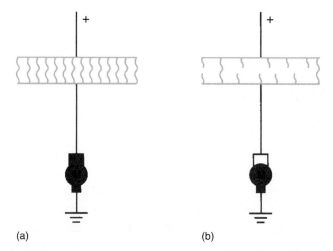

FIGURE 10–10 (a) The normal operation of a PTC circuit protector such as in a power window motor circuit showing the many conducting paths. With normal current flow, the temperature of the PTC circuit protector remains normal. (b) When current exceeds the amperage rating of the PTC circuit protector, the polymer material that makes up the electronic circuit protector increases in resistance. As shown, a high-resistance electrical path still exists even though the motor will stop operating as a result of the very low current flow through the very high resistance. The circuit protector will not reset or cool down until voltage is removed from the circuit.

may operate normally for a short time; however, the PTC circuit protector will again get hot because of too much current flow. Its resistance again increases to limit current flow.

The electronic control unit (computer) used in most vehicles today incorporates thermal overload protection devices. ● SEE FIGURE 10–11.

Therefore, when a component fails to operate, do not blame the computer. The current control device is controlling current flow to protect the computer. Components that do not operate correctly should be checked for proper resistance and current draw.

FUSIBLE LINKS
A **fusible link** is a type of fuse that consists of a short length (6 to 9 in. long) of standard copper-strand wire covered with a special nonflammable insulation. This wire is usually four wire numbers smaller than the wire of the circuits it protects. For example, a 12 gauge circuit is protected by a 16 gauge fusible link. The special thick insulation over the wire may make it look larger than other wires of the same gauge number. ● SEE FIGURE 10–12.

If excessive current flow (caused by a short-to-ground or a defective component) occurs, the fusible link will melt in half and open the circuit to prevent a fire hazard. Some fusible links are identified with "fusible link" tags at the junction between the fusible link and the standard chassis wiring, which represent only the junction. Fusible links are the backup system for circuit protection. All current except the current used by the starter motor flows through fusible links and then through individual circuit fuses. It is possible that a fusible link will melt and not blow a fuse. Fusible links are installed as close to the battery as possible so that they can protect the wiring and circuits coming directly from the battery.

MEGA FUSES
Many newer vehicles are equipped with mega fuses instead of fusible links to protect high-amperage circuits. Circuits often controlled by mega fuses include:

- Charging circuit
- HID headlights
- Heated front or rear glass
- Multiple circuits usually protected by mega fuses
- Mega fuse rating for vehicles, including 80, 100, 125, 150, 175, 200, 225, and 250 amperes
  - ● SEE FIGURE 10–13.

FIGURE 10–11 PTC circuit protectors are used extensively in the power distribution center of this Chrysler vehicle.

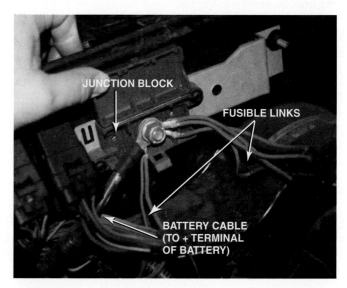

FIGURE 10–12 Fusible links are usually located close to the battery and are usually attached to a junction block. Notice that they are only 6 to 9 in. long and feed more than one fuse from each fusible link.

FIGURE 10–13 A 125 ampere rated mega fuse used to control the current from the alternator.

CHECKING FUSIBLE LINKS AND MEGA FUSES
Fusible links and mega fuses are usually located near where electrical power is sent to other fuses or circuits, such as:

- Starter solenoid battery terminals
- Power distribution centers
- Output terminals of alternators
- Positive terminals of the battery

Fusible links can melt and not show any external evidence of damage. To check a fusible link, gently pull on each end to see if it stretches. If the insulation stretches, then the wire inside has melted and the fusible link must be replaced after determining what caused the link to fail.

Another way to check a fusible link is to use a test light or a voltmeter and check for available voltage at both ends of the fusible link. If voltage is available at only one end, then the link is electrically open and should be replaced.

REPLACING A FUSIBLE LINK
If a fusible link is found to be melted, perform the following steps.

STEP 1 Determine why the fusible link failed and repair the fault.

STEP 2 Check service information for the exact length, gauge, and type of fusible link required.

STEP 3 Replace the fusible link with the specified fusible link wire and according to the instructions found in the service information.

> **CAUTION: Always use the** *exact* **length of fusible link wire required because if it is too short, it will not have enough resistance to generate the heat needed to melt the wire and protect the circuits or components. If the wire is too long, it could melt during normal operation of the circuits it is protecting. Fusible link wires are usually longer than 6 in. and shorter than 9 in.**

TECH TIP

Find the Root Cause

If a mega fuse or fusible link fails, find the root cause before replacing it. A mega fuse can fail due to vibration or physical damage as a result of a collision or corrosion. Check to see if the fuse itself is loose and can be moved by hand. If loose, then simply replace the mega fuse. If a fusible link or mega fuse has failed due to excessive current, check for evidence of a collision or any other reason that could cause an excessive amount of current to flow. This inspection should include each electrical component being supplied current from the fusible link. After being sure that the root cause has been found and corrected, then replace the fusible link or mega fuse.

TERMINALS AND CONNECTORS

A **terminal** is a metal fastener attached to the end of a wire, which makes the electrical connection. The term **connector** usually refers to the plastic portion that snaps or connects together, thereby making the mechanical connection. Wire terminal ends usually snap into and are held by a connector. Male and female connectors can then be snapped together, thereby completing an electrical connection. Connectors exposed to the environment are also equipped with a weather-tight seal. ● **SEE FIGURE 10–14.**

Terminals are retained in connectors by the use of a **lock tang.** Removing a terminal from a connector includes the following steps.

STEP 1 Release the **connector position assurance (CPA),** if equipped, that keeps the latch of the connector from releasing accidentally.

STEP 2 Separate the male and female connector by opening the lock. ● **SEE FIGURE 10–15.**

STEP 3 Release the secondary lock, if equipped. ● **SEE FIGURE 10–16.**

STEP 4 Using a pick, look for the slot in the plastic connector where the lock tang is located, depress the lock tang, and gently remove the terminal from the connector. ● **SEE FIGURE 10–17.**

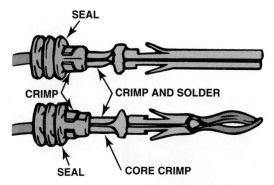

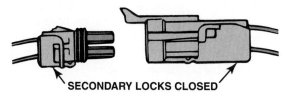

FIGURE 10–14 Some terminals have seals attached to help seal the electrical connections.

FIGURE 10–15 Separate a connector by opening the lock and pulling the two apart.

Look for the "Green Crud"

Corroded connections are a major cause of intermittent electrical problems and open circuits. The usual sequence of conditions is as follows:

1. **Heat causes expansion.** This heat can be from external sources such as connectors being too close to the exhaust system. Another possible source of heat is a poor connection at the terminal, causing a voltage drop and heat due to the electrical resistance.

2. **Condensation occurs when a connector cools.** The moisture in the condensation causes rust and corrosion.

3. **Water gets into the connector.**

The solution is, if corroded connectors are noticed, the terminal should be cleaned and the condition of the electrical connection to the wire terminal end(s) confirmed. Many vehicle manufacturers recommend using a dielectric silicone or lithium-based grease inside connectors to prevent moisture from getting into and attacking the connector.

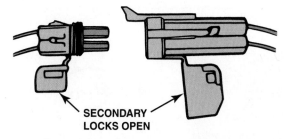

FIGURE 10–16 The secondary locks help retain the terminals in the connector.

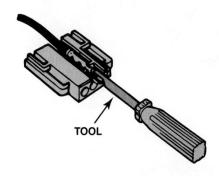

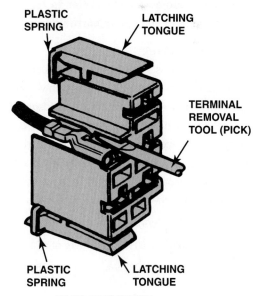

FIGURE 10–17 Use a small removal tool, sometimes called a pick, to release terminals from the connector.

FIGURE 10–18 Always use rosin-core solder for electrical or electronic soldering. Also, use small-diameter solder for small soldering irons. Use large-diameter solder only for large-diameter (large-gauge) wire and higher-wattage soldering irons (guns).

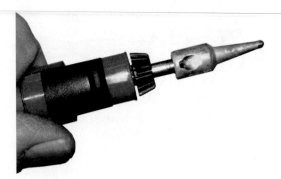

FIGURE 10–19 A butane-powered soldering tool. The cap has a built-in striker to light a converter in the tip of the tool. This handy soldering tool produces the equivalent of 60 watts of heat. It operates for about 1/2 hour on one charge from a commonly available butane refill dispenser.

WIRE REPAIR

SOLDER Many manufacturers recommend that all wiring repairs be soldered. Solder is an alloy of tin and lead used to make a good electrical contact between two wires or connections in an electrical circuit. However, a flux must be used to help clean the area and to help make the solder flow. Therefore, solder is made with a resin (rosin) contained in the center, called **rosin-core solder.**

CAUTION: Never use acid-core solder to repair electrical wiring as the acid will cause corrosion.

● **SEE FIGURE 10–18.**

An acid-core solder is also available but should only be used for soldering sheet metal. Solder is available with various percentages of tin and lead in the alloy. Ratios are used to identify these various types of solder, with the first number denoting the percentage of tin in the alloy and the second number giving the percentage of lead. The most commonly used solder is 50/50, which means that 50% of the solder is tin and the other 50% is lead. The percentages of each alloy primarily determine the melting point of the solder.

- 60/40 solder (60% tin/40% lead) melts at 361°F (183°C).
- 50/50 solder (50% tin/50% lead) melts at 421°F (216°C).
- 40/60 solder (40% tin/60% lead) melts at 460°F (238°C).

NOTE: The melting points stated here can vary depending on the purity of the metals used.

Because of the lower melting point, 60/40 solder is the most highly recommended solder to use, followed by 50/50.

SOLDERING GUNS When soldering wires, be sure to heat the wires (not the solder) using:

- An electric soldering gun or soldering pencil (60 to 150 watt rating)
- Butane-powered tool that uses a flame to heat the tip (about 60 watt rating)

● **SEE FIGURE 10–19.**

SOLDERING PROCEDURE Soldering a wiring splice includes the following steps.

STEP 1 While touching the soldering gun to the splice, apply solder to the junction of the gun and the wire.

STEP 2 The solder will start to flow. Do not move the soldering gun.

STEP 3 Just keep feeding more solder into the splice as it flows into and around the strands of the wire.

STEP 4 After the solder has flowed throughout the splice, remove the soldering gun from the splice and allow the solder to cool slowly.

The solder should have a shiny appearance. Dull-looking solder may be caused by not reaching a high enough temperature, which results in a **cold solder joint.** Reheating the splice and allowing it to cool often restores the shiny appearance.

CRIMPING TERMINALS Terminals can be crimped to create a good electrical connection if the proper type of crimping

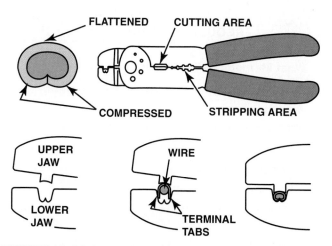

FIGURE 10–20 Notice that to create a good crimp the open part of the terminal is placed in the jaws of the crimping tool toward the anvil or the W-shape part.

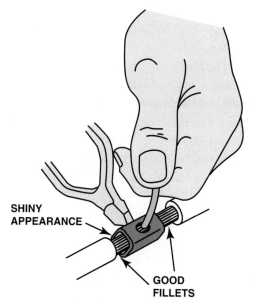

FIGURE 10–21 All hand-crimped splices or terminals should be soldered to be assured of a good electrical connection.

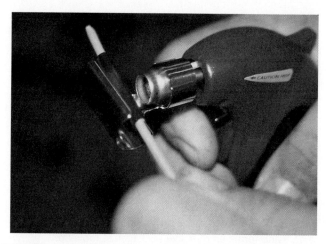

FIGURE 10–22 A butane torch especially designed for use on heat shrink applies heat without an open flame, which could cause damage.

FIGURE 10–23 A typical crimp-and-seal connector. This type of connector is first lightly crimped to retain the ends of the wires and then it is heated. The tubing shrinks around the wire splice, and thermoplastic glue melts on the inside to provide an effective weather-resistant seal.

tool is used. Most vehicle manufacturers recommend that a W-shaped crimp be used to force the strands of the wire into a tight space. ● SEE FIGURE 10–20.

Most vehicle manufacturers also specify that all hand-crimped terminals or splices be soldered. ● SEE FIGURE 10–21.

HEAT SHRINK TUBING Heat shrink tubing is usually made from polyvinyl chloride (PVC) or polyolefin and shrinks to about half of its original diameter when heated; this is usually called a 2:1 shrink ratio. Heat shrink by itself does not provide protection against corrosion, because the ends of the tubing are not sealed against moisture. DaimlerChrysler Corporation recommends that all wire repairs that may be exposed to the

elements be repaired and sealed using **adhesive-lined heat shrink tubing**. The tubing is usually made from flame-retardant flexible polyolefin with an internal layer of special thermoplastic adhesive. When heated, this tubing shrinks to one-third of its original diameter (3:1 shrink ratio) and the adhesive melts and seals the ends of the tubing. ● SEE FIGURE 10–22.

CRIMP-AND-SEAL CONNECTORS General Motors Corporation recommends the use of crimp-and-seal connectors as the method for wire repair. **Crimp-and-seal connectors** contain a sealant and shrink tubing in one piece and are not simply butt connectors. ● SEE FIGURE 10–23.

FIGURE 10–24 Heating the crimp-and-seal connector melts the glue and forms an effective seal against moisture.

WIRE REPAIR (CONTINUED)

The usual procedure specified for making a wire repair using a crimp-and-seal connector is as follows:

STEP 1   Strip the insulation from the ends of the wire (about 5/16 in., or 8 mm).

STEP 2   Select the proper size of crimp-and-seal connector for the gauge of wire being repaired. Insert the wires into the splice sleeve and crimp.

NOTE: Only use the specified crimping tool to help prevent the pliers from creating a hole in the cover.

STEP 3   Apply heat to the connector until the sleeve shrinks down around the wire and a small amount of sealant is observed around the ends of the sleeve, as shown in ● FIGURE 10–24.

ALUMINUM WIRE REPAIR   Some vehicle manufacturers used plastic-coated solid aluminum wire for some body wiring. Because aluminum wire is brittle and can break as a result of vibration, it is only used where there is no possible movement of the wire, such as along the floor or sill area. This section of wire is stationary, and the wire changes back to copper at a junction terminal after the trunk or rear section of the vehicle, where movement of the wiring may be possible.

If any aluminum wire must be repaired or replaced, the following procedure should be used to be assured of a proper repair. The aluminum wire is usually found protected in a plastic conduit. This conduit is then normally slit, after which the wires can easily be removed for repair.

STEP 1   Carefully strip only about 1/4 in. (6 mm) of insulation from the aluminum wire, being careful not to nick or damage the aluminum wire case.

STEP 2   Use a crimp connector to join two wires together. Do not solder an aluminum wire repair. Solder will not

? FREQUENTLY ASKED QUESTION

What Method of Wire Repair Should I Use?

Good question. Vehicle manufacturers recommend all wire repairs performed under the hood, or where the repair could be exposed to the elements, be weatherproof. The most commonly recommended methods include:

- **Crimp and seal connector.** These connectors are special and are not like low cost insulated-type crimp connectors. This type of connector is recommended by General Motors and others and is sealed using heat after the mechanical crimp has secured the wire ends together.
- **Solder and adhesive-lined heat shrink tubing.** This method is recommended by Chrysler and it uses the special heat shrink that has glue inside that melts when heated to form a sealed connection. Regular heat shrink tubing can be used inside a vehicle, but should not be used where it can be exposed to the elements.
- **Solder and electrical tape.** This is acceptable to use inside the vehicle where the splice will not be exposed to the outside elements. It is best to use a crimp and seal even on the inside of the vehicle for best results.

? FREQUENTLY ASKED QUESTION

What Is in Lead-Free Solder?

Lead is an environmental and a health concern and all vehicle manufacturers are switching to lead-free solder. Lead free solder does not contain lead but usually a very high percentage of tin. Several formulations of lead-free solder include:

- 95% Tin; 5% Antimony (melting temperature 450°F (245°C)
- 97% Tin; 3% Copper (melting temperature 441°F (227°C)
- 96% Tin; 4% Silver (melting temperature 443°F (228°C)

readily adhere to aluminum because the heat causes an oxide coating on the surface of the aluminum.

STEP 3   The spliced, crimped connection must be coated with petroleum jelly to prevent corrosion.

STEP 4   The coated connection should be covered with shrinkable plastic tubing or wrapped with electrical tape to seal out moisture.

FIGURE 10–25 Conduit that has a paint strip is constructed of plastic that can withstand high underhood temperatures.

(a)

(b)

FIGURE 10–26 (a) Blue conduit is used to cover circuits that carry up to 42 volts. (b) Yellow conduit can also be used to cover 42 volt wiring.

ELECTRICAL CONDUIT

The color used on electrical convoluted conduit tells the technician a lot if some information is known, such as the following:

- **Black conduit with a green or blue stripe.** This conduit is designed for high temperatures and is used under the hood and near hot engine parts. Do not replace high-temperature conduit with low-temperature conduit that does not have a strip when performing wire repairs. ● SEE FIGURE 10–25.

- **Blue or yellow conduit.** This color conduit is used to cover wires that have voltages ranging from 12 to 42 volts. Circuits that use this high voltage usually are for the electric power steering. While 42 volts does not represent a shock hazard, an arc will be maintained if a line circuit is disconnected. Use caution around these circuits. ● SEE FIGURE 10–26.

- **Orange conduit.** This color conduit is used to cover wiring that carries high-voltage current from 144 to 650 volts. These circuits are found in hybrid electric vehicles (HEVs). An electric shock from these wires can be fatal, so extreme caution has to be taken when working on or near the components that have orange conduit. Follow the vehicle manufacturer's instruction for de-powering the high-voltage circuits before work begins on any of the high-voltage components. ● SEE FIGURE 10–27.

FIGURE 10–27 Always follow the vehicle manufacturer's instructions which include the use of linesman's (high-voltage) gloves if working on circuits that are covered in orange conduit.

SUMMARY

1. The higher the AWG size number, the smaller the wire diameter.

2. Metric wire is sized in square millimeters (mm²) and the higher the number, the larger the wire.

3. All circuits should be protected by a fuse, fusible link, or circuit breaker. The current in the circuit should be about 80% of the fuse rating.

4. A terminal is the metal end of a wire, whereas a connector is the plastic housing for the terminal.

5. All wire repair should use either soldering or a crimp-and-seal connector.

REVIEW QUESTIONS

1. What is the difference between the American wire gauge (AWG) system and the metric system?

2. What is the difference between a wire and a cable?

3. What is the difference between a terminal and a connector?

4. How do fuses, PTC circuit protectors, circuit breakers, and fusible links protect a circuit?

5. How should a wire repair be done if the repair is under the hood where it is exposed to the outside?

CHAPTER QUIZ

1. The higher the AWG number, _____.
   a. The smaller the wire diameter
   b. The larger the wire diameter
   c. The thicker the insulation
   d. The more strands in the conductor core

2. Metric wire size is measured in units of _____.
   a. Meters
   b. Cubic centimeters
   c. Square millimeters
   d. Cubic millimeters

3. Which statement is true about fuse ratings?
   a. The fuse rating should be less than the maximum current for the circuit.
   b. The fuse rating should be higher than the normal current for the circuit.
   c. Of the fuse rating, 80% should equal the current in the circuit.
   d. Both b and c

4. Which statements are true about wire, terminals, and connectors?
   a. Wire is called a lead, and the metal end is a connector.
   b. A connector is usually a plastic piece where terminals lock in.
   c. A lead and a terminal are the same thing.
   d. Both a and c

5. The type of solder that should be used for electrical work is _____.
   a. Rosin core
   b. Acid core
   c. 60/40 with no flux
   d. 50/50 with acid paste flux

6. A technician is performing a wire repair on a circuit under the hood of the vehicle. Technician A says to use solder and adhesive-lined heat shrink tubing or a crimp and seal connector. Technician B says to solder and use electrical tape. Which technician is correct?
   a. Technician A only
   b. Technician B only
   c. Both Technicians A and B
   d. Neither Technician A nor B

7. Two technicians are discussing fuse testing. Technician A says that a test light should light on both test points of the fuse if it is okay. Technician B says the fuse is defective if a test light only lights on one side of the fuse. Which technician is correct?
   a. Technician A only
   b. Technician B only
   c. Both Technicians A and B
   d. Neither Technician A nor B

8. If a wire repair, such as that made under the hood or under the vehicle, is exposed to the elements, which type of repair should be used?
   a. Wire nuts and electrical tape
   b. Solder and adhesive-lined heat shrink or crimp-and-seal connectors
   c. Butt connectors
   d. Rosin-core solder and electrical tape

9. Many ground straps are uninsulated and braided because _____.
   a. They are more flexible to allow movement of the engine without breaking the wire.
   b. They are less expensive than conventional wire.
   c. They help dampen radio-frequency interference (RFI).
   d. Both a and c

10. What causes a fuse to blow?
    a. A decrease in circuit resistance
    b. An increase in the current flow through the circuit
    c. A sudden decrease in current flow through the circuit
    d. Both a and b

chapter 11
WIRING SCHEMATICS AND CIRCUIT TESTING

OBJECTIVES

After studying Chapter 11, the reader will be able to:

1. Prepare for ASE Electrical/Electronic Systems (A6) certification test content area "A" (General Electrical/Electronics System Diagnosis).
2. Interpret wiring schematics.
3. Explain how relays work.
4. Discuss the various methods that can be used to locate a short circuit.
5. List the electrical troubleshooting diagnosis steps.

KEY TERMS

Coil 151
DPDT 149
DPST 149
Gauss gauge 158
Momentary switch 150
N.C. 149
N.O. 149
Poles 149
Relay 151

Short circuit 157
SPDT 149
SPST 149
Terminal 146
Throws 149
Tone generator tester 158
Wiring schematic 144

FIGURE 11–1 The center wire is a solid color wire, meaning that the wire has no other identifying tracer or stripe color. The two end wires could be labeled "BRN/WHT," indicating a brown wire with a white tracer or stripe.

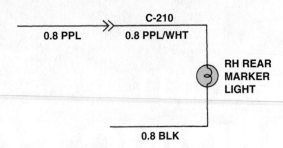

FIGURE 11–2 Typical section of a wiring diagram. Notice that the wire color changes at connection C210. The ".8" represents the metric wire size in square millimeters.

WIRING SCHEMATICS AND SYMBOLS

TERMINOLOGY The service manuals of automotive manufacturers include wiring schematics of every electrical circuit in a vehicle. A **wiring schematic**, sometimes called a *diagram*, shows electrical components and wiring using symbols and lines to represent components and wires. A typical wiring schematic may include all of the circuits combined on several large foldout sheets, or they may be broken down to show individual circuits. All circuit schematics or diagrams include:

- Power-side wiring of the circuit
- All splices
- Connectors
- Wire size
- Wire color
- Trace color (if any)
- Circuit number
- Electrical components
- Ground return paths
- Fuses and switches

CIRCUIT INFORMATION Many wiring schematics include numbers and letters near components and wires that may confuse readers of the schematic. Most letters used near or on a wire identify the color or colors of the wire.

- The first color or color abbreviation is the color of the wire insulation.
- The second color (if mentioned) is the color of the strip or tracer on the base color. ● **SEE FIGURE 11–1.**

Wires with different color tracers are indicated by both colors with a slash (/) between them. For example, BRN/WHT means a brown wire with a white stripe or tracer. ● **SEE CHART 11–1.**

WIRE SIZE Wire size is shown on all schematics. ● **FIGURE 11–2** illustrates a rear side-marker bulb circuit

ABBREVIATION	COLOR
BRN	Brown
BLK	Black
GRN	Green
WHT	White
PPL	Purple
PNK	Pink
TAN	Tan
BLU	Blue
YEL	Yellow
ORN	Orange
DK BLU	Dark blue
LT BLU	Light blue
DK GRN	Dark green
LT GRN	Light green
RED	Red
GRY	Gray
VIO	Violet

CHART 11–1

Typical abbreviations used on schematics to show wire color. Some vehicle manufacturers use two letters to represent a wire color. Check service information for the color abbreviations used.

diagram where ".8" indicates the metric wire gauge size in square millimeters (mm^2) and "PPL" indicates a solid purple wire.

The wire diagram also shows that the color of the wire changes at the number C210. This stands for "connector #210" and is used for reference purposes. The symbol for the connection can vary depending on the manufacturer. The color change from purple (PPL) to purple with a white tracer (PPL/WHT) is not important except for knowing where the wire changes color in the circuit. The wire gauge has remained the same on both sides of the connection (0.8 mm^2 or 18 gauge). The ground circuit is the ".8 BLK" wire. ● **FIGURE 11–3** shows many of the electrical and electronic symbols that are used in wiring and circuit diagrams.

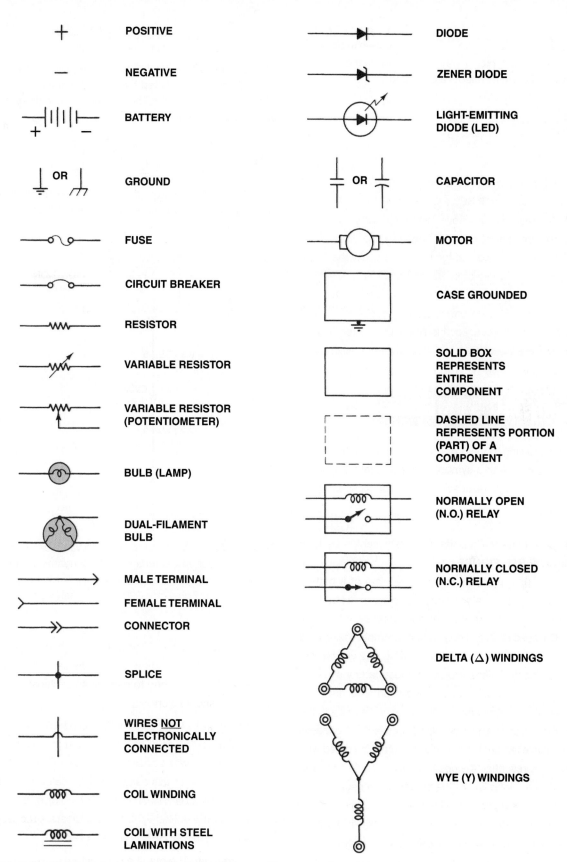

POSITIVE

NEGATIVE

BATTERY

GROUND

FUSE

CIRCUIT BREAKER

RESISTOR

VARIABLE RESISTOR

VARIABLE RESISTOR (POTENTIOMETER)

BULB (LAMP)

DUAL-FILAMENT BULB

MALE TERMINAL

FEMALE TERMINAL

CONNECTOR

SPLICE

WIRES NOT ELECTRONICALLY CONNECTED

COIL WINDING

COIL WITH STEEL LAMINATIONS

DIODE

ZENER DIODE

LIGHT-EMITTING DIODE (LED)

CAPACITOR

MOTOR

CASE GROUNDED

SOLID BOX REPRESENTS ENTIRE COMPONENT

DASHED LINE REPRESENTS PORTION (PART) OF A COMPONENT

NORMALLY OPEN (N.O.) RELAY

NORMALLY CLOSED (N.C.) RELAY

DELTA (△) WINDINGS

WYE (Y) WINDINGS

FIGURE 11–3 Typical electrical and electronic symbols used in automotive wiring and circuit diagrams.

TO BATTERY ——————————≪———————— TO ELECTRICAL COMPONENT

FIGURE 11–4 In this typical connector, note that the positive terminal is usually a female connector.

SCHEMATIC SYMBOLS

In a schematic drawing, photos or line drawings of actual components are replaced with a symbol that represents the actual component. The following discussion centers on these symbols and their meanings.

BATTERY The plates of a battery are represented by long and short lines. ● **SEE FIGURE 11–5.**

The longer line represents the positive plate of a battery and the shorter line represents the negative plate of the battery. Therefore, each pair of short and long lines represents one cell of a battery. Because each cell of a typical automotive lead-acid battery has 2.1 volts, a battery symbol showing a 12 volt battery should have six pairs of lines. However, most battery symbols simply use two or three pairs of long and short lines and then list the voltage of the battery next to the symbol. As a result, the battery symbols are shorter and yet clear, because the voltage is stated. The positive terminal of the battery is often indicated with a plus sign (+), representing the positive post of the battery, and is placed next to the long line of the end cell. The negative terminal of the battery is represented by a negative sign (−) and is placed next to the shorter cell line. The negative battery terminal is connected to ground. ● **SEE FIGURE 11–6.**

WIRING Electrical wiring is shown as straight lines and with a few numbers and/or letters to indicate the following:

- **Wire size.** This can be either AWG, such as 18 gauge, or in square millimeters, such as 0.8 mm².

FIGURE 11–5 The symbol for a battery. The positive plate of a battery is represented by the longer line and the negative plate by the shorter line. The voltage of the battery is usually stated next to the symbol.

FIGURE 11–6 The ground symbol on the left represents earth ground. The ground symbol on the right represents a chassis ground.

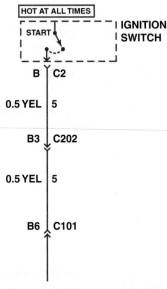

FIGURE 11–7 Starting at the top, the wire from the ignition switch is attached to terminal B of connector C2, the wire is 0.5 mm² (20 gauge AWG), and is yellow. The circuit number is 5. The wire enters connector C202 at terminal B3.

- **Circuit numbers.** Each wire in part of a circuit is labeled with the circuit number to help the service technician trace the wiring and to provide an explanation of how the circuit should work.

- **Wire color.** Most schematics also indicate an abbreviation for the color of the wire and place it next to the wire. Many wires have two colors: a solid color and a stripe color. In this case, the solid color is listed, followed by a dark slash (/) and the color of the stripe. For example, Red/Wht would indicate a red wire with a white tracer. ● **SEE FIGURE 11–7.**

- **Terminals.** The metal part attached at the end of a wire is called a **terminal.** A symbol for a terminal is shown in ● **FIGURE 11–8.**

- **Splices.** When two wires are electrically connected, the junction is shown with a black dot. The identification of

FIGURE 11–8 The electrical terminals are usually labeled with a letter.

FIGURE 11–9 Two wires that cross at the dot indicate that the two are electrically connected.

FIGURE 11–10 Wires that cross, but do not electrically contact each other, are shown with one wire bridging over the other.

the splice is an "S" followed by three numbers, such as S103. ● **SEE FIGURE 11–9.** When two wires cross in a schematic that are not electrically connected, one of the wires is shown as going over the other wire and does not connect. ● **SEE FIGURE 11–10.**

- **Connectors.** An electrical connector is a plastic part that contains one or more terminals. Although the terminals provide the electrical connection in a circuit, it is the plastic connector that keeps the terminals together mechanically.

- **Location.** Connections are usually labeled "C" and then three numbers. The three numbers indicate the general location of the connector. Normally, the connector number represents the general area of the vehicle, including:

100 to 199	Under the hood
200 to 299	Under the dash
300 to 399	Passenger compartment
400 to 499	Rear package or trunk area
500 to 599	Left-front door
600 to 699	Right-front door
700 to 799	Left-rear door
800 to 899	Right-rear door

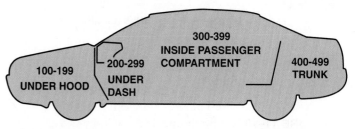

FIGURE 11–11 Connectors (C), grounds (G), and splices (S) are followed by a number, generally indicating the location in the vehicle. For example, G209 is a ground connection located under the dash.

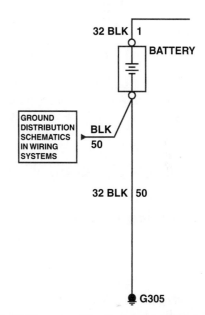

FIGURE 11–12 The ground for the battery is labeled G305 indicating the ground connector is located in the passenger compartment of the vehicle. The ground wire is black (BLK), the circuit number is 50, and the wire is 32 mm² (2 gauge AWG).

Even-numbered connectors are on the right (passenger side) of the vehicle and odd-numbered connectors are on the left (driver's side) of the vehicle. For example, C102 is a connector located under the hood (between 100 and 199) on the right side of the vehicle (even number 102). ● **SEE FIGURE 11–11.**

- **Grounds and splices.** These are also labeled using the same general format as connectors. Therefore, a ground located under the dash on the driver's side could be labeled G305 (*G* means "ground" and the "305" means that it is located in the passenger compartment). ● **SEE FIGURE 11–12.**

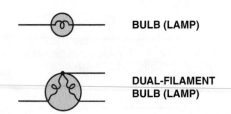

FIGURE 11–13 The symbol for light bulbs shows the filament inside a circle, which represents the glass ampoule of the bulb.

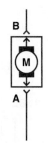

FIGURE 11–14 An electric motor symbol shows a circle with the letter *M* in the center and two black sections that represent the brushes of the motor. This symbol is used even though the motor is a brushless design.

SCHEMATIC SYMBOL (CONTINUED)

ELECTRICAL COMPONENTS Most electrical components have their own unique symbol that shows the basic function or parts.

- **Bulbs.** Light bulbs often use a filament, which heats and then gives off light when electrical current flows. The symbol used for a light bulb is a circle with a filament inside. A dual-filament bulb, such as is used for taillights and brake light/turn signals, is shown with two filaments. ● **SEE FIGURE 11–13.**

ELECTRIC MOTORS An electric motor symbol shows a circle with the letter *M* in the center and two electrical connections, one to the top and one at the bottom. ● **SEE FIGURE 11–14** for an example of a cooling fan motor.

RESISTORS Although resistors are usually part of another component, the symbol appears on many schematics and wiring diagrams. A resistor symbol is a jagged line representing resistance to current flow. If the resistor is variable, such as a thermistor, an arrow is shown running through the symbol of a fixed resistor. A potentiometer is a three-wire variable resistor, shown with an arrow pointing toward the resistance part of a fixed resistor. ● **SEE FIGURE 11–15.**

A two-wire rheostat is usually shown as part of another unit, such as a fuel level sending unit. ● **SEE FIGURE 11–16.**

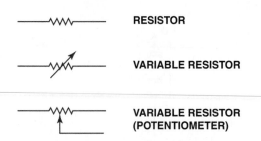

FIGURE 11–15 Resistor symbols vary depending on the type of resistor.

FIGURE 11–16 A rheostat uses only two wires—one is connected to a voltage source and the other is attached to the movable arm.

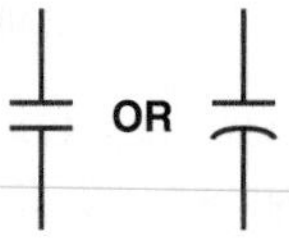

FIGURE 11–17 Symbols used to represent capacitors. If one of the lines is curved, this indicates that the capacitor being used has a polarity, while the one without a curved line can be installed in the circuit without concern about polarity.

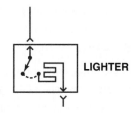

FIGURE 11–18 The gridlike symbol represents an electrically heated element.

CAPACITORS Capacitors are usually part of an electronic component, but not a replaceable component unless the vehicle is an older model. Many older vehicles used capacitors to reduce radio interference and were installed inside alternators or ignition coils, or attached to wiring connectors. ● **SEE FIGURE 11–17.**

ELECTRIC HEATED UNIT Electric grid-type rear window defoggers and cigarette lighters are shown with a square box-type symbol. ● **SEE FIGURE 11–18.**

BOXED COMPONENTS If a component is shown in a box using a solid line, the box is the entire component. If a box uses dashed lines, it represents part of a component. A commonly

FIGURE 11–19 A dashed outline represents a portion (part) of a component.

FIGURE 11–20 A solid box represents an entire component.

FIGURE 11–21 This symbol represents a component that is case grounded.

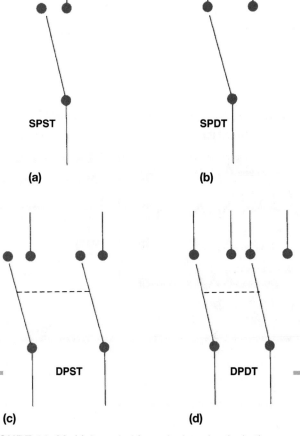

FIGURE 11–22 (a) A symbol for a single-pole, single-throw (SPST) switch. This type of switch is normally open (N.O.) because nothing is connected to the terminal that the switch is contacting in its normal position. (b) A single-pole, double-throw (SPDT) switch has three terminals. (c) A double-pole, single-throw (DPST) switch has two positions (off and on) and can control two separate circuits. (d) A double-pole, double-throw (DPDT) switch has six terminals—three for each pole. Note: Both (c) and (d) also show a dotted line between the two arms indicating that they are mechanically connected, called a "ganged switch".

used dashed-line box is a fuse panel. Often, just one or two fuses are shown in a dashed-line box. This means that a fuse panel has more fuses than shown. ● **SEE FIGURES 11–19 AND 11–20.**

SEPARATE REPLACEABLE PART Often components are shown on a schematic that cannot be replaced, but are part of a complete assembly. When looking at a schematic of General Motors vehicles, the following is shown.

- If a part name is underlined, it is a replaceable part.
- If a part is not underlined, it is not available as a replaceable part, but is included with other components shown and sold as an assembly.
- If the case itself is grounded, the ground symbol is attached to the component as shown in ● **FIGURE 11–21.**

SWITCHES Electrical switches are drawn on a wiring diagram in their normal position. This can be one of two possible positions.

- **Normally open.** The switch is not connected to its internal contacts and no current will flow. This type of switch is labeled **N.O.**
- **Normally closed.** The switch is electrically connected to its internal contacts and current will flow through the switch. This type of switch is labeled **N.C.**

  Other switches can use more than two contacts.

The **poles** refer to the number of circuits completed by the switch and the **throws** refer to the number of output circuits. A **single-pole, single-throw (SPST)** switch has only two positions, on or off. A **single-pole, double-throw (SPDT)** switch has three terminals, one wire in and two wires out. A headlight dimmer switch is an example of a typical SPDT switch. In one position, the current flows to the low-filament headlight; in the other, the current flows to the high-filament headlight.

NOTE: A SPDT switch is not an on or off type of switch but instead directs power from the source to either the high-beam lamps or the low-beam lamps.

There are also **double-pole, single-throw (DPST)** switches and **double-pole, double-throw (DPDT)** switches. ● **SEE FIGURE 11–22.**

(a)   (b)

FIGURE 11–23 (a) A symbol for a normally open (N.O.) momentary switch. (b) A symbol for a normally closed (N.C.) momentary switch.

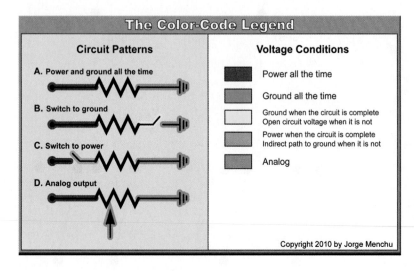

The Color-Code Legend

Circuit Patterns

A. Power and ground all the time

B. Switch to ground

C. Switch to power

D. Analog output

Voltage Conditions

Power all the time

Ground all the time

Ground when the circuit is complete
Open circuit voltage when it is not

Power when the circuit is complete
Indirect path to ground when it is not

Analog

Copyright 2010 by Jorge Menchu

FIGURE 11–24 Using a marker and color-coding the various parts of the circuit makes the circuit easier to understand and helps diagnosing electrical problems easier. (*Courtesy of Jorge Menchu.*)

SCHEMATIC SYMBOL (CONTINUED)

NOTE: All switches are shown on schematics in their normal position. This means that the headlight switch will be shown normally off, as are most other switches and controls.

MOMENTARY SWITCH A **momentary switch** is a switch primarily used to send a voltage signal to a module or controller to request that a device be turned on or off. The switch makes momentary contact and then returns to the open position. A horn switch is a commonly used momentary switch. The symbol that represents a momentary switch uses two dots for the contact with a switch above them. A momentary switch can be either normally open or normally closed. ● **SEE FIGURE 11–23.**

A momentary switch, for example, can be used to lock or unlock a door or to turn the air conditioning on or off. If the device is currently operating, the signal from the momentary switch will turn it off, and if it is off, the switch will signal the module to turn it on. The major advantage of momentary switches is that they can be lightweight and small, because the switch does not carry any heavy electrical current, just a small voltage signal. Most momentary switches use a membrane constructed of foil and plastic.

TECH TIP

Color-Coding Is Key to Understanding

Whenever diagnosing an electrical problem, it is common practice to print out the schematic of the circuit and then take it to the vehicle. A meter is then used to check for voltage at various parts of the circuit to help determine where there is a fault. The diagnosis can be made easier if the parts of the circuit are first color coded using markers or color pencils. A color-coding system that has been widely used is one developed by Jorge Menchu (**www.aeswave.com**).

The colors represent voltage conditions in various parts of a circuit. Once the circuit has been color coded, then the circuit can be tested using the factory wire colors as a guide. ● **SEE FIGURE 11–24.**

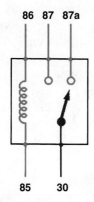

86 - POWER SIDE OF THE COIL
85 - GROUND SIDE OF THE COIL

(MOSTLY RELAY COILS
HAVE BETWEEN
50–150 OHMS
OF RESISTANCE)

30 - COMMON POWER FOR RELAY CONTACTS
87 - NORMALLY OPEN OUTPUT (N.O.)
87a - NORMALLY CLOSED OUTPUT (N.C.)

FIGURE 11–25 A relay uses a movable arm to complete a circuit whenever there is a power at terminal 86 and a ground at terminal 85. A typical relay only requires about 1/10 ampere through the relay coil. The movable arm then closes the contacts (#30 to #87) and can relay 30 amperes or more.

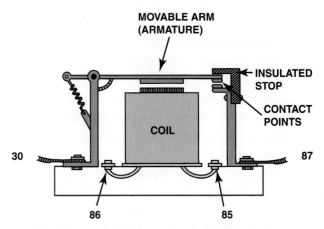

FIGURE 11–26 A cross-sectional view of a typical four-terminal relay. Current flowing through the coil (terminals 86 and 85) causes the movable arm (called the armature) to be drawn toward the coil magnet. The contact points complete the electrical circuit connected to terminals 30 and 87.

RELAY TERMINAL IDENTIFICATION

DEFINITION A **relay** is a magnetic switch that uses a movable armature to control a high-amperage circuit by using a low-amperage electrical switch.

ISO RELAY TERMINAL IDENTIFICATION Most automotive relays adhere to common terminal identification. The primary source for this common identification comes from the standards established by the International Standards Organization (ISO). Knowing this terminal information will help in the correct diagnosis and troubleshooting of any circuit containing a relay. ● SEE FIGURES 11–25 AND 11–26.

Relays are found in many circuits because they are capable of being controlled by computers, yet are able to handle enough current to power motors and accessories. Relays include the following components and terminals.

RELAY OPERATION

1. **Coil** (terminals 85 and 86)
   - A coil provides the magnetic pull to a movable armature (arm).
   - The resistance of most relay coils ranges from 50 to 150 ohms, but is usually between 60 and 100 ohms.

   - The ISO identification of the coil terminals are 86 and 85. The terminal number 86 represents the power to the relay coil and the terminal labeled 85 represents the ground side of the relay coil.
   - The relay coil can be controlled by supplying either power or ground to the relay coil winding.
   - The coil winding represents the *control circuit* which uses low current to control the higher current through the other terminals of the relay. ● SEE FIGURE 11–27.

2. Other terminals used to control the load current
   - The higher amperage current flow through a relay flows through terminals 30 and 87, and often 87a.
   - Terminal 30 is usually where power is applied to a relay. Check service information for the exact operation of the relay being tested.
   - When the relay is at rest without power and ground to the coil, the armature inside the relay electrically connects terminals 30 and 87a if the relay has five terminals. When there is power at terminal 85 and a ground at terminal 86 of the relay, a magnetic

Divide the Circuit in Half

When diagnosing any circuit that has a relay, start testing at the relay and divide the circuit in half.

- **High current portion:** Remove the relay and check that there are 12 volts at the terminal 30 socket. If there is, then the power side is okay. Use an ohmmeter and check between terminal 87 socket and ground. If the load circuit has continuity, there should be some resistance. If OL, the circuit is electrically open.

- **Control circuit (low current):** With the relay removed from the socket, check that there is 12 volts to terminal 86 with the ignition on and the control switch on. If not, check service information to see if power should be applied to terminal 86, then continue troubleshooting the switch power and related circuit.

- **Check the relay itself:** Use an ohmmeter and measure for continuity and resistance.
  - Between terminals 85 and 86 (coil), there should be 60 to 100 ohms. If not, replace the relay.
  - Between terminals 30 and 87 (high-amperage switch controls), there should be continuity (low ohms) when there is power applied to terminal 85 and a ground applied to terminal 86 that operates the relay. If OL is displayed on the meter set to read ohms, the circuit is open which requires that the reply be replaced.
  - Between terminals 30 and 87a (if equipped), with the relay tuned off, there should be low resistance (less than 5 ohms).

FIGURE 11–27 A typical relay showing the schematic of the wiring in the relay.

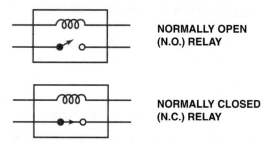

NORMALLY OPEN (N.O.) RELAY

NORMALLY CLOSED (N.C.) RELAY

FIGURE 11–28 All schematics are shown in their normal, nonenergized position.

RELAY TERMINAL IDENTIFICATION (CONTINUED)

field is created in the coil winding, which draws the armature of the relay toward the coil. The armature, when energized electrically, connects terminals 30 and 87.

The maximum current through the relay is determined by the resistance of the circuit, and relays are designed to safely handle the designed current flow. ● **SEE FIGURES 11–28 AND 11–29.**

RELAY VOLTAGE SPIKE CONTROL Relays contain a coil and when power is removed, the magnetic field surrounding the coil collapses, creating a voltage to be induced in the coil winding. This induced voltage can be as high as 100 volts or more and can cause problems with other electronic devices in the vehicle. For example, the short high-voltage surge can be heard as a "pop" in the radio. To reduce the induced voltage, some relays contain a diode connected across the coil. ● **SEE FIGURE 11–30.**

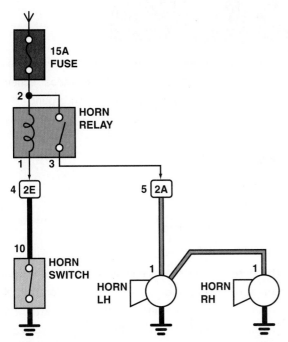

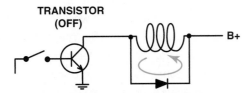

FIGURE 11–29 A typical horn circuit. Note that the relay contacts supply the heavy current to operate the horn when the horn switch simply completes a low-current circuit to ground, causing the relay contacts to close.

FIGURE 11–30 When the relay or solenoid coil current is turned off, the stored energy in the coil flows through the clamping diode and effectively reduces voltage spike.

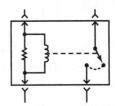

FIGURE 11–31 A resistor used in parallel with the coil windings is a common spike reduction method used in many relays.

? **FREQUENTLY ASKED QUESTION**

What Is the Difference Between a Relay and a Solenoid?

Often, these terms are used differently among vehicle manufacturers, which can lead to some confusion.

Relay: A relay is an electromagnetic switch that uses a movable arm. Because a relay uses a movable arm, it is generally limited to current flow not exceeding 30 amperes.

Solenoid: A solenoid is an electromagnetic switch that uses a movable core. Because of this type of design, a solenoid is capable of handling 200 amperes or more and is used in the starter motor circuit and other high-amperage applications, such as in the glow plug circuit of diesel engines.

When the current flows through the coil, the diode is not part of the circuit because it is installed to block current. However, when the voltage is removed from the coil, the resulting voltage induced in the coil windings has a reversed polarity to the applied voltage. Therefore, the voltage in the coil is applied to the coil in a forward direction through the diode, which conducts the current back into the winding. As a result, the induced voltage spike is eliminated.

Most relays use a resistor connected in parallel with the coil winding. The use of a resistor, typically about 400 to 600 ohms, reduces the voltage spike by providing a path for the voltage created in the coil to flow back through the coil windings when the coil circuit is opened. See ● **FIGURE 11–31.**

LOCATING AN OPEN CIRCUIT

TERMINOLOGY An open circuit is a break in the electrical circuit that prevents current from flowing and operating an electrical device. Examples of open circuits include:

- Blown (open) light bulbs
- Cut or broken wires
- Disconnected or partially disconnected electrical connectors
- Electrically open switches
- Loose or broken ground connections or wires
- Blown fuse

PROCEDURE TO LOCATE AN OPEN CIRCUIT

The typical procedure for locating an open circuit involves the following steps.

STEP 1 **Perform a thorough visual inspection.** Check the following:

- Look for evidence of a previous repair. Often, an electrical connector or ground connection can be accidentally left disconnected.
- Look for evidence of recent body damage or body repairs. Movement due to a collision can cause metal to move, which can cut wires or damage connectors or components.

STEP 2 **Print out the schematic.** Trace the circuit and check for voltage at certain places. This will help pinpoint the location of the open circuit.

STEP 3 **Check everything that does and does not work.** Often, an open circuit will affect more than one component. Check the part of the circuit that is common to the other components that do not work.

STEP 4 **Check for voltage.** Voltage is present up to the location of the open circuit fault. For example, if there is battery voltage at the positive terminal and the negative (ground) terminal of a two-wire light bulb socket with the bulb plugged in, then the ground circuit is open.

COMMON POWER OR GROUND

When diagnosing an electrical problem that affects more than one component or system, check the electrical schematic for a common power source or a common ground. ● **SEE FIGURE 11–32** for an example of lights being powered by one fuse (power source).

- Underhood light
- Inside lighted mirrors
- Dome light
- Left-side courtesy light
- Right-side courtesy light

Therefore, if a customer complains about one or more of the items listed, check the fuse and the common part of the circuit that feeds all of the affected lights. Check for a common ground if several components that seem unrelated are not functioning correctly.

 REAL WORLD FIX

The Electric Mirror Fault Story

Often, a customer will notice just one fault even though other lights or systems may not be working correctly. For example, a customer noticed that the electric mirrors stopped working. The service technician checked all electrical components in the vehicle and discovered that the interior lights were also not working.

The interior lights were not mentioned by the customer as being a problem most likely because the driver only used the vehicle in daylight hours.

The service technician found the interior light and power accessory fuse blown. Replacing the fuse restored the proper operation of the electric outside mirror and the interior lights. However, what caused the fuse to blow? A visual inspection of the dome light, next to the electric sunroof, showed an area where a wire was bare. Evidence showed the bare wire had touched the metal roof, which could cause the fuse to blow. The technician covered the bare wire with a section of vacuum hose and then taped the hose with electrical tape to complete the repair.

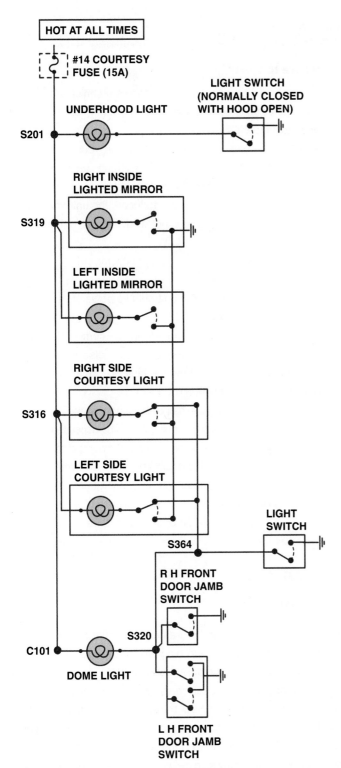

FIGURE 11–32 A typical wiring diagram showing multiple switches and bulbs powered by one fuse.

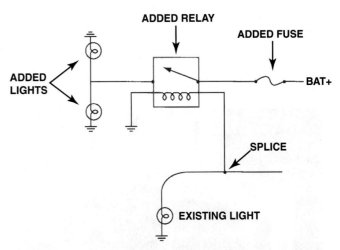

FIGURE 11–33 To add additional lighting, simply tap into an existing light wire and connect a relay. Whenever the existing light is turned on, the coil of the relay is energized. The arm of the relay then connects power from another circuit (fuse) to the auxiliary lights without overloading the existing light circuit.

TECH TIP

Do It Right—Install a Relay

Often the owners of vehicles, especially owners of pickup trucks and sport utility vehicles (SUVs), want to add additional electrical accessories or lighting. It is tempting in these cases to simply splice into an existing circuit. However, when another circuit or component is added, the current that flows through the newly added component is also added to the current for the original component. This additional current can easily overload the fuse and wiring. Do not simply install a larger amperage fuse; the wire gauge size was not engineered for the additional current and could overheat.

The solution is to install a relay, which uses a small coil to create a magnetic field that causes a movable arm to switch on a higher current circuit. The typical relay coil has from 50 to 150 ohms (usually 60 to 100 ohms) of resistance and requires just 0.24 to 0.08 ampere when connected to a 12 volt source. This small additional current will not be enough to overload the existing circuit. ● SEE FIGURE 11–33 for an example of how additional lighting can be added.

The common question is, where does a technician start the troubleshooting when using a wiring diagram (schematic)?

HINT 1 If the circuit contains a relay, start your diagnosis at the relay. The entire circuit can be tested at the terminals of the relay.

HINT 2 The easiest first step is to locate the unit on the schematic that is not working at all or not working correctly.

    a. Trace where the unit gets its ground connection.

    b. Trace where the unit gets its power connection.

Often a ground is used by more than one component. Therefore, ensure that everything else is working correctly. If not, then the fault may lie at the common ground (or power) connection.

HINT 3 Divide the circuit in half by locating a connector or a part of the circuit that can be accessed easily. Then check for power and ground at this midpoint. This step could save you much time.

HINT 4 Use a fused jumper wire to substitute a ground or a power source to replace a suspected switch or section of wire.

FIGURE 11–34 Always check the simple things first. Check the fuse for the circuit you are testing. Maybe a fault in another circuit controlled by the same fuse could have caused the fuse to blow. Use a test light to check that both sides of the fuse have voltage.

CIRCUIT TROUBLESHOOTING PROCEDURE

Follow these steps when troubleshooting wiring problems.

STEP 1 Verify the malfunction. If, for example, the backup lights do not operate, make certain that the ignition is on (key on, engine off), with the gear selector in reverse, and check for operation of the backup lights.

STEP 2 Check everything else that does or does not operate correctly. For example, if the taillights are also not working, the problem could be a loose or broken ground connection in the trunk area that is shared by both the backup lights and the taillights.

STEP 3 Check the fuse for the backup lights. ● **SEE FIGURE 11–34.**

STEP 4 Check for voltage at the backup light socket. This can be done using a test light or a voltmeter.

If voltage is available at the socket, the problem is either a defective bulb or a poor ground at the socket or a ground wire connection to the body or frame. If no voltage is available at the socket, consult a wiring diagram for the type of vehicle being tested. The wiring diagram should show all of the wiring and components included in the circuit. For example, the backup light current must flow through the fuse and ignition switch to the gear selector switch before traveling to the rear backup light socket. As stated in the second step, the fuse used for the backup lights may also be used for other vehicle circuits.

The wiring diagram can be used to determine all other components that share the same fuse. If the fuse is blown (open circuit), the cause can be a short in any of the circuits sharing the same fuse. Because the backup light circuit current must be switched on and off by the gear selector switch, an open in the switch can also prevent the backup lights from functioning.

LOCATING A SHORT CIRCUIT

TERMINOLOGY A short circuit usually blows a fuse, and a replacement fuse often also blows in the attempt to locate the source of the short circuit. A **short circuit** is an electrical connection to another wire or to ground before the current flows through some or all of the resistance in the circuit. A short-to-ground will always blow a fuse and usually involves a wire on the power side of the circuit coming in contact with metal. Therefore, a thorough visual inspection should be performed around areas involving heat or movement, especially if there is evidence of a previous collision or previous repair that may not have been properly completed.

A short-to-voltage may or may not cause the fuse to blow and usually affects another circuit. Look for areas of heat or movement where two power wires could come in contact with each other. Several methods can be used to locate the short.

FUSE REPLACEMENT METHOD Disconnect one component at a time and then replace the fuse. If the new fuse blows, continue the process until you determine the location of the short. This method uses many fuses and is *not* a preferred method for finding a short circuit.

CIRCUIT BREAKER METHOD Another method is to connect an automotive circuit breaker to the contacts of the fuse holder with alligator clips. Circuit breakers are available that plug directly into the fuse panel, replacing a blade-type fuse. The circuit breaker will alternately open and close the circuit, protecting the wiring from possible overheating damage while still providing current flow through the circuit.

NOTE: A heavy-duty (HD) flasher can also be used in place of a circuit breaker to open and close the circuit. Wires and terminals must be made to connect the flasher unit where the fuse normally plugs in.

All components included in the defective circuit should be disconnected one at a time until the circuit breaker stops clicking. The unit that was disconnected and stopped the circuit breaker clicking is the unit causing the short circuit. If the circuit breaker continues to click with all circuit components unplugged, the problem is in the wiring *from* the fuse panel *to* any one of the units in the circuit. Visual inspection of all the wiring or further disconnecting will be necessary to locate the problem.

TEST LIGHT METHOD To use the test light method, simply remove the blown fuse and connect a test light to the terminals of the fuse holder (polarity does not matter). If there is a short circuit, current will flow from the power side of the fuse holder through the test light and on to ground through the short circuit, and the test light will then light. Unplug the connectors or components protected by the fuse until the test light goes out. The circuit that was disconnected, which caused the test light to go out, is the circuit that is shorted.

BUZZER METHOD The buzzer method is similar to the test light method, but uses a buzzer to replace a fuse and act as an electrical load. The buzzer will sound if the circuit is shorted and will stop when the part of the circuit that is grounded is unplugged.

OHMMETER METHOD The fourth method uses an ohmmeter connected to the fuse holder and ground. This is the recommended method of finding a short circuit, as an ohmmeter will indicate low ohms when connected to a short circuit. However, an ohmmeter should never be connected to an operating circuit. The correct procedure for locating a short using an ohmmeter is as follows:

1. Connect one lead of an ohmmeter (set to a low scale) to a good clean metal ground and the other lead to the circuit side of the fuse holder.

    CAUTION: Connecting the lead to the power side of the fuse holder will cause current flow through and damage to the ohmmeter.

2. The ohmmeter will read zero or almost zero ohms if the circuit or a component in the circuit is shorted.

3. Disconnect one component in the circuit at a time and watch the ohmmeter. If the ohmmeter reading goes to high ohms or infinity, the component just unplugged was the source of the short circuit.

4. If all of the components have been disconnected and the ohmmeter still reads low ohms, then disconnect electrical connectors until the ohmmeter reads high ohms. The location of the short to ground is then between the ohmmeter and the disconnected connector.

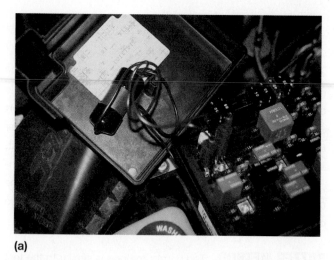

(a)

(b)

FIGURE 11–35 (a) After removing the blown fuse, a pulsing circuit breaker is connected to the terminals of the fuse. (b) The circuit breaker causes current to flow, then stop, then flow again, through the circuit up to the point of the short-to-ground. By observing the Gauss gauge, the location of the short is indicated near where the needle stops moving due to the magnetic field created by the flow of current through the wire.

LOCATING A SHORT CIRCUIT (CONTINUED)

NOTE: Some meters, such as the Fluke 87, can be set to beep (alert) when the circuit closes or when the circuit opens—a very useful feature.

GAUSS GAUGE METHOD If a short circuit blows a fuse, a special pulsing circuit breaker (similar to a flasher unit) can be installed in the circuit in place of the fuse. Current will flow through the circuit until the circuit breaker opens the circuit. As soon as the circuit breaker opens the circuit, it closes again. This on-and-off current flow creates a pulsing magnetic field around the wire carrying the current. A **Gauss gauge** is a hand-held meter that responds to weak magnetic fields. It is used to observe this pulsing magnetic field, which is indicated on the gauge as needle movement. This pulsing magnetic field will register on the Gauss gauge even through the metal body of the vehicle. A needle-type compass can also be used to observe the pulsing magnetic field. ● **SEE FIGURES 11–35 AND 11–36.**

ELECTRONIC TONE GENERATOR TESTER An electronic tone generator tester can be used to locate a short-to-ground or an open circuit. Similar to test equipment used to test telephone and cable television lines, a **tone generator tester** generates a tone that can be heard through a receiver (probe). ● **SEE FIGURE 11–37.**

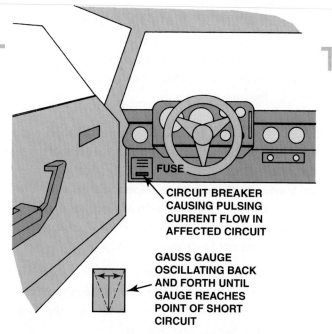

FIGURE 11–36 A Gauss gauge can be used to determine the location of a short circuit even behind a metal panel.

The tone will be generated as long as there is a continuous electrical path along the circuit. The signal will stop if there is a short-to-ground or an open in the circuit. ● **SEE FIGURE 11–38.**

The windings in the solenoids and relays will increase the strength of the signal in these locations.

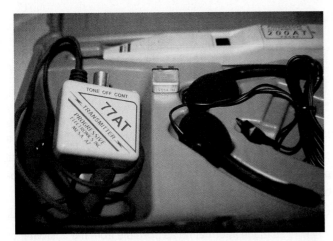

FIGURE 11–37 A tone generator-type tester used to locate open circuits and circuits that are shorted-to-ground. Included with this tester is a transmitter (tone generator), receiver probe, and headphones for use in noisy shops.

TECH TIP

Heat or Movement

Electrical shorts are commonly caused either by movement, which causes the insulation around the wiring to be worn away, or by heat melting the insulation. When checking for a short circuit, first check the wiring that is susceptible to heat, movement, and damage.

1. **Heat.** Wiring near heat sources, such as the exhaust system, cigarette lighter, or alternator
2. **Wire movement.** Wiring that moves, such as in areas near the doors, trunk, or hood
3. **Damage.** Wiring subject to mechanical injury, such as in the trunk, where heavy objects can move around and smash or damage wiring; can also occur as a result of an accident or a previous repair

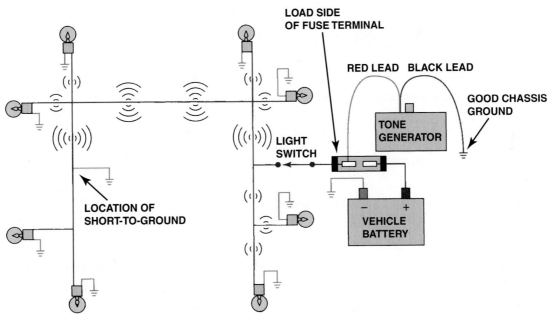

FIGURE 11–38 To check for a short-to-ground using a tone generator, connect the black transmitter lead to a good chassis ground and the red lead to the load side of the fuse terminal. Turn the transmitter on and check for tone signal with the receiver. Using a wiring diagram, follow the strongest signal to the location of the short-to-ground. There will be no signal beyond the fault, either a short-to-ground as shown or an open circuit.

TECH TIP

Wiggle Test

Intermittent electrical problems are common yet difficult to locate. To help locate these hard-to-find problems, try operating the circuit and then start wiggling the wires and connections that control the circuit. If in doubt where the wiring goes, try moving all the wiring starting at the battery. Pay particular attention to wiring running near the battery or the windshield washer container. Corrosion can cause wiring to fail, and battery acid fumes and alcohol-based windshield washer fluid can start or contribute to the problem. If you notice any change in the operation of the device being tested while wiggling the wiring, look closer in the area you were wiggling until you locate and correct the actual problem.

ELECTRICAL TROUBLE-SHOOTING GUIDE

When troubleshooting any electrical component, remember the following hints to find the problem faster and more easily.

1. For a device to work, it must have two things: power and ground.

2. If there is no power to a device, an open power side (blown fuse, etc.) is indicated.

3. If there is power on both sides of a device, an open ground is indicated.

4. If a fuse blows immediately, a grounded power-side wire is indicated.

5. Most electrical faults result from heat or movement.

6. Most noncomputer-controlled devices operate by opening and closing the power side of the circuit (power-side switch).

7. Most computer-controlled devices operate by opening and closing the ground side of the circuit (ground-side switch).

STEP-BY-STEP TROUBLESHOOTING PROCEDURE

Knowing what should be done and when it should be done is a major concern for many technicians trying to repair an electrical problem. The following field-tested procedure provides a step-by-step guide for troubleshooting an electrical fault.

STEP 1 Determine the customer concern (complaint) and get as much information as possible from the customer or service advisor.
  a. When did the problem start?
  b. Under what conditions does the problem occur?
  c. Have there been any recent previous repairs to the vehicle which could have created the problem?

STEP 2 Verify the customer's concern by actually observing the fault.

STEP 3 Perform a thorough visual inspection and be sure to check everything that does and does not work.

STEP 4 Check for technical service bulletins (TSBs).

STEP 5 Locate the wiring schematic for the circuit being diagnosed.

STEP 6 Check the factory service information and follow the troubleshooting procedure.
  a. Determine how the circuit works.
  b. Determine which part of the circuit is good, based on what works and what does not work.
  c. Isolate the problem area.

  NOTE: Split the circuit in half to help isolate the problem and start at the relay (if the circuit has a relay).

STEP 7 Determine the root cause and repair the vehicle.

STEP 8 Verify the repair and complete the work order by listing the three Cs (complaint, cause, and correction).

Shocking Experience

A customer complained that after driving for a while, he got a static shock whenever he grabbed the door handle when exiting the vehicle. The customer thought that there must be an electrical fault and that the shock was coming from the vehicle itself. In a way, the shock was caused by the vehicle, but it was not a fault. The service technician sprayed the cloth seats with an antistatic spray and the problem did not reoccur. Obviously, a static charge was being created by the movement of the driver's clothing on the seats and then discharged when the driver touched the metal door handle. ● **SEE FIGURE 11–39.**

FIGURE 11–39 Antistatic spray can be used by customers to prevent being shocked when they touch a metal object like the door handle.

SUMMARY

1. Most wiring diagrams include the wire color, circuit number, and wire gauge.

2. The number used to identify connectors, grounds, and splices usually indicates where they are located in the vehicle.

3. All switches and relays on a schematic are shown in their normal position either normally closed (N.C.) or normally open (N.O.).

4. A short-to-voltage affects the power side of the circuit and usually involves more than one circuit.

5. A short-to-ground usually causes the fuse to blow and usually affects only one circuit.

6. Most electrical faults are a result of heat or movement.

REVIEW QUESTIONS

1. List the numbers used on schematics to indicate grounds, splices, and connectors and where they are used in the vehicle.

2. List and identify the terminals of a typical ISO type relay.

3. List three methods that can be used to help locate a short circuit.

4. How can a tone generator be used to locate a short circuit?

CHAPTER QUIZ

1. On a wiring diagram, S110 with a ".8 BRN/BLK" means _____.
   a. Circuit #.8, spliced under the hood
   b. A connector with 0.8 mm² wire
   c. A splice of a brown with black stripe, wire size being 0.8 mm² (18 gauge AWG)
   d. Both a and b

2. Where is connector C250?
   a. Under the hood
   b. Under the dash
   c. In the passenger compartment
   d. In the trunk

3. All switches illustrated in schematics are _____.
   a. Shown in their normal position
   b. Always shown in their on position
   c. Always shown in their off position
   d. Shown in their on position except for lighting switches

4. When testing a relay using an ohmmeter, which two termi-nals should be touched to measure the coil resistance?
   a. 87 and 30
   b. 86 and 85
   c. 87a and 87
   d. 86 and 87

5. Technician A says that a good relay should measure between 60 and 100 ohms across the coil terminals. Technician B says that OL should be displayed on an ohmmeter when touching terminals 30 and 87. Which technician is correct?
   a. Technician A only
   b. Technician B only
   c. Both Technicians A and B
   d. Neither Technician A nor B

6. Which relay terminal is the normally closed (N.C.) terminal?
   a. 30
   b. 85
   c. 87
   d. 87a

7. Technician A says that there is often more than one cir-cuit being protected by each fuse. Technician B says that more than one circuit often shares a single ground con-nector. Which technician is correct?
   a. Technician A only
   b. Technician B only
   c. Both Technicians A and B
   d. Neither Technician A nor B

8. Two technicians are discussing finding a short-to-ground using a test light. Technician A says that the test light, con-nected in place of the fuse, will light when the circuit that has the short is disconnected. Technician B says that the test light should be connected to the positive (+) and neg-ative (−) terminals of the battery during this test. Which technician is correct?
   a. Technician A only
   b. Technician B only
   c. Both Technicians A and B
   d. Neither Technician A nor B

9. A short circuit can be located using a _____.
   a. Test light
   b. Gauss gauge
   c. Tone generator
   d. All of the above

10. For an electrical device to operate, it must have _____.
   a. Power and a ground
   b. A switch and a fuse
   c. A ground and fusible link
   d. A relay to transfer the current to the device

chapter 12
CAPACITANCE AND CAPACITORS

OBJECTIVES

After studying Chapter 12, the reader will be able to:

1. Prepare for ASE Electrical/Electronic Systems (A6) certification test content area "A" (General Electrical/Electronic Systems).

2. Explain capacitance.

3. Describe how a capacitor can be used to filter electrical noise.

4. Describe how a capacitor can store an electrical charge.

5. Explain how a capacitor circuit can be used as a timer circuit.

KEY TERMS

Capacitance 164
Condenser 164
Dielectric 164
Farads 166
Leyden jar 164

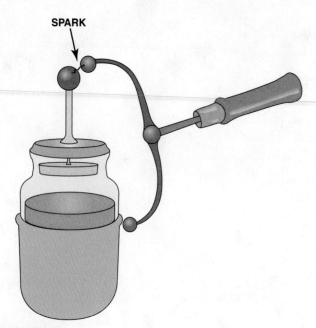

FIGURE 12–1 A Leyden jar can be used to store an electrical charge.

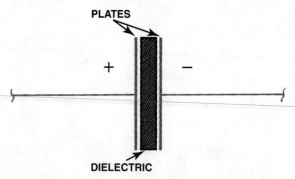

FIGURE 12–2 This simple capacitor, made of two plates separated by an insulating material, is called a dielectric.

CAPACITOR CONSTRUCTION AND OPERATION

CONSTRUCTION A capacitor (also called a condenser) consists of two conductive plates with an insulating material between them. The insulating material is commonly called a **dielectric.** This substance is a poor conductor of electricity and can include air, mica, ceramic, glass, paper, plastic, or any similar nonconductive material. The dielectric constant is the relative strength of a material against the flow of electrical current. The higher the number is, the better the insulating properties. ● **SEE CHART 12–1.**

OPERATION When a capacitor is placed in a closed circuit, the voltage source (battery) forces electrons around the circuit. Because electrons cannot flow through the dielectric of the capacitor, excess electrons collect on what becomes the negatively charged plate. At the same time, the other plate loses electrons and, therefore, becomes positively charged. ● **SEE FIGURE 12–2.**

CAPACITANCE

DEFINITION **Capacitance** is the ability of an object or surface to store an electrical charge. Around 1745, Ewald Christian von Kliest and Pieter van Musschenbroek independently discovered capacitance in an electric circuit. While engaged in separate studies of electrostatics, they discovered that an electric charge could be stored for a period of time. They used a device, now called a **Leyden jar,** for their experimentation, which consisted of a glass jar filled with water, with a nail piercing the stopper and dipping into the water. ● **SEE FIGURE 12–1.**

The two scientists connected the nail to an electrostatic charge. After disconnecting the nail from the source of the charge, they felt a shock by touching the nail, demonstrating that the device had stored the charge.

In 1747, John Bevis lined both the inside and outside of the jar with foil. This created a capacitor with two conductors (the inside and outside metal foil layers) equally separated by the insulating glass. The Leyden jar was also used by Benjamin Franklin to store the charge from lightning as well as in other experiments. The natural phenomenon of lightning includes capacitance, because huge electrical fields develop between cloud layers or between clouds and the earth prior to a lightning strike.

NOTE: Capacitors are also called condensers. This term developed because electric charges collect, or condense, on the plates of a capacitor much like water vapor collects and condenses on a cold bottle or glass.

MATERIAL	DIELECTRIC CONSTANT
Vacuum	1
Air	1.00059
Polystyrene	2.5
Paper	3.5
Mica	5.4
Flint glass	9.9
Methyl alcohol	35
Glycerin	56.2
Pure water	81

CHART 12–1

The higher the dielectric constant is, the better the insulating properties between the plates of the capacitor.

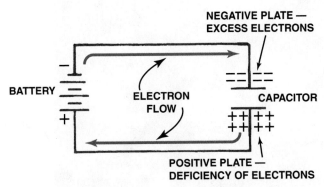

FIGURE 12–3 As the capacitor is charging, the battery forces electrons through the circuit.

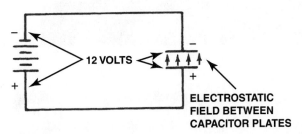

FIGURE 12–4 When the capacitor is charged, there is equal voltage across the capacitor and the battery. An electrostatic field exists between the capacitor plates. No current flows in the circuit.

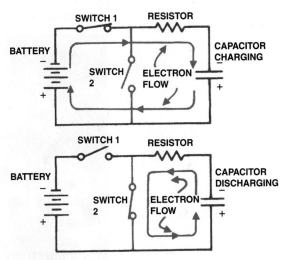

FIGURE 12–5 The capacitor is charged through one circuit (top) and discharged through another (bottom).

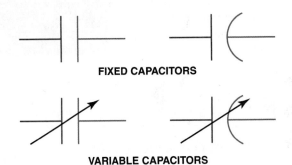

FIGURE 12–6 Capacitor symbols are shown in electrical diagrams. The negative plate is often shown curved.

Current continues until the voltage charge across the capacitor plates becomes the same as the source voltage. At that time, the negative plate of the capacitor and the negative terminal of the battery are at the same negative potential. ● SEE FIGURE 12–3.

The positive plate of the capacitor and the positive terminal of the battery are also at equal positive potentials. There is then a voltage charge across the battery terminals and an equal voltage charge across the capacitor plates. The circuit is in balance, and there is no current. An electrostatic field now exists between the capacitor plates because of their opposite charges. It is this field that stores energy. In other words, a charged capacitor is similar to a charged battery. ● SEE FIGURE 12–4.

If the circuit is opened, the capacitor will hold its charge until it is connected into an external circuit through which it can discharge. When the charged capacitor is connected to an external circuit, it discharges. After discharging, both plates of the capacitor are neutral because all the energy from a circuit stored in a capacitor is returned when it is discharged. ● SEE FIGURE 12–5.

Theoretically, a capacitor holds its charge indefinitely. Actually, the charge slowly leaks off the capacitor through the dielectric. The better the dielectric, the longer the capacitor holds its charge. To avoid an electrical shock, any capacitor should be treated as if it were charged until it is proven to be discharged. To safely discharge a capacitor, use a test light with the clip attached to a good ground, and touch the pigtail or terminal with the point of the test light. ● SEE FIGURE 12–6 for the symbol for capacitors as used in electrical schematics.

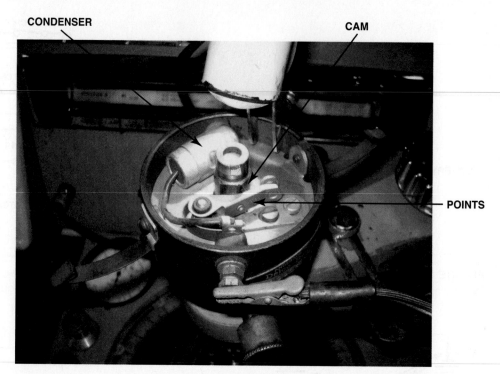

CONDENSER   CAM

POINTS

FIGURE 12–7 A point-type distributor shown with the condenser from an old vehicle being tested on a distributor machine.

What Are "Points and Condenser"?

Points and condenser are used in point-type ignition systems.

Points. A set of points uses one stationary contact and a movable contact that is opened by a cam lobe inside the ignition distributor. When the points are closed, current flows through the primary windings of the ignition coil and creates a strong magnetic field. As the engine rotates, the distributor can open the contact points, which open the circuit to the coil. The stored magnetic field in the coil collapses and generates a high-voltage arc from the secondary winding of the coil. It is this spark that is sent to the spark plugs that ignites the air-fuel mixture inside the engine.

Condenser. The condenser (capacitor) is attached to the points and the case of the condenser is grounded. When the points start to open, the charge built up in the primary winding of the coil would likely start to arc across the opening points. To prevent the points from arcing and to increase how rapidly the current is turned off, the condenser stores the current temporarily. Points and condenser were used in vehicles and small gasoline engines until the mid-1970s. ● **SEE FIGURE 12–7.**

FACTORS OF CAPACITANCE

Capacitance is governed by three factors.

- The surface area of the plates
- The distance between the plates
- The dielectric material

The larger the surface area of the plates is, the greater the capacitance, because more electrons collect on a larger plate area than on a small one. The closer the plates are to each other, the greater the capacitance, because a stronger electrostatic field exists between charged bodies that are close together. The insulating qualities of the dielectric material also affect capacitance. The capacitance of a capacitor is higher if the dielectric is a very good insulator.

MEASUREMENT OF CAPACITANCE Capacitance is measured in **farads,** which is named after Michael Faraday (1791–1867), an English physicist. The symbol for farads is the letter *F*. If a charge of 1 coulomb is placed on the plates of a capacitor and the potential difference between them is 1 volt, then the capacitance is defined to be 1 farad, or 1 F. One coulomb is equal to the charge of 6.25×10^{18} electrons. One farad is an extremely large quantity of capacitance. Microfarads (0.000001 farad), or μF, are more commonly used.

The capacitance of a capacitor is proportional to the quantity of charge that can be stored in it for each volt difference in potential.

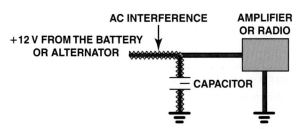

FIGURE 12–8 A capacitor blocks direct current (DC) but passes alternating current (AC). A capacitor makes a very good noise suppressor because most of the interference is AC and the capacitor will conduct this AC to ground before it can reach the radio or amplifier.

FIGURE 12–9 A 1 farad capacitor used to boost the power to large speakers.

USES FOR CAPACITORS

SPIKE SUPPRESSION A capacitor can be used in parallel to a coil to reduce the resulting voltage spike that occurs when the circuit is opened. The energy stored to the magnet field of the coil is rapidly released at this time. The capacitor acts to absorb the high voltage produced and stop it from interfering with other electronic devices, such as automotive radio and video equipment.

NOISE FILTERING Interference in a sound system or radio is usually due to alternating current (AC) voltage created somewhere in the vehicle, such as in the alternator. A capacitor does the following:

- Blocks the flow of direct current (DC)
- Allows alternating current (AC) to pass

By connecting a capacitor (condenser) to the power lead of the radio or sound system amplifier, the AC voltage passes through the capacitor to the ground where the other end of the capacitor is connected. Therefore, the capacitor provides a path for the AC without affecting the DC power circuit. ● **SEE FIGURE 12–8.**

Because a capacitor stores a voltage charge, it opposes or slows any voltage change in a circuit. Therefore, capacitors are often used as voltage "shock absorbers." You sometimes find a capacitor attached to one terminal of an ignition coil. In this application, the capacitor absorbs and dampens changes in ignition voltage that interfere with radio reception.

SUPPLEMENTAL POWER SOURCE A capacitor can be used to supply electrical power for short bursts in an audio system to help drive the speakers. Woofers and subwoofers require a lot of electrical current that often cannot be delivered by the amplifier itself. ● **SEE FIGURE 12–9.**

TIMER CIRCUITS Capacitors are used in electronic circuits as part of a timer, to control window defoggers, interior lighting, pulse wipers, and automatic headlights. The capacitors store energy and then are allowed to discharge through a resistance load. The greater the capacity of the capacitor and the higher the resistance load, the longer the time it takes for the capacitor to discharge.

COMPUTER MEMORY In most cases, the main memory of a computer is a high-speed random-access memory (RAM). One type of main memory, called dynamic random-access memory (DRAM), is the most commonly used type of RAM. A single memory chip is made up of several million memory cells. In a DRAM chip, each memory cell consists of a capacitor. When a capacitor is electrically charged, it is said to store the binary digit 1, and when discharged, it represents 0.

CONDENSER MICROPHONES A microphone converts sound waves into an electric signal. All microphones have a diaphragm that vibrates as sound waves strike. The vibrating diaphragm in turn causes an electrical component to create an output flow of current at a frequency proportional to the sound waves. A condenser microphone uses a capacitor for this purpose.

In a condenser microphone, the diaphragm is the negatively charged plate of a charged capacitor. When a sound wave compresses the diaphragm, the diaphragm is moved closer to the positive plate. Decreasing the distance between the plates increases the electrostatic attraction between them, which results in a flow of current to the negative plate. As the diaphragm moves out in response to sound waves, it also moves further from the positive plate. Increasing the distance between the plates decreases the electrostatic attraction between them. This results in a flow of current back to the positive plate. These alternating flows of current provide weak electronic signals that travel to an amplifier and then to a loudspeaker.

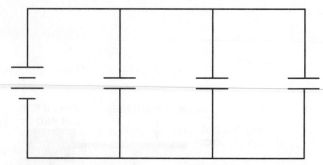

FIGURE 12–10 Capacitors in parallel effectively increase the capacitance.

CAPACITORS IN CIRCUITS

CAPACITORS IN PARALLEL CIRCUITS Capacitance can be increased in a circuit by connecting capacitors in parallel. For example, if a greater boost is needed for a sound system, then additional capacitors should be connected in parallel because their value adds together. ● **SEE FIGURE 12–10.**

We know that capacitance of a capacitor can be increased by increasing the size of its plates. Connecting two or more capacitors in parallel in effect increases plate size. Increasing plate area makes it possible to store more charge and therefore creates greater capacitance. To determine total capacitance of several parallel capacitors, simply add up their individual values. The following is the formula for calculating total capacitance in a circuit containing capacitors in parallel.

$$C_T = C_1 + C_2 + C_3 \ldots$$

For example, 220 µF + 220 µF = 440 µF when connected in parallel.

CAPACITORS IN SERIES CIRCUITS Capacitance can be decreased in a circuit by capacitors in series, as shown in ● **FIGURE 12–11.**

We know that capacitance of a capacitor can be decreased by placing the plates further apart. Connecting two or more capacitors in series in effect increases the distance between the plates and thickness of the dielectric, thereby decreasing the amount of capacitance.

Following is the formula for calculating total capacitance in a circuit containing two capacitors in series.

$$C_T = \frac{C_1 \times C_2}{C_1 + C_2}$$

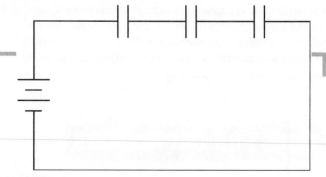

FIGURE 12–11 Capacitors in series decrease the capacitance.

For example, $\dfrac{220\ \mu F \times 220\ \mu F}{220\ \mu F + 220\ \mu F} = \dfrac{48{,}400}{440} = 110\ \mu F$

NOTE: Capacitors are often used to reduce radio interference or to improve the performance of a high-power sound system. Additional capacitance can, therefore, be added by attaching another capacitor in parallel.

SUPPRESSION CAPACITORS Capacitors are installed across many circuits and switching points to absorb voltage fluctuations. Among other applications, they are used across the following:

- The primary circuit of some electronic ignition modules
- The output terminal of most alternators
- The armature circuit of some electric motors

Radio choke coils reduce current fluctuations resulting from self-induction. They are often combined with capacitors to act as electromagnetic interference EMI filter circuits for windshield wiper and electric fuel pump motors. Filters also may be incorporated in wiring connectors.

SUMMARY

1. Capacitors (condensers) are used in numerous automotive applications.
2. Capacitors can block direct current and pass alternating current.
3. Capacitors are used to control radio-frequency interference and are installed in various electronic circuits to control unwanted noise.
4. Capacitors connected in series reduce the capacitance, whereas if connected in parallel increase the capacitance.

REVIEW QUESTIONS

1. How does a capacitor store an electrical charge?
2. How should two capacitors be electrically connected if greater capacitance is needed?
3. Where can a capacitor be used as a power source?
4. How can a capacitor be used as a noise filter?

CHAPTER QUIZ

1. A capacitor _____.
   a. Stores electrons
   b. Passes AC
   c. Blocks DC
   d. All of the above

2. To increase the capacity, capacitors should be connected in _____.
   a. Series
   b. Parallel
   c. With resistors connected between the leads
   d. Series-parallel

3. Capacitors are commonly used as a _____.
   a. Voltage supply
   b. Timer
   c. Noise filter
   d. All of the above

4. A charged capacitor acts like a _____.
   a. Switch
   b. Battery
   c. Resistor
   d. Coil

5. The unit of measurement for capacitor rating is the _____.
   a. Ohm
   b. Volt
   c. Farad
   d. Ampere

6. Two technicians are discussing the operation of a capacitor. Technician A says that a capacitor can create electricity. Technician B says that a capacitor can store electricity. Which technician is correct?
   a. Technician A only
   b. Technician B only
   c. Both Technicians A and B
   d. Neither Technician A nor B

7. Capacitors block the flow of _____ current but allow _____ current to pass.
   a. Strong; weak
   b. AC; DC
   c. DC; AC
   d. Weak; strong

8. To increase the capacity, what could be done?
   a. Connect another capacitor in series.
   b. Connect another capacitor in parallel.
   c. Add a resistor between two capacitors.
   d. Both a and b

9. A capacitor can be used in what components?
   a. Microphone
   b. Radio
   c. Speaker
   d. All of the above

10. A capacitor used for spike protection will normally be placed in _____ to the load or circuit.
    a. Series
    b. Parallel
    c. Either series or parallel
    d. Parallel with a resistor in series

chapter 13
MAGNETISM AND ELECTROMAGNETISM

OBJECTIVES

After studying Chapter 13, the reader will be able to:

1. Prepare for ASE Electrical/Electronic Systems (A6) certification test content area "A" (General Electrical/Electronic Systems).
2. Explain magnetism.
3. Describe how magnetism and voltage are related.
4. Describe how an ignition coil works.
5. Explain how an electromagnet works.

KEY TERMS

Ampere-turns 175
Counter electromotive force (CEMF) 179
Electromagnet 175
Electromagnetic induction 178
Electromagnetic interference (EMI) 182
Electromagnetism 173
Flux density 172
Flux lines 171
Ignition control module (ICM) 181
Left-hand rule 174

Lenz's law 178
Magnetic flux 171
Magnetic induction 172
Magnetism 171
Mutual induction 179
Permeability 173
Pole 171
Relay 176
Reluctance 173
Residual magnetism 172
Right-hand rule 174
Turns ratio 180

FIGURE 13–1 A freely suspended natural magnet (lodestone) will point toward the magnetic north pole.

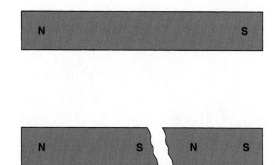

FIGURE 13–2 If a magnet breaks or is cracked, it becomes two weaker magnets.

FUNDAMENTALS OF MAGNETISM

DEFINITION   **Magnetism** is a form of energy that is caused by the motion of electrons in some materials. It is recognized by the attraction it exerts on other materials. Like electricity, magnetism cannot be seen. It can be explained in theory, however, because it is possible to see the results of magnetism and recognize the actions that it causes. Magnetite is the most naturally occurring magnet. Naturally magnetized pieces of magnetite, called *lodestone,* will attract and hold small pieces of iron.
● **SEE FIGURE 13–1.**

Many other materials can be artificially magnetized to some degree, depending on their atomic structure. Soft iron is very easy to magnetize, whereas some materials, such as aluminum, glass, wood, and plastic, cannot be magnetized at all.

🔧 **TECH TIP**

A Cracked Magnet Becomes Two Magnets

Magnets are commonly used in vehicle crankshaft, camshaft, and wheel speed sensors. If a magnet is struck and cracks or breaks, the result is two smaller-strength magnets. Because the strength of the magnetic field is reduced, the sensor output voltage is also reduced. A typical problem occurs when a magnetic crankshaft sensor becomes cracked, resulting in a no-start condition. Sometimes the cracked sensor works well enough to start an engine that is cranking at normal speeds but will not work when the engine is cold. ● **SEE FIGURE 13–2.**

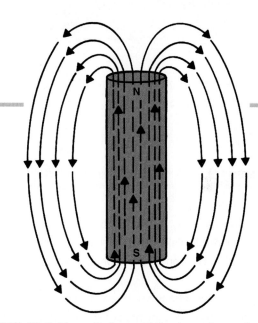

FIGURE 13–3 Magnetic lines of force leave the north pole and return to the south pole of a bar magnet.

LINES OF FORCE   The lines that create a field of force around a magnet are believed to be caused by the way groups of atoms are aligned in the magnetic material. In a bar magnet, the lines are concentrated at both ends of the bar and form closed, parallel loops in three dimensions around the magnet. Force does not flow along these lines the way electrical current flows, but the lines *do* have direction. They come out of the north end, or **pole**, of the magnet and enter at the other end.
● **SEE FIGURE 13–3.**

The opposite ends of a magnet are called its north and south poles. In reality, they should be called the "north seeking" and "south seeking" poles, because they seek the earth's North Pole and South Pole, respectively.

The more lines of force that are present, the stronger the magnet becomes. The magnetic lines of force, also called **magnetic flux** or **flux lines,** form a magnetic field. The terms *magnetic field, lines of force, flux,* and *flux lines* are used interchangeably.

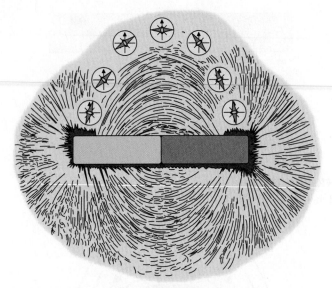

FIGURE 13–4 Iron filings and a compass can be used to observe the magnetic lines of force.

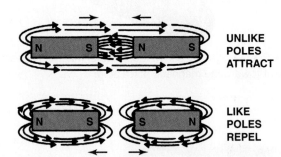

UNLIKE POLES ATTRACT

LIKE POLES REPEL

FIGURE 13–5 Magnetic poles behave like electrically charged particles—unlike poles attract and like poles repel.

FUNDAMENTALS OF MAGNETISM (CONTINUED)

Flux density refers to the number of flux lines per unit of area. A magnetic field can be measured using a Gauss gauge, named for German scientist Johann Carl Friedrick Gauss (1777–1855).

Magnetic lines of force can be seen by spreading fine iron filings or dust on a piece of paper laid on top of a magnet. A magnetic field can also be observed by using a compass. A compass is simply a thin magnet or magnetized iron needle balanced on a pivot. The needle will rotate to point toward the opposite pole of a magnet. The needle can be very sensitive to small magnetic fields. Because it is a small magnet, a compass usually has one north end (marked N) and one south end (marked S). ● **SEE FIGURE 13–4.**

MAGNETIC INDUCTION
If a piece of iron or steel is placed in a magnetic field, it will also become magnetized. This process of creating a magnet by using a magnetic field is called **magnetic induction.**

If the metal is then removed from the magnetic field, and it retains some magnetism, this is called **residual magnetism.**

ATTRACTING OR REPELLING
The poles of a magnet are called north (N) and south (S) because, when a magnet is suspended freely, the poles tend to point toward the earth's North Pole and South Pole. Magnetic flux lines exit from the north pole and bend around to enter the south pole. An equal number of

🔧 **TECH TIP**

Magnetize a Steel Needle

A piece of steel can be magnetized by rubbing a magnet in one direction along the steel. This causes the atoms to line up in the steel, so it acts like a magnet. The steel often will not remain magnetized, whereas the true magnet is permanently magnetized.

When soft iron or steel is used, such as a paper clip, it will lose its magnetism quickly. The atoms in a magnetized needle can be disturbed by heating it or by dropping the needle on a hard object, which would cause the needle to lose its magnetism. Soft iron is used inside ignition coils because it will not keep its magnetism.

lines exit and enter, so magnetic force is equal at both poles of a magnet. Flux lines are concentrated at the poles, and therefore magnetic force (flux density) is stronger at the ends.

Magnetic poles behave like positively and negatively charged particles. When unlike poles are placed close together, the lines exit from one magnet and enter the other. The two magnets are pulled together by flux lines. If like poles are placed close together, the curving flux lines meet head on, forcing the magnets apart. Therefore, like poles of a magnet repel and unlike poles attract. ● **SEE FIGURE 13–5.**

FIGURE 13–6 A crankshaft position sensor and reluctor (notched wheel).

PERMEABILITY   Magnetic flux lines cannot be insulated. There is no known material through which magnetic force does not pass, if the force is strong enough. However, some materials allow the force to pass though more easily than others. This degree of passage is called **permeability.** Iron allows magnetic flux lines to pass through much more easily than air, so iron is highly permeable.

An example of this characteristic is the use of a reluctor wheel in magnetic-type camshaft position (CMP) and crankshaft position (CKP) sensors. The teeth on a reluctor cause the magnetic field to increase as each tooth gets closer to the sensor and decrease as the tooth moves away, thus creating an AC voltage signal. ● **SEE FIGURE 13–6.**

RELUCTANCE   Although there is no absolute insulation for magnetism, certain materials resist the passage of magnetic force. This can be compared to resistance without an electrical circuit. Air does not allow easy passage, so air has a high **reluctance.** Magnetic flux lines tend to concentrate in permeable materials and avoid materials with high reluctance. As with electricity, magnetic force follows the path of least resistance.

ELECTROMAGNETISM

DEFINITION   Scientists did not discover that current-carrying conductors also are surrounded by a magnetic field until 1820. These fields may be made many times stronger than those surrounding conventional magnets. Also, the magnetic field strength around a conductor may be controlled by changing the current.

- As current increases, more flux lines are created and the magnetic field expands.
- As current decreases, the magnetic field contracts. The magnetic field collapses when the current is shut off.
- The interaction and relationship between magnetism and electricity is known as **electromagnetism.**

CREATING AN ELECTROMAGNET   An easy way to create an electromagnet is to wrap a nail with 20 turns of insulated wire and connect the ends to the terminals of a 1.5 volt dry cell battery. When energized, the nail will become a magnet and will be able to pick up tacks or other small steel objects.

STRAIGHT CONDUCTOR   The magnetic field surrounding a straight, current-carrying conductor consists of several concentric cylinders of flux that are the length of the wire. The

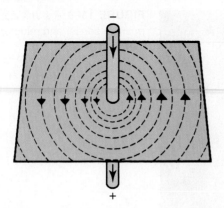

FIGURE 13–7 A magnetic field surrounds a straight, current-carrying conductor.

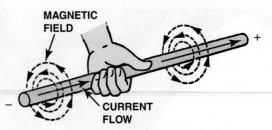

FIGURE 13–8 The left-hand rule for magnetic field direction is used with the electron flow theory.

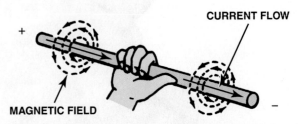

FIGURE 13–9 The right-hand rule for magnetic field direction is used with the conventional theory of electron flow.

FIGURE 13–10 Conductors with opposing magnetic fields will move apart into weaker fields.

ELECTROMAGNETISM (CONTINUED)

amount of current flow (amperes) determines how many flux lines (cylinders) there will be and how far out they extend from the surface of the wire. ● SEE FIGURE 13–7.

LEFT-HAND AND RIGHT-HAND RULES Magnetic flux cylinders have direction, just as the flux lines surrounding a bar magnet have direction. The **left-hand rule** is a simple way to determine this direction. When you grasp a conductor with your left hand so that your thumb points in the direction of electron flow (− to +) through the conductor, your fingers curl around the wire in the direction of the magnetic flux lines. ● SEE FIGURE 13–8.

Most automotive circuits use the conventional theory of current (+ to −) and, therefore, the **right-hand rule** is used to determine the direction of the magnetic flux lines. ● SEE FIGURE 13–9.

FIELD INTERACTION The cylinders of flux surrounding current-carrying conductors interact with other magnetic fields. In the following illustrations, the cross symbol (+) indicates current moving inward, or away from you. It represents the tail of an arrow. The dot symbol (●) represents an arrowhead and indicates current moving outward. If two conductors carry current in opposite directions, their magnetic fields also carry current in opposite directions (according to the left-hand rule). If they are placed side by side, then the opposing flux lines between the conductors create a strong magnetic field. Current-carrying conductors tend to move out of a strong field into a weak field, so the conductors move away from each other. ● SEE FIGURE 13–10.

If the two conductors carry current in the same direction, then their fields are in the same direction. The flux lines between the two conductors cancel each other out, leaving a very weak field between them. The conductors are drawn into this weak field, and they tend to move toward each other.

🔧 **TECH TIP**

Electricity and Magnetism

Electricity and magnetism are closely related because any electrical current flowing through a conductor creates a magnetic field. Any conductor moving through a magnetic field creates an electrical current. This relationship can be summarized as follows:

- Electricity creates magnetism.
- Magnetism creates electricity.

From a service technician's point of view, this relationship is important because wires carrying current should always be routed as the factory intended to avoid causing interference with another circuit or electronic component. This is especially important when installing or servicing spark plug wires, which carry high voltages and can cause high electromagnetic interference.

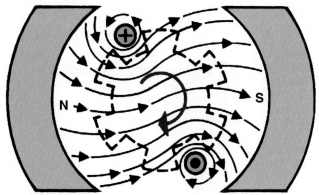

FIGURE 13-11 Electric motors use the interaction of magnetic fields to produce mechanical energy.

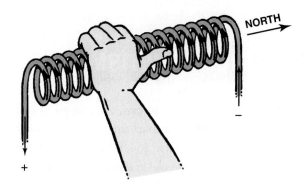

FIGURE 13-13 The left-hand rule for coils is shown.

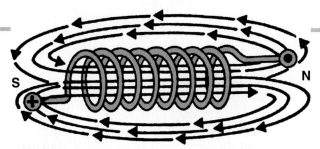

FIGURE 13-12 The magnetic lines of flux surrounding a coil look similar to those surrounding a bar magnet.

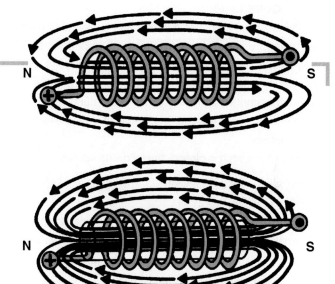

FIGURE 13-14 An iron core concentrates the magnetic lines of force surrounding a coil.

MOTOR PRINCIPLE

Electric motors, such as vehicle starter motors, use this magnetic field interaction to convert electrical energy into mechanical energy. If two conductors carrying current in opposite directions are placed between strong north and south poles, the magnetic field of the conductor interacts with the magnetic fields of the poles. The counterclockwise field of the top conductor adds to the fields of the poles and creates a strong field beneath the conductor. The conductor then tries to move up to get out of this strong field. The clockwise field of the lower conductor adds to the field of the poles and creates a strong field above the conductor. The conductor then tries to move down to get out of this strong field. These forces cause the center of the motor, where the conductors are mounted, to turn clockwise. ● SEE FIGURE 13-11.

COIL CONDUCTOR

If several loops of wire are made into a coil, then the magnetic flux density is strengthened. Flux lines around a coil are the same as the flux lines around a bar magnet. ● SEE FIGURE 13-12.

They exit from the north pole and enter at the south pole. Use the left-hand thread rule to determine the north pole of a coil, as shown in ● FIGURE 13-13.

Grasp the coil with your left hand so that your fingers point in the direction of electron flow; your thumb will point toward the north pole of the coil.

ELECTROMAGNETIC STRENGTH

The magnetic field surrounding a current-carrying conductor can be strengthened (increased) three ways.

- Place a soft iron core in the center of the coil.
- Increase the number of turns of wire in the coil.
- Increase the current flow through the coil windings.

Because soft iron is highly permeable, magnetic flux lines pass through it easily. If a piece of soft iron is placed inside a coiled conductor, the flux lines concentrate in the iron core, rather than pass through the air, which is less permeable. The concentration of force greatly increases the strength of the magnetic field inside the coil. Increasing the number of turns in a coil and/or increasing the current flow through the coil results in greater field strength and is proportional to the number of turns. The magnetic field strength is often expressed in the units called **ampere-turns**. Coils with an iron core are called **electromagnets**. ● SEE FIGURE 13-14.

USES OF ELECTROMAGNETISM

RELAYS As mentioned in the previous chapter, a **relay** is a control device that allows a small amount of current to control a large amount of current in another circuit. A simple relay contains an electromagnetic coil in series with a battery and a switch. Near the electromagnet is a movable flat arm, called an *armature*, of some material that is attracted by a magnetic field. ● **SEE FIGURE 13–15.**

The armature pivots at one end and is held a small distance away from the electromagnet by a spring (or by the spring steel of the movable arm itself). A contact point, made of a good conductor, is attached to the free end of the armature. Another contact point is fixed a small distance away. The two contact points are wired in series with an electrical load and the battery.

When the switch is closed, the following occurs.

1. Current travels from the battery through a coil, creating an electromagnet.

2. The magnetic field created by the current attracts the armature, pulling it down until the contact points close.

3. Closing the contacts allows current in the heavy current circuit from the battery to the load.

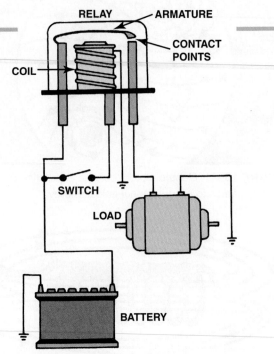

FIGURE 13–15 An electromagnetic switch that has a movable arm is referred to as a relay.

When the switch is open, the following occurs.

1. The electromagnet loses its magnetism when the current is shut off.

2. Spring pressure lifts the arm back up.

3. The heavy current circuit is broken by the opening of the contact points.

Relays also may be designed with normally closed contacts that open when current passes through the electromagnetic coil.

SOLENOID A solenoid is an example of an electromagnetic switch. A solenoid uses a movable core rather than a movable arm and is generally used in higher-amperage applications. A solenoid can be a separate unit or attached to a starter such as a starter solenoid. ● **SEE FIGURE 13–16.**

FREQUENTLY ASKED QUESTION

Solenoid or Relay?

Often, either term is used to describe the same part in service information. ● **SEE CHART 13–1** for a summary of the differences.

	CONSTRUCTION	AMPERAGE RATING	USES	CALLED IN SERVICE INFORMATION
Relay	Uses a movable arm Coil: 60 to 100 ohms requiring 0.12 to 0.20 A to energize	1 to 30 A	Lower current switching, lower cost, more commonly used	Electromagnetic switch or relay
Solenoid	Uses a movable core Coil(s): 0.2 to 0.6 ohm requiring 20 to 60 A to energize	30 to 400 A	Higher cost, used in starter motor circuits and other high-amperage applications	Solenoid, relay or electromagnetic switch

CHART 13–1

Comparison between a relay and a solenoid.

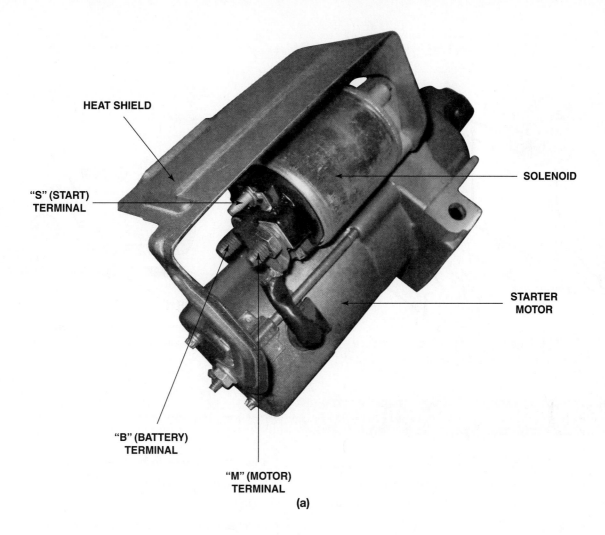

HEAT SHIELD

SOLENOID

"S" (START) TERMINAL

STARTER MOTOR

"B" (BATTERY) TERMINAL

"M" (MOTOR) TERMINAL

(a)

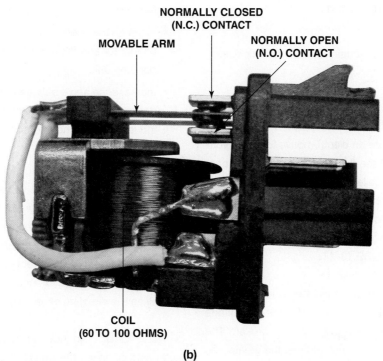

NORMALLY CLOSED (N.C.) CONTACT

MOVABLE ARM

NORMALLY OPEN (N.O.) CONTACT

COIL (60 TO 100 OHMS)

(b)

FIGURE 13–16 (a) A starter with attached solenoid. All of the current needed by the starter flows through the two large terminals of the solenoid and through the solenoid contacts inside. (b) A relay is designed to carry lower current compared to a solenoid and uses a movable arm.

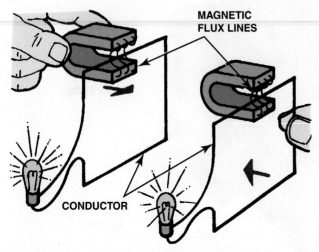

FIGURE 13–17 Voltage can be induced by the relative motion between a conductor and magnetic lines of force.

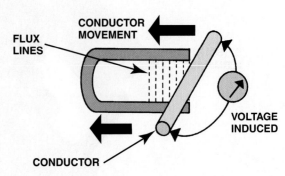

FIGURE 13–18 Maximum voltage is induced when conductors cut across the magnetic lines of force (flux lines) at a 90-degree angle.

ELECTROMAGNETIC INDUCTION

PRINCIPLES INVOLVED Electricity can be produced by using the relative movement of an electrical conductor and a magnetic field. There are three items necessary to produce electricity (voltage) from magnetism.

1. Electrical conductor (usually a coil of wire)
2. Magnetic field
3. Movement of either the conductor or the magnetic field

   Therefore:

   ■ Electricity creates magnetism.

   ■ Magnetism can create electricity.

Magnetic flux lines create an electromotive force, or voltage, in a conductor if either the flux lines or the conductor is moving. This movement is called *relative motion*. This process is called induction, and the resulting electromotive force is called *induced voltage*. This creation of a voltage (electricity) in a conductor by a moving magnetic field is called **electromagnetic induction.** ● SEE FIGURE 13–17.

VOLTAGE INTENSITY Voltage is induced when a conductor cuts across magnetic flux lines. The amount of the voltage depends on the rate at which the flux lines are broken. The more flux lines that are broken per unit of time, the greater the induced voltage. If a single conductor breaks 1 million flux lines per second, 1 volt is induced.

There are four ways to increase induced voltage.

■ Increase the strength of the magnetic field, so there are more flux lines.

■ Increase the number of conductors that are breaking the flux lines.

■ Increase the speed of the relative motion between the conductor and the flux lines so that more lines are broken per time unit.

■ Increase the angle between the flux lines and the conductor to a maximum of 90 degrees. There is no voltage induced if the conductors move parallel to, and do not break, any flux lines.

Maximum voltage is induced if the conductors break flux lines at 90 degrees. Induced voltage varies proportionately at angles between 0 and 90 degrees. ● SEE FIGURE 13–18.

Voltage can be electromagnetically induced and can be measured. Induced voltage creates current. The direction of induced voltage (and the direction in which current moves) is called *polarity* and depends upon the direction of the flux lines, as well as the direction of relative motion.

LENZ'S LAW An induced current moves so that its magnetic field opposes the motion that induced the current. This principle is called **Lenz's law.** The relative motion of a conductor and a magnetic field is opposed by the magnetic field of the current it has induced.

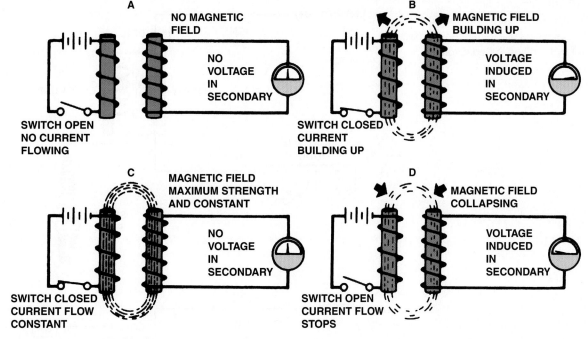

FIGURE 13–19 Mutual induction occurs when the expansion or collapse of a magnetic field around one coil induces a voltage in a second coil.

SELF-INDUCTION When current begins to flow in a coil, the flux lines expand as the magnetic field forms and strengthens. As current increases, the flux lines continue to expand, cutting across the wires of the coil and actually inducing another voltage within the same coil. Following Lenz's law, this self-induced voltage tends to *oppose* the current that produces it. If the current continues to increase, the second voltage opposes the increase. When the current stabilizes, the countervoltage is no longer induced because there are no more expanding flux lines (no relative motion). When current to the coil is shut off, the collapsing magnetic flux lines self-induce a voltage in the coil that tries to maintain the original current. The self-induced voltage *opposes* and *slows* the *decrease* in the original current. The self-induced voltage that opposes changes in current flow is an inductor called **counter electromotive force (CEMF)**.

MUTUAL INDUCTION When two coils are close together, energy may be transferred from one to the other by magnetic coupling called mutual induction. **Mutual induction** means that the expansion or collapse of the magnetic field around one coil induces a voltage in the second coil.

IGNITION COILS

IGNITION COIL WINDINGS Ignition coils use two windings and are wound on the same iron core.

- One coil winding is connected to a battery through a switch and is called the *primary winding*.

- The other coil winding is connected to an external circuit and is called the *secondary winding*.

When the switch is open, there is no current in the primary winding. There is no magnetic field and, therefore, no voltage in the secondary winding. When the switch is closed, current is introduced and a magnetic field builds up around both windings. The primary winding thus changes electrical energy from the battery into magnetic energy of the expanding field. As the field expands, it cuts across the secondary winding and induces a voltage in it. A meter connected to the secondary circuit shows current. ● **SEE FIGURE 13–19.**

When the magnetic field has expanded to its full strength, it remains steady as long as the same amount of current exists. The flux lines have stopped their cutting action. There is no relative motion and no voltage in the secondary winding, as shown on the meter.

When the switch is opened, primary current stops and the field collapses. As it does, flux lines cut across the secondary winding but in the opposite direction. This induces a secondary voltage with current in the opposite direction, as shown on the meter.

Mutual induction is used in ignition coils. In an ignition coil, low-voltage primary current induces a very high secondary

FIGURE 13–20 Some ignition coils are electrically connected, called married (top figure) whereas others use separated primary and secondary windings, called divorced (lower figure).

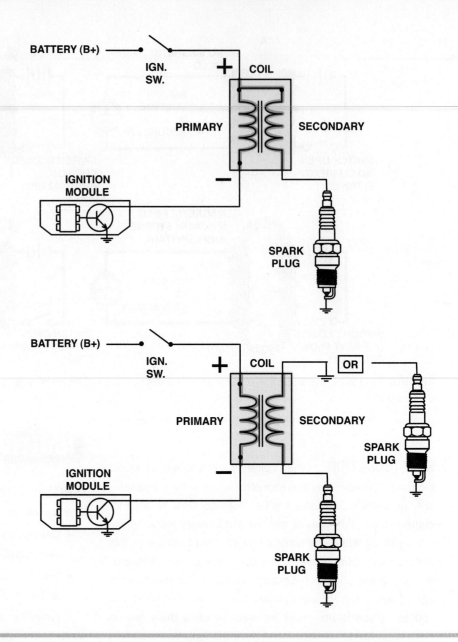

IGNITION COILS (CONTINUED)

voltage because of the different number of turns in the primary and secondary windings. Because the voltage is increased, an ignition coil is also called a *step-up transformer*.

- **Electrically connected windings.** Many ignition coils contain two separate but electrically connected windings of copper wire. This type of coil is called a "married" type and is used in older distributor-type ignition systems and in many coil-on-plug (COP) designs.

- **Electrically insulated windings.** Other coils are true transformers in which the primary and secondary windings are not electrically connected. This type of coil is often called a "divorced" type and is used in all waste-spark-type ignition systems.

  ● **SEE FIGURE 13–20.**

IGNITION COIL CONSTRUCTION The center of an ignition coil contains a core of laminated soft iron (thin strips of soft iron). This core increases the magnetic strength of the coil. Surrounding the laminated core are approximately 20,000 turns of fine wire (approximately 42 gauge). These windings are called the secondary coil windings. Surrounding the secondary windings are approximately 150 turns of heavy wire (approximately 21 gauge). These windings are called the primary coil windings. The secondary winding has about 100 times the number of turns of the primary winding, referred to as the **turns ratio** (approximately 100:1). In many coils, these windings are surrounded with a thin metal shield and insulating paper, and placed into a metal container. The metal container and shield help retain the magnetic field produced in the coil windings. The primary and secondary windings produce heat because of the electrical

FIGURE 13–21 A GM waste-spark ignition coil showing the section of laminations that is shaped like the letter *E*. These mild steel laminations improve the efficiency of the coil.

FIGURE 13–22 The coil-on-plug (COP) design typically uses a bobbin-type coil.

resistance in the turns of wire. Many coils contain oil to help cool the ignition coil. Other coil designs include the following:

- **Air-cooled, epoxy-sealed E coil.** The *E coil* is so named because the laminated, soft iron core is E shaped, with the coil wire turns wrapped around the center "finger" of the E and the primary winding wrapped inside the secondary winding. ● **SEE FIGURE 13–21.**

- **Spool design.** Used mostly for coil-on plug design, the coil windings are wrapped around a nylon or plastic spool or bobbin. ● **SEE FIGURE 13–22.**

IGNITION COIL OPERATION The negative terminal is attached to an **ignition control module (ICM,** or **igniter)**, which opens and closes the primary ignition circuit by opening or closing the ground return path of the circuit. When the ignition switch is on, voltage should be available at *both* the positive terminal and the negative terminal of the coil if the primary windings of the coil have continuity.

A spark is created by the following sequence of events.

- A magnetic field is created in the primary winding of the coil when there is 12 volts applied to the primary coil winding and the ignition control module grounds the other end on the coil.

- When the ignition control module (or powertrain control module) opens the ground circuit, the stored magnetic field collapses and creates a high voltage (up to 40,000 volts or more) in the secondary winding.

- The high-voltage pulse then flows to the spark plug and creates a spark at the ground electrode inside the engine that ignites the air-fuel mixture inside the cylinder.

ELECTROMAGNETIC INTERFERENCE

DEFINITION Until the advent of the onboard computer, **electromagnetic interference (EMI)** was not a source of real concern to automotive engineers. The problem was mainly one of *radio-frequency interference (RFI)*, caused primarily by the use of secondary ignition cables. Using spark plug wires that contained a high-resistance, nonmetallic core made of carbon, linen, or fiberglass strands impregnated with graphite mostly solved RFI from the secondary ignition system. RFI is a part of electromagnetic interference, which deals with interference that affects radio reception. All electronic devices used in vehicles are affected by EMI/RFI.

HOW EMI IS CREATED

Whenever there is current in a conductor, an electromagnetic field is created. When current stops and starts, as in a spark plug cable or a switch that opens and closes, the field strength changes. Each time this happens, it creates an electromagnetic signal wave. If it happens rapidly enough, the resulting high-frequency signal waves, or EMI, interfere with radio and television transmission or with other electronic systems such as those under the hood. This is an undesirable side effect of the phenomenon of electromagnetism.

Static electric charges caused by friction of the tires with the road, or the friction of engine drive belts contacting their pulleys, also produce EMI. Drive axles, driveshafts, and clutch or brake lining surfaces are other sources of static electric charges.

There are four ways of transmitting EMI, all of which can be found in a vehicle.

- Conductive coupling is actual physical contact through circuit conductors.
- Capacitive coupling is the transfer of energy from one circuit to another through an electrostatic field between two conductors.
- Inductive coupling is the transfer of energy from one circuit to another as the magnetic fields between two conductors form and collapse.
- Electromagnetic radiation is the transfer of energy by the use of radio waves from one circuit or component to another.

EMI SUPPRESSION DEVICES There are four general ways in which EMI is reduced.

- **Resistance suppression.** Adding resistance to a circuit to suppress RFI works only for high-voltage systems. This has been done by the use of resistance spark plug cables, resistor spark plugs, and the silicone grease used on the distributor cap and rotor of some electronic ignitions.

- **Suppression capacitors and coils.** Capacitors are installed across many circuits and switching points to absorb voltage fluctuations. Among other applications, they are used across the following:

  - The primary circuit of some electronic ignition modules
  - The output terminal of most alternators
  - The armature circuit of some electric motors

Coils reduce current fluctuations resulting from self-induction. They are often combined with capacitors to act as EMI filter circuits for windshield wiper and electric fuel pump motors. Filters also may be incorporated in wiring connectors.

- **Shielding.** The circuits of onboard computers are protected to some degree from external electromagnetic waves by their metal housings.

- **Ground wires or straps.** Ground wires or braided straps between the engine and chassis of an automobile help suppress EMI conduction and radiation by providing a low-resistance circuit ground path. Such suppression ground straps are often installed between rubber-mounted components and body parts. On some models, ground straps are installed between body parts, such as between the hood and a fender panel, where no electrical circuit exists. The strap has no other job than to suppress EMI. Without it, the sheet-metal body and hood could function as a large capacitor. The space between the fender and hood could form an electrostatic field and couple with the computer circuits in the wiring harness routed near the fender panel. ● **SEE FIGURE 13–23.**

FIGURE 13–23 To help prevent underhood electromagnetic devices from interfering with the antenna input, it is important that all ground wires, including the one from this power antenna, be properly grounded.

 TECH TIP

Cell Phone Interference

A cellular phone emits a weak signal if it is turned on, even though it is not being used. This signal is picked up and tracked by cell phone towers. When the cell phone is called, it emits a stronger signal to notify the tower that it is on and capable of receiving a phone call. It is this "handshake" signal that can cause interference in the vehicle. Often this signal causes some static in the radio speakers even though the radio is off, but it can also cause a false antilock brake (ABS) trouble code to set. These signals from the cell phone create a voltage that is induced in the wires of the vehicle. Because the cell phone usually leaves with the customer, the service technician is often unable to verify the customer concern.

Remember, the interference occurs right *before* the cell phone rings. To fix the problem, connect an external antenna to the cell phone. This step will prevent the induction of a voltage in the wiring of the vehicle.

SUMMARY

1. Most automotive electrical components use magnetism, the strength of which depends on both the amount of current (amperes) and the number of turns of wire of each electromagnet.
2. The strength of electromagnets is increased by using a soft iron core.
3. Voltage can be induced from one circuit to another.
4. Electricity creates magnetism and magnetism creates electricity.
5. Radio-frequency interference (RFI) is a part of electromagnetic interference (EMI).

REVIEW QUESTIONS

1. What is the relationship between electricity and magnetism?
2. What is the difference between mutual induction and self-induction?
3. What is the result if a magnet cracks?
4. How can EMI be reduced or controlled?

1. Technician A says that magnetic lines of force can be seen by placing iron filings on a piece of paper and then holding them over a magnet. Technician B says that the effects of magnetic lines of force can be seen using a compass. Which technician is correct?
   a. Technician A only
   b. Technician B only
   c. Both Technicians A and B
   d. Neither Technician A nor B

2. Unlike magnetic poles _____, and like magnetic poles _____.

   a. Repel; attract   c. Repel; repel
   b. Attract; repel   d. Attract; attract

3. The conventional theory for current flow is being used to determine the direction of magnetic lines of force. Technician A says that the left-hand rule should be used. Technician B says that the right-hand rule should be used. Which technician is correct?
   a. Technician A only
   b. Technician B only
   c. Both Technicians A and B
   d. Neither Technician A nor B

4. Technician A says that a relay is an electromagnetic switch. Technician B says that a solenoid uses a movable core. Which technician is correct?
   a. Technician A only
   b. Technician B only
   c. Both Technicians A and B
   d. Neither Technician A nor B

5. Two technicians are discussing electromagnetic induction. Technician A says that the induced voltage can be increased if the speed is increased between the conductor and the magnetic lines of force. Technician B says that the induced voltage can be increased by increasing the strength of the magnetic field. Which technician is correct?
   a. Technician A only
   b. Technician B only
   c. Both Technicians A and B
   d. Neither Technician A nor B

6. An ignition coil operates using the principle(s) of _____.
   a. Electromagnetic induction
   b. Self-induction
   c. Mutual induction
   d. All of the above

7. Electromagnetic interference can be reduced by using a _____.
   a. Resistance
   b. Capacitor
   c. Coil
   d. All of the above

8. An ignition coil is an example of a _____.
   a. Solenoid
   b. Step-down transformer
   c. Step-up transformer
   d. Relay

9. Magnetic field strength is measured in _____.
   a. Ampere-turns
   b. Flux
   c. Density
   d. Coil strength

10. Two technicians are discussing ignition coils. Technician A says that some ignition coils have the primary and secondary windings electrically connected. Technician B says that some coils have totally separate primary and secondary windings that are not electrically connected. Which technician is correct?
    a. Technician A only
    b. Technician B only
    c. Both Technicians A and B
    d. Neither Technician A nor B

chapter 14

ELECTRONIC FUNDAMENTALS

OBJECTIVES

After studying Chapter 14, the reader will be able to:

1. Prepare for ASE Electrical/Electronic Systems (A6) certification test content area "A" (General Electrical/Electronic Systems Diagnosis).

2. Identify semiconductor components.

3. Explain precautions necessary when working with semiconductor circuits.

4. Discuss where various electronic and semiconductor devices are used in vehicles.

5. Describe how to test diodes and transistors.

6. List the precautions that a service technician should follow to avoid damage to electronic components from electrostatic discharge.

KEY TERMS

Anode 187
Base 195
Bipolar transistor 195
Burn in 189
Cathode 187
CHMSL 193
Clamping diode 189
Collector 195
Control current 195
Darlington pair 197
Despiking diode 189
Diode 187
Doping 186
Dual inline pins (DIP) 197
Emitter 195
ESD 204
FET 196
Forward bias 188
Gate 198
Germanium 186
Heat sink 197
Holes 186
Hole theory 187
Impurities 186
Integrated circuit (IC) 197
Inverter 203
Junction 187
Light emitting diode (LED) 192

MOSFET 196
NPN transistor 195
NTC 194
N-type material 186
Op-amps 199
Photodiodes 192
Photons 192
Photoresistor 193
Phototransistor 197
Peak inverse voltage (PIV) 191
Peak reverse voltage (PRV) 191
PNP transistor 195
P-type material 186
PWM 200
Rectifier bridge 194
Reverse bias 188
SCR 193
Semiconductors 186
Silicon 186
Spike protection resistor 190
Suppression diode 189
Thermistor 194
Threshold voltage 195
Transistor 195
Zener diode 189

Electronic components are the heart of computers. Knowing how electronic components work helps take the mystery out of automotive electronics.

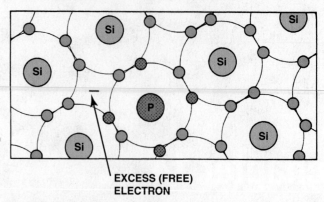

EXCESS (FREE) ELECTRON

FIGURE 14–1 N-type material. Silicon (Si) doped with a material (such as phosphorus) with five electrons in the outer orbit results in an extra free electron.

SEMICONDUCTORS

DEFINITION Semiconductors are neither conductors nor insulators. The flow of electrical current is caused by the movement of electrons in materials having *fewer* than four electrons in their atom's outer orbit. Insulators contain *more* than four electrons in their outer orbit and cannot conduct electricity because their atomic structure is stable (no free electrons).

Semiconductors are materials that contain exactly four electrons in the outer orbit of their atom structure and are, therefore, neither good conductors nor good insulators.

EXAMPLES OF SEMICONDUCTORS Two examples of semiconductor materials are **germanium** and **silicon,** which have exactly four electrons in their valance ring and no free electrons to provide current flow. However, both of these semiconductor materials can be made to conduct current if another material is added to provide the necessary conditions for electron movement.

CONSTRUCTION When another material is added to a semiconductor material in very small amounts, it is called **doping.** The doping elements are called **impurities;** therefore, after their addition, the germanium and silicon are no longer considered *pure* elements. The material added to pure silicon or germanium to make it electrically conductive represents only one atom of impurity for every *100 million* atoms of the pure semiconductor material. The resulting atoms are still electrically *neutral,* because the number of electrons still equals the number of protons of the combined materials. These combined materials are classified into two groups depending on the number of electrons in the bonding between the two materials.

- N-type materials
- P-type materials

N-TYPE MATERIAL **N-type material** is silicon or germanium that is doped with an element such as *phosphorus*, *arsenic*, or *antimony*, each having five electrons in its outer orbit. These five electrons are combined with the four electrons of the silicon or germanium to total nine electrons. There is room for only eight electrons in the bonding between the semiconductor material and the doping material. This leaves extra electrons, and even though the material is still electrically neutral, these extra electrons tend to repel other electrons outside the material. ● **SEE FIGURE 14–1.**

P-TYPE MATERIAL **P-type material** is produced by doping silicon or germanium with the element *boron* or the element *indium*. These impurities have only three electrons in their outer shell and, when combined with the semiconductor material, result in a material with seven electrons, one electron *less* than is required for atom bonding. This lack of one electron makes the material able to attract electrons, even though the material still has a neutral charge. This material tends to attract electrons to fill the **holes** for the missing eighth electron in the bonding of the materials. ● **SEE FIGURE 14–2.**

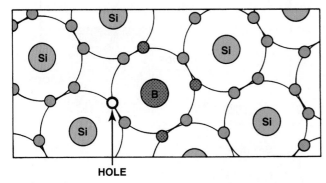

FIGURE 14–2 P-type material. Silicon (Si) doped with a material, such as boron (B), with three electrons in the outer orbit results in a hole capable of attracting an electron.

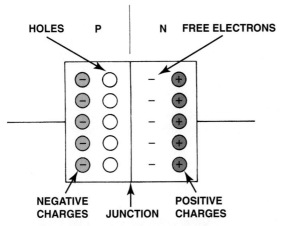

FIGURE 14–3 Unlike charges attract and the current carriers (electrons and holes) move toward the junction.

?   **FREQUENTLY ASKED QUESTION**

What Is the Hole Theory?

Current flow is expressed as the movement of electrons from one atom to another. In semiconductor and electronic terms, the movement of electrons fills the holes of the P-type material. Therefore, as the holes are filled with electrons, the unfilled holes move opposite to the flow of the electrons. This concept of hole movement is called the **hole theory** of current flow. The holes move in the direction opposite that of electron flow. For example, think of an egg carton, where if an egg is moved in one direction, the holes created move in the opposite direction. ● **SEE FIGURE 14–3.**

SUMMARY OF SEMICONDUCTORS

The following is a summary of semiconductor fundamentals.

1. The two types of semiconductor materials are P type and N type. N-type material contains extra electrons; P-type material contains holes due to missing electrons. The number of excess electrons in an N-type material must remain constant, and the number of holes in the P-type material must also remain constant. Because electrons are interchangeable, movement of electrons in or out of the material is possible to maintain a balanced material.

2. In P-type semiconductors, electrical conduction occurs mainly as the result of holes (absence of electrons). In N-type semiconductors, electrical conduction occurs mainly as the result of electrons (excess of electrons).

3. Hole movement results from the jumping of electrons into new positions.

4. Under the effect of a voltage applied to the semiconductor, electrons travel toward the positive terminal and holes move toward the negative terminal. The direction of hole current agrees with the conventional direction of current flow.

DIODES

CONSTRUCTION A **diode** is an electrical one-way check valve made by combining a P-type material and an N-type material. The word *diode* means "having two electrodes." Electrodes are electrical connections: The positive electrode is called the **anode;** the negative electrode is called the **cathode.** The point where the two types of materials join is called the **junction.** ● **SEE FIGURE 14–4.**

OPERATION The N-type material has one extra electron, which can flow into the P-type material. The P type has a need for electrons to fill its holes. If a battery were connected to the diode positive (+) to P-type material and negative (−) to N-type material, then the electrons that left the N-type material and flowed into the P-type material to fill the holes would be quickly

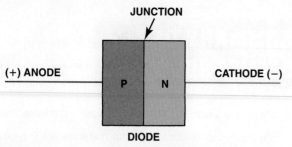

FIGURE 14–4 A diode is a component with P-type and N-type materials together. The negative electrode is called the cathode and the positive electrode is called the anode.

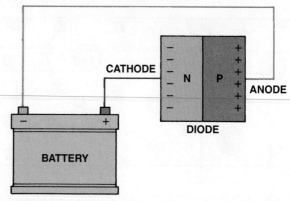

FIGURE 14–6 Diode connected with reversed polarity. No current flows across the junction between the P-type and N-type materials. This connection is called reverse bias.

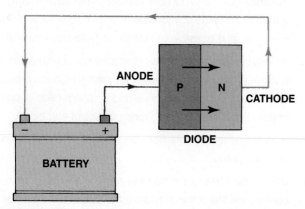

FIGURE 14–5 Diode connected to a battery with correct polarity (battery positive to P type and battery negative to N-type). Current flows through the diode. This condition is called forward bias.

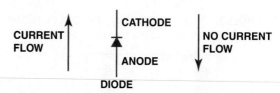

FIGURE 14–7 Diode symbol and electrode names. The stripe on one end of a diode represents the cathode end of the diode.

DIODES (CONTINUED)

replaced by the electron flow from the battery. Current flows through a forward-bias diode for the following reasons.

- Electrons move toward the holes (P-type material).
- Holes move toward the electrons (N-type material).
  ● **SEE FIGURE 14–5.**

As a result, current would flow through the diode with low resistance. This condition is called **forward bias.**

If the battery connections were reversed and the positive side of the battery was connected to the N-type material, the electrons would be pulled toward the battery and away from the junction of the N-type and P-type materials. (Remember, unlike charges attract, whereas like charges repel.) Because electrical conduction requires the flow of electrons across the junction of the N-type and P-type materials and because the battery connections are actually reversed, the diode offers very high resistance to current flow. This condition is called **reverse bias.**
● **SEE FIGURE 14–6.**

? FREQUENTLY ASKED QUESTION

What Is the Difference Between Electricity and Electronics?

Electronics usually means that solid-state devices are used in the electrical circuits. Electricity as used in automotive applications usually means electrical current flow through resistance and loads without the use of diodes, transistors, or other electronic devices.

Therefore, diodes allow current flow only when current of the correct polarity is connected to the circuit.

- Diodes are used in alternators to control current flow in one direction, which changes the AC voltage generated into DC voltage.
- Diodes are also used in computer controls, relays, air-conditioning circuits, and many other circuits to prevent possible damage due to reverse current flows that may be generated within the circuit. ● **SEE FIGURE 14–7.**

"Burn In" to Be Sure

A common term heard in the electronic and computer industry is **burn in,** which means to operate an electronic device, such as a computer, for a period from several hours to several days.

Most electronic devices fail in infancy, or during the first few hours of operation. This early failure occurs if there is a manufacturing defect, especially at the P-N junction of any semiconductor device. The junction will usually fail after only a few operating cycles.

What does this information mean to the average person? When purchasing a personal or business computer, have the computer burned in before delivery. This step helps ensure that all of the circuits have survived infancy and that the chances of chip failure are greatly reduced. Purchasing sound or television equipment that has been on display may be a good value, because during its operation as a display model, the burn-in process has been completed. The automotive service technician should be aware that if a replacement electronic device fails shortly after installation, the problem may be a case of early electronic failure.

NOTE: Whenever there is a failure of a replacement part, the technician should always check for excessive voltage or heat to and around the problem component.

ZENER DIODES

CONSTRUCTION A **zener diode** is a specially constructed diode designed to operate with a reverse-bias current. Zener diodes were named in 1934 for their inventor, Clarence Melvin Zener, an American professor of physics.

OPERATION A zener diode acts as any diode in that it blocks reverse-bias current, but only up to a certain voltage. Above this certain voltage (called the *breakdown voltage* or the *zener region*), a zener diode will conduct current without damage to the diode. A zener diode is heavily doped, and the reverse-bias voltage does not harm the material. The voltage drop across a zener diode remains practically the same before and after the breakdown voltage, and this factor makes a zener diode perfect for voltage regulation. Zener diodes can be constructed for various breakdown voltages and can be used in a variety of automotive and electronic applications, especially for electronic voltage regulators used in the charging system. ● SEE FIGURE 14–8.

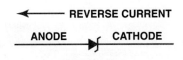

ZENER DIODE SYMBOL

FIGURE 14–8 A zener diode blocks current flow until a certain voltage is reached, then it permits current to flow.

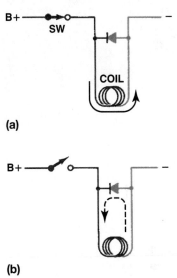

FIGURE 14–9 (a) Notice that when the coil is being energized, the diode is reverse biased and the current is blocked from passing through the diode. The current flows through the coil in the normal direction. (b) When the switch is opened, the magnetic field surrounding the coil collapses, producing a high-voltage surge in the reverse polarity of the applied voltage. This voltage surge forward biases the diode, and the surge is dissipated harmlessly back through the windings of the coil.

HIGH-VOLTAGE SPIKE PROTECTION

CLAMPING DIODES Diodes can be used as a high-voltage clamping device when the power (+) is connected to the cathode (−) of the diode. If a coil is pulsed on and off, a high-voltage spike is produced whenever the coil is turned off. To control and direct this possibly damaging high-voltage spike, a diode can be installed across the leads to the coil to redirect the high-voltage spike back through the coil windings to prevent possible damage to the rest of the vehicle's electrical or electronic circuits. A diode connected across the terminals of a coil to control voltage spikes is called a **clamping diode.** Clamping diodes can also be called **despiking** or **suppression diodes.** ● SEE FIGURE 14–9.

FIGURE 14–10 A diode connected to both terminals of the air-conditioning compressor clutch used to reduce the high-voltage spike that results when a coil (compressor clutch coil) is de-energized.

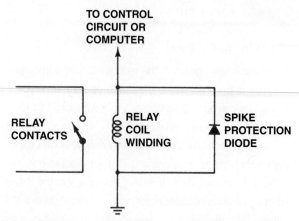

FIGURE 14–11 Spike protection diodes are commonly used in computer-controlled circuits to prevent damaging high-voltage surges that occur any time current flowing through a coil is stopped.

HIGH-VOLTAGE SPIKE PROTECTION (CONTINUED)

CLAMPING DIODE APPLICATION Diodes were first used on A/C compressor clutch coils at the same time electronic devices were first used. The diode was used to help prevent the high voltage spike generated inside the A/C clutch coil from damaging delicate to delicate electronic circuits anywhere in the vehicle's electrical system. ● **SEE FIGURE 14–10.**

Because most automotive circuits eventually are electrically connected to each other in parallel, a high-voltage surge anywhere in the vehicle could damage electronic components in other circuits.

The circuits most likely to be affected by the high-voltage surge, if the diode fails, are the circuits controlling the operation of the A/C compressor clutch and any component that uses a coil, such as those of the blower motor and climate control units.

Many relays are equipped with a diode to prevent a voltage spike when the contact points open and the magnetic field in the coil winding collapses. ● **SEE FIGURE 14–11.**

DESPIKING ZENER DIODES Zener diodes can also be used to control high-voltage spikes and keep them from damaging delicate electronic circuits. Zener diodes are most commonly used in electronic fuel-injection circuits that control the

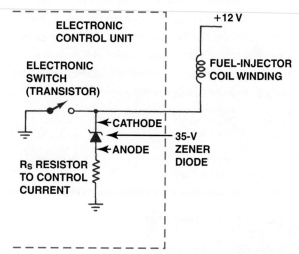

FIGURE 14–12 A zener diode is commonly used inside automotive computers to protect delicate electronic circuits from high-voltage spikes. A 35 volt zener diode will conduct any voltage spike resulting from the discharge of the fuel injector coil safely to ground through a current-limiting resistor in series with the zener diode.

firing of the injectors. If clamping diodes were used in parallel with the injection coil, the resulting clamping action would tend to delay the closing of the fuel injector nozzle. A zener diode is commonly used to clamp only the higher voltage portion of the resulting voltage spike without affecting the operation of the injector. ● **SEE FIGURE 14–12.**

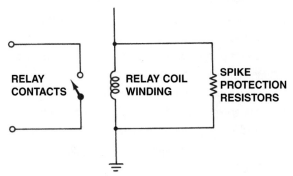

FIGURE 14–13 A despiking resistor is used in many automotive applications to help prevent harmful high-voltage surges from being created when the magnetic field surrounding a coil collapses when the coil circuit is opened.

DESPIKING RESISTORS
All coils must use some protection against high-voltage spikes that occur when the voltage is removed from any coil. Instead of a diode installed in parallel with the coil windings, a resistor can be used, called a **spike protection resistor.** ● **SEE FIGURE 14–13.**

Resistors are often preferred for two reasons.

Reason 1	Coils will usually fail when shorted rather than open, as this shorted condition results in greater current flow in the circuit. A diode installed in the reverse-bias direction cannot control this extra current, whereas a resistor in parallel can help reduce potentially damaging current flow if the coil becomes shorted.
Reason 2	The protective diode can also fail, and diodes usually fail by shorting before they blow open. If a diode becomes shorted, excessive current can flow through the coil circuit, perhaps causing damage. A resistor usually fails open and, therefore, even in failure could not in itself cause a problem.

Resistors on coils are often used in relays and in climate-control circuit solenoids to control vacuum to the various air management system doors as well as other electronically controlled applications.

DIODE RATINGS

SPECIFICATIONS Most diodes are rated according to the following:

- Maximum current flow in the forward-bias direction. Diodes are sized and rated according to the amount of current they are designed to handle in the forward-bias direction. This rating is normally from 1 to 5 amperes for most automotive applications.

- This rating of resistance to reverse-bias voltage is called the **peak inverse voltage (PIV)** rating, or the **peak reverse voltage (PRV)** rating. The peak inverse voltage is a specification for diodes. It is important that the service technician specifies and uses only a replacement diode that has the same or a higher rating than specified by the vehicle manufacturer for both amperage and PIV rating. Typical 1 A diodes use an industry numbering code that indicates the PIV rating. For example:

  1N 4001-50 V PIV

  1N 4002-100 V PIV

  1N 4003-200 V PIV (most commonly used)

  1N 4004-400 V PIV

  1N 4005-600 V PIV

- The "1N" means that the diode has one P-N junction. A higher rating diode can be used with no problems (except for slightly higher cost, even though the highest rated diode generally costs less than $1). Never substitute a *lower* rated diode than is specified.

DIODE VOLTAGE DROP The voltage drop across a diode is about the same voltage as that required to forward bias the diode. If the diode is made from germanium, the forward voltage is 0.3 to 0.5 volt. If the diode is made from silicon, the forward voltage is 0.5 to 0.7 volt.

NOTE: When diodes are tested using a digital multimeter, the meter will display the voltage drop across the P-N junction (about 0.5 to 0.7 volt) when the meter is set to the *diode-check* position.

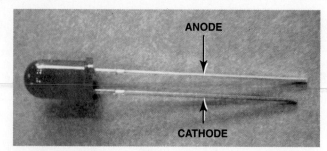

FIGURE 14–14 A typical light-emitting diode (LED). This particular LED is designed with a built-in resistor so that 12 volts DC may be applied directly to the leads without an external resistor. Normally a 300 to 500 ohm, 0.5 watt resistor is required to be attached in series with the LED, to control current flow to about 0.020 A (20 mA) or damage to the P-N junction may occur.

LIGHT-EMITTING DIODES

OPERATION All diodes radiate some energy during normal operation. Most diodes radiate heat because of the junction barrier voltage drop (typically 0.6 volt for silicon diodes). **Light emitting diode (LED)** radiate light when current flows through the diode in the forward-bias direction. ● **SEE FIGURE 14–14.**

The forward-bias voltage required for an LED ranges between 1.5 and 2.2 volts.

An LED will only light if the voltage at the anode (positive electrode) is at least 1.5 to 2.2 volts higher than the voltage at the cathode (negative electrode).

NEED FOR CURRENT LIMITING If an LED were connected across a 12 volt automotive battery, the LED would light brightly, but only for a second or two. Excessive current (amperes) that flows across the P-N junction of any electronic device can destroy the junction. A resistor *must* be connected in series with every diode (including LEDs) to control current flow across the P-N junction. This protection should include the following:

1. The value of the resistor should be from 300 to 500 ohms for each P-N junction. Commonly available resistors in this range include 470, 390, and 330 ohm resistors.

2. The resistors can be connected to either the anode or the cathode end. (Polarity of the resistor does not matter.) Current flows through the LED in series with the resistor, and the resistor will control the current flow through the LED regardless of its position in the circuit.

3. Resistors protecting diodes can be actual resistors or other current-limiting loads such as lamps or coils. With the current-limiting devices to control the current, the average LED will require about 20 to 30 milliamperes (mA), or 0.020 to 0.030 ampere.

PHOTODIODES

PURPOSE AND FUNCTION All semiconductor P-N junctions emit energy, mostly in the form of heat or light such as with an LED. In fact, if an LED is exposed to bright light, a voltage potential is established between the anode and the cathode. **Photodiodes** are specially constructed to respond to various wavelengths of light with a "window" built into the housing. ● **SEE FIGURE 14–15.**

Photodiodes are frequently used in steering wheel controls for transmitting tuning, volume, and other information from the steering wheel to the data link and the unit being controlled. If several photodiodes are placed on the steering column end and LEDs or phototransistors are placed on the steering wheel side, then data can be transmitted between the two moving points without the interference that could be caused by physical contact types of units.

CONSTRUCTION A photodiode is sensitive to light. When light energy strikes the diode, electrons are released and the diode will conduct in the forward-bias direction. (The light energy is used to overcome the barrier voltage.)

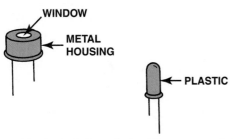

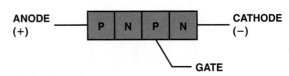

FIGURE 14–15 Typical photodiodes. They are usually built into a plastic housing so that the photodiode itself may not be visible.

FIGURE 14–18 Symbol and terminal identification of an SCR.

FIGURE 14–16 Symbol for a photodiode. The arrows represent light striking the P-N junction of the photodiode.

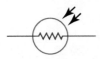

FIGURE 14–17 Either symbol may be used to represent a photoresistor.

The resistance across the photodiode decreases as the intensity of the light increases. This characteristic makes the photodiode a useful electronic device for controlling some automotive lighting systems such as automatic headlights. The symbol for a photodiode is shown in ● **FIGURE 14–16.**

PHOTORESISTORS

A **photoresistor** is a semiconductor material (usually cadmium sulfide) that changes resistance with the presence or absence of light.

Dark = High resistance

Light = Low resistance

Because resistance is reduced when the photoresistor is exposed to light, the photoresistor can be used to control headlight dimmer relays and for automotive headlights. ● **SEE FIGURE 14–17.**

SILICON-CONTROLLED RECTIFIERS

CONSTRUCTION A **silicon-controlled rectifier (SCR)** is commonly used in the electronic circuits of various automotive applications. An SCR is a semiconductor device that looks like two diodes connected end to end. ● **SEE FIGURE 14–18.**

If the anode is connected to a higher voltage source than the cathode in a circuit, no current will flow as would occur with a diode. If, however, a positive voltage source is connected to the gate of the SCR, then current can flow from anode to cathode with a typical voltage drop of 1.2 volts (double the voltage drop of a typical diode, at 0.6 volt).

Voltage applied to the gate is used to turn the SCR on. However, if the voltage source at the gate is shut off, the current will still continue to flow through the SCR until the source current is stopped.

USES OF AN SCR SCRs can be used to construct a circuit for a **center high-mounted stoplight (CHMSL).** If this third stoplight were wired into either the left- or the right-side brake light circuit, the CHMSL would also flash whenever the turn signals were used for the side that was connected to the CHMSL. When two SCRs are used, both brake lights must be activated to supply current to the CHMSL. The current to the CHMSL is shut off when both SCRs lose their power source (when the brake pedal is released, which stops the current flow to the brake lights). ● **SEE FIGURE 14–19.**

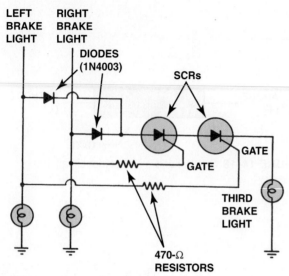

FIGURE 14–19 Wiring diagram for a center high-mounted stoplight (CHMSL) using SCRs.

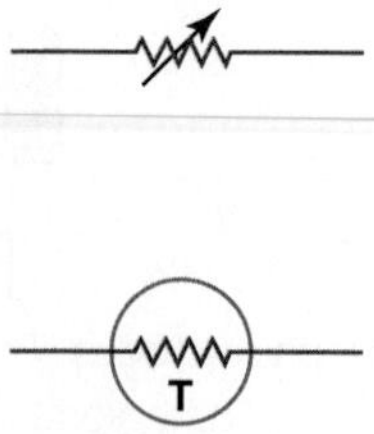

	COPPER WIRE	NTC THERMISTOR
Cold	Lower resistance	Higher resistance
Hot	Higher resistance	Lower resistance

CHART 14–1

The resistance changes opposite that of a copper wire with changes in temperature.

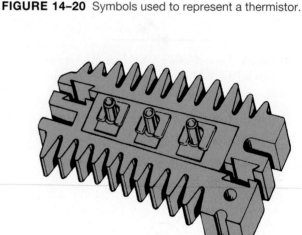

FIGURE 14–20 Symbols used to represent a thermistor.

FIGURE 14–21 This rectifier bridge contains six diodes; the three on each side are mounted in an aluminum-finned unit to help keep the diode cool during alternator operation.

THERMISTORS

CONSTRUCTION A **thermistor** is a semiconductor material such as silicon that has been doped to provide a given resistance. When the thermistor is heated, the electrons within the crystal gain energy and electrons are released. This means that a thermistor actually produces a small voltage when heated. If voltage is applied to a thermistor, its resistance decreases because the thermistor itself is acting as a current carrier rather than as a resistor at higher temperatures.

USES OF THERMISTORS A thermistor is commonly used as a temperature-sensing device for coolant temperature and intake manifold air temperature. Because thermistors operate in a manner opposite to that of a typical conductor, they are called **negative temperature coefficient (NTC)** thermistors; their resistance decreases as the temperature increases. ● **SEE CHART 14–1.**

Thermistor symbols are shown in ● **FIGURE 14–20.**

RECTIFIER BRIDGES

DEFINITION The word *rectify* means "to set straight"; therefore, a rectifier is an electronic device (such as a diode) used to convert a changing voltage into a straight or constant voltage. A **rectifier bridge** is a group of diodes that is used to change alternating current (AC) into direct current (DC). A rectifier bridge is used in alternators to rectify the AC voltage produced in the stator (stationary windings) of the alternator into DC voltage. These rectifier bridges contain six diodes: one pair of diodes (one positive and one negative) for each of the three stator windings. ● **SEE FIGURE 14–21.**

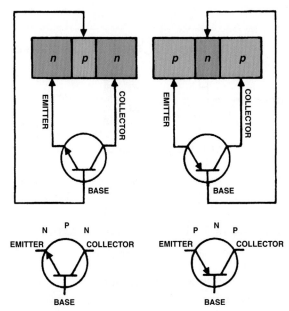

FIGURE 14–22 Basic transistor operation. A small current flowing through the base and emitter of the transistor turns on the transistor and permits a higher amperage current to flow from the collector and the emitter.

	RELAY	TRANSISTOR
Low-current circuit	Coil (terminals 85 and 86)	Base emitter
High-current circuit	Contacts terminals 30 and 87	Collector emitter

CHART 14–2

Comparison between the control (low-current) and high-current circuits of a transistor compared to a mechanical relay.

? FREQUENTLY ASKED QUESTION

Is a Transistor Similar to a Relay?

Yes, in many cases a transistor is similar to a relay. Both use a low current to control a higher current circuit. ● **SEE CHART 14–2.**

A relay can only be on or off. A transistor can provide a variable output if the base is supplied a variable current input.

TRANSISTORS

PURPOSE AND FUNCTION A **transistor** is a semiconductor device that can perform the following electrical functions.

1. Act as an electrical switch in a circuit
2. Act as an amplifier of current in a circuit
3. Regulate the current in a circuit

The word *transistor*, derived from the words *transfer* and *resistor*, is used to describe the transfer of current across a resistor. A transistor is made of three alternating sections or layers of P-type and N-type materials. This type of transistor is usually called a **bipolar transistor.**

CONSTRUCTION A transistor that has P-type material on each end, with N-type material in the center, is called a **PNP transistor.** Another type, with the exact opposite arrangement, is called an **NPN transistor.**

The material at one end of a transistor is called the **emitter** and the material at the other end is called the **collector.** The **base** is in the center and the voltage applied to the base is used to control current through a transistor.

TRANSISTOR SYMBOLS All transistor symbols contain an arrow indicating the emitter part of the transistor. The arrow points in the direction of current flow (conventional theory).

When an arrowhead appears in any semiconductor symbol, it stands for a P-N junction and it points from the P-type material toward the N-type material. The arrow on a transistor is always attached to the *emitter* side of the transistor. ● **SEE FIGURE 14–22.**

HOW A TRANSISTOR WORKS A transistor is similar to two back-to-back diodes that can conduct current in only one direction. As in a diode, N-type material can conduct electricity by means of its supply of free electrons, and P-type material conducts by means of its supply of positive holes.

A transistor will allow current flow if the electrical conditions allow it to switch on, in a manner similar to the working of an electromagnetic relay. The electrical conditions are determined, or switched, by means of the base, or *B*. The base will carry current only when the proper voltage and polarity are applied. The main circuit current flow travels through the other two parts of the transistor: the emitter *E* and the collector *C*. ● **SEE FIGURE 14–23.**

If the base current is turned off or on, the current flow from collector to emitter is turned off or on. The current controlling the base is called the **control current.** The control current must be high enough to switch the transistor on or off. (This control voltage, called the **threshold voltage,** must be above approximately

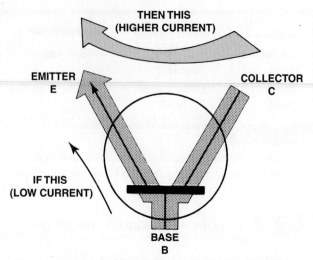

FIGURE 14–23 Basic transistor operation. A small current flowing through the base and emitter of the transistor turns on the transistor and permits a higher amperage current to flow from the collector and the emitter.

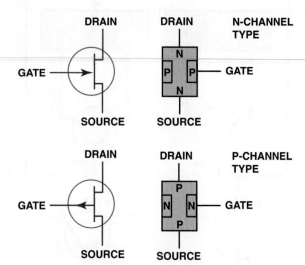

FIGURE 14–24 The three terminals of a field-effect transistor (FET) are called the source, gate, and drain.

? FREQUENTLY ASKED QUESTION

What Does the Arrow Mean on a Transistor Symbol?

The arrow on a transistor symbol is always on the emitter and points toward the N-type material. The arrow on a diode also points toward the N-type material. To know which type of transistor is being shown, note which direction the arrow points.

- PNP: pointing in
- NPN: not pointing in

TRANSISTORS (CONTINUED)

0.3 volt for germanium and 0.6 volt for silicon transistors.) This control current can also "throttle" or regulate the main circuit, in a manner similar to the operation of a water faucet.

HOW A TRANSISTOR AMPLIFIES A transistor can amplify a signal if the signal is strong enough to trigger the base of a transistor on and off. The resulting on-off current flow through the transistor can be connected to a higher powered electrical circuit. This results in a higher powered circuit being controlled by a lower powered circuit. This low-powered circuit's cycling is exactly duplicated in the higher powered circuit, and therefore any transistor can be used to amplify a signal. However, because some transistors are better than others for amplification, specialized types of transistors are used for each specialized circuit function.

FIELD-EFFECT TRANSISTORS

Field-effect transistors (FETs) have been used in most automotive applications since the mid-1980s. They use less electrical current and rely mostly on the strength of a small voltage signal to control the output. The parts of a typical FET include the *source, gate,* and *drain.* ● **SEE FIGURE 14–24.**

Many field-effect transistors are constructed of metal oxide semiconductor (MOS) materials, called **MOSFETs.** MOSFETs are highly sensitive to static electricity and can be easily damaged if exposed to excessive current or high-voltage surges (spikes). Most automotive electronic circuits use MOSFETs, which explains why it is vital for the service technician to use caution to avoid doing anything that could result in a high-voltage spike, and perhaps destroy an expensive computer module. Some vehicle manufacturers recommend that technicians wear an antistatic wristband when working with modules that contain MOSFETs. Always follow the vehicle manufacturer's instructions found in service information to avoid damaging electronic modules or circuits.

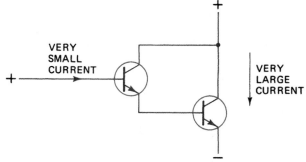

FIGURE 14–25 A Darlington pair consists of two transistors wired together, allowing for a very small current to control a larger current flow circuit.

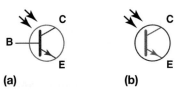

(a)   **(b)**

FIGURE 14–26 Symbols for a phototransistor. (a) This symbol uses the line for the base; (b) this symbol does not.

 FREQUENTLY ASKED QUESTION

What Is a Darlington Pair?

A **Darlington pair** consists of two transistors wired together. This arrangement permits a very small current flow to control a large current flow. The Darlington pair is named for Sidney Darlington, an American physicist for Bell Laboratories from 1929 to 1971. Darlington amplifier circuits are commonly used in electronic ignition systems, computer engine control circuits, and many other electronic applications. ● **SEE FIGURE 14–25.**

PHOTOTRANSISTORS

Similar in operation to a photodiode, a **phototransistor** uses light energy to turn on the base of a transistor. A phototransistor is an NPN transistor that has a large exposed base area to permit light to act as the control for the transistor. Therefore, a phototransistor may or may not have a base lead. If not, then it has only a collector and emitter lead. When the phototransistor is connected to a powered circuit, the light intensity is amplified by the gain of the transistor. Phototransistors, along with photo diodes, are frequently used in steering wheel controls. ● **SEE FIGURE 14–26.**

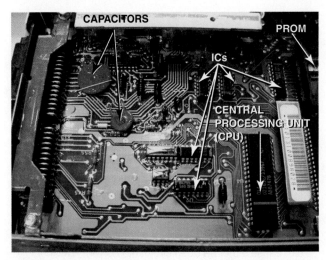

FIGURE 14–27 A typical automotive computer with the case removed to show all of the various electronic devices and integrated circuits (ICs). The CPU is an example of a DIP chip and the large red and orange devices are ceramic capacitors.

INTEGRATED CIRCUITS

PURPOSE AND FUNCTION Solid-state components are used in many electronic semiconductors and/or circuits. They are called "solid state" because they have no moving parts, just higher or lower voltage levels within the circuit. Discrete (individual) diodes, transistors, and other semiconductor devices were often used to construct early electronic ignition and electronic voltage regulators. Newer style electronic devices use the same components, but they are now combined (integrated) into one group of circuits, and are thus called an **integrated circuit (IC)**.

CONSTRUCTION Integrated circuits are usually encased in a plastic housing called a CHIP with two rows of inline pins. This arrangement is called the **dual inline pins (DIP)** chips. ● **SEE FIGURE 14–27.**

Therefore, most computer circuits are housed as an integrated circuit in a DIP chip.

HEAT SINK Heat sink is a term used to describe any area around an electronic component that, because of its shape or design, can conduct damaging heat away from electronic parts. Examples of heat sinks include the following:

1. Ribbed electronic ignition control units
2. Cooling slits and cooling fan attached to an alternator
3. Special heat-conducting grease under the electronic ignition module in General Motors HEI distributor ignition systems and other electronic systems

What Causes a Transistor or Diode to Blow?

Every automotive diode and transistor is designed to operate within certain voltage and amperage ranges for individual applications. For example, transistors used for switching are designed and constructed differently from transistors used for amplifying signals.

Because each electronic component is designed to operate satisfactorily for its particular application, any severe change in operating current (amperes), voltage, or heat can destroy the *junction.* This failure can cause either an open circuit (no current flows) or a short (current flows through the component all the time when the component should be blocking the current flow).

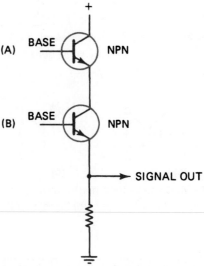

FIGURE 14–28 Typical transistor AND gate circuit using two transistors. The emitter is always the line with the arrow. Notice that both transistors must be turned on before there will be voltage present at the point labeled "signal out."

INTEGRATED CIRCUITS (CONTINUED)

Heat sinks are necessary to prevent damage to diodes, transistors, and other electronic components due to heat buildup. Excessive heat can damage the junction between the N-type and P-type materials used in diodes and transistors.

TRANSISTOR GATES

PURPOSE AND FUNCTION An understanding of the basic operation of electronic gates is important to understanding how computers work. A **gate** is an electronic circuit whose output depends on the location and voltage of two inputs.

CONSTRUCTION Whether a transistor is on or off depends on the voltage at the base of the transistor. If the voltage is at least a 0.6 volt difference from that of the emitter, the transistor is turned on. Most electronic and computer circuits use 5 volts as a power source. If two transistors are wired together, several different outputs can be received depending on how the two transistors are wired. ● **SEE FIGURE 14–28.**

OPERATION If the voltage at *A* is higher than that of the emitter, the top transistor is turned on; however, the bottom transistor is off unless the voltage at *B* is also higher. If both transistors are turned on, the output signal voltage will be high.

If only one of the two transistors is on, the output will be zero (off or no voltage). Because it requires both *A* and *B* to be on to result in a voltage output, this circuit is called an *AND gate.* In other words, both transistors have to be on before the gate opens and allows a voltage output. Other types of gates can be constructed using various connections to the two transistors. For example:

AND gate. Requires both transistors to be on to get an output.

OR gate. Requires either transistor to be on to get an output.

NAND (NOT-AND) gate. Output is on unless both transistors are on.

NOR (NOT-OR) gate. Output is on only when both transistors are off.

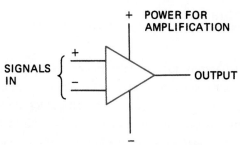

FIGURE 14–29 Symbol for an operational amplifier (op-amp).

What Are Logic Highs and Lows?

All computer circuits and most electronic circuits (such as gates) use various combinations of high and low voltages. High voltages are typically those above 5 volts, and low is generally considered zero (ground). However, high voltages do not *have* to begin at 5 volts. *High, or the number 1, to a computer is the presence of voltage above a certain level.* For example, a circuit could be constructed where any voltage higher than 3.8 volts would be considered high. *Low, or the number 0, to a computer is the absence of voltage or a voltage lower than a certain value.* For example, a voltage of 0.62 may be considered low. Various associated names and terms can be summarized.

- Logic low = Low voltage = Number 0 = Reference low
- Logic high = Higher voltage = Number 1 = Reference high

Gates represent logic circuits that can be constructed so that the output depends on the voltage (on or off; high or low) of the inputs to the bases of transistors. Their inputs can come from sensors or other circuits that monitor sensors, and their outputs can be used to operate an output device if amplified and controlled by other circuits. For example, the blower motor will be commanded on when the following events occur, to cause the control module to turn it on.

1. The ignition must be on (input).
2. The air conditioning is commanded on.
3. The engine coolant temperature is within a predetermined limit.

If all of these conditions are met, then the control module will command the blower motor on. If any of the input signals are incorrect, the control module will not be able to perform the correct command.

OPERATIONAL AMPLIFIERS

Operational amplifiers (op-amps) are used in circuits to control and amplify digital signals. Op-amps are frequently used for motor control in climate control systems (heating and air conditioning) airflow control door operation. Op-amps can provide the proper voltage polarity and current (amperes) to control the direction of permanent magnetic (PM) motors. The symbol for an op-amp is shown in ● **FIGURE 14–29.**

ELECTRONIC COMPONENT FAILURE CAUSES

Electronic components such as electronic ignition modules, electronic voltage regulators, onboard computers, and any other electronic circuit are generally quite reliable; however, failure can occur. Frequent causes of premature failure include the following:

- **Poor connections.** It has been estimated that most engine computers returned as defective have simply had poor connections at the wiring harness terminal ends. These faults are often intermittent and hard to find.

  NOTE: When cleaning electronic contacts, use a pencil eraser. This cleans the contacts without harming the thin, protective coating used on most electronic terminals.

- **Heat.** The operation and resistance of electronic components and circuits are affected by heat. Electronic components should be kept as cool as possible and never hotter than 260°F (127°C).

- **Voltage spikes.** A high-voltage spike can literally burn a hole through semiconductor material. The source of these high-voltage spikes is often the discharge of a coil without proper (or with defective) despiking protection.

A poor electrical connection at the battery or other major electrical connection can cause high-voltage spikes to occur, because the *entire wiring harness creates its own magnetic field*, similar to that formed around a coil. If the connection is loose and momentary loss of contact occurs, a high-voltage surge can occur through the entire electrical system. To help prevent this type of damage, ensure that all electrical connections, including grounds, are properly clean and tight.

CAUTION: One of the major causes of electronic failure occurs during jump starting a vehicle. Always check that the ignition switch is off on both vehicles when making the connection. Always double check that the correct polarity (+ to + and − to −) is being performed.

- **Excessive current.** All electronic circuits are designed to operate within a designated range of current (amperes). If a solenoid or relay is controlled by a computer circuit, the resistance of that solenoid or relay becomes part of that control circuit. If a coil winding inside the solenoid or relay becomes shorted, the resulting lower resistance will increase the current through the circuit. Even though individual components are used with current-limiting resistors in series, the coil winding resistance is also used as a current-control component in the circuit. If a computer fails, always measure the resistance across all computer-controlled relays and solenoids. The resistance should be within specifications (generally *over* 20 ohms) for each component that is computer controlled.

NOTE: Some computer-controlled solenoids are pulsed on and off rapidly. This type of solenoid is used in many electronically shifted transmissions. Their resistance is usually about half of the resistance of a simple on-off solenoid—usually between 10 and 15 ohms. Because the computer controls the on-time of the solenoid, the solenoid and its circuit control are called pulse-width modulated (PWM).

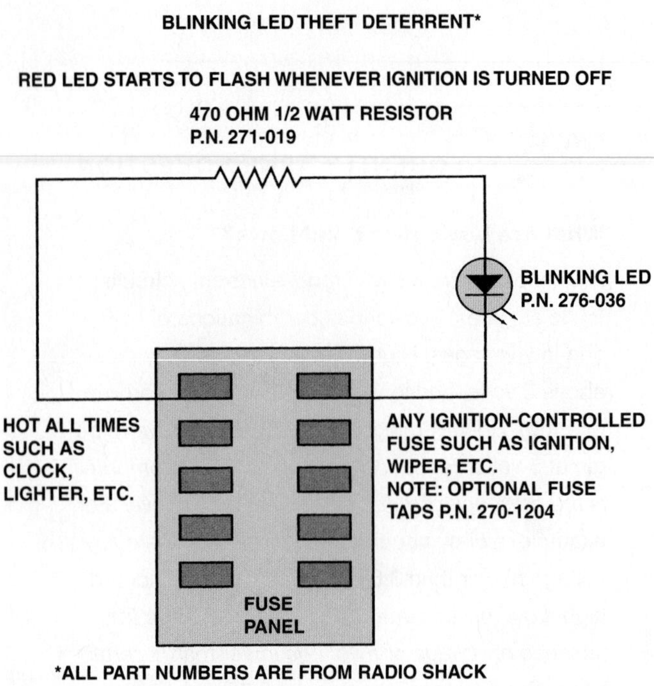

BLINKING LED THEFT DETERRENT*

RED LED STARTS TO FLASH WHENEVER IGNITION IS TURNED OFF

470 OHM 1/2 WATT RESISTOR
P.N. 271-019

BLINKING LED
P.N. 276-036

HOT ALL TIMES
SUCH AS
CLOCK,
LIGHTER, ETC.

ANY IGNITION-CONTROLLED
FUSE SUCH AS IGNITION,
WIPER, ETC.
NOTE: OPTIONAL FUSE
TAPS P.N. 270-1204

FUSE
PANEL

*ALL PART NUMBERS ARE FROM RADIO SHACK

FIGURE 14–30 Schematic for a blinking LED theft deterrent.

TECH TIP

Blinking LED Theft Deterrent

A blinking (flashing) LED consumes only about 5 milliamperes (5/1,000 of 1 ampere or 0.005 A). Most alarm systems use a blinking red LED to indicate that the system is armed. A fake alarm indicator is easy to make and install.

A 470 ohm, 0.5 watt resistor limits current flow to prevent battery drain. The positive terminal (anode) of the diode is connected to a fuse that is hot at all times, such as the cigarette lighter. The negative terminal (cathode) of the LED is connected to any ignition-controlled fuse. ● **SEE FIGURE 14–30.**

When the ignition is turned off, the power flows through the LED to ground and the LED flashes. To prevent distraction during driving, the LED goes out when the ignition is on. Therefore, this fake theft deterrent is "auto setting" and no other action is required to activate it when you leave your vehicle except to turn off the ignition and remove the key as usual.

HOW TO TEST DIODES AND TRANSISTORS

TESTERS   Diodes and transistors can be tested with an ohmmeter. The diode or transistor being tested must be disconnected from the circuit for the results to be meaningful.

- Use the *diode-check* position on a digital multimeter.

- In the diode-check position on a digital multimeter, the meter applies a higher voltage than when the ohms test function is selected.

- This slightly higher voltage (about 2 to 3 volts) is enough to forward bias a diode or the P-N junction of transistors.

DIODES   Using the diode test position, the meter applies a voltage. The display will show the voltage drop across the diode P-N junction. A good diode should give an over limit (OL) reading with the test leads attached to each lead of the diode in one way, and a voltage reading of 0.400 to 0.600 V when the leads are reversed. This reading is the voltage drop or the barrier voltage across the P-N junction of the diode.

1. A low-voltage reading with the meter leads attached both ways across a diode means that the diode is *shorted* and must be replaced.

2. An OL reading with the meter leads attached both ways across a diode means that the diode is *open* and must be replaced.

   ● **SEE FIGURE 14–31.**

TRANSISTORS   Using a digital meter set to the diode-check position, a good transistor should show a voltage drop of 0.400 to 0.600 volt between the following:

- The emitter (*E*) and the base (*B*) and between the base (*B*) and the collector (*C*) with a meter connected one way, and OL when the meter test leads are reversed.

- An OL reading (no continuity) in both directions when a transistor is tested between the emitter (*E*) and the collector (*C*) (A transistor tester can also be used if available.).

   ● **SEE FIGURE 14–32.**

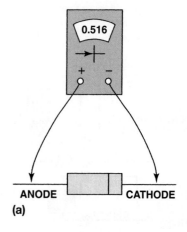
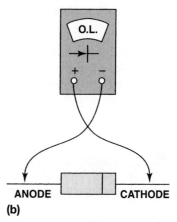

(a)

(b)

FIGURE 14–31   To check a diode, select "diode check" on a digital multimeter. The display will indicate the voltage drop (difference) between the meter leads. The meter itself applies a low-voltage signal (usually about 3 volts) and displays the difference on the display. (a) When the diode is forward biased, the meter should display a voltage between 0.500 and 0.700 V (500 to 700 mV). (b) When the meter leads are reversed, the meter should read OL (over limit) because the diode is reverse biased and blocking current flow.

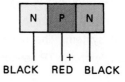

FIGURE 14–32   If the red (positive) lead of the ohmmeter (or a multimeter set to diode check) is touched to the center and the black (negative lead) touched to either end of the electrode, the meter should forward bias the P-N junction and indicate on the meter as low resistance. If the meter reads high resistance, reverse the meter leads, putting the black on the center lead and the red on either end lead. If the meter indicates low resistance, the transistor is a good PNP type. Check all P-N junctions in the same way.

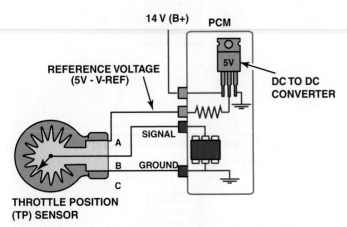

14 V (B+)   PCM

REFERENCE VOLTAGE
(5V - V-REF)

5V

DC TO DC
CONVERTER

SIGNAL

A

GROUND

B

C

THROTTLE POSITION
(TP) SENSOR

FIGURE 14–33 A DC to DC converter is built into most powertrain control modules (PCMs) and is used to supply the 5 volt reference called V-ref to many sensors used to control the internal combustion engine.

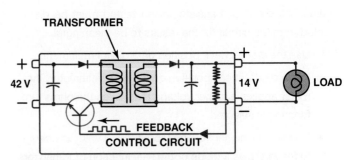

TRANSFORMER

42 V

14 V

LOAD

FEEDBACK
CONTROL CIRCUIT

FIGURE 14–34 This DC-DC converter is designed to convert 42 volts to 14 volts, to provide 14 V power to accessories on a hybrid electric vehicle operating with a 42 volt electrical system.

CONVERTERS AND INVERTERS

CONVERTERS DC to DC converters (usually written as DC-DC converter) are electronic devices used to transform DC voltage from one level of DC voltage to another higher or lower level. They are used to distribute various levels of DC voltage throughout a vehicle from a single power bus (or voltage source).

EXAMPLES OF USE One example of a DC-DC converter circuit is the circuit the PCM uses to convert 14 V to 5 V. The 5 volts is called the reference voltage, abbreviated V-ref, and is used to power many sensors in a computer-controlled engine management system. The schematic of a typical 5 volt V-ref interfacing with the TP sensor circuit is shown in
● **FIGURE 14–33.**

The PCM operates on 14 volts, using the principle of DC conversion to provide a constant 5 volts of sensor reference voltage to the TP sensor and others. The TP sensor demands little current, so the V-ref circuit is a low-power DC voltage converter in the range of 1 watt. The PCM uses a DC-DC converter, which is a small semiconductor device called a voltage regulator, and is designed to convert battery voltage to a constant 5 volts regardless of changes in the charging voltage.

Hybrid electric vehicles use DC-DC converters to provide higher or lower DC voltage levels and current requirements.

> ☠ **WARNING**
>
> Always follow the manufacturer's safety precautions for discharging capacitors in DC-DC converter circuits.

A high-power DC-DC converter schematic is shown in ● **FIGURE 14–34** and represents how a nonelectronic DC-DC converter works.

The central component of a converter is a transformer that physically isolates the input (42 V) from the output (14 V). The power transistor pulses the high-voltage coil of the transformer, and the resulting changing magnetic field induces a voltage in the coil windings of the lower voltage side of the transformer. The diodes and capacitors help control and limit the voltage and frequency of the circuit.

DC-DC CONVERTER CIRCUIT TESTING Usually a DC control voltage is used, which is supplied by a digital logic circuit to shift the voltage level to control the converter. A voltage test can indicate if the correct voltages are present when the converter is on and off.

Voltage measurements are usually specified to diagnose a DC-DC converter system. A digital multimeter (DMM) that is CAT III rated should be used.

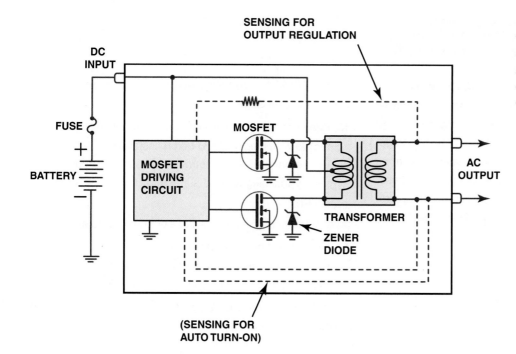

SENSING FOR
OUTPUT REGULATION

DC INPUT

FUSE

BATTERY

MOSFET DRIVING CIRCUIT

MOSFET

ZENER DIODE

TRANSFORMER

AC OUTPUT

(SENSING FOR AUTO TURN-ON)

FIGURE 14–35 A typical circuit for an inverter designed to change direct current from a battery to alternating current for use by the electric motors used in a hybrid electric vehicle.

1. Always follow the manufacturer's safety precautions when working with high-voltage circuits. These circuits are usually indicated by orange wiring.

2. Never tap into wires in a DC-DC converter circuit to access power for another circuit.

3. Never tap into wires in a DC-DC converter circuit to access a ground for another circuit.

4. Never block airflow to a DC-DC converter heat sink.

5. Never use a heat sink for a ground connection for a meter, scope, or accessory connection.

6. Never connect or disconnect a DC-DC converter while the converter is powered up.

7. Never connect a DC-DC converter to a larger voltage source than specified.

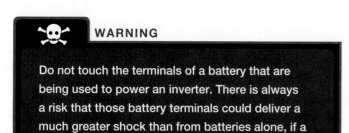

☠ **WARNING**

Do not touch the terminals of a battery that are being used to power an inverter. There is always a risk that those battery terminals could deliver a much greater shock than from batteries alone, if a motor or inverter should develop a fault.

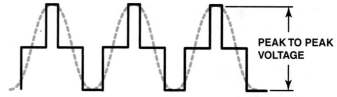

PEAK TO PEAK VOLTAGE

FIGURE 14–36 The switching (pulsing) MOSFETs create a waveform called a modified sine wave (solid lines) compared to a true sine wave (dotted lines).

INVERTERS An **inverter** is an electronic circuit that changes direct current (DC) into alternating current (AC). In most DC-AC inverters, the switching transistors, which are usually MOSFETs, are turned on alternately for short pulses. As a result, the transformer produces a modified sine wave output, rather than a true sine wave. ● **SEE FIGURE 14–35.**

The waveform produced by an inverter is not the perfect sine wave of household AC, but is rather more like a pulsing DC that reacts similar to sine wave AC in transformers and in induction motors. ● **SEE FIGURE 14–36.**

Inverters power AC motors. An inverter converts DC power to AC power at the required frequency and amplitude. The inverter consists of three half-bridge units, and the output voltage is mostly created by a pulse-width modulation (PWM) technique. The three-phase voltage waves are shifted 120 degrees to each other, to power each of the three phases.

ELECTROSTATIC DISCHARGE

DEFINITION **Electrostatic discharge (ESD)** is created when static charges build up on the human body when movement occurs. The friction of the clothing and the movement of shoes against carpet or vinyl floors cause a high voltage to build. Then when we touch a conductive material, such as a doorknob, the static charge is rapidly discharged. These charges, although just slightly painful to us, can cause severe damage to delicate electronic components. The following are typical static voltages.

- If you can feel it, it is at least 3,000 volts.
- If you can hear it, it is at least 5,000 volts.
- If you can see it, it is at least 10,000 volts.

Although these voltages seem high, the current, in amperes, is extremely low. However, sensitive electronic components such as vehicle computers, radios, and instrument panel clusters can be ruined if exposed to as little as 30 volts. This is a problem, because harm can occur to components at voltages lower than we can feel.

AVOIDING ESD To help prevent damage to components, follow these easy steps.

1. Keep the replacement electronic component in the protective wrapping until just before installation.
2. Before handling any electronic component, ground yourself by touching a metal surface to drain away any static charge.
3. Do not touch the terminals of electronic components.
4. If working in an area where touching terminals may occur, wear a static electrically grounding wrist strap available at most electronic parts stores, such as Radio Shack.

If these precautions are observed, ESD damage can be eliminated or reduced. Remember, just because the component works after being touched does not mean that damage has not occurred. Often, a section of the electronic component may be damaged, yet will not fail until several days or weeks later.

SUMMARY

1. Semiconductors are constructed by doping semiconductor materials such as silicon.
2. N-type and P-type materials can be combined to form diodes, transistors, SCRs, and computer chips.
3. Diodes can be used to direct and control current flow in circuits and to provide despiking protection.
4. Transistors are electronic relays that can also amplify signals.
5. All semiconductors can be damaged if subjected to excessive voltage, current, or heat.
6. Never touch the terminals of a computer or electronic device; static electricity can damage electronic components.

REVIEW QUESTIONS

1. What is the difference between P-type material and N-type material?
2. How can a diode be used to suppress high-voltage surges in automotive components or circuits containing a coil?
3. How does a transistor work?
4. To what precautions should all service technicians adhere, to avoid damage to electronic and computer circuits?

CHAPTER QUIZ

1. A semiconductor is a material _____.
   a. With fewer than four electrons in the outer orbit of its atoms
   b. With more than four electrons in the outer orbit of its atoms
   c. With exactly four electrons in the outer orbit of its atoms
   d. Determined by other factors besides the number of electrons

2. The arrow in a symbol for a semiconductor device _____.
   a. Points toward the negative
   b. Points away from the negative
   c. Is attached to the emitter on a transistor
   d. Both a and c

3. A diode installed across a coil with the cathode toward the battery positive is called a(n) _____.
   a. Clamping diode
   b. Forward-bias diode
   c. SCR
   d. Transistor

4. A transistor is controlled by the polarity and current at the _____.
   a. Collector
   b. Emitter
   c. Base
   d. Both a and b

5. A transistor can _____.
   a. Switch on and off
   b. Amplify
   c. Throttle
   d. All of the above

6. Clamping diodes _____.
   a. Are connected into a circuit with the positive (+) voltage source to the cathode and the negative (−) voltage to the anode
   b. Are also called despiking diodes
   c. Can suppress transient voltages
   d. All of the above

7. A zener diode is normally used for voltage regulation. A zener diode, however, can also be used for high-voltage spike protection if connected _____.
   a. Positive to anode, negative to cathode
   b. Positive to cathode, ground to anode
   c. Negative to anode, cathode to a resistor then to a lower voltage terminal
   d. Both a and c

8. The forward-bias voltage required for an LED is _____.
   a. 0.3 to 0.5 volt
   b. 0.5 to 0.7 volt
   c. 1.5 to 2.2 volts
   d. 4.5 to 5.1 volts

9. An LED can be used in a _____.
   a. Headlight
   b. Taillight
   c. Brake light
   d. All of the above

10. Another name for a ground is _____.
    a. Logic low
    b. Zero
    c. Reference low
    d. All of the above

chapter 15

COMPUTER FUNDAMENTALS

OBJECTIVES

After studying Chapter 15, the reader will be able to:

1. Prepare for ASE Electrical/Electronic Systems (A6) certification test content area "A" (General Electrical/Electronic Systems Diagnosis).
2. Explain the purpose and function of onboard computers.
3. List the various parts of an automotive computer.
4. List input sensors.
5. List output devices (actuators) controlled by the computer.

KEY TERMS

Actuator 208
Analog-to-digital (AD) converter 208
Baud rate 210
Binary system 209
Clock generator 210
Controller 207
CPU 209
Digital computer 209
Duty cycle 213
E²PROM 208
ECA 207
ECM 207
ECU 207
EEPROM 208
Engine mapping 210
Input 207
Input conditioning 207
KAM 208
Nonvolatile RAM 208
Output drivers 212
Powertrain control module (PCM) 207
PROM 208
PWM 213
RAM 208
ROM 208
SAE 207

COMPUTER FUNDAMENTALS

PURPOSE AND FUNCTION Modern automotive control systems consist of a network of electronic sensors, actuators, and computer modules designed to regulate the powertrain and vehicle support systems. The onboard automotive computer has many names. It may be called an **electronic control unit (ECU), electronic control module (ECM), electronic control assembly (ECA),** or a **controller,** depending on the manufacturer and the computer application. The **Society of Automotive Engineers (SAE)** bulletin J1930 standardizes the name as a **powertrain control module (PCM).** The PCM coordinates engine and transmission operation, processes data, maintains communications, and makes the control decisions needed to keep the vehicle operating. Not only is it capable of operating the engine and transmission, but it is also able to perform the following:

- Undergo self-tests (40% of the computing power is devoted to diagnosis)
- Set and store diagnostic trouble codes (DTCs)
- Communicate with the technician using a scan tool

VOLTAGE SIGNALS Automotive computers use voltage to send and receive information. Voltage is electrical pressure and does not flow through circuits, but voltage can be used as a signal. A computer converts input information or data into voltage signal combinations that represent number combinations. A computer processes the input voltage signals it receives by computing what they represent, and then delivering the data in computed or processed form.

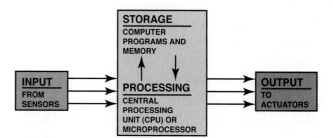

FIGURE 15–1 All computer systems perform four basic functions: input, processing, storage, and output.

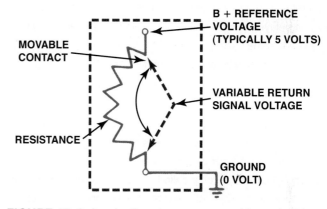

FIGURE 15–2 A potentiometer uses a movable contact to vary resistance and send an analog voltage right to the PCM.

COMPUTER FUNCTIONS

BASIC FUNCTIONS The operation of every computer can be divided into four basic functions. ● **SEE FIGURE 15–1.**

- **Input.** Receives voltage signals from sensors
- **Processing.** Performs mathematical calculations
- **Storage.** Includes short-term and long-term memory
- **Output.** Controls an output device by either turning it on or off

INPUT FUNCTIONS First, the computer receives a voltage signal (input) from an input device. **Input** is a signal from a device that can be as simple as a button or a switch on an instrument panel, or a sensor on an automotive engine. ● **SEE FIGURE 15–2** for a typical type of automotive sensor.

Vehicles use various mechanical, electrical, and magnetic sensors to measure factors such as vehicle speed, throttle position, engine RPM, air pressure, oxygen content of exhaust gas, airflow, engine coolant temperature, and status of electrical circuits (on-off). Each sensor transmits its information in the form of voltage signals. The computer receives these voltage signals, but before it can use them, the signals must undergo a process called **input conditioning.** This process includes amplifying voltage signals that are too small for the computer circuitry to handle. Input conditioners generally are located inside the computer, but a few sensors have their own input conditioning circuitry.

A digital computer changes the analog input signals (voltage) to digital bits (*bi*nary dig*its*) of information through an **analog-to-digital (AD) converter** circuit. The binary digital number is used by the computer in its calculations or logic networks. ● **SEE FIGURE 15–3.**

PROCESSING
The term *processing* is used to describe how input voltage signals received by a computer are handled through a series of electronic logic circuits maintained in its programmed instructions. These logic circuits change the input voltage signals, or data, into output voltage signals or commands.

STORAGE
Storage is the place where the program instructions for a computer are stored in electronic memory. Some programs may require that certain input data be stored for later reference or future processing. In others, output commands may be delayed or stored before they are transmitted to devices elsewhere in the system.

Computers have two types of memory.

1. Permanent memory is called **read-only memory (ROM)** because the computer can only read the contents; it cannot change the data stored in it. This data is retained even when power to the computer is shut off. Part of the ROM is built into the computer, and the rest is located in an integrated circuit (IC) chip called a **programmable read-only memory (PROM)** or calibration assembly. Many chips are erasable, meaning that the program can be changed. These chips are called erasable programmable read-only memory, or EPROM. Since the early 1990s, most programmable memory has been electronically erasable, meaning that the program in the chip can be reprogrammed by using a scan tool and the proper software. This computer reprogramming is usually called *reflashing*. These chips are electrically erasable programmable read-only memory, abbreviated **EEPROM** or **E²PROM.**

   All vehicles equipped with onboard diagnosis second generation, called OBD-II, are equipped with EEPROMs.

2. Temporary memory is called **random-access memory (RAM),** because the computer can write or store new data into it as directed by the computer program, as well as read the data already in it. Automotive computers use two types of RAM memory.

   ▪ Volatile RAM memory is lost whenever the ignition is turned off. However, a type of volatile RAM called **keep-alive memory (KAM)** can be wired directly

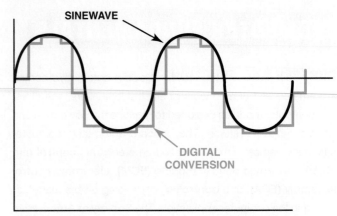

FIGURE 15–3 An AD converter changes analog (variable) voltage signals into digital signals that the PCM can process.

to battery power. This prevents its data from being erased when the ignition is turned off. One example of RAM and KAM is the loss of station settings in a programmable radio when the battery is disconnected. Because all the settings are stored in RAM, they have to be reset when the battery is reconnected. System trouble codes are commonly stored in RAM and can be erased by disconnecting the battery.

▪ **Nonvolatile RAM** memory can retain its information even when the battery is disconnected. One use for this type of RAM is the storage of odometer information in an electronic speedometer. The memory chip retains the mileage accumulated by the vehicle. When speedometer replacement is necessary, the odometer chip is removed and installed in the new speedometer unit. KAM is used primarily in conjunction with adaptive strategies.

OUTPUT FUNCTIONS
After the computer has processed the input signals, it sends voltage signals or commands to other devices in the system, such as system actuators. An **actuator** is an electrical or mechanical output device that converts electrical energy into a mechanical action, such as:

- Adjusting engine idle speed
- Operating fuel injectors
- Ignition timing control
- Altering suspension height

COMPUTER COMMUNICATION
A typical vehicle can have many computers, also called modules or controllers. Computers also can communicate with, and control, each other through their output and input functions. This means that the output signal from one computer system can be the input signal for another computer system through a data network. See Chapter 16 for details on network communications.

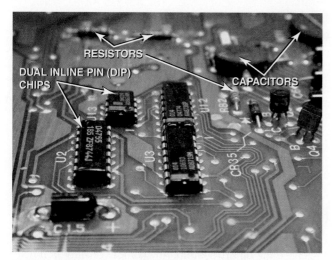

FIGURE 15–4 Many electronic components are used to construct a typical vehicle computer including chips, resistors, and capacitors.

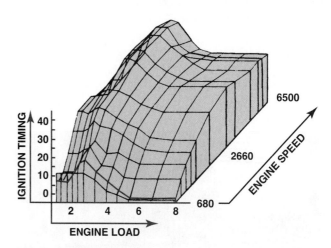

FIGURE 15–5 Typical engine map developed from testing and used by the vehicle computer to provide the optimum ignition timing for all engine speeds and load combinations.

DIGITAL COMPUTERS

PARTS OF A COMPUTER   The software consists of the programs and logic functions stored in the computer's circuitry. The hardware is the mechanical and electronic parts of a computer.

- **Central processing unit.** The microprocessor is the **central processing unit (CPU)** of a computer. Because it performs the essential mathematical operations and logic decisions that make up its processing function, the CPU can be considered the brain of a computer. Some computers use more than one microprocessor, called a coprocessor. The digital computer can process thousands of digital signals per second because its circuits are able to switch voltage signals on and off in billionths of a second. It is called a **digital computer** because it processes zeros and ones (digits) and needs to have any variable input signals, called analog inputs, converted to digital form before it can function. ● **SEE FIGURE 15–4.**

- **Computer memory.** Other integrated circuit (IC) devices store the computer operating program, system sensor input data, and system actuator output data—information that is necessary for CPU operation.

- **Computer programs.** By operating a vehicle on a dynamometer and manually adjusting the variable factors

such as speed, load, and spark timing, it is possible to determine the optimum output settings for the best driveability, economy, and emission control. This is called engine mapping. ● **SEE FIGURE 15–5.**

Engine mapping creates a three-dimensional performance graph that applies to a given vehicle and powertrain combination. Each combination is mapped in this manner to produce a PROM or EEPROM calibration. This allows an automaker to use one basic computer for all models.

Many older-vehicle computers used a single PROM that plugged into the computer.

NOTE: If the computer needs to be replaced, the PROM or calibration module must be removed from the defective unit and installed in the replacement computer. Since the mid-1990s, PCMs do not have removable calibration PROMs, and must be programmed or *flashed* using a scan tool before being put into service.

CLOCK RATES AND TIMING   The microprocessor receives sensor input voltage signals, processes them by using information from other memory units, and then sends voltage signals to the appropriate actuators. The microprocessor communicates by transmitting long strings of 0s and 1s in a language called binary code; but the microprocessor must have

FIGURE 15–6 The clock generator produces a series of pulses that are used by the microprocessor and other components to stay in step with each other at a steady rate.

? **FREQUENTLY ASKED QUESTION**

What Is a Binary System?

In a digital computer the signals are simple high-low, yes-no, on-off signals. The digital signal voltage is limited to two voltage levels: high voltage and low voltage. Since there is no stepped range of voltage or current in between, a digital binary signal is a "square wave." The signal is called "digital" because the on and off signals are processed by the computer as the digits or numbers 0 and 1. The number system containing only these two digits is called the **binary system.** Any number or letter from any number system or language alphabet can be translated into a combination of binary 0s and 1s for the digital computer. A digital computer changes the analog input signals (voltage) to digital bits (*binary digits*) of information through an analog-to-digital (AD) converter circuit. The binary digital number is used by the computer in its calculations or logic networks. Output signals usually are digital signals that turn system actuators on and off.

DIGITAL COMPUTERS (CONTINUED)

some way of knowing when one signal ends and another begins. That is the job of a crystal oscillator called a **clock generator.**
● **SEE FIGURE 15–6.**

The computer's crystal oscillator generates a steady stream of one-bit-long voltage pulses. Both the microprocessor and the memories monitor the clock pulses while they are communicating. Because they know how long each voltage pulse should be, they can distinguish between a 01 and a 0011. To complete the process, the input and output circuits also watch the clock pulses.

COMPUTER SPEEDS Not all computers operate at the same speed; some are faster than others. The speed at which a computer operates is specified by the cycle time, or clock speed, required to perform certain measurements. Cycle time or clock speed is measured in megahertz (4.7 MHz, 8 MHz, 15 MHz, 18 MHz, and 32 Hz, which is the clock speed of most vehicle computers today).

BAUD RATE The computer transmits bits of a serial data-stream at precise intervals. The computer's speed is called the **baud rate,** or bits per second. The term *baud* was named after J. M. Emile Baudot (1845–1903), a French telegraph operator who developed a five-bit-per-character code of telegraph. Just as mph helps in estimating the length of time required to travel a certain distance, the baud rate is useful in estimating how long a given computer will need to transmit a specified amount of data to another computer.

Automotive computers have evolved from a baud rate of 160 used in the early 1980s to a baud rate as high as 500,000 for some networks. The speed of data transmission is an important factor both in system operation and in system troubleshooting.

CONTROL MODULE LOCATIONS The computer hardware is all mounted on one or more circuit boards and installed in a metal case to help shield it from electromagnetic interference (EMI). The wiring harnesses that link the computer to sensors and actuators connect to multipin connectors or edge connectors on the circuit boards.

FIGURE 15–7 This powertrain control module (PCM) is located under the hood on this Chevrolet pickup truck.

FIGURE 15–8 This PCM on a Chrysler vehicle can only be seen by hoisting the vehicle, because it is located next to the radiator and in the airflow to help keep it cool.

Onboard computers range from single-function units that control a single operation to multifunction units that manage all of the separate (but linked) electronic systems in the vehicle. They vary in size from a small module to a notebook-size box. Most other engine computers are installed in the passenger compartment either under the instrument panel or in a side kick panel where they can be shielded from physical damage caused by temperature extremes, dirt, and vibration, or interference by the high currents and voltages of various underhood systems. ● **SEE FIGURES 15–7 AND 15–8.**

COMPUTER INPUT SENSORS

The vehicle computer uses signals (voltage levels) from the following sensors.

- **Engine speed (revolutions per minute, or RPM) sensor.** This signal comes from the primary ignition signal in the ignition control module (ICM) or directly from the crankshaft position (CKP) sensor.
- **Switches or buttons for accessory operation.** Many accessories use control buttons that signal the body computer to turn on or off an accessory such as the windshield wiper or heated seats.
- **Manifold absolute pressure (MAP) sensor.** This sensor detects engine load by using a signal from a sensor that measures the vacuum in the intake manifold.
- **Mass airflow (MAF) sensor.** This sensor measures the mass (weight and density) of the air flowing through the sensor and entering the engine.
- **Engine coolant temperature (ECT) sensor.** This sensor measures the temperature of the engine coolant. This is a sensor used for engine controls and for automatic air-conditioning control operation.
- **Oxygen sensor (O2S).** This sensor measures the oxygen in the exhaust stream. There are as many as four oxygen sensors in some vehicles.
- **Throttle position (TP) sensor.** This sensor measures the throttle opening and is used by the computer for engine control and the shift points of the automotive transmission/transaxle.
- **Vehicle speed (VS) sensor.** This sensor measures the vehicle speed using a sensor located at the output of the transmission/transaxle or by monitoring sensors at the wheel speed sensors. This sensor is used by the speedometer, cruise control, and airbag systems.

OUTPUT CONTROLS After the computer has processed the input signals, it sends voltage signals or commands to other devices in the system, as follows:

- **Operate actuators.** An actuator is an electrical or mechanical device that converts electrical energy into heat, light, or motion to control engine idle speed, suspension height, ignition timing, and other output devices.

- **Network communication.** Computers also can communicate with another computer system through a network.

A vehicle computer can do only two things.

1. Turn a device on.
2. Turn a device off.

Typical output devices include the following:

- **Fuel injectors.** The computer can vary the amount of time in milliseconds the injectors are held open, thereby controlling the amount of fuel supplied to the engine.

- **Blower motor control.** Many blower motors are controlled by the body computer by pulsing the current on and off to maintain the desired speed.

- **Transmission shifting.** The computer provides a ground to the shift solenoids and torque converter clutch (TCC) solenoid. The operation of the automatic transmission/ transaxle is optimized based on vehicle sensor information.

- **Idle speed control.** The computer can control the idle air control (IAC) or electronic throttle control (ETC) to maintain engine idle speed and to provide an increased idle speed as needed.

- **Evaporative emission control solenoids.** The computer can control the flow of gasoline fumes from the charcoal canister to the engine and seal off the system to perform a fuel system leak detection test as part of the OBD-II system requirements.

Most outputs work electrically in one of three ways:

1. Digital
2. Pulse-width modulated
3. Switched

Digital control is mostly used for computer communications and involves voltage signals that are transmitted and received in packets.

Pulse-width control allows a device, such as a blower motor, to be operated at variable speed by changing the amount of time electrical power is supplied to the device.

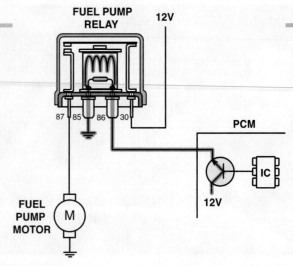

FIGURE 15–9 A typical output driver. In this case, the PCM applies voltage to the fuel pump relay coil to energize the fuel pump.

A switched output is an output that is either on or off. In many circuits, the PCM uses a relay to switch a device on or off, because the relay is a low-current device that can switch to a higher current device. Most computer circuits cannot handle high amounts of current. By using a relay circuit, the PCM provides the output control to the relay, which in turn provides the output control to the device.

The relay coil, which the PCM controls, typically draws less than 0.5 ampere. The device that the relay controls may draw 30 amperes or more. The PCM switches are actually transistors, and are often called **output drivers.** ● SEE FIGURE 15–9.

OUTPUT DRIVERS There are two basic types of output drivers.

1. **Low-side drivers.** The low-side drivers (LSDs) are transistors inside the computer that complete the ground path of relay coil. Ignition (key-on) voltage and battery voltage are supplied to the relay. The ground side of the relay coil is connected to the transistor inside the computer. In the example of a fuel pump relay, when the transistor turns "on," it will complete the ground for the relay coil, and the relay will then complete the power circuit between the battery power and the fuel pump. A relatively low current flows through the relay coil and transistor that is inside the computer. This causes the relay to switch and provides the fuel pump with battery voltage. The majority of switched outputs have typically been low-side drivers. ● SEE FIGURE 15–10.

Low-side drivers can often perform a diagnostic circuit check by monitoring the voltage from the relay to check

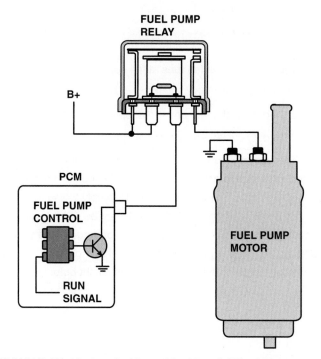

FIGURE 15–10 A typical low-side driver (LSD) which uses a control module to control the ground side of the relay coil.

that the control circuit for the relay is complete. A low-side driver, however, cannot detect a short-to-ground.

2. **High-side drivers.** The high-side drivers (HSDs) control the power side of the circuit. In these applications when the transistor is switched on, voltage is applied to the device. A ground has been provided to the device so when the high-side driver switches, the device will be energized. In some applications, high-side drivers are used instead of low-side drivers to provide better circuit protection. General Motors vehicles have used a high-side driver to control the fuel pump relay instead of a low-side driver. In the event of an accident, should the circuit to the fuel pump relay become grounded, a high-side driver would cause a short circuit, which would cause the fuel pump relay to de-energize. High-side drivers inside modules can detect electrical faults such as a lack of continuity when the circuit is not energized. ● **SEE FIGURE 15–11.**

PULSE-WIDTH MODULATION
Pulse-width modulation (PWM) is a method of controlling an output using a digital signal. Instead of just turning devices on or off, the computer can control the amount of on-time. For example, a solenoid could be a PWM device. If, for example, a vacuum solenoid is controlled by a switched driver, switching either on or off would mean that either full vacuum would flow through the solenoid or no vacuum would flow through the solenoid. However, to

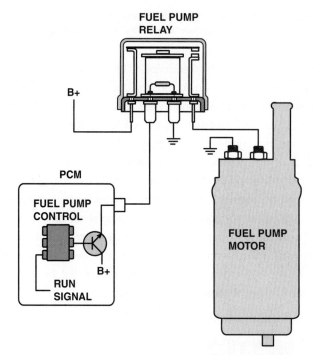

FIGURE 15–11 A typical module-controlled high-side driver (HSD) where the module itself supplies the electrical power to the device. The logic circuit inside the module can detect circuit faults including continuity of the circuit and if there is a short-to-ground in the circuit being controlled.

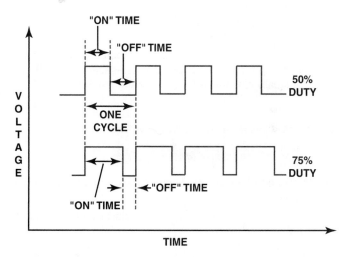

FIGURE 15–12 Both the top and bottom pattern have the same frequency. However, the amount of on-time varies. Duty cycle is the percentage of the time during a cycle that the signal is turned on.

control the amount of vacuum that flows through the solenoid, pulse-width modulation could be used. A PWM signal is a digital signal, usually 0 volt and 12 volts, which is cycling at a fixed frequency. Varying the length of time that the signal is on provides a signal that can vary the on- and off-time of an output. The ratio of on-time relative to the period of the cycle is referred to as **duty cycle.** ● **SEE FIGURE 15–12.**

Depending on the frequency of the signal, which is usually fixed, this signal would turn the device on and off a fixed number of times per second. When, for example, the voltage is high (12 volts) 90% of the time and low (0 volt) the other 10% of the time, the signal has a 90% duty cycle. In other words, if this signal were applied to the vacuum solenoid, the solenoid would be on 90% of the time. This would allow more vacuum to flow through the solenoid. The computer has the ability to vary this on- and off-time or pulse-width modulation at any rate between 0% and 100%. A good example of pulse-width modulation is the cooling fan speed control. The speed of the cooling fan is controlled by varying the amount of on-time that the battery voltage is applied to the cooling fan motor.

- 100% duty cycle: fan runs at full speed
- 75% duty cycle: fan runs at 3/4 speed
- 50% duty cycle: fan runs at 1/2 speed
- 25% duty cycle: fan runs at 1/4 speed

The use of PWM, therefore, results in precise control of an output device to achieve the amount of cooling needed and conserve electrical energy compared to simply timing the cooling fan on high when needed. PWM may be used to control vacuum through a solenoid, the amount of purge of the evaporative purge solenoid, the speed of a fuel pump motor, control of a linear motor, or even the intensity of a light bulb.

SUMMARY

1. The Society of Automotive Engineers (SAE) standard J1930 specifies that the term powertrain control module (PCM) be used for the computer that controls the engine and transmission in a vehicle.
2. The four basic computer functions are input, processing, storage, and output.
3. Types of memory include read-only memory (ROM) which can be programmable (PROM), erasable (EPROM), or electrically erasable (EEPROM); RAM; and KAM.
4. Computer input sensors include engine speed (RPM), MAP, MAF, ECT, O2S, TP, and VS.
5. A computer can only turn a device on or turn a device off, but it can do either operation rapidly.

REVIEW QUESTIONS

1. What part of the vehicle computer is considered to be the brain?
2. What is the difference between volatile and nonvolatile RAM?
3. What are the four input sensors?
4. What are the four output devices?

CHAPTER QUIZ

1. What unit of electricity is used as a signal for a computer?
   a. Volt
   b. Ohm
   c. Ampere
   d. Watt
2. The four basic computer functions include _____.
   a. Writing, processing, printing, and remembering
   b. Input, processing, storage, and output
   c. Data gathering, processing, output, and evaluation
   d. Sensing, calculating, actuating, and processing
3. All OBD-II vehicles use what type of read-only memory?
   a. ROM
   b. PROM
   c. EPROM
   d. EEPROM
4. The "brain" of the computer is the _____.
   a. PROM
   b. RAM
   c. CPU
   d. AD converter

5. Computer speed is measured in _____.
   a. Baud rate
   b. Clock speed (Hz)
   c. Voltage
   d. Bytes

6. Which item is a computer input sensor?
   a. RPM
   b. Throttle position
   c. Engine coolant temperature
   d. All of the above

7. Which item is a computer output device?
   a. Fuel injector
   b. Transmission shift solenoid
   c. Evaporative emission control solenoid
   d. All of the above

8. The SAE term for the vehicle computer is _____.
   a. PCM
   b. ECM
   c. ECA
   d. Controller

9. What two things can a vehicle computer actually perform (output)?
   a. Store and process information
   b. Turn something on or turn something off
   c. Calculate and vary temperature
   d. Control fuel and timing only

10. Analog signals from sensors are changed to digital signals for processing by the computer through which type of circuit?
    a. Digital
    b. Analog
    c. Analog-to-digital converter
    d. PROM

chapter 16

CAN AND NETWORK COMMUNICATIONS

OBJECTIVES

After studying Chapter 16, the reader will be able to:

1. Prepare for ASE Electrical/Electronic Systems (A6) certification test content area "A" (General Electrical/Electronic Systems Diagnosis).

2. Describe the types of networks and serial communications used on vehicles.

3. Discuss how the networks connect to the data link connector and to other modules.

4. Explain how to diagnose module communication faults.

KEY TERMS

Breakout box (BOB) 228
BUS 218
CAN 221
Class 2 222
E & C 221
GMLAN 222
Keyword 222
Multiplexing 218
Network 218
Node 217
Plastic optical fiber (POF) 228
Programmable controller interface (PCI) 224
Protocol 221
Serial communications interface (SCI) 225
Serial data 218
Splice pack 218
Standard corporate protocol (SCP) 223
State of health (SOH) 230
SWCAN 222
Terminating resistors 230
Twisted pair 218
UART 221
UART-based protocol (UBP) 224

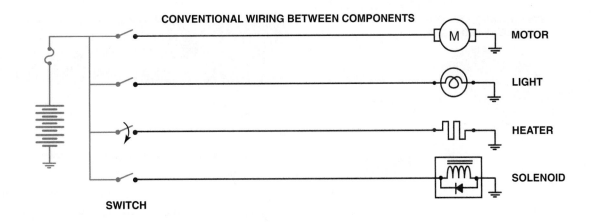

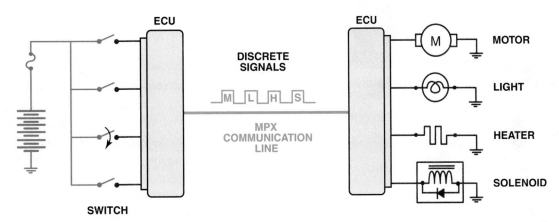

FIGURE 16-1 Module communications makes controlling multiple electrical devices and accessories easier by utilizing simple low-current switches to signal another module, which does the actual switching of the current to the device.

MODULE COMMUNICATIONS AND NETWORKS

NEED FOR NETWORK Since the 1990s, vehicles have used modules to control the operation of most electrical components. A typical vehicle will have 10 or more modules and they communicate with each other over data lines or hard wiring, depending on the application.

ADVANTAGES Most modules are connected together in a network because of the following advantages.

- A decreased number of wires are needed, thereby saving weight and cost, as well as helping with installation at the factory and decreased complexity, making servicing easier.
- Common sensor data can be shared with those modules that may need the information, such as vehicle speed, outside air temperature, and engine coolant temperature.
- **SEE FIGURE 16-1.**

NETWORK FUNDAMENTALS

MODULES AND NODES Each module, also called a **node,** must communicate to other modules. For example, if the driver depresses the window-down switch, the power window switch sends a window-down message to the body control module. The body control module then sends the request to the driver's side window module. This module is responsible for actually performing the task by supplying power and ground to the window lift motor in the current polarity to cause the window to go down. The module also contains a circuit that monitors the current flow through the motor and will stop and/or reverse the window motor if an obstruction causes the window motor to draw more than the normal amount of current.

TYPES OF COMMUNICATION The types of communications include the following:

- **Differential.** In the differential form of BUS communication, a difference in voltage is applied to two wires, which

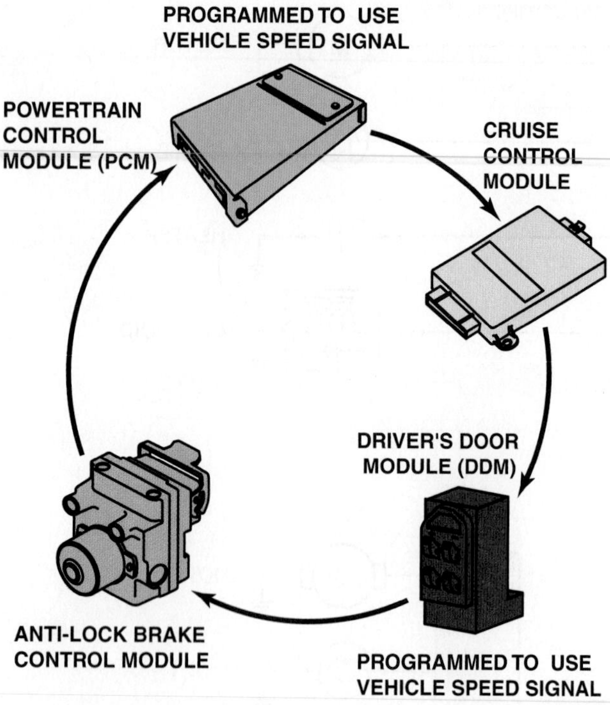

PROGRAMMED TO USE
VEHICLE SPEED SIGNAL

POWERTRAIN
CONTROL
MODULE (PCM)

CRUISE
CONTROL
MODULE

DRIVER'S DOOR
MODULE (DDM)

ANTI-LOCK BRAKE
CONTROL MODULE

PROGRAMMED TO USE
VEHICLE SPEED SIGNAL

FIGURE 16–2 A network allows all modules to communicate with other modules.

NETWORK FUNDAMENTALS (CONTINUED)

are twisted to help reduce electromagnetic interference (EMI). These transfer wires are called a **twisted pair.**

- **Parallel.** In the parallel type of BUS communication, the send and receive signals are on different wires.

- **Serial data.** The **serial data** is data transmitted by a series of rapidly changing voltage signals pulsed from low to high or from high to low.

- **Multiplexing.** The process of **multiplexing** involves the sending of multiple signals of information at the same time over a signal wire and then separating the signals at the receiving end.

This system of intercommunication of computers or processors is referred to as a **network.** ● SEE FIGURE 16–2.

By connecting the computers together on a communications network, they can easily share information back and forth. This multiplexing has the following advantages.

- Elimination of redundant sensors and dedicated wiring for these multiple sensors

- Reduction of the number of wires, connectors, and circuits

- Addition of more features and option content to new vehicles

- Weight reduction due to fewer components, wires, and connectors, thereby increasing fuel economy

- Changeable features with software upgrades versus component replacement

MODULE COMMUNICATIONS CONFIGURATION

The three most common types of networks used on vehicles include:

1. **Ring link networks.** In a ring-type network, all modules are connected to each other by a serial data line (in a line) until all are connected in a ring. ● SEE FIGURE 16–3.

2. **Star link networks.** In a star link network, a serial data line attaches to each module and then each is connected to a central point. This central point is called a **splice pack**, abbreviated SP such as in "SP 306." The splice pack uses a bar to splice all of the serial lines together. Some GM vehicles use two or more splice packs to tie the modules together. When more than one splice pack is used, a serial data line connects one splice pack to the others. In most applications, the BUS bar used in each splice pack can be removed. When the BUS bar is removed, a special tool (J 42236) can be installed in place of the removed BUS bar. Using this tool, the serial data line for each module can be isolated and tested for a possible problem. Using the special tool at the splice pack makes diagnosing this type of network easier than many others. ● SEE FIGURE 16–4.

3. **Ring/star hybrid.** In a ring/star network, the modules are connected using both types of network configurations. Check service information (SI) for details on how this network is connected on the vehicle being diagnosed and always follow the recommended diagnostic steps.

? **FREQUENTLY ASKED QUESTION**

What Is a BUS?

A **BUS** is a term used to describe a communications network. Therefore, there are *connections to the BUS* and *BUS communications*, both of which refer to digital messages being transmitted among electronic modules or computers.

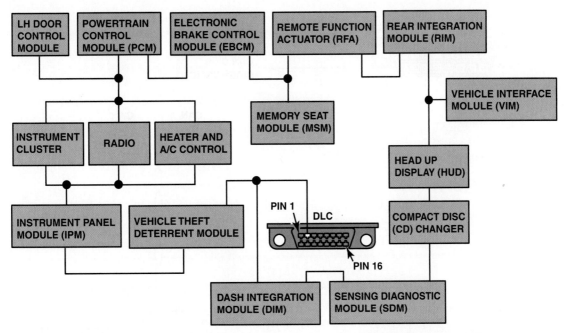

FIGURE 16–3 A ring link network reduces the number of wires it takes to interconnect all of the modules.

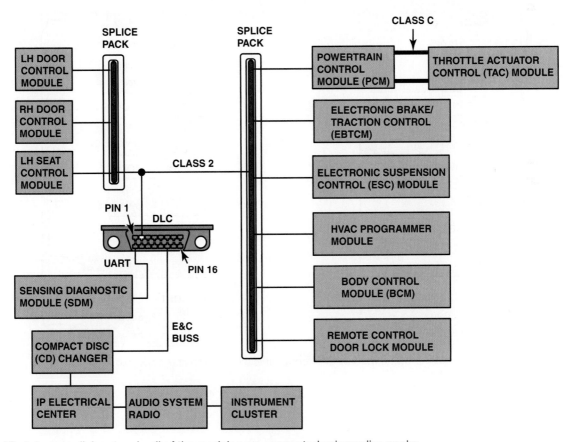

FIGURE 16–4 In a star link network, all of the modules are connected using splice packs.

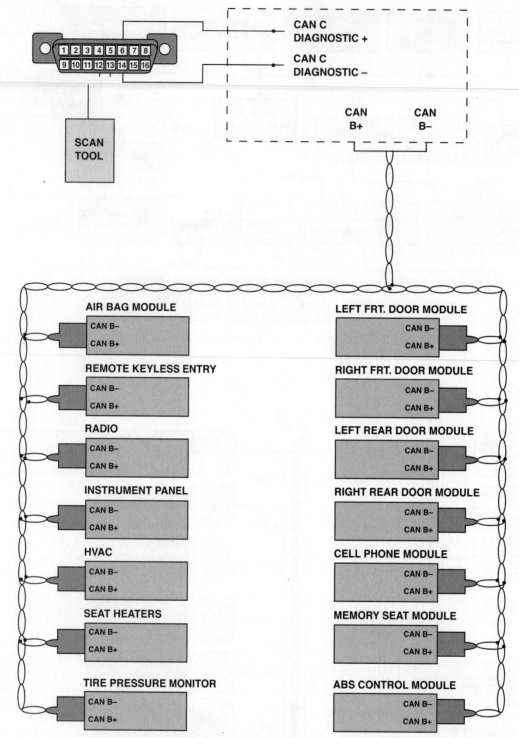

FIGURE 16–5 A typical BUS system showing module CAN communications and twisted pairs of wire.

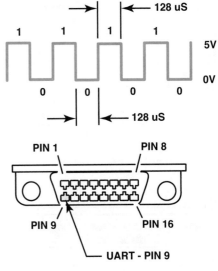

FIGURE 16-6 UART serial data master control module is connected to the data link connector at pin 9.

NETWORK COMMUNICATIONS CLASSIFICATIONS

The Society of Automotive Engineers (SAE) standards include the following three categories of in-vehicle network communications.

CLASS A Low-speed networks, meaning less than 10,000 bits per second (bps, or 10 Kbs), are generally used for trip computers, entertainment, and other convenience features.

CLASS B Medium-speed networks, meaning 10,000 to 125,000 bps (10 to 125 Kbs), are generally used for information transfer among modules, such as instrument clusters, temperature sensor data, and other general uses.

CLASS C High-speed networks, meaning 125,000 to 1,000,000 bps, are generally used for real-time powertrain and vehicle dynamic control. High-speed BUS communication systems now use a **controller area network (CAN).** ● SEE FIGURE 16-5.

GENERAL MOTORS COMMUNICATIONS PROTOCOLS

UART General Motors and others use UART communications for some electronic modules or systems. **UART** is a serial data communications protocol that stands for **universal asynchronous receive and transmit.** UART uses a master control module connected to one or more remote modules. The master control module is used to control message traffic on the data line by poling all of the other UART modules. The remote modules send a response message back to the master module.

UART uses a fixed pulse-width switching between 0 and 5 V. The UART data BUS operates at a baud rate of 8,192 bps. ● **SEE FIGURE 16-6.**

ENTERTAINMENT AND COMFORT COMMUNICATION

The GM **entertainment and comfort (E & C)** serial data is similar to UART, but uses a 0 to 12 V toggle. Like UART, the E & C serial data uses a master control module connected to other remote modules, which could include the following:

- Compact disc (CD) player
- Instrument panel (IP) electrical center
- Audio system (radio)

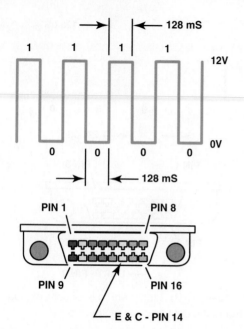

FIGURE 16–7 The E & C serial data is connected to the data link connector (DLC) at pin 14.

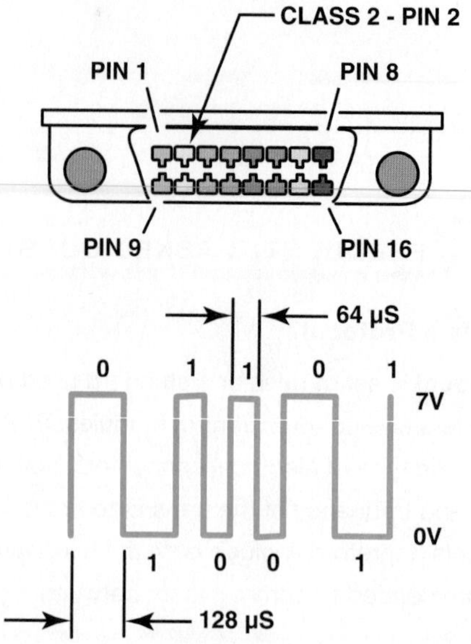

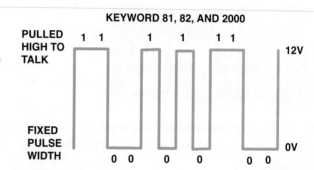

FIGURE 16–8 Class 2 serial data communication is accessible at the data link connector (DLC) at pin 2.

GENERAL MOTORS COMMUNICATIONS PROTOCOLS (CONTINUED)

- Heating, ventilation, and air-conditioning (HVAC) programmer and control head
- Steering wheel controls
  - ● **SEE FIGURE 16–7.**

CLASS 2 COMMUNICATIONS **Class 2** is a serial communications system that operates by toggling between 0 and 7 V at a transfer rate of 10.4 Kbs. Class 2 is used for most high-speed communications between the powertrain control module (PCM) and other control modules, plus to the scan tool. Class 2 is the primary high-speed serial communications system used by GMCAN (CAN). ● **SEE FIGURE 16–8.**

KEYWORD COMMUNICATION **Keyword** 81, 82, and 2000 serial data are also used for some module-to-module communication on GM vehicles. Keyword data BUS signals are toggled from 0 to 12 V when communicating. The voltage or the datastream is zero volt when not communicating. Keyword serial communication is used by the seat heater module and others, but is not connected to the data link connector (DLC). ● **SEE FIGURE 16–9.**

GMLAN General Motors, like all vehicle manufacturers, must use high-speed serial data to communicate with scan tools on all vehicles effective with the 2008 model year. As mentioned, the

FIGURE 16–9 Keyword 82 operates at a rate of 8,192 bps, similar to UART, and keyword 2000 operates at a baud rate of 10,400 bps (the same as a Class 2 communicator).

standard is called controller area network (CAN), which General Motors calls **GMLAN,** which stands for **GM local area network.**

General Motors uses two versions of GMLAN.

- **Low-speed GMLAN.** The low-speed version is used for driver-controlled functions such as power windows and door locks. The baud rate for low-speed GMLAN is 33,300 bps. The GMLAN low-speed serial data is not connected directly to the data link connector and uses one wire. The voltage toggles between 0 and 5 V after an initial 12 V spike, which indicates to the modules to turn on or wake up and listen for data on the line. Low-speed GMLAN is also known as **single-wire CAN,** or **SWCAN.**

- **High-speed GMLAN.** The baud rate is almost real time at 500 Kbs. This serial data method uses a two-twisted-wire circuit which is connected to the data link connector on pins 6 and 14. ● **SEE FIGURE 16–10.**

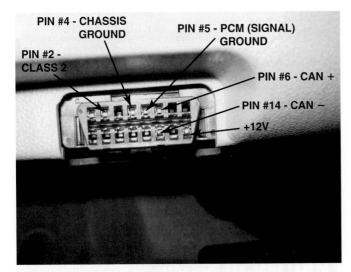

FIGURE 16–10 GMLAN uses pins at terminals 6 and 14.

FIGURE 16–12 A CANDi module will flash the green LED rapidly if communication is detected.

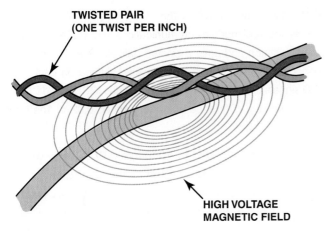

FIGURE 16–11 A twisted pair is used by several different network communications protocols to reduce interference that can be induced in the wiring from nearby electromagnetic sources.

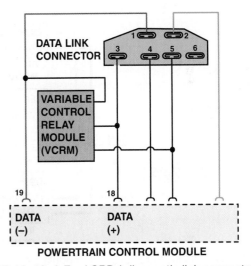

FIGURE 16–13 A Ford OBD-I diagnostic link connector showing that SCP communication uses terminals in cavities 1 (upper left) and 3 (lower left).

FREQUENTLY ASKED QUESTION

Why Is a Twisted Pair Used?

A twisted pair is where two wires are twisted to prevent electromagnetic radiation from affecting the signals passing through the wires. By twisting the two wires about once every inch (9 to 16 times per foot), the interference is canceled by the adjacent wire. ● **SEE FIGURE 16–11.**

A CANDi (CAN diagnostic interface) module is required to be used with the Tech 2 to be able to connect a GM vehicle equipped with GMLAN. ● **SEE FIGURE 16–12.**

FORD NETWORK COMMUNICATIONS PROTOCOLS

STANDARD CORPORATE PROTOCOL Only a few Fords had scan tool data accessible through the OBD-I data link connector. To identify an OBD-I (1988–1995) on a Ford vehicle that is equipped with **standard corporate protocol (SCP)** and be able to communicate through a scan tool, look for terminals in cavities 1 and 3 of the DLC. ● **SEE FIGURE 16–13.**

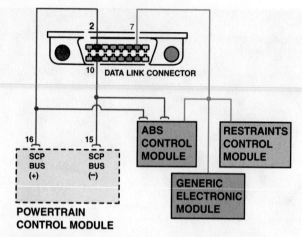

FIGURE 16–14 A scan tool can be used to check communications with the SCP BUS through terminals 2 and 10 and to the other modules connected to terminal 7 of the data link connector (DLC).

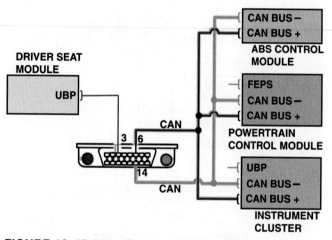

FIGURE 16–15 Many Fords use UBP module communications along with CAN.

FORD NETWORK COMMUNICATIONS PROTOCOLS (CONTINUED)

SCP uses the J-1850 protocol and is active with the key on. The SCP signal is from 4 V negative to 4.3 V positive, and a scan tool does not have to be connected for the signal to be detected on the terminals. OBD-II (EECV) Ford vehicles use terminals 2 (positive) and 10 (negative) of the 16 pin data link connector (DLC) for network communication, using the SCP module communications.

UART-BASED PROTOCOL Newer Fords use the CAN for scan tool diagnosis, but still retain SCP and **UART-based protocol (UBP)** for some modules. ● **SEE FIGURES 16–14 AND 16–15.**

? **FREQUENTLY ASKED QUESTION**

What Are U Codes?

The U diagnostic trouble codes were at first "undefined" but are now network-related codes. Use the network codes to help pinpoint the circuit or module that is not working correctly.

CHRYSLER COMMUNICATIONS PROTOCOLS

CCD Since the late 1980s, the CCD multiplex network is used for scan tool and module communications. It is a differential-type communication and uses a twisted pair of wires. The modules connected to the network apply a bias voltage on each wire. CCD signals are divided into plus and minus (CCD+ and CCD−) and the voltage difference does not exceed 0.02 V. The baud rate is 7,812.5 bps.

NOTE: The "collision" in CCD-type BUS communications refers to the program that avoids conflicts of information exchange within the BUS, and does not refer to airbags or other accident-related circuits of the vehicle.

The circuit is active without a scan tool command. ● **SEE FIGURE 16–16.**

The modules on the CCD BUS apply a bias voltage on each wire by using termination resistors. ● **SEE FIGURE 16–17.**

The difference in voltage between CCD+ and CCD− is less than 20 mV. For example, using a digital meter with the black meter lead attached to ground and the red meter lead attached at the data link connector (DLC), a normal reading could include:

- Terminal 3 = 2.45 volts
- Terminal 11 = 2.47 volts

This is an acceptable reading because the readings are 20 mV (0.020 volt) of each other. If both had been exactly 2.5 volts, then this could indicate that the two data lines are shorted together. The module providing the bias voltage is usually the body control module on passenger cars and the front control module on Jeeps and trucks.

PROGRAMMABLE CONTROLLER INTERFACE The Chrysler **programmable controller interface (PCI)** is a one-wire communication protocol that connects at the OBD-II DLC

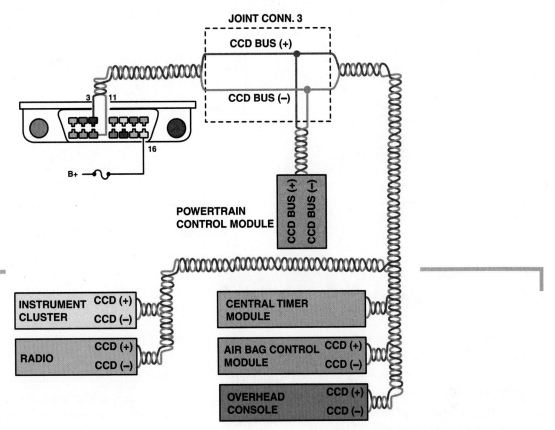

FIGURE 16–16 CCD signals are labeled plus and minus and use a twisted pair of wires. Notice that terminals 3 and 11 of the data link connector are used to access the CCD BUS from a scan tool. Pin 16 is used to supply 12 volts to the scan tool.

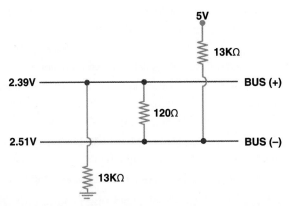

FIGURE 16–17 The differential voltage for the CCD BUS is created by using resistors in a module.

at terminal 2. The PCI BUS is connected to all modules on the BUS in a star configuration and operates at a baud rate of 10,200 bps. The voltage signal toggles between 7.5 and 0 V. If this voltage is checked at terminal 2 of the OBD-II DLC, a voltage of about 1 V indicates the average voltage and means that the BUS is functioning and is not shorted-to-ground. PCI and CCD are often used in the same vehicle. ● **SEE FIGURE 16–18.**

SERIAL COMMUNICATIONS INTERFACE Chrysler used **serial communications interface (SCI)** for most scan tool and flash reprogramming functions until it was replaced

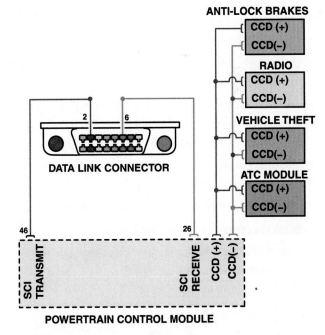

FIGURE 16–18 Many Chrysler vehicles use both SCI and CCD for module communication.

with CAN. SCI is connected at the OBD-II diagnostic link connector (DLC) at terminals 6 (SCI receive) and 7 (SCI transmit). A scan tool must be connected to test the circuit.

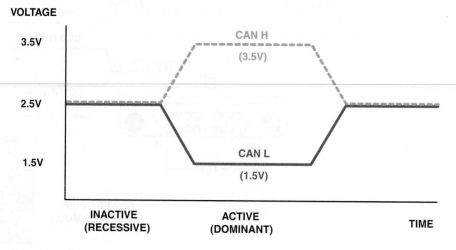

FIGURE 16–19 CAN uses a differential type of module communication where the voltage on one wire is the equal but opposite voltage on the other wire. When no communication is occurring, both wires have 2.5 volts applied. When communication is occurring, CAN H goes up 1 volt to 3.5 volts and CAN L goes down 1 volt to 1.5 volts.

CONTROLLER AREA NETWORK

BACKGROUND Robert Bosch Corporation developed the CAN protocol, which was called CAN 1.2, in 1993. The CAN protocol was approved by the Environmental Protection Agency (EPA) for 2003 and newer vehicle diagnostics, and a legal requirement for all vehicles by 2008. The CAN diagnostic systems use pins 6 and 14 in the standard 16 pin OBD-II (J-1962) connector. Before CAN, the scan tool protocol had been manufacturer specific.

CAN FEATURES The CAN protocol offers the following features.

- Faster than other BUS communication protocols
- Cost effective because it is an easier system than others to use
- Less effected by electromagnetic interference (Data is transferred on two wires that are twisted together, called twisted pair, to help reduce EMI interference.)
- Message based rather than address based which makes it easier to expand
- No wakeup needed because it is a two-wire system
- Supports up to15 modules plus a scan tool
- Uses a 120 ohm resistor at the ends of each pair to reduce electrical noise
- Applies 2.5 volts on both wires:

    H (high) goes to 3.5 volts when active

    L (low) goes to 1.5 volts when active

    ● SEE FIGURE 16–19.

CAN CLASS A, B, AND C There are three classes of CAN and they operate at different speeds. The CAN A, B, and C networks can all be linked using a gateway within the same

vehicle. The gateway is usually one of the many modules in the vehicle.

- **CAN A.** This class operates on only one wire at slow speeds and is therefore less expensive to build. CAN A operates a data transfer rate of 33.33 Kbs in normal mode and up to 83.33 Kbs during reprogramming mode. CAN A uses the vehicle ground as the signal return circuit.

- **CAN B.** This class operates on a two-wire network and does not use the vehicle ground as the signal return circuit. CAN B uses a data transfer rate of 95.2 Kbs. Instead, CAN B (and CAN C) uses two network wires for differential signaling. This means that the two data signal voltages are opposite to each other and used for error detection by constantly being compared. In this case, when the signal voltage at one of the CAN data wires goes high (CAN H), the other one goes low (CAN L), hence the name *differential signaling*. Differential signaling is also used for redundancy, in case one of the signal wires shorts out.

- **CAN C.** This class is the highest speed CAN protocol with speeds up to 500 Kbs. Beginning with 2008 models, all vehicles sold in the United States must use CAN BUS for scan tool communications. Most vehicle manufacturers started using CAN in older models; and it is easy to determine if a vehicle is equipped with CAN. The CAN BUS communicates to the scan tool through terminals 6 and 14 of the DLC indicating that the vehicle is equipped with CAN. ● **SEE FIGURE 16–20.**

The total voltage remains constant at all times and the electromagnetic field effects of the two data BUS lines cancel each other out. The data BUS line is protected against received radiation and is virtually neutral in sending radiation.

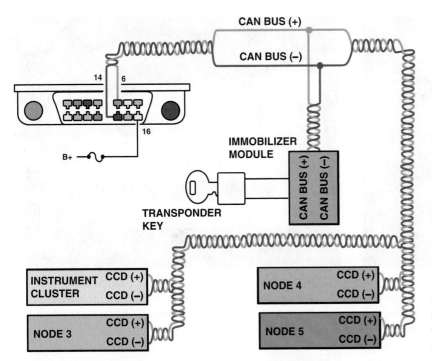

FIGURE 16–20 A typical (generic) system showing how the CAN BUS is connected to various electrical accessories and systems in the vehicle.

FIGURE 16–21 A DLC from a pre-CAN Acura. It shows terminals in cavities 4, 5 (grounds), 7, 10, 14, and 16 (B+).

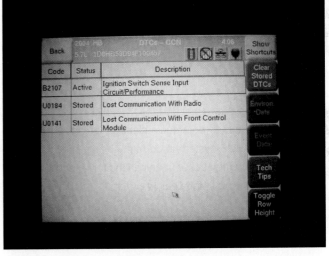

FIGURE 16–22 A Honda scan display showing a B and two U codes, all indicating a BUS-related problem(s).

HONDA/TOYOTA COMMUNICATIONS

The primary BUS communications on pre-CAN-equipped vehicles is ISO 9141-2 using terminals 7 and 15 at the OBD-II DLC. ● SEE FIGURE 16–21.

A factory scan tool or an aftermarket scan tool equipped with enhanced original equipment (OE) software is needed to access many of the BUS messages. ● SEE FIGURE 16–22.

EUROPEAN BUS COMMUNICATIONS

UNIQUE DIAGNOSTIC CONNECTOR   Many different types of module communications protocols are used on European vehicles such as Mercedes and BMW.

Most of these communication BUS messages cannot be accessed through the data link connector (DLC). To check the operation of the individual modules, a scan tool equipped with

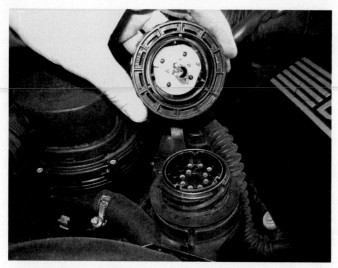

FIGURE 16–23 A typical 38-cavity diagnostic connector as found on many BMW and Mercedes vehicles under the hood. The use of a breakout box (BOB) connected to this connector can often be used to gain access to module BUS information.

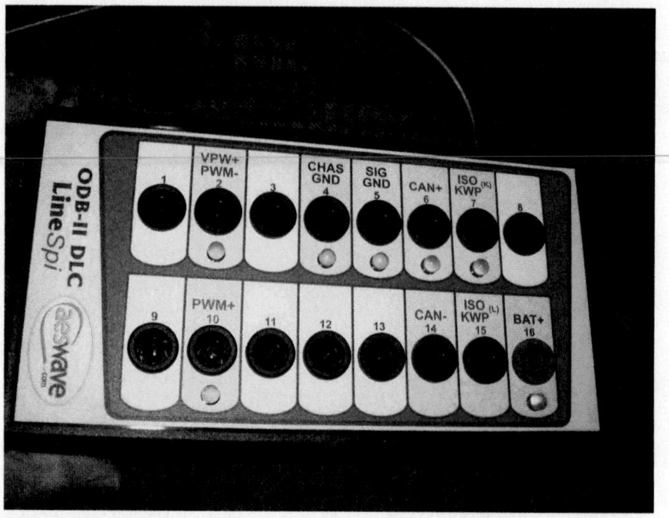

FIGURE 16–24 A breakout box (BOB) used to access the BUS terminals while using a scan tool to activate the modules. This breakout box is equipped with LEDs that light when circuits are active.

EUROPEAN BUS COMMUNICATIONS (CONTINUED)

factory-type software will be needed to communicate with the module through the gateway module. ● **SEE FIGURE 16–23** for an alternative access method to the modules.

MEDIA ORIENTED SYSTEM TRANSPORT BUS The media oriented system transport (MOST) BUS uses fiber optics for module-to-module communications in a ring or star configuration. This BUS system is currently being used for entertainment equipment data communications for videos, CDs, and other media systems in the vehicle.

MOTOROLA INTERCONNECT BUS Motorola interconnect (MI) is a single-wire serial communications protocol, using one master control module and many slave modules. Typical application of the MI BUS protocol is with power and memory mirrors, seats, windows, and headlight levelers.

DISTRIBUTED SYSTEM INTERFACE BUS Distributed system interface (DSI) BUS protocol was developed by Motorola and uses a two-wire serial BUS. This BUS protocol is currently being used for safety-related sensors and components.

BOSCH-SIEMANS-TEMIC BUS The Bosch-Siemans-Temic (BST) BUS is another system that is used for safety-related components and sensors in a vehicle, such as airbags. The BST BUS is a two-wire system and operates up to 250,000 bps.

? FREQUENTLY ASKED QUESTION

How Do You Know What System Is Used?

Use service information to determine which network communication protocol is used. However, due to the various systems on some vehicles, it may be easier to look at the data link connection to determine the system. All OBD-II vehicles have terminals in the following cavities.

Terminal 4: chassis ground

Terminal 5: computer (signal) ground

Terminal 16: 12 V positive

The terminals in cavities 6 and 14 mean that this vehicle is equipped with CAN as the only module communication protocol available at the DLC. To perform a test of the BUS, use a **breakout box (BOB)** to gain access to the terminals while connecting to the vehicle, using a scan tool. ● **SEE FIGURE 16–24** or a typical OBD-II connector breakout box.

BYTEFLIGHT BUS The byteflight BUS is used in safety critical systems, such as airbags, and uses the time division multiple access (TDMA) protocol, which operates at 10 million bps using a **plastic optical fiber (POF).**

FLEXRAY BUS FlexRay BUS is a version of byteflight, and is a high-speed serial communication system for in-vehicle networks. FlexRay is commonly used for steer-by-wire and brake-by-wire systems.

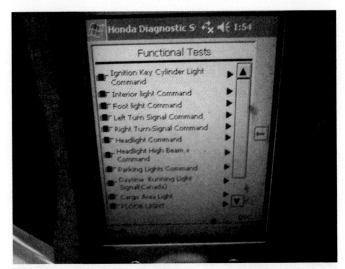

FIGURE 16–25 This Honda scan tool allows the technician to turn on individual lights and operate individual power windows and other accessories that are connected to the BUS system.

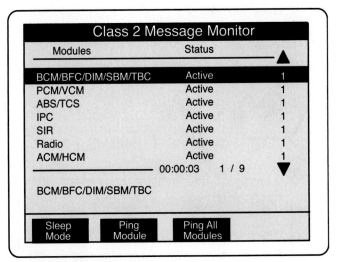

FIGURE 16–26 Modules used in a General Motors vehicle can be "pinged" using a Tech 2 scan tool.

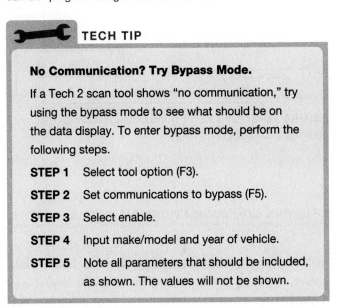

DOMESTIC DIGITAL BUS The domestic digital BUS, commonly designated D2B, is an optical BUS system connecting audio, video, computer, and telephone components in a single-ring structure with a speed of up to 5,600,000 bps.

LOCAL INTERCONNECT NETWORK BUS Local interconnect network (LIN) is a BUS protocol used between intelligent sensors and actuators, and has a BUS speed of 19,200 bps.

TECH TIP

No Communication? Try Bypass Mode.

If a Tech 2 scan tool shows "no communication," try using the bypass mode to see what should be on the data display. To enter bypass mode, perform the following steps.

STEP 1 Select tool option (F3).

STEP 2 Set communications to bypass (F5).

STEP 3 Select enable.

STEP 4 Input make/model and year of vehicle.

STEP 5 Note all parameters that should be included, as shown. The values will not be shown.

NETWORK COMMUNICATIONS DIAGNOSIS

STEPS TO FINDING A FAULT When a network communications fault is suspected, perform the following steps.

STEP 1 **Check everything that does and does not work.** Often accessories that do not seem to be connected can help identify which module or BUS circuit is at fault.

STEP 2 **Perform module status test.** Use a factory level scan tool or an aftermarket scan tool equipped with enhanced software that allows OE-like functions. Check if the components or systems can be operated through the scan tool. ● **SEE FIGURE 16–25.**

- **Ping modules.** Start the Class 2 diagnosis by using a scan tool and select *diagnostic circuit check*. If no diagnostic trouble codes (DTCs) are shown, there could be a communication problem. Select *message monitor,* which will display the status of all of the modules on the Class 2 BUS circuit. The modules that are awake will be shown as active and the scan tool can be used to ping individual modules or command all modules. The ping command should change the status from "active" to "inactive." ● **SEE FIGURE 16–26.**

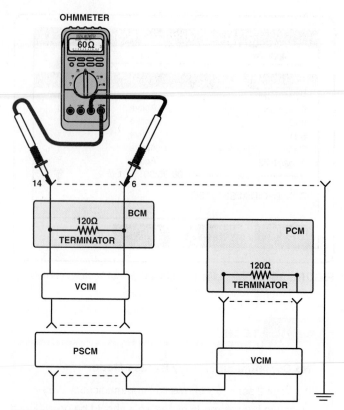

FIGURE 16–27 Checking the terminating resistors using an ohmmeter at the DLC.

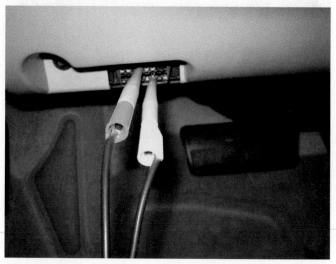

FIGURE 16–28 Use front-probe terminals to access the data link connector. Always follow the specified back-probe and front-probe procedures as found in service information.

NETWORK COMMUNICATIONS DIAGNOSIS (CONTINUED)

NOTE: If an excessive parasitic draw is being diagnosed, use a scan tool to ping the modules in one way to determine if one of the modules is not going to sleep and causing the excessive battery drain.

- **Check state of health.** All modules on the Class 2 BUS circuit have at least one other module responsible for reporting **state of health (SOH)**. If a module fails to send a state of health message within five seconds, the companion module will set a diagnostic trouble code for the module that did not respond. The defective module is not capable of sending this message.

STEP 3 **Check the resistance of the terminating resistors.** Most high-speed BUS systems use resistors at each end, called **terminating resistors**. These resistors are used to help reduce interference into other systems in the vehicle. Usually two 120 ohm resistors are installed at each end and are therefore connected electrically in parallel. Two 120 ohm resistors connected in parallel would measure 60 ohms if being tested using an ohmmeter. ● **SEE FIGURE 16–27.**

STEP 4 **Check data BUS for voltages.** Use a digital multimeter set to DC volts, to monitor communications and check the BUS for proper operation. Some BUS conditions and possible causes include:

- **Signal is zero volt all of the time.** Check for short-to-ground by unplugging modules one at a time to check if one module is causing the problem.
- **Signal is high or 12 volts all of the time.** The BUS circuit could be shorted to 12 V. Check with the customer to see if any service or body repair work was done recently. Try unplugging each module one at a time to pin down which module is causing the communications problem.
- **A variable voltage usually indicates that messages are being sent and received.** CAN and Class 2 can be identified by looking at the data link connector (DLC) for a terminal in cavity number 2. Class 2 is active all of the time the ignition is on, and therefore voltage variation between 0 and 7 V can be measured using a DMM set to read DC volts. ● **SEE FIGURE 16–28.**

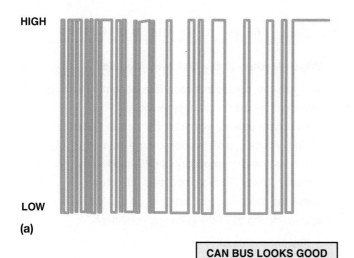

HIGH

LOW

(a)

CAN BUS LOOKS GOOD

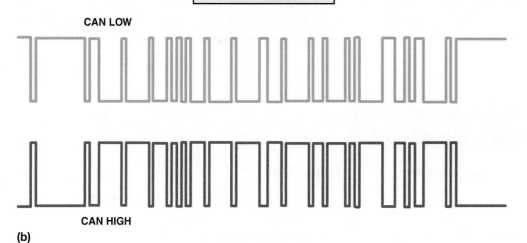

CAN LOW

CAN HIGH

(b)

FIGURE 16–29 (a) Data is sent in packets, so it is normal to see activity then a flat line between messages. (b) A CAN BUS should show voltages that are opposite when there is normal communications. CAN H circuit should go from 2.5 volts at rest to 3.5 volts when active. The CAN L circuit goes from 2.5 volts at rest to 1.5 volts when active.

STEP 5 **Use a digital storage oscilloscope to monitor the waveforms of the BUS circuit.** Using a scope on the data line terminals can show if communication is being transmitted. Typical faults and their causes include:

- **Normal operation.** Normal operation shows variable voltage signals on the data lines. It is impossible to know what information is being transmitted, but if there is activity with short sections of inactivity, this indicates normal data line transmission activity. ● **SEE FIGURE 16–29.**
- **High voltage.** If there is a constant high-voltage signal without any change, this indicates that the data line is shorted to voltage.
- **Zero or low voltage.** If the data line voltage is zero or almost zero and not showing any higher voltage signals, then the data line is short-to-ground.

STEP 6 **Follow factory service information instructions to isolate the cause of the fault.** This step often involves disconnecting one module at a time to see if it is the cause of a short-to-ground or an open in the BUS circuit.

REAL WORLD FIX

The Radio Caused No-Start Story

A 2005 Chevrolet Cobalt did not start. A technician checked with a subscription-based helpline service and discovered that a fault with the Class 2 data circuit could prevent the engine from starting. The advisor suggested that a module should be disconnected one at a time to see if one of them was taking the data line to ground. The two most common components on the Class 2 serial data line that have been known to cause a lack of communication and become shorted-to-ground are the radio and electronic brake control module (EBCM). The first one the technician disconnected was the radio. The engine started and ran. Apparently the Class 2 serial data line was shorted-to-ground inside the radio, which took the entire BUS down. When BUS communication is lost, the PCM is not able to energize the fuel pump, ignition, or fuel injectors so the engine would not start. The radio was replaced to solve the no-start condition.

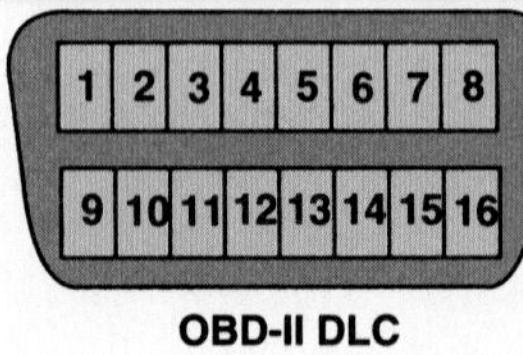

PIN NO.	ASSIGNMENTS
1.	MANUFACTURER'S DISCRETION
2.	BUS + LINE, SAE J1850
3.	MANUFACTURER'S DISCRETION
4.	CHASSIS GROUND
5.	SIGNAL GROUND
6.	MANUFACTURER'S DISCRETION
7.	K LINE, ISO 9141
8.	MANUFACTURER'S DISCRETION
9.	MANUFACTURER'S DISCRETION
10.	BUS – LINE, SAE J1850
11.	MANUFACTURER'S DISCRETION
12.	MANUFACTURER'S DISCRETION
13.	MANUFACTURER'S DISCRETION
14.	MANUFACTURER'S DISCRETION
15.	L LINE, ISO 9141
16.	VEHICLE BATTERY POSITIVE (4A MAX)

OBD-II DLC

FIGURE 16–30 A 16 pin OBD-II DLC with terminals identi-fied. Scan tools use the power pin (16) and ground pin (4) for power so that a separate cigarette lighter plug is not neces-sary on OBD-II vehicles.

? FREQUENTLY ASKED QUESTION

Which Module Is the Gateway Module?

The gateway module is responsible for communicating with other modules and acts as the main commu-nications module for scan tool data. Most General Motors vehicles use the body control module (BCM) or the instrument panel control (IPC) module as the gateway. To verify which module is the gateway, check the schematic and look for one that has voltage applied during all of the following conditions.

- Key on, engine off
- Engine cranking
- Engine running

OBD-II DATA LINK CONNECTOR

All OBD-II vehicles use a 16 pin connector that includes:

Pin 4 = chassis ground

Pin 5 = signal ground

Pin 16 = battery power (4 A max)

● **SEE FIGURE 16–30.**

GENERAL MOTORS VEHICLES

- SAE J-1850 (VPW, Class 2, 10.4 Kbs) standard, which uses pins 2, 4, 5, and 16, but not 10
- GM Domestic OBD-II

Pin 1 and 9: CCM (comprehensive component monitor) slow baud rate, 8,192 UART

Pins 2 and 10: OEM enhanced, fast rate, 40,500 baud rate

Pins 7 and 15: generic OBD-II, ISO 9141, 10,400 baud rate

Pins 6 and 14: GMLAN

ASIAN, CHRYSLER, AND EUROPEAN VEHICLES

- ISO 9141-2 standard, which uses pins 4, 5, 7, 15, and 16
- Chrysler Domestic Group OBD-II

Pins 2 and 10: CCM

Pins 3 and 14: OEM enhanced, 60,500 baud rate

Pins 7 and 15: generic OBD-II, ISO 9141, 10,400 baud rate

FORD VEHICLES

- SAE J-1850 (PWM) (PWM, 41.6 Kbs) standard, which uses pins 2, 4, 5, 10, and 16
- Ford Domestic OBD-II

Pins 2 and 10: CCM

Pins 6 and 14: OEM enhanced, Class C, 40,500 baud rate

Pins 7 and 15: generic OBD-II, ISO 9141, 10,400 baud rate

 TECH TIP

Check Computer Data Line Circuit Schematic

Many General Motors vehicles use more than one type of BUS communications protocol. Check service information (SI) and look at the schematic for compu-ter data line circuits which should show all of the data BUSes and their connectors to the diagnostic link connector (DLC). ● **SEE FIGURE 16–31.**

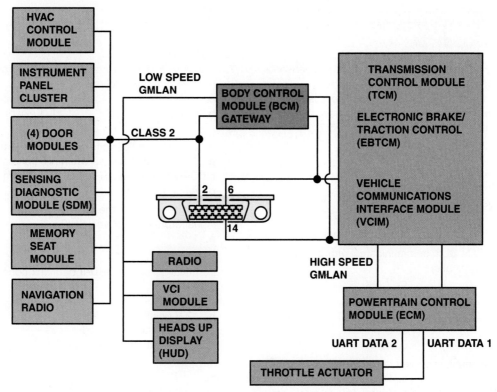

FIGURE 16–31 This schematic of a Chevrolet Equinox shows that the vehicle uses a GMLAN BUS (DLC pins 6 and 14), plus a Class 2 (pin 2) and UART.

SUMMARY

1. The use of a network for module communications reduces the number of wires and connections needed.
2. Module communication configurations include ring link, star link, and ring/star hybrid systems.
3. The SAE communication classifications for vehicle communications systems include Class A (low speed), Class B (medium speed), and Class C (high speed).
4. Various module communications used on General Motors vehicles include UART, E & C, Class 2, keyword communications, and GMLAN (CAN).
5. Types of module communications used on Ford vehicles include SCP, UBP, and CAN.
6. Chrysler brand vehicles use SCI, CCD, PCI, and CAN communications protocols.
7. Many European vehicles use an underhood electrical connector that can be used to access electrical components and modules using a breakout box (BOB) or special tester.
8. Diagnosis of network communications includes checking the terminating resistor value and checking for charging voltage signals at the DLC.

REVIEW QUESTIONS

1. Why is a communication network used?
2. Why are the two wires twisted if used for network communications?
3. Why is a gateway module used?
4. What are U codes?

1. Technician A says that module communications networks are used to reduce the number of wires in a vehicle. Technician B says that a communications network is used to share data from sensors, which can be used by many different modules. Which technician is correct?
   a. Technician A only
   b. Technician B only
   c. Both Technicians A and B
   d. Neither Technician A nor B

2. A module is also known as a _____.
   a. BUS
   b. Node
   c. Terminator
   d. Resistor pack

3. A high-speed CAN BUS communicates with a scan tool through which terminal(s)?
   a. 6 and 14
   b. 2
   c. 7 and 15
   d. 4 and 16

4. UART uses a _____ signal that toggles 0 V.
   a. 5 V
   b. 7 V
   c. 8 V
   d. 12 V

5. GM Class 2 communication toggles between _____.
   a. 5 and 7 V
   b. 0 and 12 V
   c. 7 and 12 V
   d. 0 and 7 V

6. Which terminal of the data link connector does General Motors use for Class 2 communication?
   a. 1
   b. 2
   c. 3
   d. 4

7. GMLAN is the General Motors term for which type of module communication?
   a. UART
   b. Class 2
   c. High-speed CAN
   d. Keyword 2000

8. CAN H and CAN L operate how?
   a. CAN H is at 2.5 volts when not transmitting.
   b. CAN L is at 2.5 volts when not transmitting.
   c. CAN H goes to 3.5 volts when transmitting.
   d. All of the above

9. Which terminal of the OBD-II data link connector is the signal ground for all vehicles?
   a. 1
   b. 3
   c. 4
   d. 5

10. Terminal 16 of the OBD-II data link connector is used for what?
   a. Chassis ground
   b. 12 V positive
   c. Module (signal ground)
   d. Manufacturer's discretion

chapter 17
BATTERIES

OBJECTIVES

After studying Chapter 17, the reader will be able to:

1. Prepare for ASE Electrical/Electronic Systems (A6) certification test content area "B" (Battery Diagnosis and Service).
2. Describe how a battery works.
3. List battery ratings.
4. Describe deep cycling.
5. Discuss how charge indicators work.

KEY TERMS

AGM 241
Ampere hour 242
Battery Council International (BCI) 243
CA 242
CCA 242
Cells 237
Deep cycling 243
Electrolyte 238
Element 237
Flooded cell battery 241
Gassing 236
Gel battery 241
Grid 236
Low-water-loss battery 236

Maintenance-free battery 236
MCA 242
Partitions 238
Porous lead 236
Recombinant battery 241
Reserve capacity 242
Sediment chamber 236
SLA 241
SLI 236
Specific gravity 239
Sponge lead 236
SVR 241
VRLA 241

INTRODUCTION

PURPOSE AND FUNCTION Everything electrical in a vehicle is supplied current from the battery. The battery is one of the most important parts of a vehicle because it is the heart or foundation of the electrical system. The primary purpose of an automotive battery is to provide a source of electrical power for starting and for electrical demands that exceed alternator output.

WHY BATTERIES ARE IMPORTANT The battery also acts as a stabilizer to the voltage for the entire electrical system. The battery is a voltage stabilizer because it acts as a reservoir where large amounts of current (amperes) can be removed quickly during starting and replaced gradually by the alternator during charging.

■ The battery *must* be in good (serviceable) condition before the charging system and the cranking system can be tested. For example, if a battery is discharged, the cranking circuit (starter motor) could test as being defective because the battery voltage might drop below specifications.

■ The charging circuit could also test as being defective because of a weak or discharged battery. It is important to test the vehicle battery before further testing of the cranking or charging system.

FREQUENTLY ASKED QUESTION

What Is an SLI Battery?

Sometimes the term *SLI* is used to describe a type of battery. **SLI** means **starting, lighting, and ignition,** and describes the use of a typical automotive battery. Other types of batteries used in industry are usually batteries designed to be deep cycled and are usually not as suitable for automotive needs.

BATTERY CONSTRUCTION

CASE Most automotive battery cases (container or covers) are constructed of polypropylene, a thin (approximately 0.08 in., or 0.02 mm, thick), strong, and lightweight plastic. In contrast, containers for industrial batteries and some truck batteries are constructed of a hard, thick rubber material.

Inside the case are six cells (for a 12 volt battery). Each cell has positive and negative plates. Built into the bottom of many batteries are ribs that support the lead-alloy plates and provide a space for sediment to settle, called the **sediment chamber.** This space prevents spent active material from causing a short circuit between the plates at the bottom of the battery. ● **SEE FIGURE 17–1.**

A **maintenance-free battery** uses little water during normal service because of the alloy material used to construct the battery plate grids. Maintenance-free batteries are also called **low-water-loss batteries.**

GRIDS Each positive and negative plate in a battery is constructed on a framework, or **grid,** made primarily of lead. Lead is a soft material and must be strengthened for use in an automotive battery grid. Adding antimony or calcium to the pure lead adds strength to the lead grids. ● **SEE FIGURE 17–2.**

Battery grids hold the active material and provide the electrical pathways for the current created in the plate.

Maintenance-free batteries use calcium instead of antimony, because 0.2% calcium has the same strength as 6% antimony. A typical lead-calcium grid uses only 0.09% to 0.12% calcium. Using low amounts of calcium instead of higher amounts of antimony reduces **gassing.** Gassing is the release of hydrogen and oxygen from the battery that occurs during charging and results in water usage.

Low-maintenance batteries use a low percentage of antimony (about 2% to 3%), or use antimony only in the positive grids and calcium for the negative grids. *The percentages that make up the alloy of the plate grids constitute the major difference between standard and maintenance-free batteries.* The chemical reactions that occur inside each battery are identical regardless of the type of material used to construct the grid plates.

POSITIVE PLATES The positive plates have *lead dioxide (peroxide)* placed onto the grid framework. This process is called *pasting*. This active material can react with the sulfuric acid of the battery and is dark brown in color.

NEGATIVE PLATES The negative plates are pasted to the grid with a pure **porous lead,** called **sponge lead,** and are gray in color.

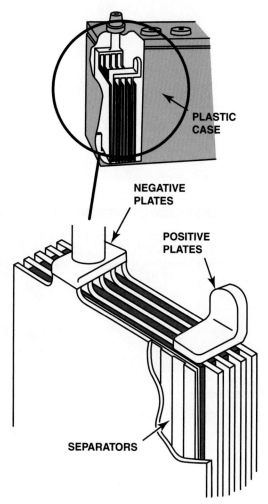

FIGURE 17–1 Batteries are constructed of plates grouped into cells and installed in a plastic case.

FIGURE 17–2 A grid from a battery used in both positive and negative plates.

SEPARATORS

The positive and the negative plates must be installed alternately next to each other without touching. Nonconducting *separators* are used, which allow room for the reaction of the acid with both plate materials, yet insulate the

FIGURE 17–3 Two groups of plates are combined to form a battery element.

plates to prevent shorts. These separators are porous (with many small holes) and have ribs facing the positive plate. Separators can be made from resin-coated paper, porous rubber, fiberglass, or expanded plastic. Many batteries use envelope-type separators that encase the entire plate and help prevent any material that may shed from the plates from causing a short circuit between plates at the bottom of the battery.

CELLS

Cells are constructed of positive and negative plates with insulating separators between each plate. Most batteries use one more negative plate than positive plate in each cell; however, many newer batteries use the same number of positive and negative plates. A cell is also called an **element.** Each cell is actually a 2.1 volt battery, regardless of the number of positive or negative plates used. The greater the number of plates used in each cell, the greater the amount of *current* that can be produced. Typical batteries contain four positive plates and five negative plates per cell. A 12 volt battery contains six cells connected in series, which produce 12.6 volts ($6 \times 2.1 = 12.6$) and contain 54 plates (9 plates per cell $\times$ 6 cells). If the same 12 volt battery had five positive plates and six negative plates, for a total of 11 plates per cell (5 + 6), or 66 plates (11 plates $\times$ 6 cells), then it would have the same voltage, but the amount of current that the battery could produce would be increased. ● **SEE FIGURE 17–3.**

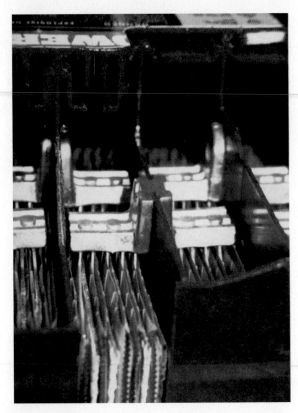

FIGURE 17-4 A cutaway battery showing the connection of the cells to each other through the partition.

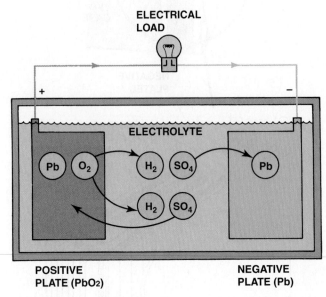

FIGURE 17-5 Chemical reaction for a lead-acid battery that is fully charged being discharged by the attached electrical load.

BATTERY CONSTRUCTION (CONTINUED)

The amperage capacity of a battery is determined by the amount of active plate material in the battery and the area of the plate material exposed to the electrolyte in the battery.

PARTITIONS Each cell is separated from the other cells by **partitions,** which are made of the same material as that used for the outside case of the battery. Electrical connections between cells are provided by lead connectors that loop over the top of the partition and connect the plates of the cells together. Many batteries connect the cells directly through the partition connectors, which provide the shortest path for the current and the lowest resistance. ● **SEE FIGURE 17-4.**

ELECTROLYTE **Electrolyte** is the term used to describe the acid solution in a battery. The electrolyte used in automotive batteries is a solution (liquid combination) of 36% sulfuric acid and 64% water. This electrolyte is used for both lead-antimony and lead-calcium (maintenance-free) batteries. The chemical symbol for this sulfuric acid solution is H_2SO_4.

H_2 = Symbol for hydrogen (the subscript 2 means that there are two atoms of hydrogen)

S = Symbol for sulfur

O_4 = Symbol for oxygen (the subscript 4 indicates that there are four atoms of oxygen)

Electrolyte is sold premixed in the proper proportion and is factory installed or added to the battery when the battery is sold. Additional electrolyte must *never* be added to any battery after the original electrolyte fill. It is normal for some water (H_2O) to escape during charging as a result of the chemical reactions. The escape of gases from a battery during charging or discharging is called gassing. Only pure distilled water should be added to a battery. If distilled water is not available, clean drinking water can be used.

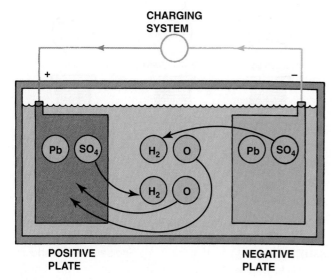

FIGURE 17–6 Chemical reaction for a lead-acid battery that is fully discharged being charged by the attached generator.

? FREQUENTLY ASKED QUESTION

Is There an Easy Way to Remember How a Battery Works?

Yes. Think of the sulfuric acid solution in the electrolyte being deposited, then removed from the plates.

- **During discharge.** The acid (SO_4) is leaving the electrolyte and getting onto both plates.
- **During charging.** The acid (SO_4) is being forced from both plates and enters the electrolyte.

HOW A BATTERY WORKS

PRINCIPLE INVOLVED The principle of how a battery works is based on a scientific principle discovered years ago that states:

- When two dissimilar metals are placed in an acid, electrons flow between the metals if a circuit is connected between them.
- This can be demonstrated by pushing a steel nail and a piece of solid copper wire into a lemon. Connect a voltmeter to the ends of the copper wire and nail, and voltage will be displayed.

A fully charged lead-acid battery has a positive plate of lead dioxide (peroxide) and a negative plate of lead surrounded by a sulfuric acid solution (electrolyte). The difference in potential (voltage) between lead peroxide and lead in acid is approximately 2.1 volts.

DURING DISCHARGING The positive plate lead dioxide (PbO_2) combines with the SO_4, forming $PbSO_4$ from the electrolyte and releases its O_2 into the electrolyte, forming H_2O. The negative plate also combines with the SO_4 from the electrolyte and becomes lead sulfate ($PbSO_4$). ● **SEE FIGURE 17–5.**

FULLY DISCHARGED STATE When the battery is fully discharged, both the positive and the negative plates are $PbSO_4$ (lead sulfate) and the electrolyte has become water (H_2O). As the battery is being discharged, the plates and elec-

trolyte approach the completely discharged state. There is also the danger of freezing when a battery is discharged, because the electrolyte is mostly water.

CAUTION: Never charge or jump start a frozen battery because the hydrogen gas can get trapped in the ice and ignite if a spark is caused during the charging process. The result can be an explosion.

DURING CHARGING During charging, the sulfate from the acid leaves both the positive and the negative plates and returns to the electrolyte, where it becomes normal-strength sulfuric acid solution. The positive plate returns to lead dioxide (PbO_2), the negative plate is again pure lead (Pb), and the electrolyte becomes H_2SO_4. ● **SEE FIGURE 17–6.**

SPECIFIC GRAVITY

DEFINITION The amount of sulfate in the electrolyte is determined by the electrolyte's **specific gravity,** which is the ratio of the weight of a given volume of a liquid to the weight of an equal volume of water. In other words, the more dense the liquid is, the higher its specific gravity. Pure water is the basis for this measurement and is given a specific gravity of 1.000 at 80°F (27°C). Pure sulfuric acid has a specific gravity of 1.835; the *correct* concentration of water and sulfuric acid

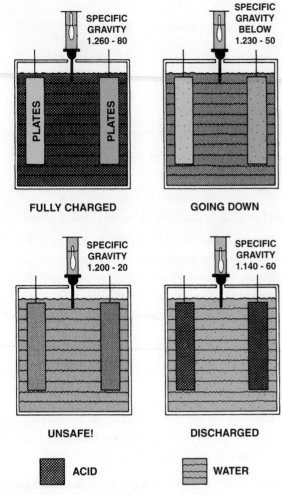

FIGURE 17–7 As the battery becomes discharged, the specific gravity of the battery acid decreases.

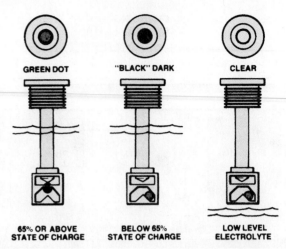

FIGURE 17–8 Typical battery charge indicator. If the specific gravity is low (battery discharged), the ball drops away from the reflective prism. When the battery is charged enough, the ball floats and reflects the color of the ball (usually green) back up through the sight glass and the sight glass is dark.

SPECIFIC GRAVITY	STATE OF CHARGE	BATTERY VOLTAGE (V)
1.265	Fully charged	12.6 or higher
1.225	75% charged	12.4
1.190	50% charged	12.2
1.155	25% charged	12.0
Lower than 1.120	Discharged	11.9 or lower

CHART 17–1

A comparison showing the relationship among specific gravity, battery voltage, and state of charge.

SPECIFIC GRAVITY (CONTINUED)

(called electrolyte—64% water, 36% acid) is 1.260 to 1.280 at 80°F. The higher the battery's specific gravity, the more fully it is charged. ● **SEE FIGURE 17–7.**

CHARGE INDICATORS Some batteries are equipped with a built-in state-of-charge indicator, commonly called *green eyes*. This indicator is simply a small, ball-type hydrometer that is installed in one cell. This hydrometer uses a plastic ball that floats if the electrolyte density is sufficient (which it is when the battery is about 65% charged). When the ball floats, it appears in the hydrometer's sight glass, changing its color. ● **SEE FIGURE 17–8.**

Because the hydrometer is only testing one cell (out of six on a 12 volt battery), and because the hydrometer ball can easily stick in one position, do not trust that this is accurate information about a state of charge (SOC) of the battery.

Values of specific gravity, state of charge, and battery voltage at 80°F (27°C) are given in ● **CHART 17–1.**

VALVE REGULATED LEAD-ACID BATTERIES

TERMINOLOGY There are two basic types of **valve regulated lead-acid (VRLA)**, also called **sealed valve-regulated (SVR)** or **sealed lead-acid (SLA)**, batteries. These batteries use a low-pressure venting system that releases excess gas and automatically reseals if a buildup of gas is created due to overcharging. The two types include the following:

- **Absorbed glass mat.** The acid used in an **absorbed glass mat (AGM)** battery is totally absorbed into the separator, making the battery leakproof and spillproof. The battery is assembled by compressing the cell about 20%, then inserting it into the container. The compressed cell helps reduce damage caused by vibration and helps keep the acid tightly against the plates. The sealed maintenance-free design uses a pressure release valve in each cell. Unlike conventional batteries that use a liquid electrolyte, called **flooded cell batteries,** most of the hydrogen and oxygen given off during charging remains inside the battery. The separator or mat is only 90% to 95% saturated with electrolyte, thereby allowing a portion of the mat to be filled with gas. The gas spaces provide channels to allow the hydrogen and oxygen gases to recombine rapidly and safely. Because the acid is totally absorbed into the glass mat separator, an AGM battery can be mounted in any direction. AGM batteries also have a longer service life, often lasting 7 to 10 years. Absorbed glass mat batteries are used as standard equipment in some vehicles such as the Chevrolet Corvette and in most Toyota hybrid electric vehicles. ● **SEE FIGURE 17–9.**

- **Gelled electrolyte batteries.** In a gelled electrolyte battery, silica is added to the electrolyte, which turns the electrolyte into a substance similar to gelatin. This type of battery is also called a **gel battery.**

Both types of valve-regulated, lead-acid batteries are also called **recombinant battery** design. A recombinant-type battery means that the oxygen gas generated at the positive plate travels through the dense electrolyte to the negative plate. When the oxygen reaches the negative plate, it reacts with the lead, which consumes the oxygen gas and prevents the formation of hydrogen gas. It is because of this oxygen recombination that VRLA batteries do not use water.

FIGURE 17–9 An absorbed glass mat battery is totally sealed and is more vibration resistant than conventional lead-acid batteries.

CAUSES AND TYPES OF BATTERY FAILURE

NORMAL LIFE Most automotive batteries have a useful service life of three to seven years; however, proper care can help increase the life of a battery, but abuse can shorten it. The major cause of premature battery failure is overcharging.

CHARGING VOLTAGE The automotive charging circuit, consisting of an alternator and connecting wires, must be operating correctly to prevent damage to the battery.

- Charging voltages higher than 15.5 volts can damage a battery by warping the plates as a result of the heat of overcharging.

- AGM batteries can be damaged if charged at a voltage higher than 14.5 volts.

Overcharging also causes the active plate material to disintegrate and fall out of the supporting grid framework. Vibration or bumping can also cause internal damage similar to that caused by overcharging. It is important, therefore, to ensure that all automotive batteries are securely clamped down in the vehicle. The shorting of cell plates can occur without notice. If one of the six cells of a 12 volt battery is shorted, the resulting voltage of the battery is only 10 volts ($12 - 2 = 10$). With only 10 volts available, the starter *usually* will not be able to start the engine.

BATTERY HOLD-DOWNS

BATTERY HOLD-DOWNS All batteries must be attached securely to the vehicle to prevent battery damage. Normal vehicle vibrations can cause the active materials inside the battery to shed. Battery hold-down clamps or brackets help reduce vibration, which can greatly reduce the capacity and life of any battery. ● **SEE FIGURE 17–10.**

BATTERY RATINGS

Batteries are rated according to the amount of current they can produce under specific conditions.

COLD-CRANKING AMPERES Every automotive battery must be able to supply electrical power to crank the engine in cold weather and still provide battery voltage high enough to operate the ignition system for starting. The cold-cranking ampere rating of a battery is the number of amperes that can be supplied by a battery at 0°F (−18°C) for 30 seconds while the battery still maintains a voltage of 1.2 volts per cell or higher. This means that the battery voltage would be 7.2 volts for a 12 volt battery and 3.6 volts for a 6 volt battery. The cold-cranking performance rating is called **cold-cranking amperes (CCA).** Try to purchase a battery with the highest CCA for the money. See the vehicle manufacturer's specifications for recommended battery capacity.

CRANKING AMPERES The designation **CA** refers to the number of amperes that can be supplied by a battery at 32°F (0°C). This rating results in a higher number than the more stringent CCA rating. ● **SEE FIGURE 17–11.**

MARINE CRANKING AMPERES **Marine cranking amperes (MCA)** is similar to cranking amperes and is tested at 32°F (0°C).

RESERVE CAPACITY The **reserve capacity** rating for batteries is *the number of minutes* for which the battery can produce 25 amperes and still have a battery voltage of 1.75 volts per cell (10.5 volts for a 12 volt battery). This rating is actually

BATTERY HOLD DOWN BRACKET

FIGURE 17–10 A typical battery hold-down bracket. All batteries should use a bracket to prevent battery damage due to vibration and shock.

FIGURE 17–11 This battery has a cranking amperes (CA) rating of 1,000. This means that this battery is capable of cranking an engine for 30 seconds at a temperature of 32°F (0°C) at a minimum of 1.2 volts per cell (7.2 volts for a 12 volt battery).

a measurement of the time for which a vehicle can be driven in the event of a charging system failure.

AMPERE HOUR **Ampere hour** is an older battery rating system that measures how many amperes of current the battery can produce over a period of time. For example, a battery that has a 50 amp-hour (A-H) rating can deliver 50 amperes for one hour or 1 ampere for 50 hours or any combination that equals 50 amp-hours.

What Determines Battery Capacity?

The capacity of any battery is determined by the amount of active plate material in the battery. A battery with a large number of thin plates can produce high current for a short period. If a few thick plates are used, the battery can produce low current for a long period. A trolling motor battery used for fishing must supply a low current for a long period of time. An automotive battery is required to produce a high current for a short period for cranking. Therefore, every battery is designed for a specific application.

What Is Deep Cycling?

Deep cycling is almost fully discharging a battery and then completely recharging it. Golf cart batteries are an example of lead-acid batteries that must be designed to be deep cycled. A golf cart must be able to cover two 18-hole rounds of golf and then be fully recharged overnight. Charging is hard on batteries because the internal heat generated can cause plate warpage, so these specially designed batteries use thicker plate grids that resist warpage. Normal automotive batteries are not designed for repeated deep cycling.

BATTERY SIZES

BCI GROUP SIZES   Battery sizes are standardized by the **Battery Council International (BCI).** When selecting a replacement battery, check the specified group number in service information, battery application charts at parts stores, or the owner's manual.

TYPICAL GROUP SIZE APPLICATIONS

- **24/24F (top terminals).** Fits many Honda, Acura, Infinity, Lexus, Nissan, and Toyota vehicles.

- **34/78 (dual terminals, both side and top posts).** Fits many General Motors pickups and SUVs, as well as midsize and larger GM sedans and large Chrysler/Dodge vehicles.

- **35 (top terminals).** Fits many Japanese brand vehicles.

- **65 (top terminals).** Fits most large Ford/Mercury passenger cars, trucks, and SUVs.

- **75 (side terminals).** Fits some General Motors small and midsize cars and some Chrysler/ Dodge vehicles.

- **78 (side terminals).** Fits many General Motors pickups and SUVs, as well as midsize and larger GM sedans.

Exact dimensions can be found on the Internet by searching for BCI battery sizes.

SUMMARY

1. Maintenance-free batteries use lead-calcium grids instead of lead-antimony grids to reduce gassing.
2. When a battery is being discharged, the acid (SO_4) is leaving the electrolyte and being deposited on the plates. When the battery is being charged, the acid (SO_4) is forced off the plates and back into the electrolyte.
3. All batteries give off hydrogen and oxygen when being charged.
4. Batteries are rated according to CCA and reserve capacity.

REVIEW QUESTIONS

1. Why can discharged batteries freeze?
2. What are the battery-rating methods?
3. Why can a battery explode if it is exposed to an open flame or spark?

1. When a battery becomes completely discharged, both positive and negative plates become _____ and the electrolyte becomes _____.
   a. H_2SO_4 / Pb
   b. $PbSO_4$ / H_2O
   c. PbO_2 / H_2SO_4
   d. $PbSO_4$ / H_2SO_4

2. A fully charged 12 volt battery should indicate _____.
   a. 12.6 volts or higher
   b. A specific gravity of 1.265 or higher
   c. 12 volts
   d. Both a and b

3. Deep cycling means _____.
   a. Overcharging the battery
   b. Overfilling or underfilling the battery with water
   c. The battery is fully discharged and then recharged
   d. The battery is overfilled with acid (H_2SO_4)

4. What makes a battery "low maintenance" or "maintenance free"?
   a. Material is used to construct the grids.
   b. The plates are constructed of different metals.
   c. The electrolyte is hydrochloric acid solution.
   d. The battery plates are smaller, making more room for additional electrolytes.

5. The positive battery plate is _____.
   a. Lead dioxide
   b. Brown in color
   c. Sometimes called lead peroxide
   d. All of the above

6. Which battery rating is tested at 0°F (−18°C)?
   a. Cold-cranking amperes (CCA)
   b. Cranking amperes (CA)
   c. Reserve capacity
   d. Battery voltage test

7. Which battery rating is expressed in minutes?
   a. Cold-cranking amperes (CCA)
   b. Cranking amperes (CA)
   c. Reserve capacity
   d. Battery voltage test

8. What battery rating is tested at 32°F (0°C)?
   a. Cold-cranking amperes (CCA)
   b. Cranking amperes (CA)
   c. Reserve capacity
   d. Battery voltage test

9. What gases are released from a battery when it is being charged?
   a. Oxygen
   b. Hydrogen
   c. Nitrogen and oxygen
   d. Hydrogen and oxygen

10. A charge indicator (eye) operates by showing green or red when the battery is charged and dark if the battery is discharged. This charge indicator detects _____.
    a. Battery voltage
    b. Specific gravity
    c. Electrolyte water pH
    d. Internal resistance of the cells

chapter 18

BATTERY TESTING AND SERVICE

OBJECTIVES

After studying Chapter 18, the reader will be able to:

1. Prepare for ASE Electrical/Electronic Systems (A6) certification test content area "B" (Battery Diagnosis and Service).

2. List the precautions necessary when working with batteries.

3. Explain how to safely charge a battery.

4. Discuss how to perform a battery drain test.

5. Describe how to perform a battery load test and a conductance test.

6. Discuss how to test batteries for open-circuit voltage and specific gravity.

KEY TERMS

Battery electrical drain test 256

Dynamic voltage 247

Hydrometer 249

IOD 256

Load test 249

Open circuit voltage 247

Parasitic load test 256

Three-minute charge test 249

BATTERY SERVICE SAFETY CONSIDERATIONS

HAZARDS Batteries contain acid and release explosive gases (hydrogen and oxygen) during normal charging and discharging cycles.

SAFETY PROCEDURES To help prevent physical injury or damage to the vehicle, always adhere to the following safety procedures.

1. When working on any electrical component on a vehicle, disconnect the negative battery cable from the battery. When the negative cable is disconnected, all electrical circuits in the vehicle will be open, which will prevent accidental electrical contact between an electrical component and ground. Any electrical spark has the potential to cause explosion and personal injury.

2. Wear eye protection (goggles preferred) when working around any battery.

3. Wear protective clothing to avoid skin contact with battery acid.

4. Always adhere to all safety precautions as stated in the service procedures for the equipment used for battery service and testing.

5. Never smoke or use an open flame around any battery.

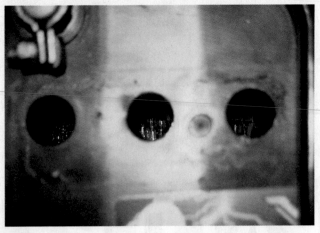

FIGURE 18–1 A visual inspection on this battery shows the electrolyte level was below the plates in all cells.

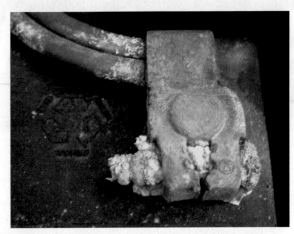

FIGURE 18–2 Corrosion on a battery cable could be an indication that the battery itself is either being overcharged or is sulfated, creating a lot of gassing of the electrolyte.

SYMPTOMS OF A WEAK OR DEFECTIVE BATTERY

The following warning signs indicate that a battery is near the end of its useful life.

- **Uses water in one or more cells.** This indicates that the plates are sulfated and that during the charging process, the water in the electrolyte is being turned into separate hydrogen and oxygen gases. ● **SEE FIGURE 18–1.**

- **Excessive corrosion on battery cables or connections.** Corrosion is more likely to occur if the battery is sulfated, creating hot spots on the plates. When the battery is being charged, the acid fumes are forced out of the vent holes and onto the battery cables, connections, and even on the battery tray underneath the battery. ● **SEE FIGURE 18–2.**

- **Slower than normal engine cranking.** When the capacity of the battery is reduced due to damage or age, it is less likely to be able to supply the necessary current for starting the engine, especially during cold weather.

Dynamic versus Open Circuit Voltage

Open circuit voltage is the voltage (usually of a battery) that exists *without* a load being applied. **Dynamic voltage** is the voltage of the power source (battery) with the circuit in operation. A vehicle battery, for example, may indicate that it has 12.6 volts or more, but that voltage will drop when the battery is put under a load such as cranking the engine. If the battery voltage drops too much, the starter motor will rotate more slowly and the engine may not start.

If the dynamic voltage is lower than specified, the battery may be weak or defective or the circuit may be defective, resulting in too much current being drawn from the battery.

FIGURE 18–3 Besides baking soda and water, a sugar-free diet soft drink can also be used to neutralize the battery acid.

BATTERY MAINTENANCE

NEED FOR MAINTENANCE Most new-style batteries are of a maintenance-free design that uses lead-calcium instead of lead-antimony plate grid construction. Because lead-calcium batteries do not release as much gas as the older-style, lead-antimony batteries, there is less consumption of water during normal service. Also, with less gassing, less corrosion is observed on the battery terminals, wiring, and support trays. If the electrolyte level can be checked, and if it is low, add only distilled water. Distilled water is recommended by all battery manufacturers, but if distilled water is not available, clean ordinary drinking water, low in mineral content, can be used.

Battery maintenance includes making certain that the battery case is clean and checking that the battery cables and hold-down fasteners are clean and tight.

BATTERY TERMINAL CLEANING Many battery-related faults are caused by poor electrical connections at the battery. Battery cable connections should be checked and cleaned to prevent voltage drop at the connections. One common reason for an engine to not start is loose or corroded battery cable connections. Replacement battery cable terminal ends are

available at most automotive parts stores. Perform an inspection and check for the following conditions.

- Loose or corroded connections at the battery terminals (should not be able to be moved by hand)
- Loose or corroded connections at the ground connector on the engine block
- Wiring that has been modified to add auxiliary power for a sound system, or other electrical accessory

If the connections are loose or corroded, use 1 tablespoon of baking soda in 1 quart (liter) of water and brush this mixture onto the battery and housing to neutralize the acid. Mechanically clean the connections and wash the area with water. ● **SEE FIGURE 18–3.**

BATTERY HOLD-DOWN The battery should also be secured with a hold-down bracket to prevent vibration from damaging the plates inside the battery. The hold-down bracket should be snug enough to prevent battery movement, yet not so tight as to cause the case to crack. Factory-original hold-down brackets are often available through local automobile dealers, and universal hold-down units are available through local automotive parts stores.

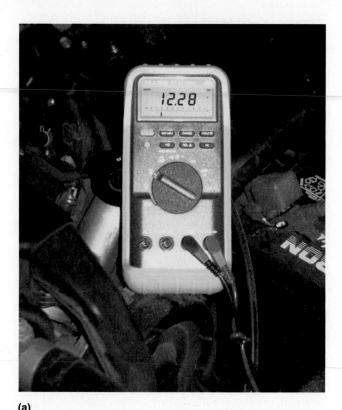

(a)

(b)

FIGURE 18–4 (a) A battery voltage of 12.28 volts is definitely not fully charged and should be charged before testing. (b) A battery that measures 12.6 volts or higher after the surface charge has been removed is 100% charged.

BATTERY VOLTAGE TEST

STATE OF CHARGE Testing the battery voltage with a voltmeter is a simple method for determining the state of charge of any battery. ● **SEE FIGURE 18–4.**

The voltage of a battery does not necessarily indicate whether the battery can perform satisfactorily, but it does indicate to the technician more about the battery's condition than a simple visual inspection. A battery that "looks good" may not be good. This test is commonly called an *open circuit battery voltage test* because it is conducted with an open circuit, no current flowing, and no load applied to the battery.

1. If the battery has just been charged or the vehicle has recently been driven, it is necessary to remove the surface charge from the battery before testing. A surface charge is a charge of higher-than-normal voltage that is just on the surface of the battery plates. The surface charge is quickly removed when the battery is loaded and therefore does not accurately represent the true state of charge of the battery.

2. To remove the surface charge, turn the headlights on high beam (brights) for one minute, then turn the headlights off and wait two minutes.

BATTERY VOLTAGE (V)	STATE OF CHARGE
12.6 or higher	100% charged
12.4	75% charged
12.2	50% charged
12.0	25% charged
11.9 or lower	Discharged

CHART 18–1

The estimated state of charge of a 12 volt battery after the surface charge has been removed.

3. With the engine and all electrical accessories off, and the doors shut (to turn off the interior lights), connect a voltmeter to the battery posts. Connect the red positive lead to the positive post and the black negative lead to the negative post.

   NOTE: If the meter reads negative (−), the battery has been reverse charged (has reversed polarity) and should be replaced, or the meter has been connected incorrectly.

4. Read the voltmeter and compare the results with the state of charge. The voltages shown are for a battery at or near room temperature (70°F to 80°F, or 21°C to 27°C). ● **SEE CHART 18–1.**

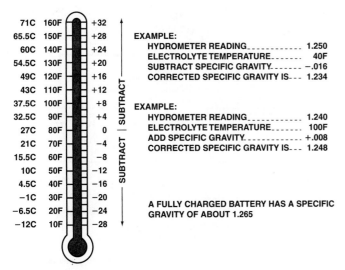

71C	160F	+32
65.5C	150F	+28
60C	140F	+24
54.5C	130F	+20
49C	120F	+16
43C	110F	+12
37.5C	100F	+8
32.5C	90F	+4
27C	80F	0
21C	70F	−4
15.5C	60F	−8
10C	50F	−12
4.5C	40F	−16
−1C	30F	−20
−6.5C	20F	−24
−12C	10F	−28

EXAMPLE:
HYDROMETER READING _ _ _ _ _ _ _ _ _ _ 1.250
ELECTROLYTE TEMPERATURE _ _ _ _ _ _ _ 40F
SUBTRACT SPECIFIC GRAVITY _ _ _ _ _ _ −.016
CORRECTED SPECIFIC GRAVITY IS _ _ _ 1.234

EXAMPLE:
HYDROMETER READING _ _ _ _ _ _ _ _ _ _ 1.240
ELECTROLYTE TEMPERATURE _ _ _ _ _ _ _ 100F
ADD SPECIFIC GRAVITY _ _ _ _ _ _ _ _ _ +.008
CORRECTED SPECIFIC GRAVITY IS _ _ _ 1.248

A FULLY CHARGED BATTERY HAS A SPECIFIC GRAVITY OF ABOUT 1.265

FIGURE 18–5 When testing a battery using a hydrometer, the reading must be corrected if the temperature is above or below 80°F (27°C).

SPECIFIC GRAVITY	BATTERY VOLTAGE (V)	STATE OF CHARGE
1.265	12.6 or higher	100% charged
1.225	12.4	75% charged
1.190	12.2	50% charged
1.155	12.0	25% charged
Lower than 1.120	11.9 or lower	Discharged

CHART 18–2

Measuring the specific gravity can detect a defective battery. A battery should be at least 75% charged before being load tested.

HYDROMETER TESTING

If the battery has removable filler caps, the specific gravity of the electrolyte can also be checked. A **hydrometer** is a tester that measures the specific gravity. ● **SEE FIGURE 18–5.**

This test can also be performed on most maintenance-free batteries because their filler caps are removable, except for those produced by Delco (Delphi) Battery. The specific gravity test indicates the state of battery charge and can indicate a defective battery if the specific gravity of one or more cells varies by more than 0.050 from the value of the highest-reading cell. ● **SEE CHART 18–2.**

? **FREQUENTLY ASKED QUESTION**

What Is the Three-Minute Charge Test?

A **three-minute charge test** is used to check if a battery is sulfated, and is performed as follows:

- Connect a battery charger and a voltmeter to the battery terminals.
- Charge the battery at a rate of 40 amperes for three minutes.
- At the end of three minutes, read the voltmeter.

Results: If the voltage is above 15.5 volts, replace the battery. If the voltage is below 15.5 volts, the battery is not sulfated and should be charged and retested.

This is *not* a valid test of many maintenance-free batteries, such as the Delphi Freedom. Due to the high internal resistance, a discharged Delphi Freedom battery may not start to accept a charge for several hours. Always use another alternative battery test before discarding a battery based on the results of the three-minute charge test.

BATTERY LOAD TESTING

TERMINOLOGY One test to determine the condition of any battery is the **load test.** Most automotive starting and charging testers use a carbon pile to create an electrical load on the battery. The amount of the load is determined by the original CCA rating of the battery, which should be at least 75% charged before performing a load test. The capacity is measured in cold-cranking amperes, which is the number of amperes that a battery can supply at 0°F (−18°C) for 30 seconds.

TEST PROCEDURE To perform a battery load test, take the following steps.

STEP 1 **Determine the CCA rating of the battery.** The proper electrical load used to test a battery is half of the CCA rating or three times the ampere-hour rating, with a minimum 150 ampere load. ● **SEE FIGURE 18–6.**

STEP 2 **Connect the load tester to the battery.** Follow the instructions for the tester being used.

STEP 3 **Apply the load for a full 15 seconds.** Observe the voltmeter during the load testing and check the voltage at the end of the 15 sec. period while the battery is still under load. A good battery should indicate above 9.6 V.

FIGURE 18–6 This battery has cold-cranking amperes (CCA) of 550 A, cranking amperes (CA) of 680 A, and load test amperes of 270 A listed on the top label. Not all batteries have this complete information.

FIGURE 18–7 An alternator regulator battery starter tester (ARBST) automatically loads the battery with a fixed load for 15 sec. to remove the surface charge, then removes the load for 30 sec. to allow the battery to recover, and then reapplies the load for another 15 sec. The results of the test are then displayed.

BATTERY LOAD TESTING (CONTINUED)

STEP 4 Repeat the test. Many battery manufacturers recommend performing the load test twice, using the first load period to remove the surface charge on the battery and the second test to provide a truer indication of the condition of the battery. Wait 30 seconds between tests to allow time for the battery to recover. ● **SEE FIGURE 18–7.**

Results: If the battery fails the load test, recharge the battery and retest. If the load test is failed again, replacement of the battery is required.

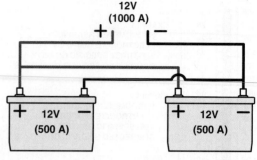

FIGURE 18–8 Most light-duty vehicles equipped with two batteries are connected in parallel as shown. Two 500 A, 12 volt batteries are capable of supplying 1,000 A at 12 volts, which is needed to start many diesel engines.

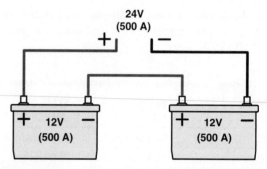

FIGURE 18–9 Many heavy-duty trucks and buses use two 12 volt batteries connected in series to provide 24 volts.

<table>
<tr><td>**?**</td><td>**FREQUENTLY ASKED QUESTION**</td></tr>
</table>

How Should You Test a Vehicle Equipped with Two Batteries?

Many vehicles equipped with a diesel engine use two batteries. These batteries are usually electrically connected in parallel to provide additional current (amperes) at the same voltage. ● **SEE FIGURE 18–8.**

Some heavy-duty trucks and buses connect two batteries in series to provide about the same current as one battery, but with twice the voltage, as shown in ● **FIGURE 18–9.**

To successfully test the batteries, they should be disconnected and tested separately. If just one battery is found to be defective, most experts recommend that both be replaced to help prevent future problems. Because the two batteries are electrically connected, a fault in one battery can cause the good battery to discharge into the defective battery, thereby affecting both even if just one battery is at fault.

FIGURE 18–10 A conductance tester is very easy to use and has proved to accurately determine battery condition if the connections are properly made. Follow the instructions on the display exactly for best results.

ELECTRONIC CONDUCTANCE TESTING

TERMINOLOGY General Motors Corporation, Chrysler Corporation, and Ford specify that an electronic conductance tester be used to test batteries in vehicles still under factory warranty. Conductance is a measure of how well a battery can create current. This tester sends a small signal through the battery and then measures a part of the AC response. As a battery ages, the plates can become sulfated and shed active materials from the grids, reducing the battery capacity. Conductance testers can be used to test flooded or absorbed glass (AGM) type batteries. The unit can determine the following information about a battery.

- CCA
- State of charge
- Voltage of the battery
- Defects such as shorts and opens

However, a conductance tester is not designed to accurately determine the state of charge or CCA rating of a new battery. Unlike a battery load test, a conductance tester can be used on a battery that is discharged. This type of tester should only be used to test batteries that have been in service. ● **SEE FIGURE 18–10.**

TEST PROCEDURE

STEP 1 Connect the unit to the positive and negative terminals of the battery. If testing a side post battery, always use the lead adapters and *never* use steel bolts as these can cause an incorrect reading.

NOTE: Test results can be incorrectly reported on the display if proper, clean connections to the battery are not made. Also be sure that all accessories and the ignition switch are in the off position.

STEP 2 Enter the CCA rating (if known) and push the arrow keys.

STEP 3 The tester determines and displays one of the following:
- **Good battery.** The battery can return to service.
- **Charge and retest.** Fully recharge the battery and return it to service.
- **Replace the battery.** The battery is not serviceable and should be replaced.
- **Bad cell—replace.** The battery is not serviceable and should be replaced.

Some conductance testers can check the charging and cranking circuits, too.

OPEN CIRCUIT VOLTAGE	BATTERY SPECIFIC GRAVITY*	STATE OF CHARGE	CHARGING TIME TO FULL CHARGE AT 80° F**					
			at 60 amps	at 50 amps	at 40 amps	at 30 amps	at 20 amps	at 10 amps
12.6	1.265	100%	FULL CHARGE					
12.4	1.225	75%	15 min.	20 min.	27 min.	35 min.	48 min.	90 min.
12.2	1.190	50%	35 min.	45 min.	55 min.	75 min.	95 min.	180 min.
12.0	1.155	25%	50 min.	65 min.	85 min.	115 min.	145 min.	260 min.
11.8	1.120	0%	65 min.	85 min.	110 min.	150 min.	195 min.	370 min.

CHART 18–3

Battery charging guideline showing the charging times that vary according to state of charge, temperature, and charging rate. It may take eight hours or more to charge a fully discharged battery.
*Correct for temperature
**If colder, it'll take longer

BATTERY CHARGING

CHARGING PROCEDURE If the state of charge of a battery is low, it must be recharged. It is best to slow charge any battery to prevent possible overheating damage to the battery. Perform the following steps.

STEP 1 **Determine the charge rate.** The charge rate is based on the current state of charge (SOC) and charging rate.
● **SEE CHART 18–3** for the recommended charging rate.

STEP 2 **Connect a battery charger to the battery.** Be sure the charger is not plugged in when connecting a charger to a battery. Always follow the battery charger's instructions for proper use.

STEP 3 **Set the charging rate.** The initial charge rate should be about 35 A for 30 minutes to help start the charging process. Fast charging a battery increases the temperature of the battery and can cause warping of the plates inside the battery. Fast charging also increases the amount of gassing (release of hydrogen and oxygen), which can create a health and fire hazard. The battery temperature should not exceed 125°F (hot to the touch).
  • Fast charge: 15 A maximum
  • Slow charge: 5 A maximum
● **SEE FIGURE 18–11.**

CHARGING AGM BATTERIES Charging an absorbed glass mat (AGM) battery requires a different charger than is used to recharge a flooded-type battery. The differences include:

  ▪ The AGM can be charged with high current, up to 75% of the ampere-hour rating due to lower internal resistance.

  ▪ The charging voltage has to be kept at or below 14.4 volts to prevent damage.

FIGURE 18–11 A typical industrial battery charger. Be sure that the ignition switch is in the off position before connecting any battery charger. Connect the cables of the charger to the battery before plugging the charger into the outlet. This helps prevent a voltage spike that could occur if the charger happened to be accidentally left on. Always follow the battery charger manufacturer's instructions.

Because most conventional battery chargers use a charging voltage of 16 volts or higher, a charger specifically designed to charge AGM batteries must be used.

Absorbed glass mat batteries are often used as auxiliary batteries in hybrid electric vehicles when the battery is located inside the vehicle. ● **SEE CHART 18–4** for a summary of the locations of the 12 volt auxiliary battery and high-voltage battery and safety switch/plug.

MAKE, MODEL (YEARS)	AUXILIARY 12 V BATTERY LOCATION	HV BATTERY PACK LOCATION (VOLTAGE)	TYPE OF 12 V BATTERY
Cadillac Escalade (2008+) (two mode)	Under the hood; driver's side	Under second row seat (300 volts)	Flooded lead-acid
Chevrolet Malibu (2008+)	Under the hood; driver's side	Mounted behind rear seat under vehicle floor (36 volts)	Flooded lead-acid
Chevrolet Silverado (2004–2008) (PHT)	Under the hood; driver's side	Under second row seat (42 volts)	Flooded lead-acid
Chevrolet Tahoe (two mode)	Under the hood; driver's side	Under second row seat (300 volts)	Flooded lead-acid
Chrysler Aspen (2009)	Under driver's side door, under vehicle	Under rear seat; driver's side (288 volts)	Flooded lead-acid
Dodge Durango (2009)	Under driver's side door, under vehicle	Under rear seat; driver's side (288 volts)	Flooded lead-acid
Ford Escape (2005+)	Under the hood; driver's side	Cargo area in the rear under carpet (300 volts)	Flooded lead-acid
GMC Sierra (2004–2008) (PHT)	Under the hood; driver's side	Under second row seat (42 volts)	Flooded lead-acid
GMC Yukon (2008+) (two mode)	Under the hood; driver's side	Under second row seat (300 volts)	Flooded lead-acid
Honda Accord (2005–2007)	Under the hood; driver's side	Behind rear seat (144 volts)	Flooded lead-acid
Honda Civic (2003+)	Under the hood; driver's side	Behind rear seat (144 to 158 volts, 2006+)	Flooded lead-acid
Honda Insight (1999–2005)	Under the hood; center under windshield	144 volts; under hatch floor in the rear	Flooded lead-acid
Honda Insight (2010+)	Under the hood; driver's side	144 volts; under floor behind rear seat	Flooded lead-acid
Lexus GS450h (2007+)	In the trunk; driver's side, behind interior panel	Trunk behind rear seat (288 volts)	Absorbed glass mat (AGM)
Lexus LS 600h (2006+)	In the trunk; driver's side, behind interior panel	Trunk behind rear seat (288 volts)	Absorbed glass mat (AGM)
Lexus RX400h (2006–2009)	Under the hood; passenger side	Under the second row seat (288 volts)	Flooded lead-acid
Mercury Mariner (2005+)	Under the hood; driver's side	Cargo area in the rear under carpet (300 volts)	Flooded lead-acid
Nissan Altima (2007+)	In the trunk; driver's side	Behind rear seat (245 volts)	Absorbed glass mat (AGM)
Saturn AURA Hybrid (2007+)	Under the hood; driver's side	Behind the rear seat; under the vehicle floor (36 volts)	Flooded lead-acid
Saturn VUE Hybrid (2007+)	Under the hood; driver's side	Behind the rear seat; under the vehicle floor (36 volts)	Flooded lead-acid
Toyota Camry Hybrid (2007+)	In the trunk; passenger side	Behind the rear seat; under the vehicle floor (245 volts)	Absorbed glass mat (AGM)
Toyota Highlander Hybrid (2006–2009)	Under the hood; passenger side	Under the second row seat (288 volts)	Flooded lead-acid
Toyota Prius (2001–2003)	In the trunk; driver's side	Behind rear seat (274 volts)	Absorbed glass mat (AGM)
Toyota Prius (2004–2009)	In the trunk; driver's side	Behind rear seat (201 volts)	Absorbed glass mat (AGM)
Toyota Prius (2010+)	In the trunk; driver's side	Behind rear seat (201.6 volts)	Absorbed glass mat (AGM)

CHART 18–4

A summary chart showing where the 12 volt and high-voltage batteries and shut-off switch/plugs are located. Only the auxiliary 12 volt batteries can be serviced or charged.

Charge Batteries at 1% of Their CCA Rating

Many batteries are damaged due to being over-charged. To help prevent damage such as warped plates and excessive release of sulfur smell gases, charge batteries at a rate equal to 1% of the battery's CCA rating. For example, a battery with a 700 CCA rating should be charged at 7 amperes (700 × 0.01 = 7 amperes). No harm will occur to the battery at this charge rate even though it may take longer to achieve a full charge. This means that a battery may require eight or more hours to become fully charged depending on the battery capacity and state of charge (SOC).

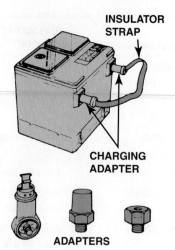

FIGURE 18–12 Adapters should be used on side terminal batteries whenever charging.

 TECH TIP

Always Use Adapters on Side Post Batteries

Side post batteries require that an adapter be used when charging the battery, if it is removed from the vehicle. Do not use steel bolts. If a bolt is threaded into the terminal, only the parts of the threads that contact the battery terminal will be conducting all of the charging current. An adapter or a bolt with a nut attached is needed to achieve full contact with the battery terminals. ● **SEE FIGURE 18–12.**

BATTERY CHARGE TIME

The time needed to charge a completely discharged battery can be estimated by using the reserve capacity rating of the battery in minutes divided by the charging rate.

Hours needed to charge the battery = Reserve capacity ÷ Charge current

For example, if a 10 A charge rate is applied to a discharged battery that has a 90-minute reserve capacity, the time needed to charge the battery will be nine hours.

90 minutes ÷ 10 A = 9 hours

 FREQUENTLY ASKED QUESTION

Should Batteries Be Kept Off of Concrete Floors?

All batteries should be stored in a cool, dry place when not in use. Many technicians have been warned not to store or place a battery on concrete. According to battery experts, it is the temperature difference between the top and the bottom of the battery that causes a difference in the voltage potential between the top (warmer section) and the bottom (colder section). It is this difference in temperature that causes self-discharge to occur.

In fact, submarines cycle seawater around their batteries to keep all sections of the battery at the same temperature to help prevent self-discharge.

Therefore, always store or place batteries up off the floor and in a location where the entire battery can be kept at the same temperature, avoiding extreme heat and freezing temperatures. Concrete cannot drain the battery direction, because the case of the battery is a very good electrical insulator.

FIGURE 18–13 A typical battery jump box used to jump start vehicles. These hand-portable units have almost made jumper cables obsolete.

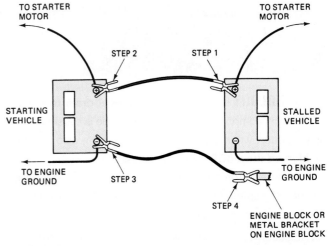

FIGURE 18–14 Jumper cable usage guide. Notice that the last connection should be the engine block of the disabled vehicle to help prevent the spark that normally occurs from igniting the gases from the battery.

JUMP STARTING

To jump start another vehicle with a dead battery, connect good-quality copper jumper cables or a jump box to the good battery and the dead battery, as shown in ● **FIGURE 18–13.**

When using jumper cables or a battery jump box, the last connection made should always be on the engine block or an engine bracket on the dead vehicle as far from the battery as possible. ● **SEE FIGURE 18–14.**

It is normal for a spark to be created when the jumper cables finally complete the jumping circuit, and this spark could cause an explosion of the gases around the battery. Many newer vehicles have special ground and/or positive power connections built away from the battery just for the purpose of jump starting. Check the owner's manual or service information for the exact location.

FIGURE 18–15 The code on the Delphi battery indicates that it was built in 2005 (5), in February (B), on the eleventh day (11), during third shift (C), and in the Canadian plant (Z).

🔧 **TECH TIP**

Look at the Battery Date Code

All major battery manufacturers stamp codes on the battery case that give the date of manufacture and other information. Most battery manufacturers use a number to indicate the year of manufacture and a letter to indicate the month of manufacture, except the letter I, because it can be confused with the number 1. For example:

A = January	G = July
B = February	H = August
C = March	J = September
D = April	K = October
E = May	L = November
F = June	M = December

The shipping date from the manufacturing plant is usually indicated by a *sticker* on the end of the battery. Almost every battery manufacturer uses just one letter and one number to indicate the month and year. ● **SEE FIGURE 18–15.**

BATTERY ELECTRICAL DRAIN TEST

TERMINOLOGY The **battery electrical drain test** determines if any component or circuit in a vehicle is causing a drain on the battery when everything is off. This test is also called the **ignition off draw (IOD)** or **parasitic load test.**

Many electronic components draw a continuous, slight amount of current from the battery when the ignition is off. These components include:

1. Electronically tuned radios for station memory and clock circuits

2. Computers and controllers, through slight diode leakage

3. The alternator, through slight diode leakage

These components may cause a voltmeter to read full battery voltage if it is connected between the negative battery terminal and the removed end of the negative battery cable. Because of this fact, voltmeters should not be used for battery drain testing. This test should be performed when one of the following conditions exists.

1. When a battery is being charged or replaced (a battery drain could have been the cause for charging or replacing the battery)

2. When the battery is suspected of being drained

PROCEDURE FOR BATTERY ELECTRICAL DRAIN TEST

- **Inductive DC ammeter.** The fastest and easiest method to measure battery electrical drain is to connect an inductive DC ammeter that is capable of measuring low current (10 mA). ● **SEE FIGURE 18–16** for an example of a clamp-on digital multimeter being used to measure battery drain.

- **DMM set to read milliamperes.** Following is the procedure for performing the battery electrical drain test using a DMM set to read DC amperes.

    STEP 1 Make certain that all lights, accessories, and ignition are off.

    STEP 2 Check all vehicle doors to be certain that the interior courtesy (dome) lights are off.

    STEP 3 Disconnect the *negative* (−) battery cable and install a parasitic load tool, as shown in ● **FIGURE 18–17.**

    STEP 4 Start the engine and drive the vehicle about 10 minutes, being sure to turn on all the lights and accessories including the radio.

FIGURE 18–16 This mini clamp-on digital multimeter is being used to measure the amount of battery electrical drain that is present. In this case, a reading of 20 mA (displayed on the meter as 00.02 A) is within the normal range of 20 to 30 mA. Be sure to clamp around all of the positive battery cable or all of the negative battery cable, whichever is easiest to get the clamp around.

FIGURE 18–17 After connecting the shut-off tool, start the engine and operate all accessories. Stop the engine and turn off everything. Connect the ammeter across the shut-off switch in parallel. Wait 20 minutes. This time allows all electronic circuits to "time out" or shut down. Open the switch—all current now will flow through the ammeter. A reading greater than specified (usually greater than 50 mA, or 0.05 A) indicates a problem that should be corrected.

STEP 5 Turn the engine and all accessories off including the underhood light.

STEP 6 Connect an ammeter across the parasitic load tool switch and wait 20 minutes for all computers and circuits to shut down.

STEP 7 Open the switch on the load tool and read the battery electrical drain on the meter display.

FIGURE 18–18 The battery was replaced in this Acura and the radio displayed "code" when the replacement battery was installed. Thankfully, the owner had the five-digit code required to unlock the radio.

 REAL WORLD FIX

The Chevrolet Battery Story

A 2005 Chevrolet Impala was being diagnosed for a dead battery. Testing for a battery drain (parasitic draw) showed 2.25 A, which was clearly over the acceptable value of 0.050 or less. At the suggestion of the shop foreman, the technician used a Tech 2 scan tool to check if all of the computers and modules went to sleep after the ignition was turned off. The scan tool display indicated that the instrument panel (IP) showed that it remained awake after all of the others had gone into sleep mode. The IP cluster was unplugged and the vehicle was tested for an electrical drain again. This time, it was only 32 mA (0.032 A), well within the normal range. Replacing the IP cluster solved the excessive battery drain.

NOTE: Using a voltmeter or test light to measure battery drain is *not* recommended by most vehicle manufacturers. The high internal resistance of the voltmeter results in an irrelevant reading that does not provide the technician with adequate information about a problem.

SPECIFICATIONS   Results:

- Normal = 20 to 30 mA (0.02 to 0.03 A)
- Maximum allowable = 50 mA (0.05 A)

RESET ALL MEMORY FUNCTIONS   Be sure to reset the clock, "auto up" windows, and antitheft radio if equipped.
● **SEE FIGURE 18–18.**

BATTERY DRAIN AND RESERVE CAPACITY   It is normal for a battery to self-discharge even if there is not an electrical load such as computer memory to drain the battery. According to General Motors, this self-discharge is about 13 mA (0.013 A).

Some vehicle manufacturers specify a maximum allowable parasitic draw or battery drain be based on the reserve capacity of the battery. The calculation used is the reserve capacity of the battery divided by 4; this equals the maximum allowable battery drain. For example, a battery rated at 120 minutes reserve capacity should have a maximum battery drain of 30 mA.

120 minutes reserve capacity ÷ 4 = 30 mA

FINDING THE SOURCE OF THE DRAIN   If there is a drain, check and temporarily disconnect the following components.

1. Underhood light
2. Glove compartment light
3. Trunk light

If after disconnecting these three components the battery drain draws more than 50 mA (0.05 A), disconnect one fuse at a time from the fuse box until the excessive drain drops to normal.

NOTE: Do not reinsert fuses after they have been removed as this action can cause modules to "wake up," leading to an inconclusive test.

If the excessive battery drain stops after one fuse is disconnected, the source of the drain is located in that particular circuit, as labeled on the fuse box. Continue to disconnect the *power-side* wire connectors from each component included in that particular circuit until the test light goes off. The source of the battery drain can then be traced to an individual component or part of one circuit.

WHAT TO DO IF A BATTERY DRAIN STILL EXISTS
If all the fuses have been disconnected and the drain still exists, the source of the drain has to be between the battery and the fuse box. The most common sources of drain under the hood include the following:

1. **The alternator.** Disconnect the alternator wires and retest. If the ammeter now reads a normal drain, the problem is a defective diode(s) in the alternator.
2. **The starter solenoid (relay) or wiring near its components.** These are also a common source of battery drain, due to high current flows and heat, which can damage the wire or insulation.

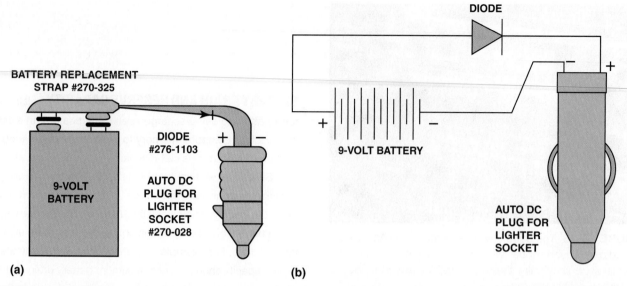

FIGURE 18–19 (a) Memory saver. The part numbers represent components from Radio Shack. (b) A schematic drawing of the same memory saver. Some experts recommend using a 12 volt lantern battery instead of a small 9 volt battery to help ensure that there will be enough voltage in the event that a door is opened while the vehicle battery is disconnected. Interior lights could quickly drain a small 9 volt battery.

TECH TIP

It Could Happen to You!

The owner of a Toyota replaced the battery. After doing so, the owner noted that the "airbag" amber warning lamp was lit and the radio was locked out. The owner had purchased the vehicle used and did not know the four-digit security code needed to unlock the radio. Determined to fix the problem, the owner tried three four-digit numbers, hoping that one of them would work. However, after three tries, the radio became permanently disabled.

Frustrated, the owner went to a dealer. It cost over $300 to fix the problem. A special tool was required to easily reset the airbag lamp. The radio had to be removed and sent out of state to an authorized radio service center and then reinstalled into the vehicle.

Therefore, before disconnecting the battery, check to be certain that the owner has the security code for a security-type radio. A "memory saver" may be needed to keep the radio powered up when the battery is being disconnected. ● SEE FIGURE 18–19.

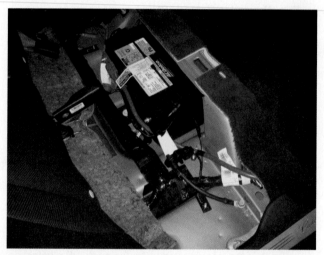

FIGURE 18–20 Many newer vehicles have batteries that are sometimes difficult to find. Some are located under plastic panels under the hood, under the front fender, or even under the rear seat. The jump-start instructions indicate that the spare tire hold-down bolt is to be used as the ground connection if jump starting is necessary.

 FREQUENTLY ASKED QUESTION

Where Is the Battery?

Many vehicle manufacturers today place the battery under the backseat, under the front fender, or in the trunk, as shown in ● FIGURE 18–20.

Often, the battery is not visible even if it is located under the hood. When testing or jump starting a vehicle, look for a battery access point.

Check the Battery Condition First

A discharged or defective battery has lower voltage potential than a good battery that is at least 75% charged. This lower battery voltage cannot properly power the starter motor. A weak battery could also prevent the charging voltage from reaching the voltage regulator cutoff point. This lower voltage could be interpreted as indicating a defective alternator and/or voltage regulator. If the vehicle continues to operate with low system voltage, the stator winding in the alternator can be overheated, causing alternator failure.

BATTERY SYMPTOM GUIDE

The following list will assist technicians in troubleshooting batteries.

Problem	Possible Causes and/or Solutions
1. Headlights are dimmer than normal.	1. Discharged battery or poor connections on the battery, engine, or body
2. Solenoid clicks.	2. Discharged battery or poor connections on the battery or an engine fault, such as coolant on top of the pistons, causing a hydrostatic lock
3. Engine is slow in cranking.	3. Discharged battery, high-resistance battery cables, or defective starter or solenoid
4. Battery will not accept a charge.	4. Possible loose battery cable connections (If the battery is a maintenance-free type, attempt to fast charge the battery for several hours. If the battery still will not accept a charge, replace the battery.)
5. Battery is using water.	5. Check charging system for too high a voltage (If the voltage is normal, the battery is showing signs of gradual failure. Load test and replace the battery, if necessary.)

SUMMARY

1. All batteries should be securely attached to the vehicle with hold-down brackets to prevent vibration damage.

2. Batteries can be tested with a voltmeter to determine the state of charge. A battery load test loads the battery to half of its CCA rating. A good battery should be able to maintain higher than 9.6 volts for the entire 15 sec. test period.

3. Batteries can be tested with a conductance tester even if discharged.

4. A battery drain test should be performed if the battery runs down.

5. Be sure that a battery charger is unplugged from a power outlet when making connections to a battery.

REVIEW QUESTIONS

1. What are the results of a voltmeter test of a battery and its state of charge?

2. What are the steps for performing a battery load test?

3. How is a battery drain test performed?

4. Why should a battery not be fast charged?

1. Technician A says that distilled or clean drinking water should be added to a battery when the electrolyte level is low. Technician B says that fresh electrolyte (solution of acid and water) should be added. Which technician is correct?
   a. Technician A only
   b. Technician B only
   c. Both Technicians A and B
   d. Neither Technician A nor B

2. All batteries should be in a secure bracket that is bolted to the vehicle to prevent physical damage to the battery.
   a. True
   b. False

3. A battery date code sticker indicates D6. What does this mean?
   a. The date it was shipped from the factory was December 2006.
   b. The date it was shipped from the factory was April 2006.
   c. The battery expires in December 2002.
   d. It was built the second day of the week (Tuesday).

4. Many vehicle manufacturers recommend that a special electrical connector be installed between the battery and the battery cable when testing for _____.
   a. Battery drain (parasitic drain)
   b. Specific gravity
   c. Battery voltage
   d. Battery charge rate

5. When load testing a battery, which battery rating is often used to determine how much load to apply to the battery?
   a. CA   c. MCA
   b. RC   d. CCA

6. When measuring the specific gravity of the electrolyte, the maximum allowable difference between the highest and lowest hydrometer reading is _____.
   a. 0.010   c. 0.050
   b. 0.020   d. 0.50

7. A battery high-rate discharge (load capacity) test is being performed on a 12 volt battery. Technician A says that a good battery should have a voltage reading of higher than 9.6 volts while under load at the end of the 15 sec. test. Technician B says that the battery should be discharged (loaded) to twice its CCA rating. Which technician is correct?
   a. Technician A only
   b. Technician B only
   c. Both Technicians A and B
   d. Neither Technician A nor B

8. When charging a lead-acid (flooded-type) battery, _____.
   a. The initial charging rate should be about 35 amperes for 30 minutes
   b. The battery may not accept a charge for several hours, yet may still be a good (serviceable) battery
   c. The battery temperature should not exceed 125°F (hot to the touch)
   d. All of the above

9. Normal battery drain (parasitic drain) in a vehicle with many computer and electronic circuits is _____.
   a. 20 to 30 milliamperes
   b. 2 to 3 amperes
   c. 150 to 300 milliamperes
   d. None of the above

10. When jump starting, _____.
    a. The last connection should be the positive post of the dead battery
    b. The last connection should be the engine block of the dead vehicle
    c. The alternator must be disconnected on both vehicles
    d. Both a and c

chapter 19
CRANKING SYSTEM

OBJECTIVES

After studying Chapter 19, the reader will be able to:

1. Prepare for ASE Electrical/Electronic Systems (A6) certification test content area "C" (Starting System Diagnosis and Repair).

2. Describe how the cranking circuit works.

3. Discuss how a starter motor converts electrical power into mechanical power.

4. Describe the hold-in and pull-in windings of a starter solenoid.

KEY TERMS

Armature 267
Brush-end housing 266
Brushes 268
CEMF 265
Commutator-end housing 266
Commutator segments 268
Compression spring 270
Drive-end housing 266
Field coils 267
Field housing 266
Field poles 267
Ground brushes 268

Hold-in winding 272
Insulated brushes 268
Mesh spring 270
Neutral safety switch 262
Overrunning clutch 270
PM starter 266
Pole shoes 266
Pull-in winding 272
RVS 263
Starter drive 269
Starter solenoid 271
Through bolts 266

FIGURE 19-1 A typical solenoid-operated starter.

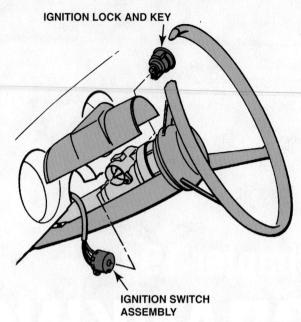

FIGURE 19-2 Some column-mounted ignition switches act directly on the electrical ignition switch itself, whereas others use a link from the lock cylinder to the ignition switch.

CRANKING CIRCUIT

PARTS INVOLVED For any engine to start, it must first be rotated using an external power source. It is the purpose and function of the cranking circuit to create the necessary power and transfer it from the battery to the starter motor, which rotates the engine.

The cranking circuit includes those mechanical and electrical components required to crank the engine for starting. The cranking force in the early 1900s was the driver's arm, because the driver had to physically crank the engine until it started. Modern cranking circuits include the following:

1. **Starter motor.** The starter is normally a 0.5 to 2.6 horsepower (0.4 to 2 kilowatts) electric motor that can develop nearly 8 horsepower (6 kilowatts) for a very short time when first cranking a cold engine. ● **SEE FIGURE 19-1.**

2. **Battery.** The battery must be of the correct capacity and be at least 75% charged to provide the necessary current and voltage for correct starter operation.

3. **Starter solenoid or relay.** The high current required by the starter must be able to be turned on and off. A large switch would be required if the current were controlled by the driver directly. Instead, a small current switch (ignition switch) operates a solenoid or relay that controls the high current to the starter.

4. **Starter drive.** The starter drive uses a small pinion gear that contacts the engine flywheel gear teeth and transmits starter motor power to rotate the engine.

5. **Ignition switch.** The ignition switch and safety control switches control the starter motor operation. ● **SEE FIGURE 19-2.**

CONTROL CIRCUIT PARTS AND OPERATION The engine is cranked by an electric motor that is controlled by a key-operated ignition switch. The ignition switch will not operate the starter unless the automatic transmission is in neutral or park, or the clutch pedal is depressed on manual transmission/transaxle vehicles. This is to prevent an accident that might result from the vehicle moving forward or rearward when the engine is started. The types of controls that are used to be sure that the vehicle will not move when being cranked include the following:

- Many automobile manufacturers use an electric switch called a **neutral safety switch,** which opens the circuit between the ignition switch and the starter to prevent starter motor operation, unless the gear selector is in neutral or park. The safety switch can be attached either to the steering column inside the vehicle near the floor or on the side of the transmission.

- Many manufacturers use a mechanical blocking device in the steering column to prevent the driver from turning the key switch to the start position unless the gear selector is in neutral or park.

- Many manual transmission vehicles also use a safety switch to permit cranking only if the clutch is depressed. This switch is commonly called the *clutch safety switch.* ● **SEE FIGURE 19-3.**

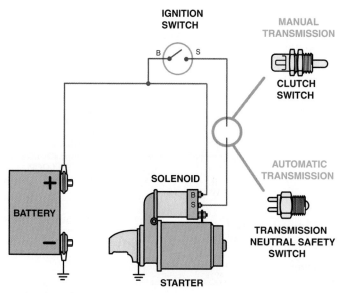

FIGURE 19-3 To prevent the engine from cranking, an electrical switch is usually installed to open the circuit between the ignition switch and the starter solenoid.

FIGURE 19-4 Instead of using an ignition key to start the engine, some vehicles are using a start button which is also used to stop the engine, as shown on this Jaguar.

COMPUTER-CONTROLLED STARTING

OPERATION Some key-operated ignition systems and most push-button-to-start systems use the computer to crank the engine. The ignition switch start position on the push-to-start button is used as an input signal to the powertrain control module (PCM). Before the PCM cranks the engine, the following conditions must be met.

- The brake pedal is depressed.
- The gear selector is in park or neutral.
- The correct key fob (code) is present in the vehicle.

A typical push-button start system includes the following sequence.

- The ignition key can be turned to the start position, released, and the PCM cranks the engine until it senses that the engine has started.
- The PCM can detect that the engine has started by looking at the engine speed signal.
- Normal cranking speed can vary between 100 and 250 RPM. If the engine speed exceeds 400 RPM, the PCM determines that the engine started and opens the circuit to the "S" (start) terminal of the starter solenoid that stops the starter motor.

FIGURE 19-5 The top button on this key fob is the remote start button.

Computer-controlled starting is almost always part of the system if a push-button start is used. ● **SEE FIGURE 19-4.**

REMOTE STARTING Remote starting, sometimes called **remote vehicle start (RVS),** is a system that allows the driver to start the engine of the vehicle from inside the house or a building at a distance of about 200 ft (65 m). The doors remain locked to reduce the possibility of theft. This feature allows the heating or air-conditioning system to start before the driver arrives. ● **SEE FIGURE 19-5.**

NOTE: Most remote start systems will turn off the engine after 10 minutes of run time unless reset by using the remote.

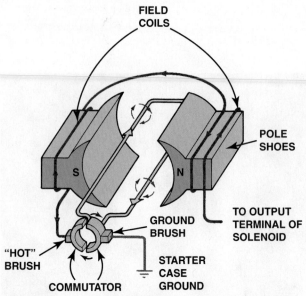

FIGURE 19–6 This series-wound electric motor shows the basic operation with only two brushes: one hot brush and one ground brush. The current flows through both field coils, then through the hot brush and the loop winding of the armature, before reaching ground through the ground brush.

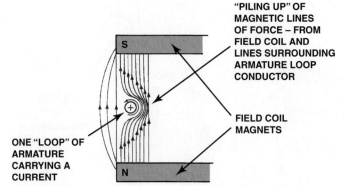

FIGURE 19–7 The interaction of the magnetic fields of the armature loops and field coils creates a stronger magnetic field on the right side of the conductor, causing the armature loop to move toward the left.

STARTER MOTOR OPERATION

PRINCIPLES A starter motor uses electromagnetic principles to convert electrical energy from the battery (up to 300 amperes) to mechanical power (up to 8 horsepower [6 kilowatts]) to crank the engine. Current for the starter motor or power circuit is controlled by a solenoid or relay, which is itself controlled by the driver-operated ignition switch.

The current travels through the brushes and into the armature windings, where other magnetic fields are created around each copper wire loop in the armature. The two strong magnetic fields created inside the starter housing create the force that rotates the armature.

Inside the starter housing is a strong magnetic field created by the field coil magnets. The armature, a conductor, is installed inside this strong magnetic field, with little clearance between the armature and the field coils.

The two magnetic fields act together, and their lines of force "bunch up" or are strong on one side of the armature loop wire and become weak on the other side of the conductor. This causes the conductor (armature) to move from the area of strong magnetic field strength toward the area of weak magnetic field strength. ● SEE FIGURES 19–6 AND 19–7.

The difference in magnetic field strength causes the armature to rotate. This rotation force (torque) is increased as the current flowing through the starter motor increases. The torque of a starter is determined by the strength of the magnetic fields inside the starter. Magnetic field strength is measured in ampere-turns. If the current or the number of turns of wire is increased, the magnetic field strength is increased.

The magnetic field of the starter motor is provided by two or more pole shoes and field windings. The pole shoes are made of iron and are attached to the frame with large screws. ● SEE FIGURE 19–8.

● FIGURE 19–9 shows the paths of magnetic flux lines within a four-pole motor.

The field windings are usually made of a heavy copper ribbon to increase their current-carrying capacity and electromagnetic field strength. ● SEE FIGURE 19–10.

Automotive starter motors usually have four pole shoes and two to four field windings to provide a strong magnetic field within the motor. Pole shoes that do not have field windings are magnetized by flux lines from the wound poles.

SERIES MOTORS A series motor develops its maximum torque at the initial start (0 RPM) and develops less torque as the speed increases.

■ A series motor is commonly used for an automotive starter motor because of its high starting power characteristics.

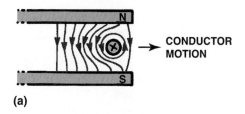

(a)

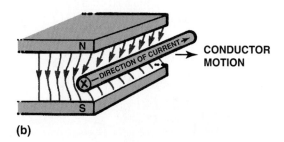

(b)

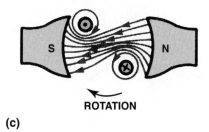

ROTATION

(c)

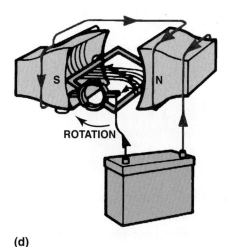

ROTATION

(d)

FIGURE 19–8 The armature loops rotate due to the difference in the strength of the magnetic field. The loops move from a strong magnetic field strength toward a weaker magnetic field strength.

- A series starter motor develops less torque at high RPM, because a current is produced in the starter itself that acts against the current from the battery. Because this current works against battery voltage, it is called **counterelectromotive force,** or **CEMF.** This CEMF is produced by electromagnetic induction in the armature conductors, which are cutting across the magnetic lines of force formed by the field coils. This induced voltage operates against the

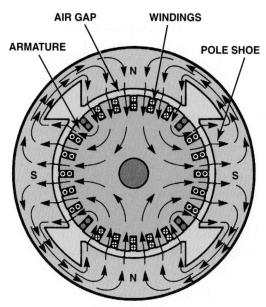

FIGURE 19–9 Magnetic lines of force in a four-pole motor.

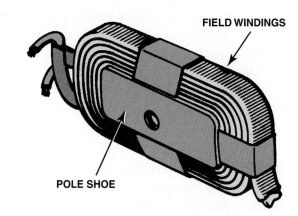

FIGURE 19–10 A pole shoe and field winding.

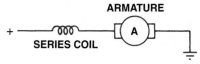

FIGURE 19–11 This wiring diagram illustrates the construction of a series-wound electric motor. Notice that all current flows through the field coils, then through the armature (in series) before reaching ground.

applied voltage supplied by the battery, which reduces the strength of the magnetic field in the starter.

- Because the power (torque) of the starter depends on the strength of the magnetic fields, the torque of the starter decreases as the starter speed increases. A series-wound starter also draws less current at higher speeds and will keep increasing in speed under light loads. This could lead to the destruction of the starter motor unless controlled or prevented. ● **SEE FIGURE 19–11.**

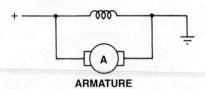

FIGURE 19–12 This wiring diagram illustrates the construction of a shunt-type electric motor, and shows the field coils in parallel (or shunt) across the armature.

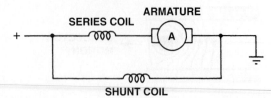

FIGURE 19–13 A compound motor is a combination of series and shunt types, using part of the field coils connected electrically in series with the armature and some in parallel (shunt).

STARTER MOTOR OPERATION (CONTINUED)

SHUNT MOTORS Shunt-type electric motors have the field coils in parallel (or shunt) across the armature.

A shunt-type motor has the following features.

- A shunt motor does not decrease in torque at higher motor RPM, because the CEMF produced in the armature does not decrease the field coil strength.

- A shunt motor, however, does not produce as high a starting torque as that of a series-wound motor, and is not used for starters. Many small electric motors used in automotive blower motors, windshield wipers, power windows, and power seats use permanent magnets rather than electromagnets.

● **SEE FIGURE 19–12.**

PERMANENT MAGNET MOTORS A **permanent magnet (PM) starter** uses permanent magnets that maintain constant field strength, the same as a shunt-type motor, so they have similar operating characteristics. To compensate for the lack of torque, all PM starters use gear reduction to multiply starter motor torque. The permanent magnets used are an alloy of neodymium, iron, and boron, and are almost 10 times more powerful than previously used permanent magnets.

COMPOUND MOTORS A compound-wound, or compound, motor has the operating characteristics of a series motor *and* a shunt-type motor, because some of the field coils are connected to the armature in series and some (usually only one) are connected directly to the battery in parallel (shunt) with the armature.

Compound-wound starter motors are commonly used in Ford, Chrysler, and some GM starters. The shunt-wound field coil is called a shunt coil and is used to limit the maximum speed of the starter. Because the shunt coil is energized as soon as the battery current is sent to the starter, it is used to engage the starter drive on older Ford positive engagement–type starters.
● **SEE FIGURE 19–13.**

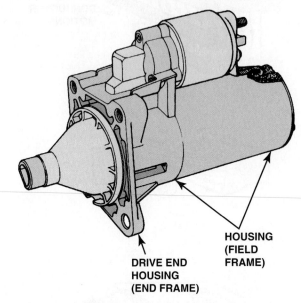

HOUSING (FIELD FRAME)

DRIVE END HOUSING (END FRAME)

FIGURE 19–14 A typical starter motor showing the drive-end housing.

HOW THE STARTER MOTOR WORKS

PARTS INVOLVED A starter consists of the main structural support of a starter called the main **field housing,** one end of which is called a **commutator-end (or brush-end) housing** and the other end a **drive-end housing.** The drive-end housing contains the drive pinion gear, which meshes with the engine flywheel gear teeth to start the engine. The commutator-end plate supports the end containing the starter brushes. **Through bolts** hold the three components together. ● **SEE FIGURE 19–14.**

- **Field coils.** The steel housing of the starter motor contains four electromagnets that are connected directly to the positive post of the battery to provide a strong magnetic field inside the starter. The four electromagnets use heavy copper or aluminum wire wrapped around a soft-iron core, which is contoured to fit against the rounded internal surface of the starter frame. The soft-iron cores are called **pole shoes.** Two of the four pole shoes are

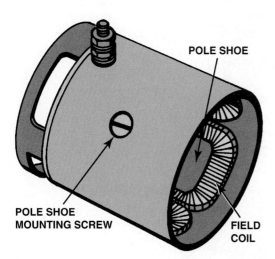

FIGURE 19–15 Pole shoes and field windings installed in the housing.

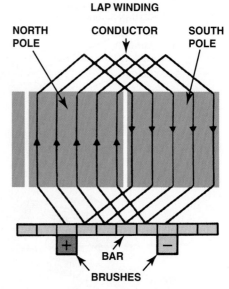

FIGURE 19–17 An armature showing how its copper wire loops are connected to the commutator.

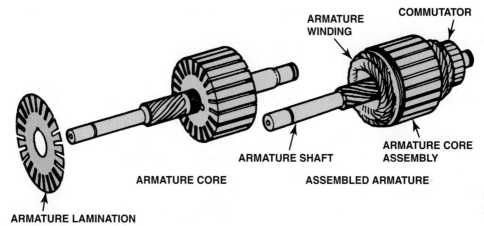

FIGURE 19–16 A typical starter motor armature. The armature core is made from thin sheet metal sections assembled on the armature shaft, which is used to increase the magnetic field strength.

wrapped with copper wire in one direction to create a north pole magnet, and the other two pole shoes are wrapped in the opposite direction to create a south pole magnet. These magnets, when energized, create strong magnetic fields inside the starter housing and, therefore, are called **field coils.** The soft-iron cores (pole shoes) are often called **field poles.** ● SEE FIGURE 19–15.

■ **Armature.** Inside the field coils is an **armature** that is supported with either bushings or ball bearings at both ends, which permit it to rotate. The armature is constructed of thin, circular disks of steel laminated together and wound lengthwise with heavy-gauge insulated copper wire. The laminated iron core supports the copper loops of wire and helps concentrate the magnetic field produced by the coils. ● SEE FIGURE 19–16.

Insulation between the laminations helps to increase the magnetic efficiency in the core. For reduced resistance, the armature conductors are made of a thick copper wire. The two ends of each conductor are attached to two adjacent commutator bars.

The commutator is made of copper bars insulated from each other by mica or some other insulating material. ● SEE FIGURE 19–17.

The armature core, windings, and commutator are assembled on a long armature shaft. This shaft also carries the pinion gear that meshes with the engine flywheel ring gear. The shaft is supported by bearings or bushings in the end housings.

STARTER BRUSHES To supply the proper current to the armature, a four-pole motor must have four brushes riding on the commutator. Most automotive starters have two grounded

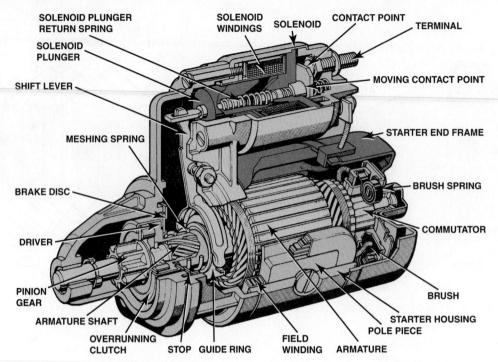

SOLENOID PLUNGER RETURN SPRING
SOLENOID PLUNGER
SHIFT LEVER
MESHING SPRING
BRAKE DISC
DRIVER
PINION GEAR
ARMATURE SHAFT
OVERRUNNING CLUTCH
STOP
GUIDE RING
FIELD WINDING
ARMATURE
SOLENOID WINDINGS
SOLENOID
CONTACT POINT
TERMINAL
MOVING CONTACT POINT
STARTER END FRAME
BRUSH SPRING
COMMUTATOR
BRUSH
STARTER HOUSING
POLE PIECE

FIGURE 19–18 A cutaway of a typical starter motor showing the commutator, brushes, and brush spring.

HOW THE STARTER MOTOR WORKS (CONTINUED)

and two insulated brushes, which are held against the commutator by spring force.

The ends of the copper armature windings are soldered to **commutator segments.** The electrical current that passes through the field coils is then connected to the commutator of the armature by brushes that can move over the segments of the rotating armature. These **brushes** are made of a combination of copper and carbon.

- The copper is a good conductor material.

- The carbon added to the starter brushes helps provide the graphite-type lubrication needed to reduce wear of the brushes and the commutator segments.

The starter uses four brushes—two brushes to transfer the current from the field coils to the armature, and two brushes to provide the ground return path for the current that flows through the armature.

The two sets of brushes include:

1. Two **insulated brushes,** which are in holders and are insulated from the housing.

2. Two **ground brushes,** which use bare, stranded copper wire connections to the brushes. The ground brush holders are not insulated and attach directly to the field housing or brush-end housing.

● **SEE FIGURE 19–18.**

PERMANENT MAGNET FIELDS Permanent magnets are used in place of the electromagnetic field coils and pole shoes. This eliminates the motor field circuit, which in turn eliminates the potential for field coil faults and other electrical problems. The motor has only an armature circuit.

 **TECH TIP**

Don't Hit That Starter!

In the past, it was common to see service technicians hitting a starter in their effort to diagnose a no-crank condition. Often the shock of the blow to the starter aligned or moved the brushes, armature, and bushings. Many times, the starter functioned after being hit, even if only for a short time.

However, most starters today use permanent magnet fields, and the magnets can be easily broken if hit. A magnet that is broken becomes two weaker magnets. Some early PM starters used magnets that were glued or bonded to the field housing. If struck with a heavy tool, the magnets could be broken with parts of the magnet falling onto the armature and into the bearing pockets, making the starter impossible to repair or rebuild. ● **SEE FIGURE 19–19.**

FIGURE 19–19 This starter permanent magnet field housing was ruined when someone used a hammer on the field housing in an attempt to "fix" a starter that would not work. A total replacement is the only solution in this case.

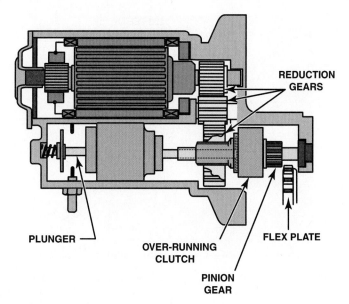

FIGURE 19–20 A typical gear-reduction starter.

GEAR-REDUCTION STARTERS

PURPOSE AND FUNCTION Gear-reduction starters are used by many automotive manufacturers. The purpose of the gear reduction (typically 2:1 to 4:1) is to increase starter motor speed and provide the torque multiplication necessary to crank an engine.

As a series-wound motor increases in rotational speed, the starter produces less power, and less current is drawn from the battery because the armature generates greater CEMF as the starter speed increases. However, a starter motor's maximum torque occurs at 0 RPM and torque decreases with increasing RPM. A smaller starter using a gear-reduction design can produce the necessary cranking power with reduced starter amperage requirements. Lower current requirements mean that smaller battery cables can be used. Many permanent magnet starters use a planetary gear set (a type of gear reduction) to provide the necessary torque for starting. ● **SEE FIGURE 19–20.**

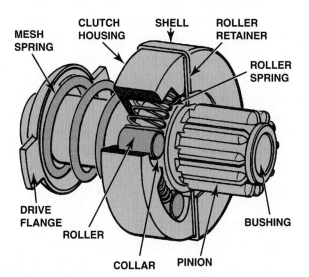

FIGURE 19–21 A cutaway of a typical starter drive showing all of the internal parts.

STARTER DRIVES

PURPOSE AND FUNCTION A **starter drive** includes small pinion gears that mesh with and rotate the larger gear on the engine flywheel or flex plate for starting. The pinion gear must engage with the engine gear slightly *before* the starter motor rotates, to prevent serious damage to either the starter gear or the engine, but must be disengaged after the engine starts. The ends of the starter pinion gear are tapered to help the teeth mesh more easily without damaging the flywheel ring gear teeth. ● **SEE FIGURE 19–21.**

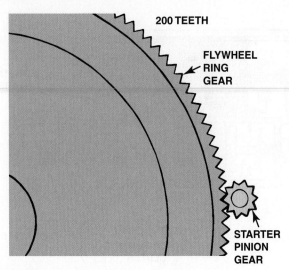

FIGURE 19–22 The ring gear to pinion gear ratio is usually 15:1 to 20:1.

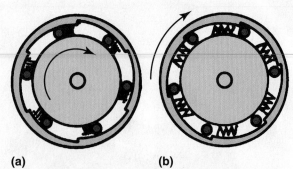

(a)   (b)

FIGURE 19–23 Operation of the overrunning clutch. (a) Starter motor is driving the starter pinion and cranking the engine. The rollers are wedged against spring force into their slots. (b) The engine has started and is rotating faster than the starter armature. Spring force pushes the rollers so they can rotate freely.

STARTER DRIVES (CONTINUED)

STARTER DRIVE GEAR RATIO The ratio of the number of teeth on the engine ring gear to the number on the starter pinion is between 15:1 and 20:1. A typical small starter pinion gear has 9 teeth that turn an engine ring gear with 166 teeth. This provides an 18:1 gear reduction; thus, the starter motor is rotating approximately 18 times faster than the engine. Normal cranking speed for the engine is 200 RPM (varies from 70 to 250 RPM). This means that the starter motor speed is 18 times faster, or 3600 starter RPM (200 × 18 = 3600). If the engine starts and is accelerated to 2000 RPM (normal cold engine speed), the starter will be destroyed by the high speed (36,000 RPM) if the starter was not disengaged from the engine. ● SEE FIGURE 19–22.

STARTER DRIVE OPERATION All starter drive mechanisms use a type of one-way clutch that allows the starter to rotate the engine, but that turns freely if the engine speed is greater than the starter motor speed. This clutch, called an **overrunning clutch,** protects the starter motor from damage if the ignition switch is held in the start position after the engine starts. The overrunning clutch, which is built in as a part of the starter drive unit, uses steel balls or rollers installed in tapered notches. ● SEE FIGURE 19–23.

This taper forces the balls or rollers tightly into the notch, when rotating in the direction necessary to start the engine. When the engine rotates faster than the starter pinion, the balls or rollers are forced out of the narrow tapered notch, allowing the pinion gear to turn freely (overrun).

The spring between the drive tang or pulley and the overrunning clutch and pinion is called a **mesh spring.** It helps to cushion and control the engagement of the starter drive pinion with the engine flywheel gear. This spring is also called a **compression spring,** because the starter solenoid or starter yoke compresses the spring and the spring tension causes the starter pinion to engage the engine flywheel.

FAILURE MODE A starter drive is generally a dependable unit and does not require replacement unless defective or worn. The major wear occurs in the overrunning clutch section of the starter drive unit. The steel balls or rollers wear and often do not wedge tightly into the tapered notches as is necessary for engine cranking. A worn starter drive can cause the starter motor to operate and then stop cranking the engine and creating a "whining" noise. The whine indicates that the starter motor is operating and that the starter drive is not rotating the engine flywheel. The entire starter drive is replaced as a unit. The overrunning clutch section of the starter drive cannot be serviced or repaired separately because the drive is a sealed unit. Starter drives are most likely to fail intermittently at first and then more frequently, until replacement becomes necessary to start the engine. Intermittent starter drive failure (starter whine) is often most noticeable during cold weather.

FREQUENTLY ASKED QUESTION

What Is a Bendix?

Older-model starters often used a Bendix drive mechanism, which used inertia to engage the starter pinion with the engine flywheel gear. Inertia is the tendency of a stationary object to remain stationary, because of its weight, unless forced to move. On these older-model starters, the small starter pinion gear was attached to a shaft with threads, and the weight of this gear caused it to be spun along the threaded shaft and mesh with the flywheel whenever the starter motor spun. If the engine speed was greater than the starter speed, the pinion gear was forced back along the threaded shaft and out of mesh with the flywheel gear. The Bendix drive mechanism has generally not been used since the early 1960s, but some technicians use this term when describing a starter drive.

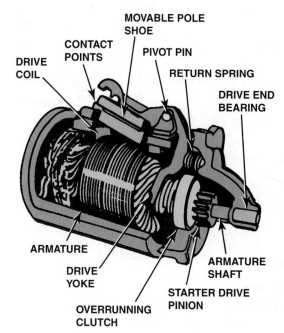

FIGURE 19–24 A Ford movable pole shoe starter.

POSITIVE ENGAGEMENT STARTERS

OPERATION Positive engagement starters (direct drive) were used on Ford engines from 1973 to 1990. These starters use the shunt coil winding and a movable pole shoe to engage the starter drive. The high starting current is controlled by an ignition switch–operated starter solenoid, usually mounted near the positive post of the battery. When this control circuit is closed, current flows through a hollow coil (called a drive coil) that attracts a movable pole shoe.

As soon as the starter drive has engaged the engine flywheel, a tang on the movable pole shoe "opens" a set of contact points. The contact points provide the ground return path for the drive coil operation. After these grounding contacts are opened, all of the starter current can flow through the remaining three field coils and through the brushes to the armature, causing the starter to operate.

The movable pole shoe is held down (which keeps the starter drive engaged) by a smaller coil on the inside of the main drive coil. This coil, called the *holding coil,* is strong enough to hold the starter drive engaged while permitting the flow of the maximum possible current to operate the starter. ● **SEE FIGURE 19–24.**

ADVANTAGES The movable metal pole shoe is attached to and engages the starter drive with a lever (called the plunger lever). As a result, this type of starter does not use a solenoid to engage the starter drive.

DISADVANTAGES If the grounding contact points are severely pitted, the starter may not operate the starter drive or the starter motor because of the resulting poor ground for the drive coil. If the contact points are bent or damaged enough to prevent them from opening, the starter will "clunk" the starter drive into engagement but will not allow the starter motor to operate.

SOLENOID-OPERATED STARTERS

SOLENOID OPERATION A **starter solenoid** is an electromagnetic switch containing two separate, but connected, electromagnetic windings. This switch is used to engage the starter drive and control the current from the battery to the starter motor.

SOLENOID WINDINGS The two internal windings contain approximately the same number of turns but are made from different-gauge wire. Both windings together produce a strong magnetic field that pulls a metal plunger into the solenoid. The plunger is attached to the starter drive through a shift fork lever. When the ignition switch is turned to the start position, the

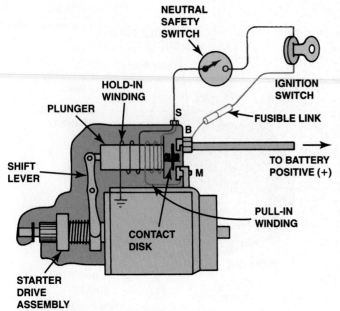

FIGURE 19–25 Wiring diagram of a typical starter solenoid. Notice that both the pull-in winding and the hold-in winding are energized when the ignition switch is first turned to the "start" position. As soon as the solenoid contact disk makes electrical contact with both the B and M terminals, the battery current is conducted to the starter motor and electrically neutralizes the pull-in winding.

SOLENOID-OPERATED STARTERS (CONTINUED)

motion of the plunger into the solenoid causes the starter drive to move into mesh with the flywheel ring gear.

1. The heavier-gauge winding (called the **pull-in winding**) is needed to draw the plunger into the solenoid and is grounded through the starter motor.

2. The lighter-gauge winding (called the **hold-in winding**), which is grounded through the starter frame, produces enough magnetic force to keep the plunger in position. The main purpose of using two separate windings is to permit as much current as possible to operate the starter and yet provide the strong magnetic field required to move the starter drive into engagement. ● SEE FIGURE 19–25.

OPERATION

1. The solenoid operates as soon as the ignition or computer-controlled relay energizes the "S" (start) terminals. At that instant, the plunger is drawn into the solenoid enough to engage the starter drive.

FIGURE 19–26 A palm-size starter armature.

? FREQUENTLY ASKED QUESTION

How Are Starters Made So Small?

Starters and most components in a vehicle are being made as small and as light in weight as possible to help increase vehicle performance and fuel economy. A starter can be constructed smaller due to the use of gear reduction and permanent magnets to achieve the same cranking torque as a straight drive starter, but using much smaller components. ● SEE FIGURE 19–26 for an example of an automotive starter armature that is palm size.

2. The plunger makes contact with a metal disk that connects the battery terminal post of the solenoid to the motor terminal. This permits full battery current to flow through the solenoid to operate the starter motor.

3. The contact disk also electrically disconnects the pull-in winding. The solenoid *has* to work to supply current to the starter. Therefore, if the starter motor operates at all, the solenoid is working, even though it may have high external resistance that could cause slow starter motor operation.

SUMMARY

1. All starter motors use the principle of magnetic interaction between the field coils attached to the housing and the magnetic field of the armature.

2. The control circuit includes the ignition switch, neutral safety (clutch) switch, and solenoid.

3. The power circuit includes the battery, battery cables, solenoid, and starter motor.

4. The parts of a typical starter include the main field housing, commutator-end (or brush-end) housing, drive-end housing, brushes, armature, and starter drive.

REVIEW QUESTIONS

1. What is the difference between the control circuit and the power (motor) circuit sections of a typical cranking circuit?

2. What are the parts of a typical starter?

3. Why does a gear-reduction unit reduce the amount of current required by the starter motor?

4. What are the symptoms of a defective starter drive?

CHAPTER QUIZ

1. Starter motors operate on the principle that _____.
   a. The field coils rotate in the opposite direction from the armature
   b. Opposite magnetic poles repel
   c. Like magnetic poles repel
   d. The armature rotates from a strong magnetic field toward a weaker magnetic field

2. Series-wound electric motors _____.
   a. Produce electrical power
   b. Produce maximum power at 0 RPM
   c. Produce maximum power at high RPM
   d. Use a shunt coil

3. Technician A says that a defective solenoid can cause a starter whine. Technician B says that a defective starter drive can cause a starter whining noise. Which technician is correct?
   a. Technician A only
   b. Technician B only
   c. Both Technicians A and B
   d. Neither Technician A nor B

4. The neutral safety switch is located _____.
   a. Between the starter solenoid and the starter motor
   b. Inside the ignition switch itself
   c. Between the ignition switch and the starter solenoid
   d. In the battery cable between the battery and the starter solenoid

5. The brushes are used to transfer electrical power between _____.
   a. Field coils and the armature
   b. The commutator segments
   c. The solenoid and the field coils
   d. The armature and the solenoid

6. The faster a starter motor rotates, _____.
   a. The more current it draws from the battery
   b. The less CEMF is generated
   c. The less current it draws from the battery
   d. The greater the amount of torque produced

7. Normal cranking speed of the engine is about _____.
   a. 2000 RPM   c. 1000 RPM
   b. 1500 RPM   d. 200 RPM

8. A starter motor rotates about _____ times faster than the engine.
   a. 18   c. 5
   b. 10   d. 2

9. Permanent magnets are commonly used for what part of the starter?
   a. Armature   c. Field coils
   b. Solenoid   d. Commutator

10. What unit contains a hold-in winding and a pull-in winding?
    a. Field coil   c. Armature
    b. Starter solenoid d. Ignition switch

CRANKING SYSTEM DIAGNOSIS AND SERVICE

OBJECTIVES

After studying Chapter 20, the reader will be able to:

1. Prepare for ASE Electrical/Electronic Systems (A6) certification test content area "C" (Starting System Diagnosis and Repair).

2. Explain how to disassemble and reassemble a starter motor and solenoid.

3. Discuss how to perform a voltage drop test on the cranking circuit.

4. Describe how to perform cranking system repair procedures.

5. Describe testing and repair procedures of the cranking circuit and components.

KEY TERMS

Bench testing 281
Growler 280

Shims 282
Voltage drop 276

STARTING SYSTEM TROUBLE-SHOOTING PROCEDURE

OVERVIEW The proper operation of the starting system depends on a good battery, good cables and connections, and a good starter motor. Because a starting problem can be caused by a defective component anywhere in the starting circuit, it is important to check for the proper operation of each part of the circuit to diagnose and repair the problem quickly.

STEPS INVOLVED Following are the steps involved in the diagnosis of a fault in the cranking circuit.

STEP 1 **Verify the customer concern.** Sometimes the customer is not aware of how the cranking system is supposed to work, especially if it is computer controlled.

STEP 2 **Visually inspect the battery and battery connections.** The starter is the highest amperage draw device used in a vehicle and any faults, such as corrosion on battery terminals, can cause cranking system problems.

STEP 3 **Test battery condition.** Perform a battery load or conductance test on the battery to be sure that the battery is capable of supplying the necessary current for the starter.

STEP 4 **Check the control circuit.** An open or high resistance anywhere in the control circuit can cause the starter motor to not engage. Items to check include:
- "S" terminal of the starter solenoid
- Neutral safety or clutch switch

THEFT DETERRENT INDICATOR LAMP

FIGURE 20–1 A theft deterrent indicator lamp of the dash. A flashing lamp usually indicates a fault in the system, and the engine may not start.

- Starter enable relay (if equipped)
- Antitheft system fault (If the engine does not crank or start and the theft indicator light is on or flashing, there is likely a fault in the theft deterrent system. Check service information for the exact procedures to follow before attempting to service the cranking circuit. ● **SEE FIGURE 20–1.**)

STEP 5 **Check voltage drop of the starter circuit.** Any high resistance in either the power side or ground side of the starter circuit will cause the starter to rotate slowly or not at all.

 TECH TIP

Voltage Drop Is Resistance

Many technicians have asked, "Why measure voltage drop when the resistance can be easily measured using an ohmmeter?" Think of a battery cable with all the strands of the cable broken, except for one strand. If an ohmmeter were used to measure the resistance of the cable, the reading would be very low, probably less than 1 ohm. However, the cable is not capable of conducting the amount of current necessary to crank the engine. In less severe cases, several strands can be broken, thereby affecting the operation of the starter motor. Although the resistance of the battery cable will not indicate an increase, the restriction to current flow will cause heat and a drop of voltage available at the starter. Because resistance is not effective until current flows, measuring the voltage drop (differences in voltage between two points) is the most accurate method of determining the true resistance in a circuit.

How much is too much? According to Bosch Corporation, all electrical circuits should have a maximum of 3% loss of the circuit voltage to resistance. Therefore, in a 12 volt circuit, the maximum loss of voltage in cables and connections should be 0.36 volt (12 × 0.03 = 0.36 volt). The remaining 97% of the circuit voltage (11.64 volts) is available to operate the electrical device (load). Just remember:

- Low-voltage drop = Low resistance
- High-voltage drop = High resistance

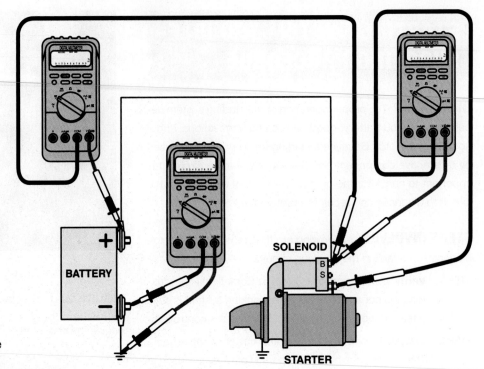

FIGURE 20–2 Voltmeter hookups for voltage drop testing of a solenoid-type cranking circuit.

VOLTAGE DROP TESTING

PURPOSE **Voltage drop** is the drop in voltage that occurs when current is flowing through a resistance. For example, a voltage drop is the difference between voltage at the source and voltage at the electrical device to which it is flowing. The higher the voltage drop is, the greater the resistance in the circuit. Even though voltage drop testing can be performed on any electrical circuit, the most common areas of testing include the cranking circuit and the charging circuit wiring and connections. Voltage drop testing should be performed on both the power side and ground side of the circuit.

A high voltage drop (high resistance) in the cranking circuit wiring can cause slow engine cranking with less than normal starter amperage drain as a result of the excessive circuit resistance. If the voltage drop is high enough, such as that caused by dirty battery terminals, the starter may not operate. A typical symptom of high resistance in the cranking circuit is a "clicking" of the starter solenoid.

TEST PROCEDURE Voltage drop testing of the wire involves connecting a voltmeter set to read DC volts to the suspected high-resistance cable ends and cranking the engine. ● **SEE FIGURES 20–2 THROUGH 20–4.**

NOTE: Before a difference in voltage (voltage drop) can be measured between the ends of a battery cable, current must be flowing through the cable. Resistance is not effective unless current is flowing. If the engine is not being cranked, current is not flowing through the battery cables and the voltage drop cannot be measured.

STEP 1 Disable the ignition or fuel injection as follows:
- Disconnect the primary (low-voltage) electrical connection(s) from the ignition module or ignition coils.
- Remove the fuel-injection fuse or relay, or the electrical connection leading to all of the fuel injectors.

CAUTION: Never disconnect the high-voltage ignition wires unless they are connected to ground. The high voltage that could occur when cranking can cause the ignition coil to fail (arc internally).

STEP 2 Connect one lead of the voltmeter to the starter motor battery terminal and the other end to the positive battery terminal.

STEP 3 Crank the engine and observe the reading while cranking. (Disregard the first higher reading.) The reading should be less than 0.20 volt (200 mV).

STEP 4 If accessible, test the voltage drop across the "B" and "M" terminals of the starter solenoid with the engine cranking. The voltage drop should be less than 0.20 volt (200 mV).

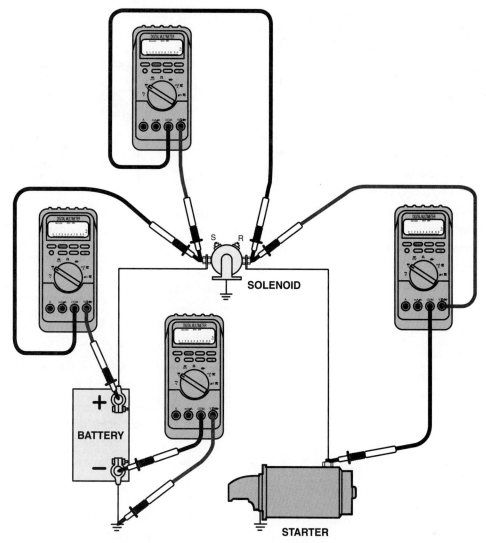

FIGURE 20–3 Voltmeter hookups for voltage drop testing of a Ford cranking circuit.

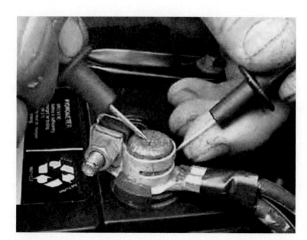

FIGURE 20–4 To test the voltage drop of the battery cable connection, place one voltmeter lead on the battery terminal and the other voltmeter lead on the cable end and crank the engine. The voltmeter will read the difference in voltage between the two leads, which should not exceed 0.20 volt (200 mV).

STEP 5 Repeat the voltage drop on the ground side of the cranking circuit by connecting one voltmeter lead to the negative battery terminal and the other at the starter housing. Crank the engine and observe the voltmeter display. The voltage drop should be less than 0.2 volt (200 mV).

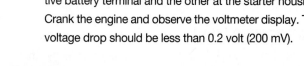 **TECH TIP**

A Warm Cable Equals High Resistance

If a cable or connection is warm to the touch, there is electrical resistance in the cable or connection. The resistance changes electrical energy into heat energy. Therefore, if a voltmeter is not available, touch the battery cables and connections while cranking the engine. If any cable or connection is hot to the touch, it should be cleaned or replaced.

CONTROL CIRCUIT TESTING

PARTS INVOLVED The control circuit for the starting circuit includes the battery, ignition switch, neutral or clutch safety switch, theft deterrent system, and starter solenoid. When the ignition switch is rotated to the start position, current flows through the ignition switch and neutral safety switch to activate the solenoid. High current then flows directly from the battery through the solenoid and to the starter motor. Therefore, an open or break anywhere in the control circuit will prevent the operation of the starter motor.

If a starter is inoperative, first check for voltage at the "S" (start) terminal of the starter solenoid. Check for faults with the following:

- Neutral safety or clutch switch
- Blown crank fuse
- Open at the ignition switch in the crank position

Some models with antitheft controls use a relay to open this control circuit to prevent starter operation.

STARTER AMPERAGE TEST

REASON FOR A STARTER AMPERAGE TEST A starter should be tested to see if the reason for slow or no cranking is due to a fault with the starter motor or another problem. A voltage drop test is used to find out if the battery cables and connections are okay. A starter amperage draw test determines if the starter motor is the cause of a no or slow cranking concern.

TEST PREPARATION Before performing a starter amperage test, be certain that the battery is sufficiently charged (75% or more) and capable of supplying adequate starting current. Connect a starter amperage tester following the tester's instructions. ● **SEE FIGURE 20–5.**

A starter amperage test should be performed when the starter fails to operate normally (is slow in cranking) or as part of a routine electrical system inspection.

SPECIFICTIONS Some service manuals specify normal starter amperage for starter motors being tested on the vehicle; however, most service manuals only give the specifications for bench testing a starter without a load applied. These

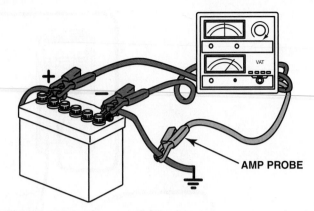

FIGURE 20–5 A starter amperage tester uses an amp probe around the positive or negative battery cables.

AMP PROBE

🔧 **TECH TIP**

Watch the Dome Light

When diagnosing any starter-related problem, open the door of the vehicle and observe the brightness of the dome or interior light(s).

The brightness of any electrical lamp is proportional to the voltage of the battery.

Normal operation of the starter results in a slight dimming of the dome light.

If the light remains bright, the problem is usually an open in the control circuit.

If the light goes out or almost goes out, there could be a problem with the following:

- A shorted or grounded armature of field coils inside the starter
- Loose or corroded battery connections or cables
- Weak or discharged battery

---

specifications are helpful in making certain that a repaired starter meets exact specifications, but they do not apply to starter testing on the vehicle. If exact specifications are not available, the following can be used as general *maximum* amperage draw specifications for testing a starter on the vehicle.

- **4-cylinder engines** = 150 to 185 amperes (normally less than 100 A) at room temperature
- **6-cylinder engines** = 160 to 200 amperes (normally less than 125 A) at room temperature
- **8-cylinder engines** = 185 to 250 amperes (normally less than 150 A) at room temperature

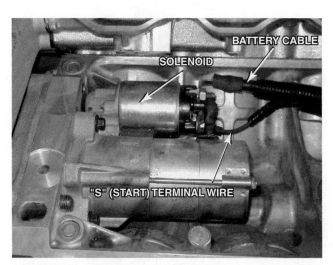

FIGURE 20–6 The starter is located under the intake manifold on this Cadillac Northstar engine.

Excessive current draw may indicate one or more of the following:

1. Binding of starter armature as a result of worn bushings

2. Oil too thick (viscosity too high) for weather conditions

3. Shorted or grounded starter windings or cables

4. Tight or seized engine

5. Shorted starter motor (usually caused by fault with the field coils or armature)

   - High mechanical resistance = High starter amperage draw
   - High electrical resistance = Low starter amperage draw

Lower amperage draw and slow or no cranking may indicate one or more of the following:

- Dirty or corroded battery connections
- High internal resistance in the battery cable(s)
- High internal starter motor resistance
- Poor ground connection between the starter motor and the engine block

STARTER REMOVAL

PROCEDURE After testing has confirmed that a starter motor may need to be replaced, most vehicle manufacturers recommend the following general steps and procedures.

STEP 1 Disconnect the negative battery cable.

STEP 2 Hoist the vehicle safely.

> **NOTE: This step may not be necessary. Check service information for the specified procedure for the vehicle being serviced. Some starters are located under the intake manifold. ● SEE FIGURE 20–6.**

STEP 3 Remove the starter retaining bolts and lower the starter to gain access to the wire(s) connection(s) on the starter.

STEP 4 Disconnect and label the wire(s) from the starter and remove the starter.

STEP 5 Inspect the flywheel (flexplate) for ring gear damage. Also check that the mounting holes are clean and the mounting flange is clean and smooth. Service as needed.

STARTER MOTOR SERVICE

PURPOSE Most starter motors are replaced as an assembly or not easily disassembled or serviced. However, some starters, especially on classic muscle or collector vehicles, can be serviced.

DISASSEMBLY PROCEDURE Disassembly of a starter motor usually includes the following steps.

STEP 1 Remove the starter solenoid assembly.

STEP 2 Mark the location of the through bolts on the field housing to help align them during reassembly.

STEP 3 Remove the drive-end housing and then the armature assembly.

   ● **SEE FIGURE 20–7.**

INSPECTION AND TESTING The various parts should be inspected and tested to see if the components can be used to restore the starter to serviceable condition.

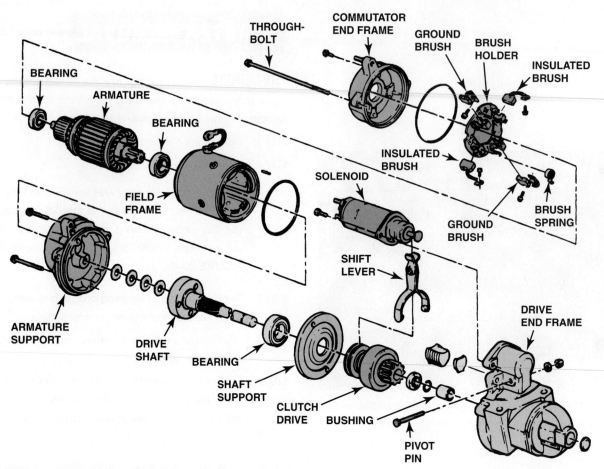

FIGURE 20–7 An exploded view of a typical solenoid-operated starter.

STARTER MOTOR SERVICE (CONTINUED)

- **Solenoid.** Check the resistance of the solenoid winding. The solenoid can be tested using an ohmmeter to check for the proper resistance in the hold-in and pull-in windings. ● **SEE FIGURE 20–8.**

  Most technicians replace the solenoid whenever the starter is replaced and is usually included with a replacement starter.

- **Starter armature.** After the starter drive has been removed from the armature, it can be checked for runout using a dial indicator and V-blocks, as shown in ● **FIGURE 20–9.**

- **Growler.** Because the loops of copper wire are interconnected in the armature of a starter, an armature can be accurately tested only by use of a **growler**. A growler is a 110 volt AC test unit that generates an alternating (60 hertz) magnetic field around an armature. A starter armature is placed into the V-shaped top portion of a laminated soft-iron core surrounded by a coil of copper wire. When the growler is plugged into a 110 volt outlet and switched on, the moving magnetic field creates an alternating current in the armature windings.

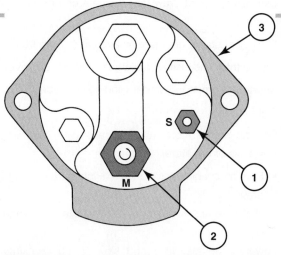

FIGURE 20–8 GM solenoid ohmmeter check. The reading between 1 and 3 (S terminal and ground) should be 0.4 to 0.6 ohm (hold-in winding). The reading between 1 and 2 (S terminal and M terminal) should be 0.2 to 0.4 ohm (pull-in winding).

- **Starter motor field coils.** With the armature removed from the starter motor, the field coils should be tested for opens and grounds using a powered test light or an ohmmeter. To test for a grounded field coil, touch one lead of the tester to a

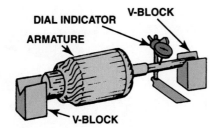

FIGURE 20–9 Measuring an armature shaft for runout using a dial indicator and V-blocks.

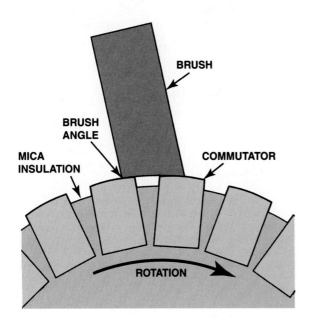

FIGURE 20–10 Replacement starter brushes should be installed so the beveled edge matches the rotation of the commutator.

field brush (insulated or hot) and the other end to the starter field housing. The ohmmeter should indicate infinity (no continuity), and the test light should *not* light. If there is continuity, replace the field coil housing assembly. The ground brushes should show continuity to the starter housing.

NOTE: Many starters use removable field coils. These coils must be rewound using the proper equipment and insulating materials. Usually, the cost involved in replacing defective field coils exceeds the cost of a replacement starter.

- **Starter brush inspection.** Starter brushes should be replaced if the brush length is less than half of its original length (less than 0.5 in. [13 mm]). On some models of starter motors, the field brushes are serviced with the field coil assembly and the ground brushes with the brush holder. Many starters use brushes that are held in with screws and are easily replaced, whereas other starters may require soldering to remove and replace the brushes. ● **SEE FIGURE 20–10.**

BENCH TESTING

Every starter should be tested before installation in a vehicle. **Bench testing** is the usual method and involves clamping the starter in a vise to prevent rotation during operation and connecting heavy-gauge jumper wires (minimum 4 gauge) to both a battery known to be good and the starter. The starter motor should rotate as fast as specifications indicate and not draw more than the free-spinning amperage permitted. A typical amperage specification for a starter being tested on a bench (not installed in a vehicle) usually ranges from 60 to 100 amperes.

STARTER INSTALLATION

After verifying that the starter assembly is functioning correctly, verify that the negative battery cable has been disconnected. Then safely hoist the vehicle, if necessary. Following are the usual steps to install a starter. Be sure to check service information for the exact procedures to follow for the vehicle being serviced.

STEP 1 Check service information for the exact wiring connections to the starter and/or solenoid.

STEP 2 Verify that all electrical connections on the starter motor and/or solenoid are correct for the vehicle and that they are in good condition.

> **NOTE: Be sure that the locking nuts for the studs are tight. Often, the retaining nut that holds the wire to the stud will be properly tightened, but if the stud itself is loose, cranking problems can occur.**

STEP 3 Attach the power and control wires.

STEP 4 Install the starter, and torque all the fasteners to factory specifications and tighten evenly.

STEP 5 Perform a starter amperage draw test and check for proper engine cranking.

> **CAUTION: Be sure to install all factory heat shields to help ensure problem starter operation under all weather and driving conditions.**

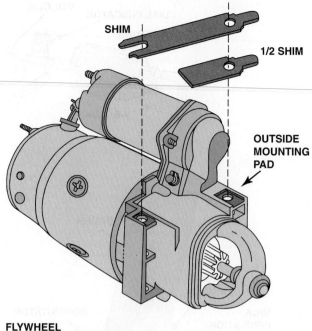

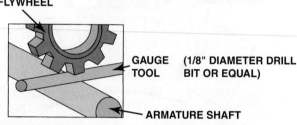

FIGURE 20–11 A shim (or half shim) may be needed to provide the proper clearance between the flywheel teeth of the engine and the pinion teeth of the starter.

STARTER DRIVE-TO-FLYWHEEL CLEARANCE

NEED FOR SHIMS   For the proper operation of the starter and absence of abnormal starter noise, there must be a slight clearance between the starter pinion and the engine flywheel ring gear. Many starters use **shims,** which are thin metal strips between the flywheel and the engine block mounting pad to provide the proper clearance. ● **SEE FIGURE 20–11.**

Some manufacturers use shims under the starter drive-end housings during production. Other manufacturers *grind* the mounting pads at the factory for proper starter pinion gear clearance. If a GM starter is replaced, the starter pinion should be checked and corrected as necessary to prevent starter damage and excessive noise.

SYMPTOMS OF CLEARANCE PROBLEMS

- If the clearance is too great, the starter will produce a high-pitched whine *during* cranking.

- If the clearance is too small, the starter may bind, crank slowly, or produce a high-pitched whine *after* the engine starts, just as the ignition key is released.

PROCEDURE FOR PROPER CLEARANCE   To be sure that the starter is shimmed correctly, use the following procedure.

STEP 1   Place the starter in position and finger-tighten the mounting bolts.

TECH TIP

Reuse Drive-End Housing to Be Sure

Most GM starter motors use a pad mount and attach to the engine with bolts through the drive-end (nose) housing. Many times when a starter is replaced on a GM vehicle, the starter makes noise because of improper starter pinion-to-engine flywheel ring gear clearance. Instead of spending a lot of time shimming the new starter, simply remove the drive-end housing from the original starter and install it on the replacement starter. Service the bushing in the drive-end housing if needed. Because the original starter did not produce excessive gear engagement noise, the replacement starter will also be okay. Reuse any shims that were used with the original starter. This is preferable to removing and reinstalling the replacement starter several times until the proper clearance is determined.

The following list will assist technicians in troubleshooting starting systems.

Problem	Possible Causes
1. Starter motor whines	1. Possible defective starter drive; worn starter drive engagement yoke; defective flywheel; improper starter drive to flywheel clearance
2. Starter rotates slowly	2. Possible high resistance in the battery cables or connections; possible defective or discharged battery; possible worn starter bushings, causing the starter armature to drag on the field coils; possible worn starter brushes or weak brush springs; possible defective (open or shorted) field coil
3. Starter fails to rotate	3. Possible defective ignition switch or neutral safety switch, or open in the starter motor control circuit; theft deterrent system fault; possible defective starter solenoid
4. Starter produces grinding noise	4. Possible defective starter drive unit; possible defective flywheel; possible incorrect distance between the starter pinion and the flywheel; possible cracked or broken starter drive-end housing; worn or damaged flywheel or ring gear teeth
5. Starter clicks when engaged	5. Low battery voltage; loose or corroded battery connections

STEP 2   Use a 1/8 in. diameter drill bit (or gauge tool) and insert between the armature shaft and a tooth of the engine flywheel.

STEP 3   If the gauge tool cannot be inserted, use a full-length shim across both mounting holes to move the starter away from the flywheel.

STEP 4   Remove a shim (or shims) if the gauge tool is loose between the shaft and the tooth of the engine flywheel.

STEP 5   If no shims have been used and the fit of the gauge tool is too loose, add a half shim to the outside pad only. This moves the starter closer to the teeth of the engine flywheel.

1 This dirty and greasy starter can be restored to useful service.

2 The connecting wire between the solenoid and the starter is removed.

3 An old starter field housing is being used to support the drive-end housing of the starter as it is being disassembled. This rebuilder is using an electric impact wrench to remove the solenoid fasteners.

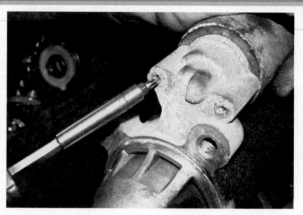

4 A Torx driver is used to remove the solenoid attaching screws.

5 After the retaining screws have been removed, the solenoid can be separated from the starter motor. This rebuilder always replaces the solenoid.

6 The through-bolts are being removed.

7 The brush end plate is removed.

8 The armature assembly is removed from the field frame.

9 Notice that the length of a direct-drive starter armature (top) is the same length as the overall length of a gear-reduction armature except smaller in diameter.

10 A light tap with a hammer dislodges the armature thrust ball (in the palm of the hand) from the center of the gear reduction assembly.

11 This figure shows the planetary ring gear and pinion gears.

12 A close-up of one of the planetary gears, which shows the small needle bearings on the inside.

CONTINUED ▶

13 The clip is removed from the shaft so the planetary gear assembly can be separated and inspected.

14 The shaft assembly is being separated from the stationary gear assembly.

15 The commutator on the armature is discolored and the brushes may not have been making good contact with the segments.

16 All of the starter components are placed in a tumbler with water-based cleaner. The armature is installed in a lathe and the commutator is resurfaced using emery cloth.

17 The finished commutator looks like new.

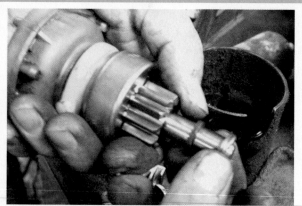

18 Starter reassembly begins by installing a new starter drive on the shaft assembly. The stop ring and stop ring retainer are then installed.

19 The gear-reduction assembly is positioned along with the shift fork (drive lever) into the cleaned drive-end housing.

20 After gear retainer has been installed over the gear reduction assembly, the armature is installed.

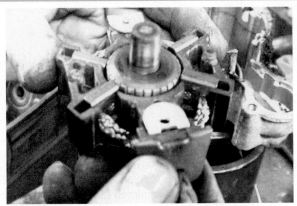

21 New brushes are being installed into the brush holder assembly.

22 The brush end plate and the through-bolts are installed, being sure that the ground connection for the brushes is clean and tight.

23 This starter was restored to useful service by replacing the solenoid, the brushes, and the starter drive assembly plus a thorough cleaning and attention to detail in the reassembly.

1. Proper operation and testing of the starter motor depends on the battery being at least 75% charged and the battery cables being of the correct size (gauge) and having no more than a 0.2 volt drop.

2. Voltage drop testing includes cranking the engine, measuring the drop in voltage from the battery to the starter, and measuring the drop in voltage from the negative terminal of the battery to the engine block.

3. The cranking circuit should be tested for proper amperage draw.

4. An open in the control circuit can prevent starter motor operation.

REVIEW QUESTIONS

1. What are the parts of the cranking circuit?

2. What are the steps taken to perform a voltage drop test of the cranking circuit?

3. What are the steps necessary to replace a starter?

CHAPTER QUIZ

1. A growler is used to test what starter component?
   a. Field coils
   b. Armatures
   c. Commutator
   d. Solenoid

2. Two technicians are discussing what could be the cause of slow cranking and excessive current draw. Technician A says that an engine mechanical fault could be the cause. Technician B says that the starter motor could be binding or defective. Which technician is correct?
   a. Technician A only
   b. Technician B only
   c. Both Technicians A and B
   d. Neither Technician A nor B

3. A V-6 is being checked for starter amperage draw. The initial surge current was about 210 amperes and about 160 amperes during cranking. Technician A says the starter is defective and should be replaced because the current flow exceeds 200 amperes. Technician B says this is normal current draw for a starter motor on a V-6 engine. Which technician is correct?
   a. Technician A only
   b. Technician B only
   c. Both Technicians A and B
   d. Neither Technician A nor B

4. What component or circuit can keep the engine from cranking?
   a. Antitheft
   b. Solenoid
   c. Ignition switch
   d. All of the above

5. Technician A says that a discharged battery (lower than normal battery voltage) can cause solenoid clicking. Technician B says that a discharged battery or dirty (corroded) battery cables can cause solenoid clicking. Which technician is correct?
   a. Technician A only
   b. Technician B only
   c. Both Technicians A and B
   d. Neither Technician A nor B

6. Slow cranking by the starter can be caused by all except _____.
   a. A low or discharged battery
   b. Corroded or dirty battery cables
   c. Engine mechanical problems
   d. An open neutral safety switch

7. Bench testing of a starter should be done _____.
   a. After reassembling an old starter
   b. Before installing a new starter
   c. After removing the old starter
   d. Both a and b

8. If the clearance between the starter pinion and the engine flywheel is too great, _____.
   a. The starter will produce a high-pitched whine during cranking
   b. The starter will produce a high-pitched whine after the engine starts
   c. The starter drive will not rotate at all
   d. The solenoid will not engage the starter drive unit

9. A technician connects one lead of a digital voltmeter to the positive (+) terminal of the battery and the other meter lead to the battery terminal (B) of the starter solenoid and then cranks the engine. During cranking, the voltmeter displays a reading of 878 mV. Technician A says that this reading indicates that the positive battery cable has too high resistance. Technician B says that this reading indicates that the starter is defective. Which technician is correct?
   a. Technician A only
   b. Technician B only
   c. Both Technicians A and B
   d. Neither Technician A nor B

10. A vehicle equipped with a V-8 engine does not crank fast enough to start. Technician A says the battery could be discharged or defective. Technician B says that the negative cable is loose at the battery. Which technician is correct?
   a. Technician A only
   b. Technician B only
   c. Both Technicians A and B
   d. Neither Technician A nor B

CHARGING SYSTEM

OBJECTIVES

After studying Chapter 21, the reader will be able to:

1. Prepare for ASE Electrical/Electronic Systems (A6) certification test content area "D" (Charging System Diagnosis and Repair).

2. List the parts of a typical alternator.

3. Describe how an alternator works.

4. Explain how the powertrain control module (PCM) controls the charging circuit.

KEY TERMS

Alternator 291	OAD 292
Claw poles 293	OAP 291
Delta winding 297	Rectifier 294
Diodes 294	Rotor 293
Drive-end (DE) housing 291	Slip-ring-end (SRE) housing 291
Duty cycle 301	Stator 294
EPM 300	Thermistor 300
IDP 292	

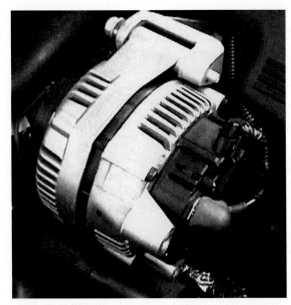

FIGURE 21–1 A typical alternator on a Chevrolet V-8 engine.

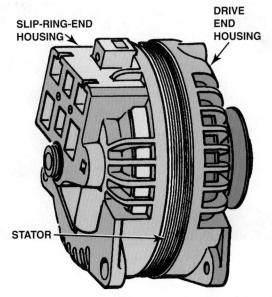

FIGURE 21–2 The end frame toward the drive belt is called the drive-end housing and the rear section is called the slip-ring-end housing.

PRINCIPLES OF ALTERNATOR OPERATION

TERMINOLOGY It is the purpose and function of the charging system to keep the battery fully charged. The Society of Automotive Engineers (SAE) term for the unit that generates electricity is *generator.* The term **alternator** is most commonly used in the trade and will be used in this title.

PRINCIPLES All electrical alternators use the principle of electromagnetic induction to generate electrical power from mechanical power. Electromagnetic induction involves the generation of an electrical current in a conductor when the conductor is moved through a magnetic field. The amount of current generated can be increased by the following factors.

1. Increasing the *speed* of the conductors through the magnetic field

2. Increasing the *number* of conductors passing through the magnetic field

3. Increasing the *strength* of the magnetic field

CHANGING AC TO DC An alternator generates an alternating current because the current changes polarity during the alternator's rotation. However, a battery cannot "store" alternating current; therefore, this alternating current is changed to direct current (DC) by diodes inside the alternator. Diodes are one-way electrical check valves that permit current to flow in only one direction. Most vehicle manufacturers call an AC generator an alternator, a common term in the automotive industry.

ALTERNATOR CONSTRUCTION

HOUSING An alternator is constructed using a two-piece cast aluminum housing. Aluminum is used because of its lightweight, nonmagnetic properties and heat transfer properties needed to help keep the alternator cool. A front ball bearing is pressed into the front housing, called the **drive-end (DE) housing,** to provide the support and friction reduction necessary for the belt-driven rotor assembly. The rear housing, or the **slip-ring-end (SRE) housing,** usually contains either a roller bearing or ball bearing support for the rotor and mounting for the brushes, diodes, and internal voltage regulator (if so equipped). ● **SEE FIGURES 21–1 AND 21–2.**

ALTERNATOR OVERRUNNING PULLEYS

PURPOSE AND FUNCTION Many alternators are equipped with an **overrunning alternator pulley (OAP),** also called an *overrunning clutch pulley* or an *alternator clutch pulley.* The purpose of this pulley is to help eliminate noise and vibration in the accessory drive belt system, especially when the engine is at idle speed. At idle, engine impulses are transmitted to the alternator through the accessory drive belt. The mass of the rotor of the alternator tends to want to keep spinning, but the engine crankshaft speeds up and slows down slightly due to the power

FIGURE 21–3 An OAP on a Chevrolet Corvette alternator.

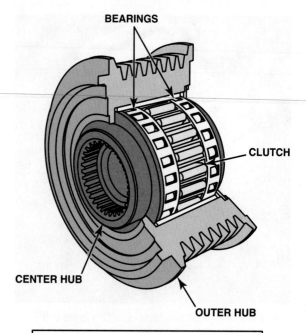

OVERRUNNING ALTERNATOR PULLEY (OAP)

FIGURE 21–4 An exploded view of an overrunning alternator pulley showing all of the internal parts.

ALTERNATOR OVERRUNNING PULLEYS (CONTINUED)

impulses. Using a one-way clutch in the alternator pulley allows the belt to apply power to the alternator in only one direction, thereby reducing fluctuations in the belt. ● **SEE FIGURES 21–3 AND 21-4.**

A conventional drive pulley attaches to the alternator (rotor) shaft with a nut and lock washer. In the overrunning clutch pulley, the inner race of the clutch acts as the nut as it screws on to the shaft. Special tools are required to remove and install this type of pulley.

Another type of alternator pulley uses a dampener spring inside, plus a one-way clutch. These units have the following names.

- **Isolating Decoupler Pulley (IDP)**
- **Active Alternator Pulley (AAP)**
- **Alternator Decoupler Pulley (ADP)**
- **Alternator Overrunning Decoupler Pulley**
- **Overrunning Alternator Dampener (OAD)** (most common term)

OAP or OAD pulleys are primarily used on vehicles equipped with diesel engines or on luxury vehicles where noise and vibration need to be kept at a minimum. Both are designed to:

- Reduce accessory drive belt noise
- Improve the life of the accessory drive belt
- Improve fuel economy by allowing the engine to be operated at a low idle speed

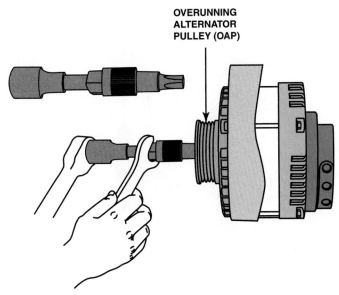

FIGURE 21–5 A special tool is needed to remove and install overrunning alternator pulleys or dampeners.

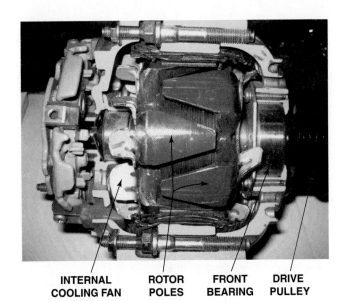

INTERNAL COOLING FAN   ROTOR POLES   FRONT BEARING   DRIVE PULLEY

FIGURE 21–6 A cutaway of an alternator, showing the rotor and cooling fan that is used to force air through the unit to remove the heat created when it is charging the battery and supplying electrical power for the vehicle.

 FREQUENTLY ASKED QUESTION

Can I Install an OAP or an OAD to My Alternator?

Usually, no. An alternator needs to be equipped with the proper shaft to allow the installation of an OAP or OAD. This also means that a conventional pulley often cannot be used to replace a defective overrunning alternator pulley or dampener with a conventional pulley. Check service information for the exact procedure to follow.

 TECH TIP

Always Check the OAP or OAD First

Overrunning alternator pulleys and overrunning alternator dampeners can fail. The most common factor is the one-way clutch. If it fails, it can freewheel and not power the alternator or it can lock up and not provide the dampening as designed. If the charging system is not working, the OAP or OAD could be the cause, rather than a fault in the alternator itself.

In most cases, the entire alternator assembly will be replaced because each OAP or OAD is unique for each application and both require special tools to remove and replace.
● **SEE FIGURE 21–5.**

ALTERNATOR COMPONENTS AND OPERATION

ROTOR CONSTRUCTION The **rotor** is the rotating part of the alternator and is driven by the accessory drive belt. The rotor creates the magnetic field of the alternator and produces a current by electromagnetic induction in the stationary stator windings. The rotor is constructed of many turns of copper wire coated with a varnish insulation wound over an iron core. The iron core is attached to the rotor shaft.

At both ends of the rotor windings are heavy-gauge metal plates bent over the windings with triangular fingers called **claw poles.** These pole fingers do not touch, but alternate or interlace, as shown in ● **FIGURE 21–6.**

HOW ROTORS CREATE MAGNETIC FIELDS The two ends of the rotor winding are connected to the rotor's slip rings. Current for the rotor flows from the battery into one brush that rides on one of the slip rings, then flows through the rotor winding, then exits the rotor through the other slip ring and brush. One alternator brush is considered to be the "positive" brush and one is considered to be the "negative" or "ground" brush. The voltage regulator is connected to either the positive or the negative brush and controls the field current through the rotor that controls the output of the alternator.

If current flows through the rotor windings, the metal pole pieces at each end of the rotor become electromagnets. Whether a north or a south pole magnet is created depends on the

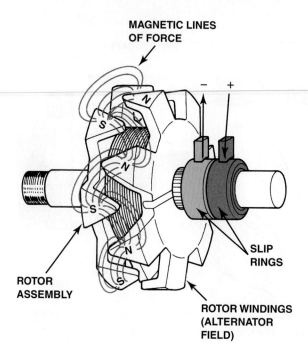

FIGURE 21-7 Rotor assembly of a typical alternator. Current through the slip rings causes the "fingers" of the rotor to become alternating north and south magnetic poles. As the rotor revolves, these magnetic lines of force induce a current in the stator windings.

MAGNETIC LINES OF FORCE

SLIP RINGS

ROTOR ASSEMBLY

ROTOR WINDINGS (ALTERNATOR FIELD)

ALTERNATOR COMPONENTS AND OPERATION (CONTINUED)

direction in which the wire coil is wound. Because the pole pieces are attached to each end of the rotor, one pole piece will be a north pole magnet. The other pole piece is on the opposite end of the rotor and therefore is viewed as being wound in the opposite direction, creating a south pole. Therefore, the rotor fingers are alternating north and south magnetic poles. The magnetic fields are created between the alternating pole piece fingers. These individual magnetic fields produce a current by electromagnetic induction in the stationary stator windings. ● **SEE FIGURE 21-7.**

ROTOR CURRENT The current necessary for the field (rotor) windings is conducted through slip rings with carbon brushes. The maximum rated alternator output in amperes depends on the number and gauge of the rotor windings. Substituting rotors from one alternator to another can greatly affect maximum output. Many commercially rebuilt alternators are tested and then display a sticker to indicate their tested output. The original rating stamped on the housing is then ground off.

The current for the field is controlled by the voltage regulator and is conducted to the slip rings through carbon brushes. The brushes conduct only the field current that is just 2 to 5 amperes.

STATOR CONSTRUCTION The **stator** consists of the stationary coil windings inside the alternator. The stator is supported between the two halves of the alternator housing, with three copper wire windings that are wound on a laminated metal core.

As the rotor revolves, its moving magnetic field induces a current in the stator windings. ● **SEE FIGURE 21-8.**

DIODES **Diodes** are constructed of a semiconductor material (usually silicon) and operate as a one-way electrical check valve that permits the current to flow in only one direction. Alternators often use six diodes (one positive and one negative set for each of the three stator windings) to convert alternating current to direct current.

Diodes used in alternators are included in a single part called a **rectifier,** or *rectifier bridge*. A rectifier not only includes the diodes (usually six), but also the cooling fins and connections for the stator windings and the voltage regulator. ● **SEE FIGURE 21-9.**

DIODE TRIO Some alternators are equipped with a diode trio that supplies current to the brushes from the stator windings. A diode trio uses three diodes, in one housing, with one diode for each of the three stator windings and then one output terminal.

HOW AN ALTERNATOR WORKS

FIELD CURRENT IS PRODUCED A rotor inside an alternator is turned by a belt and drive pulley which are turned by the engine. The magnetic field of the rotor generates a current in the stator windings by electromagnetic induction. ● **SEE FIGURE 21-10.**

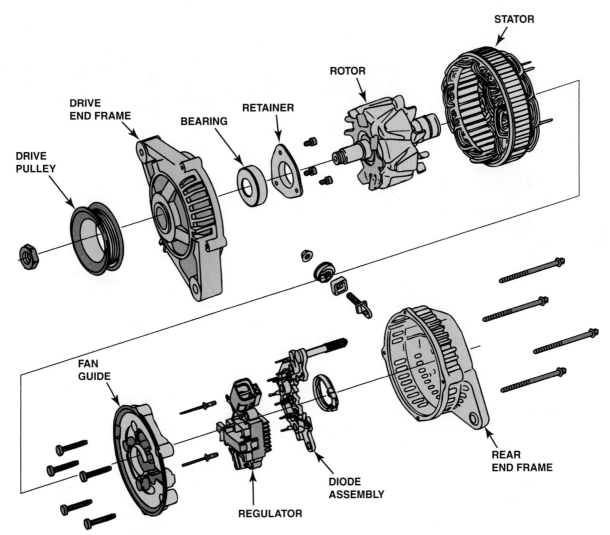

FIGURE 21–8 An exploded view of a typical alternator showing all of its internal parts including the stator windings.

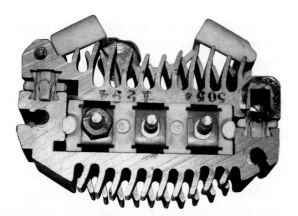

FIGURE 21–9 A rectifier usually includes six diodes in one assembly and is used to rectify AC voltage from the stator windings into DC voltage suitable for use by the battery and electrical devices in the vehicle.

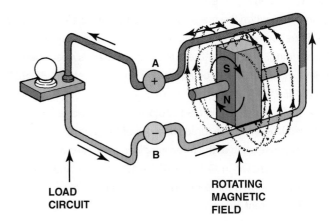

FIGURE 21–10 Magnetic lines of force cutting across a conductor induce a voltage and current in the conductor.

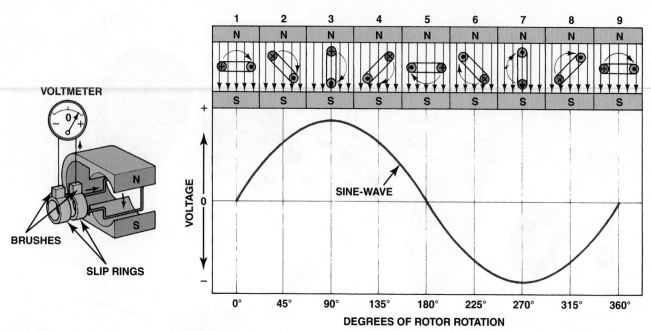

FIGURE 21–11 A sine wave (shaped like the letter *S* on its side) voltage curve is created by one revolution of a winding as it rotates in a magnetic field.

HOW AN ALTERNATOR WORKS (CONTINUED)

Field current flowing through the slip rings to the rotor creates an alternating north and south pole on the rotor, with a magnetic field between each finger of the rotor.

CURRENT IS INDUCED IN THE STATOR
The induced current in the stator windings is an alternating current because of the alternating magnetic field of the rotor. The induced current starts to increase as the magnetic field starts to induce current in each winding of the stator. The current then peaks when the magnetic field is the strongest and starts to decrease as the magnetic field moves away from the stator winding. Therefore, the current generated is described as being of a sine wave or alternating current pattern. ● SEE FIGURE 21–11.

As the rotor continues to rotate, this sine wave current is induced in each of the three windings of the stator.

Because each of the three windings generates a sine wave current, as shown in ● FIGURE 21–12, the resulting currents combine to form a three-phase voltage output.

The current induced in the stator windings connects to diodes (one-way electrical check valves) that permit the alternator output current to flow in only one direction. All alternators contain six diodes, one pair (a positive and a negative diode)

for each of the three stator windings. Some alternators contain eight diodes with another pair connected to the center connection of a wye-type stator.

WYE-CONNECTED STATORS
The Y (pronounced "wye" and generally so written) type or star pattern is the most commonly used alternator stator winding connection. ● SEE FIGURE 21–13.

The output current with a wye-type stator connection is constant over a broad alternator speed range.

Current is induced in each winding by electromagnetic induction from the rotating magnetic fields of the rotor. In a wye-type stator connection, the currents must combine because two windings are always connected in series. ● SEE FIGURE 21–14.

The current produced in each winding is added to the other windings' current and then flows through the diodes to the alternator output terminal. One-half of the current produced is available at the neutral junction (usually labeled "STA" for stator). The voltage at this center point is used by some alternator manufacturers (especially Ford) to control the charge indicator light or is used by the voltage regulator to control the rotor field current.

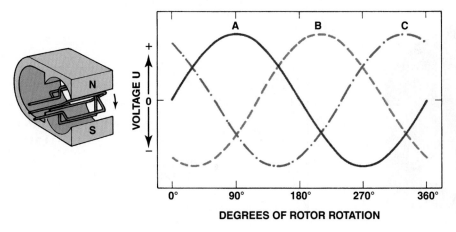

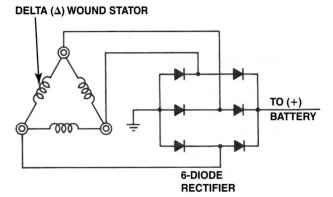

FIGURE 21–12 When three windings (A, B, and C) are present in a stator, the resulting current generation is represented by the three sine waves. The voltages are 120 degrees out of phase. The connection of the individual phases produces a three-phase alternating voltage.

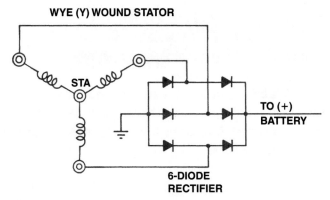

FIGURE 21–13 Wye-connected stator winding.

FIGURE 21–15 Delta-connected stator winding.

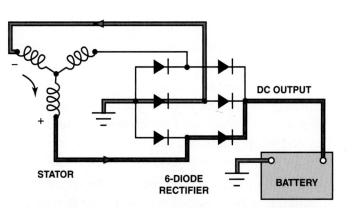

FIGURE 21–14 As the magnetic field, created in the rotor, cuts across the windings of the stator, a current is induced. Notice that the current path includes passing through one positive (+) diode on the way to the battery and one negative (−) diode as a complete circuit is completed through the rectifier and stator.

DELTA-CONNECTED STATORS The **delta winding** is connected in a triangular shape. Delta is a Greek letter shaped like a triangle. ● **SEE FIGURE 21–15.**

Current induced in each winding flows to the diodes in a parallel circuit. More current can flow through two parallel circuits than can flow through a series circuit (as in a wye-type stator connection).

Delta-connected stators are used on alternators where high output at high-alternator RPM is required. The delta-connected alternator can produce 73% more current than the same alternator with wye-type stator connections. For example, if an alternator with a wye-connected stator can produce 55 A, the *same* alternator with delta-connected stator windings can produce 73% more current, or 95 A (55 × 1.73 = 95). The delta-connected alternator, however, produces lower current at low speed and must be operated at high speed to produce its maximum output.

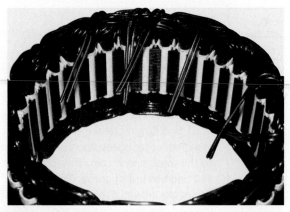

FIGURE 21–16 A stator assembly with six, rather than the normal three, windings.

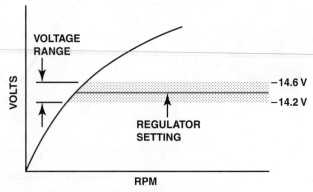

FIGURE 21–17 Typical voltage regulator range.

ALTERNATOR OUTPUT FACTORS

The output voltage and current of an alternator depend on the following factors.

1. **Speed of rotation.** Alternator output is increased with alternator rotational speed up to the alternator's maximum possible ampere output. Alternators normally rotate at a speed two to three times faster than engine speed, depending on the relative pulley sizes used for the belt drive. For example, if an engine is operating at 5000 RPM, the alternator will be rotating at about 15,000 RPM.

2. **Number of conductors.** A high-output alternator contains more turns of wire in the stator windings. Stator winding connections (whether wye or delta) also affect the maximum alternator output. ● **SEE FIGURE 21–16** for an example of a stator that has six rather than three windings, which greatly increases the amperage output of the alternator.

3. **Strength of the magnetic field.** If the magnetic field is strong, a high output is possible because the current generated by electromagnetic induction is dependent on the number of magnetic lines of force that are cut.

   a. The strength of the magnetic field can be increased by increasing the number of turns of conductor wire wound on the rotor. A higher output alternator has more turns of wire than an alternator with a low rated output.

   b. The strength of the magnetic field also depends on the current through the field coil (rotor). Because magnetic field strength is measured in ampere-turns, the greater the amperage or the number of turns, or both, the greater the alternator output.

ALTERNATOR VOLTAGE REGULATION

PRINCIPLES An automotive alternator must be able to produce electrical pressure (voltage) higher than battery voltage to charge the battery. Excessively high voltage can damage the battery, electrical components, and the lights of a vehicle. Basic principles include the following:

- If no (zero) amperes of current existed throughout the field coil of the alternator (rotor), alternator output would be zero because without field current a magnetic field does not exist.

- The field current required by most automotive alternators is less than 3 amperes. It is the *control* of the *field* current that controls the output of the alternator.

- Current for the rotor flows from the battery positive post, through the rotor positive brush, into the rotor field winding, and exits the rotor winding through the rotor ground brush. Most voltage regulators control field current by controlling the amount of field current through the ground brush.

- The voltage regulator simply opens the field circuit if the voltage reaches a predetermined level, then closes the field circuit again as necessary to maintain the correct charging voltage. ● **SEE FIGURE 21–17.**

- The electronic circuit of the voltage regulator cycles between 10 and 7,000 times per *second* as needed to accurately control the field current through the rotor, and therefore control the alternator output.

FIGURE 21–18 A typical electronic voltage regulator with the cover removed showing the circuits inside.

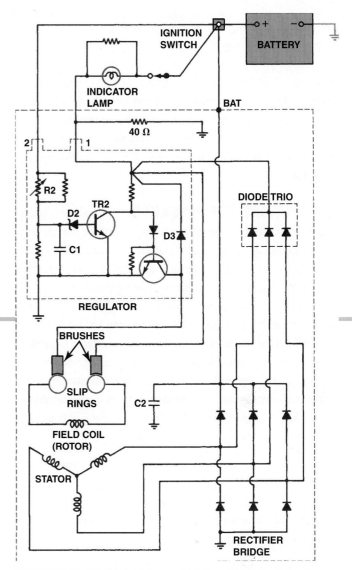

FIGURE 21–19 Typical General Motors SI-style alternator with an integral voltage regulator. Voltage present at terminal 2 is used to reverse bias the zener diode (D2) that controls TR2. The positive brush is fed by the ignition current (terminal I) plus current from the diode trio.

REGULATOR OPERATION

- The control of the field current is accomplished by opening and closing the *ground* side of the field circuit through the rotor of the alternator.

- The zener diode is a major electronic component that makes voltage regulation possible. A zener diode blocks current flow until a specific voltage is reached, then it permits current to flow. Alternator voltage from the stator and diodes is first sent through a thermistor, which changes resistance with temperature, and then to a zener diode. When the upper-limit voltage is reached, the zener diode conducts current to a transistor, which then opens the field (rotor) circuit. The electronics are usually housed in a separate part inside the alternator.
  ● **SEE FIGURES 21–18 AND 21–19.**

BATTERY CONDITION AND CHARGING VOLTAGE If the automotive battery is discharged, its voltage will be lower than the voltage of a fully charged battery. The alternator will supply charging current, but it may not reach the maximum charging voltage. For example, if a vehicle is jump started and run at a fast idle (2000 RPM), the charging voltage may be only 12 volts. In this case, the following may occur.

- As the battery becomes charged and the battery voltage increases, the charging voltage will also increase, until the voltage regulator limit is reached.

- Then the voltage regulator will start to control the charging voltage. A good, but discharged, battery should be able to convert into chemical energy all the current the

alternator can produce. As long as alternator voltage is higher than battery voltage, current will flow from the alternator (high voltage) to the battery (lower voltage).

- Therefore, if a voltmeter is connected to a discharged battery with the engine running, it may indicate charging voltage that is lower than normally acceptable.

In other words, the condition and voltage of the battery *do* determine the charging rate of the alternator. It is often stated that the battery is the true "voltage regulator" and that the voltage regulator simply acts as the upper-limit voltage control.

This is the reason why all charging system testing *must* be performed with a reliable and known to be good battery, at least 75% charged, to be assured of accurate test results. If a discharged battery is used during charging system testing, tests could mistakenly indicate a defective alternator and/or voltage regulator.

TEMPERATURE COMPENSATION All voltage regulators (mechanical or electronic) provide a method for increasing the charging voltage slightly at low temperatures and for lowering the charging voltage at high temperatures. A battery requires a higher charging voltage at low temperatures because of the resistance to chemical reaction changes. However, the battery would be overcharged if the charging voltage were not reduced during warm weather. Electronic voltage regulators use a temperature-sensitive resistor in the regulator circuit. This resistor, called a **thermistor,** provides lower resistance as the temperature increases. A thermistor is used in the electronic circuits of the voltage regulator to control charging voltage over a wide range of underhood temperatures.

NOTE: Voltmeter test results may vary according to temperature. Charging voltage tested at 32°F (0°C) will be higher than for the same vehicle tested at 80°F (27°C) because of the temperature-compensation factors built into voltage regulators.

ALTERNATOR COOLING

Alternators create heat during normal operation and this heat must be removed to protect the component inside, especially the diodes and voltage regulator. The types of cooling include:

- External fan
- Internal fan(s)
- Both an external fan and an internal fan
- Coolant cooled (● **SEE FIGURE 21–20.**)

COOLANT CONNECTIONS

FIGURE 21–20 A coolant-cooled alternator showing the hose connections where coolant from the engine flows through the rear frame of the alternator.

COMPUTER-CONTROLLED ALTERNATORS

TYPES OF SYSTEMS Computers can interface with the charging system in three ways.

1. The computer can *activate* the charging system by turning on and off the field current to the rotor. In other words, the computer, usually the powertrain control module (PCM), controls the field current to the rotor.

2. The computer can *monitor* the operation of the alternator and increase engine speed if needed during conditions when a heavy load is demanded by the alternator.

3. The computer can *control* the alternator by controlling alternator output to match the needs of the electrical system. This system detects the electrical needs of the vehicle and commands the alternator to charge only when needed to improve fuel economy.

GM ELECTRICAL POWER MANAGEMENT SYSTEM A typical system used on some General Motors vehicles is called **electrical power management (EPM)**. It uses a Hall-effect sensor attached to the negative or positive battery cable to measure the current leaving and entering the battery. ● **SEE FIGURE 21–21.**

The engine control module (ECM) controls the alternator by changing the on-time of the current through the rotor. ● **SEE FIGURE 21–22.**

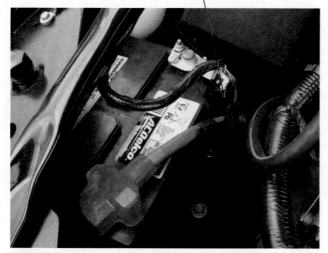

CURRENT SENSOR

FIGURE 21–21 A Hall-effect current sensor attached to the positive battery cable is used as part of the EPM system.

COMMAND DUTY CYCLE	ALTERNATOR OUTPUT VOLTAGE
10%	11.0 V
20%	11.6 V
30%	12.1 V
40%	12.7 V
50%	13.3 V
60%	13.8 V
70%	14.4 V
80%	14.9 V
90%	15.5 V

CHART 21–1

The output voltage is controlled by varying the duty cycle as controlled by the PCM.

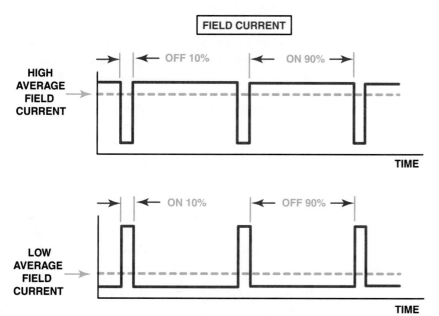

FIELD CURRENT

OFF 10%   ON 90%

HIGH AVERAGE FIELD CURRENT

TIME

ON 10%   OFF 90%

LOW AVERAGE FIELD CURRENT

TIME

FIGURE 21–22 The amount of time current is flowing through the field (rotor) determines the alternator output.

The on-time, called **duty cycle,** varies from 5% to 95%.
● **SEE CHART 21–1.**

This system has six modes of operation.

1. **Charge mode.** The charge mode is activated when any of the following occurs.
   - Electric cooling fans are on high speed.
   - Rear window defogger is on.
   - Battery state of charge (SOC) is less than 80%.
   - Outside (ambient) temperature is less than 32°F (0°C).

2. **Fuel economy mode.** This mode reduces the load on the engine from the alternator for maximum fuel economy. This mode is activated when the following conditions are met.
   - Ambient temperature is above 32°F (0°C).
   - The state of charge of the battery is 80% or higher.
   - The cooling fans and rear defogger are off.

   The target voltage is 13 volts and will return to the charge mode, if needed.

3. **Voltage reduction mode.** This mode is commanded to reduce the stress on the battery during low-load conditions. This mode is activated when the following conditions are met.
   - Ambient temperature is above 32°F (0°C).
   - Battery discharge rate is less than 7 amperes.
   - Rear defogger is off.
   - Cooling fans are on low or off.
   - Target voltage is limited to 12.7 volts.

4. **Start-up mode.** This mode is selected after engine start and commands a charging voltage of 14.5 volts for 30 seconds. After 30 seconds, the mode is changed depending on conditions.

5. **Battery sulfation mode.** This mode is commanded if the output voltage is less than 13.2 volts for 45 minutes, which can indicate that sulfated plates could be the cause. The target voltage is 13.9 to 15.5 volts for three minutes. After three minutes, the system returns to another mode based on conditions.

6. **Headlight mode.** This mode is selected when the headlights are on and the target voltage is 14.5 volts.

COMPUTER-CONTROLLED CHARGING SYSTEMS

Computer control of the charging system has the following advantages.

1. The computer controls the field of the alternator, which can pulse it on or off as needed for maximum efficiency, thereby saving fuel.

   NOTE: Some vehicle manufacturers, such as Honda/ Acura, use an *electronic load control (ELC)*, which turns on the alternator when decelerating, where the additional load on the engine is simply used to help slow the vehicle. This allows the battery to be charged without placing a load on the engine, helping to increase fuel economy.

TECH TIP

The Voltage Display Can Be a Customer Concern

A customer may complain that the voltmeter reading on the dash fluctuates up and down. This may be normal as the computer-controlled charging system commands various modes of operation based on the operating conditions. Follow the vehicle manufacturer's recommended procedures to verify proper operation.

2. Engine idle can also be improved by turning on the alternator slowly, rather than all at once, if an electrical load is switched on, such as the air-conditioning system.

3. Most computers can also reduce the load on the electrical system if the demand exceeds the capacity of the charging system by reducing fan speed, shutting off rear window defoggers, or increasing engine speed to cause the alternator to increase the amperage output.

   NOTE: A commanded higher-than-normal idle speed may be the result of the computer compensating for an abnormal electrical load. This higher idle speed could indicate a defective battery or other electrical system faults.

4. The computer can monitor the charging system and set diagnostic trouble codes (DTCs) if a fault is detected. Many systems allow the service technician to control the charging of the alternator using a scan tool.

5. Because the charging system is computer controlled, it can be checked using a scan tool. Some vehicle systems allow the scan tool to activate the alternator field and then monitor the output to help detect fault locations. Always follow the vehicle manufacturer's diagnostic procedure.

SUMMARY

1. Alternator output is increased if the speed of the alternator is increased.

2. The parts of a typical alternator include the drive-end (DE) housing, slip-ring-end (SRE) housing, rotor assembly, stator, rectifier bridge, brushes, and voltage regulator.

3. The magnetic field is created in the rotor.

4. The alternator output current is created in the stator windings.

5. The voltage regulator controls the current flow through the rotor winding.

1. How can a small electronic voltage regulator control the output of a typical 100 ampere alternator?

2. What are the component parts of a typical alternator?

3. How is the computer used to control an alternator?

4. Why do voltage regulators include temperature compensation?

5. How is AC voltage inside the alternator changed to DC voltage at the output terminal?

6. What is the purpose of an OAP or OAD?

CHAPTER QUIZ

1. Technician A says that the diodes regulate the alternator output voltage. Technician B says that the field current can be computer controlled. Which technician is correct?
   a. Technician A only
   b. Technician B only
   c. Both Technicians A and B
   d. Neither Technician A nor B

2. A magnetic field is created in the _____ in an alternator (AC alternator).
   a. Stator
   b. Diodes
   c. Rotor
   d. Drive-end frame

3. The voltage regulator controls current through the _____.
   a. Alternator brushes
   b. Rotor
   c. Alternator field
   d. All of the above

4. Technician A says that two diodes are required for each stator winding lead. Technician B says that diodes change alternating current into direct current. Which technician is correct?
   a. Technician A only
   b. Technician B only
   c. Both Technicians A and B
   d. Neither Technician A nor B

5. The alternator output current is produced in the _____.
   a. Stator
   b. Rotor
   c. Brushes
   d. Diodes (rectifier bridge)

6. Alternator brushes are constructed from _____.
   a. Copper
   b. Aluminum
   c. Carbon
   d. Silver-copper alloy

7. How much current flows through the alternator brushes?
   a. All of the alternator output flows through the brushes
   b. 25 to 35 A, depending on the vehicle
   c. 10 to 15 A
   d. 2 to 5 A

8. Technician A says that an alternator overrunning pulley is used to reduce vibration and noise. Technician B says that an overrunning alternator pulley or dampener uses a one-way clutch. Which technician is correct?
   a. Technician A only
   b. Technician B only
   c. Both Technicians A and B
   d. Neither Technician A nor B

9. Operating an alternator in a vehicle with a defective battery can harm the _____.
   a. Diodes (rectifier bridge)
   b. Stator
   c. Voltage regulator
   d. Brushes

10. Technician A says that a wye-wound stator produces more maximum output than the same alternator equipped with a delta-wound stator. Technician B says that an alternator equipped with a delta-wound stator produces more maximum output than a wye-wound stator. Which technician is correct?
    a. Technician A only
    b. Technician B only
    c. Both Technicians A and B
    d. Neither Technician A nor B

CHARGING SYSTEM DIAGNOSIS AND SERVICE

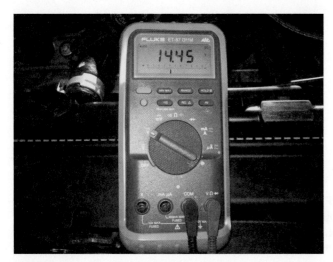

FIGURE 22–1 The digital multimeter should be set to read DC volts, with the red lead connected to the positive (+) battery terminal and the black meter lead connected to the negative (−) battery terminal.

FIGURE 22–2 A scan tool can be used to diagnose charging system problems.

CHARGING SYSTEM TESTING AND SERVICE

BATTERY STATE OF CHARGE

The charging system can be tested as part of a routine vehicle inspection or to determine the reason for a no-charge or reduced charging circuit performance. The battery *must* be at least 75% charged before testing the alternator and the charging system. A weak or defective battery will cause inaccurate test results. If in doubt, replace the battery with a known good shop battery for testing.

CHARGING VOLTAGE TEST

The **charging voltage test** is the easiest way to check the charging system voltage at the battery. Use a digital multimeter to check the voltage, as follows:

STEP 1 Select DC volts.

STEP 2 Connect the red meter lead to the positive (+) terminal of the battery and the black meter lead to the negative (−) terminal of the battery.

> **NOTE: The polarity of the meter leads is not too important when using a digital multimeter. If the meter leads are connected backward on the battery, the resulting readout will simply have a negative (−) sign in front of the voltage reading.**

STEP 3 Start the engine and increase the engine speed to about 2000 RPM (fast idle) and record the charging voltage. ● **SEE FIGURE 22–1.**

Specifications for charging voltage = 13.5 to 15 V

- If the voltage is too high, check that the alternator is properly grounded.

- If the voltage is lower than specifications, then there is a fault with the wiring or the alternator.

- If the wiring and the connections are okay, then additional testing is required to help pinpoint the root cause. Replacement of the alternator and/or battery is often required if the charging voltage is not within factory specifications.

SCAN TESTING THE CHARGING CIRCUIT

Most vehicles that use a computer-controlled charging system can be diagnosed using a scan tool. Not only can the charging voltage be monitored, but also in many vehicles, the field circuit can be controlled and the output voltage monitored to check that the system is operating correctly. ● **SEE FIGURE 22–2.**

> **NOTE: Some charging systems, such as those on many Honda/Acura vehicles, use an electronic load detection circuit that energizes the field circuit only when an electrical load is detected. For example, if the engine is running and there are no accessories on, the voltage read at the battery may be 12.6 V, which could indicate that the charging system is not operating. In this situation, turning on the headlights or an accessory should cause the computer to activate the field circuit, and the alternator should produce normal charging voltage.**

FREQUENTLY ASKED QUESTION

What Is a Full-Fielding Test?

Full fielding is a procedure used on older noncomputerized vehicles for bypassing the voltage regulator that could be used to determine if the alternator is capable of producing its designed output. This test is no longer performed for the following reasons.

- The voltage regulator is built into the alternator, therefore requiring that the entire assembly be replaced even if just the regulator is defective.
- When the regulator is bypassed, the alternator can produce a high voltage (over 100 volts in some cases) which could damage all of the electronic circuits in the vehicle.

    Always follow the vehicle manufacture's recommended testing procedures.

TECH TIP

Use a Test Light to Check for a Defective Fusible Link

Most alternators use a fusible link or mega fuse between the output terminal and the positive (+) terminal of the battery. If this fusible link or fuse is defective (blown), then the charging system will not operate at all. Many alternators have been replaced repeatedly because of a blown fusible link that was not discovered until later. A quick and easy test to check if the fusible link is okay is to touch a test light to the output terminal. With the other end of the test light attached to a good ground, the fusible link or mega fuse is okay if the light lights. This test confirms that the circuit between the alternator and the battery has continuity. ● **SEE FIGURE 22–3.**

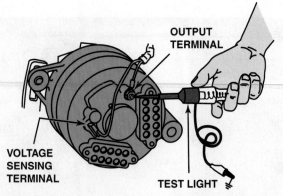

FIGURE 22–3 Before replacing an alternator, the wise technician checks that battery voltage is present at the output and battery voltage sense terminals. If not, then there is a fault in the wiring.

DRIVE BELT INSPECTION AND ADJUSTMENT

BELT VISUAL INSPECTION   It is generally recommended that all belts be inspected regularly and replaced as needed. Replace any serpentine belt that has more than three cracks in any one rib that appears in a 3 in. span. Check service information for the specified procedure and recommended replacement interval. ● **SEE FIGURE 22–4.**

BELT TENSION MEASUREMENT   If the vehicle does not use a belt tensioner, then a belt tension gauge is needed to achieve the specified belt tension. Install the belt and operate the engine with all of the accessories turned on to "run-in" the belt for at least five minutes. Adjust the tension of the accessory drive belt to factory specifications or use the following table for an example of the proper tension based on the size of the belt.

There are four ways that vehicle manufacturers specify that the belt tension is within factory specifications.

1. **Belt tension gauge.** A belt tension gauge is needed to determine if it is at the specified belt tension. Install the belt and operate the engine with all of the accessories turned on to "run-in" the belt for at least five minutes. Adjust the tension of the accessory drive belt to factory specifications, or see ● **CHART 22–1** for an example of the proper tension based on the size of the belt.

2. **Marks on a tensioner.** Many tensioners have marks that indicate the normal operating tension range for the accessory drive belt. Check service information for the preferred location of the tensioner mark. ● **SEE FIGURE 22–5.**

FIGURE 22–4 This accessory drive belt is worn and requires replacement. Newer belts are made from ethylene propylene diene monomer (EPDM). This rubber does not crack like older belts and may not show wear even though the ribs do wear and can cause slippage.

 TECH TIP

The Hand Cleaner Trick

Lower-than-normal alternator output could be the result of a loose or slipping drive belt. All belts (V and serpentine multigroove) use an interference angle between the angle of the Vs of the belt and the angle of the Vs on the pulley. As the belt wears, the interference angles are worn off of both edges of the belt. As a result, the belt may start to slip and make a squealing sound even if tensioned properly.

A common trick used to determine if the noise is belt related is to use grit-type hand cleaner or scouring powder. With the engine off, sprinkle some powder onto the pulley side of the belt. Start the engine. The excess powder will fly into the air, so get away from under the hood when the engine starts. If the belts are now quieter, you know that it was the glazed belt that made the noise.

The noise can sound exactly like a noisy bearing. Therefore, before you start removing and replacing parts, try the hand cleaner trick.

Often, the grit from the hand cleaner will remove the glaze from the belt and the noise will not return. However, if the belt is worn or loose, the noise will return and the belt should be replaced. A fast, alternative method to see if the noise is from the belt is to spray water from a squirt bottle at the belt with the engine running. If the noise stops, the belt is the cause of the noise. The water quickly evaporates and, therefore, unlike the gritty hand cleaner, water simply finds the problem—it does not provide a short-term fix.

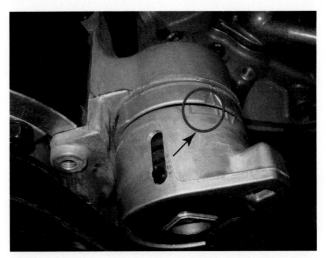

FIGURE 22–5 Check service information for the exact marks where the tensioner should be located for proper belt tension.

SERPENTINE BELTS	
NUMBER OF RIBS USED	TENSION RANGE (LB)
3	45–60
4	60–80
5	75–100
6	90–125
7	105–145
V-BELTS	
V-BELT TOP WIDTH (IN.)	TENSION RANGE (LB)
1/4	45–65
5/16	60–85
25/64	85–115
31/64	105–145

CHART 22–1

Typical belt tension for various widths of belts. Tension is the force needed to depress the belt as displayed on a belt tension gauge.

3. **Torque wrench reading.** Some vehicle manufacturers specify that a beam-type torque wrench be used to determine the torque needed to rotate the tensioner. If the torque reading is below specifications, the tensioner must be replaced.

4. **Deflection.** Depress the belt between the two pulleys that are the farthest apart; the flex or deflection should be 1/2 in. (13 mm).

FIGURE 22–6 This overrunning alternator dampener (OAD) is longer than an overrunning alternator pulley (OAP) because it contains a dampener spring as well as a one way clutch. Be sure to check that it locks in one direction.

🔧 **TECH TIP**

Check the Overrunning Clutch

If low or no alternator output is found, remove the alternator drive belt and check the overrunning alternator pulley (OAP) or overrunning alternator dampener (OAD) for proper operation. Both types of overrunning clutches use a one-way clutch. Therefore, the pulley should freewheel in one direction and rotate the alternator rotor when rotated in the opposite direction. ● **SEE FIGURE 22–6.**

MEASURING THE AC RIPPLE FROM THE ALTERNATOR TELLS A LOT ABOUT ITS CONDITION. IF THE AC RIPPLE IS ABOVE 500 MILLIVOLTS, OR .5 VOLTS, LOOK FOR A PROBLEM IN THE DIODES OR STATOR. IF THE RIPPLE IS BELOW 500 MILLIVOLTS, CHECK THE ALTERNATOR OUTPUT TO DETERMINE ITS CONDITION.

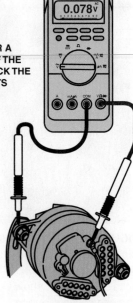

FIGURE 22–7 AC ripple at the output terminal of the alternator is more accurate than testing at the battery due to the resistance of the wiring between the alternator and the battery. The reading shown on the meter, set to AC volts, is only 78 mV (0.078 V), far below what the reading would be if a diode were defective.

AC RIPPLE VOLTAGE CHECK

PRINCIPLES A good alternator should produce very little AC voltage or current output. It is the purpose of the diodes in the alternator to rectify or convert most AC voltage into DC voltage. While it is normal to measure some AC voltage from an alternator, excessive AC ripple is undesirable and indicates a fault with the rectifier diodes or stator windings inside the alternator.

TESTING AC RIPPLE VOLTAGE The procedure to check for **AC ripple voltage** includes the following steps.

STEP 1 Set the digital meter to read AC volts.

STEP 2 Start the engine and operate it at 2000 RPM (fast idle).

STEP 3 Connect the voltmeter leads to the positive and negative battery terminals.

STEP 4 Turn on the headlights to provide an electrical load on the alternator.

NOTE: A more accurate reading can be obtained by touching the meter lead to the output or "battery" terminal of the alternator. ● SEE FIGURE 22–7.

The results should be interpreted as follows: If the rectifier diodes are good, the voltmeter should read *less* than 400 mV (0.4 volt) AC. If the reading is over 500 mV (0.5 volt) AC, the rectifier diodes are defective.

NOTE: Many conductance testers, such as Midtronic and Snap-On, automatically test for AC ripple.

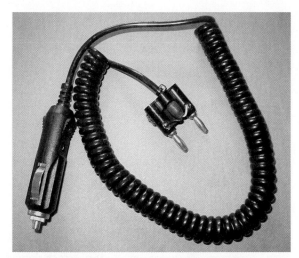

FIGURE 22–8 Charging system voltage can be easily checked at the lighter plug by connecting a lighter plug to the voltmeter through a double banana plug.

FIGURE 22–9 A mini clamp-on meter can be used to measure alternator output as shown here (105.2 Amp.). Then the meter can be used to check AC current ripple by selecting AC Amps on the rotary dial. AC ripple current should be less than 10% of the DC current output.

TESTING AC RIPPLE CURRENT

All alternators should create direct current (DC) if the diodes and stator windings are functioning correctly. A mini clamp-on meter capable of measuring AC amperes can be used to check the alternator. A good alternator should produce less than 10% of its rated amperage output in AC ripple amperes. For example, an alternator rated at 100 amperes should not produce more than 10 amperes AC ripple (100 × 10% = 10). It is normal for a good alternator to produce 3 or 4 A of AC ripple current to the battery. Only if the AC ripple current exceeds 10% of the rating of the alternator should the alternator be repaired or replaced.

TEST PROCEDURE To measure the AC current to the battery, perform the following steps.

STEP 1 Start the engine and turn on the lights to create an electrical load on the alternator.

STEP 2 Using a mini clamp-on digital multimeter, place the clamp around either all of the positive (+) battery cables or all of the negative (−) battery cables.

An AC/DC current clamp adapter can also be used with a conventional digital multimeter set on the DC millivolts scale.

STEP 3 To check for AC current ripple, switch the meter to read AC amperes and record the reading. Read the meter display.

STEP 4 The results should be within 10% of the specified alternator rating. A reading of greater than 10 amperes AC indicates defective alternator diodes. ● **SEE FIGURE 22–9.**

 **TECH TIP**

The Lighter Plug Trick

Battery voltage measurements can be read through the lighter socket. Simply construct a test tool using a lighter plug at one end of a length of two-conductor wire and the other end connected to a double banana plug. The double banana plug will fit most meters in the common (COM) terminal and the volt terminal of the meter. This is handy to use while road testing the vehicle under real-life conditions. Both DC voltage and AC ripple voltage can be measured. ● **SEE FIGURE 22–8.**

CHARGING SYSTEM VOLTAGE DROP TESTING

ALTERNATOR WIRING For the proper operation of any charging system, there must be good electrical connections between the battery positive terminal and the alternator output terminal. The alternator must also be properly grounded to the engine block.

Many manufacturers of vehicles run the lead from the output terminal of the alternator to other connectors or junction

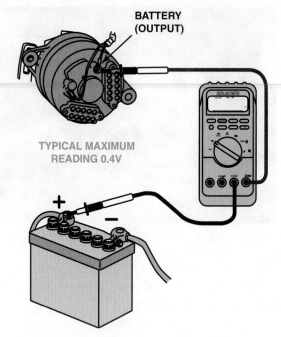

BATTERY
(OUTPUT)

TYPICAL MAXIMUM
READING 0.4V

+   −

VOLTAGE DROP - INSULATED CHARGING CIRCUIT

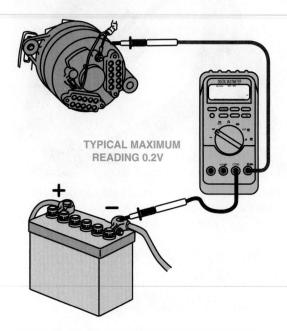

ENGINE AT 2,000 RPM.
CHARGING SYSTEM
LOADED TO 20A

TYPICAL MAXIMUM
READING 0.2V

+   −

VOLTAGE DROP - CHARGING GROUND CIRCUIT

FIGURE 22–10 Voltmeter hookup to test the voltage drop of the charging circuit.

CHARGING SYSTEM VOLTAGE DROP TESTING (CONTINUED)

blocks that are electrically connected to the positive terminal of the battery. If there is high resistance (a high voltage drop) in these connections or in the wiring itself, the battery will not be properly charged.

VOLTAGE DROP TEST PROCEDURE When there is a suspected charging system problem (with or without a charge indicator light on), simply follow these steps to measure the voltage drop of the insulated (power-side) charging circuit.

STEP 1 Start the engine and run it at a fast idle (about 2000 engine RPM).

STEP 2 Turn on the headlights to ensure an electrical load on the charging system.

STEP 3 Using any voltmeter set to read DC volts, connect the positive test lead (red) to the output terminal of the alternator. Attach the negative test lead (black) to the positive post of the battery.

The results should be interpreted as follows:

1. If there is less than a 0.4 volt (400 mV) reading, then all wiring and connections are satisfactory.

2. If the voltmeter reads higher than 0.4 volt, there is excessive resistance (voltage drop) between the alternator output terminal and the positive terminal of the battery.

3. If the voltmeter reads battery voltage (or close to battery voltage), there is an open circuit between the battery and the alternator output terminal.

To determine whether the alternator is correctly grounded, maintain the engine speed at 2000 RPM with the headlights on. Connect the positive voltmeter lead to the case of the alternator and the negative voltmeter lead to the negative terminal of the battery. The voltmeter should read less than 0.2 volt (200 mV) if the alternator is properly grounded. If the reading is over 0.2 volt, connect one end of an auxiliary ground wire to the case of the alternator and the other end to a good engine ground. ● **SEE FIGURE 22–10.**

Use a Fused Jumper Wire as a Diagnostic Tool

When diagnosing an alternator charging problem, try using a fused jumper wire to connect the positive and negative terminals of the alternator directly to the positive and negative terminals of the battery. If a definite improvement is noticed, the problem is in the wiring of the vehicle. High resistance, due to corroded connections or loose grounds, can cause low alternator output, repeated regulator failures, slow cranking, and discharged batteries. A voltage drop test of the charging system can also be used to locate excessive resistance (high voltage drop) in the charging circuit, but using a fused jumper wire is often faster and easier.

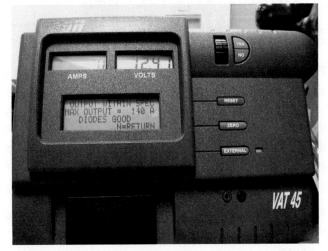

FIGURE 22–11 A typical tester used to test batteries as well as the cranking and charging system. Always follow the operating instructions.

ALTERNATOR OUTPUT TEST

PRELIMINARY CHECKS   An **alternator output test** measures the current (amperes) of the alternator. A charging circuit may be able to produce correct charging circuit voltage, but not be able to produce adequate amperage output. If in doubt about charging system output, first check the condition of the alternator drive belt. With the engine off, attempt to rotate the fan of the alternator by hand. Replace or tighten the drive belt if the alternator fan can be rotated this way.

CARBON PILE TEST PROCEDURE   A carbon pile tester uses plates of carbon to create an electrical load. A carbon pile test is used to load test a battery and/or an alternator. ● **SEE FIGURE 22–11.**

The testing procedure for alternator output is as follows:

STEP 1   Connect the starting and charging test leads according to the manufacturer's instructions, which usually include installing the amp clamp around the output wire near the alternator.

STEP 2   Turn off all electrical accessories to be sure that the tester is measuring the true output of the alternator.

STEP 3   Start the engine and operate it at 2000 RPM (fast idle). Turn the load increase control slowly to obtain the highest reading on the ammeter scale. Do not allow the voltage to drop below 12.6 volts. Note the ampere reading.

STEP 4   Add 5 to 7 amperes to the reading because this amount of current is used by the ignition system to operate the engine.

STEP 5   Compare the output reading to factory specifications. The rated output may be stamped on the alternator or can be found in service information.

CAUTION: *NEVER* disconnect a battery cable with the engine running. All vehicle manufacturers warn not to do this, because this was an old test, before alternators, to see if a generator could supply current to operate the ignition system without a battery. When a battery cable is removed, the alternator (or PCM) will lose the battery voltage sense signal. Without a battery voltage sense circuit, the alternator will do one of two things, depending on the make and model of vehicle.

- **The alternator output can exceed 100 volts. This high voltage may not only damage the alternator but also electrical components in the vehicle, including the PCM and all electronic devices.**
- **The alternator stops charging as a fail safe measure to protect the alternator and all of the electronics in the vehicle from being damaged due to excessively high voltage.**

MINIMUM REQUIRED ALTERNATOR OUTPUT

PURPOSE All charging systems must be able to supply the electrical demands of the electrical system. If lights and accessories are used constantly and the alternator cannot supply the necessary ampere output, the battery will be drained. To determine the minimum electrical load requirements, connect an inductive ammeter probe around either battery cable or the alternator output cable. ● **SEE FIGURE 22–12.**

NOTE: If using an inductive pickup ammeter, be certain that the pickup is over *all* the wires leaving the battery terminal.

Failure to include the small body ground wire from the negative battery terminal to the body or the small positive wire (if testing from the positive side) will *greatly* *decrease* the current flow readings.

PROCEDURE After connecting an ammeter correctly in the battery circuit, continue as follows:

1. Start the engine and operate to about 2000 RPM (fast idle).
2. Turn the heat selector to air conditioning (if the vehicle is so equipped).
3. Turn the blower motor to high speed.
4. Turn the headlights on bright.
5. Turn on the rear defogger.
6. Turn on the windshield wipers.
7. Turn on any other accessories that may be used continuously (do not operate the horn, power door locks, or other units that are not used for more than a few seconds).

Observe the ammeter. The current indicated is the electrical load that the alternator is able to exceed to keep the battery fully charged.

TEST RESULTS The minimum acceptable alternator output is 5 amperes greater than the accessory load. A negative (discharge) reading indicates that the alternator is not capable of supplying the current (amperes) that may be needed.

FIGURE 22–12 The best place to install a charging system tester amp probe is around the generator output terminal wire, as shown.

 TECH TIP

Bigger Is Not Always Better

Many technicians are asked to install a higher output alternator to allow the use of emergency equipment or other high-amperage equipment such as a high-wattage sound system.

Although many higher output units can be physically installed, it is important not to forget to upgrade the wiring and the fusible link(s) in the alternator circuit. Failure to upgrade the wiring could lead to overheating. The usual failure locations are at junctions or electrical connectors.

ALTERNATOR REMOVAL

After diagnosis of the charging system has determined that there is a fault with the alternator, it must be removed safely from the vehicle. Always check service information for the exact procedure to follow on the vehicle being serviced. A typical removal procedure includes the following steps.

STEP 1 Before disconnecting the negative battery cable, use a test light or a voltmeter and check for battery voltage at the output terminal of the alternator. A complete circuit must exist between the alternator and the battery. If there is no voltage at the alternator output terminal, check for a blown fusible link or other electrical circuit fault.

STEP 2 Disconnect the negative (−) terminal from the battery. (Use a memory saver to maintain radio, memory seats, and other functions.)

FIGURE 22–13 Replacing an alternator is not always as easy as it is from a Buick with a 3800 V-6, where the alternator is easy to access. Many alternators are difficult to access, and require the removal of other components.

FIGURE 22–14 Always mark the case of the alternator before disassembly to be assured of correct reassembly.

TECH TIP

The Sniff Test

When checking for the root cause of an alternator failure, one test that a technician could do is to sniff (smell) the alternator. If the alternator smells like a dead rat (rancid smell), the stator windings have been overheated by trying to charge a discharged or defective battery. If the battery voltage is continuously low, the voltage regulator will continue supplying full-field current to the alternator. The voltage regulator is designed to cycle on and off to maintain a narrow charging system voltage range.

If the battery voltage is continually below the cutoff point of the voltage regulator, the alternator is continually producing current in the stator windings. This constant charging can often overheat the stator and burn the insulating varnish covering the stator windings. If the alternator fails the sniff test, the technician should replace the stator and other alternator components that are found to be defective and replace or recharge and test the battery.

STEP 3 Remove the accessory drive belt that drives the alternator.

STEP 4 Remove the fasteners, spacers, and brackets, as necessary, and remove the alternator from the vehicle. ● **SEE FIGURE 22–13**.

ALTERNATOR DISASSEMBLY

DISASSEMBLY PROCEDURE

STEP 1 Mark the case with a scratch or with chalk to ensure proper reassembly of the alternator case. ● **SEE FIGURE 22–14**.

STEP 2 After the through bolts have been removed, carefully separate the two halves. The stator windings must stay with the rear case. When this happens, the brushes and springs will fall out.

STEP 3 Remove the rectifier assembly and voltage regulator.

ROTOR TESTING The slip rings on the rotor should be smooth and round (within 0.002 in. of being perfectly round).

- If grooved, the slip rings can be machined to provide a suitable surface for the brushes. Do not machine beyond the minimum slip-ring dimension as specified by the manufacturer.

- If the slip rings are discolored or dirty, they can be cleaned with 400-grit or fine emery (polishing) cloth. The rotor must be turned while being cleaned to prevent flat spots on the slip rings.

- Measure the resistance between the slip rings using an ohmmeter. Typical resistance values and results include the following:

    1. The resistance measured between either slip ring and the steel rotor shaft should be infinity (OL). If there is continuity, then the rotor is shorted to ground.

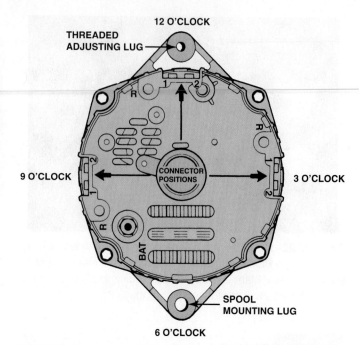

12 O'CLOCK

THREADED ADJUSTING LUG

9 O'CLOCK

CONNECTOR POSITIONS

3 O'CLOCK

BAT

SPOOL MOUNTING LUG

6 O'CLOCK

FIGURE 22–15 Explanation of clock positions. Because the four through bolts are equally spaced, it is possible for an alternator to be installed in one of four different clock positions. The connector position is determined by viewing the generator from the diode end with the threaded adjusting lug in the up or 12 o'clock position. Select the 3 o'clock, 6 o'clock, 9 o'clock, or 12 o'clock position to match the unit being replaced.

ALTERNATOR DISASSEMBLY (CONTINUED)

2. Rotor resistance range is normally between 2.4 and 6 ohms.

3. If the resistance is below specification, the rotor is shorted.

4. If the resistance is above specification, the rotor connections are corroded or open.

If the rotor is found to be bad, it must be replaced or repaired at a specialized shop. ● **SEE FIGURE 22–16.**

NOTE: The cost of a replacement rotor may exceed the cost of an entire rebuilt alternator. Be certain, however, that the rebuilt alternator is rated at the same output as the original or higher.

STATOR TESTING
The stator must be disconnected from the diodes (rectifiers) before testing. Because all three windings of the stator are electrically connected (either wye or delta), an ohmmeter can be used to check a stator.

- There should be low resistance at all three stator leads (continuity).

- There should *not* be continuity (in other words, there should be a meter reading of infinity ohms) when the stator is tested between any stator lead and the metal stator core.

- If there is continuity, the stator is shorted-to-ground and must be repaired or replaced. ● **SEE FIGURE 22–17.**

TESTING AN ALTERNATOR ROTOR USING AN OHMMETER

CHECKING FOR GROUNDS (SHOULD READ INFINITY IF ROTOR IS NOT GROUNDED)

OHMMETER

OL

3.1 Ω

OHMMETER

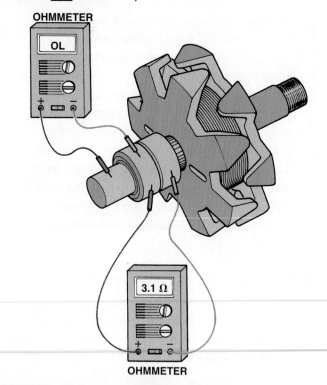

FIGURE 22–16 Testing an alternator rotor using an ohmmeter.

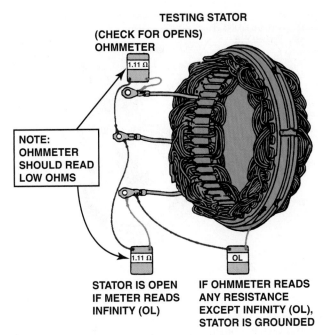

TESTING STATOR
(CHECK FOR OPENS)
OHMMETER

1.11 Ω

NOTE:
OHMMETER
SHOULD READ
LOW OHMS

1.11 Ω

OL

STATOR IS OPEN
IF METER READS
INFINITY (OL)

IF OHMMETER READS
ANY RESISTANCE
EXCEPT INFINITY (OL),
STATOR IS GROUNDED

FIGURE 22–17 If the ohmmeter reads infinity between any two of the three stator windings, the stator is open and, therefore, defective. The ohmmeter should read infinity between any stator lead and the steel laminations. If the reading is less than infinity, the stator is grounded. Stator windings can be tested if shorted because the normal resistance is very low.

NOTE: **Because the resistance is very low for a normal stator, it is generally *not* possible to test for a *shorted* (copper-to-copper) stator. A shorted stator will, however, greatly reduce alternator output. An ohmmeter cannot detect an open stator if the stator is delta wound. The ohmmeter will still indicate low resistance because all three windings are electrically connected.**

TESTING THE DIODE TRIO

Many alternators are equipped with a diode trio. A diode is an electrical one-way check valve that permits current to flow in only one direction. Because *trio* means "three," a diode trio is three diodes connected together. ● SEE FIGURE 22–18.

The diode trio is connected to all three stator windings. The current generated in the stator flows through the diode trio to the internal voltage regulator. The diode trio is designed to supply current for the field (rotor) and turns off the charge indicator light when the alternator voltage equals or exceeds the battery voltage. If one of the three diodes in the diode trio is defective (usually open), the alternator may produce close-to-normal output; however, the charge indicator light will be on dimly.

A diode trio should be tested with a digital multimeter. The meter should be set to the diode-check position. The multimeter should indicate 0.5 to 0.7 V (500 to 700 mV) one way and OL (overlimit) after reversing the test leads and touching all three connectors of the diode trio.

FIGURE 22–18 Typical diode trio. If one leg of a diode trio is open, the alternator may produce close to normal output, but the charge indicator light on the dash will be on dimly.

TESTING THE RECTIFIER

TERMINOLOGY The rectifier assembly usually is equipped with six diodes including three positive diodes and three negative diodes (one positive and one negative for each winding of the stator).

METER SETUP The rectifier(s) (diodes) should be tested using a multimeter that is set to "diode check" position on the digital multimeter (DMM).

Because a diode (rectifier) should allow current to flow in only one direction, each diode should be tested to determine if the diode allows current flow in one direction and blocks current flow in the opposite direction. To test some alternator diodes, it may be necessary to unsolder the stator connections. ● SEE FIGURE 22–19.

Accurate testing is not possible unless the diodes are separated electrically from other alternator components.

TESTING PROCEDURE Connect the leads to the leads of the diode (pigtail and housing of the rectifier bridge). Read the meter. Reverse the test leads. A good diode should have high resistance (OL) one way (reverse bias) and low voltage drop of 0.5 to 0.7 V (500 to 700 mV) the other way (forward bias).

RESULTS Open or shorted diodes must be replaced. Most alternators group or combine all positive and all negative diodes in the one replaceable rectifier component.

FIGURE 22–19 A typical rectifier bridge that contains all six diodes in one replaceable assembly.

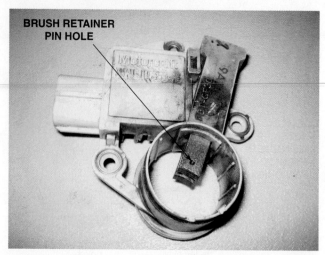

BRUSH RETAINER
PIN HOLE

FIGURE 22–20 A brush holder assembly with new brushes installed. The holes in the brushes are used to hold the brushes up in the holder when it is installed in the alternator. After the rotor has been installed, the retaining pin is removed which allows the brushes to contact the slip rings of the rotor.

REASSEMBLING THE ALTERNATOR

BRUSH HOLDER REPLACEMENT Alternator carbon brushes often last for many years and require no scheduled maintenance. The life of the alternator brushes is extended because they conduct only the field (rotor) current, which is normally only 2 to 5 amperes. The alternator brushes should be inspected when the alternator is disassembled and should be replaced when worn to less than 1/2 in. long. Brushes are commonly purchased assembled together in a brush holder. After the brushes are installed (usually retained by two or three screws) and the rotor is installed in the alternator housing, a brush retainer pin can be pulled out through an access hole in the rear of the alternator, allowing the brushes to be pressed against the slip rings by the brush springs. ● **SEE FIGURE 22–20.**

BEARING SERVICE AND REPLACEMENT The bearings of an alternator must be able to support the rotor and reduce friction. An alternator must be able to rotate at up to 15,000 RPM and withstand the forces created by the drive belt. The front bearing is usually a ball bearing type and the rear can be either a smaller roller or ball bearing.

The old or defective bearing can sometimes be pushed out of the front housing and the replacement pushed in by applying pressure with a socket or pipe against the outer edge of the bearing (outer race). Replacement bearings are usually prelubricated and seated. Many alternator front bearings must be removed from the rotor using a special puller.

ALTERNATOR ASSEMBLY After testing or servicing, the alternator rectifier(s), regulator, stator, and brush holder must be reassembled using the following steps.

STEP 1 If the brushes are internally mounted, insert a wire through the holes in the brush holder to hold the brushes against the springs.

STEP 2 Install the rotor and front-end frame in proper alignment with the mark made on the outside of the alternator housing. Install the through bolts. Before removing the wire pin holding the brushes, spin the alternator pulley. If the alternator is noisy or not rotating freely, the alternator can easily be disassembled again to check for the cause. After making certain the alternator is free to rotate, remove the brush holder pin and spin the alternator again by hand. The noise level may be slightly higher with the brushes released onto the slip rings.

STEP 3 Alternators should be tested on a bench tester, if available, before they are reinstalled on a vehicle. When installing the alternator on the vehicle, be certain that all mounting bolts and nuts are tight. The battery terminal should be covered with a plastic or rubber protective cap to help prevent accidental shorting to ground, which could seriously damage the alternator.

REMANUFACTURED ALTERNATORS

Remanufactured or rebuilt alternators are totally disassembled and rebuilt. Even though there are many smaller rebuilders who may not replace all worn parts, the major national remanufacturers *totally* remanufacture the alternator. Old alternators (called **cores**) are totally disassembled and cleaned. Both bearings are replaced and all components are tested. Rotors are rewound to original specifications if required. The rotor windings are not counted but are rewound on the rotor "spool," using the correct-gauge copper wire, to the *weight* specified by the original manufacturer. New slip rings are replaced as required, soldered to the rotor spool windings, and machined. The rotors are also balanced and measured to ensure that the outside diameter of the rotor meets specifications. An undersized rotor will produce less alternator output because the field must be close to the stator windings for maximum output. Bridge rectifiers are replaced, if required. Every alternator is then assembled and tested for proper output, boxed, and shipped to a warehouse. Individual parts stores (called jobbers) purchase parts from various regional or local warehouses.

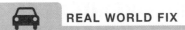

REAL WORLD FIX

The Two-Minute Alternator Repair

A Chevrolet pickup truck was brought to a shop for routine service. The customer stated that the battery required a jump start after a weekend of sitting. The technician tested the battery and charging system voltage using a small handheld digital multimeter. The battery voltage was 12.4 volts (about 75% charged), but the charging voltage was also 12.4 volts at 2000 RPM. Because normal charging voltage should be 13.5 to 15 volts, it was obvious that the charging system was not operating correctly.

The technician checked the dash and found that the "charge" light was *not* on. Before removing the alternator for service, the technician checked the wiring connection on the alternator. When the connector was removed, it was discovered to be rusty. After the contacts were cleaned, the charging system was restored to normal operation. The technician had learned that the simple things should always be checked first before tearing into a big (or expensive) repair.

ALTERNATOR INSTALLATION

Before installing a replacement alternator, check service information for the exact procedure to follow for the vehicle being serviced. A typical installation procedure includes the following steps.

STEP 1 Verify that the replacement alternator is the correct unit for the vehicle.

STEP 2 Install the alternator wiring on the alternator and install the alternator.

STEP 3 Check the condition of the drive belt and replace, if necessary. Install the drive belt over the drive pulley.

STEP 4 Properly tension the drive belt.

STEP 5 Tighten all fasteners to factory specifications.

STEP 6 Double-check that all fasteners are correctly tightened and remove all tools from the engine compartment area.

STEP 7 Reconnect the negative battery cable.

STEP 8 Start the engine and verify proper charging circuit operation.

ALTERNATOR OVERHAUL

1 Before the generator (alternator) is disassembled, it is spin tested and connected to a scope to check for possible defective components.

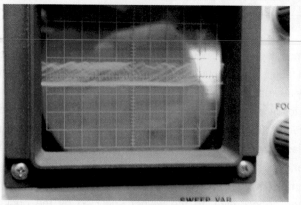

2 The scope pattern shows that the voltage output is far from being a normal pattern. This pattern indicates serious faults in the rectifier diodes.

3 The first step is to remove the drive pulley. This rebuilder is using an electric impact wrench to accomplish the task.

4 Carefully inspect the drive galley for damage of embedded rubber from the drive belt. The slightest fault can cause a vibration, noise, or possible damage to the generator (alternator).

5 Remove the external fan (if equipped) and then the spacers as shown.

6 Next pop off the plastic cover (shield) covering the stator/rectifier connection.

7 After the cover has been removed, the stator connections to the rectifier can be seen.

8 Using a diagonal cutter, cut the weld to separate the stator from the rectifier.

9 Before separating the halves of the case, this technician uses a punch to mark both halves.

10 After the case has been marked, the through-bolts are removed.

11 The drive-end housing and the stator are being separated from the rear (slip-ring-end) housing.

12 The stator is checked by visual inspection for discoloration or other physical damage, and then checked with an ohmmeter to see if the windings are shorted-to-ground.

CONTINUED ▶

13 The front bearing is removed from the drive-end housing using a press.

14 A view of the slip-ring-end (SRE) housing showing the black plastic shield, which helps direct air flow across the rectifier.

15 A punch is used to dislodge the plastic shield retaining clips.

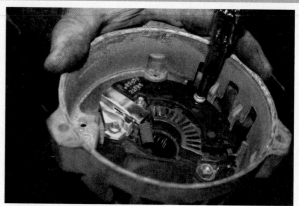

16 After the shield has been removed, the rectifier, regulator, and brush holder assembly can be removed by removing the retaining screws.

17 The hear transfer grease is visible when the rectifier assembly is lifted out of the rear housing.

18 The parts are placed into a tumbler where ceramic stones and a water-based solvent are used to clean the parts.

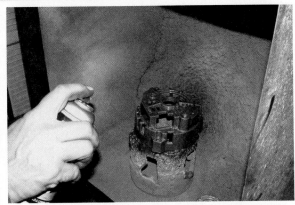

19 This rebuilder is painting the housing using a high-quality industrial grade spray paint to make the rebuilt generator look like new.

20 The slip rings on the rotor are being machined on a lathe.

21 The rotor is being tested using an ohmmeter. The specifications for the resistance between the slip rings on the CS-130 are 2.2 to 3.5 ohms.

22 The rotor is also tested between the slip ring and the rotor shaft. This reading should be infinity.

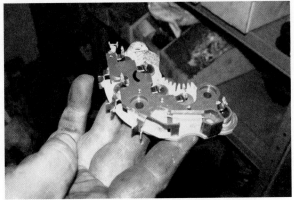

23 A new rectifier. This replacement unit is significantly different than the original but is designed to replace the original unit and meets the original factory specifications.

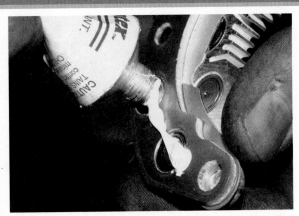

24 Silicone heat transfer compound is applied to the heat sink of the new rectifier.

CONTINUED ▶

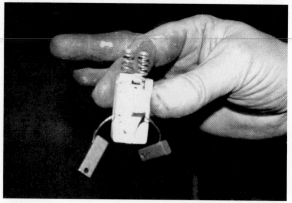

25 Replacement brushes and springs are assembled into the brush holder.

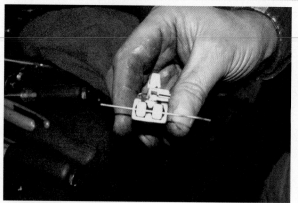

26 The brushes are pushed into the brush holder and retained by a straight wire, which extends through the rear housing of the generator. This wire is then pulled out when the unit is assembled.

27 Here is what the CS generator looks like after installing the new brush holder assembly, rectifier bridge, and voltage regulator.

28 The junction between the rectifier bridge and the voltage regulator is soldered.

29 The plastic deflector shield is snapped back into location using a blunt chisel and a hammer. This shield directs the airflow from the fan over the rectifier bridge and voltage regulator.

30 Before the stator windings can be soldered to the rectifier bridge, the varnish insulation is removed from the ends of the leads.

31 After the stator has been inserted into the rear housing the stator leads are soldered to the copper lugs of the rectifier bridge.

32 New bearings are installed. A spacer is placed between the bearing and the slip rings to help prevent the possibility that the bearing could move on the shaft and short against the slip ring.

33 The slip-ring-end (SRE) housing is aligned with the marks made during disassembly and is pressed into the drive-end (DE) housing.

34 The retaining bolts, which are threaded into the drive-end housing from the back of the generator are installed.

35 The external fan and drive pulley are installed and the retaining nut is tightened on the rotor shaft.

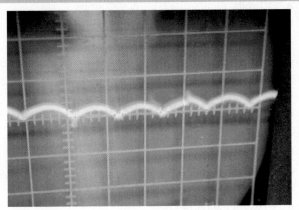

36 The scope pattern shows that the diodes and stator are functioning correctly and voltage check indicates that the voltage regulator is also functioning correctly.

1. Charging system testing requires that the battery be at least 75% charged to be assured of accurate test results. The charge indicator light should be on with the ignition switch on, but should go out when the engine is running. Normal charging voltage (at 2000 engine RPM) is 13.5 to 15 volts.

2. To check for excessive resistance in the wiring between the alternator and the battery, a voltage drop test should be performed.

3. Alternators do not produce their maximum rated output unless required by circuit demands. Therefore, to test for maximum alternator output, the battery must be loaded to force the alternator to produce its maximum output.

4. Each alternator should be marked across its case before disassembly to ensure proper clock position during reassembly. After disassembly, all alternator internal components should be tested using a continuity light or an ohmmeter. The following components should be tested.
   a. Stator
   b. Rotor
   c. Diodes
   d. Diode trio (if the alternator is so equipped)
   e. Bearings
   f. Brushes (should be more than 1/2 in. long)

REVIEW QUESTIONS

1. How does a technician test the voltage drop of the charging circuit?

2. How does a technician measure the amperage output of an alternator?

3. What tests can be performed to determine whether a diode or stator is defective before removing the alternator from the vehicle?

CHAPTER QUIZ

1. To check the charging voltage, connect a digital multimeter (DMM) to the positive (+) and the negative (−) terminals of the battery and select _____.
   a. DC volts
   b. AC volts
   c. DC amps
   d. AC amps

2. To check for ripple voltage from the alternator, connect a digital multimeter (DMM) and select _____.
   a. DC volts
   b. AC volts
   c. DC amps
   d. AC amps

3. The maximum allowable alternating current (AC) in amperes that is being sent to the battery from the alternator is _____.
   a. 0.4 A
   b. 1 to 3 A
   c. 3 to 4 A
   d. 10% of the rated output of the alternator

4. Why should the lights be turned on when checking for ripple voltage or alternating current from the alternator?
   a. To warm the battery
   b. To check that the battery is fully charged
   c. To create an electrical load for the alternator
   d. To test the battery before conducting other tests

5. An acceptable charging circuit voltage on a 12 volt system is _____.
   a. 13.5 to 15 volts
   b. 12.6 to 15.6 volts
   c. 12 to 14 volts
   d. 14.9 to 16.1 volts

6. Technician A says that the computer can be used to control the output of the alternator by controlling the field current. Technician B says that voltage regulators control the alternator output by controlling the field current through the rotor. Which technician is correct?
   a. Technician A only
   b. Technician B only
   c. Both Technicians A and B
   d. Neither Technician A nor B

7. Technician A says that a voltage drop test of the charging circuit should only be performed when current is flowing through the circuit. Technician B says to connect the leads of a voltmeter to the positive and negative terminals of the battery to measure the voltage drop of the charging system. Which technician is correct?
   a. Technician A only
   b. Technician B only
   c. Both Technicians A and B
   d. Neither Technician A nor B

8. When testing an alternator rotor, if an ohmmeter shows zero ohms with one meter lead attached to the slip rings and the other meter lead touching the rotor shaft, the rotor is _____.

   a. Okay (normal)
   b. Defective (shorted-to-ground)
   c. Defective (shorted-to-voltage)
   d. Okay (rotor windings are open)

9. An alternator diode is being tested using a digital multimeter set to the diode-check position. A good diode will read _____ if the leads are connected one way across the diode and _____ if the leads are reversed.

   a. 300/300   c. OL/OL
   b. 0.475/0.475   d. 0.551/OL

10. An alternator could test as producing lower-than-normal output, yet be okay, if the _____.

   a. Battery is weak or defective
   b. Engine speed is not high enough during testing
   c. Drive belt is loose or slipping
   d. All of the above

chapter 23

LIGHTING AND SIGNALING CIRCUITS

OBJECTIVES

After studying Chapter 23, the reader will be able to:

1. Prepare for ASE Electrical/Electronic Systems (A6) certification test content area "E" (Lighting System Diagnosis and Repair).
2. Determine which replacement bulb to use on a given vehicle.
3. Describe how interior and exterior lighting systems work.
4. Read and interpret a bulb chart.
5. Discuss troubleshooting procedures for lighting and signaling circuits.

KEY TERMS

INTRODUCTION

The vehicle has many different lighting and signaling systems, each with its own specific components and operating characteristics. The major light-related circuits and systems covered include:

- Exterior lighting
- Headlights (halogen, HID, and LED)
- Bulb trade numbers
- Brake lights
- Turn signals and flasher units
- Courtesy lights
- Light-dimming rearview mirrors

EXTERIOR LIGHTING

HEADLIGHT SWITCH CONTROL Exterior lighting is controlled by the headlight switch, which is connected directly to the battery on most vehicles. Therefore, if the light switch is left on manually, the lights could drain the battery. Older headlight switches contained a built-in circuit breaker. If excessive current flows through the headlight circuit, the circuit breaker will momentarily open the circuit, then close it again. The result is headlights that flicker on and off rapidly. This feature allows the headlights to function, as a safety measure, in spite of current overload.

The headlight switch controls the following lights on most vehicles, usually through a module.

1. Headlights
2. Taillights
3. Side-marker lights
4. Front parking lights
5. Dash lights
6. Interior (dome) light(s)

COMPUTER-CONTROLLED LIGHTS Because these lights can easily drain the battery if accidentally left on, many newer vehicles control these lights through computer modules. The computer module keeps track of the time the lights are on and can turn them off if the time is excessive. The computer can control either the power side or the ground side of the circuit.

For example, a typical computer-controlled lighting system usually includes the following steps.

STEP 1 The driver depresses or rotates the headlight switch.

STEP 2 The signal from the headlight switch is sent to the nearest control module.

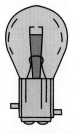
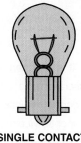

DOUBLE CONTACT 1157/2057 BULBS   **SINGLE CONTACT 1156 BULBS**

WEDGE 194 BULB

FIGURE 23–1 Dual-filament (double-contact) bulbs contain both a low-intensity filament for taillights or parking lights and a high-intensity filament for brake lights and turn signals. Bulbs come in a variety of shapes and sizes. The numbers shown are the trade numbers.

STEP 3 The control module then sends a request to the headlight control module to turn on the headlights as well as the front park and side-marker lights.

Through the data BUS, the rear control module receives the lights on signal and turns on the lights at the rear of the vehicle.

STEP 4 All modules monitor current flow through the circuit and will turn on a bulb failure warning light if it detects an open bulb or a fault in the circuit.

STEP 5 After the ignition has been turned off, the modules will turn off the lights after a time delay to prevent the battery from being drained.

BULB NUMBERS

TRADE NUMBER The number used on automotive bulbs is called the bulb **trade number**, as recorded with the American National Standards Institute (ANSI). The number is the same regardless of the manufacturer. ● **SEE FIGURE 23–1.**

CANDLEPOWER The trade number also identifies the size, shape, number of filaments, and amount of light produced, measured in **candlepower**. For example, the 1156 bulb, commonly used for backup lights, is 32 candlepower. A 194 bulb, commonly used for dash or side-marker lights, is rated at only 2 candlepower. The amount of light produced by a bulb is determined by the resistance of the filament wire, which also affects the amount of current (in amperes) required by the bulb.

It is important that the correct trade number of bulb always be used for replacement to prevent circuit or component damage. The correct replacement bulb for a vehicle is usually listed in the owner or service manual. ● **REFER TO CHART 23–1** for a listing of common bulbs and their specifications used in most vehicles.

BULB NUMBER SUFFIXES   Many bulbs have suffixes that indicate some feature of the bulb, while keeping the same size and light output specifications.

Typical bulb suffixes include:

- NA: natural amber (amber glass)
- A: amber (painted glass)
- HD: heavy duty
- LL: long life
- IF: inside frosted
- R: red
- B: blue
- G: green

● **SEE FIGURE 23–2** on page 330.

BULB NUMBER	FILAMENTS	AMPERAGE LOW/HIGH	WATTAGE LOW/HIGH	CANDLEPOWER LOW/HIGH
Headlights				
1255/H1	1	4.58	55.00	129.00
1255/H3	1	4.58	55.00	121.00
6024	2	2.73/4.69	35.00/60.00	27,000/35,000
6054	2	2.73/5.08	35.00/65.00	35,000/40,000
9003	2	4.58/5.00	55.00/60.00	72.00/120.00
9004	2	3.52/5.08	45.00/65.00	56.00/95.00
9005	1	5.08	65.00	136.00
9006	1	4.30	55.00	80.00
9007	2	4.30/5.08	55.00/65.00	80.00/107.00
9008	2	4.30/5.08	55.00/65.00	80.00/107.00
9011	1	5.08	65.00	163.50
Headlights (HID—Xenon)				
D2R	Air Gap	0.41	35.00	222.75
D2S	Air Gap	0.41	35.00	254.57

CHART 23–1

Bulb chart sorted by typical applications. Check the owner's manual, service information, or a bulb manufacturer's application chart for the exact bulb to use.

BULB NUMBER	FILAMENTS	AMPERAGE LOW/HIGH	WATTAGE LOW/HIGH	CANDLEPOWER LOW/HIGH
Taillights, Stop, and Turn Lamps				
1156	1	2.10	26.88	32.00
1157	2	0.59/2.10	8.26/26.88	3.00/32.00
2057	2	0.49/2.10	6.86/26.88	2.00/32.00
3057	2	6.72/26.88	0.48/2.10	1.50/24.00
3155	1	1.60	20.48	21.00
3157	2	0.59/2.10	8.26/26.88	2.20/24.00
4157	2	0.59/2.10	8.26/26.88	3.00/32.00
7440	1	1.75	21.00	36.60
7443	2	0.42/1.75	5.00/21.00	2.80/36.60
17131	1	0.33	4.00	2.80
17635	1	1.75	21.00	37.00
17916	2	0.42/1.75	5.00/21.00	1.20/35.00
Parking, Daytime Running Lamps				
24	1	0.24	3.36	2.00
67	1	0.59	7.97	4.00
168	1	0.35	4.90	3.00
194	1	0.27	3.78	2.00
889	1	3.90	49.92	43.00
912	1	1.00	12.80	12.00
916	1	0.54	7.29	2.00
1034	2	0.59/1.80	8.26/23.04	3.00/32.00
1156	1	2.10	26.88	32.00
1157	2	0.59/2.10	8.26/26.88	3.00/32.00
2040	1	0.63	8.00	10.50
2057	2	0.49/2.10	6.86/26.88	1.50/24.00
2357	2	0.59/2.23	8.26/28.54	3.00/40.00
3157	2	0.59/2.10	8.26/26.88	3.00/32.00
3357	2	0.59/2.23	8.26/28.54	3.00/40.00
3457	2	0.59/2.23	8.26/28.51	3.00/40.00
3496	2	0.66/2.24	8.00/27.00	3.00/45.00
3652	1	0.42	5.00	6.00
4114	2	0.59/2/23	8.26/31.20	3.00/32.00
4157	2	0.59/2.10	8.26/26/88	3.00/32.00
7443	2	0.42/1.75	5.00/21.00	2.80/36.60
17131	1	0.33	4.00	2.80
17171	1	0.42	5.00	4.00
17177	1	0.42	5.00	4.00
17311	1	0.83	10.00	10.00

CONTINUED

BULB NUMBER	FILAMENTS	AMPERAGE LOW/HIGH	WATTAGE LOW/HIGH	CANDLEPOWER LOW/HIGH
17916	2	0.42/1.75	5.00/21.00	1.20/35.00
68161	1	0.50	6.00	10.00

Center High-Mounted Stop Lamp (CHMSL)

BULB NUMBER	FILAMENTS	AMPERAGE LOW/HIGH	WATTAGE LOW/HIGH	CANDLEPOWER LOW/HIGH
70	1	0.15	2.10	1.50
168	1	0.35	4.90	3.00
175	1	0.58	8.12	5.00
211-2	1	0.97	12.42	12.00
577	1	1.40	17.92	21.00
579	1	0.80	10.20	9.00
889	1	3.90	49.92	43.00
891	1	0.63	8.00	11.00
906	1	0.69	8.97	6.00
912	1	1.00	12.80	12.00
921	1	1.40	17.92	21.00
922	1	0.98	12.54	15.00
1141	1	1.44	18.43	21.00
1156	1	2.10	26.88	32.00
2723	1	0.20	2.40	1.50
3155	1	1.60	20.48	21.00
3156	1	2.10	26.88	32.00
3497	1	2.24	27.00	45.00
7440	1	1.75	21.00	36.60
17177	1	0.42	5.00	4.00
17635	1	1.75	21.00	37.00

License Plate, Glove Box, Dome, Side Marker, Trunk, Map, Ashtray, Step/Courtesy, Underhood

BULB NUMBER	FILAMENTS	AMPERAGE LOW/HIGH	WATTAGE LOW/HIGH	CANDLEPOWER LOW/HIGH
37	1	0.09	1.26	0.50
67	1	0.59	7.97	4.00
74	1	0.10	1.40	.070
98	1	0.62	8.06	6.00
105	1	1.00	12.80	12.00
124	1	0.27	3.78	1.50
161	1	0.19	2.66	1.00
168	1	0.35	4.90	3.00
192	1	0.33	4.29	3.00
194	1	0.27	3.78	2.00
211-1	1	0.968	12.40	12.00
212-2	1	0.74	9.99	6.00
214-2	1	0.52	7.02	4.00

CONTINUED

BULB NUMBER	FILAMENTS	AMPERAGE LOW/HIGH	WATTAGE LOW/HIGH	CANDLEPOWER LOW/HIGH
293	1	0.33	4.62	2.00
561	1	0.97	12.42	12.00
562	1	0.74	9.99	6.00
578	1	0.78	9.98	9.00
579	1	0.80	10.20	9.00
PC579	1	0.80	10.20	9.00
906	1	0.69	8.97	6.00
912	1	1.00	12.80	12.00
917	1	1.20	14.40	10.00
921	1	1.40	17.92	21.00
1003	1	0.94	12.03	15.00
1155	1	0.59	7.97	4.00
1210/H2	1	8.33	100.00	239.00
1210/H3	1	8.33	100.00	192.00
1445	1	0.14	2.02	0.70
1891	1	0.24	3.36	2.00
1895	1	0.27	3.78	2.00
3652	1	0.42	5.00	6.00
11005	1	0.39	5.07	4.00
11006	1	0.24	3.36	2.00
12100	1	0.77	10.01	9.55
13050	1	0.38	4.94	3.00
17036	1	0.10	1.20	0.48
17097	1	0.25	3.00	1.76
17131	1	0.33	4.00	2.80
17177	1	0.42	5.00	4.00
17314	1	0.83	10.00	8.00
17916	2	0.42/1.75	5.00/21.00	1.20/35.00
47830	1	0.39	5.00	6.70

Instrument Panel

BULB NUMBER	FILAMENTS	AMPERAGE LOW/HIGH	WATTAGE LOW/HIGH	CANDLEPOWER LOW/HIGH
37	1	0.09	1.26	0.50
73	1	0.08	1.12	0.30
74	1	0.10	1.40	0.70
PC74	1	0.10	1.40	0.70
PC118	1	0.12	1.68	0.70
124	1	0.27	3.78	1.50
158	1	0.24	3.36	2.00
161	1	0.19	2.66	1.00
192	1	0.33	4.29	3.00

CONTINUED

BULB NUMBER	FILAMENTS	AMPERAGE LOW/HIGH	WATTAGE LOW/HIGH	CANDLEPOWER LOW/HIGH
194	1	0.27	3.78	2.00
PC194	1	0.27	3.78	2.00
PC195	1	0.27	3.78	1.80
1210/H1	1	8.33	100.00	217.00
1210/H3	1	8.33	100.00	192.00
17037	1	0.10	1.20	0.48
17097	1	0.25	3.00	1.76
17314	1	0.83	10.00	8.00
Backup, Cornering, Fog/Driving Lamps				
67	1	0.59	7.97	4.00
579	1	0.80	10.20	9.00
880	1	2.10	26.88	43.00
881	1	2.10	26.88	43.00
885	1	3.90	49.92	100.00
886	1	3.90	49.92	100.00
893	1	2.93	37.50	75.00
896	1	2.93	37.50	75.00
898	1	2.93	37.50	60.00
899	1	2.93	37.50	60.00
921	1	1.40	17.92	21.00
1073	1	1.80	23.04	32.00
1156	1	2.10	26.88	32.00
1157	2	0.59/2.10	8.26/26.88	3.00/32.00
1210/H1	1	8.33	100.00	217.00
1255/H1	1	4.58	55.00	129.00
1255/H3	1	4.58	55.00	121.00
1255/H11	1	4.17	55.00	107.00
2057	2	0.49/2.10	6.86/26.88	1.50/24.00
3057	2	0.48/2.10	6.72/26.88	2.00/32.00
3155	1	1.60	20.48	21.00
3156	1	2.10	26.88	32.00
3157	2	0.59/2.10	8.26/26.88	3.00/32.00
4157	2	0.59/2.10	8.26/26/88	3.00/32.00
7440	1	1.75	21.00	36.00
9003	2	4.58/5.00	55.00/60.00	72.00/120.00
9006	1	4.30	55.00	80.00
9145	1	3.52	45.00	65.00
17635	1	1.75	21.00	37.00

FIGURE 23–2 Bulbs that have the same trade number have the same operating voltage and wattage. The NA means that the bulb uses a natural amber glass ampoule with clear turn signal lenses.

 REAL WORLD FIX

Weird Problem—Easy Solution

A General Motors minivan had the following electrical problems.

- The turn signals flashed rapidly on the left side.
- With the ignition key off, the lights-on warning chime sounded if the brake pedal was depressed.
- When the brake pedal was depressed, the dome light came on.

All of these problems were caused by *one* defective 2057 dual-filament bulb, as shown in
● **FIGURE 23–3**.

Apparently, the two filaments were electrically connected when one filament broke and then welded to the other filament. This caused the electrical current to feed back from the brake light filament into the taillight circuit, causing all the problems.

TESTING BULBS   Bulbs can be tested using two basic tests.

1. Perform a visual inspection of any bulb. Many faults, such as a shorted filament, corroded connector, or water, can cause weird problems that are often thought to be wiring issues.

● **SEE FIGURES 23–4 AND 23–5.**

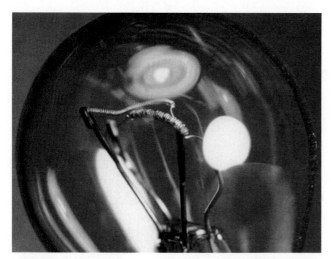

FIGURE 23–3 Close-up a 2057 dual-filament (double-contact) bulb that failed. Notice that the top filament broke from its mounting and melted onto the lower filament. This bulb caused the dash lights to come on whenever the brakes were applied.

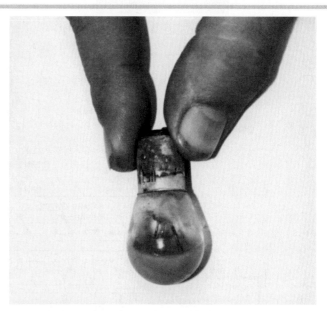

FIGURE 23–5 Often the best diagnosis is a thorough visual inspection. This bulb was found to be filled with water, which caused weird problems.

FIGURE 23–4 Corrosion caused the two terminals of this dual-filament bulb to be electrically connected.

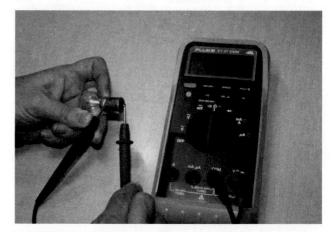

FIGURE 23–6 This single-filament bulb is being tested with a digital multimeter set to read resistance in ohms. The reading of 1.1 ohms is the resistance of the bulb when cold. As soon as current flows through the filament, the resistance increases about 10 times. It is the initial surge of current flowing through the filament when the bulb is cool that causes many bulbs to fail in cold weather as a result of the reduced resistance. As the temperature increases, the resistance increases.

2. Bulbs can be tested using an ohmmeter and checking the resistance of the filaments(s). Most bulbs will read low resistance at room temperature between 0.5 and 20 ohms depending on the bulb. Test results include:

- **Normal resistance.** The bulb is good. Check both filaments if it is a two-filament bulb.
  - **SEE FIGURE 23–6.**

- **Zero ohms.** It is unlikely but possible for the bulb filament to be shorted.
- **OL (electrically open).** The reading indicates that the bulb filament is broken.

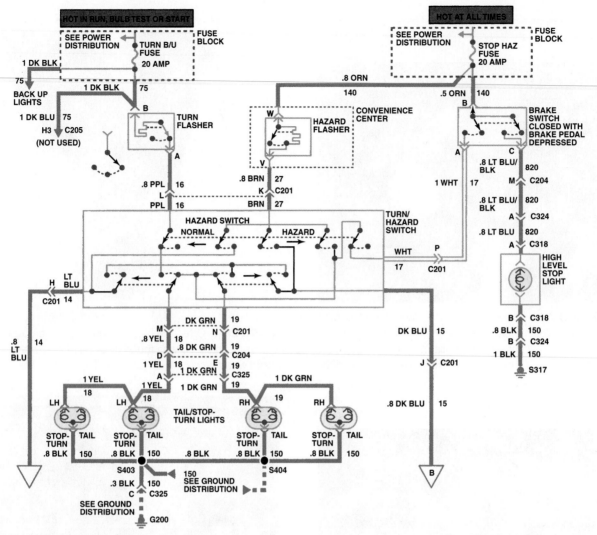

FIGURE 23–7 Typical brake light and taillight circuit showing the brake switch and all of the related circuit components.

BRAKE LIGHTS

OPERATION **Brake lights**, also called stop lights, use the high-intensity filament of a double-filament bulb. (The low-intensity filament is for the taillights.) When the brakes are applied, the brake switch is closed and the brake lamps light. The brake switch receives current from a fuse that is hot all the time. The brake light switch is a normally open (N.O.) switch, but is closed when the driver depresses the brake pedal. Since 1986, all vehicles sold in the United States have a third brake light commonly referred to as the **center high-mounted stop light** **(CHMSL)**. ● **SEE FIGURE 23–7.**

The brake switch is also used as an input switch (signal) for the following:

1. Cruise control (deactivates when the brake pedal is depressed)

2. Antilock brakes (ABS)

3. Brake shift interlock (prevents shifting from park position unless the brake pedal is depressed)

FIGURE 23–8 A replacement LED taillight bulb is constructed of many small, individual light-emitting diodes.

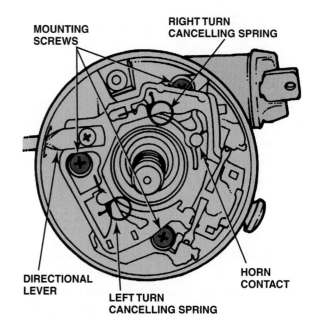

FIGURE 23–9 The typical turn signal switch includes various springs and cams to control the switch and to cause the switch to cancel after a turn has been completed.

? FREQUENTLY ASKED QUESTION

Why Are LEDs Used for Brake Lights?

Light-emitting diode (LED) brake lights are frequently used for high-mounted stop lamps (CHMSLs) for the following reasons.

1. **Faster illumination.** An LED will light up to 200 milliseconds faster than an incandescent bulb, which requires some time to heat the filament before it is hot enough to create light. This faster illumination can mean the difference in stopping distances at 60 mph (100 km/h) by about 18 ft (6 m) due to the reduced reaction time for the driver of the vehicle behind.

2. **Longer service life.** LEDs are solid-state devices that do not use a filament to create light. As a result, they are less susceptible to vibration and will often last the life of the vehicle.

NOTE: Aftermarket replacement LED bulbs that are used to replace conventional bulbs may require the use of a different type of flasher unit due to the reduced current draw of the LED bulbs. ● **SEE FIGURE 23–8.**

TURN SIGNALS

OPERATION The turn signal circuit is supplied power from the ignition switch and operated by a lever and switch. ● **SEE FIGURE 23–9.**

When the turn signal switch is moved in either direction, the corresponding turn signal lamps receive current through the flasher unit. The flasher unit causes the current to start and stop as the turn signal lamp flashes on and off with the interrupted current.

ONE-FILAMENT STOP/TURN BULBS In many vehicles, the stop and turn signals are both provided by one filament. When the turn signal switch is turned on (closed), the filament receives interrupted current through the flasher unit. When the brakes are applied, the current first flows to the turn signal switch, except for the high-mounted stop, which is fed directly from the brake switch. If neither turn signal is on, then current through the turn signal switch flows to both rear brake lights. If the turn signal switch is operated (turned to either left or right), current flows through the flasher unit on the side that was selected and directly to the brake lamp on the opposite side. If the brake pedal is not depressed, then current flows through the flasher and only to one side. ● **SEE FIGURE 23-10.**

Moving the lever up or down completes the circuit through the flasher unit and to the appropriate turn signal lamps. A turn signal switch includes cams and springs that cancel the signal after the turn has been completed. As the steering wheel is turned in the signaled direction and then returns to its normal position, the cams and springs cause the turn signal switch contacts to open and break the circuit.

TWO-FILAMENT STOP/TURN BULBS

In systems using separate filaments for the stop and turn lamps, the brake and turn signal switches are not connected. If the vehicle uses the same filament for both purposes, then brake switch current is routed through contacts within the turn signal switch. By linking certain contacts, the bulbs can receive either brake switch current or flasher current, depending upon which direction is being signaled. For example, ● **FIGURE 23-11** shows current flow through the switch when the brake switch is closed and a right turn is signaled.

Steady current through the brake switch is sent to the left brake lamp. Interrupted current from the turn signal is sent to the right turn lamps.

FLASHER UNITS

A turn signal flasher unit is a metal or plastic can containing a switch that opens and closes the turn signal circuit. Vehicles can be equipped with many different types of flasher units. ● **SEE FIGURE 23-12.**

- **DOT flashers.** This turn signal flasher unit is often installed in a metal clip attached to the dash panel to allow the "clicking" noise of the flasher to be heard by the driver. The turn signal flasher is designed to transmit the current to light the front and rear bulbs on only one side at a time. The U.S. **Department of Transportation (DOT)** regulation requires that the driver be alerted when a turn signal bulb is not working. This is achieved by using a series-type flasher unit. The flasher unit requires current flow through two bulbs (one in the front and one in the rear) in order to flash. If one bulb burns out, the current flow through only one bulb is not sufficient to make the unit flash; it will be a steady light. These turn signal units are often called DOT flashers.

- **Bimetal flashers.** The bimetal flashers have a lower cost and shorter life expectancy than hybrid or solid-state flashers. The operation of this flasher is current sensitive, which means that the flasher will stop flashing when one of the light bulbs is out and that it will flash at a faster rate when adding additional load, such as a trailer. The bimetal element is a sandwich of two different

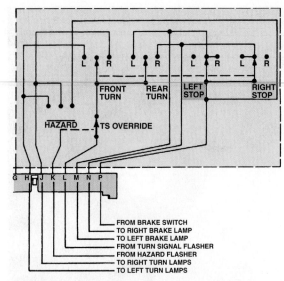

FIGURE 23-10 When the stop lamps and turn signals share a common bulb filament, stop light current flows through the turn signal switch.

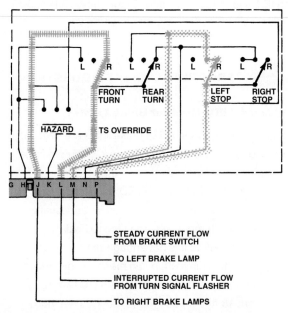

FIGURE 23-11 When a right turn in signaled, the turn signal switch contacts send flasher current to the right-hand filament and brake switch current to the left-hand filament.

FIGURE 23-12 Two styles of two-prong flasher units.

metals that distorts with temperature changes similar to a circuit breaker. The turn signal lamp current is passed through the bimetal element and causes heating. When the element is hot enough, the bimetal distorts, opening the contacts and turning off the lamps. After the bimetal cools, it returns to the original shape, closing the contacts and turning on the lamps again. This sequence is repeated until the load is removed. If one bulb burns out, the turn signal indicator lamp on the dash will remain lighted. The flasher will not flash because there is not enough current flow through the one remaining bulb to cause the flasher to become heated enough to open.

- **Hybrid flashers.** The **hybrid flashers** have an electronic flasher control circuit to operate the internal electromechanical relay and are commonly called a *flasher relay.* This type of flasher has a stable electronic timing circuitry that enables a wide operating voltage and temperature range with a reasonable cost. The life expectancy is considerably longer compared to bimetal units and is dependent on the load and relay used internally for switching the load. The hybrid flasher has a lamp current-sensing circuit which will cause the flash rate to double when a bulb is burned out.

- **Solid-state flashers.** The solid-state flashers have an internal electronic circuit for timing and solid-state power output devices for load switching. Life expectancy is longer than other flashers because there are no moving parts for mechanical breakdown. The biggest disadvantage of solid state is the higher cost. Solid-state units cause the turn indicator to flash rapidly if a bulb is burned out.

ELECTRONIC FLASHER REPLACEMENT UNITS Older vehicles (and a few newer ones) use thermal (bimetal) flashers that use heat to switch on and off. Most turn signal flasher units are mounted in a metal clip that is attached to the dash. The dash panel acts as a sounding board, increasing the sound of the flasher unit. Most four-way hazard flasher units are plugged into the fuse panel. Some turn signal flasher units are plugged into the fuse panel. How do you know for sure where the flasher unit is located? With both the turn signal and the ignition on, listen and/ or feel for the clicking of the flasher unit. Some service manuals also give general locations for the placement of flasher units.

Newer vehicles have electronic flashers that use microchips to control the on/off function. Electronic flashers are compatible with older systems and are wise to use for the following reasons.

FIGURE 23–13 A hazard warning flasher uses a parallel resistor across the contacts to provide a constant flashing rate regardless of the number of bulbs used in the circuit.

? **FREQUENTLY ASKED QUESTION**

How Do You Tell What Type of Flasher Is Being Used?

The easiest way to know which type of flasher can be used is to look at the type of bulb used in the tail lamps and turn signals. If it is a "wedge" style (plastic base, flat and rectangular), the vehicle has an electronic flasher. If it is a "twist and turn" bayonet-style (brass base) bulb, then either type of flasher can be used.

1. Electronic flashers do not burn out, and they provide a faster "flash" of the turn signals.

2. If upgrading to LED tail lamps, or lights, the LED bulbs only work with electronic flashers unless a resistor is added in the circuit.

HAZARD WARNING FLASHER The **hazard warning** flasher is a device installed in a vehicle lighting system with the primary function of causing both the left and right turn signal lamps to flash when the hazard warning switch is activated. Secondary functions may include visible dash indicators for the hazard system and an audible signal to indicate when the flasher is operating. A typical hazard warning flasher is also called a *parallel* or *variable-load* flasher because there is a resistor in parallel with the contacts to provide a control load and, therefore, a constant flash rate, regardless of the number of bulbs being flashed. **SEE FIGURE 23–13.**

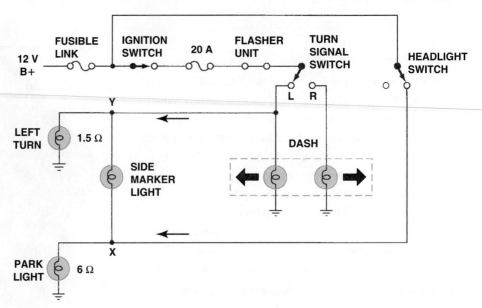

FIGURE 23-14 The side-marker light goes out whenever there is voltage at both points X and Y. These opposing voltages stop current flow through the side-marker light. The left turn light and left park light are actually the same bulb (usually 2057) and are shown separately to help explain how the side-marker light works on many vehicles.

COMBINATION TURN SIGNAL AND HAZARD WARNING

FLASHER The combination flasher is a device that combines the functions of a turn signal flasher and a hazard warning flasher into one package, which often uses three electrical terminals.

 FREQUENTLY ASKED QUESTION

Why Does the Side-Marker Light Alternately Flash?

A question that service technicians are asked frequently is why the side-marker light alternately goes out when the turn signal is on, and is on when the turn signal is off. Some vehicle owners think that there is a fault with the vehicle, but this is normal operation. The side-marker light goes out when the lights are on and the turn signal is flashing because there are 12 volts on both sides of the bulb (see points X and Y in ● **FIGURE 23-14**).

Normally, the side-marker light gets its ground through the turn signal bulb.

HEADLIGHTS

HEADLIGHT SWITCHES The headlight switch operates the exterior and interior lights of most vehicles. On noncomputer-controlled lighting systems, the headlight switch is connected directly to the battery through a fusible link, and has continuous power or is "hot" all the time. A circuit breaker is built into most older model headlight switches to protect the headlight circuit. ● **SEE FIGURE 23-15.**

The headlight switch may include the following:

- The interior dash lights can often be dimmed manually by rotating the headlight switch knob or by another rotary knob that controls a variable resistor (called a **rheostat**). The rheostat drops the voltage sent to the dash lights. Whenever there is a voltage drop (increased resistance), there is heat. A coiled resistance wire is built into a ceramic housing that is designed to insulate the rest of the switch from the heat and allow heat to escape.

- The headlight switch also contains a built-in circuit breaker that will rapidly turn the headlights on and off in the event of a short circuit. This prevents a total loss of headlights. If the headlights are rapidly flashing on and off, check the entire headlight circuit for possible shorts. The circuit breaker controls only the headlights. The other lights controlled by the headlight switch (taillights, dash lights, and parking lights) are fused separately. Flashing headlights also may be caused by a failure in the built-in circuit breaker, requiring replacement of the switch assembly.

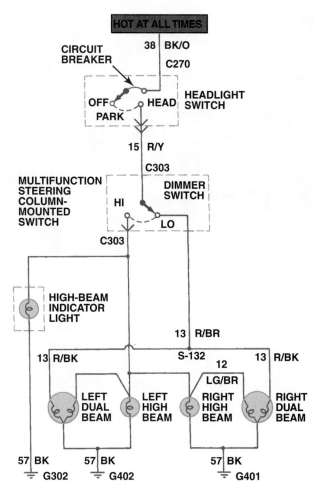

FIGURE 23–15 Typical headlight circuit diagram. Note that the headlight switch is represented by a dotted outline indicating that other circuits (such as dash lights) also operate from the switch.

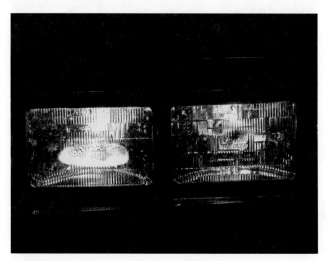

FIGURE 23–16 A typical four-headlight system using sealed beam headlights.

AUTOMATIC HEADLIGHTS
Computer-controlled lights use a light sensor that signals when to have the computer turn on the headlights. The sensor is mounted on the dashboard or mirror. Often these systems have a driver-adjusted sensitivity control that allows for the lights to be turned on at various levels of light. Most systems also have a computer module control over the time that the lights remain on after the ignition has been turned off and the last door has been closed. A scan tool is often needed to change this driver selectable time delay.

SEALED BEAM HEADLIGHTS
A sealed beam headlight consists of a sealed glass or plastic assembly containing the bulb, reflective surface, and prism lenses to properly focus the light beam. Low-beam headlights contain two filaments and three electrical terminals.

- One for low beam
- One for high beam

High-beam headlights contain only one filament and two terminals. Because low-beam headlights also contain a high-beam filament, the entire headlight assembly must be replaced if either filament is defective. ● **SEE FIGURE 23–16.**

A sealed beam headlight can be tested with an ohmmeter. A good bulb should indicate low ohms between the ground terminal and both power-side (hot) terminals. If either the high-beam or the low-beam filament is burned out, the ohmmeter will indicate infinity (OL).

HALOGEN SEALED BEAM HEADLIGHTS
Halogen sealed beam headlights are brighter and more expensive than normal headlights. Because of their extra brightness, it is common practice to have only two headlights on at any one time, because the candlepower output would exceed the maximum U.S. federal standards if all four halogen headlights were on. Therefore, before trying to repair the problem that only two of the four lamps are on, check the owner or shop manual for proper operation.

CAUTION: Do not attempt to wire all headlights together. The extra current flow could overheat the wiring from the headlight switch through the dimmer switch and to the headlights. The overloaded circuit could cause a fire.

COMPOSITE HEADLIGHTS
Composite headlights are constructed using a replaceable bulb and a fixed lens cover that is part of the vehicle. Composite headlights are the result

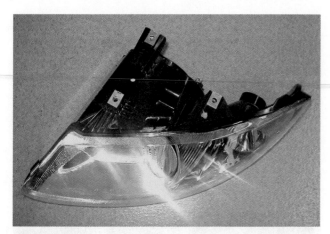

FIGURE 23–17 A typical composite headlamp assembly. The lens, housing, and bulb sockets are usually included as a complete assembly.

FIGURE 23–18 Handle a halogen bulb by the base to prevent the skin's oil from getting on the glass.

HEADLIGHTS (CONTINUED)

of changes in the aerodynamic styling of vehicles where sealed beam lamps could no longer be used. ● **SEE FIGURE 23–17.**

The replaceable bulbs are usually bright halogen bulbs. Halogen bulbs get very hot during operation, between 500°F and 1,300°F (260°C and 700°C). It is important never to touch the glass of any halogen bulb with bare fingers because the natural oils of the skin on the glass bulb can cause the bulb to break when it heats during normal operation.

 **TECH TIP**

Diagnose Bulb Failure

Halogen bulbs can fail for various reasons. Some causes for halogen bulb failure and their indications are as follows:

- **Gray color.** Low voltage to bulb (check for corroded socket or connector)
- **White (cloudy) color.** Indication of an air leak
- **Broken filament.** Usually caused by excessive vibration
- **Blistered glass.** Indication that someone has touched the glass

NOTE: *Never touch the glass (called the ampoule) of any halogen bulb. The oils from your fingers can cause unequal heating of the glass during operation, leading to a shorter-than-normal service life.* ● **SEE FIGURE 23–18.**

HIGH-INTENSITY DISCHARGE HEADLIGHTS

PARTS AND OPERATION High-intensity discharge (HID) headlights produce a distinctive blue-white light that is crisper, clearer, and brighter than light produced by a halogen headlight.

High-intensity discharge lamps do not use a filament like conventional electrical bulbs, but contain two electrodes about 0.2 in. (5 mm) apart. A high-voltage pulse is sent to the bulb which arcs across the tips of electrodes producing light.

It creates light from an electrical discharge between two electrodes in a gas-filled arc tube. It produces twice the light with less electrical input than conventional halogen bulbs.

The HID lighting system consists of the discharge arc source, igniter, ballast, and headlight assembly. ● **SEE FIGURE 23–19.**

The two electrodes are contained in a tiny quartz capsule filled with xenon gas, mercury, and metal halide salts. HID headlights are also called **xenon headlights**. The lights and support electronics are expensive, but they should last the life of the vehicle unless physically damaged.

HID headlights produce a white light giving the lamp a blue-white color. The color of light is expressed in temperature using the Kelvin scale. **Kelvin (K)** temperature is the Celsius temperature plus 273 degrees. Typical color temperatures include:

- Daylight: 5,400°K
- HID: 4,100°K

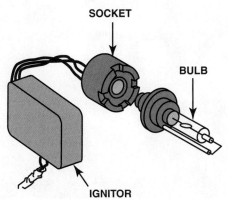

FIGURE 23–19 The igniter contains the ballast and transformer needed to provide high-voltage pulses to the arc tube bulb.

FIGURE 23–20 HID (xenon) headlights emit a whiter light than halogen headlights and usually look blue compared to halogen bulbs.

- Halogen: 3,200°K
- Incandescent (tungsten): 2,800°K
  - ● SEE FIGURE 23–20.

The HID ballast is powered by 12 volts from the headlight switch on the body control module. The HID headlights operate in three stages or states.

1. Start-up or stroke state
2. Run-up state
3. Steady state

START-UP OR STROKE STATE When the headlight switch is turned to the on position, the ballast may draw up to 20 amperes at 12 volts. The ballast sends multiple high-voltage pulses to the arc tube to start the arc inside the bulb. The voltage provided by the ballast during the start-up state ranges from −600 volts to +600 volts, which is increased by a transformer to about 25,000 volts. The increased voltage is used to create an arc between the electrodes in the bulb.

RUN-UP STATE After the arc is established, the ballast provides a higher than steady state voltage to the arc tube to keep the bulb illuminated. On a cold bulb, this state could last as long as 40 seconds. On a hot bulb, the run-up state may last only 15 seconds. The current requirements during the run-up

? FREQUENTLY ASKED QUESTION

What Is the Difference Between the Temperature of the Light and the Brightness of the Light?

The temperature of the light indicates the color of the light. The brightness of the light is measured in lumens. A standard 100 watt incandescent light bulb emits about 1,700 lumens. A typical halogen headlight bulb produces about 2,000 lumens, and a typical HID bulb produces about 2,800 lumens.

state are about 360 volts from the ballast and a power level of about 75 watts.

STEADY STATE The steady state phase begins when the power requirement of the bulb drops to 35 watts. The ballast provides a minimum of 55 volts to the bulb during steady state operation.

BI-XENON HEADLIGHTS Some vehicles are equipped with bi-xenon headlights, which use a shutter to block some of the light during low-beam operation and then mechanically move to expose more of the light from the bulb for high-beam operation. Because xenon lights are relatively slow to start working, vehicles equipped with bi-xenon headlights use two halogen lights for the "flash-to-pass" feature.

FAILURE SYMPTOMS   The following symptoms indicate bulb failure.

- A light flickers

- Lights go out (caused when the ballast assembly detects repeated bulb restrikes)

- Color changes to a dim pink glow

Bulb failures are often intermittent and difficult to repeat. However, bulb failure is likely if the symptoms get worse over time. Always follow the vehicle manufacturer's recommended testing and service procedures.

DIAGNOSIS AND SERVICE   High-intensity discharge head-lights will change slightly in color with age. This **color shift** is usu-ally not noticeable unless one headlight arc tube assembly has been replaced due to a collision repair, and then the difference in color may be noticeable. The difference in color will gradually change as the arc tube ages and should not be too noticeable by most customers. If the arc tube assembly is near the end of its life, it may not light immediately if it is turned off and then back on immediately. This test is called a "hot restrike" and if it fails, a replacement arc tube assembly may be needed or there is another fault, such as a poor electrical connection, that should be checked.

 WARNING:

Always adhere to all warnings because the high-voltage output of the ballast assembly can cause personal injury or death.

LED HEADLIGHTS

Some vehicles, including several Lexus models, use LED head-lights either as standard equipment (Lexus LS600h) or optional. ● **SEE FIGURE 23–21**.

Advantages include:

- Long service life

- Reduced electrical power required

Disadvantages include:

- High cost

- Many small LEDs required to create the necessary light output

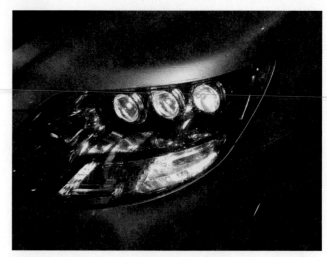

FIGURE 23–21 LED headlights usually require multiple units to provide the needed light as seen on this Lexus LS600h.

HEADLIGHT AIMING

According to U.S. federal law, all headlights, regardless of shape, must be able to be aimed using headlight aiming equip-ment. Older vehicles equipped with sealed beam headlights used a headlight aiming system that attached to the headlight itself. ● **SEE FIGURES 23–22 AND 23–23.** Also see the photo sequence on headlight aiming at the end of the chapter.

ADAPTIVE FRONT LIGHTING SYSTEM

PARTS AND OPERATION   A system that mechanically moves the headlights to follow the direction of the front wheels is called **adaptive (or advanced) front light system,** or **AFS**. The AFS provides a wide range of visibility during cornering. The headlights are usually capable of rotating 15 degrees to the left and 5 degrees to the right (some systems rotate 14 degrees and 9 degrees, respectively). Vehicles that use AFS include Lexus, Mercedes, and certain domestic models, usually as an extra cost option. ● **SEE FIGURE 23–24.**

NOTE: These angles are reversed on vehicles sold in countries that drive on the left side of the road, such as Great Britain, Japan, Australia, and New Zealand.

The vehicle has to be moving above a predetermined speed, usually above 20 mph (30 km/h) and the lights stop mov-ing when the speed drops below about 3 mph (5 km/h).

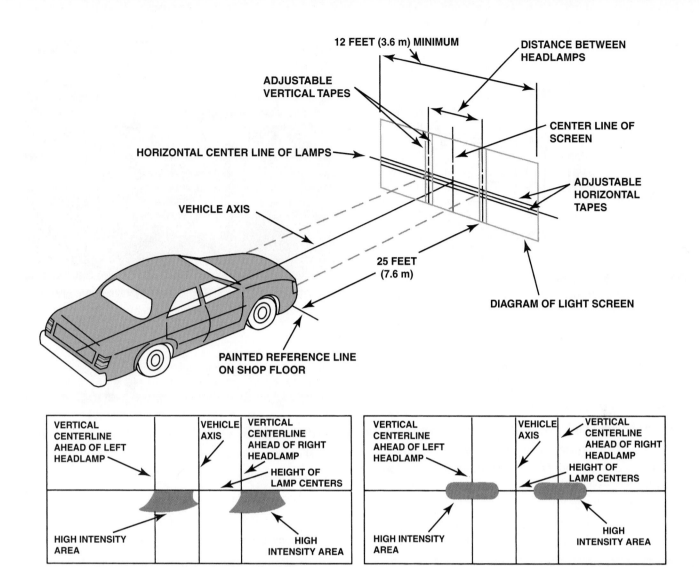

FIGURE 23–22 Typical headlight aiming diagram as found in service information.

FIGURE 23–23 Many composite headlights have a built-in bubble level to make aiming easy and accurate.

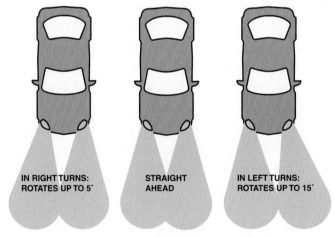

FIGURE 23–24 Adaptive front lighting systems rotate the low-beam headlight in the direction of travel.

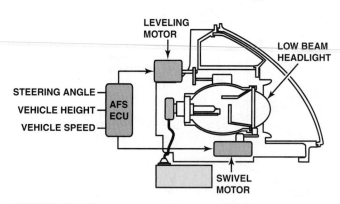

FIGURE 23–25 A typical adaptive front lighting system uses two motors: one for the up and down movement and the other for rotating the low-beam headlight to the left and right.

FIGURE 23–26 Typical dash-mounted switch that allows the driver to disable the front lighting system.

ADAPTIVE FRONT LIGHTING SYSTEM (CONTINUED)

AFS is often used in addition to self-leveling motors so that the headlights remain properly aimed regardless of how the vehicle is loaded. Without self-leveling, headlights would shine higher than normal if the rear of the vehicle is heavily loaded. ● **SEE FIGURE 23–25.**

When a vehicle is equipped with an adaptive front lighting system, the lights are moved by the headlight controller outward, and then inward as well as up and down as a test of the system. This action is quite noticeable to the driver, and is normal operation of the system.

DIAGNOSIS AND SERVICE The first step when diagnosing an AFS fault is to perform the following visual inspection.

- Start by checking that the AFS is switched on. Most AFS headlights are equipped with a switch that allows the driver to turn the system on and off. ● **SEE FIGURE 23–26.**

- Check that the system performs a self-test during start-up.

- Verify that both low-beam and high-beam lights function correctly. The system may be disabled if a fault with one of the headlights is detected.

- Use a scan tool to test for any AFS-related diagnostic trouble codes. Some systems allow the AFS to be checked and operated using a scan tool.

Always follow the recommended testing and service procedures as specified by the vehicle manufacturer in service information.

DAYTIME RUNNING LIGHTS

PURPOSE AND FUNCTION Daytime running lights **(DRLs)** involve operation of the following:

- Front parking lights

- Separate DRL lamps

- Headlights (usually at reduced current and voltage) when the vehicle is running

Canada has required daytime running lights on all new vehicles since 1990. Studies have shown that DRLs have reduced accidents where used.

Daytime running lights primarily use a control module that turns on either the low- or high-beam headlights or separate daytime running lights. The lights on some vehicles come on when the engine starts. Other vehicles will turn on the lamps when the engine is running but delay their operation until a signal from the vehicle speed sensor indicates that the vehicle is moving.

To avoid having the lights on during servicing, some systems will turn off the headlights when the parking brake is applied and the ignition switch is cycled off then back on. Others will only light the headlights when the vehicle is in a drive gear. ● **SEE FIGURE 23–27.**

CAUTION: Most factory daytime running lights operate the headlights at reduced intensity. These are *not* designed to be used at night. Normal intensity of the headlights (and operation of the other external lamps) is actuated by turning on the headlights as usual.

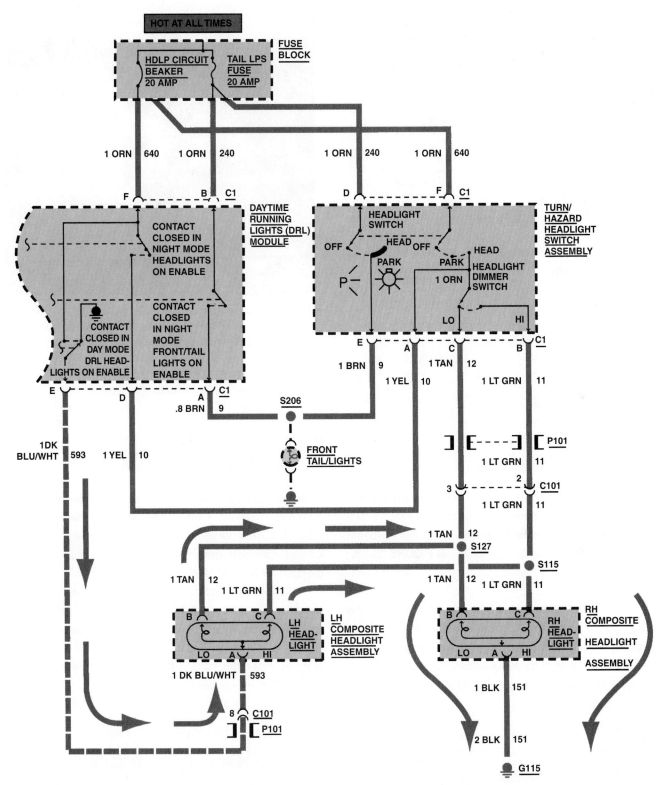

FIGURE 23–27 Typical daytime running light (DRL) circuit. Follow the arrows from the DRL module through both headlights. Notice that the left and right headlights are connected in series, resulting in increased resistance, less current flow, and dimmer than normal lighting. When the normal headlights are turned on, both headlights receive full battery voltage, with the left headlight grounding through the DRL module.

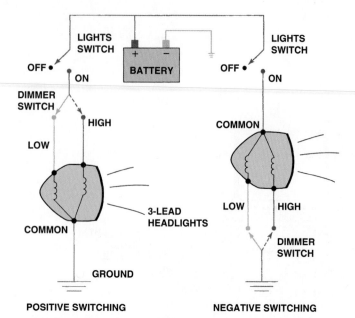

FIGURE 23–28 Most vehicles use positive switching of the high- and low-beam headlights. Notice that both filaments share the same ground connection. Some vehicles use negative switching and place the dimmer switch between the filaments and the ground.

FIGURE 23–29 A typical courtesy light doorjamb switch. Newer vehicles use the door switch as an input to the vehicle computer and the computer turns the interior lights on or off. By placing the lights under the control of the computer, the vehicle engineers have the opportunity to delay the lights after the door is closed and to shut them off after a period of time to avoid draining the battery.

DIMMER SWITCHES

The headlight switch controls the power or hot side of the headlight circuit. The current is then sent to the dimmer switch, which allows current to flow to either the high-beam or the low-beam filament of the headlight bulb, as shown in ● **FIGURE 23–28.**

An indicator light illuminates on the dash when the high beams are selected.

The dimmer switch is usually hand operated by a lever on the steering column. Some steering column switches are actually attached to the *outside* of the steering column and are spring loaded. To replace these types of dimmer switches, the steering column needs to be lowered slightly to gain access to the switch itself.

🔧 TECH TIP

Checking a Dome Light Can Be Confusing

If a technician checks a dome light with a test light, both sides of the bulb will "turn on the light" if the bulb is good. This will be true if the system's "ground switched" doors are closed and the bulb is good. This confuses many technicians because they do not realize that the ground will not be sensed unless the door is open.

COURTESY LIGHTS

Courtesy light is a generic term primarily used for interior lights, including overhead (dome) and under-the-dash (courtesy) lights. These interior lights are controlled by operating switches located in the doorjambs of the vehicle doors or by a switch on the dash. ● **SEE FIGURE 23–29.**

Many Ford vehicles use the door switches to open and close the power side of the circuit. Many newer vehicles operate the interior lights through the vehicle computer or through an electronic module. Because the exact wiring and operation of these units differ, consult the service literature for the exact model of the vehicle being serviced.

ILLUMINATED ENTRY

Some vehicles are equipped with illuminated entry, meaning the interior lights are turned on for a given amount of time when the outside door handle is operated while the doors are locked. Most vehicles equipped with illuminated entry also light the exterior door keyhole. Vehicles equipped with body computers use the input from the key fob remote to "wake up" the power supply for the body computer.

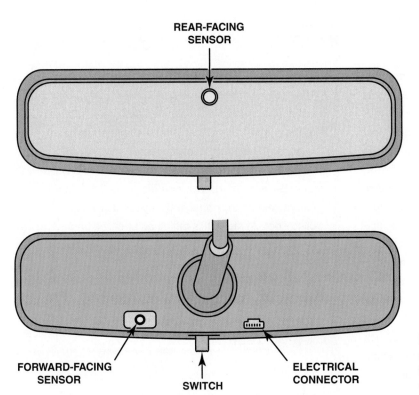

REAR-FACING SENSOR

FORWARD-FACING SENSOR

SWITCH

ELECTRICAL CONNECTOR

FIGURE 23–30 An automatic dimming mirror compares the amount of light toward the front of the vehicle to the rear of the vehicle and allies a voltage to cause the gel to darken the mirror.

FIBER OPTICS

Fiber optics is the transmission of light through special plastic (polymethyl methacrylate) that keeps the light rays parallel even if the plastic is tied in a knot. These strands of plastic are commonly used in automotive applications as indicators for the driver that certain lights are functioning. For example, some vehicles are equipped with fender-mounted units that light when the lights or turn signals are operating. Plastic fiber-optic strands, which often look like standard electrical wire, transmit the light at the bulb to the indicator on top of the fender so that the driver can determine if a certain light is operating. Fiber-optic strands also can be run like wires to indicate the operation of all lights on the dash or console. Fiber-optic strands are also commonly used to light ashtrays, outside door locks, and other areas where a small amount of light is required. The source of the light can be any normally operating light bulb, which means that one bulb can be used to illuminate many areas. A special bulb clip is normally used to retain the fiber-optic plastic tube near the bulb.

AUTOMATIC DIMMING MIRRORS

PARTS AND OPERATION Automatic dimming mirrors use electrochromic technology to dim the mirror in proportion to the amount of headlight glare from other vehicles at the rear. The electrochromic technology developed by Gentex Corporation uses a gel that changes with light between two pieces of glass. One piece of glass acts as a reflector and the other has a transparent (clear) electrically conductive coating. The inside rearview mirror also has a forward-facing light sensor that is used to detect darkness and signal the rearward-facing sensor to begin to check for excessive glare from headlights behind the vehicle. The rearward-facing sensor sends a voltage to the electrochromic gel in the mirror that is in proportion to the amount of glare detected. The mirror dims in proportion to the glare and then becomes like a standard rearview mirror when the glare is no longer detected. If automatic dimming mirrors are used on the exterior, the sensors in the interior mirror and electronics are used to control both the interior and exterior mirrors. ● **SEE FIGURE 23–30.**

DIAGNOSIS AND SERVICE If a customer concern states that the mirrors do not dim when exposed to bright headlights from the vehicle behind, the cause could be sensors or the mirror itself. Be sure that the mirror is getting electrical power. Most automotive dimming mirrors have a green light to indicate the presence of electrical power. If no voltage is found at the mirror, follow standard troubleshooting procedures to find the cause. If the mirror is getting voltage, start the diagnosis by placing a strip of tape over the forward-facing light sensor. Turn the ignition key off, engine off (KOEO), and observe the operation of the mirror when a flashlight or trouble light is directed onto the mirror. If the mirror reacts and dims, the forward-facing sensor is defective. Most often, the entire mirror assembly has to be replaced if any sensor or mirror faults are found.

One typical fault with automatic dimming mirrors is a crack can occur in the mirror assembly, allowing the gel to escape from between the two layers of glass. This gel can drip onto the dash or center console and harm these surfaces. The mirror should be replaced at the first sign of any gel leakage.

FEEDBACK

DEFINITION When current that lacks a good ground goes backward along the power side of the circuit in search of a return path (ground) to the battery, this reverse flow is called **feedback**, or *reverse-bias* current flow. Feedback can cause other lights or gauges that should not be working to actually turn on.

FEEDBACK EXAMPLE A customer complained that when the headlights were on, the left turn signal indicator light on the dash remained on. The cause was found to be a poor ground connection for the left front parking light socket. The front parking light bulb is a dual filament: one filament for the parking light (dim) and one filament for the turn signal operation (bright). A corroded socket did not provide a good enough ground to conduct all current required to light the dim filament of the bulb.

The two filaments of the bulb share the same ground connection and are electrically connected. When all the current could not flow through the bulb's ground in the socket, it caused a feedback or reversed its flow through the other filament, looking for ground. The turn signal filament is electrically connected to the dash indicator light; therefore, the reversed current on its path toward ground could light the turn signal indicator light. Cleaning or replacing the socket usually solves the problem if the ground wire for the socket is making a secure chassis ground connection.

? FREQUENTLY ASKED QUESTION

What Is the Troxler Effect?

The **Troxler effect**, also called *Troxler fading,* is a visual effect where an image remains on the retina of the eye for a short time after the image has been removed. The effect was discovered in 1804 by Igney Paul Vital Troxler (1780–1866), a Swiss physician. Because of the Troxler effect, headlight glare can remain on the retina of the eye and create a blind spot. At night, this fading away of the bright lights from the vehicle in the rear reflected by the rearview mirror can cause a hazard.

 TECH TIP

The Weirder the Problem, the More Likely It Is a Poor Ground Connection

Bad grounds are often the cause for feedback or lamps operating at full or partial brilliance. At first the problem looks weird because often the switch for the lights that are on dimly is not even turned on. When an electrical device is operating and it lacks a proper ground connection, the current will try to find ground and will often cause other circuits to work. Check all grounds before replacing parts.

LIGHTING SYSTEM DIAGNOSIS

Diagnosing any faults in the lighting and signaling systems usually includes the following steps.

STEP 1 Verify the customer concern.

STEP 2 Perform a visual inspection, checking for collision damage or other possible causes that would affect the operation of the lighting circuit.

STEP 3 Connect a factory or enhanced scan tool with bidirectional control of the computer modules to check for proper operation of the affected lighting circuit.

STEP 4 Follow the diagnostic procedure as found in service information to determine the root cause of the problem.

LIGHTING SYSTEM SYMPTOM GUIDE

The following list will assist technicians in troubleshooting lighting systems.

Problem	Possible Causes and/or Solutions
One headlight dim	1. Poor ground connection on body 2. Corroded connector
One headlight out (low or high beam)	1. Burned out headlight filament (Check the headlight with an ohmmeter. There should be a low-ohm reading between the power-side connection and the ground terminal of the bulb.) 2. Open circuit (no 12 volts to the bulb)
Both high- and low-beam headlights out	1. Burned out bulbs (Check for voltage at the wiring connector to the headlights for a possible open circuit to the headlights or open [defective] dimmer switch.) 2. Open circuit (no 12 volts to the bulb)
All headlights inoperative	1. Burned out filaments in all headlights (Check for excessive charging system voltage.) 2. Defective dimmer switch 3. Defective headlight switch
Slow turn signal operation	1. Defective flasher unit 2. High resistance in sockets or ground wire connections 3. Incorrect bulb numbers
Turn signals operating on one side only	1. Burned out bulb on affected side 2. Poor ground connection or defective socket on affected side 3. Incorrect bulb number on affected side 4. Defective turn signal switch

Problem	Possible Causes and/or Solutions
Interior light(s) inoperative	1. Burned out bulb(s) 2. Open in the power-side circuit (blown fuse) 3. Open in doorjamb switch(es)
Interior lights on all the time	1. Shorted doorjamb switch 2. Shorted control switch
Brake lights inoperative	1. Defective brake switch 2. Defective turn signal switch 3. Burned out brake light bulbs 4. Open circuit or poor ground connection 5. Blown fuse
Hazard warning lights inoperative	1. Defective hazard flasher unit 2. Open in hazard circuit 3. Blown fuse 4. Defective hazard switch
Hazard warning lights blinking too rapidly	1. Incorrect flasher unit 2. Shorted wiring to front or rear lights 3. Incorrect bulb numbers

TAILLIGHT BULB REPLACEMENT

1 The driver noticed that the taillight fault indicator (icon) on the dash was on any time the lights were on.

2 A visual inspection at the rear of the vehicle indicated that the right rear taillight bulb did not light. Removing a few screws from the plastic cover revealed the taillight assembly.

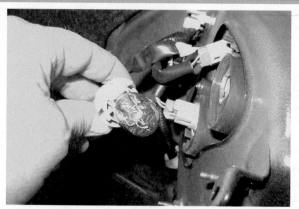

3 The bulb socket is removed from the taillight assembly by gently twisting the base of the bulb counterclockwise.

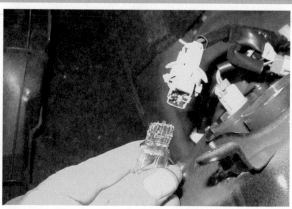

4 The bulb is removed from the socket by gently grasping the bulb and pulling the bulb straight out of the socket. Many bulbs required that you rotate the bulb 90° (1/4 turn) to release the retaining bulbs.

5 The new 7443 replacement bulb is being checked with an ohmmeter to be sure that it is okay before it is installed in the vehicle.

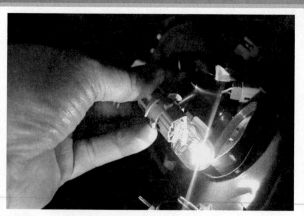

6 The replacement bulb in inserted into the taillight socket and the lights are turned on to verify proper operation before putting the components back together.

1 Before checking the vehicle for headlight aim, be sure that all the tires are at the correct inflation pressure, and that the suspension is in good working condition.

2 The headlight aim equipment will have to be adjusted for the slope of the floor in the service bay. Start the process by turning on the laser light generator on the side of the aimer body.

3 Place a yardstick or measuring tape vertically in front of the center of the front wheel, noting the height of the laser beam.

4 Move the yardstick to the center of the rear wheel and measure the height of the laser beam at this point. The height at the front and rear wheels should be the same.

5 If the laser beam height measurements are not the same, the floor slope of the aiming equipment must be adjusted. Turn the floor slope knob until the measurements are equal.

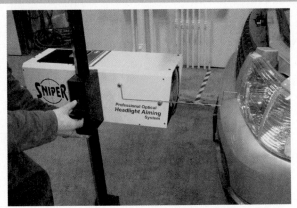

6 Place the aimer in front of the headlight to be checked, at a distance of 10 to 14 inches (25 to 35 cm). Use the aiming pointer to adjust the height of the aimer to the middle of the headlight.

CONTINUED ▶

7 Align the aimer horizontally, using the pointer to place the aimer at the center of the headlight.

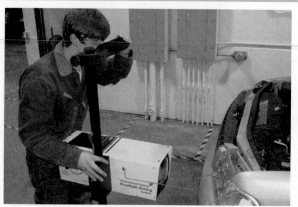

8 Lateral alignment (aligning the body of the aimer with the body of the vehicle) is done by looking through the upper visor. The line in the upper visor is aligned with symmetrical points on the vehicle body.

9 Turn on the vehicle headlights, being sure to select the correct beam position for the headlight to be aimed.

10 View the light beam through the aimer window. The position of the light pattern will be different for high and low beams.

11 If the first headlight is aimed adequately, move the aimer to the headlight on the opposite side of the vehicle. Follow the previous steps to position the aimer accurately.

12 If adjustment is required, move the headlight adjusting screws using a special tool or a 1/4-in. drive ratchet/socket combination. Watch the light beam through the aimer window to verify the adjustment.

1. Automotive bulbs are identified by trade numbers.

2. The trade number is the same regardless of manufacturer for the exact same bulb specification.

3. Daytime running lights (DRLs) are used on many vehicles.

4. High-intensity discharge (HID) headlights are brighter and have a blue tint.

5. Turn signal flashers come in many different types and construction.

REVIEW QUESTIONS

1. Why should the exact same trade number of bulb be used as a replacement?

2. Why is it important to avoid touching a halogen bulb with your fingers?

3. How do you diagnose a turn signal operating problem?

4. How do you aim headlights on a vehicle equipped with aerodynamic-style headlights?

CHAPTER QUIZ

1. Technician A says that the bulb trade number is the same for all bulbs of the same size. Technician B says that a dual-filament bulb has different candlepower ratings for each filament. Which technician is correct?
   a. Technician A only
   b. Technician B only
   c. Both Technicians A and B
   d. Neither Technician A nor B

2. Two technicians are discussing flasher units. Technician A says that only a DOT-approved flasher unit should be used for turn signals. Technician B says that a parallel (variable-load) flasher will function for turn signal usage, although it will not warn the driver if a bulb burns out. Which technician is correct?
   a. Technician A only
   b. Technician B only
   c. Both Technicians A and B
   d. Neither Technician A nor B

3. Interior overhead lights (dome lights) are operated by doorjamb switches that _____.
   a. Complete the power side of the circuit
   b. Complete the ground side of the circuit
   c. Move the bulb(s) into contact with the power and ground
   d. Complete either a or b depending on application

4. Electrical feedback is usually a result of _____.
   a. Too high a voltage in a circuit
   b. Too much current (in amperes) in a circuit
   c. Lack of a proper ground
   d. Both a and b

5. According to Chart 23–1, which bulb is brightest?
   a. 194
   b. 168
   c. 194NA
   d. 1157

6. If a 1157 bulb were to be installed in a left front parking light socket instead of a 2057 bulb, what would be the most likely result?
   a. The left turn signal would flash faster.
   b. The left turn signal would flash slower.
   c. The left parking light would be slightly brighter.
   d. The left parking light would be slightly dimmer.

7. A technician replaced a 1157NA with a 1157A bulb. Which is the most likely result?
   a. The bulb is brighter because the 1157A candlepower is higher.
   b. The amber color of the bulb is a different shade.
   c. The bulb is dimmer because the 1157A candlepower is lower.
   d. Both b and c

8. A customer complained that every time he turned on his vehicle's lights, the left-side turn signal indicator light on the dash remained on. The most likely cause is a _____.

   a. Poor ground to the parking light (or taillight) bulb on the *left* side

   b. Poor ground to the parking light (or taillight) bulb on the *right* side, causing current to flow to the left-side lights

   c. Defective (open) parking light (or taillight) bulb on the left side

   d. Both a and c

9. A defective taillight or front park light bulb could cause the _____.

   a. Turn signal indicator on the dash to light when the lights are turned on

   b. Dash lights to come on when the brake lights are on

   c. Lights-on warning chime to sound if the brake pedal is depressed

   d. All of the above

10. A defective brake switch could prevent proper operation of the _____.

    a. Cruise control

    b. ABS brakes

    c. Shift interlock

    d. All of the above

DRIVER INFORMATION AND NAVIGATION SYSTEMS

After studying Chapter 24, the reader will be able to:

1. Prepare for ASE Electrical/Electronic Systems (A6) certification test content area "F" (Gauges, Warning Devices, and Driver Information System Diagnosis and Repair).
2. Be able to identify the meaning of dash warning symbols.
3. Discuss how a fuel gauge works.
4. Explain how to use a service manual to trouble-shoot a malfunctioning dash instrument.
5. Describe how a navigation system works.
6. List the various types of dash instrument displays.

Backup camera 374
CFL 365
Combination valve 358
CRT 365
EEPROM 368
GPS 370
HUD 361
IP 359
LCD 364
LDWS 376

LED 376
NVRAM 368
Phosphor 365
PM generator 367
Pressure differential switch 358
RPA 374
Stepper motor 359
VTF 365
WOW display 366

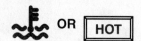

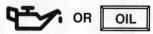

FIGURE 24–1 Engine coolant temperature is too high.

FIGURE 24–3 Water detected in fuel. Notice to drain the water from the fuel filter assembly on a vehicle equipped with a diesel engine.

FIGURE 24–2 Engine oil pressure too low.

FIGURE 24–4 Maintenance required. This usually means that the engine oil is scheduled to be changed or other routine service items replaced or checked.

DASH WARNING SYMBOLS

PURPOSE AND FUNCTION   All vehicles are equipped with warning lights that are often confusing to drivers. Because many vehicles are sold throughout the world, symbols instead of words are being used as warning lights. The dash warning lights are often called *telltale* lights as they are used to notify the driver of a situation or fault.

BULB TEST   When the ignition is first turned on, all of the warning lights come on as part of a self-test and to help the driver or technician spot any warning light that may be burned out. Technicians or drivers who are familiar with what lights should light may be able to determine if one or more warning lights are not on when the ignition is first turned on. Most factory scan tools can be used to command all of the warning lights on to help determine if one is not working.

ENGINE FAULT WARNING   Engine fault warning lights include the following:

- **Engine coolant temperature.** This warning lamp should come on when the ignition is first turned on as a bulb check and if the coolant temperature reaches 248°F to 258°F (120°C to 126°C), depending on the make and model of the vehicle. ● SEE FIGURE 24–1.

  If the engine coolant temperature warning lamp comes on while driving, perform the following in an attempt to reduce the temperature.

  1. Turn off the air conditioning.
  2. Turn on the heater.
  3. If the hot light remains on, drive to a safe location and shut off the engine and allow it to cool to help avoid serious engine damage.

- **Engine oil pressure.** This warning lamp should light when the ignition is first turned on as a bulb check; or

if the engine oil pressure light comes on when driving, perform the following:

1. Pull off the road as soon as possible.
2. Shut off the engine.
3. Check the oil level.
4. Do not drive the vehicle with the engine oil light on or severe engine damage can occur.

● **SEE FIGURE 24–2.**

- **Water in diesel fuel warning.** This warning lamp will light when the ignition is first turned on as a bulb check and if water is detected in the diesel fuel. This lamp is only used or operational in vehicles equipped with a diesel engine. If the water in diesel fuel warning lamp comes on, do the following:

  1. Remove the water using the built-in drain, usually part of the fuel filter.
  2. Check service information for the exact procedure to follow.

● **SEE FIGURE 24–3.**

- **Maintenance required warning.** The maintenance required lamp comes on when the ignition is first turned on as a bulb check and if the vehicle requires service. The service required could include:

  1. Oil and oil filter change
  2. Tire rotation
  3. Inspection

  Check service information for the exact service required. ● **SEE FIGURE 24–4.**

- **Malfunction indicator lamp (MIL), also called a check engine or service engine soon (SES) light.** This warning lamp comes on when the ignition is first turned on as a bulb test and then only if a fault in the powertrain control

FIGURE 24–5 Malfunction indicator lamp (MIL), also called a check engine light. The light means the engine control computer has detected a fault.

FIGURE 24–6 Charging system fault detected.

FIGURE 24–7 Fasten safety belt warning light.

FIGURE 24–8 Fault detected in the supplemental restraint system.

FIGURE 24–9 Fault detected in base brake system.

module (PCM) has been detected. If the MIL comes on when driving, it is not necessary to stop the vehicle, but the cause for why the warning lamp came on should be determined as soon as possible to avoid harming the engine or engine control systems. The MIL could come on if any of the following has been detected.

1. A sensor or actuator is electrically open or shorted.
2. A sensor is out of range for expected values.
3. An emission control system failure occurs, such as a loose gas cap.

If the MIL is on, a diagnostic trouble code has been set. Use a scan tool to retrieve the code(s) and follow service information for the exact procedure to follow. ● **SEE FIGURE 24–5.**

ELECTRICAL SYSTEM–RELATED WARNING LIGHTS

- **Charging system fault.** This warning lamp will come on when the ignition is first turned on as a bulb check and if a fault in the charging system has been detected. The lamp could include a fault with any of the following:

  1. Battery state of charge (SOC), electrical connections, or the battery itself
  2. Alternator or related wiring
  ● **SEE FIGURE 24–6.**

If the charge system warning lamp comes on, continue to drive until it is safe to pull over. The vehicle can usually be driven for several miles using battery power alone.

Check the following by visible inspection.

1. Alternator drive belt
2. Loose or corroded electrical connections at the battery
3. Loose or corroded wiring to the alternator
4. Defective alternator

SAFETY-RELATED WARNING LAMPS
Safety-related warning lamps include the following

- **Safety belt warning lamp.** The safety belt warning lamp will light and sound an alarm to notify the driver if the driver's side or passenger's side safety belt is not fastened. It is also used to indicate a fault in the safety belt circuit. Check service information for the exact procedure to follow if the safety belt warning light remains on even when the belts are fastened. ● **SEE FIGURE 24–7.**

- **Airbag warning lamp.** The airbag warning lamp comes on and flashes when the ignition is first turned on as part of a self-test of the system. If the airbag warning lamp remains on after the self-test, then the airbag controller has detected a fault. Check service information for the exact procedure to follow if the airbag warning lamp is on. ● **SEE FIGURE 24–8.**

NOTE: **The passenger side airbag light may indicate that it is on or off, depending if there is a passenger or an object heavy enough to trigger the seat sensor.**

- **Red brake fault warning light.** All vehicles are equipped with a red brake warning (RBW) lamp that lights if a fault in the base (hydraulic) brake system is detected. Three types of sensors are used to light this warning light.

  1. A brake fluid level sensor located in the master cylinder brake fluid reservoir
  2. A pressure switch located in the pressure differential switch, which detects a difference in pressure between the front and rear or diagonal brake systems
  3. The parking brake could be applied. ● **SEE FIGURE 24–9.**

If the red brake warning light comes on, do not drive the vehicle until the cause is determined and corrected.

FIGURE 24–10 Brake light bulb failure detected.

FIGURE 24–11 Exterior light bulb failure detected.

FIGURE 24–12 Worn brake pads or linings detected.

 OR OR

FIGURE 24–13 Fault detected in antilock brake system.

FIGURE 24–14 Low tire pressure detected.

 OR

FIGURE 24–15 Door open or ajar.

 OR

FIGURE 24–16 Windshield washer fluid low.

 OR

FIGURE 24–17 Low fuel level.

DASH WARNING SYMBOLS (CONTINUED)

- **Brake light bulb failure.** Some vehicles are able to detect if a brake light is burned out. The warning lamp will warn the driver when a situation like this occurs. ● SEE **FIGURE 24–10.**

- **Exterior light bulb failure.** Many vehicles use the body control module (BCM) to monitor current flow through all of the exterior lights and therefore can detect if a bulb is not working. ● SEE **FIGURE 24–11.**

- **Worn brake pads.** Some vehicles are equipped with sensors built into the disc brake pads that are used to trigger a dash warning light. The warning light often comes on when the ignition is first turned on as a bulb check and then goes out. If the brake pad warning lamp is on, check service information for the exact service procedure to follow. ● SEE **FIGURE 24–12.**

- **Antilock brake system (ABS) fault.** The amber antilock brake system warning light comes on if the ABS controller detects a fault in the antilock braking system. Examples of what could trigger the warning light include:

  1. Defective wheel speed sensor
  2. Low brake fluid level in the hydraulic control unit assembly
  3. Electrical fault detected anywhere in the system
     ● SEE **FIGURE 24–13.**

  If the amber ABS warning lamp is on, it is safe to drive the vehicle, but the antilock portion may not function.

TECH TIP

Check the Spare

Some vehicles that are equipped with a full-size spare tire also have a sensor in the spare. If the warning lamp is on and all four tires are properly inflated, check the spare.

- **Low tire pressure warning.** A tire pressure monitoring system (TPMS) warns if the inflation pressure of a tire has decreased by 25% (about 8 psi). If the warning lamp or message of a low tire is displayed, check the tire pressures before driving. If the inflation pressure is low, repair or replace the tire. ● SEE **FIGURE 24–14.**

DRIVER INFORMATION SYSTEM

- **Door open or ajar warning light.** If a door is open or ajar, a warning light is used to notify the driver. Check and close all doors and tailgates before driving. ● SEE **FIGURE 24–15.**

- **Windshield washer fluid low.** A sensor in the windshield washer fluid reservoir is used to turn on the low washer fluid warning lamp. ● SEE **FIGURE 24–16.**

- **Low fuel warning.** A low fuel indicator light is used to warn the driver that the fuel level is low. In most vehicles, the light comes on when there is between 1 and 3 gallons (3.8 and 11 liters) of fuel remaining. ● SEE **FIGURE 24–17.**

FIGURE 24–18 Headlights on.

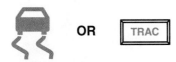

FIGURE 24–19 Low traction detected. Traction control system is functioning to restore traction (usually flashes when actively working to restore traction).

VSC

FIGURE 24–20 Vehicle stability control system either off or working if flashing.

TRAC OFF

FIGURE 24–21 Traction control system has been turned off.

- **Headlights on light.** This dash indicator lights whenever the headlights are on. ● SEE FIGURE 24–18.

  NOTE: This light may or may not indicate that the headlights are on if the headlight switch is set to the automatic position.

- **Low traction detected.** On a vehicle equipped with a traction control system (TCS), a dash indicator light is flashed whenever the system is working to restore traction. If the low traction warning light is flashing, reduce the rate of acceleration to help the system restore traction of the drive wheels with the road surface. ● SEE FIGURE 24–19.

- **Electronic stability control.** If a vehicle is equipped with electronic stability control (ESC), also called vehicle stability control (VSC), the dash indicator lamp will flash if the system is trying to restore vehicle stability. ● SEE FIGURE 24–20.

- **Traction off.** If the traction control system (TCS) is turned off by the driver, an indicator lamp lights to help remind the driver that this system has been turned off and will not be able to restore traction when lost. The system reverts to on, when the ignition is turned off, and then back on as the traction off button is depressed. ● SEE FIGURE 24–21.

- **Cruise indicator lamp.** Most vehicles are equipped with a switch that turns on the cruise control. The cruise (speed) control system does not work unless it has been turned on to help prevent accidental engagement. When the cruise control has been turned on, the cruise indicator light is on. ● SEE FIGURE 24–22.

CRUISE

FIGURE 24–22 Indicates that the cruise control is on and able to maintain vehicle speed if set.

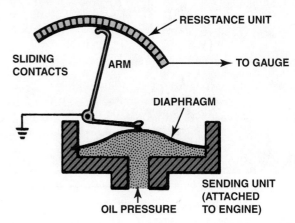

FIGURE 24–23 A typical oil pressure sending unit provides a varying amount of resistance as engine oil pressure changes. The output from the sensor is a variable voltage.

OIL PRESSURE WARNING DEVICES

OPERATION The oil pressure lamp operates through use of an oil pressure sensor unit, which is screwed into the engine block, and grounds the electrical circuit and lights the dash warning lamp in the event of low oil pressure, that is, 3 to 7 psi (20 to 50 kilopascals [kPa]). Normal oil pressure is generally between 10 and 60 psi (70 and 400 kPa). Some vehicles are equipped with a variable voltage oil pressure senors rather than a simple pressure switch. ● SEE FIGURE 24–23.

OIL PRESSURE LAMP DIAGNOSIS To test the operation of the oil pressure warning circuit, unplug the wire from the oil pressure sending unit, usually located near the oil filter, with the ignition switch on. With the wire disconnected from the sending unit, the warning lamp should be off. If the wire is touched to a ground, the warning lamp should be on. If there is *any* doubt of the operation of the oil pressure warning lamp, always check the actual engine oil pressure using a gauge that can be screwed into the opening that is left after unscrewing the oil pressure sending unit. For removing the sending unit, special sockets are available at most auto parts stores, or a 1 in. or 1 1/16 in. 6-point socket may be used for most units.

FIGURE 24–24 A temperature gauge showing normal operating temperature between 180°F and 215°F, depending on the specific vehicle and engine.

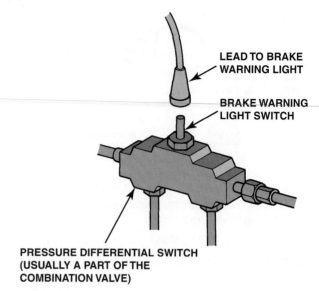

PRESSURE DIFFERENTIAL SWITCH (USUALLY A PART OF THE COMBINATION VALVE)

FIGURE 24–25 Typical brake warning light switch located on or near the master brake cylinder.

 REAL WORLD FIX

The Low Oil Pressure Story

After replacing valve cover gaskets on a Chevrolet V-8, the technician discovered that the oil pressure warning lamp was on. After checking the oil level and finding everything else okay, the technician discovered a wire pinched under the valve cover.

The wire went to the oil pressure sending unit. The edge of the valve cover had cut through the insulation and caused the current from the oil lamp to go to ground through the engine. Normally the oil lamp comes on when the sending unit grounds the wire from the lamp.

The technician freed the pinched wire and covered the cut with silicone sealant to prevent corrosion damage.

TEMPERATURE LAMP DIAGNOSIS

The "hot" lamp, or engine coolant overheat warning lamp, warns the driver whenever the engine coolant temperature is between 248°F and 258°F (120°C and 126°C). This temperature is slightly below the boiling point of the coolant in a properly operating cooling system. The temperature sensor on older models was separate from the sensor used by the engine computer. However, most vehicles now use the engine coolant temperature (ECT) sensor for engine temperature gauge operation. To test this sensor, use a scan tool to verify proper engine temperature and follow the vehicle manufacturer's recommended testing procedures. ● **SEE FIGURE 24–24.**

BRAKE WARNING LAMP

All vehicles sold in the United States after 1967 must be equipped with a dual braking system and a dash-mounted warning lamp to signal the driver of a failure in one part of the hydraulic brake system. The switch that operates the warning lamp is called a **pressure differential switch**. This switch is usually the center portion of a multipurpose brake part called a **combination valve**. If there is unequal hydraulic pressure in the braking system, the switch usually provides a ground path for the brake warning lamp, and the lamp comes on. ● **SEE FIGURE 24–25.**

Unfortunately, the dash warning lamp is often the same lamp as that used to warn the driver that the parking brake is on. The warning lamp is usually operated by using the parking brake lever or brake hydraulic pressure switch to complete the ground for the warning lamp circuit. If the warning lamp is on, first check if the parking brake is fully released. If the parking brake is fully released, the problem could be a defective parking brake switch or a hydraulic brake problem. To test for which system is causing the lamp to remain on, simply unplug the wire from the valve or switch. If the wire on the pressure differential switch is disconnected and the warning lamp remains on, then the problem is due to a defective or misadjusted parking brake switch. If, however, the warning lamp goes out when the wire is removed from the brake switch, then the problem is due to a hydraulic brake fault that caused the pressure differential switch to complete the warning lamp circuit. The red brake warning lamp also can be turned on if the brake fluid is low. ● **SEE FIGURE 24–26** for an example of a brake fluid level sensor.

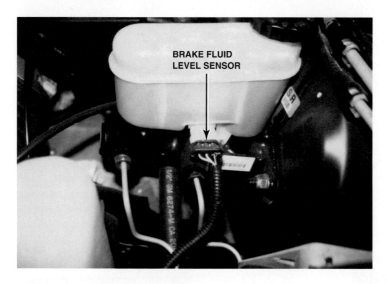

FIGURE 24–26 The red brake warning lamp can be turned on if the brake fluid level is low.

ANALOG DASH INSTRUMENTS

An analog display uses a needle to show the value, whereas a digital display uses numbers. Analog electromagnetic dash instruments use small electromagnetic coils that are connected to a sending unit for such things as fuel level, water temperature, and oil pressure. The sensors are the same regardless of the type of display used. The resistance of the sensor varies with what is being measured. ● **SEE FIGURE 24–27** for typical electromagnetic fuel gauge operation.

NETWORK COMMUNICATION

DESCRIPTION Many instrument panels are operated by electronic control units that communicate with the engine control computer for engine data such as revolutions per minute (RPM) and engine temperature. These electronic **instrument panels (IPs)** use the voltage changes from variable-resistance sensors, such as that of the fuel gauge, to determine fuel level. Therefore, even though the sensor in the fuel tank is the same, the display itself may be computer controlled. The data is transmitted to the instrument cluster as well as to the powertrain control module through serial data lines. Because all sensor inputs are interconnected, the technician should always follow the factory recommended diagnostic procedures. ● **SEE FIGURE 24–28** on page 361.

STEPPER MOTOR ANALOG GAUGES

DESCRIPTION Most analog dash displays use a stepper motor to move the needle. A **stepper motor** is a type of electric motor that is designed to rotate in small steps based on the signal from a computer. This type of gauge is very accurate.

OPERATION A digital output is used to control stepper motors. Stepper motors are direct current motors that move in fixed steps or increments from de-energized (no voltage) to fully energized (full voltage). A stepper motor often has as many as 120 steps of motion. When using a stepper motor that is controlled by the PCM, it is very easy for the PCM to keep track of the stepper motor's position. By counting the number of steps that have been sent to the stepper motor, the PCM can determine its relative position. While the PCM does not actually receive a feedback signal from the stepper motor, it knows how many steps forward or backward the motor should have moved.

A typical stepper motor uses a permanent magnet and two electromagnets. Each of the two electromagnetic windings is controlled by the computer. The computer pulses the windings and changes the polarity of the windings to cause the armature of the stepper motor to rotate 90 degrees at a time. Each 90-degree pulse is recorded by the computer as a "count" or "step," which explains the name given to this type of motor. ● **SEE FIGURE 24–29.**

NOTE: Many electronic gauge clusters are checked at key on where the dash display needles will be commanded to 1/4, 1/2, 3/4, and full positions before returning to their normal readings. This self-test allows the service technician to check the operation of each individual gauge, even though replacing the entire instrument panel cluster is usually necessary to repair an inoperative gauge.

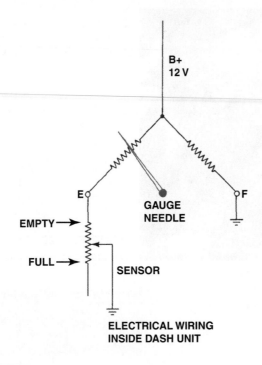

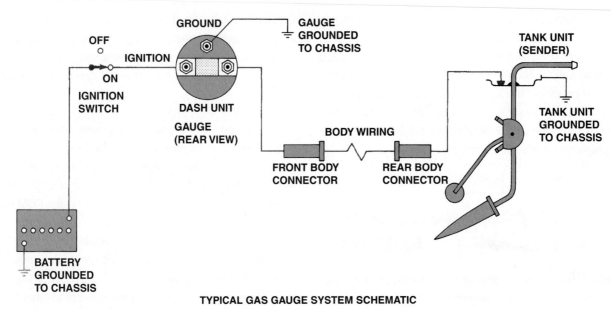

TYPICAL GAS GAUGE SYSTEM SCHEMATIC

FIGURE 24–27 Electromagnetic fuel gauge wiring. If the sensor wire is unplugged and grounded, the needle should point to "E" (empty). If the sensor wire is unplugged and held away from ground, the needle should point to "F" (full).

STEPPER MOTOR ANALOG GAUGES (CONTINUED)

DIAGNOSIS The dash electronic circuits are often too complex to show on a wiring diagram. Instead, all related electronic circuits are simply indicated as a solid box with "electronic module" printed on the diagram. Even if all the electronic circuits were shown on the wiring diagram, it would require the skill of an electronics engineer to determine exactly how the circuit was designed to work. ● **SEE FIGURE 24–30.**

Note that the grounding for the "check oil" dash indicator lamp is accomplished through an electronic buffer. The exact conditions, such as amount of time since the ignition was shut off, are unknown to the technician. To correctly diagnose problems with this type of circuit, technicians must read, understand, and follow the written diagnostic procedures specified by the vehicle manufacturer.

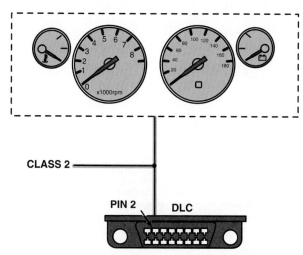

COOLANT
TEMPERATURE   TACHOMETER   SPEEDOMETER

CLASS 2

PIN 2   DLC

FIGURE 24–28 A typical instrument display uses data from the sensors over serial data lines to the individual gauges.

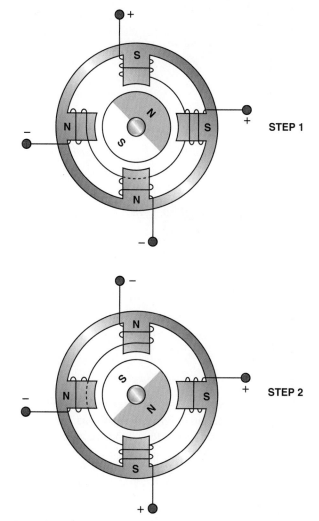

STEP 1

STEP 2

FIGURE 24–29 Most stepper motors use four wires which are pulsed by the computer to rotate the armature in steps.

The **head-up display (HUD)** is a supplemental display that projects the vehicle speed and sometimes other data, such as turn signal information, onto the windshield. The projected image looks as if it is some distance ahead, making it easy for the driver to see without having to refocus on a closer dash display. ● **SEE FIGURES 24–31 AND 24–32** on page 363.

The head-up display can also have the brightness controlled on most vehicles that use this type of display. The HUD unit is installed in the instrument panel (IP) and uses a mirror to project vehicle information onto the inside surface of the windshield. ● **SEE FIGURE 24–33** on page 363.

Follow the vehicle manufacturer's recommended diagnostic and testing procedures if any faults are found with the head-up display.

NIGHT VISION

PARTS AND OPERATION   Night vision systems use a camera that is capable of observing objects in the dark to assist the driver while driving at night. The primary night viewing illumination devices are the headlights. The night vision option uses a head-up display (HUD) to improve the vision of the driver beyond the scope of the headlights. Using a HUD display allows the driver to keep eyes on the road and hands on the wheel for maximum safety.

Besides the head-up display, the night vision camera uses a special thermal imaging or infrared technology. The camera is mounted behind the grill in the front of the vehicle. ● **SEE FIGURE 24–34** on page 363.

The camera creates pictures based on the heat energy emitted by objects rather than from light reflected on an object as in a normal optical camera. The image looks like a black and white photo negative when hot objects (higher thermal energy) appear light or white, and cool objects appear dark or black. Other parts of the night vision system include:

■ **On/off and dimming switch.** This allows the driver to adjust the brightness of the display and to turn it on or off as needed.

■ **Up/down switch.** The night vision HUD system has an electric tilt adjust motor that allows the driver to adjust the image up or down on the windshield within a certain image.

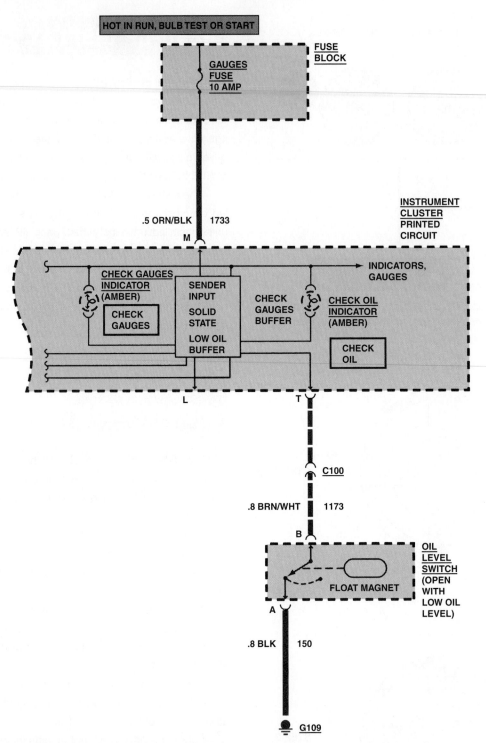

FIGURE 24–30 The ground for the "check oil" indicator lamp is controlled by the electronic low-oil buffer. Even though this buffer is connected to an oil level sensor, the buffer also takes into consideration the amount of time the engine has been stopped and the temperature of the engine. The only way to properly diagnose a problem with this circuit is to use the procedures specified by the vehicle manufacturer. Besides, only the engineer who designed the circuit knows for sure how it is supposed to work.

FIGURE 24–31 A typical head-up display showing zero miles per hour, which is actually projected on the windshield from the head-up display in the dash.

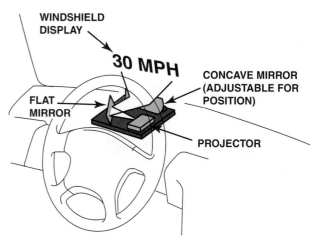

FIGURE 24–33 A typical head-up display (HUD) unit.

FIGURE 24–32 The dash-mounted control for the head-up display on this Cadillac allows the driver to move the image up and down on the windshield for best viewing.

FIGURE 24–34 A night vision camera behind the grille of a Cadillac.

NIGHT VISION (CONTINUED)

CAUTION: Becoming accustomed to night vision can be difficult and may take several nights to get used to looking at the head-up display.

DIAGNOSIS AND SERVICE The first step when diagnosing a fault with the night vision system is to verify the concern. Check the owner manual or service information for proper operation. For example, the Cadillac night vision system requires the following actions to function.

1. The ignition has to be in the on (run) position.
2. The Twilight Sentinel photo cell must indicate that it is dark.
3. The headlights must be on.
4. The switch for the night vision system must be on and the brightness adjusted so the image is properly displayed.

The night vision system uses a camera in the front of the vehicle that is protected from road debris by a grille. However, small stones or other debris can get past the grille and damage the lens of the camera. If the camera is damaged, it must be replaced as an assembly because no separate parts are available. Always follow the vehicle manufacturer's recommended testing and servicing procedures.

DIGITAL ELECTRONIC DISPLAY OPERATION

TYPES

- Mechanical or electromechanical dash instruments use cables, mechanical transducers, and sensors to operate a particular dash instrument.

- Digital dash instruments use various electric and electronic sensors that activate segments or sections of an electronic display. Most electronic dash clusters use a computer chip and various electronic circuits to operate and control the internal power supply, sensor voltages, and display voltages.

- Electronic dash display systems may use one or more of several types of displays: light-emitting diode (LED), liquid crystal display (LCD), vacuum tube fluorescent (VTF), and cathode ray tube (CRT).

LED DIGITAL DISPLAYS   All diodes emit some form of energy during operation; the **light-emitting diode (LED)** is a semiconductor that is constructed to release energy in the form of light. Many colors of LEDs can be constructed, but the most popular are red, green, and yellow. Red is difficult to see in direct sunlight; therefore, if an LED is used, most vehicle manufacturers use yellow. Light-emitting diodes can be arranged in a group of seven, which then can be used to display both numbers and letters. ● **SEE FIGURE 24–35.**

An LED display requires more electrical power than other types of electronic displays. A typical LED display requires 30 mA for each *segment;* therefore, each number or letter displayed could require 210 mA (0.210 A).

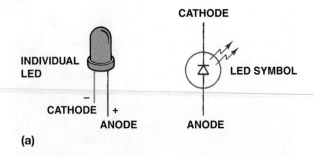

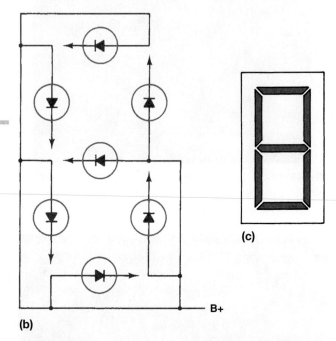

FIGURE 24–35 (a) Symbol and line drawing of a typical light-emitting diode (LED). (b) Grouped in seven segments, this array is called a seven-segment LED display with a common anode (positive connection). The dash computer toggles the cathode (negative) side of each individual segment to display numbers and letters. (c) When all segments are turned on, the number 8 is displayed.

LIQUID CRYSTAL DISPLAYS   **Liquid crystal displays (LCDs)** can be arranged into a variety of forms, letters, numbers, and bar graph displays.

- LCD construction consists of a special fluid sandwiched between two sheets of polarized glass. The special fluid between the glass plates will permit light to pass if a small voltage is applied to the fluid through a conductive film laminated to the glass plates.

- The light from a very bright halogen bulb behind the LCD shines through those segments of the LCD that have been polarized to let the light through, which then show numbers or letters. Color filters can be placed in front of

FIGURE 24–36 A typical navigation system. This Honda/Acura system uses some of the climate control functions as well as the trip information on the display. This particular unit uses a DVD unit in the trunk along with a global positioning satellite (GPS) to display a map and your exact location for the entire country.

the display to change the color of certain segments of the display, such as the maximum engine speed on a digital tachometer.

CAUTION: Be careful, when cleaning an LCD, not to push on the glass plate covering the special fluid. If excessive pressure is exerted on the glass, the display may be permanently distorted. If the glass breaks, the fluid will escape and could damage other components in the vehicle as a result of its strong alkaline nature. Use only a soft, damp cloth to clean these displays.

■ The major disadvantage of an LCD digital dash is that the numbers or letters are slow to react or change at low temperatures. ● **SEE FIGURE 24–36.**

VACUUM TUBE FLUORESCENT DISPLAYS The **vacuum tube fluorescent (VTF)** display is a popular automotive and household appliance display because it is very bright and can easily be viewed in strong sunlight. The usual VTF display is green, but white is often used for home appliances.

■ The VTF display generates its bright light in a manner similar to that of a TV screen, where a chemical-coated light-emitting element called a **phosphor** is hit with high-speed electrons.

■ VTF displays are very bright and must be dimmed by use of dense filters or by controlling the voltage applied to the display. A typical VTF dash is dimmed to 75% brightness whenever the parking lights or headlights are turned on. Some displays use a photocell to monitor and adjust the intensity of the display during daylight viewing. Most VTF displays are green for best viewing under most lighting conditions.

CATHODE RAY TUBE A **cathode ray tube (CRT)** dash display, which is similar to a television tube or LCD display, permits the display of hundreds of controls and diagnostic messages in one convenient location.

Using the touch-sensitive cathode ray tube, the driver or technician can select from many different displays, including those of radio, climate, trip, and dash instrument information. The driver can readily access all of these functions. Further diagnostic information can be displayed on the CRT if the proper combination of air-conditioning controls is touched. The diagnostic procedures for these displays involve pushing two or more buttons at the same time to access the diagnostic menu. Always follow the factory service manual recommendations.

COLD CATHODE FLUORESCENT DISPLAYS Cold **cathode fluorescent lighting (CFL)** models are used by many vehicle manufacturers for backlighting. Current consumption ranges from 3 to 5 mA (0.003 to 0.005 A) with an average life of 40,000 hours. CFL is replacing conventional incandescent light bulbs.

ELECTRONIC ANALOG DISPLAYS Most analog dash displays since the early 1990s are electronically or computer controlled. The sensors may be the same, but the sensor information is sent to the body or vehicle computer through a data BUS, and then the computer controls current through small electromagnets that move the needle of the

(a)

(b)

(c)

FIGURE 24–37 (a) View of the vehicle dash with the instrument cluster removed. Sometimes the dash instruments can be serviced by removing the padded dash cover (crash pad) to gain access to the rear of the dash. (b) The front view of the electronic analog dash display. (c) The rear view of the dash display showing that there are a few bulbs that can be serviced, but otherwise the unit is serviced as an assembly.

DIGITAL ELECTRONIC DISPLAY OPERATION (CONTINUED)

gauge. ● **SEE FIGURE 24–37.** A scan tool often is needed to diagnosis the operation of a computer-controlled analog dash instrument display.

WOW DISPLAY When a vehicle equipped with a digital dash is started, all segments of the electronic display are turned on at full brilliance for 1 or 2 seconds. This is commonly called the **WOW display,** and is used to show off the brilliance of the display. If numbers are part of the display, the number 8 is shown, because this number uses all segments of a number display. Technicians can also use the WOW display to determine if all segments of the electronic display are functioning correctly.

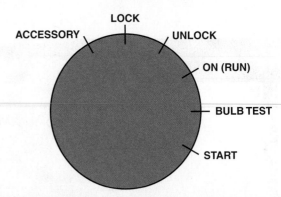

FIGURE 24–38 Typical ignition switch positions. Notice the bulb check position between "on" (run) and "start." These inputs are often just voltage signal to the body control module and can be checked using a scan tool.

FIGURE 24–39 Many newer vehicles place the ignition switch on the dash and incorporate antitheft controls. Note the location of the accessory position.

 TECH TIP

The Bulb Test

Many ignition switches have six positions. Notice the *bulb test* position (between "on" and "start"). When the ignition is turned to "on" (run), some dash warning lamps are illuminated. When the bulb test position is reached, additional dash warning lamps often are lighted. Technicians use this ignition switch position to check the operation of fuses that protect various circuits. Dash warning lamps are not all powered by the same fuses. If an electrical component or circuit does not work, the power side (fuse) can be quickly checked by observing the operation of the dash lamps that share a common fuse with the problem circuit. Consult a wiring diagram for fuse information on the exact circuit being tested. ● **SEE FIGURES 24–38 AND 24–39.**

FIGURE 24–40 A vehicle speed sensor located in the extension housing of the transmission. Some vehicles use the wheel speed sensors for vehicle speed information.

 REAL WORLD FIX

The Speedometer Works as if It Is a Tachometer

The owner of a Lincoln Town Car complained that all of a sudden the speedometer needle went up and down with engine speed rather than vehicle speed. In fact, the speedometer needle went up and down with engine speed even though the gear selector was in "park" and the vehicle was not moving. After hours of troubleshooting, the service technician went back and started checking the basics and discovered that the generator (alternator) had a bad diode. The technician measured over 1 volt AC and over 10 amperes AC ripple current using a clamp-on AC/DC ammeter. Replacing the generator restored the proper operation of the speedometer.

ELECTRONIC SPEEDOMETERS

OPERATION Electronic dash displays ordinarily use an electric vehicle speed sensor driven by a small gear on the output shaft of the transmission. These speed sensors contain a permanent magnet and generate a voltage in proportion to the vehicle speed. These speed sensors are commonly called **permanent magnet (PM) generators**. ● **SEE FIGURE 24–40.**

The output of a PM generator speed sensor is an AC voltage that varies in frequency and amplitude with increasing vehicle speed. The PM generator speed signal is sent to the

 **TECH TIP**

The Soldering Gun Trick

Diagnosing problems with digital or electronic dash instruments can be difficult. Replacement parts generally are expensive and usually not returnable if installed in the vehicle. A popular trick that helps isolate the problem is to use a soldering gun near the PM generator.

A PM generator contains a coil of wire. As the magnet inside revolves, a voltage is produced. It is the *frequency* of this voltage that the dash (or engine) computer uses to calculate vehicle speed.

A soldering gun plugged into 110 volts AC will provide a strong *varying* magnetic field around the soldering gun. This magnetic field is constantly changing at the rate of 60 cycles per second. This frequency of the magnetic field induces a voltage in the windings of the PM generator. This induced voltage at 60 hertz (Hz) is converted by the computer circuits to a miles per hour (mph) reading on the dash.

To test the electronic speedometer, turn the ignition to "on" (engine off) and hold a soldering gun near the PM generator.

CAUTION: The soldering gun tip can get hot, so hold it away from wiring or other components that may be damaged by the hot tip.

If the PM generator, wiring, computer, and dash are okay, the speedometer should register a speed, usually 54 mph (87 km/h). If the speedometer does not work when the vehicle is driven, the problem is in the PM generator drive.

If the speedometer does not register a speed when the soldering gun is used, the problem could be caused by the following:
1. Defective PM generator (check the windings with an ohmmeter)
2. Defective (open or shorted) wiring from the PM generator to the computer
3. Defective computer or dash circuit

instrument cluster electronic circuits. These specialized electronic circuits include a buffer amplifier circuit that converts the variable sine wave voltage from the speed sensor to an on/off signal that can be used by other electronic circuits to indicate a vehicle's speed. The vehicle speed is then displayed by either an electronic needle-type speedometer or by numbers on a digital display.

The Toyota Truck Story

The owner of a Toyota truck complained that several electrical problems plagued the truck, including the following:

1. The cruise (speed) control would kick out intermittently.
2. The red brake warning lamp would come on, especially during cold weather.

The owner had replaced the parking brake switch, thinking that was the cause of the red brake warning lamp coming on.

An experienced technician checked the wiring diagram in service information. Checking the warning lamp circuit, the technician noticed that the same wire went to the brake fluid level sensor. The brake fluid was at the minimum level. Filling the master cylinder to the maximum level with clean brake fluid solved both problems. The electronics of the cruise control stopped operation when the red brake warning lamp was on as a safety measure.

(a)

(b)

FIGURE 24–41 (a) Some odometers are mechanical and are operated by a stepper motor. (b) Many vehicles are equipped with an electronic odometer.

ELECTRONIC ODOMETERS

PURPOSE AND FUNCTION An odometer is a dash display that indicates the total miles traveled by the vehicle. Some dash displays also include a trip odometer that can be reset and used to record total miles traveled on a trip or the distance traveled between fuel stops. Electronic dash displays can use either an electrically driven mechanical odometer or a digital display odometer to indicate miles traveled. On mechanical type odometers, a small electric motor, called a stepper motor, is used to turn the number wheels of a mechanical-style odometer. A pulsed voltage is fed to this stepper motor, which moves in relation to the miles traveled. ● **SEE FIGURE 24–41.**

Digital odometers use LED, LCD, or VTF displays to indicate miles traveled. Because total miles must be retained when the ignition is turned off or the battery is disconnected, a special electronic chip must be used that will retain the miles traveled.

These special chips are called **nonvolatile random-access memory (NVRAM).** *Nonvolatile* means that the information stored in the electronic chip is not lost when electrical power is removed. Some vehicles use a chip called **electronically**

erasable programmable read-only memory (EEPROM). Most digital odometers can read up to 999,999.9 miles or kilometers (km), and then the display indicates error. If the chip is damaged or exposed to static electricity, it may fail to operate and "error" may appear.

SPEEDOMETER/ODOMETER SERVICE If the speedometer and odometer fail to operate, check the following:

- The speed sensor should be the first item checked. With the vehicle safely raised off the ground and supported, check vehicle speed using a scan tool. If a scan tool is not available, disconnect the wires from the speed sensor near the output shaft of the transmission. Connect a multimeter set on AC volts to the terminals of the speed

Look for Previous Repairs

A technician was asked to fix the speedometer on a Pontiac Grand Am that showed approximately double the actual speed. Previous repairs had included a new vehicle speed (VS) sensor and computer. Nothing made any difference. The customer stated that the problem happened all of a sudden. After hours of troubleshooting, the customer just happened to mention that the automatic transaxle had been repaired shortly before the speedometer problem. The root cause of the problem was discovered when the technician learned that a final drive assembly from a 4T60-E transaxle had been installed on the 3T-40 transaxle. The 4T60-E final drive assembly has 13 reluctor teeth whereas the 3T-40 has 7 teeth. This difference in the number of teeth caused the speedometer to read almost double the actual vehicle speed. After the correct part was installed, the speedometer worked correctly. The technician now always asks if there has been any recent work performed in the vehicle prior to any diagnosis.

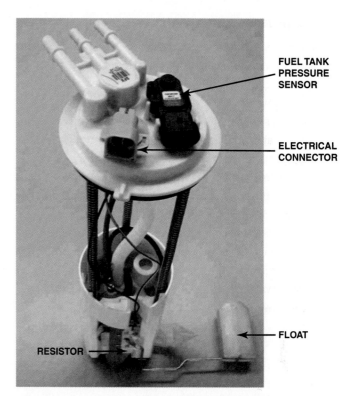

FIGURE 24–42 A fuel tank module assembly that contains the fuel pump and fuel level sensor in one assembly.

sensor and rotate the drive wheels with the transmission in neutral. A good speed sensor should indicate approximately 2 volts AC if the drive wheels are rotated by hand.

- If the speed sensor is working, check the wiring from the speed sensor to the dash cluster. If the wiring is good, the instrument panel (IP) should be sent to a specialty repair facility.

- If the speedometer operates correctly but the mechanical odometer does not work, the odometer stepper motor, the number wheel assembly, or the circuit controlling the stepper motor is defective. If the digital odometer does not operate but the speedometer operates correctly, then the dash cluster must be removed and sent to a specialized repair facility. A replacement chip is available only through authorized sources; if the odometer chip is defective, the original number of miles must be programmed into the replacement chip.

ELECTRONIC FUEL LEVEL GAUGES

OPERATION Electronic fuel level gauges ordinarily use the same fuel tank sending unit as that used on conventional fuel gauges. The tank unit consists of a float attached to a variable resistor. As the fuel level changes, the resistance of the sending unit changes. As the resistance of the tank unit changes, the dash-mounted gauge also changes. The only difference between a digital fuel level gauge and a conventional needle type is in the display. Digital fuel level gauges can be either numerical (indicating gallons or liters remaining in the tank) or a bar graph display. ● **SEE FIGURE 24–42.**

The diagnosis of a problem is the same as that described earlier for conventional fuel gauges. If the tests indicate that the dash unit is defective, usually the *entire* dash gauge assembly must be replaced.

Electronic Devices Cannot Swim

The owner of a Dodge minivan complained that after the vehicle was cleaned inside and outside, the temperature gauge, fuel gauge, and speedometer stopped working. The vehicle speed sensor was checked and found to be supplying a square wave signal that changed with vehicle speed. A scan tool indicated a speed, yet the speedometer displayed zero all the time. Finally, the service technician checked the body computer to the right of the accelerator pedal and noticed that it had been wet, from the interior cleaning. Drying the computer did not fix the problem, but a replacement body computer fixed all the problems. The owner discovered that electronic devices do not like water and that computers cannot swim.

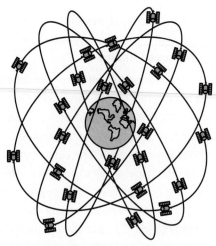

FIGURE 24–43 Global positioning systems use 24 satellites in high earth orbit whose signals are picked up by navigation systems. The navigation system computer then calculates the location based on the position of the satellite overhead.

 FREQUENTLY ASKED QUESTION

Does the Government Know Where I Am?

No. The navigation system uses signals from the satellites and uses the signals from three or more to determine position. If the vehicle is equipped with OnStar, then the vehicle position can be monitored by the use of the cellular telephone link to OnStar call centers. Unless the vehicle has a cellular phone connection to the outside world, the only people who will know the location of the vehicle are the persons inside the vehicle viewing the navigation screen.

NAVIGATION AND GPS

PURPOSE AND FUNCTION The **global positioning system (GPS)** uses 24 satellites in orbit around the earth to provide signals for navigation devices. GPS is funded and controlled by the U.S. Department of Defense (DOD). While the system can be used by anyone with a GPS receiver, it was designed for and is operated by the U.S. military. ● **SEE FIGURE 24–43.**

BACKGROUND The current global positioning system was developed after a civilian airplane from Korean Airlines, Flight 007, was shot down as it flew over Soviet territory in 1983. The system became fully operational in 1991. Civilians were granted use of GPS that same year, but with less accuracy than the system used by the military.

Until 2000, the nonmilitary use of GPS was purposely degraded by a computer program called selection availability (S/A) built into the satellite transmission signals. After 2000, the S/A has been officially turned off, allowing nonmilitary users more accurate position information from the GPS receivers.

NAVIGATION SYSTEM PARTS AND OPERATION
Navigation systems use the GPS satellites for basic location information. The navigation controller located in the rear of the vehicle uses other sensors, including a digitized map to display the location of the vehicle.

- **GPS satellite signals.** These signals from at least three satellites are needed to locate the vehicle.

- **Yaw sensor.** This sensor is often used inside the navigation unit to detect movement of the vehicle during cornering. This sensor is also called a "g" sensor because it measures force; 1 g is the force of gravity.

- **Vehicle speed sensor.** This sensor input is used by the navigation controller to determine the speed and distance the vehicle travels. This information is compiled and compared to the digital map and GPS satellite inputs to locate the vehicle.

- **Audio output/input.** Voice-activated factory units use a built-in microphone at the center top of the windshield and the audio speakers speech output.

FIGURE 24–44 A typical GPS display screen showing the location of the vehicle.

FIGURE 24–45 A typical navigation display showing various options. Some systems do not allow access to these functions if the vehicle is in gear and/or moving.

TECH TIP

Window Tinting Can Hurt GPS Reception

Most factory-installed navigation systems use a GPS antenna inside the rear back glass or under the rear package shelf. If a metalized window tint is applied to the rear glass, the signal strength from the GPS satellites can be reduced. If the customer concern includes inaccurate or nonfunctioning navigation, check for window tint.

TECH TIP

Touch Screen Tip

Most vehicle navigation systems use a touch screen for use by the driver (or passenger) to input information or other on-screen prompts. Most touch screens use infrared beams projected from the top and bottom plus across the screen to form a grid. The system detects where on the screen a finger is located by the location of the beams that are cut. Do not push harder on the display if the unit does not respond, or damage to the display unit may occur. If no response is detected when lightly depressing the screen, rotate the finger to cause the infrared beams to be cut.

Navigation systems include the following components.

1. Screen display ● **SEE FIGURE 24–44.**

2. GPS antenna

3. Navigation control unit, usually with map information on a DVD

   The DVD includes street names and the following information.

1. Points of interest (POI), including automated teller machines (ATMs), restaurants, schools, colleges, museums, shopping, and airports, as well as vehicle dealer locations.

2. Business addresses and telephone numbers, including hotels and restaurants (If the telephone number is listed in the business telephone book, it can usually be displayed on the navigation screen. If the telephone number of the business is known, the location can be displayed.)

NOTE: Private residences or cellular telephone numbers are not included in the database of telephone numbers stored on the navigation system DVD.

3. Turn-by-turn directions to addresses that are selected by:

   ■ Points of interest (POI)

   ■ Typed in using a keyboard shown on the display

   The navigation unit then often allows the user to select the fastest way to the destination, as well as the shortest way, or how to avoid toll roads. ● **SEE FIGURE 24–45.**

DIAGNOSIS AND SERVICE For the correct functioning of the navigation system, three inputs are needed.

■ Location

■ Direction

■ Speed

What Is Navigation Enhanced Climate Control?

Some vehicles, such as the Acura RL, use data from the navigation system to help control the automatic climate control system. Data about the location of the vehicle includes:

- **Time and date.** This information allows the automatic climate control system to determine where the sun is located.
- **Direction of travel.** The navigation system can also help the climate control system determine the direction of travel.

As a result of the input from the navigation system, the automatic climate control system can control cabin temperature in addition to various other sensors in the vehicle. For example, if the vehicle was traveling south in the late afternoon in July, the climate control system could assume that the passenger side of the vehicle would be warmed more by the sun than the driver's side and could increase the airflow to the passenger side to help compensate for the additional solar heating.

NAVIGATION AND GPS (CONTINUED)

The navigation system uses the GPS satellite and map data to determine a location. Direction and speed are determined by the navigation computer from inputs from the satellite, plus the yaw sensor and vehicle speed sensor. The following symptoms may occur and be a customer complaint. Knowing how the system malfunctions helps to determine the most likely cause.

- If the vehicle icon jumps down the road, a fault with the vehicle speed (VS) sensor input is usually indicated.

- If the icon rotates on the screen, but the vehicle is not being driven in circles, a fault with the yaw sensor or yaw sensor input to the navigation controller is likely.

- If the icon goes off course and shows the vehicle on a road that it is not on, a fault with the GPS antenna is the most common reason for this situation.

Sometimes the navigation system itself will display a warning that views from the satellite are not being received. Always follow the displayed instructions. ● **SEE FIGURE 24–46.**

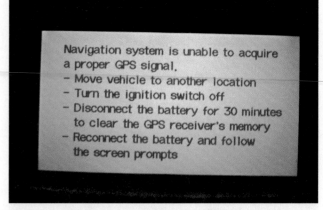

FIGURE 24–46 A screen display of a navigation system that is unable to acquire usable signals from GPS satellites.

ONSTAR

PARTS AND OPERATION OnStar is a system that includes the following functions.

1. Cellular telephone
2. Global positioning antenna and computer

OnStar is standard or optional on most General Motors vehicles and selected other brands and models, to help the driver in an emergency or to provide other services. The cellular telephone is used to communicate with the driver from advisors at service centers. The advisor at the service center is able to see the location of the vehicle as transmitted from the GPS antenna and computer system in the vehicle on a display. OnStar does not display the location of the vehicle to the driver unless the vehicle is also equipped with a navigation system.

Unlike most navigation systems, the OnStar system requires a monthly fee. OnStar was first introduced in 1996 as an option on some Cadillac models. Early versions used a handheld cellular telephone while later units used a group of three buttons mounted on the inside rearview mirror and a hands-free cellular telephone. ● **SEE FIGURE 24–47.**

The first version used analog cellular service while later versions used a dual mode (analog and digital) service until 2007. Since 2007, all OnStar systems use digital cellular service, which means that older systems that were analog only need to be upgraded.

The OnStar system includes the following features, which can vary depending on the level of service desired and cost per month.

- **Automatic notification of airbag deployment.** If the airbag is deployed, the advisor is notified immediately and attempts to call the vehicle. If there is no reply, or if the

FIGURE 24-47 The three-button OnStar control is located on the inside rearview mirror. The left button (telephone handset icon) is pushed if a hands-free cellular call is to be made. The center button is depressed to contact an OnStar advisor and the right emergency button is used to request that help be sent to the vehicle's location.

occupants report an emergency, the advisor will contact emergency services and give them the location of the vehicle.

- **Emergency services.** If the red button is pushed, OnStar immediately locates the vehicle and contacts the nearest emergency service agency.

- **Stolen vehicle location assistance.** If a vehicle is reported stolen, a call center advisor can track the vehicle.

- **Remote door unlock.** An OnStar advisor can send a cellular telephone message to the vehicle to unlock the vehicle if needed.

- **Roadside assistance.** When called, an OnStar advisor can locate a towing company or locate a provider who can bring gasoline or change a flat tire.

- **Accident assistance.** An OnStar advisor is able to help with the best way to handle an accident. The advisor can supply a step-by-step checklist of the things that should be done plus call the insurance company, if desired.

- **Remote horn and lights.** The OnStar system is tied into the lights and horn circuits so an advisor can activate them if requested to help the owner locate the vehicle in a parking lot or garage.

- **Vehicle diagnosis.** Because the OnStar system is tied to the PCM, an OnStar advisor can help with diagnosis if there is a fault detected. The system works as follows:

  - The malfunction indicator light (MIL) (check engine) comes on to warn the driver that a fault has been detected.

  - The driver can depress the OnStar button to talk to an advisor and ask for a diagnosis.

  - The OnStar advisor will send a signal to the vehicle requesting the status from the powertrain control module (PCM), as well as the controller for the antilock brakes and the airbag module.

  - The vehicle then sends any diagnostic trouble codes to the advisor. The advisor can then inform the driver about the importance of the problem and give advice as to how to resolve the problem.

DIAGNOSIS AND SERVICE The OnStar system can fail to meet the needs of the customer if any of the following conditions occur.

1. Lack of cellular telephone service in the area

2. Poor global positioning system (GPS) signals, which can prevent an OnStar advisor from determining the position of the vehicle

3. Transport of the vehicle by truck or ferry so that it is out of contact with the GPS satellite in order for an advisor to properly track the vehicle

If all of the above are okay and the problem still exists, follow service information diagnostic and repair procedures. If a new vehicle communication interface module (VCIM) is installed in the vehicle, the electronic serial number (ESN) must be tied to the vehicle. Follow service information instructions for the exact procedures to follow.

FIGURE 24–48 A typical view displayed on the navigation screen from the backup camera.

FIGURE 24–49 A typical fisheye-type backup camera usually located near the center on the rear of the vehicle near the license plate.

BACKUP CAMERA

PARTS AND OPERATION A **backup camera** is used to display the area at the rear of the vehicle in a screen display on the dash when the gear selector is placed in reverse. Backup cameras are also called *reversing cameras* or *rearview cameras*.

Backup cameras are different from normal cameras because the image displayed on the dash is flipped so it is a mirror image of the scene at the rear of the vehicle. This reversing of the image is needed because the driver and the camera are facing in opposite directions. Backup cameras were first used in large vehicles with limited rearward visibility, such as motor homes. Many vehicles equipped with navigation systems today include a backup camera for added safety while backing. ● **SEE FIGURE 24–48.**

The backup camera contains a wide-angle or fisheye lens to give the largest viewing area. Most backup cameras are pointed downward so that objects on the ground, as well as walls, are displayed. ● **SEE FIGURE 24–49.**

DIAGNOSIS AND SERVICE Faults in the backup camera system can be related to the camera itself, the display, or the connecting wiring. The main input to the display unit comes from the transmission range switch which signals the backup camera when the transmission is shifted into reverse.

To check the transmission range switch, perform the following:

1. Check if the backup (reverse) lights function when the gear selector is placed in reverse with the key on, engine off (KOEO).

2. Check that the transmission/transaxle is fully engaged in reverse when the selector is placed in reverse.

Most of the other diagnosis involves visual inspection, including:

1. Check the backup camera for damage.

2. Check the screen display for proper operation.

3. Check that the wiring from the rear camera to the body is not cut or damaged.

Always follow the vehicle manufacturer's recommended diagnosis and repair procedures.

BACKUP SENSORS

COMPONENTS Backup sensors are used to warn the driver if there is an object behind the vehicle while backing. The system used in General Motors vehicles is called **rear park assist (RPA),** and includes the following components.

- Ultrasonic object sensors built into the rear bumper assembly
- A display with three lights usually located inside the vehicle above the rear window and visible to the driver in the rearview mirror
- An electronic control module that uses an input from the transmission range switch and lights the warning lamps needed when the vehicle gear selector is in reverse

OPERATION The three-light display includes two amber lights and one red light. The following lights are displayed depending on the distance from the rear bumper.

- One amber lamp will light when the vehicle is in reverse and traveling at less than 3 mph (5 km/h) and the sensors

FIGURE 24–50 A typical backup sensor display located above the rear window inside the vehicle. The warning lights are visible in the inside rearview mirror.

FIGURE 24–51 The small round buttons in the rear bumper are ultrasonic sensors used to sense distance to an object.

 TECH TIP

Check for Repainted Bumper

The ultrasonic sensors embedded in the bumper are sensitive to paint thickness because the paint covers the sensors. If the system does not seem to be responding to objects, and if the bumper has been repainted, measure the paint thickness using a nonferrous paint thickness gauge. The maximum allowable paint thickness is 6 mils (0.006 inch or 0.15 mm).

detect an object 40 to 60 in. (102 to 152 cm) from the rear bumper. A chime also sounds once when an object is detected, to warn the driver to look at the rear parking assist display. ● **SEE FIGURE 24–50.**

- Two amber lamps light when the distance between the rear bumper and an object is between 20 and 40 in. (50 and 100 cm) and the chime will sound again.

- Two amber lamps and the red lamp light and the chime sounds continuously when the distance between the rear bumper and the object is between 11 and 20 in. (28 and 50 cm).

If the distance between the rear bumper and the object is less than 11 in. (28 cm), all indicator lamps flash and the chime will sound continuously.

The ultrasonic sensors embedded in the rear bumper "fire" individually every 150 milliseconds (27 times per second). ● **SEE FIGURE 24–51.**

The sensors fire and then receive a return signal and arm to fire again in sequence from the left sensor to the right sensor. Each sensor has the following three wires.

1. An 8 volt supply wire from the RPA module, used to power the sensor

2. A reference low or ground wire

3. A signal line, used to send and receive commands to and from the RPA module

DIAGNOSIS The rear parking assist control module is capable of detecting faults and storing diagnostic trouble codes (DTCs). If a fault has been detected by the control module, the red lamp flashes and the system is disabled. Follow service information diagnostic procedures because the rear parking assist module cannot usually be accessed using a scan tool. Most systems use the warning lights to indicate trouble codes.

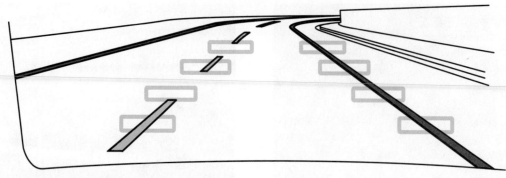

FIGURE 24–52 A lane departure warning system often uses cameras to sense the road lines and warns the driver if the vehicle is not staying within the lane, unless the turn signal is on.

LANE DEPARTURE WARNING SYSTEM

PARTS AND OPERATION The **lane departure warning system (LDWS)** uses cameras to detect if the vehicle is crossing over lane marking lines on the pavement. Some systems use two cameras, one mounted on each outside rearview mirror. Some systems use infrared sensors located under the front bumper to monitor the lane markings on the road surface.

The system names also vary according to vehicle manufacturer, including:

Honda/Acura: lane keep assist system (LKAS)

Toyota/Lexus: lane monitoring system (LMS)

General Motors: lane departure warning (LDW)

Ford: lane departure warning (LDW)

Nissan/Infinity: lane departure prevention (LDP) system

If the cameras detect that the vehicle is starting to cross over a lane dividing line, a warning chime will sound or a vibrating mechanism mounted in the driver's seat cushion is triggered on the side where the departure is being detected. This warning will not occur if the turn signal is on in the same direction as detected. ● **SEE FIGURE 24–52.**

DIAGNOSIS AND SERVICE Before attempting to service or repair a lane departure warning system fault, check service information for an explanation on how the system is supposed to work. If the system is not working as designed, perform a visual inspection of the sensors or cameras, checking for damage from road debris or evidence of body damage, which could affect the sensors. After a visual inspection, follow the vehicle manufacturer's recommended diagnosis procedures to locate and repair the fault in the system.

ELECTRONIC DASH INSTRUMENT DIAGNOSIS AND TROUBLESHOOTING

If one or more electronic dash gauges do not work correctly, first check the WOW display that lights all segments to full brilliance whenever the ignition switch is first switched on. If *all* segments of the display do *not* operate, then the entire electronic cluster must be replaced in most cases. If all segments operate during the WOW display but do not function correctly afterwards, the problem is most often a defective sensor or defective wiring to the sensor.

All dash instruments except the voltmeter use a variable-resistance unit as a sensor for the system being monitored. Most new-vehicle dealers are required to purchase essential test equipment, including a test unit that permits the technician to insert various fixed-resistance values in the suspected circuit. For example, if a 45 ohm resistance is put into the fuel gauge circuit that reads from 0 to 90 ohms, a properly operating dash unit should indicate one-half tank. The same tester can produce a fixed signal to test the operation of the speedometer and tachometer. If this type of special test equipment is not available, the electronic dash instruments can be tested using the following procedure.

1. With the ignition switched off, unplug the wire(s) from the sensor for the function being tested. For example, if the oil pressure gauge is not functioning correctly, unplug the wire connector at the oil pressure sending unit.

2. With the sensor wire unplugged, turn the ignition switch on and wait until the WOW display stops. The display for the affected unit should show either fully lighted segments or no lighted segments, depending on the make of the vehicle and the type of sensor.

TECH TIP

Keep Stock Overall Tire Diameter

Whenever larger (or smaller) wheels or tires are installed, the speedometer and odometer calibration are also thrown off. This can be summarized as follows:

- **Larger diameter tires.** The speed showing on the speedometer is slower than the actual speed. The odometer reading will show fewer miles than actual.
- **Smaller diameter tires.** The speed showing on the speedometer is faster than the actual speed. The odometer reading will show more miles than actual.

General Motors trucks can be recalibrated with a recalibration kit (1988–1991) or with a replacement controller assembly called a digital ratio adapter controller (DRAC) located under the dash. It may be possible to recalibrate the speedometer and odometer on earlier models, before 1988, or vehicles that use speedometer cables by replacing the drive gear in the transmission. Check service information for the procedure on the vehicle being serviced.

3. Turn the ignition switch off. Connect the sensor wire lead to ground and turn the ignition switch on. After the WOW display, the display should be the opposite (either fully on or fully off) of the results in step 2.

TESTING RESULTS If the electronic display functions fully on and fully off with the sensor unplugged and then grounded, the problem is a defective sensor. If the electronic display fails to function fully on and fully off when the sensor wire(s) are opened and grounded, the problem is usually in the wiring from the sensor to the electronic dash or it is a defective electronic cluster.

CAUTION: Whenever working on or *near* any type of electronic dash display, always wear a wire attached to your wrist (wrist strap) connected to a good body ground to prevent damaging the electronic dash with static electricity.

MAINTENANCE REMINDER LAMPS

Maintenance reminder lamps indicate that the oil should be changed or that other service is required. There are numerous ways to extinguish a maintenance reminder lamp. Some require the use of a special tool. Always check the owner manual or service information for the exact procedure for the vehicle being serviced. For example, to reset the oil service reminder light on many General Motors vehicles, you have to perform the following:

STEP 1 Turn the ignition key on (engine off).

STEP 2 Depress the accelerator pedal three times and hold it down on the fourth.

STEP 3 When the reminder light flashes, release the accelerator pedal.

STEP 4 Turn the ignition key to the off position.

STEP 5 Start the engine and the light should be off.

FUEL GAUGE DIAGNOSIS

1 Observe the fuel gauge. This General Motors vehicle shows an indicated reading of slightly above one-half tank.

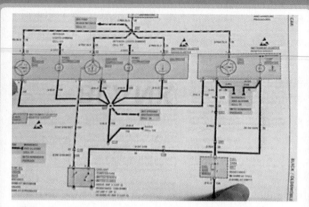

2 Consult the factory service manual for the specifications, wire color, and recommended test procedure.

3 From the service manual, the connector for the fuel gauge-sending unit was located under the vehicle near the rear. A visual inspection indicated that the electrical wiring and connector were not damaged or corroded.

4 To test resistance of the sending unit (tank unit) use a digital multimeter and select ohms (Ω).

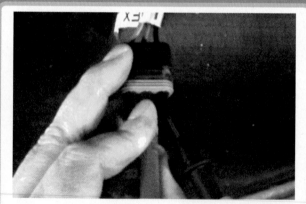

5 Following the schematic in the service manual the sending unit resistance can be measured between the pink and the black wires in the connector.

6 The meter displays 50 ohms or slightly above the middle of the normal resistance value for the vehicle of 0Ω (empty) to 90Ω (full).

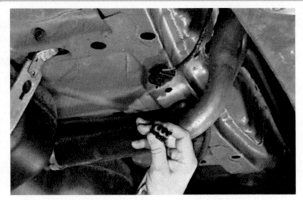

7 To check if the dash unit can move, the connector is unplugged with the ignition key on (engine off).

8 As the connector is disconnected, the needle of the dash unit moves toward full.

9 After a couple of seconds, the needle disappears above the full reading. The open connector represented infinity ohms and normal maximum reading occurs when the tank unit reads 90 ohms. If the technician does not realize that the needle could disappear, an incorrect diagnosis could be made.

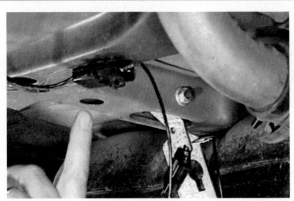

10 To check if the dash unit is capable of reading empty, a fuse jumper wire is connected between the signal wire at the dash end of the connector and a good chassis ground.

11 A check of a dash unit indicated that the needle does accurately read empty.

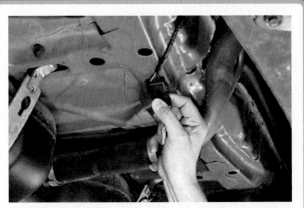

12 After testing, reconnect the electrical connectors and verify for proper operation of the fuel level gauge.

SUMMARY

1. Most digital and analog (needle-type) dash gauges use variable-resistance sensors.

2. Dash warning lamps are called telltale lamps.

3. Many electronically operated or computer-operated dash indicators require that a service manual be used to perform accurate diagnosis.

4. Permanent magnet (PM) generators produce an AC signal and are used for vehicle speed and wheel speed sensors.

5. Navigation systems and warning systems are part of the driver information system on many vehicles.

REVIEW QUESTIONS

1. How does a stepper motor analog dash gauge work?

2. What are LED, LCD, VTF, and CRT dash displays? Describe each.

3. How do you diagnose a problem with a red brake warning lamp?

4. How do you test the dash unit of a fuel gauge?

5. How does a navigation system determine the location of the vehicle?

CHAPTER QUIZ

1. Two technicians are discussing a fuel gauge on a General Motors vehicle. Technician A says that if the ground wire connection to the fuel tank sending unit becomes rusty or corroded, the fuel gauge will read lower than normal. Technician B says that if the power lead to the fuel tank sending unit is disconnected from the tank unit and grounded (ignition on), the fuel gauge should go to empty. Which technician is correct?
   a. Technician A only
   b. Technician B only
   c. Both Technicians A and B
   d. Neither Technician A nor B

2. If an oil pressure warning lamp on a General Motors vehicle is on all the time, yet the engine oil pressure is normal, the problem could be a _____.
   a. Defective (shorted) oil pressure sending unit (sensor)
   b. Defective (open) oil pressure sending unit (sensor)
   c. Wire shorted-to-ground between the sending unit (sensor) and the dash warning lamp
   d. Both a and c

3. When the oil pressure drops to between 3 and 7 psi, the oil pressure lamp lights by _____.
   a. Opening the circuit
   b. Shorting the circuit
   c. Grounding the circuit
   d. Conducting current to the dash lamp by oil

4. A brake warning lamp on the dash remains on whenever the ignition is on. If the wire to the pressure differential switch (usually a part of a combination valve or built into the master cylinder) is unplugged, the dash lamp goes out. Technician A says that this is an indication of a fault in the hydraulic brake system. Technician B says that the problem is probably due to a stuck parking brake cable switch. Which technician is correct?
   a. Technician A only
   b. Technician B only
   c. Both Technicians A and B
   d. Neither Technician A nor B

5. A customer complains that every time the lights are turned on in the vehicle, the dash display dims. What is the most probable explanation?
   a. Normal behavior for LED dash displays
   b. Normal behavior for VTF dash displays
   c. Poor ground in lighting circuit causing a voltage drop to the dash lamps
   d. Feedback problem most likely caused by a short-to-voltage between the headlights and dash display

6. Technician A says that LCDs may be slow to work at low temperatures. Technician B says that an LCD dash display can be damaged if pressure is exerted on the front of the display during cleaning. Which technician is correct?
   a. Technician A only
   b. Technician B only
   c. Both Technicians A and B
   d. Neither Technician A nor B

7. Technician A says that backup sensors use LEDs to detect objects. Technician B says that a backup sensor will not work correctly if the paint is thicker than 0.006 in. Which technician is correct?

   a. Technician A only
   b. Technician B only
   c. Both Technicians A and B
   d. Neither Technician A nor B

8. Technician A says that metal-type tinting can affect the navigation system. Technician B says most navigation systems require a monthly payment for use of the GPS satellite. Which technician is correct?

   a. Technician A only
   b. Technician B only
   c. Both Technicians A and B
   d. Neither Technician A nor B

9. Technician A says that the data displayed on the dash can come from the engine computer. Technician B says that the entire dash assembly may have to be replaced even if just one unit fails. Which technician is correct?

   a. Technician A only
   b. Technician B only
   c. Both Technicians A and B
   d. Neither Technician A nor B

10. How does changing the size of the tires affect the speedometer reading?

    a. A smaller diameter tire causes the speedometer to read faster than actual speed and more than actual mileage on the odometer.
    b. A smaller diameter tire causes the speedometer to read slower than the actual speed and less than the actual mileage on the odometer.
    c. A larger diameter tire causes the speedometer to read faster than the actual speed and more than the actual mileage on the odometer.
    d. A larger diameter tire causes the speedometer to read slower than the actual speed and more than the actual mileage on the odometer.

HORN, WIPER, AND BLOWER MOTOR CIRCUITS

HORNS

PURPOSE AND FUNCTION **Horns** are electric devices that emit a loud sound used to alert other drivers or persons in the area. Horns are manufactured in several different tones ranging from 1,800 to 3,550 Hz. Vehicle manufacturers select from various horn tones for a particular vehicle sound. ● **SEE FIGURE 25–1.**

When two horns are used, each has a different tone when operated separately, yet the sound combines when both are operated.

HORN CIRCUITS Automotive horns usually operate on full battery voltage wired from the battery, through a fuse, switch, and then to the horns. Most vehicles use a horn *relay*. With a relay, the horn button on the steering wheel or column completes a circuit to ground that closes a relay, and the heavy current flow required by the horn then travels from the relay to the horn. Without a horn relay, the high current of the horns must flow through the steering wheel horn switch. ● **SEE FIGURE 25–2.**

The horn relay is also connected to the body control module, which "beeps" the horn when the vehicle is locked or unlocked, using the key fob remote.

HORN OPERATION A vehicle horn is an actuator that converts an electrical signal to sound. The horn circuit includes an armature (a coil of wire) and contacts that are attached to a diaphragm. When energized, the armature causes the diaphragm to move up which then opens a set of contact points that de-energize the armature circuit. As the diaphragm moves down, the contact points close, re-energize the armature circuit, and the diaphragm moves up again. This rapid opening and closing of the contact points causes the diaphragm to vibrate at an audible frequency. The sound created by the diaphragm is magnified as it travels through a trumpet attached to the diaphragm chamber. Most horn systems typically use one or two horns, but some have up to four. Those with multiple horns use both high- and low-pitch units to achieve a harmonious tone. Only a high-pitched unit is used in single-horn applications. The horn assembly is marked with an "H" or "L" for pitch identification.

HORN SYSTEM DIAGNOSIS There are three types of horn failure.

- No horn operation
- Intermittent operation
- Constant operation
- weak or low volume sound

If a horn does not operate at all, check for the following:

- Burned fuse or fusible link
- Open circuit

FIGURE 25–1 Two horns are used on this vehicle. Many vehicles use only one horn, often hidden underneath the vehicle.

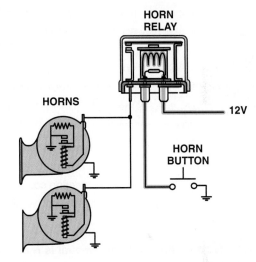

FIGURE 25–2 A typical horn circuit. Note that the horn button completes the ground circuit for the relay.

- Defective horn
- Faulty relay
- Defective horn switch
- Poor ground (horn mounting)
- Corroded or rusted electrical connector

If a horn operates intermittently, check for the following:

- Loose contact at the switch
- Loose, frayed, or broken wires
- Defective relay

HORN SOUNDS CONTINUOUSLY A horn that sounds continuously and cannot be shut off is caused by horn switch contacts that are stuck closed, or a short-to-ground on the control circuit. This may be the result of a defective horn switch or a faulty relay. Stuck relay contacts keep the circuit complete so the horn sounds constantly. Disconnect the horn and check continuity through the horn switch and relay to locate the source of the problem.

INOPERATIVE HORN To help determine the cause of an inoperative horn, use a fused jumper wire and connect one end to the positive post of the battery and the other end to the wire terminal of the horn itself. Also use a fused jumper wire to substitute a ground path to test or confirm a potential bad ground circuit. If the horn works with jumper wires connected, check ground wires and connections.

- If the horn works, the problem is in the circuit supplying current to the horn.

- If the horn does not work, the horn itself could be defective or the mounting bracket may not be providing a good ground.

HORN SERVICE When a horn malfunctions, circuit tests are made to determine if the horn, relay, switch, or wiring is the source of the failure. Typically, a digital multimeter (DMM) is used to perform voltage drop and continuity checks to isolate the failure.

- **Switch and relay.** A momentary contact switch is used to sound the horn. The horn switch is mounted to the steering wheel in the center of the steering column on some models, and is part of a multifunction switch installed on the steering column.

CAUTION: If steering wheel removal is required for diagnosis or repair of the horn circuit, follow service information procedures for disarming the airbag circuit prior to steering wheel removal, and for the specified test equipment to use.

On most late-model vehicles, the horn relay is located in a centralized power distribution center along with other relays, circuit breakers, and fuses. The horn relay bolts onto an inner fender or the bulkhead in the engine compartment of older vehicles. Check the relay to determine if the coil is being energized and if current passes through the power circuit when the horn switch is depressed.

Obtain an electrical schematic of the horn circuit and use a voltmeter to test input, output, and control voltage.

- **Circuit testing.** Circuit testing involves the following steps.

STEP 1 Make sure the fuse or fusible link is good before attempting to troubleshoot the circuit.

STEP 2 Check that the ground connections for the horn are clean and tight. Most horns ground to the chassis

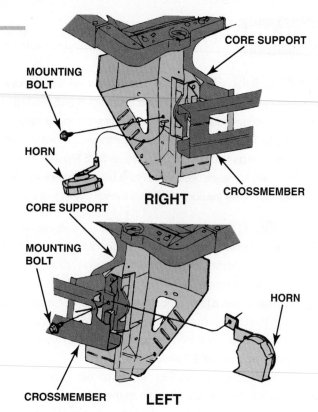

FIGURE 25–3 Horns typically mount to the radiator core support or bracket at the front of the vehicle.

through the mounting bolts. High ground circuit resistance due to corrosion, road dirt, or loose fasteners may cause no, or intermittent, horn operation.

STEP 3 On a system with a relay, test the power output circuit and the control circuit. Check for voltage available at the horn, voltage available at the relay, and continuity through the switch. When no relay is used, there are two wires leading to the horn switch, and a connection to the steering wheel is made with a double contact slip ring. Test points on this system are similar to those of a system with a relay, but there is no control circuit.

HORN REPLACEMENT Horns are generally mounted on the radiator core support by bolts and nuts or sheet metal screws. It may be necessary to remove the grille or other parts to access the horn mounting screws. If a replacement horn is required, attempt to use a horn of the same tone as the original. The tone is usually indicated by a number or letter stamped on the body of the horn. To replace a horn, simply remove the fasteners and lift the old horn from its mounting bracket.

Clean the attachment area on the mounting bracket and chassis before installing the new horn. Some models use a corrosion-resistant mounting bolt to ensure a ground connection. ● **SEE FIGURE 25–3.**

WINDSHIELD WIPER AND WASHER SYSTEM

PURPOSE AND FUNCTION **Windshield wipers** are used to keep the viewing area of the windshield clean of rain. Windshield wiper systems and circuits vary greatly between manufacturers as well as between models. Some vehicles combine the windshield wiper and windshield washer functions into a single system. Many minivans and sport utility vehicles (SUVs) also have a rear window wiper and washer system that works independently of the windshield system. In spite of the design differences, all windshield and rear window wiper and washer systems operate in a similar fashion.

COMPUTER CONTROLLED Most wipers since the 1990s have used the body computer to control the actual operation of the wiper. The wiper controls are simply a command to the computer. The computer may also turn on the headlights whenever the wipers are on, which is the law in some states. ● **SEE FIGURE 25–4.**

WIPER AND WASHER COMPONENTS A typical combination wiper and washer system consists of the following:

- Wiper motor
- Gearbox
- Wiper arms and linkage
- Washer pump
- Hoses and jets (nozzles)
- Fluid reservoir
- Combination switch
- Wiring and electrical connectors
- Electronic control module

The motor and gearbox assembly is wired to the wiper switch on the instrument panel or steering column or to the wiper control module. ● **SEE FIGURE 25–5.**

Some systems use either a one- or two-speed wiper motor, whereas others have a variable-speed motor.

WINDSHIELD WIPER MOTORS The windshield wipers ordinarily use a special two-speed electric motor. Most are compound-wound motors, a motor type, which provides for two different speeds.

- **Series-wound field**
- **Shunt field**

One speed is achieved in the series wound field and the other speed in the shunt wound field. The wiper switch provides the necessary electrical connections for either motor speed. Switches

in the mechanical wiper motor assembly provide the necessary operation for "parking" and "concealing" of the wipers. ● **SEE FIGURE 25–6** for a typical wiper motor assembly.

- **Wiper motor operation.** Most wiper motors use a permanent magnet motor with a low speed + brush and a high speed + brush. The brushes connect the battery to the internal windings of the motor, and the two brushes provide for two different motor speeds.

  The ground brush is directly opposite the low-speed brush. The high-speed brush is off to the side of the low-speed brush. When current flows through the high-speed brush, there are fewer turns on the armature between the hot and ground brushes, and therefore the resistance is less. With less resistance, more current flows and the armature revolves faster. ● **SEE FIGURES 25–7 AND 25–8.**

- **Variable wipers.** The **variable-delay wipers** (also called **pulse wipers**) use an electronic circuit with a variable resistor that controls the time of the charge and discharge of a capacitor. The charging and discharging of the capacitor controls the circuit for the operation of the wiper motor. ● **SEE FIGURE 25–9.**

HIDDEN WIPERS Some vehicles are equipped with wipers that become hidden when turned off. These wipers are also called *depressed wipers*. The gearbox has an additional linkage arm to provide depressed parking for hidden wipers. This link extends to move the wipers into the park position when the motor turns in reverse of operating direction. With depressed park, the motor assembly includes an internal park switch. The park switch completes a circuit to reverse armature polarity in the motor when the windshield wiper switch is turned off. The park circuit opens once the wiper arms are in the park position. Instead of a depressed park feature, some systems simply extend the cleaning arc below the level of the hood line.

WINDSHIELD WIPER DIAGNOSIS Windshield wiper failure may be the result of an electrical fault or a mechanical problem, such as binding linkage. Generally, if the wipers operate at one speed setting but not another, the problem is electrical.

To determine if there is an electrical or mechanical problem, access the motor assembly and disconnect the wiper arm linkage from the motor and gearbox. Depending on the type of vehicle, this procedure may involve:

- Removing body trim panels from the covered areas at the base of the windshield to gain access to the linkage connectors

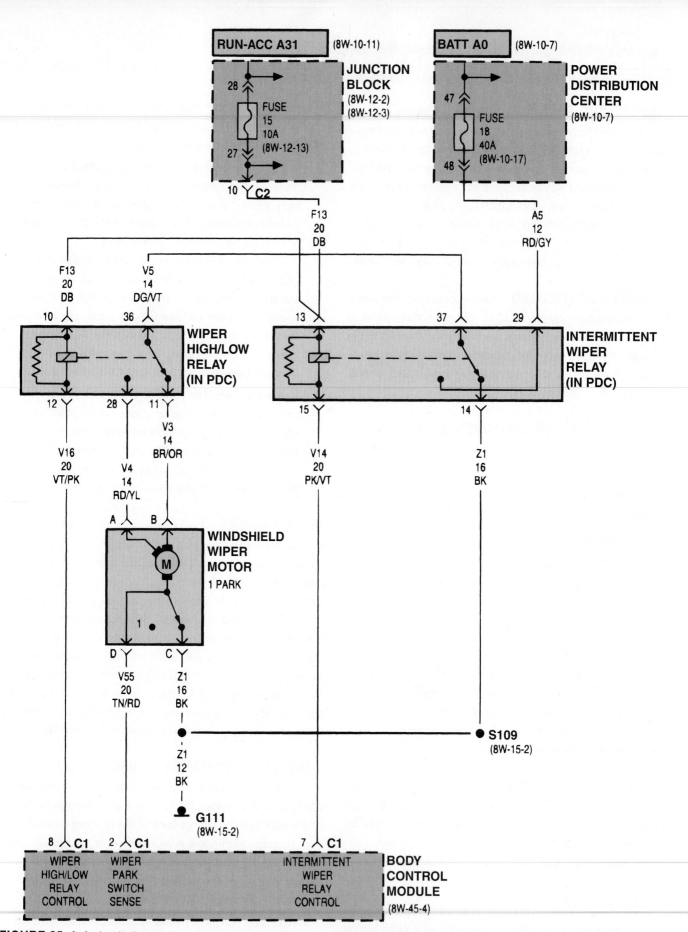

FIGURE 25-4 A circuit diagram is necessary to troubleshoot a windshield wiper problem.

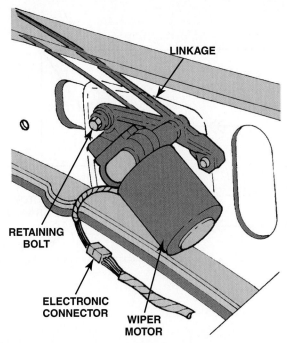

FIGURE 25–5 The motor and linkage bolt to the body and connect to the switch with a wiring harness.

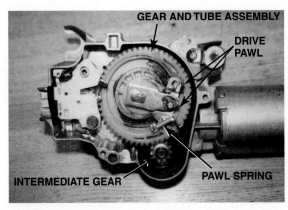

FIGURE 25–6 A typical wiper motor with the housing cover removed. The motor itself has a worm gear on the shaft that turns the small intermediate gear, which then rotates the gear and tube assembly, which rotates the crank arm (not shown) that connects to the wiper linkage.

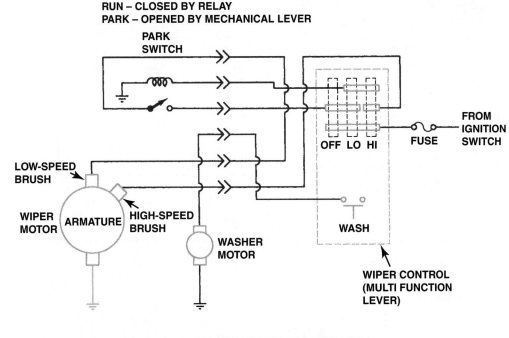

FIGURE 25–7 A wiring diagram of a two-speed windshield wiper circuit using a three-brush, two-speed motor. The dashed line for the multifunction lever indicates that the circuit shown is only part of the total function of the steering column lever.

WINDSHIELD WIPER AND WASHER SYSTEM (CONTINUED)

- Switching the motor on to each speed (If the motor operates at all speeds, the problem is mechanical. If the motor still does not operate, the problem is electrical.)

If the wiper motor does not run at all, check for the following:

- Grounded or inoperative switch
- Defective motor
- Circuit wiring fault
- Poor electrical ground connection

If the motor operates but the wipers do not, check for the following:

- Stripped gears in the gearbox or stripped linkage connection
- Loose or separated motor-to-gearbox connection
- Loose linkage to the motor connection

If the motor does not shut off, check for the following:

- Defective park switch inside the motor
- Defective wiper switch
- Poor ground connection at the wiper switch

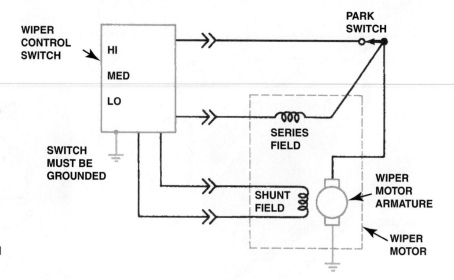

FIGURE 25–8 A wiring diagram of a three-speed windshield wiper circuit using a two-brush motor, but both a series-wound and a shunt field coil.

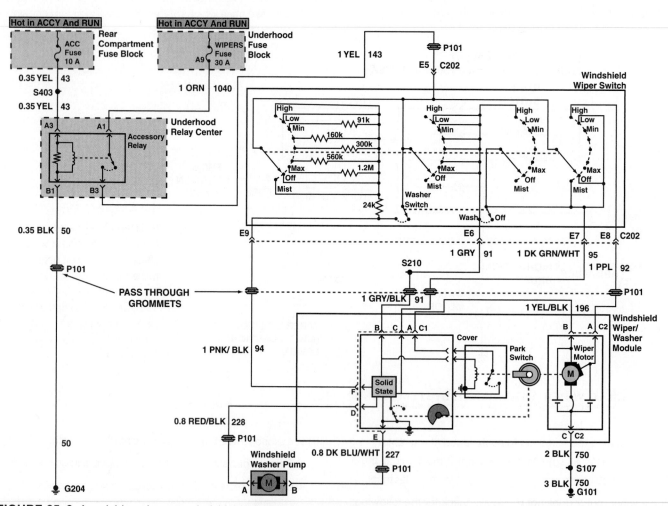

FIGURE 25–9 A variable pulse rate windshield wiper circuit. Notice that the wiring travels from the passenger compartment through pass-through grommets to the underhood area.

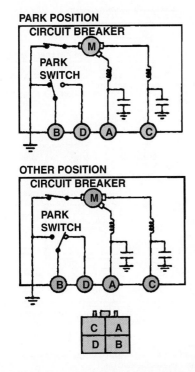

PARK POSITION

OTHER POSITION

TERMINAL	OPERATION SPEED
C	LOW
A	HIGH

FIGURE 25–10 A wiper motor connector pin chart.

WINDSHIELD WIPER AND WASHER SYSTEM (CONTINUED)

WINDSHIELD WIPER TESTING When the wiper motor does not operate with the linkage disconnected, perform the following steps to determine the fault. ● **SEE FIGURE 25–10.**

To test the wiper system, perform the following steps.

STEP 1 Refer to the circuit diagram or a connector pin chart for the vehicle being serviced to determine the test points for voltage measurements.

STEP 2 Switch the ignition on and set the wiper switch to a speed at which the motor does not operate.

STEP 3 Check for battery voltage available at the appropriate wiper motor terminal for the selected speed. If voltage is available to the motor, an internal motor problem is indicated. No voltage available indicates a switch or circuit failure.

STEP 4 Check for proper ground connections.

STEP 5 Check that battery voltage is available at the motor side of the wiper switch. If battery voltage is available, the circuit is open between the switch and motor. No voltage available indicates either a faulty switch or a power supply problem.

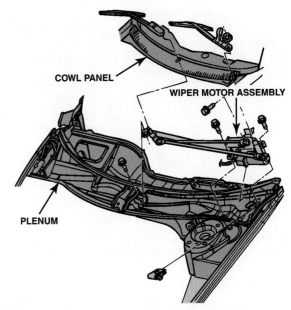

FIGURE 25–11 The wiper motor and linkage mount under the cowl panel on many vehicles.

? **FREQUENTLY ASKED QUESTION**

How Do Wipers Park?

Some vehicles have wiper arms that park lower than the normal operating position so that they are hidden below the hood when not in operation. This is called a *depressed park position*. When the wiper motor is turned off, the park switch allows the motor to continue to turn until the wiper arms reach the bottom edge of the windshield. Then the park switch reverses the current flow through the wiper motor, which makes a partial revolution in the opposite direction. The wiper linkage pulls the wiper arms down below the level of the hood and the park switch is opened, stopping the wiper motor.

STEP 6 Check for battery voltage available at the power input side of the wiper switch. If voltage is available, the switch is defective. Replace the switch. No voltage available to the switch indicates a circuit problem between the battery and switch.

WINDSHIELD WIPER SERVICE Wiper motors are replaced if defective. The motor usually mounts on the bulkhead (firewall). Bulkhead-mounted units are accessible from under the hood, while the cowl panel needs to be removed to service a motor mounted in the cowl. ● **SEE FIGURE 25–11.**

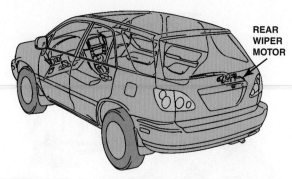

FIGURE 25–12 A single wiper arm mounts directly to the motor on most rear wiper applications.

WINDSHIELD WIPER AND WASHER SYSTEM (CONTINUED)

After gaining access to the motor, removal is simply a matter of disconnecting the linkage, unplugging the electrical connectors, and unbolting the motor. Move the wiper linkage through its full travel by hand to check for any binding before installing the new motor.

Rear window wiper motors are generally located inside the rear door panel of station wagons, or the rear hatch panel on vehicles with a hatchback or liftgate. ● **SEE FIGURE 25–12.**

After removing the trim panel covering the motor, replacement is essentially the same as replacing the front wiper motor.

Wiper control switches are either installed on the steering column or on the instrument panel.

Steering column wiper switches, which are operated by controls on the end of a switch stalk (usually called a *multifunction switch*), require partial disassembly of the steering column for replacement.

PULSE WIPE SYSTEMS
Windshield wipers may also incorporate a delay, or intermittent operation, feature commonly called pulse wipe. The length of the delay, or the frequency of the intermittent operation, is adjustable on some systems. Pulse wipe systems may rely on simple electrical controls, such as a variable-resistance switch, or be controlled electronically through a control module.

With any electronic control system, it is important to follow the diagnosis and test procedures recommended by the manufacturer for that specific vehicle.

A typical pulse, or interval, wiper system uses either a governor or a solid-state module that contains either a variable resistor or rheostat and capacitor. The module connects into the electrical circuitry between the wiper switch and wiper motor. The variable resistor or rheostat controls the length of the interval between wiper pulses. A solid-state pulse wipe timer regulates the control circuit of the pulse relay to direct current to the motor at the prescribed interval. ● **SEE FIGURE 25–13.**

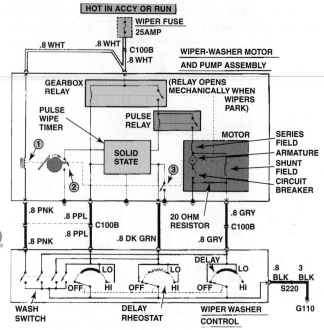

① RATCHET RELEASE SOLENOID
   (OPERATED WHEN WASH SWITCH DEPRESSED)
② WASHER OVERRIDE SWITCH
   (CLOSED DURING WASH CYCLE)
③ HOLDING SWITCH
   (OPEN AT THE END OF EACH SWEEP)

FIGURE 25–13 Circuit diagram of a rheostat-controlled, electronically timed interval wiper.

The following troubleshooting procedure applies to most models.

STEP 1 If the wipers do not run at all, check the wiper fuse, fusible link, or circuit breaker and verify that voltage is available to the switch.

STEP 2 Refer to a wiring diagram of the switch to determine how current is routed through it to the motor in the different positions.

STEP 3 Disconnect the switch and use fused jumper wires to apply power directly to the motor on the different speed circuits.
- If the motor now runs, the problem is in the switch or module.
- Check for continuity in the circuit for each speed through the control-to-ground if the wiper motor runs at some, but not all, speeds.

WINDSHIELD WASHER OPERATION
Most vehicles use a positive-displacement or centrifugal-type washer pump located in the washer reservoir. A momentary contact switch, which is often part of a steering column–mounted combination switch assembly, energizes the washer pump. Washer pump switches are installed either on the steering column or on the instrument panel. The nozzles can be located on the bulkhead or in the hood depending on the vehicle.

Use a Scan Tool to Check Accessories

Most vehicles built since 2000 can have the lighting and accessory circuits checked using a scan tool. A technician can use the following:

- Factory scan tool, such as:
  - Tech 2 or Multiple Diagnostic Interface (MDI) (General Motors vehicle)
  - DRB III or Star Scan or Star Mobile or WiTech (Chrysler-Jeep vehicles)
  - New Generation Star or IDS (Ford)
  - Honda Diagnostic System (HDS)
  - TIS Tech Stream (Toyota/Lexus)
- Enhanced aftermarket scan tool that has body bidirectional control capability, including:
  - Snap-on Modis, Solus, or Verus
  - OTC Genisys
  - Autoengenuity

Using a bidirectional scan tool allows the technician to command the operation of electrical accessories such as windows, lights, and wipers. If the circuit operates correctly when commanded by the scan tool and does not function using the switche(s), follow service information instructions to diagnose the switch circuits.

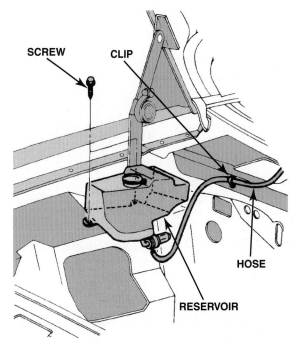

FIGURE 25–14 Disconnect the hose at the pump and operate the switch to check a washer pump.

NOTE: Always use good-quality windshield washer fluid from a closed container to prevent contaminated fluid from damaging the washer pump. Radiator antifreeze (ethylene glycol) should never be used in any windshield wiper system.

● **SEE FIGURE 25–14.**

STEP 2 If fluid squirts from the pump, the delivery system is at fault, not the motor, switch, or circuitry.

STEP 3 If no fluid squirts from the pump, the problem is most likely a circuit failure, defective pump, or faulty switch.

STEP 4 A clogged reservoir screen also may be preventing fluid from entering the pump.

WINDSHIELD WASHER DIAGNOSIS Inoperative windshield washers may be caused by the following:

- Blown fuse or open circuit
- Empty reservoir
- Clogged nozzle
- Broken, pinched, or clogged hose
- Loose or broken wire
- Blocked reservoir screen
- Leaking reservoir
- Defective pump

To diagnose the washer system, follow service information procedures that usually include the following steps.

STEP 1 To quick check any washer system, make sure the reservoir has fluid and is not frozen, and then disconnect the pump hose and operate the washer switch.

WINDSHIELD WASHER SERVICE When a fluid delivery problem is indicated, check for:

- Blocked, pinched, broken, or disconnected hose
- Clogged nozzles
- Blocked washer pump outlet

If the pump motor does not operate, check for battery voltage available at the pump while operating the washer switch. If voltage is available and the pump does not run, check for continuity on the pump ground circuit. If there is no voltage drop on the ground circuit, replace the pump motor.

If battery voltage is not available at the motor, check for power through the washer switch. If voltage is available at and

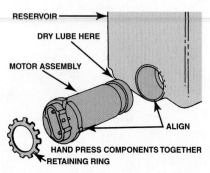

FIGURE 25–15 Washer pumps usually install into the reservoir and are held in place with a retaining ring.

FIGURE 25–16 A typical rain sensing module located on the inside of the windshield near the inside rearview mirror.

WINDSHIELD WIPER AND WASHER SYSTEM (CONTINUED)

through the switch, there is a problem in the wiring between the switch and pump. Perform voltage drop tests to locate the fault. Repair the wiring as needed and retest.

Washer motors are not repairable and are simply replaced if defective. Centrifugal or positive-displacement pumps are located on or inside the washer reservoir tank or cover and secured with a retaining ring or nut. ● **SEE FIGURE 25–15.**

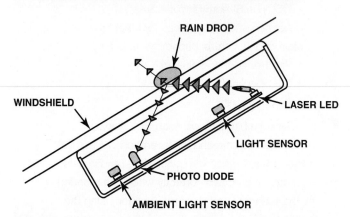

FIGURE 25–17 The electronics in the rain sense wiper module can detect the presence of rain drops under various lighting conditions.

RAIN SENSE WIPER SYSTEM

PARTS AND OPERATION   **Rain sense wiper** systems use a sensor located at the top of the windshield on the inside to detect rain droplets. This sensor is called the *rain sense module (RSM)* by General Motors. It determines and adjusts the time delay of the wiper based on how much moisture it detects on the windshield. The wiper switch can be left on the sense position all of the time and if no rain is sensed, the wipers will not swipe. ● **SEE FIGURES 25–16 AND 25–17.**

The control knob is rotated to the desired wiper sensibility level.

The microprocessor in the RSM sends a command to the body control module (BCM). RSM is a triangular-shaped black plastic housing. Fine openings on the windshield side of the housing are fitted with eight convex clear plastic lenses. The unit contains four infrared (IR) diodes, two photocells, and a microprocessor.

The IR diodes generate IR beams that are aimed by four of the convex optical lenses near the base of the module

through the windshield glass. Four additional convex lenses near the top of the RSM are focused on the IR light beam on the outside of the windshield glass and allow the two photocells to sense changes in the intensity of the IR light beam. When sufficient moisture accumulates, the RSM detects a change in the monitored IR light beam intensity. The RSM processes the signal BCM over the data BUS to command a swipe of the wiper.

DIAGNOSIS AND SERVICE   If there is a complaint about the rain sense wipers not functioning correctly, check the owner manual to be sure that they are properly set and adjusted. Also, verify that the windshield wipers are functioning correctly on all speeds before diagnosing the rain sensor circuits. Always follow the vehicle manufacturer's recommended diagnosis and testing procedures.

BLOWER MOTOR

PURPOSE AND FUNCTION

The same blower motor moves air inside the vehicle for:

1. Air conditioning
2. Heat
3. Defrosting
4. Defogging
5. Venting of the passenger compartment

The motor turns a squirrel cage-type fan. A squirrel cage-type fan is able to move air without creating a lot of noise. The fan switch controls the path that the current follows to the blower motor. ● **SEE FIGURE 25–18.**

PARTS AND OPERATION

The motor is usually a permanent magnet, one-speed motor that operates at its maximum speed with full battery voltage. The switch gets current from the fuse panel with the ignition switch on, and then directs full battery voltage to the blower motor for high speed and to the blower motor through resistors for lower speeds.

VARIABLE SPEED CONTROL

The fan switch controls the path of current through a resistor pack to obtain different fan speeds of the blower motor. The electrical path can be:

- Full battery voltage for high-speed operation
- Through one or more resistors to reduce the voltage and the current to the blower motor which then rotates at a slower speed

The resistors are located near the blower motor and mounted in the duct where the airflow from the blower can cool the resistors. The current flow through the resistor is controlled by the switch and often uses a relay to carry the heavy current (10 to 12 amperes) needed to power the fan. Normal operation includes:

- **Low speed.** Current flows through three resistors in series to drop the voltage to about 4 volts and 4 amperes.
- **Medium speed.** Current is directed through two resistors in series to lower the voltage to about 6 volts and 6 amperes.
- **Medium-high speed.** Current is directed through one resistor resulting in a voltage of about 9 volts and 9 amperes.
- **High speed.** Full battery voltage, usually through a relay, is applied to the blower motor resulting in a current of about 12 amperes.

● **SEE FIGURES 25–19 AND 25–20.**

FIGURE 25–18 A squirrel cage blower motor. A replacement blower motor usually does not come equipped with the squirrel cage blower, so it has to be switched from the old motor.

NOTE: Most Ford and some other vehicles place the blower motor resistors on the ground side of the motor circuit. The location of the resistors does not affect the operation because they are connected in series.

Some blower motors are electronically controlled by the body control module (BCM) and include electronic circuits to achieve a variable speed. ● **SEE FIGURE 25–21.**

BLOWER MOTOR DIAGNOSIS

If the blower motor does not operate at any speed, the problem could be any of the following:

1. Defective ground wire or ground wire connection
2. Defective blower motor (not repairable; must be replaced)
3. Open circuit in the power-side circuit, including fuse, wiring, or fan switch

If the blower works on lower speeds but not on high speed, the problem is usually an inline fuse or high-speed relay that controls the heavy current flow for high-speed operation. The high-speed fuse or relay usually fails as a result of internal blower motor bushing wear, which causes excessive resistance to motor rotation. At slow blower speeds, the resistance is not as noticeable and the blower operates normally. The blower motor is a sealed unit, and if defective, must be replaced as a unit. The squirrel cage fan usually needs to be removed from the old motor and attached to the replacement motor. If the blower motor operates normally at high speed but not at any of the lower speeds, the problem could be melted wire resistors or a defective switch.

The blower motor can be tested using a clamp-on DC ammeter. ● **SEE FIGURE 25–22.**

Most blower motors do not draw more than 15 A on high speed. A worn or defective motor usually draws more current than normal and could damage the blower motor resistors or blow a fuse if not replaced.

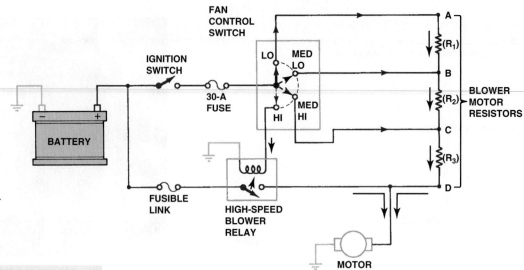

FIGURE 25–19 A typical blower motor circuit with four speeds. The three lowest fan speeds (low, medium-low, and medium-high) use the blower motor resistors to drop the voltage to the motor and reduce current to the motor. On high, the resistors are bypassed. The "high" position on the fan switch energizes a relay, which supplies the current for the blower on high through a fusible link.

FIGURE 25–20 A typical blower motor resistor pack used to control blower motor speed. Some blower motor resistors are flat and look like a credit card and are called "credit card resistors".

FIGURE 25–21 A brushless DC motor that uses the body computer to control the speed. *(Courtesy of Sammy's Auto Service, Inc.)*

 TECH TIP

The 20 Ampere Fuse Test

Most blower motors operate at about 12 A on high speed. If the bushings (bearings) on the armature of the motor become worn or dry, the motor turns more slowly. Because a motor also produces counterelectromotive force (CEMF) as it spins, a slower-turning motor will actually draw more amperes than a fast-spinning motor.

If a blower motor draws too many amperes, the resistors or the electronic circuit controlling the blower motor can fail. Testing the actual current draw of the motor is sometimes difficult because the amperage often exceeds the permissible amount for most digital meters.

One test recommended by General Motors Co. is to unplug the power lead to the motor (retain the ground on the motor) and use a fused jumper lead with one end connected to the battery's positive terminal and the other end to the motor terminal. Use a 20 A fuse in the test lead, and operate the motor for several minutes. If the blower motor is drawing more than 20 A, the fuse will blow. Some experts recommend using a 15 A fuse. If the 15 A fuse blows and the 20 A fuse does not, then you know the approximate blower motor current draw.

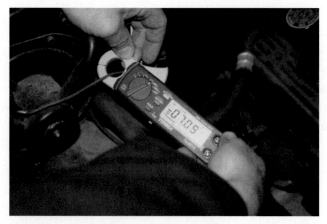

FIGURE 25–22 Using a mini AC/DC clamp-on multimeter to measure the current draw of a blower motor.

ELECTRICAL ACCESSORY SYMPTOM GUIDE

The following list will assist technicians in troubleshooting electrical accessory systems.

Blower Motor Problem	Possible Causes and/or Solutions
Blower motor does not operate.	1. Blown fuse 2. Poor ground connection on blower motor 3. Defective motor (Use a fused jumper wire connected between the positive terminal of the battery and the blower motor power lead connection [lead disconnected] to check for blower motor operation.) 4. Defective control switch 5. Resistor block open
Blower motor operates only on high speed.	1. Open in the resistors located in the air box near the blower motor 2. Stuck or defective high-speed relay 3. Defective blower motor control switch
Blower motor operates in lower speed(s) only, no high speed.	1. Defective high-speed relay or blower high-speed fuse NOTE: If the high-speed fuse blows a second time, check the current draw of the motor and replace the blower motor if the current draw is above specifications. Check for possible normal operation if the rear window defogger is not in operation; some vehicles electrically prevent simultaneous operation of the high-speed blower and rear window defogger to help reduce the electrical loads.

Windshield Wiper or Washer Problem	Possible Causes and/or Solutions
Windshield wipers are inoperative.	1. Blown fuse 2. Poor ground on the wiper motor or the control switch 3. Defective motor or linkage problem
Windshield wipers operate on high speed or low speed only.	1. Defective switch 2. Defective motor assembly 3. Poor ground on the wiper control switch
Windshield washers are inoperative.	1. Defective switch 2. Empty reservoir or clogged lines or discharge nozzles 3. Poor ground on the washer pump motor

Horn Problem	Possible Causes and/or Solutions
Horn(s) are inoperative.	1. Poor ground on horn(s) 2. Defective relay (if used); open circuit in the steering column 3. Defective horn (Use a fused jumper wire connected between the positive terminal of the battery and the horn [horn wire disconnected] to check for proper operation of the horn.)
Horn(s) produce low volume or wrong sound.	1. Poor ground at horn 2. Incorrect frequency of horn
Horn blows all the time.	1. Stuck horn relay (if used) 2. Short-to-ground in the wire to the horn button

1. Horn frequency can range from 1,800 to 3,550 Hz.

2. Most horn circuits use a relay, and the current through the relay coil is controlled by the horn switch.

3. Most windshield wipers use a three-brush, two-speed motor.

4. Windshield washer diagnosis includes checking the pump both electrically and mechanically for proper operation.

5. Most blower motors use resistors wired in series to control blower motor speed.

6. A good blower motor should draw less than 20 A.

REVIEW QUESTIONS

1. What are the three types of horn failure?

2. How is the horn switch used to operate the horn?

3. How do you determine if a windshield wiper problem is electrical or mechanical?

4. Why does a defective blower motor draw more current (amperes) than a good motor?

CHAPTER QUIZ

1. Technician A says that a defective high-speed blower motor relay could prevent high-speed blower operation, yet allows normal operation at low speeds. Technician B says that a defective (open) blower motor resistor can prevent low-speed blower operation, yet permit normal high-speed operation. Which technician is correct?
   a. Technician A only
   b. Technician B only
   c. Both Technicians A and B
   d. Neither Technician A nor B

2. To determine if a windshield wiper problem is electrical or mechanical, the service technician should _____.
   a. Disconnect the linkage arm from the windshield wiper motor and operate the windshield wiper
   b. Check to see if the fuse is blown
   c. Check the condition of the wiper blades
   d. Check the washer fluid for contamination

3. A weak-sounding horn is being diagnosed. Technician A says that a poor ground connector at the horn itself can be the cause. Technician B says an open relay can be the cause. Which technician is correct?
   a. Technician A only
   b. Technician B only
   c. Both Technicians A and B
   d. Neither Technician A nor B

4. What controls the operation of a pulse wiper system?
   a. Resistor that controls current flow to the wiper motor
   b. Solid-state (electronic) module
   c. Variable-speed gem set
   d. Transistor

5. Which pitch horn is used for a single horn application?
   a. High pitch
   b. Low pitch

6. The horn switch on the steering wheel on a vehicle that uses a horn relay _____.
   a. Sends electrical power to the horns
   b. Provides the ground circuit for the horn
   c. Grounds the horn relay coil
   d. Provides power (12 V) to the horn relay

7. A rain sense wiper system uses a rain sensor that is usually mounted _____.
   a. Behind the grille
   b. Outside of the windshield at the top
   c. Inside the windshield at the top
   d. On the roof

8. Technician A says a blower motor can be tested using a fused jumper lead. Technician B says a blower motor can be tested using a clamp-on ammeter. Which technician is correct?
   a. Technician A only
   b. Technician B only
   c. Both Technicians A and B
   d. Neither Technician A nor B

9. A defective blower motor draws more current than a good motor because the _____.
   a. Speed of the motor increases
   b. CEMF decreases
   c. Airflow slows down, which decreases the cooling of the motor
   d. Both a and c

10. Windshield washer pumps can be damaged if _____.
    a. Pure water is used in freezing weather
    b. Contaminated windshield washer fluid is used
    c. Ethylene glycol (antifreeze) is used
    d. All of the above

chapter 26

ACCESSORY CIRCUITS

OBJECTIVES

After studying Chapter 26, the reader will be able to:

1. Prepare for ASE Electrical/Electronic Systems (A6) certification test content area "H" (Accessories Diagnosis and Repair).

2. Explain how the body control module or body computer controls the operation of electrical accessories.

3. Explain how cruise control operates and how to diagnose the circuit.

4. Describe how power door locks, windows, and seats operate.

5. Describe how a keyless remote can be reprogrammed.

6. Explain how the theft deterrent system works.

KEY TERMS

Adjustable pedals 413
Backlight 403
CHMSL 400
Control wires 408
Cruise control 398
Direction wires 408
Electric adjustable
   pedals (EAP) 413
ETC 400
HomeLink 405
Independent
   switches 406
Key fob 415

Lockout switch 406
Lumbar 409
Master control
   switch 406
Peltier effect 412
Permanent magnet
   electric motors 406
Rubber coupling 409
Screw jack
   assembly 409
Thermoelectric device
   (TED) 412
Window regulator 406

CRUISE CONTROL
SERVO UNIT

FIGURE 26–1 This cruise control servo unit has an electrical connection with wires that go to the cruise control module or the vehicle computer, depending on the vehicle. The vacuum hoses supply engine manifold vacuum to the rubber diaphragm that moves the throttle linkage to maintain the preset speed.

CRUISE CONTROL

PARTS INVOLVED **Cruise control** (also called *speed control*) is a combination of electrical and mechanical components designed to maintain a constant, set vehicle speed without driver pressure on the accelerator pedal. Major components of a typical cruise control system include the following:

1. **Servo unit.** The servo unit attaches to the throttle linkage through a cable or chain.

   The servo unit controls the movement of the throttle by receiving a controlled amount of vacuum from a control module. ● **SEE FIGURE 26–1.**

   Some systems use a stepper motor and do not use engine vacuum.

2. **Computer or cruise control module.** This unit receives inputs from the brake switch, throttle position (TP) sensor, and vehicle speed sensor. It operates the solenoids or stepper motor to maintain the set speed.

3. **Speed set control.** A speed set control is a switch or control located on the steering column, steering wheel, dash, or console. Many cruise control units feature coast, accelerate, and resume functions. ● **SEE FIGURE 26–2.**

4. **Safety release switches.** When the brake pedal is depressed, the cruise control system is disengaged through use of an electrical or vacuum switch, usually located on the brake pedal bracket. Both electrical and vacuum releases are

FIGURE 26–2 A cruise control used on a Toyota/Lexus.

 **WARNING**

Most vehicle manufacturers warn in the owner manual that cruise control should not be used when it is raining or if the roads are slippery. Cruise control systems operate the throttle and, if the drive wheels start to hydroplane, the vehicle slows, causing the cruise control unit to accelerate the engine. When the engine is accelerated and the drive wheels are on a slippery road surface, vehicle stability will be lost and might possibly cause a crash.

used to be certain that the cruise control system is released, even in the event of failure of one of the release switches.

CRUISE CONTROL OPERATION A typical cruise control system can be set only if the vehicle speed is 30 mph or more. In a noncomputer-operated system, the transducer contains a low-speed electrical switch that closes when the speed-sensing section of the transducer senses a speed exceeding the minimum engagement speed.

NOTE: Toyota-built vehicles do not retain the set speed in memory if the vehicle speed drops below 25 mph (40 km/h). The driver is required to set the desired speed again. This is normal operation and not a fault with the cruise control system.

When the set button is depressed on the cruise control, solenoid values on the servo unit allow engine vacuum to be applied to one side of the diaphragm, which is attached to the throttle plate of the engine through a cable or linkage. The servo unit usually contains two solenoids to control the opening and closing of the throttle.

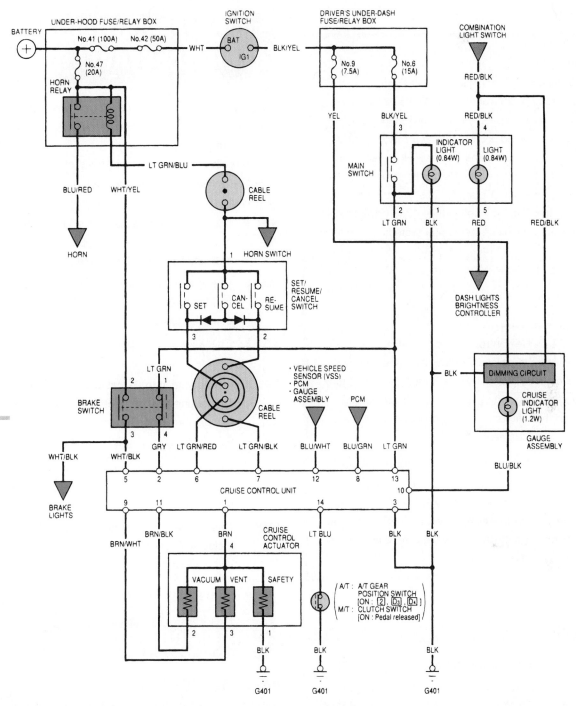

FIGURE 26–3 Circuit diagram of a typical electronic cruise control system.

■ One solenoid opens and closes to control the passage, which allows engine vacuum to be applied to the diaphragm of the servo unit, increasing the throttle opening.

■ One solenoid bleeds air back into the sensor chamber to reduce the throttle opening.

The throttle position (TP) sensor or a position sensor, inside the servo unit, sends the throttle position information to the cruise control module.

Most computer-controlled cruise control systems use the vehicle's speed sensor input to the engine control computer for speed reference. Computer-controlled cruise control units also use servo units for throttle control, control switches for driver control of cruise control functions, and both electrical and vacuum brake pedal release switches. ● **SEE FIGURE 26–3.**

TECH TIP

Bump Problems

Cruise control problem diagnosis can involve a complex series of checks and tests. The troubleshooting procedures vary among manufacturers (and year), so a technician should always consult a service manual for the exact vehicle being serviced. However, every cruise control system uses a brake safety switch and, if the vehicle has manual transmission, a clutch safety switch. The purpose of these safety switches is to ensure that the cruise control system is disabled if the brakes or the clutch is applied. Some systems use redundant brake pedal safety switches, one electrical to cut off power to the system and the other a vacuum switch used to bleed vacuum from the actuating unit.

If the cruise control "cuts out" or disengages itself while traveling over bumpy roads, the most common cause is a misadjusted brake (and/or clutch) safety switch(es). Often, a simple readjustment of these safety switches will cure the intermittent cruise control disengagement problems.

CAUTION: Always follow the manufacturer's recommended safety switch adjustment procedures. If the brake safety switch(es) is misadjusted, it could keep pressure applied to the master brake cylinder, resulting in severe damage to the braking system.

TECH TIP

Check the Third Brake Light

On many General Motors vehicles, the cruise control will not work if the third brake light is out. This third brake light is called the **center high-mounted stop light (CHMSL).** Always check the brake lights first if the cruise control does not work on a General Motors vehicle.

TROUBLESHOOTING CRUISE CONTROL

Cruise control system troubleshooting is usually performed using the step-by-step procedure as specified by the vehicle manufacturer.

The usual steps in the diagnosis of an inoperative or incorrectly operating mechanical-type cruise control include the following:

STEP 1 Use a factory or enhanced scan tool to retrieve any cruise control diagnostic trouble codes (DTCs). Perform bidirectional testing if possible using the scan tool.

STEP 2 Check that the cruise control fuse is not blown and that the cruise control dash light is on when the cruise control is turned on.

STEP 3 Check for proper operation of the brake and/or clutch switch.

STEP 4 Inspect the throttle cable and linkage between the sensor unit and the throttle plate for proper operation without binding or sticking.

STEP 5 Check the vacuum hoses for cracks or other faults.

STEP 6 Check that the vacuum servo unit (if equipped), using a hand-operated vacuum pump, can hold vacuum without leaking.

STEP 7 Check the servo solenoids for proper operation, including a resistance measurement check.

ELECTRONIC THROTTLE CRUISE CONTROL

PARTS AND OPERATION Many vehicles are equipped with an **electronic throttle control (ETC)** system. Vehicles equipped with such a system do not use throttle actuators for the cruise control. The ETC system operates the throttle under all engine operating conditions. An ETC system uses a DC electric motor to move the throttle plate that is spring loaded to a partially open position. The motor actually closes the throttle at idle against spring pressure. The spring-loaded position is the default position and results in a high idle speed. The powertrain control module (PCM) uses the input signals from the *accelerator pedal position (APP)* sensor to determine the desired throttle position. The PCM then commands the throttle to the necessary position of the throttle plate. ● **SEE FIGURE 26–4.**

FIGURE 26–4 A typical electronic throttle with the protective covers removed.

FIGURE 26–5 A trailer icon lights on the dash of this Cadillac when the transmission trailer towing mode is selected.

The cruise control on a vehicle equipped with an electronic throttle control system consists of a switch to set the desired speed. The PCM receives the vehicle speed information from the vehicle speed (VS) sensor and uses the ETC system to maintain the set speed.

DIAGNOSIS AND SERVICE   Any fault in the APP sensor or ETC system will disable the cruise control function. Always follow the specified troubleshooting procedures, which will usually include the use of a scan tool to properly diagnose the ETC system.

RADAR CRUISE CONTROL

PURPOSE AND FUNCTION   The purpose of a radar cruise control system is to give the driver more control over the vehicle by keeping an assured clear distance behind the vehicle in front. If the vehicle in front slows, the radar cruise control detects the slowing vehicle and automatically reduces the speed of the vehicle to keep a safe distance. Then if the vehicle speeds up, the radar cruise control also allows the vehicle to increase to the preset speed. This makes driving in congested areas easier and less tiring.

TERMINOLOGY   Depending on the manufacturer, radar cruise control is also referred to as the following:

- **Adaptive cruise control** (Audi, Ford, General Motors, and Hyundai)
- **Dynamic cruise control** (BMW, Toyota/Lexus)
- **Active cruise control** (Mini Cooper, BMW)
- **Autonomous cruise control** (Mercedes)

It uses forward-looking radar to sense the distance to the vehicle in front and maintains an assured clear distance. This type of cruise control system works within the following conditions.

1. Speeds from 20 to 100 mph (30 to 161 km/h)
2. Designed to detect objects as far away as 500 ft (150 m)

The cruise control system is able to sense both distance and relative speed. ● **SEE FIGURE 26–6.**

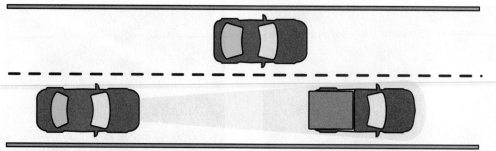

FIGURE 26–6 Radar cruise control uses sensors to keep the distance the same even when traffic slows ahead.

? **FREQUENTLY ASKED QUESTION**

Will Radar Cruise Control Set Off My Radar Detector?

It is doubtful. The radar used for radar cruise control systems operates on frequencies that are not detectable by police radar detector units. Cruise control radar works on the following frequencies.

- 76 to 77 GHz (long range)
- 24 GHz (short range)

The frequencies used for the various types of police radar include:

- X-band: 8 to 12 GHz
- K-band: 24 GHz
- Ka-band: 33 to 36 GHz

The only time there may be interference is when the radar cruise control, as part of a precollision system, starts to use short-range radar (SRR) in the 24 GHz frequency. This would trigger the radar detector but would be an unlikely event and just before a possible collision with a vehicle coming toward you.

RADAR CRUISE CONTROL (CONTINUED)

PARTS AND OPERATION Radar cruise control systems use long-range radar (LRR) to detect faraway objects in front of the moving vehicle. Some systems use a short-range radar (SRR) and/or infrared (IR) or optical cameras to detect distances for when the distance between the moving vehicle and another vehicle in front is reduced. ● **SEE FIGURE 26–7.**

The radar frequencies include:

- 76 to 77 GHz (long-range radar)
- 24 GHz (short-range radar)

PRECOLLISION SYSTEM

PURPOSE AND FUNCTION The purpose and function of a precollision system is to monitor the road ahead and prepare to avoid a collision, and to protect the driver and passengers. A precollision system uses components of the following systems.

1. The long-range and short-range radar or detection systems used by a radar cruise control system to detect objects in front of the vehicle

2. Antilock brake system (ABS)

3. Adaptive (radar) cruise control

4. Brake assist system

TERMINOLOGY Precollision systems can be called various names depending on the make of the vehicle. Some commonly used names for a precollision or precrash system include:

- **Ford/Lincoln:** Collision Warning with Brake Support
- **Honda/Acura:** Collision Mitigation Brake System (CMBS)
- **Mercedes-Benz:** Pre-Safe or Attention Assist
- **Toyota/Lexus:** Pre-Collision System (PCS) or Advanced Pre-Collision System (APCS)
- **General Motors:** Pre-Collision System (PCS)
- **Volvo:** Collision Warning with Brake Support or Collision Warning with Brake Assist

OPERATION The system functions by monitoring objects in front of the vehicle and can act to avoid a collision by the following actions.

- Sounds an alarm
- Flashes a warning lamp
- Applies the brakes and brings the vehicle to a full stop (if needed), if the driver does not react

● **SEE FIGURE 26–8.**

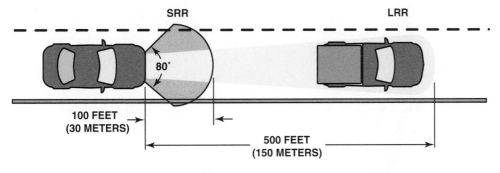

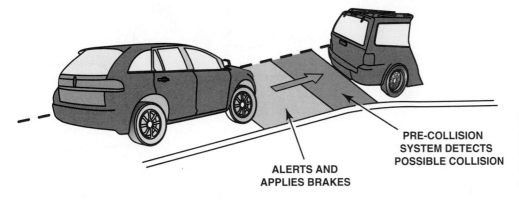

FIGURE 26–7 Most radar cruise control systems use radar, both long and short range. Some systems use optical or infrared cameras to detect objects.

SRR

LRR

80°

100 FEET
(30 METERS)

500 FEET
(150 METERS)

PRE-COLLISION
SYSTEM DETECTS
POSSIBLE COLLISION

ALERTS AND
APPLIES BRAKES

FIGURE 26–8 A precollision system is designed to prevent a collision first, and then interacts to prepare for a collision if needed.

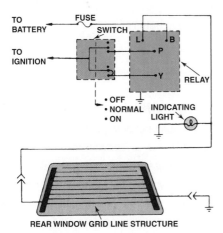

FIGURE 26–9 A switch and relay control current through the heating grid of a rear window defogger.

If the system is unable to prevent a collision, the system will perform the following actions.

1. Apply the brakes full force to reduce vehicle speed as much as possible

2. Close all windows and the sunroof to prevent the occupants from being ejected from the vehicle

3. Move the seats to an upright position

4. Raise the headrest (if electrically powered)

5. Pretension the seat belts

6. Airbags and seat belt tensioners function as designed during the collision

HEATED REAR WINDOW DEFOGGERS

PARTS AND OPERATION An electrically heated rear window defogger system uses an electrical grid baked on the glass that warms the glass to about 85°F (29°C) and clears it of fog or frost. The rear window is also called a **backlight**. The rear window defogger system is controlled by a driver-operated switch and a timer relay. ● **SEE FIGURE 26–9.**

The timer relay is necessary because the window grid can draw up to 30 A, and continued operation would put a strain on the battery and the charging system. Generally, the timer relay permits current to flow through the rear window grid for only 10 minutes. If the window is still not clear of fog after 10 minutes, the driver can turn the defogger on again, but after the first 10 minutes any additional defogger operation is limited to 5 minutes.

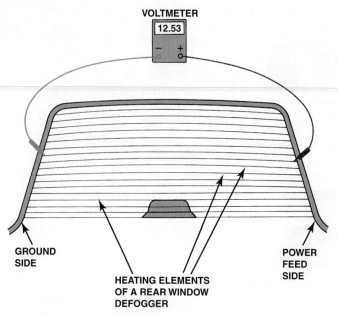

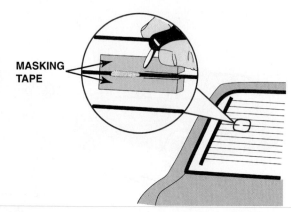

FIGURE 26–10 A rear window defogger electrical grid can be tested using a voltmeter to check for a decreasing voltage as the meter lead is moved from the power side toward the ground side. As the voltmeter positive lead is moved along the grid (on the inside of the vehicle), the voltmeter reading should steadily decrease as the meter approaches the ground side of the grid.

FIGURE 26–11 The typical repair material contains conductive silver-filled polymer, which dries in 10 minutes and is usable in 30 minutes.

HEATED REAR WINDOW DEFOGGERS (CONTINUED)

PRECAUTION Electric grid-type rear window defoggers can be damaged easily by careless cleaning or scraping of the inside of the rear window glass. Short, broken sections of the rear window grid can be repaired using a special epoxy-based electrically conductive material. If more than one section is damaged or if the damaged grid length is greater than approximately 1.5 in. (3.8 cm), a replacement rear window glass may be required to restore proper defogger operation.

The electrical current through the grids depends, in part, on the temperature of the conductor grids. As the temperature decreases, the resistance of the grids decreases and the current flow increases, helping to warm the rear glass. As the temperature of the glass increases, the resistance of the conductor grids increases and the current flow decreases. Therefore, the defogger system tends to self-regulate the electrical current requirements to match the need for defogging.

NOTE: Some vehicles use the wire grid of the rear window defogger as the radio antenna. Therefore, if the grid is damaged, radio reception can also be affected.

HEATED REAR WINDOW DEFOGGER DIAGNOSIS

Troubleshooting a nonfunctioning rear window defogger unit involves using a test light or a voltmeter to check for voltage to the grid. If no voltage is present at the rear window, check for voltage at the switch and relay timer assembly. A poor ground connection on the opposite side of the grid from the power side can also cause the rear defogger not to operate. Because most defogger circuits use an indicator light switch and a relay timer, it is possible to have the indicator light on, even if the wires are disconnected at the rear window grid. A voltmeter can be used to test the operation of the rear window defogger grid. ● **SEE FIGURE 26–10.**

With the negative test terminal attached to a good body ground, carefully probe the grid conductors. There should be a decreasing voltage reading as the probe is moved from the power ("hot") side of the grid toward the ground side of the grid.

REPAIR OR REPLACEMENT If there is a broken grid wire, it can be repaired using an electrically conductive substance available in a repair kit.

Most vehicle manufacturers recommend that grid wire less than 2 in. (5 cm) long be repaired. If a bad section is longer than 2 in., the entire rear window will need to be replaced. ● **SEE FIGURE 26–11.**

The Breath Test

It is difficult to test for the proper operation of all grids of a rear window defogger unless the rear window happens to be covered with fog. A common trick that works is to turn on the rear defogger and exhale onto the outside of the rear window glass. In a manner similar to that of people cleaning eyeglasses with their breath, this procedure produces a temporary fog on the glass so that all sections of the rear grids can quickly be checked for proper operation.

FIGURE 26–12 Typical HomeLink garage door opener buttons. Notice that three different units can be controlled from the vehicle using the HomeLink system.

HEATED MIRRORS

PURPOSE AND FUNCTION The purpose and function of heated outside mirrors is to heat the surface of the mirror, which evaporates moisture on the surface. The heat helps keep ice and fog off the mirrors, to allow for better driver visibility.

PARTS AND OPERATION Heated outside mirrors are often tied into the same electrical circuit as the rear window defogger. Therefore, when the rear defogger is turned on, the heating grid on the backside of the mirror is also turned on. Some vehicles use a switch for each mirror.

DIAGNOSIS The first step in any diagnosis procedure is to verify the customer concern. Check the owner's manual or service information for the proper method to use to turn on the heated mirrors.

NOTE: Heated mirrors are not designed to melt snow or a thick layer of ice.

If a fault has been detected, follow service information instructions for the exact procedure to follow. If the mirror itself is found to be defective, it is usually replaced as an assembly instead of being repaired.

HOMELINK GARAGE DOOR OPENER

OPERATION **HomeLink** is a device installed in many new vehicles that duplicates the radio-frequency code of the original garage door opener. The frequency range which HomeLink is able to operate is 288 to 418 MHz. The typical vehicle garage door opening system has three buttons that can be used to operate one or more of the following devices.

1. Garage doors equipped with a radio transmitter electric opener
2. Gates
3. Entry door locks
4. Lighting or small appliances

The devices include both fixed-frequency devices, usually older units, and rolling (encrypted) code devices. ● **SEE FIGURE 26–12.**

PROGRAMMING A VEHICLE GARAGE DOOR OPENER

When a vehicle is purchased, it must be programmed using the transmitter for the garage door opener or other device.

NOTE: The HomeLink garage door opening controller can only be programmed by using a transmitter. If an automatic garage door system does not have a remote transmitter, HomeLink cannot be programmed.

Normally, the customer is responsible for programming the HomeLink to the garage door opener. However, some customers may find that help is needed from the service department. The steps that are usually involved in programming HomeLink in the vehicle to the garage door opener are as follows:

STEP 1 Unplug the garage door opener during programming to prevent it from being cycled on and off, which could damage the motor.

STEP 2 Check that the frequency of the handheld transmitter is between 288 and 418 MHz.

STEP 3 Install new batteries in the transmitter to be assured of a strong signal being transmitted to the HomeLink module in the vehicle.

STEP 4 Turn the ignition on, engine off (KOEO).

STEP 5 While holding the transmitter 4 to 6 in. away from the HomeLink button, press and hold the HomeLink button while pressing and releasing the handheld transmitter every two seconds. Continue pressing and releasing the transmitter until the indicator light near the HomeLink button changes from slow blink to a rapid flash.

STEP 6 Verify that the vehicle garage door system (HomeLink) button has been programmed. Press and hold the garage door button. If the indicator light blinks rapidly for two seconds and then comes on steady, the system has been successfully programmed using a rolling code design. If the indicator light is on steady, then it has been successfully programmed to a fixed-frequency device.

DIAGNOSIS AND SERVICE
If a fault occurs with the HomeLink system, first verify that the garage door opener is functioning correctly. Also, check if the garage door opener remote control is capable of operating the door. Repair the garage door opener system as needed.

If the problem still exists, attempt reprogramming the HomeLink vehicle system, being sure that the remote has a newly purchased battery.

POWER WINDOWS

SWITCHES AND CONTROLS
Power windows use electric motors to raise and lower door glass. They can be operated by both a **master control switch** located beside the driver and additional **independent switches** for each electric window. Some power window systems use a **lockout switch** located on the driver's controls to prevent operation of the power windows from the independent switches. Power windows are designed to operate only with the ignition switch in the on (run) position, although some manufacturers use a time delay for accessory power after the ignition switch is turned off. This feature permits the driver and passengers an opportunity to close all windows or operate other accessories for about 10 minutes or until a vehicle door is opened after the ignition has been turned off. This feature is often called *retained accessory power*.

POWER WINDOW MOTORS
Most power window systems use **permanent magnet (PM) electric motors**. It is possible to run a PM motor in the reverse direction simply by reversing the polarity of the two wires going to the motor. Most power window motors do not require that the motor be grounded to the body (door) of the vehicle. The ground for all the power windows is most often centralized near the driver's master control switch. The up-and-down motion of the individual window motors is controlled by double-pole, double-throw (DPDT) switches. These DPDT switches have five contacts and permit battery voltage to be applied to the power window motor, as well as reverse the polarity and direction of the motor. Each motor is protected by an electronic circuit breaker. These circuit breakers are built into the motor assembly and are not a separate replaceable part. ● **SEE FIGURE 26–13.**

The power window motors rotate a mechanism called a **window regulator.** The window regulator is attached to the door glass and controls opening and closing of the glass. Door glass adjustments such as glass tilt and upper and lower stops are usually the same for both power and manual windows. ● **SEE FIGURE 26–14.**

AUTO DOWN/UP FEATURES
Many power windows are equipped with an auto down feature that allows windows to be lowered all of the way if the control switch is moved to a detent or held down for longer than 0.3 second. The window will then move down all the way to the bottom, and then the motor stops.

Many vehicles are equipped with the auto up feature that allows the driver to raise the driver's side or all windows in some cases, with just one push of the button. A sensor in the window

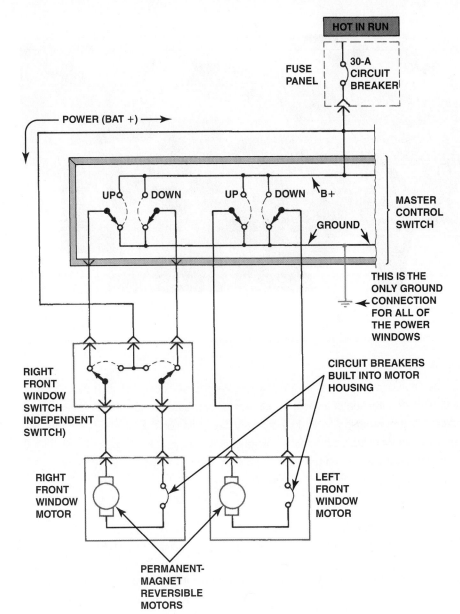

FIGURE 26–13 A typical power window circuit using PM motors. Control of the direction of window operation is achieved by directing the polarity of the current through the nongrounded motors. The only ground for the entire system is located at the master control (driver's side) switch assembly.

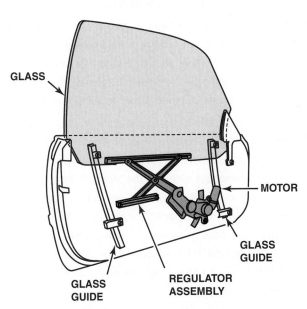

FIGURE 26–14 An electric motor and a regulator assembly raise and lower the glass on a power window.

motor circuit measures the current through the motor. The circuit is opened if the window touches an object, such as a hand or finger. When the window reaches the top or hits an object, the current through the window motor increases. When the upper limit amperage draw is reached, the motor circuit is opened and the window either stops or reverses. Most newer power windows use network communications modules to operate the power windows, and the switches are simply voltage signals to the module which supplies current to the individual window motors. ● **SEE FIGURE 26–15.**

TROUBLESHOOTING POWER WINDOWS Before troubleshooting a power window problem, check for proper operation of all power windows. Check service information for the

FIGURE 26–15 A master power window control panel with the buttons and the cover removed.

 TECH TIP

Programming Auto Down Power Windows

Many vehicles are equipped with automatic operation that can cause the window to go all the way down (or up) if the switch is depressed beyond a certain point or held for a fraction of a second. Sometimes this feature is lost if the battery in the vehicle has been disconnected. Although this programming procedure can vary depending on the make and model, many times the window(s) can be reprogrammed without using a scan tool by simply depressing and holding the down button for 10 seconds. If the vehicle is equipped with an auto up feature, repeat the procedure by holding the button up for 10 seconds. Always check exact service information for the vehicle being serviced.

POWER WINDOWS (CONTINUED)

exact procedure to follow. In a newer system, a scan tool can be used to perform the following:

- Check for B (body) or U (network) diagnostic trouble codes (DTCs)
- Operate the power windows using the bidirectional control feature
- Relearn or program the operation of the power windows after a battery disconnect

For older systems, if one of the **control wires** that run from the independent switch to the master switch is cut (open), the power window may operate in only one direction. The window may go down but not up, or vice versa. However, if one of the **direction wires** that run from the independent switch to the motor is cut (open), the window will not operate in either direction. The direction wires and the motor must be electrically connected to permit operation and change of direction of the electric lift motor in the door.

1. If *both* rear door windows fail to operate from the independent switches, check the operation of the window lockout (if the vehicle is so equipped) and the master control switch.

2. If one window can move in one direction only, check for continuity in the control wires (wires between the independent control switch and the master control switch).

3. If *all* windows fail to work or fail to work occasionally, check, clean, and tighten the ground wire(s) located either behind the driver's interior door panel or under the dash on the driver's side. A defective fuse or circuit breaker could also cause all the windows to fail to operate.

4. If one window fails to operate in both directions, the problem could be a defective window lift motor. The window could be stuck in the track of the door, which could cause the circuit breaker built into the motor to open the circuit to protect the wiring, switches, and motor from damage. To check for a stuck door glass, attempt to move (even slightly) the door glass up and down, forward and back, and side to side. If the window glass can move slightly in all directions, the power window motor should be able to at least move the glass.

5. Always refer to and follow service information when diagnosing power window circuits.

FIGURE 26–16 A power seat uses electric motors under the seat, which drive cables that extend to operate screw jacks (up and down) or gears to move the seat forward and back.

POWER SEATS

PARTS AND OPERATION A typical power-operated seat includes a reversible electric motor and a transmission assembly that may have three solenoids and six *drive cables* that turn the six seat adjusters. A six-way power seat offers seat movement forward and backward, plus seat cushion movement up and down at the front and the rear. The drive cables are similar to speedometer cables because they rotate inside a cable housing and connect the power output of the seat transmission to a gear or screw jack assembly that moves the seat. ● **SEE FIGURE 26–16.**

A **screw jack assembly** is often called a *gear nut*. It is used to move the front or back of the seat cushion up and down.

A **rubber coupling**, usually located between the electric motor and the transmission, and prevents electric motor damage in the event of a jammed seat. This coupling is designed to prevent motor damage.

Most power seats use a permanent magnet motor that can be reversed by simply reversing the polarity of the current sent to the motor by the seat switch. ● **SEE FIGURE 26–17.**

POWER SEAT MOTOR(S)
Most PM motors have a built-in circuit breaker or PTC circuit protector to protect the motor from overheating. Many Ford power seat motors use three separate armatures inside one large permanent magnet field housing. Some power seats use a series-wound electric motor with two separate field coils, one field coil for each direction of rotation. This type of power seat motor typically uses a relay to control the direction of current from the seat switch to the corresponding field coil of the seat motor. This type of power seat can be identified by the "click" heard when the seat switch is changed from up to down or front to back, or vice versa. The click is the sound of the relay switching the field coil current. Some power seats use as many as eight separate PM motors that operate all functions of the seat, including headrest height, seat length, and side bolsters, in addition to the usual six-way power seat functions.

NOTE: Some power seats use a small air pump to inflate a bag (or bags) in the lower part of the back of the seat, called the lumbar, because it supports the lumbar section of the spine. The lumbar section of the seat can also be changed, using a lever or knob that the driver can move to change the seat section for the lower back.

MEMORY SEAT
Memory seats use a potentiometer to sense the position of the seat. The seat position can be programmed into the body control module (BCM) or memory seat module and stored by position number 1, 2, or 3. The driver pushes the desired button and the seat moves to the stored position. ● **SEE FIGURE 26–18** on page 411.

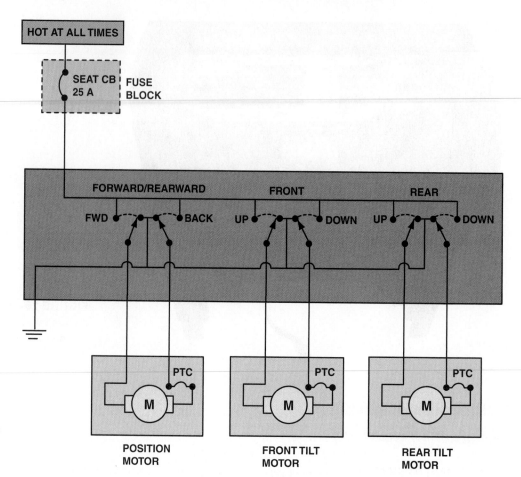

FIGURE 26–17 A typical power seat circuit diagram. Notice that each motor has a built-in electronic (solid-state) PTC circuit protector. The seat control switch can change the direction in which the motor(s) runs by reversing the direction in which the current flows through the motor.

POWER SEATS (CONTINUED)

On some vehicles, the memory seat position is also programmed into the remote keyless entry key fob.

TROUBLESHOOTING POWER SEATS Power seats are usually wired from the fuse panel so they can be operated without having to turn the ignition switch to on (run). If a power seat does not operate or make any noise, the circuit breaker (or fuse, if the vehicle is so equipped) should be checked first. The steps usually include:

STEP 1 Check service information for the exact procedure to follow when diagnosing power seats. If the seat relay clicks, the circuit breaker is functioning, but the relay or electric motor may be defective.

STEP 2 Remove the screws or clips that retain the controls to the inner door panel or seat and check for voltage at the seat control.

STEP 3 Check the ground connection(s) at the transmission and clutch control solenoids (if equipped). The solenoids must be properly grounded to the vehicle body for the power seat circuit to operate.

 **TECH TIP**

Easy Exit Seat Programming

Some vehicles are equipped with memory seats that allow the seat to move rearward when the ignition is turned off to allow easy exit from the vehicle. Vehicles equipped with this feature include an *exit/entry* button that is used to program the desired exit/entry position of the seat for each of two drivers.

If the vehicle is not equipped with this feature and only one driver primarily uses the vehicle, the second memory position can be programmed for easy exit and entry. Simply set position 1 to the desired seat position and position 2 to the entry/exit position. Then, when exiting the vehicle, press memory 2 to allow easy exit and easy entry the next time. Press memory 1 when in the vehicle to return the seat memory to the desired driving position.

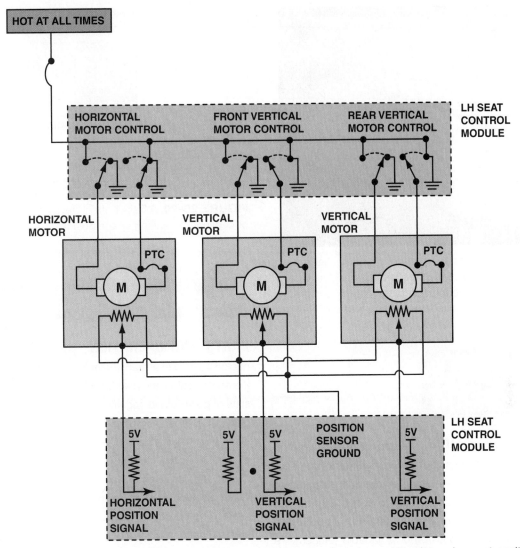

FIGURE 26–18 A typical memory seat module showing the three-wire potentiometer used to determine seat position.

If the power seat motor runs but does not move the seat, the most likely fault is a worn or defective rubber clutch sleeve between the electric seat motor and the transmission.

If the seat relay clicks but the seat motor does not operate, the problem is usually a defective seat motor or defective wiring between the motor and the relay. If the power seat uses a motor relay, the motor has a double reverse-wound field for reversing the motor direction. This type of electric motor must be properly grounded. Permanent magnet motors do not require grounding for operation.

NOTE: Power seats are often difficult to service because of restricted working room. If the entire seat cannot be removed from the vehicle because the track bolts are covered, attempt to remove the seat from the top of the power seat assembly. These bolts are almost always accessible regardless of seat position.

TECH TIP

What Every Driver Should Know About Power Seats

Power seats use an electric motor or motors to move the position of the seat. These electric motors turn small cables that operate mechanisms that move the seat. *Never* place rags, newspapers, or any other object under a power seat. Even ice scrapers can get caught between moving parts of the seat and can often cause serious damage or jamming of the power seat.

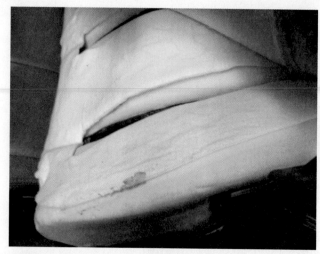

FIGURE 26–19 The heating element of a heated seat is a replaceable part, but service requires that the upholstery be removed. The yellow part is the seat foam material and the entire white cover is the replaceable heating element. This is then covered by the seat material.

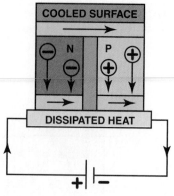

FIGURE 26–20 A Peltier effect device is capable of heating or cooling, depending on the polarity of the applied current.

ELECTRICALLY HEATED SEATS

PARTS AND OPERATION Heated seats use electric heating elements in the seat bottom, as well as in the seat back in many vehicles. The heating element is designed to warm the seat and/or back of the seat to about 100°F (37°C) or close to normal body temperature (98.6°F). Many heated seats also include a high-position or a variable temperature setting, so the temperature of the seats can therefore be as high as 110°F (44°C).

A temperature sensor in the seat cushion is used to regulate the temperature. The sensor is a variable resistor which changes with temperature and is used as an input signal to a heated seat control module. The heated seat module uses the seat temperature input, as well as the input from the high-low (or variable) temperature control, to turn the current on or off to the heating element in the seat. Some vehicles are equipped with heated seats in both the rear and the front seats.

DIAGNOSIS AND SERVICE When diagnosing a heated seat concern, start by verifying that the switch is in the on position and that the temperature of the seat is below normal body temperature. Using service information, check for power and ground at the control module and to the heating element in the seat. Most vehicle manufacturers recommend replacing the entire heating element if it is defective. ● **SEE FIGURE 26–19.**

HEATED AND COOLED SEATS

PARTS AND OPERATION Most electrically heated and cooled seats use a **thermoelectric device (TED)** located under the seat cushion and seat back. The thermoelectric device consists of positive and negative connections between two ceramic plates. Each ceramic plate has copper fins to allow the transfer of heat to air passing over the device and directed into the seat cushion. The thermoelectric device uses the **Peltier effect,** named after the inventor, Jean C. A. Peltier, a French clockmaker. When electrical current flows through the module, one side is heated and the other side is cooled. Reversing the polarity of the current changes which side is heated. ● **SEE FIGURE 26–20.**

Most vehicles equipped with heated and cooled seats use two modules per seat, one for the seat cushion and one for the seat back. When the heated and cooled seats are turned on, air is forced through a filter and then through the thermoelectric modules. The air is then directed through passages in the foam of the seat cushion and seat back. Each thermoelectric device has a temperature sensor, called a thermistor. The control module uses sensors to determine the temperature of the fins in the thermoelectric device so the controller can maintain the set temperature.

DIAGNOSIS AND SERVICE The first step in any diagnosis is to verify that the heated-cooled seat system is not functioning. Check the owner's manual or service information for the specified procedures. If the system works partially, check the air filter, usually located under the seat for each thermoelectric device. A partially clogged filter can restrict airflow and reduce the heating or cooling effect. If the system control indicator light is not on or the system does not work at all, check for power and ground at the thermoelectric devices. Always follow the vehicle manufacturer's recommended diagnosis and service procedures.

TECH TIP

Check the Seat Filter

Heated and cooled seats often use a filter to trap dirt and debris to help keep the air passages clean. If a customer complains of a slow heating or cooling of the seat, check the air filter and replace or clean as necessary. Check service information for the exact location of the seat filter and for instructions on how to remove and/or replace it.

HEATED STEERING WHEEL

PARTS INVOLVED A heated steering wheel usually consists of the following components.

- Steering wheel with a built-in heater in the rim
- Heated steering wheel control switch
- Heated steering wheel control module

OPERATION When the steering wheel heater control switch is turned on, a signal is sent to the control module and electrical current flows through the heating element in the rim of the steering wheel. ● **SEE FIGURE 26–21.**

The system remains on until the ignition switch is turned off or the driver turns off the control switch. The temperature of the steering wheel is usually calibrated to stay at about 90°F (32°C), and it requires three to four minutes to reach that temperature depending on the outside temperature.

DIAGNOSIS AND SERVICE Diagnosis of a heated steering wheel starts with verifying that the heated steering wheel is not working as designed.

NOTE: **Most heated steering wheels do not work if the temperature inside the vehicle is about 90°F (32°C) or higher.**

If the heated steering wheel is not working, follow the service information testing procedures which would include a check of the following:

1. Check the heated steering wheel control switch for proper operation. This is usually done by checking for voltage at both terminals of the switch. If voltage is available at only one of the two terminals of the switch and the switch has been turned on and off, an open (defective) switch is indicated.

2. Check for voltage and ground at the terminals leading to the heating element. If voltage is available at the heating

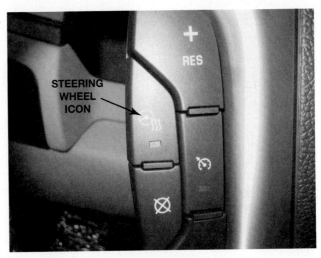

FIGURE 26–21 The heated steering wheel is controlled by a switch on the steering wheel in this vehicle.

element and the ground has less than 0.2 volt drop to a good chassis ground, the heating element is defective. The entire steering wheel has to be replaced if the element is defective.

Always follow the vehicle manufacturer's recommended diagnosis and testing procedures.

ADJUSTABLE PEDALS

PURPOSE AND FUNCTION **Adjustable pedals**, also called **electric adjustable pedals (EAP)**, place the brake pedal and the accelerator pedal on movable brackets that are motor operated. A typical adjustable pedal system includes the following components.

- **Adjustable pedal position switch.** Allows the driver to position the pedals
- **Adjustable pedal assembly.** Includes the motor, threaded adjustment rods, and a pedal position sensor

  ● **SEE FIGURE 26–22.**

The position of the pedals, as well as the position of the seat system, is usually included as part of the memory seat function and can be set for two or more drivers.

DIAGNOSIS AND SERVICE The first step when there is a customer concern about the functioning of the adjustable pedals is to verify that the unit is not working as designed. Check the owner manual or service information for the proper operation. Follow the vehicle manufacturer's recommended troubleshooting procedure. Many diagnostic procedures include the use of a factory scan tool with bidirectional control capabilities to test this system.

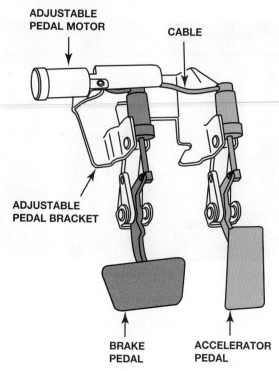

FIGURE 26–22 A typical adjustable pedal assembly. Both the accelerator and the brake pedal can be moved forward and rearward by using the adjustable pedal position switch.

FIGURE 26–23 Electrically folded mirror in the folded position.

FIGURE 26–24 The electric mirror control is located on the driver's side door panel on this Cadillac Escalade.

 **TECH TIP**

Check the Remote

The memory function may be programmed to a particular key fob remote, which would command the adjustable pedals to move to the position set in memory. Always check both remote settings before attempting to repair a problem that may not be a problem.

OUTSIDE FOLDING MIRRORS

Mirrors that can be electrically folded inward are a popular feature, especially on larger sport utility vehicles. A control inside is used to fold both mirrors inward when needed, such as when entering a garage or close parking spot. For diagnosis and servicing of outside folding mirrors, check service information for details.

 REAL WORLD FIX

The Case of the Haunted Mirrors

The owner complained that while driving, either one or the other outside mirror would fold in without any button being depressed. Unable to verify the customer concern, the service technician looked at the owner's manual to find out exactly how the mirrors were supposed to work. In the manual, a caution statement said that if the mirror is electrically folded inward and then manually pushed out, the mirror will not lock into position. The power folding mirrors must be electrically cycled outward, using the mirror switches to lock them in position. After cycling both mirrors inward and outward electrically, the problem was solved. ● **SEE FIGURES 26–23 AND 26–24.**

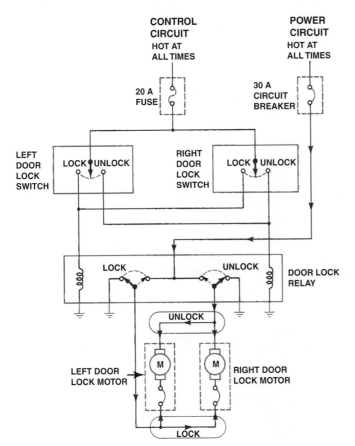

FIGURE 26–25 A typical electric power door lock circuit diagram. Note that the control circuit is protected by a fuse, whereas the power circuit is protected by a circuit breaker. As with the operation of power windows, power door locks typically use reversible permanent magnet (PM) nongrounded electric motors. These motors are geared mechanically to the lock-unlock mechanism.

ELECTRIC POWER DOOR LOCKS

Electric power door locks use a permanent magnet (PM) reversible motor to lock or unlock all vehicle door locks from a control switch or switches.

The electric motor uses a built-in circuit breaker and operates the lock-activating rod. PM reversible motors do not require grounding because, as with power windows, the motor control is determined by the polarity of the current through the two motor wires. ● **SEE FIGURE 26–25.**

Some two-door vehicles do *not* use a power door lock relay because the current flow for only two PM motors can be handled through the door lock switches. However, most four-door vehicles and vans with power locks on rear and side doors use a relay to control the current flow necessary to operate four or more power door lock motors. The door lock relay is controlled by the door lock switch and is commonly the location of the one and only *ground* connection for the entire door lock circuit.

FIGURE 26–26 A key fob remote with the cover removed showing the replaceable battery.

KEYLESS ENTRY

Even though some Ford vehicles use a keypad located on the outside of the door, most keyless entry systems use a wireless transmitter built into the key or key fob. A **key fob** is a decorative tab or item on a key chain. ● **SEE FIGURE 26–26.**

The transmitter broadcasts a signal that is received by the electronic control module, which is generally mounted in the trunk or under the instrument panel. ● **SEE FIGURE 26–27.**

The electronic control unit sends a voltage signal to the door lock actuator(s) located in the doors. Generally, if the transmitter unlock button is depressed once, only the driver's door is unlocked. If the unlock button is depressed twice, then all doors unlock.

ROLLING CODE RESET PROCEDURE Many keyless remote systems use a rolling code type of transmitter and receiver. In a conventional system, the transmitter emits a certain fixed frequency, which is received by the vehicle control module. This single frequency can be intercepted and rebroadcast to open the vehicle.

A rolling code type of transmitter emits a different frequency every time the transmitter button is depressed and then rolls over to another frequency so that it cannot be intercepted. Both the transmitter and the receiver must be kept in synchronized order so that the remote will function correctly.

If the transmitter is depressed when it is out of range from the vehicle, the proper frequency may not be recognized by the receiver, which did not roll over to the new frequency when the transmitter was depressed. If the transmitter does not work, try to resynchronize the transmitter to the receiver by depressing and holding both the lock and the unlock button for 10 seconds when within range of the receiver.

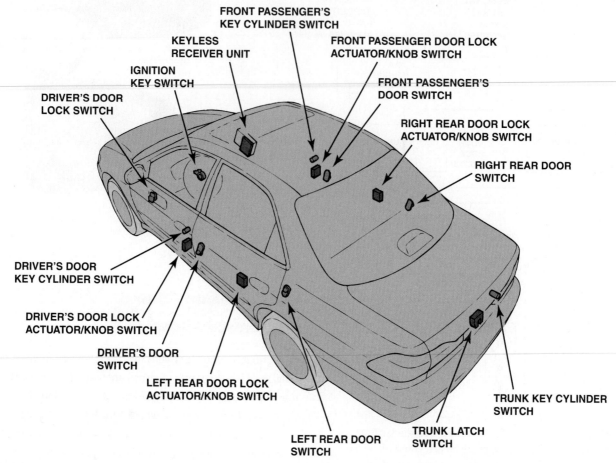

FRONT PASSENGER'S
KEY CYLINDER SWITCH

KEYLESS
RECEIVER UNIT

FRONT PASSENGER DOOR LOCK
ACTUATOR/KNOB SWITCH

IGNITION
KEY SWITCH

FRONT PASSENGER'S
DOOR SWITCH

DRIVER'S DOOR
LOCK SWITCH

RIGHT REAR DOOR LOCK
ACTUATOR/KNOB SWITCH

RIGHT REAR DOOR
SWITCH

DRIVER'S DOOR
KEY CYLINDER SWITCH

DRIVER'S DOOR LOCK
ACTUATOR/KNOB SWITCH

DRIVER'S DOOR
SWITCH

LEFT REAR DOOR LOCK
ACTUATOR/KNOB SWITCH

TRUNK KEY CYLINDER
SWITCH

LEFT REAR DOOR
SWITCH

TRUNK LATCH
SWITCH

FIGURE 26–27 A typical vehicle showing the location of the various components of the remote keyless entry system.

KEYLESS ENTRY (CONTINUED)

KEYLESS ENTRY DIAGNOSIS
A small battery powers the transmitter, and a weak battery is a common cause of remote power locks failing to operate. If the keyless entry system fails to operate after the transmitter battery has been replaced, check the following items.

- Mechanical binding in the door lock
- Low vehicle battery voltage
- Blown fuse
- Open circuit to the control module
- Defective control module
- Defective transmitter

PROGRAMMING A NEW REMOTE
If a new or additional remote transmitter is to be used, it must be programmed to the vehicle. The programming procedure varies and may require the use of a scan tool. Check service information for the exact procedure to follow. ● **SEE CHART 26–1.**

ANTITHEFT SYSTEMS

PARTS AND OPERATION
Antitheft devices flash lights or sound an alarm if the vehicle is broken into or vandalized. In addition to the alarm, some systems prevent the engine from starting by disabling the starter, ignition, or fuel system once the antitheft device is activated. Others permit the engine to start, but then disable it after several seconds. Switches in the door-jambs, trunk, and hood provide an input signal to the control module should an undesirable entry occur on a typical system. Some antitheft systems are more complex and also have electronic sensors that trigger the alarm if there is a change in battery current draw, a violent vehicle motion, or if glass is broken. These sensors also provide an input signal to the control module, which may be a separate antitheft unit or incorporated into the PCM or BCM. ● **SEE FIGURE 26–28** on page 424 for an example of a shock sensor used in an antitheft alarm system.

MAKE/MODEL	NOTES	PROCEDURE
Mazda 5 6	Start with the key out and all doors, trunk lid, and lift gate closed. A total of three transmitters can be programmed. Previously programmed transmitters may be erased during this procedure. If possible, program all desired transmitters at the same time.	1. Open the driver's side door. 2. Put the key in the ignition lock and turn the ignition to on and back to lock, three times (ending in the lock position with the key in the ignition). 3. Close and then open the driver's door three times, ending with the door open. The door locks will lock and unlock. 4. Push the unlock button on the transmitter twice. Door locks will lock and unlock to verify programming is okay. 5. Repeat step 4 for any additional transmitter to be programmed. 6. When the last transmitter to be programmed has been learned, push the unlock button twice on that transmitter to exit programming mode.
Mazda 626 Millenia Protégé	Start with the key out and all doors, trunk lid, and lift gate closed. A total of three transmitters can be programmed. Previously programmed transmitters may be erased during this procedure. If possible, program all desired transmitters at the same time. Protégé will cycle locks instead of sounding a buzzer.	1. Open the driver's side door. 2. Put the key in the ignition lock and turn the ignition to on and back to lock, three times, then remove the key. 3. Close and then open the driver's door three times, ending with the door open. A buzzer will sound from the CPU. 4. Push any button on the transmitter twice. Buzzer will sound once to verify programming is okay. 5. Repeat step 4 for any additional transmitter to be programmed. 6. When the last transmitter to be programmed has been learned, push any button twice on that transmitter. The buzzer will sound twice to exit programming mode.
Nissan Altima Armada Frontier Maxima Murano Titan	Key fob codes can also be checked and changed using a scan tool. If step 2 is done too fast, the system will not enter programming mode. Up to five key fobs can be registered. If more than five are input, the oldest ID code will be overwritten. It is possible to enter the same key code into all five memories. This can be used to erase the ID code of a fob that has been lost, if needed.	1. Enter the vehicle and close all doors. 2. Insert and then completely remove key from the ignition cylinder more than six times within 10 seconds. Hazard warning lamps will flash twice to indicate programming mode is active. 3. Insert the key and turn the ignition to ACC. 4. Press any key on the fob once. The hazard warning lamps will flash twice to indicate that the code is stored. 5. To end programming mode, open the driver's door. If programming additional fobs proceed to step 6 (don't open the driver's door). 6. To enter an additional code unlock and then lock the driver's door using the window main switch. 7. Press any button on the additional fob. The hazard warning lamps will flash twice to indicate the code is learned. 8. To enter another key fob code repeat steps 6 and 7. 9. Open the driver's door to end programming mode.
Pontiac Vibe **Scion** xB	Up to four transmitters can be programmed. If more than four transmitters are programmed, the oldest transmitter code will be overwritten.	1. Enter the vehicle, key out of ignition, close all doors except the driver's door. 2. Insert and remove the key from the ignition twice within 5 seconds. 3. Close and open the driver's door twice within 40 seconds and then insert the key and remove it.

CHART 26–1

Continued

(*CONTINUED*)

MAKE/MODEL	NOTES	PROCEDURE

Toyota
Camry
Corolla
	There are four programming modes:
	• Add mode: Used to program additional transmitters
	• Rewrite mode: Erases all previously programmed transmitters
	• Confirmation mode: Indicates how many transmitters are already programmed
	• Prohibition mode: Erases all learned codes and disables the wireless entry system
	
	In confirmation mode, if no codes are stored the door locks will cycle five times.
	
	Open any door to exit the programming mode.
		4. Close and open the driver's door twice again, then insert the ignition key and close the door.
		5. Turn the key from lock to on and back to lock to select the programming mode:
		  • One time for add mode (go to step 6)
		  • Two times for rewrite mode (go to step 6)
		  • Three times for confirmation mode (go to step 10)
		  • Five times for prohibition mode (see step 11)
		6. Remove the key from the ignition.
		7. The doors will lock-unlock once for add mode or twice for rewrite mode.
		8. To program a transmitter, press lock and unlock buttons for 1.5 seconds and release; then within 3 seconds press either button for more than 1 second to confirm programming:
		  • One lock-unlock cycle indicates okay.
		  • Two lock-unlock cycles indicates not okay; repeat this step.
		9. Repeat step 8 to program additional transmitters.
		10. In confirmation mode the number of lock-unlock cycles will indicate the number of codes already stored and programming mode will exit. Example: Two cycles indicates two codes are stored.
		11. If prohibition mode is selected the locks will cycle five times and programming mode will exit.

Pontiac G6 **Saturn** Ion L300	A scan tool is used to program key fobs. Up to four transmitters can be programmed. If any key fob is programmed, all fobs must be programmed at the same time. On vehicles with personalization features, the transmitters are numbered 1 and 2. The first transmitter programmed will become driver 1 and the second will become driver 2.	1. Install the scan tool and navigate to the Program Key Fobs menu. 2. Select the number of fobs to be programmed. 3. Press and hold the lock and unlock buttons on the first fob to be programmed. The locks should cycle to indicate okay. NOTE: This fob becomes driver 1 key fob. 4. Repeat step 3 for the second fob. This fob becomes driver 2 key fob. 5. Repeat step 3 for any other key fobs to be programmed. 6. Turn off and remove the scan tool to exit programming.
Saab 9-2	Up to four transmitters can be programmed.	1. Sit in the driver's seat and close all doors. 2. Open and close the driver's door. 3. Turn the ignition switch from on to lock, 10 times within 15 seconds. The horn will chirp to indicate programming mode. 4. Open and close the driver's door. 5. Press any button on the fob to be programmed. 6. The horn will chirp two times to indicate that the transmitter has been learned. 7. Repeat steps 4, 5, and 6 for any additional transmitters. 8. To exit from programming mode remove the key from the ignition. The horn should chirp three times to confirm.

CHART 26–1

Remote keyless programming steps for popular vehicles. Procedures may also apply to similar vehicles by the same manufacturer. Always refer to service information for specific vehicles.

MAKE/MODEL	NOTES	PROCEDURE
Subaru Forester Impreza Legacy Outback Tribeca	A scan tool is used to program RKE codes. Up to four RKE transmitters can be registered. The eight-digit code is on the plastic bag of a new transmitter on the circuit board inside the transmitter.	1. Install the scan tool and navigate to the keyless transmitter ID registration menu. 2. Input the transmitter eight-digit ID number into the scan tool. 3. When the number is correct, press yes. 4. The scan tool will display "ID registration done" when the ID is programmed. 5. Follow the scan tool menus to program additional transmitters.
Toyota Tundra Sequoia **Lexus** GS 430 RX 300	Up to four transmitters can be programmed. If more than four transmitters are programmed, the oldest transmitter code will be overwritten. There are four programming modes: • Add mode: Used to program additional transmitters • Rewrite mode: Erases all previously programmed transmitters • Confirmation mode: Indicates how many transmitters are already programmed • Prohibition mode: Erases all learned codes and disables the wireless entry system In confirmation mode, if no codes are stored the door locks will cycle five times. Open any door to exit the programming mode.	1. Enter the vehicle, key out of ignition, close all doors except the driver's door. 2. Insert and remove the key from the ignition key cylinder. 3. Use the driver's door lock control switch to lock and unlock the doors five times, at about 1 second intervals. 4. Close and open the driver's door. 5. Use the driver's door lock control switch to lock and unlock the doors fivetimes, at about 1 second intervals. 6. Insert the ignition key. 7. Turn the key from lock to on and back to lock to select the programming mode: • One time for add mode (go to step 10) • Two times for rewrite mode (go to step 10) • Three times for confirmation mode (go to step 12) • Five times for prohibition mode (see step 13) 8. Remove the key from the ignition. 9. The doors will lock-unlock once, twice, three times of five times to confirm the mode. 10. To program a transmitter press lock and unlock buttons for 1.5 seconds and release; then within 3 seconds press either button for more than 1 second to confirm programming: One lock-unlock cycle indicates okay. Two lock-unlock cycles indicates not okay; repeat this step. 11. Repeat step 10 to program additional transmitters. 12. In confirmation mode the number of lock-unlock cycles will indicate the number of codes already stored and programming mode will exit. Example: Two cycles indicates two codes are stored. 13. If prohibition mode is selected the locks will cycle five times and programming mode will exit.

CHART 26-1

Continued

ANTITHEFT SYSTEMS (CONTINUED)

ANTITHEFT SYSTEM DIAGNOSIS Most factory-installed antitheft systems are integrated with several other circuits to form a complex, multiple-circuit system. The major steps are as follows:

1. It is essential to have accurate diagrams, specifications, and test procedures for the specific model being serviced.

2. The easiest way to reduce circuit complexity is to use the wiring diagram to break the entire system into its subcircuits, then check only those related to the problem.

3. If any step indicates that a subcircuit is not complete, check the power source, ground, components, and wiring in that subcircuit.

FIGURE 26–28 A shock sensor used in alarm and antitheft systems. If the vehicle is moved, the magnet will move relative to the coil, inducing a small voltage that will trigger the alarm.

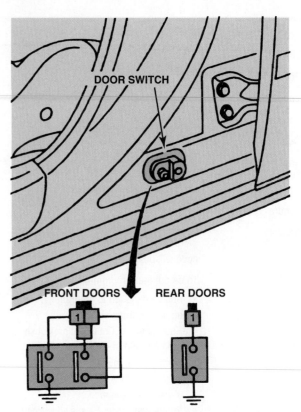

FIGURE 26–29 Door switches, which complete the ground circuit with the door open, are a common source of high resistance.

ANTITHEFT SYSTEMS (CONTINUED)

Many systems use a computer chip in the plastic part of the key. Most systems are electronically regulated and have a self-diagnostic program. This self-diagnostic program is generally accessed and activated using a scan tool. Diagnostic and test procedures are similar as for any of the other electronic control systems used on the vehicle.

ANTITHEFT SYSTEM TESTING AND SERVICE Before performing any diagnostic checks, make sure that all of the following electrical devices function correctly.

- Parking and low-beam headlights
- Dome and courtesy lights
- Horn
- Electric door locks

Circuit information from these devices often provides basic inputs to the control module. If a problem is detected in any of these circuits, such as a missing signal or a signal that is out of range, the control module disables the antitheft system and may record a diagnostic trouble code (DTC).

If all of the previously mentioned devices are operational, check all the circuits leading to the antitheft control module. Make sure all switches are in their normal or off positions. Doorjamb switches complete the ground circuit when a door is opened. ● **SEE FIGURE 26–29.**

Frequently, corrosion that builds up on the switch contacts prevents the switch from operating properly. Conduct voltage

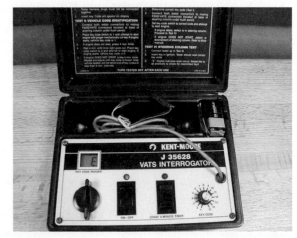

FIGURE 26–30 A special tool is needed to diagnose a General Motors VATS security system and special keys that contain a resistor pellet.

drop tests to isolate faulty components and circuit problems. Repair as needed and retest to confirm that the system is operational. Follow procedures from the manufacturer to clear DTC records, and then run the self-diagnostic program to verify repairs. Some system diagnostic procedures specify the use of special testers. ● **SEE FIGURE 26–30.**

● **SEE CHART 26–2** for programming procedures for selected vehicles.

MAKE/MODEL	NOTES	PROCEDURES

Chrysler
  Pacifica
  Town and Country
  PT Cruiser
  Sebring
  300
  Some other models
 	
Dodge
  Caravan
  Durango
  Magnum
  Neon
  Pickup
  Stratus
 	
Jeep
  Liberty
  Grand Cherokee
  Some other models
	Programming is by scan tool or by "customer learn" mode.
	
	Customer learn mode requires at least two functioning Sentry keys.
	
	If no functioning Sentry keys are available, the scan tool and the vehicle PIN number are required for programming.
	
	Both the immobilizer and RKE are programmed with this procedure.
	
	Only a blank key transponder can be programmed. Once programmed, the key cannot be used in another vehicle.
	
	The customer learn mode will exit after each key is programmed. The complete procedure must be completed for each key to be programmed.
	
	A total of eight keys can be programmed by the Sentry Key Remote Entry Module (four on some models).
		CUSTOMER LEARN MODE
		
		1. Using a blank Sentry key, cut the key to match the lock cylinder code.
		2. Insert one of the two valid keys into the ignition and turn the ignition on.
		3. After 3 seconds, but before 15 seconds expire, turn off the ignition and remove the key.
		4. Within 15 seconds insert the second valid key and turn the ignition on.
		5. Within 10 seconds a chime will sound and/or the indicator lamp will flash, indicating customer learn mode is active.
		6. Within 60 seconds turn the ignition off, insert the blank Sentry key, and turn the ignition on.
		7. After about 10 seconds a single chime will sound and the indicator lamp will stay on solid for about 3 seconds; this indicates the key has been programmed.

Ford
  Taurus
  Some other models
 	
Lincoln
  Some models
 	
Mercury
  Grand Marquis
  Milan
  Montego
	This procedure requires two or more programmed keys.
	
	If two programmed keys are not available a scan tool must be used.
	
	Maximum of eight keys can be programmed.
	
	Repeat the complete procedure for each key to be learned.
	
	If the programming is not successful the antitheft indicator will flash and the vehicle will not start. Leave the key on for 30 seconds and then retry the procedure.
		1. Using the first programmed key, turn the ignition from off to run. Leave the switch in run for at least 3 seconds but not more than 10 seconds.
		2. Turn the switch to off. Within 10 seconds repeat step 1 with the second programmed key.
		3. Turn the ignition switch off.
		4. Within 20 seconds, insert the un-programmed key and turn the ignition switch from off to run.
		5. After 3 seconds, attempt to start the vehicle. If the programming is successful the vehicle will start and the antitheft indicator will light for 3 seconds and go out.

Ford
  Crown Victoria
  Some other models
	This procedure requires two or more programmed keys.
	
	If two programmed keys are not available a scan tool must be used.
	
	Maximum of eight keys can be programmed.
		1. Using the first programmed key, turn the ignition from off to run. Leave the switch in run for 1 second.
		2. Turn the switch to off. Within 5 seconds repeat step 1 with the second programmed key.
		3. Turn the ignition switch off.

CHART 26–2

(CONTINUED)

Immobilizer or vehicle theft deterrent key learn procedures for some popular vehicles.

MAKE/MODEL	NOTES	PROCEDURES
	Repeat the complete procedure for each key to be learned. If the programming is not successful the antitheft indicator will flash and the vehicle will not start. Leave the key on for 30 seconds and then retry the procedure.	4. Within 10 seconds, insert the un-programmed key and turn the ignition switch from off to run. 5. After 1 second, attempt to start the vehicle. If the programming is successful the vehicle will start and the antitheft indicator will light for 3 seconds and go out.

General Motors

Passkey

Passkey II

(except vehicles with BCM)

The Passkey decoder will learn the first pellet read when the decoder module is first installed. This learned value cannot be changed.

A Passkey Interrogator special tool is needed to read key pellet resistance when replacing keys. The tool will read out a code number related to the pellet resistance.

PELLET CODE	RESISTANCE
1	402
2	523
3	681
4	887
5	1,130
6	1,470
7	1,870
8	2,370
9	3,010
10	3,740
11	4,750
12	6,040
13	7,500
14	9,530
15	11,800

NEW DECODER MODULE

1. Install the new decoder module.

2. Insert the key and start the vehicle to program the pellet code into the new module.

DUPLICATE KEY

1. Use the Interrogator tool to read the existing key code.

2. Obtain a key with the matching pellet code and cut the key to match the original key.

LOST KEY

1. The Interrogator tool must be used to determine the stored code.

2. Cut a blank key so that the ignition can be turned.

3. Access the lock cylinder 2 wire connector and connect it to the Interrogator.

4. Alternately select each of the 15 code positions on the Interrogator until the vehicle starts. This is then the correct pellet code.

5. Obtain the correct coded key and cut it to fit.

General Motors

Passkey II

(vehicles with BCM)

On vehicles with a body control module (BCM) the Passkey II pellet code is stored in the BCM. The BCM can learn the pellet code of a replacement key using a scan tool or this procedure.

Make sure that the battery is fully charged.

If the learning procedure is not successful check the system for codes and repair.

1. Insert the key to be learned and turn the ignition on. Leave the switch on for 11 minutes. The security lamp will be on or flashing during this time.

2. When the security lamp goes off turn the ignition off for 30 seconds.

3. Repeat step 1 two more times.

4. Turn the ignition off for 30 seconds.

5. Attempt to start the vehicle. The vehicle should start and run if the learn is successful.

CHART 26–2

Immobilizer or vehicle theft deterrent key learn procedures for some popular vehicles.

MAKE/MODEL	NOTES	PROCEDURES
General Motors Passkey III Passkey III+	Quick-Learn requires at least one programmed master (black) key. Keys can be learned with a scan tool. If no programmed master key is available the 30 minute Auto Learn procedure must be used. Auto Learn procedure will erase all learned keys. Make sure that the battery is fully charged. On vehicles with a driver information center (DIC) a "STARTING DISABLED DUE TO THEFT" message will display during the 10 minute timer.	QUICK LEARN 1. Insert a programmed master key and turn on the ignition. 2. Turn the ignition off and remove the key. 3. Within 10 seconds insert the key to be learned and turn the ignition on. 4. The key is now programmed. 30 MINUTE AUTO LEARN 1. Insert the new master key and turn on the ignition. The security lamp should be on and then turn it off after 10 minutes. 2. Turn the ignition off for 5 seconds. 3. Repeat steps 1 and 2 two more times (30 minutes total). 4. From the off position turn on and start the vehicle. 5. The vehicle should start and run, indicating the key has been learned.
General Motors Passlock (early systems)	Passlock systems do not have coded keys. Replacement or new keys do not have to be learned. Early Passlock systems pass an "R" code to the instrument cluster and then the IPC sends a password on to the PCM. Perform this procedure if replacing the instrument cluster, lock cylinder, or PCM.	1. After parts are installed, attempt to start the vehicle. 2. The vehicle should start and stall. 3. Leave the key on and wait until the flashing theft lamp stays on steady. 4. Attempt to start the vehicle again. It should start and continue to run. 5. The theft lamp should flash for 10 seconds and then go out to indicate the password has been learned.
General Motors Passlock (later models)	Replacement or additional keys do not have to be learned. Programming is necessary if the Passlock sensor, BCM, or PCM has been replaced. A scan tool can also be used to program the Passlock system. ● **SEE FIGURE 26–31** on page 428.	1. Turn the ignition on and attempt to start the vehicle. 2. The vehicle will not start. Release the key to on. Wait about 10 minutes for the security lamp to go off. 3. Turn off the ignition for 5 seconds. 4. Repeat steps 1 through 3 two more times. 5. For a fourth time turn the key on and start the vehicle. The vehicle should start and run, indicating that the lock code has been learned.
Honda	A programmed key, scan tool, and password are required to program keys.	1. Connect the scan tool and navigate to the ADD and DELETE KEYS menu. 2. Follow the instructions on the scan tool to add or delete keys as needed.
Hyundai	A scan tool can be used to program keys. A special ID key is needed to program new or additional keys.	1. Using the ID key, turn the ignition on then off. 2. Using the key to be programmed, turn the ignition on then off. This will program the key. 3. Repeat step 2 for any additional keys.

CHART 26–2

Continued

(CONTINUED)

MAKE/MODEL	NOTES	PROCEDURES
Toyota Camry Land Cruiser Some other earlier models	Up to seven master (black) keys can be learned. An already learned master key must be used to initiate the procedure. Keys can also be programmed with a scan tool.	1. Insert a programmed master key into the ignition switch. 2. Within 15 seconds, press and release the accelerator pedal five times. 3. Within 20 seconds, press and release the brake pedal six times. 4. Remove the master key. 5. Within 10 seconds, insert the key to be programmed into the lock cylinder and press and release the accelerator pedal one time. 6. The security indicator should flash for about 1 minute and then go out to indicate that the key has been learned. 7. To program additional keys repeat steps 5 and 6 within 10 seconds.
Toyota Corolla Matrix Tacoma Sienna RAV4 Some other late models **Lexus** LS430 Some other models	Up to five keys can be learned. A scan tool should be used to register keys.	1. Insert a programmed master key into the ignition and turn the ignition on. 2. Install the scan tool and navigate to the IMMOBILIZER, TRANSP CODE REG. screen. Follow the instructions on the scan tool. 3. The security indicator will turn on. Within 20 seconds, remove the master key. 4. Within 10 seconds, insert the new key to be programmed. 5. The security indicator will blink for 60 seconds and then go off when the key is learned.

CHART 26–2

Immobilizer or vehicle theft deterrent key learn procedures for some popular vehicles.

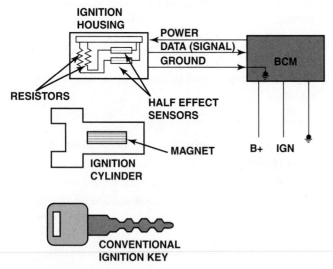

FIGURE 26–31 The Passlock series of General Motors security systems uses a conventional key. The magnet is located in the ignition lock cylinder and triggers the Hall-effect sensors.

FIGURE 26–32 Corrosion or faults at the junction between the wiring and the rear window electrical grid are the source of many rear window defogger problems.

ELECTRICAL ACCESSORY SYMPTOM GUIDE

Cruise Control

Problem	Possible Causes and/or Solutions
Cruise (speed) control is inoperative.	1. Blown fuse 2. Defective or misadjusted electrical or vacuum safety switch near the brake pedal arm 3. Lack of engine vacuum to servo or transducer 4. Defective transducer; defective speed control switch
Cruise (speed) control speed is incorrect or variable.	1. Misadjusted activation cable 2. Defective or pinched vacuum hose 3. Misadjustment of transducer

Power Windows

Problem	Possible Causes and/or Solutions
Power windows are inoperative.	1. Defective (blown) fuse (circuit breaker) 2. Defective relay (if used) 3. Poor ground for master control switch 4. Poor connections at switch(es) or motor(s) 5. Open circuit (usually near the master control switch) 6. Defective lockout switch
One power window is inoperative.	1. Defective motor; defective or open control switch 2. Open or loose wiring to the switch or the motor
Only one power window can be operated from the master switch.	1. Poor connection or open circuit in the control wire(s)

Power Seats

Problem	Possible Causes and/or Solutions
Power seats are inoperative, no click or noise.	1. Defective circuit breaker 2. Poor ground at the switch or relay (if used) 3. Open in the wiring between the switch and relay (if used); defective switch 4. Defective solenoid(s) or wiring 5. Defective door switch

Problem	Possible Causes and/or Solutions
Power seats are inoperative, click is heard.	1. "Flex" in the cables from the motor(s) to check for motor operation (If flex is felt, the motor is trying to operate the gear nut or the screw jack.) 2. Binding or obstruction 3. Defective motor (The click is generally the relay sound.) 4. Defective solenoid(s) or wiring to the solenoid(s)
All power seat functions are operative except one.	1. Defective motor 2. Defective solenoid or wiring to the solenoid

Electric Power Door Lock

Problem	Possible Causes and/or Solutions
Power door locks are inoperative.	1. Defective circuit breaker, fuse, or wiring to the switch or relay (if used) 2. Defective relay (if used); defective switch 3. Defective door lock solenoid or ground for solenoid (if solenoid operated) 4. Open in the wiring to the door lock solenoid or the motor 5. Mechanical obstruction of the door lock mechanism
Only one door lock is inoperative.	1. Defective switch; poor ground on the solenoid (if solenoid operated) 2. Defective door lock solenoid or motor; poor electrical connection at the motor or solenoid

Rear Window Defogger

Problem	Possible Causes and/or Solutions
Rear window defogger is inoperative.	1. Proper operation by performing breath test and/or voltmeter (Check at the power side of the rear window grid.); defective relay or timer assembly 2. Defective switch 3. Open ground connection at the rear window grid (● SEE FIGURE 26–32.) NOTE: If there is an open circuit (power side or ground side), the dash indicator light will still operate in most cases.
Rear window defogger cleans only a portion of the rear window.	1. Broken grid wire(s) or poor electrical connections at either the power side or the ground side of the wire grid

DOOR PANEL REMOVAL

1 Looking at the door panel there appears to be no visible fasteners.

2 Gently prying at the edge of the light shows that it snaps in place and can be easily removed.

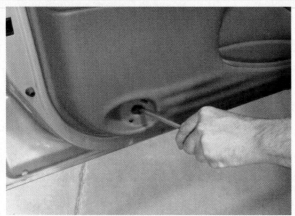

3 Under the red "door open" warning light is a fastener.

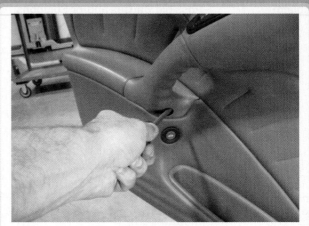

4 Another screw is found under the armrest.

5 A screw is removed from the bezel around the interior door handle.

6 The electric control panel is held in by clips.

7 Another screw is found after the control panel is removed.

8 The panel beside the outside mirror is removed by gently prying.

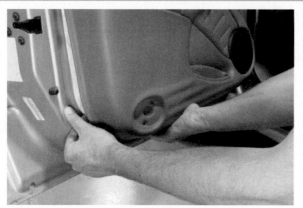

9 A gentle tug and the door panel is removed.

10 The sound-deadening material also acts as a moisture barrier and would need to be removed to gain access to the components inside the door.

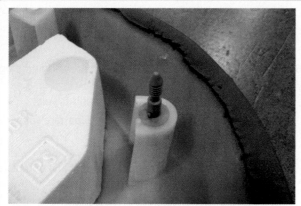

11 Carefully inspect the door panel clips before reinstalling the door panel.

12 Align and press the door panel clips into the openings and reinstall all of the fasteners and components.

SUMMARY

1. Most power windows and power door locks use a permanent magnet motor that has a built-in circuit breaker and is reversible. The control switches and relays direct the current through the motors.

2. The current flow through a rear window defogger is often self-regulating. As the temperature of the grid increases, its resistance increases, reducing current flow. Some rear window defoggers are also used as radio antennas.

3. Radar cruise control systems use many of the same components as the precollision system.

4. Remote keyless entry systems use a wireless transmitter built into the key fob to operate the power door lock.

5. Factory antitheft systems must function properly to allow the engine to crank and/or start.

REVIEW QUESTIONS

1. How do power door locks on a four-door vehicle function with only one ground wire connection?

2. How does a rear window defogger regulate how much current flows through the grids based on temperature?

3. What is the usual procedure to follow to resynchronize a remote keyless entry transmitter?

4. How do heated and cooled seats operate?

CHAPTER QUIZ

1. The owner of a vehicle equipped with cruise control complains that the cruise control often stops working when driving over rough or bumpy pavement. Technician A says the brake switch may be out of adjustment. Technician B says a defective servo unit is the most likely cause. Which technician is correct?
   a. Technician A only
   b. Technician B only
   c. Both Technicians A and B
   d. Neither Technician A nor B

2. Technician A says that the cruise control on a vehicle that uses an electronic throttle control (ETC) system uses a servo to move the throttle. Technician B says that the cruise control on a vehicle with ETC uses the APP sensor to set the speed. Which technician is correct?
   a. Technician A only
   b. Technician B only
   c. Both Technicians A and B
   d. Neither Technician A nor B

3. All power windows fail to operate from the independent switches but all power windows operate from the master switch. Technician A says the window lockout switch may be on. Technician B says the power window relay could be defective. Which technician is correct?
   a. Technician A only
   b. Technician B only
   c. Both Technicians A and B
   d. Neither Technician A nor B

4. Technician A says that a defective ground connection at the master control switch (driver's side) could cause the failure of all power windows. Technician B says that if *one* control wire is disconnected, all windows will fail to operate. Which technician is correct?
   a. Technician A only
   b. Technician B only
   c. Both Technicians A and B
   d. Neither Technician A nor B

5. A typical radar cruise control system uses _____.
   a. Long-range radar (LRR)
   b. Short-range radar (SRR)
   c. Electronic throttle control system to control vehicle speed
   d. All of the above

6. When checking the operation of a rear window defogger with a voltmeter, _____.
   a. The voltmeter should be set to read AC volts
   b. The voltmeter should read close to battery voltage anywhere along the grid
   c. Voltage should be available anytime at the power side of the grid because the control circuit just completes the ground side of the heater grid circuit
   d. The voltmeter should indicate decreasing voltage when the grid is tested across the width of the glass

7. PM motors used in power windows, mirrors, and seats can be reversed by _____.

   a. Sending current to a reversed field coil
   b. Reversing the polarity of the current to the motor
   c. Using a reverse relay circuit
   d. Using a relay and a two-way clutch

8. If only one power door lock is inoperative, a possible cause is a _____.

   a. Poor ground connection at the power door lock relay
   b. Defective door lock motor (or solenoid)
   c. Defective (open) circuit breaker for the power circuit
   d. Defective (open) fuse for the control circuit

9. A keyless remote control stops working. Technician A says the battery in the remote could be dead. Technician B says that the key fob may have to be resynchronized. Which technician is correct?

   a. Technician A only
   b. Technician B only
   c. Both Technicians A and B
   d. Neither Technician A nor B

10. Two technicians are discussing antitheft systems. Technician A says that some systems require a special key. Technician B says that some systems use a computer chip in the key. Which technician is correct?

    a. Technician A only
    b. Technician B only
    c. Both Technicians A and B
    d. Neither Technician A nor B

AIRBAG AND PRETENSIONER CIRCUITS

After studying Chapter 27, the reader will be able to:

1. Prepare for ASE Electrical/Electronic Systems (A6) certification test content area "H" (Accessories Diagnosis and Repair).

2. List the appropriate safety precautions to be followed when working with airbag systems.

3. Describe the procedures to diagnose and repair common faults in airbag systems.

4. Explain how the passenger presence system works.

Airbag 436

Arming sensor 437

Clockspring 440

Deceleration sensor 439

Dual-stage airbags 440

EDR 447

Integral sensor 439

Knee airbags 443

Occupant detection systems (ODS) 445

Passenger presence system (PPS) 445

Pretensioners 436

SAR 436

Side airbags 447

SIR 436

Squib 437

SRS 436

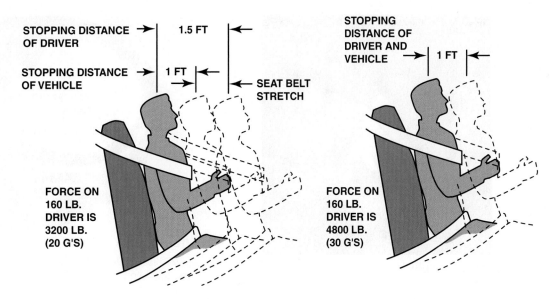

STOPPING DISTANCE OF DRIVER → 1.5 FT ←

STOPPING DISTANCE OF VEHICLE → 1 FT ←

STOPPING DISTANCE OF DRIVER AND VEHICLE → 1 FT ←

SEAT BELT STRETCH

FORCE ON 160 LB. DRIVER IS 3200 LB. (20 G'S)

FORCE ON 160 LB. DRIVER IS 4800 LB. (30 G'S)

FIGURE 27–1 (a) Safety belts are the primary restraint system. (b) During a collision the stretching of the safety belt slows the impact to help reduce bodily injury.

CRASH SCENARIO WITH VEHICLE STOPPING IN ONE FOOT DISTANCE FROM A SPEED OF 30 MPH.

SAFETY BELTS AND RETRACTORS

SAFETY BELTS   Safety belts are used to keep the driver and passengers secured to the vehicle in the event of a collision. Most safety belts include three-point support and are constructed of nylon webbing about 2 in. (5 cm) wide. The three support points include two points on either side of the seat for the belt over the lap and one crossing over the upper torso, which is attached to the "B" pillar or seat back. Every crash consists of three types of collisions.

Collision 1: The vehicle strikes another vehicle or object.

Collision 2: The driver and/or passengers hit objects inside the vehicle if unbelted.

Collision 3: The internal organs of the body hit other organs or bones, which causes internal injuries.

If a safety belt is being worn, the belt stretches, absorbing a lot of the impact, thereby preventing collision with other objects in the vehicle and reducing internal injuries. ● **SEE FIGURE 27–1.**

BELT RETRACTORS   Safety belts are also equipped with one of the following types of retractors.

- Nonlocking retractors, which are used primarily on recoiling
- Emergency locking retractors, which lock the position of the safety belt in the event of a collision or rollover

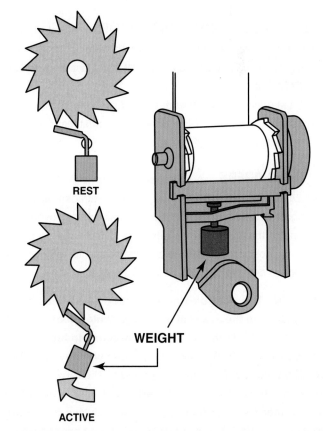

REST

WEIGHT

ACTIVE

FIGURE 27–2 Most safety belts have an inertia-type mechanism that locks the belt in the event of rapid movement.

- Emergency and web speed-sensitive retractors, which allow freedom of movement for the driver and passenger but lock if the vehicle is accelerating too fast or if the vehicle is decelerating too fast

● **SEE FIGURE 27–2** for an example of an inertia-type seat belt locking mechanism.

FIGURE 27–3 A typical safety belt warning light.

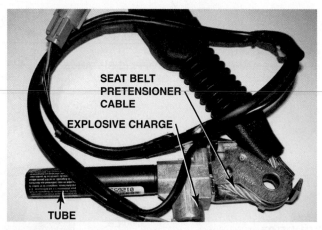

FIGURE 27–4 A small explosive charge in the pre-tensioner forces the end of the seat belt down the tube, which removes any slack in the seat belt.

SAFETY BELTS AND RETRACTORS (CONTINUED)

SAFETY BELT LIGHTS AND CHIMES All late-model vehicles are equipped with a safety belt warning light on the dash and a chime that sounds if the belt is not fastened. ● **SEE FIGURE 27–3.**

Some vehicles will intermittently flash the reminder light and sound a chime until the driver and sometimes the front passenger fasten their safety belts.

PRETENSIONERS A **pretensioner** is an explosive (pyrotechnic) device that is part of the seat belt retractor assembly and tightens the seat belt as the airbag is being deployed. The purpose of the pretensioning device is to force the occupant back into position against the seat back and to remove any slack in the seat belt. ● **SEE FIGURE 27–4.**

CAUTION: The seat belt pretensioner assemblies must be replaced in the event of an airbag deployment. Always follow the vehicle manufacturer's recommended service procedure. Pretensioners are explosive devices that could be ignited if voltage is applied to the terminals. Do not use a jumper wire or powered test light around the wiring near the seat belt latch wiring. Always follow the vehicle manufacturer's recommended test procedures.

FRONT AIRBAGS

PURPOSE AND FUNCTION **Airbag** passive restraints are designed to cushion the driver (or passenger, if the passenger side is so equipped) during a frontal collision. The system consists of one or more nylon bags folded up in compartments located in the steering wheel, dashboard, interior panels, or side pillars of the vehicle. During a crash of sufficient force, pressurized gas instantly fills the airbag and then deploys out of the storage compartment to protect the occupant from serious injury. These airbag systems may be known by many different names, including the following:

1. **Supplemental restraint system (SRS)**
2. **Supplemental inflatable restraints (SIR)**
3. **Supplemental air restraints (SAR)**

Most airbags are designed to supplement the safety belts in the event of a collision, and front airbags are meant to be deployed only in the event of a frontal impact within 30 degrees of center. Front (driver and passenger side) airbag systems are *not* designed to inflate during side or rear impact. The force required to deploy a typical airbag is approximately equal to the force of a vehicle hitting a wall at over 10 mph (16 km/hr).

The force required to trigger the sensors within the system prevents accidental deployment if curbs are hit or the brakes are rapidly applied. The system requires a substantial force to deploy the airbag to help prevent accidental inflation.

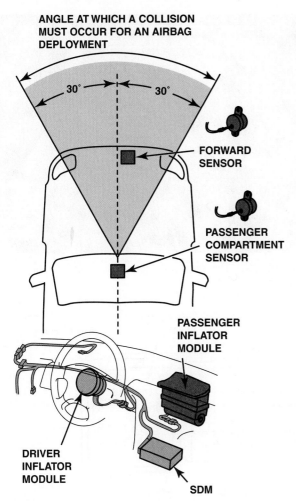

FIGURE 27–5 A typical airbag system showing many of the components. The SDM is the "sensing and diagnostic module" and includes the arming sensor as well as the electronics that keep checking the circuits for continuity and the capacitors that are discharged to deploy the air bags.

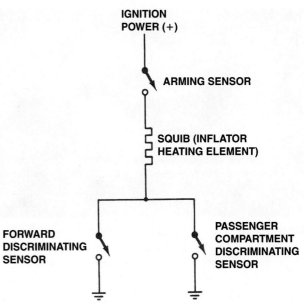

FIGURE 27–6 A simplified airbag deployment circuit. Note that both the arming sensor and at least one of the discriminating sensors must be activated at the same time. The arming sensor provides the power, and either one of the discriminating sensors can provide the ground for the circuit.

- The arming sensor provides the electrical power to the airbag heating unit, called a **squib**, inside the inflator module.
- The squib uses electrical power and converts it into heat for ignition of the propellant used to inflate the airbag.
- Before the airbag can inflate, however, the squib circuit also must have a ground provided by the forward or the discriminating sensor. In other words, two sensors (arming and forward sensors) *must* be triggered *at the same time* before the airbag will be deployed. ● **SEE FIGURE 27–6.**

PARTS INVOLVED ● SEE FIGURE 27–5 for an overall
view of the parts included in a typical airbag system.

The parts include:

1. Sensors
2. Airbag (inflator) module
3. Clockspring wire coil in the steering column
4. Control module
5. Wiring and connectors

OPERATION To cause inflation, the following events must
occur.

- To cause a deployment of the airbag, two sensors must be triggered at the same time. The **arming sensor** is used to provide electrical power, and a *forward* or *discriminating sensor* is used to provide the ground connection.

TYPES OF AIRBAG INFLATORS There are two different
types of inflators used in airbags.

1. **Solid fuel.** This type uses sodium azide pellets and, when ignited, generates a large quantity of nitrogen gas that quickly inflates the airbag. This was the first type used and is still commonly used in driver and passenger side airbag inflator modules. ● **SEE FIGURE 27–7.** The squib is the electrical heating element used to ignite the gas-generating material, usually sodium azide. It requires about 2 A of current to heat the heating element and ignite the inflator.

2. **Compressed gas.** Commonly used in passenger side airbags and roof-mounted systems, the compressed gas system uses a canister filled with argon gas, plus a small percentage of helium at 3,000 psi (435 kPa). A small igniter ruptures a burst disc to release the gas when energized. The compressed gas inflators are long cylinders that can

FIGURE 27-7 The inflator module is being removed from the airbag housing. The squib, inside the inflator module, is the heating element that ignites the pyrotechnic gas generator that rapidly produces nitrogen gas to fill the airbag.

FRONT AIRBAGS (CONTINUED)

be installed inside the instrument panel, seat back, door panel, or along any side rail or pillar of the vehicle. ● SEE FIGURE 27-8.

Once the inflator is ignited, the nylon bag quickly inflates (in about 30 ms or 0.030 second) with nitrogen gas generated by the inflator. During an actual frontal collision accident, the driver is being thrown forward by the driver's own momentum toward the steering wheel. The strong nylon bag inflates at the same time. Personal injury is reduced by the spreading of the stopping force over the entire upper-body region. The normal collapsible steering column remains in operation and collapses in a collision when equipped with an airbag system. The bag is equipped with two large side vents that allow the bag to deflate immediately after inflation, once the bag has cushioned the occupant in a collision.

TIMELINE FOR AIRBAG DEPLOYMENT Following are the times necessary for an airbag deployment in milliseconds (each millisecond is equal to 0.001 second or 1/1,000 of a second).

1. Collision occurs: 0.0 ms
2. Sensors detect collision: 16 ms (0.016 second)
3. Airbag is deployed and seam cover rips: 40 ms (0.040 second)
4. Airbag is fully inflated: 100 ms (0.100 second)
5. Airbag deflated: 250 ms (0.250 second)

In other words, an airbag deployment occurs and is over in about a quarter of a second.

SENSOR OPERATION All three sensors are basically switches that complete an electrical circuit when activated. The sensors are similar in construction and operation, and the *location* of the sensor determines its name. All airbag sensors are

FIGURE 27-8 This shows a deployed side curtain airbag on a training vehicle.

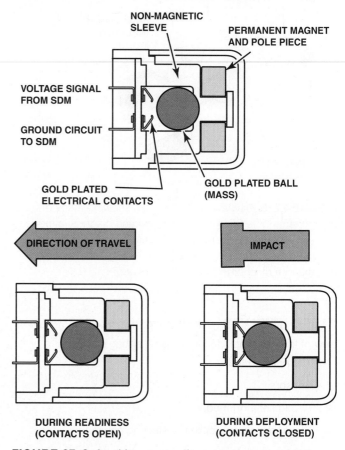

FIGURE 27-9 An airbag magnetic sensor.

rigidly mounted to the vehicle and *must* be mounted with the arrow pointing toward the front of the vehicle to ensure that the sensor can detect rapid forward deceleration.

There are three basic styles (designs) of airbag sensors.

1. **Magnetically retained gold-plated ball sensor.** This sensor uses a permanent magnet to hold a gold-plated steel ball away from two gold-plated electrical contacts. ● SEE FIGURE 27-9.

CRASH SENSOR

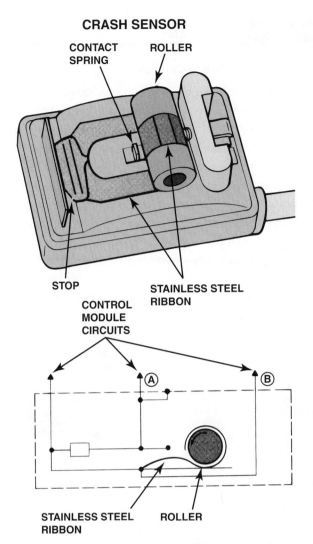

FIGURE 27–10 Some vehicles use a ribbon-type crash sensor.

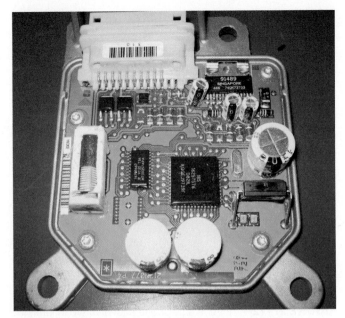

FIGURE 27–11 A sensing and diagnostic module that includes an accelerometer.

If the vehicle (and the sensor) stops rapidly enough, the steel ball is released from the magnet because the inertia force of the crash was sufficient to overcome the magnetic pull on the ball and then makes contact with the two gold-plated electrodes. The steel ball only remains in contact with the electrodes for a relatively short time because the steel ball is drawn back into contact with the magnet.

2. **Rolled up stainless-steel ribbon-type sensor.** This sensor is housed in an airtight package with nitrogen gas inside to prevent harmful corrosion of the sensor parts. If the vehicle (and the sensor) stops rapidly, the stainless-steel roll "unrolls" and contacts the two gold-plated contacts. Once the force is stopped, the stainless-steel roll will roll back into its original shape. ● **SEE FIGURE 27–10.**

3. **Integral sensor.** Some vehicles use electronic **deceleration sensors** built into the inflator module, called **integral sensors**. For example, General Motors uses the term *sensing and diagnostic module (SDM)* to describe their integrated sensor/module assembly. These units contain an accelerometer-type sensor which measures the rate of deceleration and, through computer logic, determines if the airbags should be deployed. ● **SEE FIGURE 27–11.**

TWO-STAGE AIRBAGS Two-stage airbags, often called advanced airbags or smart airbags, use an accelerometer-type of sensor to detect force of the impact. This type of sensor measures the actual amount of deceleration rate of the vehicle and is used to determine whether one or both elements of a two-stage airbag should be deployed.

- **Low-stage deployment.** This lower force deployment is used if the accelerometer detects a low-speed crash.
- **High-stage deployment.** This stage is used if the accelerometer detects a higher speed crash or a more rapid deceleration rate.
- **Both low- and high-stage deployment.** Under severe high-speed crashes, both stages can be deployed. ● **SEE FIGURE 27–12.**

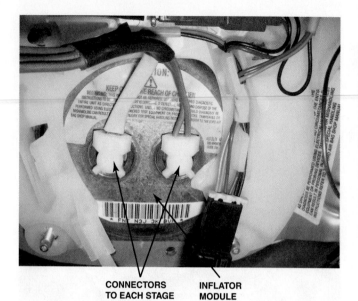

CONNECTORS TO EACH STAGE **INFLATOR MODULE**

FIGURE 27–12 A driver's side airbag showing two inflator connectors. One is for the lower force inflator and the other is for the higher force inflator. Either can be ignited or both at the same time if the deceleration sensor detects a severe impact.

FRONT AIRBAGS (CONTINUED)

WIRING Wiring and connectors are very important for proper identification and long life. Airbag-related circuits have the following features.

- All electrical wiring connectors and conduit for airbags are colored yellow.

- To ensure proper electrical connection to the inflator module in the steering wheel, a coil assembly is used in the steering column. This coil is a ribbon of copper wires that operates much like a window shade when the steering wheel is rotated. As the steering wheel is rotated, this coil, usually called a **clockspring,** prevents the lack of continuity between the sensors and the inflator assembly that might result from a horn-ring type of sliding conductor.

- Inside the yellow plastic airbag connectors are gold-plated terminals which are used to prevent corrosion.

  ● **SEE FIGURE 27–13.**

Most airbag systems also contain a diagnostic unit that often includes an auxiliary power supply, which is used to provide the current to inflate the airbag if the battery is disconnected from the vehicle during a collision. This auxiliary power supply normally uses capacitors that are discharged through the squib of the inflation module. When the ignition is turned off these capacitors are discharged. Therefore, after a few minutes an airbag system will not deploy if the vehicle is hit while parked.

AIRBAG DIAGNOSIS TOOLS AND EQUIPMENT

SELF-TEST PROCEDURE The electrical portion of airbag systems is constantly checked by the circuits within the airbag-energizing power unit or through the airbag controller. The electrical airbag components are monitored by applying a small-signal voltage from the airbag controller through the various sensors and components. Each component and sensor uses a resistor in parallel with the load or open sensor switch for use by the diagnostic signals. If continuity exists, the testing circuits will measure a small voltage drop. If an open or short circuit occurs, a dash warning light is lighted and a possible diagnostic trouble code (DTC) is stored. Follow exact manufacturer's recommended procedures for accessing and erasing airbag diagnostic trouble codes.

Diagnosis and service of airbag systems usually require some or all of the following items.

- Digital multimeter (DMM)
- Airbag simulator, often called a load tool
- Scan tool
- Shorting bar or shorting connector(s)
- Airbag system tester
- Vehicle-specific test harness

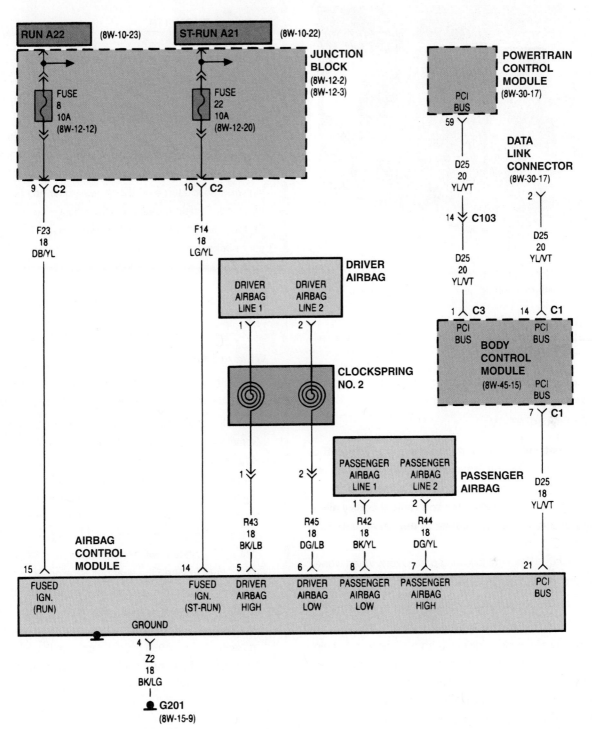

FIGURE 27–13 The airbag control module is linked to the powertrain control module (PCM) and the body control module (BCM) on this Chrysler system. Notice the airbag wire connecting the module to the airbag through the clockspring. Both power, labeled "driver airbag high" and ground, labeled "driver airbag low" are conducted through the clockspring.

FIGURE 27–14 An airbag diagnostic tester. Included in the plastic box are electrical connectors and a load tool that substitutes for the inflator module during troubleshooting.

AIRBAG DIAGNOSIS TOOLS
AND EQUIPMENT (CONTINUED)

- Special wire repair tools or connectors, such as crimp-and-seal weatherproof connectors
  - **SEE FIGURE 27–14.**

CAUTION: Most vehicle manufacturers specify that the negative battery terminal be removed when testing or working around airbags. Be aware that a memory saver device used to keep the computer and radio memory alive can supply enough electrical power to deploy an airbag.

PRECAUTIONS Take the following precautions when working with or around airbags.

1. Always follow all precautions and warning stickers on vehicles equipped with airbags.

2. Maintain a safe working distance from all airbags to help prevent the possibility of personal injury in the unlikely event of an unintentional airbag deployment.
   - Side impact airbag: 5 in. (13 cm) distance
   - Driver front airbag: 10 in. (25 cm) distance
   - Passenger front airbag: 20 in. (50 cm) distance

3. In the event of a collision in which the bag(s) is deployed, the inflator module *and* all sensors usually must be replaced to ensure proper future operation of the system.

4. Avoid using a self-powered test light around the yellow airbag wiring. Even though it is highly unlikely, a self-powered test light could provide the necessary current to accidentally set off the inflator module and cause an airbag deployment.

5. Use care when handling the inflator module section when it is removed from the steering wheel. Always hold the inflator away from your body.

6. If handling a deployed inflator module, always wear gloves and safety glasses to avoid the possibility of skin irritation from the sodium hydroxide dust, which is used as a lubricant on the bag(s), that remains after deployment.

7. Never jar or strike a sensor. The contacts inside the sensor may be damaged, preventing the proper operation of the airbag system in the event of a collision.

8. When mounting a sensor in a vehicle, make certain that the arrow on the sensor is pointing toward the front of the vehicle. Also be certain that the sensor is securely mounted.

AIRBAG SYSTEM SERVICE

DIS-ARMING The airbags should be dis-armed, (temporarily disconnected), whenever performing service work on any of the follow locations.

- Steering wheel
- Dash or instrument panel
- Glove box (instrument panel storage compartment)

Check service information for the exact procedure, which usually includes the following steps.

STEP 1 Disconnect the negative battery cable.

STEP 2 Remove the airbag fuse (has a yellow cover).

STEP 3 Disconnect the yellow electrical connector located at the base of the steering column to disable the driver's side airbag.

STEP 4 Disconnect the yellow electrical connector for the passenger side airbag.

This procedure is called "disabling air bags" in most service information. Always follow the vehicle manufacturer's specified procedures.

DIAGNOSTIC AND SERVICE PROCEDURE

Airbag system components and their location in the vehicle vary according to system design, but the basic principles of testing are the same as for other electrical circuits. Use service information to determine how the circuit is designed and the correct sequence of tests to be followed.

- Some airbag systems require the use of special testers. The built-in safety circuits of such testers prevent accidental deployment of the airbag.
- If such a tester is not available, follow the recommended alternative test procedures specified by the manufacturer.
- Access the self-diagnostic system and check for diagnostic trouble code (DTC) records.
- The scan tool is needed to access the data stream on most systems.

SELF-DIAGNOSIS

All airbag systems can detect system electrical faults, and if found will disable the system and notify the driver through an airbag warning lamp in the instrument cluster. Depending on circuit design, a system fault may cause the warning lamp to fail to illuminate, remain lit continuously, or flash. Some systems use a tone generator that produces an audible warning when a system fault occurs or if the warning lamp is inoperative.

? **FREQUENTLY ASKED QUESTION**

Why Change Knee Bolsters If Switching to Larger Wheels?

Larger wheels and tires can be installed on vehicles, but the powertrain control module (PCM) needs to be reprogrammed so the speedometer and other systems that are affected by a change in wheel/tire size can work effectively. When 20 in. wheels are installed on General Motors trucks or sport utility vehicles (SUVs), GM specifies that replacement knee bolsters be installed. Knee bolsters are the padded area located on the lower part of the dash where a driver or passenger's knees would hit in the event of a front collision. The reason for the need to replace the knee bolsters is to maintain the crash testing results. The larger 20 in. wheels would tend to be forced further into the passenger compartment in the event of a front-end collision. Therefore to maintain the frontal crash rating standard, the larger knee bolsters are required.

WARNING: Failure to perform the specified changes when changing wheels and tires could result in the vehicle not being able to provide occupant protection as designed by the crash test star rating that the vehicle originally achieved.

The warning lamp should illuminate with the ignition key on and engine off as a bulb check. If not, the diagnostic module is likely disabling the system. If the airbag warning light remains on, the airbags may or may not be disabled, depending on the specific vehicle and the fault detected. Some warning lamp circuits have a timer that extinguishes the lamp after a few seconds. The airbag system generally does not require service unless there is a failed component. However, a steering wheel–mounted airbag module is routinely removed and replaced in order to service switches and other column-mounted devices.

KNEE AIRBAGS

Some vehicles are equipped with **knee airbags** usually on the driver's side. Use caution if working under the dash and always follow the vehicle manufacturer's specified service procedures.

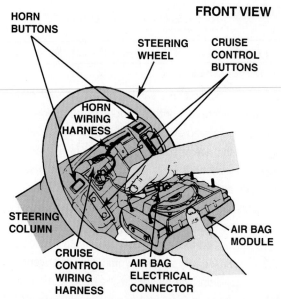

HORN
BUTTONS

STEERING
WHEEL

CRUISE
CONTROL
BUTTONS

HORN
WIRING
HARNESS

STEERING
COLUMN

CRUISE
CONTROL
WIRING
HARNESS

AIR BAG
ELECTRICAL
CONNECTOR

AIR BAG
MODULE

FIGURE 27–15 After disconnecting the battery and the yellow connector at the base of the steering column, the airbag inflator module can be removed from the steering wheel and the yellow airbag electrical connector at the inflator module disconnected.

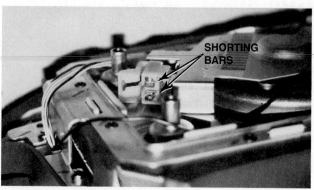

SHORTING
BARS

FIGURE 27–16 Shorting bars are used in most airbag connectors. These spring-loaded clips short across both terminals of an airbag connector when it is disconnected to help prevent accidental deployment of the airbag. If electrical power was applied to the terminals, the shorting bars would simply provide a low-resistance path to the other terminal and not allow current to flow past the connector. The mating part of the connector has a tapered piece that spreads apart the shorting bars when the connector is reconnected.

DRIVER SIDE AIRBAG MODULE REPLACEMENT

For the specific model being serviced, carefully follow the procedures provided by the vehicle manufacturer to disable and remove the airbag module. Failure to do so may result in serious injury and extensive damage to the vehicle. Replacing a discharged airbag is costly. The following procedure reviews the basic steps for removing an airbag module. Do not substitute these general instructions for the specific procedure recommended by the manufacturer.

1. Turn the steering wheel until the front wheels are positioned straight ahead. Some components on the steering column are removed only when the front wheels are straight.

2. Switch the ignition off and disconnect the negative battery cable, which cuts power to the airbag module.

3. Once the battery is disconnected, wait as long as recommended by the manufacturer before continuing. When in doubt, wait at least 10 minutes to make sure the capacitor is completely discharged.

4. Loosen and remove the nuts or screws that hold the airbag module in place. On some vehicles, these fasteners are located on the back of the steering wheel. On other vehicles, they are located on each side of the steering wheel. The fasteners may be concealed with plastic finishing covers that must be pried off with a small screwdriver to access them.

5. Carefully lift the airbag module from the steering wheel and disconnect the electrical connector. Connector location varies: Some are below the steering wheel behind a plastic trim cover; others are at the top of the column under the module. ● **SEE FIGURES 27–15 AND 27–16.**

6. Store the module pad side up in a safe place where it will not be disturbed or damaged while the vehicle is being serviced. Do not attempt to disassemble the airbag module. If the airbag is defective, replace the entire assembly.

When installing the airbag module, make sure the clockspring is correctly positioned to ensure module-to-steering-column continuity. ● **SEE FIGURE 27–17.**

Always route the wiring exactly as it was before removal. Also, make sure the module seats completely into the steering wheel. Secure the assembly using new fasteners, if specified.

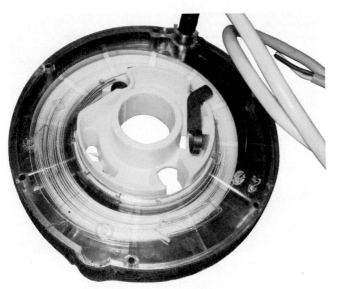

FIGURE 27-17 An airbag clockspring showing the flat conductor wire. It must be properly positioned to ensure proper operation.

FIGURE 27-18 An airbag being deployed as part of a demonstration in an automotive laboratory.

SAFETY WHEN MANUALLY DEPLOYING AIRBAGS

Airbag modules cannot be disposed of unless they are deployed. Do the following to prevent injury when manually deploying an airbag.

- When possible, deploy the airbag outside of the vehicle. Follow the vehicle manufacturer's recommendations.
- Follow the vehicle manufacturer's procedures and equipment recommendations.
- Wear the proper hearing and eye protection.
- Deploy the airbag with the trim cover facing up.
- Stay at least 20 ft (6 m) from the airbag. (Use long jumper wires attached to the wiring and routed outside the vehicle to a battery.)
- Allow the airbag module to cool.
  - ● **SEE FIGURE 27-18.**

FIGURE 27-19 A dash warning lamp will light if the passenger side airbag is off because no passenger was detected by the seat sensor.

OCCUPANT DETECTION SYSTEMS

PURPOSE AND FUNCTION The U.S. Federal Motor Vehicle Safety Standard 208 (FMVSS) specifies that the passenger side airbag be disabled or deployed with reduced force under the following conditions. This system is referred to as an **occupant detection system (ODS)** or the **passenger presence system (PPS)**.

- When there is no weight on the seat and no seat belt is fastened, the passenger side airbag will not deploy and the passenger airbag light should be off. ● **SEE FIGURE 27-19.**

- The passenger side airbag will be disabled and the disabled airbag light will be on if only 10 to 37 lb (4.5 to 17 kg) is on the passenger seat, which would generally represent a seated child.

FIGURE 27–20 The passenger side airbag "on" lamp will light if a passenger is detected on the passenger seat.

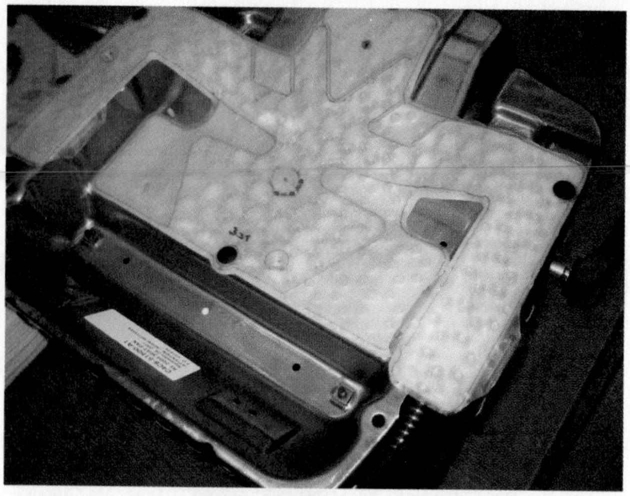

FIGURE 27–21 A gel-filled (bladder-type) occupant detection sensor showing the pressure sensor and wiring.

OCCUPANT DETECTION SYSTEMS (CONTINUED)

- If 38 to 99 lb (17 to 45 kg) is detected on the passenger seat, which represents a child or small adult, the airbag will deploy at a decreased force.

- If 99 lb (45 kg) or more is detected on the passenger seat, the airbag will deploy at full force, depending on the severity of the crash, speed of the vehicle, and other factors which may result in the airbag deploying at a reduced force.
  ● SEE FIGURE 27–20.

TYPE OF SEAT SENSOR The passenger presence system (PPS) uses one of three types of sensors.

- **Gel-filled bladder sensor.** This type of occupant sensor uses a silicone-filled bag that has a pressure sensor attached. The weight of the passenger is measured by the pressure sensor, which sends a voltage signal to the module controlling the airbag deployment. A safety belt tension sensor is also used with a gel-filled bladder system to monitor the tension on the belt. The module then uses the information from both the bladder and the seat belt sensor to determine if a tightened belt may be used to restrain a child seat. ● SEE FIGURE 27–21.

- **Capacitive strip sensors.** This type of occupant sensor uses several flexible conductive metal strips under the seat cushion. These sensor strips transmit and receive a low-level electric field, which changes due to the weight of the front passenger seat occupant. The module determines the weight of the occupant based on the sensor values.

FIGURE 27–22 A resistor-type occupant detection sensor. The weight of the passenger strains these resistors, which are attached to the seat, thereby signaling to the module the weight of the occupant.

- **Force-sensing resistor sensors.** This type of occupant sensor uses resistors, which change their resistance based on the stress that is applied. These resistors are part of the seat structure, and the module can determine the weight of the occupant based on the change in the resistance of the sensors. ● SEE FIGURE 27–22.

CAUTION: Because the resistors are part of the seat structure, it is very important that all seat fasteners be torqued to factory specifications to ensure proper operation of the occupant detection system. A *seat track position (STP) sensor* is used by the airbag controller to determine the position of the seat. If the seat is too close to the airbag, the controller may disable the airbag.

DIAGNOSING OCCUPANT DETECTION SYSTEMS

A fault in the system may cause the passenger side airbag light to turn on when there is no weight on the seat. A scan tool is often used to check or calibrate the seat, which must be empty, by commanding the module to rezero the seat sensor. Some systems, such as those on Chrysler vehicles, use a unit that has various weights along with a scan tool to calibrate and diagnose the occupant detection system. ● SEE FIGURE 27–23.

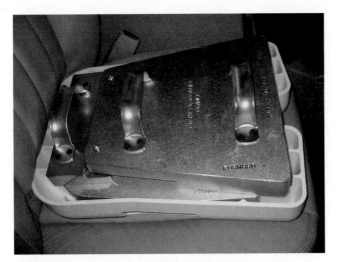

FIGURE 27–23 A test weight is used to calibrate the occupant detection system on a Chrysler vehicle.

FIGURE 27–24 A typical seat (side) airbag that deploys from the side of the seat.

SEAT AND SIDE CURTAIN AIRBAGS

SEAT AIRBAGS Side and/or *curtain airbags* use a variety of sensors to determine if they need to be deployed. **Side airbags** are mounted in one of two general locations.

- In the side bolster of the seat (**SEE FIGURE 27–24.**)

- In the door panel

Most side airbag sensors use an electronic accelerometer to detect when to deploy the airbags, which are usually mounted to the bottom of the left and right "B" pillars (where the front doors latch) behind a trim panel on the inside of the vehicle.

CAUTION: Avoid using a lockout tool (e.g., a "slim jim") in vehicles equipped with side airbags to help prevent damage to the components and wiring in the system.

SIDE CURTAIN AIRBAGS Side curtain airbags are usually deployed by a module based on input from many different sensors, including a lateral acceleration sensor and wheel speed sensors. For example, in one system used by Ford, the ABS controller commands that the brakes on one side of the vehicle be applied, using down pressure while monitoring the wheel speed sensors. If the wheels slow down with little brake pressure, the controller assumes that the vehicle could roll over, thereby deploying the side curtain airbags.

EVENT DATA RECORDERS

PARTS AND OPERATION As part of the airbag controller on many vehicles, the **event data recorder (EDR)** is used to record parameters just before and slightly after an airbag deployment. The following parameters are recorded.

- Vehicle speed

- Brake on/off

- Seat belt fastened

- G-forces as measured by the accelerometer

Unlike an airplane event data recorder, a vehicle unit is not a separate unit and does not record voice conversations and does not include all crash parameters. This means that additional crash data, such as skid marks and physical evidence at the crash site, will be needed to fully reconstruct the incident.

The EDR is embedded into the airbag controller and receives data from many sources and at varying sample rates. The data is constantly being stored in a memory buffer and not recorded into the EPROM unless an airbag deployment has been commanded. The combined data is known as an *event file*. The airbag is commanded on, based on input mainly from the accelerometer sensor. This sensor, usually built into the airbag controller, is located inside the vehicle. The accelerometer calculates the rate of change of the speed of the vehicle. This determines the acceleration rate and is used to predict if that rate is high enough to deploy the frontal airbags. The airbags will be deployed if the threshold g-value is exceeded. The passenger side airbag will also be deployed unless it is suppressed by either of the following:

- No passenger is detected.
- The passenger side airbag switch is off.

DATA EXTRACTION   Data extraction from the event data recorder in the airbag controller can only be achieved using a piece of equipment known as the Crash Data Retrieval System, manufactured by Vetronics Corporation. This is the only authorized method for retrieving event files and only certain organizations are allowed access to the data. These groups or organizations include:

- Original equipment manufacturer's representatives
- National Highway Traffic Safety Administration
- Law enforcement agencies
- Accident reconstruction companies

Crash data retrieval must only be done by a trained crash data retrieval (CDR) technician or analyst. A technician undergoes specialized training and must pass an examination. An analyst must attend additional training beyond that of a technician to achieve CDR analyst certification.

SUMMARY

1. Airbags use a sensor(s) to determine if the rate of deceleration is enough to cause bodily harm.

2. All airbag electrical connectors and conduit are yellow and all electrical terminals are gold plated to protect against corrosion.

3. Always follow the manufacturer's procedure for disabling the airbag system prior to any work performed on the system.

4. Frontal airbags only operate within 30 degrees from center and do not deploy in the event of a rollover, side, or rear collision.

5. Two sensors must be triggered at the same time for an airbag deployment to occur. Many newer systems use an accelerometer-type crash sensor that actually measures the amount of deceleration.

6. Pretensioners are explosive (pyrotechnic) devices which remove the slack from the seat belt and help position the occupant.

7. Occupant detection systems use sensors in the seat to determine whether the airbag will be deployed and with full or reduced force.

REVIEW QUESTIONS

1. What are the safety precautions to follow when working around an airbag?

2. What sensor(s) must be triggered for an airbag deployment?

3. How should deployed inflation modules be handled?

4. What is the purpose of pretensioners?

1. A vehicle is being repaired after an airbag deployment. Technician A says that the inflator module should be handled as if it is still live. Technician B says rubber gloves should be worn to prevent skin irritation. Which technician is correct?
   a. Technician A only
   b. Technician B only
   c. Both Technicians A and B
   d. Neither Technician A nor B

2. A seat belt pretensioner is _____.
   a. A device that contains an explosive charge
   b. Used to remove slack from the seat belt in the event of a collision
   c. Used to force the occupant back into position against the seat back in the event of a collision
   d. All of the above

3. What conducts power and ground to the driver's side airbag?
   a. Twisted-pair wires
   b. Clockspring
   c. Carbon contact and brass surface plate on the steering column
   d. Magnetic reed switch

4. Two technicians are discussing dual-stage airbags. Technician A says that a deployed airbag is safe to handle regardless of which stage caused the deployment of the airbag. Technician B says that both stages ignite, but at different speeds depending on the speed of the vehicle. Which technician is correct?
   a. Technician A only
   b. Technician B only
   c. Both Technicians A and B
   d. Neither Technician A nor B

5. Where are shorting bars used?
   a. In pretensioners
   b. At the connectors for airbags
   c. In the crash sensors
   d. In the airbag controller

6. Technician A says that a deployed airbag can be repacked, reused, and reinstalled in the vehicle. Technician B says that a deployed airbag should be discarded and replaced with an entire new assembly. Which technician is correct?
   a. Technician A only
   b. Technician B only
   c. Both Technicians A and B
   d. Neither Technician A nor B

7. What color are the airbag electrical connectors and conduit?
   a. Blue
   b. Red
   c. Yellow
   d. Orange

8. Driver and/or passenger side airbags will only deploy if a collision occurs how many degrees from straight ahead?
   a. 10 degrees
   b. 30 degrees
   c. 60 degrees
   d. 90 degrees

9. How many sensors must be triggered at the same time to cause an airbag deployment?
   a. One
   b. Two
   c. Three
   d. Four

10. The electrical terminals used for airbag systems are unique because they are _____.
    a. Solid copper
    b. Tin-plated heavy-gauge steel
    c. Silver plated
    d. Gold plated

AUDIO SYSTEM OPERATION AND DIAGNOSIS

OBJECTIVES

After studying Chapter 28, the reader will be able to:

1. Prepare for ASE Electrical/Electronic Systems (A6) certification test content area "H" (Accessories Diagnosis and Repair).
2. Describe how AM and FM radio works.
3. Explain how to test speaker polarity.
4. Explain how to match speaker impedance.
5. Explain how crossovers work.
6. List causes and corrections of radio noise and interference.

KEY TERMS

Active crossover 459	Modulation 452
Alternator whine 464	Powerline capacitor 459
AM 452	Radio choke 464
Bluetooth 462	Radio frequency
Crossover 459	(RF) 451
Decibels (dB) 458	RMS 460
Floating ground	SDARS 462
system 457	Skin effect 457
FM 452	Speakers 456
Frequency 451	Stiffening capacitor 459
Ground plane 464	Subwoofer 458
Hertz 451	THD 460
High-pass filter 459	Tweeter 458
Impedance 456	Voice recognition 461
Low-pass filter 459	Wavelength 451

AUDIO FUNDAMENTALS

INTRODUCTION The audio system of today's vehicles is a complex combination of antenna system, receiver, amplifier, and speakers all designed to provide living room–type music reproduction while the vehicle is traveling in city traffic or at highway speed.

Audio systems produce audible sounds and include:

- Radio (AM, FM, and satellite)
- Antenna systems that are used to capture electronic energy broadcast to radios
- Speaker systems
- Aftermarket enhancement devices that increase the sound energy output of an audio system
- Diagnosis of audio-related problems

Many audio-related problems can be addressed and repaired by a service technician.

TYPES OF ENERGY There are two types of energy that affect audio systems.

- **Electromagnetic energy or radio waves.** Antennas capture the radio waves which are then sent to the radio or receiver to be amplified.
- **Acoustical energy, usually called sound.** Radios and receivers amplify the radio wave signals and drive speakers which reproduce the original sound as transmitted by radio waves.
  - ● **SEE FIGURE 28–1.**

TERMINOLOGY Radio waves travel at approximately the speed of light (186,282,000 miles per second) and are electromagnetic. Radio waves are measured in two ways, wavelength and frequency. A radio wave has a series of high points and low points. A **wavelength** is the time and distance between two consecutive points, either high or low. A wavelength is measured in meters. **Frequency**, also known as **radio frequency (RF)**, is the number of times a particular waveform repeats itself in a given amount of time, and is measured in **hertz (Hz)**. A signal with a frequency of 1 Hz is one radio wavelength per second. Radio frequencies are measured in kilohertz (kHz), thousands of wavelengths per second, and megahertz (MHz), millions of wavelengths per second. ● **SEE FIGURE 28–2.**

- The higher the frequency, the shorter the wavelength.
- The lower the frequency, the longer the wavelength.

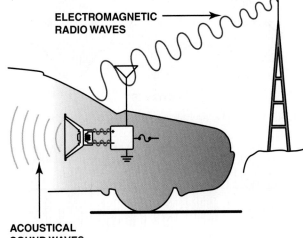

FIGURE 28–1 Audio systems use both electromagnetic radio waves and sound waves to reproduce sound inside the vehicle.

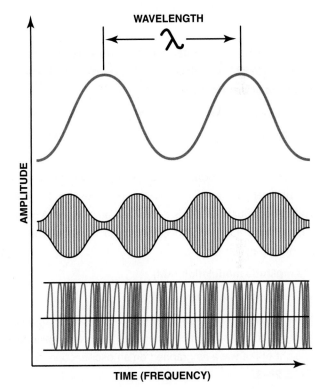

FIGURE 28–2 The relationship among wavelength, frequency, and amplitude.

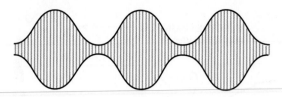

AM WAVES

FIGURE 28–3 The amplitude changes in AM broadcasting.

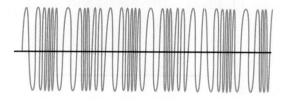

FM WAVES

FIGURE 28–4 The frequency changes in FM broadcasting and the amplitude remains constant.

AUDIO FUNDAMENTALS (CONTINUED)

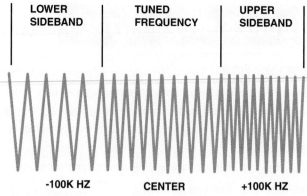

| LOWER SIDEBAND | TUNED FREQUENCY | UPPER SIDEBAND |

-100K HZ   CENTER   +100K HZ

FIGURE 28–5 Using upper and lower sidebands allows stereo to be broadcast. The receiver separates the signals to provide left and right channels.

A longer wavelength can travel a further distance than a shorter wavelength. Therefore, lower frequencies provide better reception at further distances.

- AM radio frequencies range from 530 to 1,710 kHz.
- FM radio frequencies range from 87.9 to 107.9 MHz.

MODULATION

Modulation is the term used to describe when information is added to a constant frequency. The base radio frequency used for RF is called the *carrier wave*. A carrier is a radio wave that is changed to carry information. The two types of modulation are:

- **Amplitude modulation (AM)**
- **Frequency modulation (FM)**

AM waves are radio waves that have amplitude that can be varied, transmitted, and detected by a receiver. Amplitude is the height of the wave as graphed on an oscilloscope. ● **SEE FIGURE 28–3.**

FM waves are also radio waves that have a frequency that can be varied, transmitted, and detected by a receiver. This type of modulation changes the number of cycles per second, or frequency, to carry the information. ● **SEE FIGURE 28–4.**

RADIO WAVE TRANSMISSION

More than one signal can be carried by a radio wave. This process is called *sideband operation.* Sideband frequencies are measured in kilohertz. The amount of the signal above the assigned frequency is referred to as the upper sideband. The amount of the signal below the assigned frequency is called the lower sideband. This capability allows radio signals to carry stereo broadcasts. Stereo broadcasts use the upper sideband to carry one channel of the stereo signal, and the lower sideband to carry the other channel. When the signal is decoded by the radio, these two signals become the right and left channels. ● **SEE FIGURE 28–5.**

NOISE

Because radio waves are a form of electromagnetic energy, other forms of energy can impact them. For example, a bolt of lightning generates broad radio-frequency bandwidths known as radio-frequency interference (RFI). RFI is one type of electromagnetic interference (EMI) and is the frequency that interferes with radio transmission.

AM CHARACTERISTICS

AM radio reception can be achieved over long distances from the transmitter because the waves can bounce off the ionosphere, usually at night. Even during the day, the AM signals can be picked up some distance from the transmitter. AM radio reception depends on a good antenna. If there is a fault in the antenna circuit, AM reception is affected the most.

FM CHARACTERISTICS

Because FM waves have a high RF and a short wavelength, they travel only a short distance. The waves cannot follow the shape of the earth but instead travel in a straight line from the transmitter to the receiver. FM waves will travel through the ionosphere and into space and do not reflect back to earth like AM waves.

What Does a "Capture" Problem Mean?

A capture problem affects only FM reception and means that the receiver is playing more than one station if two stations are broadcasting at the same frequency. Most radios capture the stronger signal and block the weaker signal. However, if the stronger signal is weakened due to being blocked by buildings or mountains, the weaker signal will then be used. When this occurs, it will sound as if the radio is changing stations by itself. This is not a fault with the radio, but simply a rare occurrence with FM radio.

MULTIPATH   Multipath is caused by reflected, refracted, or line of sight signals reaching an antenna at different times. Multipath results from the radio receiving two signals to process on the same frequency. This causes an echo effect in the speakers. *Flutter,* or *picket fencing* as it is sometimes called, is caused by the blocking of part of the FM signal. This blocking causes a weakening of the signal resulting in only part of the signal getting to the antenna, causing an on-again off-again radio sound. Flutter also occurs when the transmitter and the receiving antenna are far apart.

RADIOS AND RECEIVERS

The antenna receives the radio wave where it is converted into very weak fluctuating electrical current. This current travels along the antenna lead-in to the radio that amplifies the signal and sends the new signal to the speakers where it is converted into acoustical energy.

Most late-model radios and receivers use five input/output circuits.

1. **Power.** Usually a constant 12 volt feed to keep the internal clock alive
2. **Ground.** This is the lowest voltage in the circuit and connects indirectly to the negative terminal of the battery.
3. **Serial data.** Used to turn the unit on and off and provide other functions such as steering wheel control operation
4. **Antenna input.** From one or more antennas
5. **Speaker outputs.** These wires connect the receiver to the speakers or as an input to an amplifier.

ANTENNAS

TYPES OF ANTENNAS   The typical radio electromagnetic energy from the broadcast antenna induces a signal in the antenna that is very small, only about 25 microvolts AC (0.000025 VAC) in strength. The radio contains amplifier circuits that increase the received signal strength into usable information.

For example, the five types of antennas used on vehicles include:

- **Slot antenna.** The slot antenna is concealed in the roof of some plastic body vehicles such as older General Motors plastic body vans. This antenna is surrounded by metal on a Mylar sheet.

- **Rear window defogger grid.** This type of system uses the heating wires to receive the signals and special circuitry to separate the RF from the DC heater circuit.

- **Powered mast.** These antennas are controlled by the radio. When the radio is turned on, the antenna is raised; when the radio is shut off, the antenna is retracted. The antenna system consists of an antenna mast and a drive motor controlled by the radio "on" signal through a relay.

- **Fixed mast antenna.** This antenna offers the best overall performance currently available. The mast is simply a vertical rod. Mast antennas are typically located on the fender or rear quarter panel of the vehicle.

- **Integrated antenna.** This type of antenna is sandwiched in the windshield and an appliqué on the rear window glass. The antenna in the rear window is the primary antenna and receives both AM and FM signals. The secondary antenna is located in the front windshield typically on the passenger side of the vehicle. This antenna receives only FM signals.

● **SEE FIGURE 28–6.**

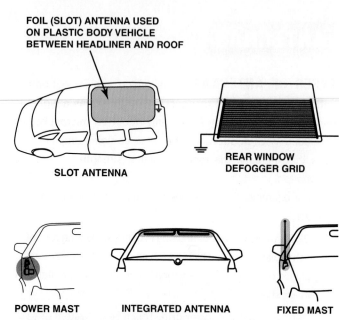

FOIL (SLOT) ANTENNA USED ON PLASTIC BODY VEHICLE BETWEEN HEADLINER AND ROOF

SLOT ANTENNA

REAR WINDOW DEFOGGER GRID

POWER MAST   INTEGRATED ANTENNA   FIXED MAST

FIGURE 28–6 The five types of antennas used on General Motors vehicles include the slot antenna, fixed mast antenna, rear window defogger grid antenna, a powered mast antenna, and an integrated antenna.

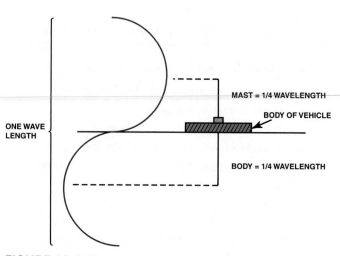

ONE WAVE LENGTH

MAST = 1/4 WAVELENGTH

BODY OF VEHICLE

BODY = 1/4 WAVELENGTH

FIGURE 28–7 The ground plane is actually one-half of the antenna.

ANTENNA DIAGNOSIS

ANTENNA HEIGHT The antenna collects all radio-frequency signals. An AM radio operates best with as long an antenna as possible, but FM reception is best when the antenna height is exactly 31 in. (79 cm). Most fixed-length antennas are, therefore, exactly this height. Even the horizontal section of a windshield antenna is 31 in. (79 cm) long.

A defective antenna will:

- Greatly affect AM radio reception
- May affect FM radio reception

ANTENNA TESTING If the antenna or lead-in cable is broken (open), FM reception will be heard but may be weak, and there will be *no* AM reception. An ohmmeter should read infinity between the center antenna lead and the antenna case. For proper reception and lack of noise, the case of the antenna must be properly grounded to the vehicle body. ● SEE **FIGURE 28–8.**

POWER ANTENNA TESTING AND SERVICE Most power antennas use a circuit breaker and a relay to power a reversible, permanent magnet (PM) electric motor that moves a nylon cord attached to the antenna mast. Some vehicles have a dash-mounted control that can regulate antenna mast height and/or operation, whereas many operate automatically when the radio is turned on and off. The power antenna assembly is usually mounted between the outer and inner front fender or in the rear quarter panel. The unit contains the motor, a spool for the cord, and upper- and lower-limit switches. The power antenna mast is tested in the same way as a fixed-mast

 FREQUENTLY ASKED QUESTION

What Is a Ground Plane?

Antennas designed to pick up the electromagnetic energy that is broadcast through the air to the transmitting antenna are usually one-half wavelength high, and the other half of the wavelength is the **ground plane**. This one-half wavelength in the ground plane is literally underground.

For ideal reception, the receiving antenna should also be the same as the wavelength of the signal. Because this length is not practical, a design compromise uses the length of the antenna as one-fourth of the wavelength; in addition, the body of the vehicle itself is one-fourth of the wavelength. The body of the vehicle, therefore, becomes the ground plane. ● SEE **FIGURE 28–7.**

Any faulty condition in the ground plane circuit will cause the ground plane to lose effectiveness, such as:

- Loose or corroded battery cable terminals
- Acid buildup on battery cables
- Engine grounds with high resistance
- Loss of antenna or audio system grounds
- Defective alternator, causing an AC ripple exceeding 50 mV (0.050 V)

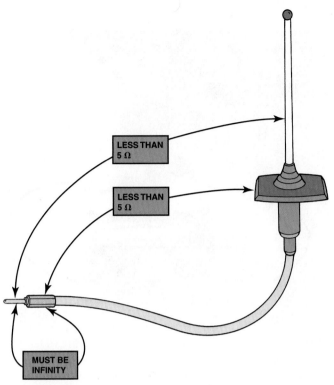

FIGURE 28–8 If all ohmmeter readings are satisfactory, the antenna is good.

FIGURE 28–9 Cutting a small hole in a fender cover helps to protect the vehicle when replacing or servicing an antenna.

> 🔧 **TECH TIP**
>
> **The Hole in the Fender Cover Trick**
>
> A common repair is to replace the mast of a power antenna. To help prevent the possibility of causing damage to the body or paint of the vehicle, cut a hole in a fender cover and place it over the antenna.
> ● **SEE FIGURE 28–9.**
>
> If a wrench or tool slips during the removal or installation process, the body of the vehicle will be protected.

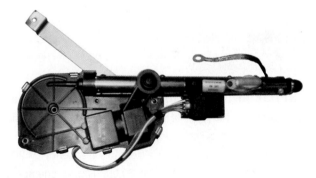

FIGURE 28–10 A typical power antenna assembly. Note the braided ground wire used to ensure that the antenna has a good ground plane.

antenna. (An infinity reading should be noted on an ohmmeter when the antenna is tested between the center antenna terminal and the housing or ground.) Except in the case of cleaning or mast replacement, most power antennas are either replaced as a unit or repaired by specialty shops. ● **SEE FIGURE 28–10.**

Making certain that the drain holes in the motor housing are not plugged with undercoating, leaves, or dirt can prevent many power antenna problems. All power antennas should be kept clean by wiping the mast with a soft cloth and lightly oiling with light oil such as WD-40 or similar.

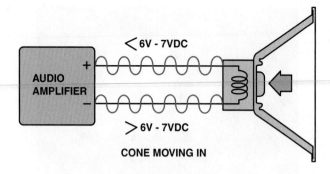

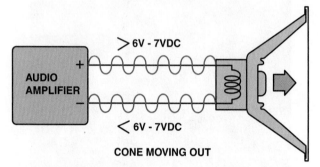

FIGURE 28–11 Between 6 and 7 volts is applied to each speaker terminal, and the audio amplifier then increases the voltage on one terminal and at the same time decreases the voltage on the other terminal causing the speaker cone to move. The moving cone then moves the air, causing sound.

FIGURE 28–12 A typical automotive speaker with two terminals. The polarity of the speakers can be identified by looking at the wiring diagram in the service manual or by using a 1.5 volt battery to check. When the battery positive is applied to the positive terminal of the speaker, the cone will move outward. When the battery leads are reversed, the speaker cone will move inward.

SPEAKERS

PURPOSE AND FUNCTION The purpose of any **speaker** is to reproduce the original sound as accurately as possible. Speakers are also called *loudspeakers*. The human ear is capable of hearing sounds from a very low frequency of 20 Hz (cycles per seconds) to as high as 20,000 Hz. No one speaker is capable of reproducing sound over such a wide frequency range. ● SEE FIGURE 28–11.

Good-quality speakers are the key to a proper sounding radio or sound system. Replacement speakers should be securely mounted and wired according to the correct *polarity*. ● SEE FIGURE 28–12.

IMPEDANCE MATCHING All speakers used on the same radio or amplifier should have the same internal coil resistance, called **impedance**. If unequal-impedance speakers are used,

sound quality may be reduced and serious damage to the radio may result. ● SEE FIGURE 28–13.

All speakers should have the same impedance. For example, if two 4 ohm speakers are being used for the rear and they are connected in parallel, the total impedance is 2 ohms.

$$R_T = \frac{4\Omega\,(\text{impedance of each speaker})}{2\,(\text{number of speakers in parallel})} = 2 \text{ ohms}$$

The front speakers should also represent a 2 ohm load from the radio or amplifier. See the following example.

Two front speakers: each 2 ohms

Two rear speakers: each 8 ohms

Solution: Connect the front speakers in series (connect the positive [+] of one speaker to the negative [−] of the other) for a total impedance of 4 ohms (2 Ω + 2 Ω = 4 Ω).

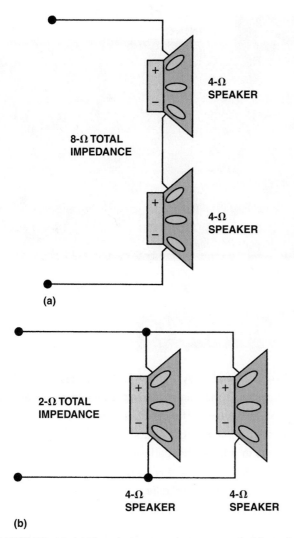

(a)

(b)

FIGURE 28–13 (a) Two 4 ohm speakers connected in series result in total impedance of 8 ohms. (b) Two 4 ohm speakers connected in parallel result in total impedance of 2 ohms.

Connect the two rear speakers in parallel (connect the positive [+] of each speaker together and the negative [−] of each speaker together) for a total impedance of 4 ohms ($8 \, \Omega \div 2 = 4 \, \Omega$).

SPEAKER WIRING The wire used for speakers should be as large a wire (as low an AWG gauge number) as is practical in order to be assured that full power is reaching the speakers. Typical "speaker wire" is about 22 gauge (0.35 mm^2), yet tests conducted by audio engineers have concluded that increasing the wire gauge—up to 4 gauge (19 mm^2) or larger—greatly increases sound quality. All wiring connections should be soldered after making certain that all speaker connections have the correct polarity.

CAUTION: Be careful when installing additional audio equipment on a General Motors vehicle system that uses a two-wire speaker connection called a floating ground system. Other systems run only one power (hot) lead to each speaker and ground the other speaker lead to the body of the vehicle.

This arrangement helps prevent interference and static that could occur if these components were connected to a chassis (vehicle) ground. If the components are chassis grounded, there may be a difference in the voltage potential (voltage); this condition is called a *ground loop*.

CAUTION: Regardless of radio speaker connections used, *never* operate any radio without the speakers connected, or the speaker driver section of the radio may be damaged as a result of the open speaker circuit.

SPEAKER TYPES

INTRODUCTION   No one speaker is capable of reproducing sound over such a wide frequency range. Therefore, speakers are available in three basic types.

1. Tweeters are for high-frequency ranges.
2. Midrange are for mid-frequency ranges.
3. Woofers and subwoofers are for low-frequency ranges.

TWEETER   A **tweeter** is a speaker designed to reproduce high-frequency sounds, usually between 4,000 and 20,000 Hz (4 and 20 kHz). Tweeters are very directional. This means that the human ear is most likely to be able to detect the location of the speaker while listening to music. This also means that a tweeter should be mounted in the vehicle where the sound can be directed in line of sight to the listener. Tweeters are usually mounted on the inside door near the top, windshield "A" pillar, or similar locations.

MIDRANGE   A midrange speaker is designed and manufactured to be able to best reproduce sounds in the middle of the human hearing range, from 400 to 5,000 Hz. Most people are sensitive to the sound produced by these midrange speakers. These speakers are also directional in that the listener can usually locate the source of the sound.

SUBWOOFER   A **subwoofer**, sometimes called a *woofer*, produces the lowest frequency of sounds, usually 125 Hz and lower. A *midbass* speaker may also be used to reproduce those frequencies between 100 and 500 Hz. Low-frequency sounds from these speakers are *not* directional. This means that the listener usually cannot detect the source of the sound from these speakers. The low-frequency sounds seem to be everywhere in the vehicle, so the location of the speakers is not as critical as with the higher frequency speakers.

The subwoofer can be placed almost anywhere in the vehicle. Most subwoofers are mounted in the rear of the vehicle where there is more room for the larger subwoofer speakers.

SPEAKER FREQUENCY RESPONSE   Frequency response is how a speaker responds to a range of frequencies. A typical frequency response for a midrange speaker may be 500 to 4,000 Hz.

 WARNING

Hearing loss is possible if exposed to loud sounds. According to noise experts (audiologists), hearing protection should be used whenever the following occurs.

1. You must raise your voice to be heard by others next to you.
2. You cannot hear someone else speaking who is less than 3 ft (1 m) away.
3. You are operating power equipment, such as a lawnmower.

SOUND LEVELS

DECIBEL SCALE   A **decibel (dB)** is a measure of sound power, and it is the faintest sound a human can hear in the midband frequencies. The dB scale is not linear (straight line) but logarithmic, meaning that a small change in the dB reading results in a large change in volume of noise. An increase of 10 dB in sound pressure is equal to doubling the perceived volume. Therefore, a small difference in dB rating means a big difference in the sound volume of the speaker.

EXAMPLES   Some examples of decibel sound levels include:

- Quiet, faint   30 dB: whisper, quiet library
                          40 dB: quiet room
- Moderate   50 dB: moderate range sound
                          60 dB: normal conversation
- Loud   70 dB: vacuum cleaner, city traffic
                          80 dB: busy noisy traffic, vacuum cleaner
- Extremely loud   90 dB: lawnmower, shop tools
                          100 dB: chain saw, air drill
- Hearing loss possible   110 dB: loud rock music

What Is a Bass Blocker?

A bass blocker is a capacitor and coil assembly that effectively blocks low frequencies. A bass blocker is normally used to block low frequencies being sent to the smaller front speakers. Using a bass blocker allows the smaller front speakers to more efficiently reproduce the midrange and high-range frequency sounds.

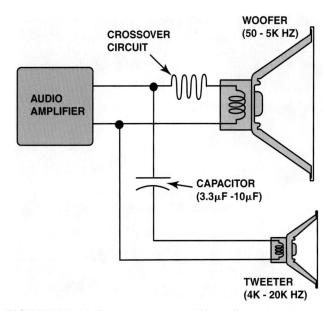

FIGURE 28–14 Crossovers are used in audio systems to send high-frequency sounds to the small (tweeter) speakers and low-frequency sounds to larger (woofer) speakers.

CROSSOVERS

DEFINITION A **crossover** is designed to separate the frequency of a sound and send a certain frequency range, such as low bass sounds, to a woofer designed to reproduce these low-frequency sounds. There are two types of crossovers: passive and active.

PASSIVE CROSSOVER A passive crossover does not use an external power source. Rather it uses a coil and a capacitor to block certain frequencies that a particular type of speaker cannot handle and allow just those frequencies that it can handle to be applied to the speaker. For example, a 6.6 millihenry coil and a 200 microfarad capacitor can effectively pass 100 Hz frequency sound to a large 10 in. subwoofer. This type of passive crossover is called a **low-pass filter**, because it passes (transfers) only the low-frequency sounds to the speaker and blocks all other frequencies. A **high-pass filter** is used to transfer higher frequency (over 100 Hz) to smaller speakers.

ACTIVE CROSSOVER **Active crossovers** use an external power source and produce superior performance. An active crossover is also called an *electronic crossover* or *crossover network.* These units include many powered filters and are considerably more expensive than passive crossovers. Two amplifiers are necessary to fully benefit from an active crossover. One amplifier is for the higher frequencies and midrange and the other amplifier is for the subwoofers. If you are on a budget and plan to use just one amplifier, then use passive crossover. If you can afford to use two or more amplifiers, then consider using the electronic (active) crossover. ● **SEE FIGURE 28–14** for an example of crossovers used in factory-installed systems.

AFTERMARKET SOUND SYSTEM UPGRADE

POWER AND GROUND UPGRADES If adding an amplifier and additional audio components, be sure to include the needed power and ground connections. These upgrades can include:

- A separate battery for the audio system
- An inline fuse near the battery to protect the wiring and the components
- Wiring that is properly sized to the amperage draw of the system and the length of wire (The higher the output wattage the greater the amperage required and the larger the wire gauge needed. The longer the distance between the battery and the components, the larger the wire gauge needed for best performance.)
- Ground wires at least the same gauge as the power side wiring (Some experts recommend using extra ground wires for best performance.)

Read, understand, and follow all instructions that come with audio system components.

POWERLINE CAPACITOR A **powerline capacitor**, also called a **stiffening capacitor**, refers to a large capacitor (often abbreviated CAP) of 0.25 farad or larger connected to an amplifier power wire. The purpose and function of this capacitor is to provide the electrical reserve energy needed by the amplifier to provide deep bass notes. ● **SEE FIGURE 28–15.**

POWERLINE (STIFFENING) CAPACITORS

FIGURE 28–15 Two capacitors connected in parallel provide the necessary current flow to power large subwoofer speakers.

POWERLINE CAPACITOR USAGE GUIDE

WATTS (AMPLIFIER)	RECOMMENDED CAPACITOR IN FARADS (MICROFARADS)
100 W	0.10 farad (100,000 μF)
200 W	0.20 farad (200,000 μF)
250 W	0.25 farad (250,000 μF)
500 W	0.50 farad (500,000 μF)
750 W	0.75 farad (750,000 μF)
1,000 W	1.00 farad (1,000,000 μF)

CHART 28–1

The rating of the capacitor needed to upgrade an audio system is directly related to the wattage of the system.

AFTERMARKET SOUND SYSTEM UPGRADE (CONTINUED)

Battery power is often slow to respond; and when the amplifier attempts to draw a large amount of current, the capacitor will try to stabilize the voltage level at the amplifier by discharging stored current as needed.

A rule of thumb is to connect a capacitor with a capacity of 1 farad for each 1,000 watts of amplifier power. ● **SEE CHART 28–1.**

CAPACITOR INSTALLATION A powerline capacitor connects to the power leads between the inline fuse and the amplifier. ● **SEE FIGURE 28–16.**

If the capacitor were connected to the circuit as shown without "precharging," the capacitor would draw so much current that it would blow the inline fuse. To safely connect a large capacitor, it must be *precharged*. To precharge the capacitor, follow these steps.

STEP 1 Connect the negative (−) terminal of the capacitor to a good chassis ground.

STEP 2 Insert an automotive 12 V light bulb, such as a headlight or parking light, between the positive (+) terminal of the capacitor and the positive terminal of the battery. The light will light as the capacitor is being charged and then go out when the capacitor is fully charged.

STEP 3 Disconnect the light from the capacitor, then connect the power lead to the capacitor. The capacitor is now fully charged and ready to provide the extra power necessary to supplement battery power to the amplifier.

? FREQUENTLY ASKED QUESTION

What Do the Amplifier Specifications Mean?

RMS power	**RMS** means root-mean-square and is the rating that indicates how much power the amplifier is capable of producing continuously.
RMS power at 2 ohms	This specification in watts indicates how much power the amplifier delivers into a 2 ohm speaker load. This 2 ohm load is achieved by wiring two 4 ohm speakers in parallel or by using 2 ohm speakers.
Peak power	Peak power is the maximum wattage an amplifier can deliver in a short burst during a musical peak.
THD	**Total harmonic distortion (THD)** represents the amount of change of the signal as it is being amplified. The lower the number, the better the amplifier (e.g., a 0.01% rating is better than a 0.07% rating).
Signal-to-noise ratio	This specification is measured in decibels (dB) and compares the strength of the signal with the level of the background noise (hiss). A higher volume indicates less background noise (e.g., a 105 dB rating is better than a 100 dB rating).

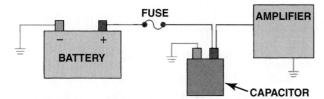

FIGURE 28–16 A powerline capacitor should be connected through the power wire to the amplifier as shown. When the amplifier requires more electrical power (watts) than the battery can supply, the capacitor will discharge into the amplifier and supply the necessary current for the fraction of a second it is needed by the amplifier. At other times when the capacitor is not needed, it draws current from the battery to keep it charged.

FIGURE 28–17 Voice commands can be used to control many functions, including navigation systems, climate control, telephone, and radio.

VOICE RECOGNITION

PARTS AND OPERATION **Voice recognition** is an expanding technology. It allows the driver of a vehicle to perform tasks, such as locate an address in a navigation system by using voice commands rather than buttons. In the past, users had to say the exact words to make it work such as the following examples listed from an owner manual for a vehicle equipped with a voice-actuated navigation system.

"Go home"

"Repeat guidance"

"Nearest ATM"

The problem with these simple voice commands was that the exact wording had to be spoken. The voice recognition software would compare the voice command to a specific list of words or phrases stored in the system in order for a match to occur. Newer systems recognize speech patterns and take action based on learned patterns. Voice recognition can be used for the following functions.

1. Navigation system operation (● **SEE FIGURE 28–17.**)
2. Sound system operation
3. Climate control system operation
4. Telephone dialing and other related functions (● **SEE FIGURE 28–18.**)

A microphone is usually placed in the driver's side sun visor or in the overhead console in the center top portion of the windshield area.

FIGURE 28–18 The voice command icon on the steering wheel of a Cadillac.

DIAGNOSIS AND SERVICE Voice recognition is usually incorporated into many functions of the vehicle. If a problem occurs with the system, perform the following steps.

1. Verify the customer complaint (concern). Check the owner manual or service information for the proper voice commands and verify that the system is not functioning correctly.
2. Check for any aftermarket accessories that may interfere or were converted to components used by the voice recognition system, such as remote start units, MP3 players, or any other electrical component.
3. Check for stored diagnostic trouble codes (DTCs) using a scan tool.
4. Follow the recommended troubleshooting procedures as stated in service information.

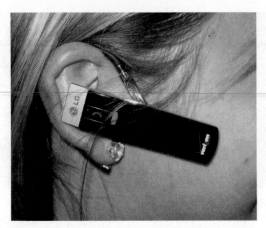

FIGURE 28–19 Bluetooth earpiece that contains a microphone and speaker unit that is paired to a cellular phone. The telephone has to be within 33 ft (10 m) of the earpiece.

BLUETOOTH

OPERATION **Bluetooth** is a (radio frequency) standard for short-range communications. The range of a typical Bluetooth device is 33 ft (10 m) and it operates in the ISM (industrial, scientific, and medical) band between 2.4000 and 2.4835 MHz.

Bluetooth is a wireless standard that works on two levels.

- It provides physical communication using low power, requiring only about 1 milliwatt (1/1,000 of a watt) of electrical power, making it suitable for use with small handheld or portable devices, such as an ear-mounted speaker/microphone.

- It provides a standard protocol for how bits of data are sent and received.

The Bluetooth standard is an advantage because it is wireless, low cost, and automatic. The automotive use of Bluetooth technology is in the operation of a cellular telephone being tied into the vehicle. The vehicle allows the use of hands-free telephone usage. A vehicle that is Bluetooth telephone equipped has the following components.

- A Bluetooth receiver can be built into the navigation or existing sound system.

- A microphone allows the driver to use voice commands as well as telephone conversations from the vehicle to the cell via Bluetooth wireless connections.

Many cell phones are equipped with Bluetooth which may allow the caller to use an ear-mounted microphone and speaker. ● **SEE FIGURE 28–19.**

If the vehicle and the cell phone are equipped with Bluetooth, the speaker and microphone can be used as a hands-free telephone when the phone is in the vehicle. The cell phone can be activated in the vehicle by using voice commands.

? FREQUENTLY ASKED QUESTION

Where Did Bluetooth Get Its Name?

The early adopters of the standard used the term Bluetooth, and they named it for Harold Bluetooth, the king of Denmark in the late 900s. The king was able to unite Denmark and part of Norway into a single kingdom.

? FREQUENTLY ASKED QUESTION

Can Two Bluetooth Telephones Be Used in a Vehicle?

Usually. In order to use two telephones, the second phone needs to be given a name. When both telephones enter the vehicle, check which one is recognized. Say "phone status" and the system will tell you to which telephone the system is responding. If it is not the one you want, simply say, "next phone" and it will move to the other one.

SATELLITE RADIO

PARTS AND OPERATION Satellite radio, also called **Satellite Digital Audio Radio Services** or **SDARS**, is a fee-based system that uses satellites to broadcast high-quality radio. SDARS broadcasts on the S-band of 2.1320 to 2.345 GHz.

SIRIUS/XM RADIO Sirius/XM radio is standard equipment or optional in most vehicles. XM radio uses two satellites launched in 2001 called Rock (XM-2) and Roll (XM-1) in a geosynchronous orbit above North America. Two replacement satellites, Rhythm (XM-3) and Blues (XM-4) were launched in 2006. Sirius and XM radio combined in 2008 and now share some programming. The two types of satellite radios use different protocols and, therefore, require separate radios unless a combination unit is purchased.

RECEPTION Reception from satellites can be affected by tall buildings and mountains. To help ensure consistent reception, both SDARS providers do the following:

- Include in the radio itself a buffer circuit that can store several seconds of broadcasts to provide service when traveling out of a service area

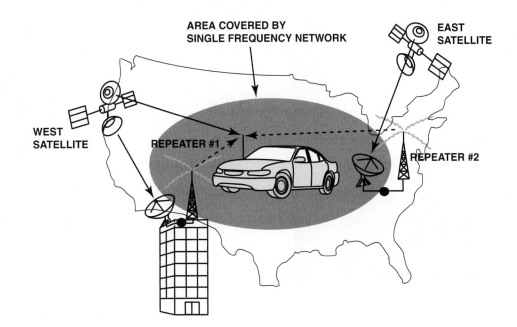

FIGURE 28–20 SDARS uses satellites and repeater stations to broadcast radio.

FIGURE 28–21 An aftermarket XM radio antenna mounted on the rear deck lid. The deck lid acts as the ground plane for the antenna.

FIGURE 28–22 A shark-fin-type factory antenna used for both XM and OnStar.

- Provide land-based repeater stations in most cities
  (● **SEE FIGURE 28–20.**)

ANTENNA   To be able to receive satellite radio, the antenna needs to be able to receive signals from both the satellite and the repeater stations located in many large cities. There are various types and shapes of antennas, including those shown in ● **FIGURES 28–21 AND 28–22.**

DIAGNOSIS AND SERVICE   The first step in any diagnosis is to verify the customer complaint (concern). If no satellite service is being received, first check with the customer to verify

that the monthly service fee has been paid and the account is up to date. If poor reception is the cause, carefully check the antenna for damage or faults with the lead-in wire. The antennas must be installed on a metal surface to provide the proper ground plane.

For all other satellite radio fault problems, check service information for the exact tests and procedures. Always follow the factory recommended procedures. Check the following websites for additional information.

- www.xmradio.com
- www.sirius.com
- www.siriusxm.com

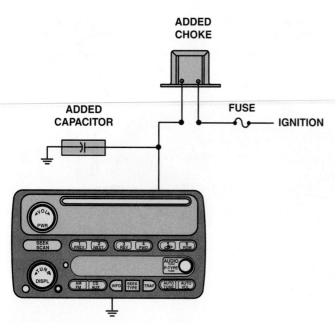

FIGURE 28–23 A radio choke and/or a capacitor can be installed in the power feed lead to any radio, amplifier, or equalizer.

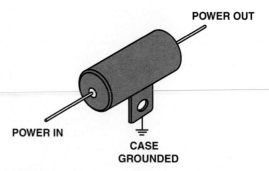

FIGURE 28–24 Many automobile manufacturers install a co-axial capacitor, like this one, in the power feed wire to the blower motor to eliminate interference caused by the blower motor.

? FREQUENTLY ASKED QUESTION

What Does ESN Mean?

ESN means electronic serial number. This is necessary information to know when reviewing satellite radio subscriptions. Each radio has its own unique ESN, often found on a label at the back or bottom of the unit. It is also often shown on scan tools or test equipment designed to help diagnose faults in the units.

RADIO INTERFERENCE

DEFINITION Radio interference is caused by variations in voltage in the powerline or picked up by the antenna. A "whine" that increases in frequency with increasing engine speed is usually referred to as an **alternator whine** and is eliminated by installing a radio choke or a filter capacitor in the power feed wire to the radio. ● **SEE FIGURE 28–23.**

CAPACITOR USAGE Ignition noise is usually a raspy sound that varies with the speed of the engine. This noise is usually eliminated by the installation of a capacitor on the positive side of the ignition coil. The capacitor should be connected to the power feed wire to either the radio or the amplifier, or both. The capacitor *has* to be grounded. A capacitor allows AC interference to pass through to ground while blocking the flow of DC current. Use a 470 μF, 50 volt electrolytic capacitor, which is readily available from most radio supply stores. A special coaxial capacitor can also be used in the powerline. ● **SEE FIGURE 28–24.**

RADIO CHOKE A **radio choke**, which is a coil of wire, can also be used to reduce or eliminate radio interference. Again, the radio choke is installed in the power feed wire to the radio equipment. Radio interference being picked up by the antenna can best be eliminated by stopping the source of the interference and making certain that all units containing a coil, such as electric motors, have a capacitor or diode attached to the power-side wire.

BRAIDED GROUND WIRE Using a braided ground wire is usually specified when electrical noise is a concern. The radio-frequency signals travel on the surface of a conductor rather than through the core of the wire. A braided ground strap is used because the overlapped wires short out any radio-frequency signals traveling on the surface.

AUDIO NOISE SUMMARY In summary:

- Radio noise can be broadcast or caused by noise (voltage variations) in the power circuit to the radio.
- Most radio interference complaints come when someone installs an amplifier, power booster, equalizer, or other radio accessory.
- *A major cause of this interference is the variation in voltage through the ground circuit wires. To prevent or reduce this interference, make sure all ground connections are clean and tight.*
- Placing a capacitor in the ground circuit also may be beneficial.

CAUTION: Amplifiers sold to boost the range or power of an antenna often increase the level of interference and radio noise to a level that disturbs the driver.

FIGURE 28–25 A "sniffer" can be made from an old antenna lead-in cable by removing about 3 in. of the outer shielding from the end. Plug the lead-in cable into the antenna input of the radio and tune the radio to a weak station. Move the end of the antenna wire around the vehicle dash area. The sniffer is used to locate components that may not be properly shielded or grounded and can cause radio interference through the case (housing) of the radio itself.

 TECH TIP

The Separate Battery Trick

Whenever diagnosing sound system interference, try running separate 14 gauge wire(s) from the sound system power lead and ground to a separate battery outside of the vehicle. If the noise is still heard, the interference is *not* due to an alternator diode or other source in the wiring of the vehicle.

AUDIO NOISE CONTROL SYMPTOM CHART		
NOISE SOURCE	**WHAT IT SOUNDS LIKE**	**WHAT TO TRY**
Alternator	A whine whose pitch changes with engine speed	Install a capacitor to a ground at the alternator output
Ignition	Ticking that changes with engine speed	Use a sniffer to further localize the source of the problem
Turn signals	Popping in time with the turn signals	Install a capacitor across the turn signal flasher
Brake lights	Popping whenever the brake pedal is depressed	Install a capacitor across the brake light switch contacts
Blower motor	Ticking in time with the blower motor	Install a capacitor to ground at the motor hot lead
Dash lamp dimmer	A buzzy whine whose pitch changes with the dimmer setting	Install a capacitor to ground at the dimmer hot lead
Horn switch	Popping when the horn is sounded	Install a capacitor between the hot lead and horn lead at the horn relay
Horn	Buzzing synchronized with the horn	Install a capacitor to ground at each horn hot lead
Amplifier power supply	A buzz, not affected by engine speed	Ground the amplifier chassis using a braided ground strap

CHART 28–2

Radio noise can have various causes, and knowing where or when the noise occurs helps pin down the location.

Capacitor and/or radio chokes are the most commonly used components. Two or more capacitors can be connected in parallel to increase the capacity of the original capacitor. A "sniffer" can be used to locate the source of the radio noise. A sniffer is a length of antenna wire with a few inches of insulation removed from the antenna end. The sniffer is attached to the antenna input terminal of the radio, and the radio is turned on and set to a weak station. The other end of the sniffer is then moved around areas of the dash to locate where the source of the interference originates. The radio noise will greatly increase if the end of the sniffer comes close to where electromagnetic leakage is occurring. ● **SEE FIGURE 28–25.**

● **SEE CHART 28–2.**

Lightning Damage

A radio failed to work in a vehicle that was outside during a thunderstorm. The technician checked the fuses and verified that power was reaching the radio. Then the technician noticed the antenna. It had been struck by lightning. Obviously, the high voltage from the lightning strike traveled to the radio receiver and damaged the circuits. Both the radio and the antenna were replaced to correct the problem.

● **SEE FIGURE 28–26.**

FIGURE 28–26 The tip of this antenna was struck by lightning.

 REAL WORLD FIX

The General Motors Security Radio Problem

A customer replaced the battery in a General Motors vehicle and now the radio display shows "LOC." This means that the radio is locked and there is a customer code stored in the radio.

Other displays and their meaning include:

"InOP" This display indicates that too many incorrect codes have been entered and the radio must be kept powered for one hour and the ignition turned on before any more attempts can be made.

"SEC" This display means there is a customer's code stored and the radio is unlocked, secured and operable.

"---" This means there is no customer code stored and the radio is unlocked.

"REP" This means the customer's code has been entered once and the radio now is asking that the code be repeated to verify it was entered correctly the first time.

To unlock the radio, the technician used the following steps (the code number being used is 4321).

STEP 1 Press the "HR" (hour) button: "000" is displayed.

STEP 2 Set the first two digits using the hour button: "4300" is displayed.

STEP 3 Set the last two digits of the code using the "MIN" (minutes) button: "4321" is displayed.

STEP 4 Press the AM-FM button to enter the code. The radio is unlocked and the clock displays "1:00."

Thankfully, the owner had the security code. If the owner had lost the code, the technician would have to secure a scrambled factory backup code from the radio and then call a toll-free number to obtain another code for the customer. The code will only be given to authorized dealers or repair facilities.

SUMMARY

1. Radios receive AM (amplitude modulation) and FM (frequency modulation) signals that are broadcast through the air.

2. The radio antenna is used to induce a very small voltage signal as an input into the radio from the electromagnetic energy via the broadcast station.

3. AM requires an antenna whereas FM may be heard from a radio without an antenna.

4. Speakers reproduce the original sound, and the impedance of all speakers should be equally matched.

5. Crossovers are used to block certain frequencies to allow each type of speaker to perform its job better. A low-pass filter is used to block high-frequency sounds being sent to large woofer speakers, and a high-pass filter blocks low-frequency sounds being sent to tweeters.

6. Radio interference can be caused by many different things, such as a defective alternator, a fault in the ignition system, a fault in a relay or solenoid, or a poor electrical ground connection.

1. Why do AM signals travel farther than FM signals?

2. What are the purpose and function of the ground plane?

3. How do you match the impedance of speakers?

4. What two items may need to be added to the wiring of a vehicle to control or reduce radio noise?

CHAPTER QUIZ

1. Technician A says that a radio can receive AM signals, but not FM signals, if the antenna is defective. Technician B says that a good antenna should give a reading of about 500 ohms when tested with an ohmmeter between the center antenna wire and ground. Which technician is correct?

   a. Technician A only
   b. Technician B only
   c. Both Technicians A and B
   d. Neither Technician A nor B

2. An antenna lead-in wire should have how many ohms of resistance between the center terminal and the grounded outer covering?

   a. Less than 5 ohms
   b. 5 to 50 ohms
   c. 300 to 500 ohms
   d. Infinity (OL)

3. Technician A says that a braided ground wire is best to use for audio equipment to help reduce interference. Technician B says to use insulated 14 gauge or larger ground wire to reduce interference. Which technician is correct?

   a. Technician A only
   b. Technician B only
   c. Both Technicians A and B
   d. Neither Technician A nor B

4. What maintenance should be performed to a power antenna to help keep it working correctly?

   a. Remove it from the vehicle and lubricate the gears and cable.
   b. Clean the mast with a soft cloth and lubricate with a light oil.
   c. Disassemble the mast and pack the mast with silicone grease (or equal).
   d. Loosen and then retighten the retaining nut.

5. If two 4 ohm speakers are connected in parallel, meaning positive (+) to positive (+) and negative (−) to negative (−), the total impedance will be _____.

   a. 8 ohms
   b. 4 ohms
   c. 2 ohms
   d. 1 ohm

6. If two 4 ohm speakers are connected in series, meaning the positive (+) of one speaker connected to the negative (−) of the other speaker, the total impedance will be _____.

   a. 8 ohms
   b. 4 ohms
   c. 5 ohms
   d. 1 ohm

7. An aftermarket satellite radio has poor reception. Technician A says that a lack of a proper ground plane on the antenna could be the cause. Technician B says that mountains or tall buildings can interfere with reception. Which technician is correct?

   a. Technician A only
   b. Technician B only
   c. Both Technicians A and B
   d. Neither Technician A nor B

8. 100,000 μF means _____.

   a. 0.10 farad
   b. 0.01 farad
   c. 0.001 farad
   d. 0.0001 farad

9. A radio choke is actually a _____.

   a. Resistor
   b. Capacitor
   c. Coil (inductor)
   d. Transistor

10. What device passes AC interference to ground and blocks DC voltage, and is used to control radio interference?

    a. Resistor
    b. Capacitor
    c. Coil (inductor)
    d. Transistor

NATEF TASK CORRELATION CHART

For every task in Electrical/Electronic Systems, the following safety requirements must be strictly enforced: Comply with personal and environmental safety practices associated with clothing; eye protection; hand tools; power equipment; proper ventilation; and the handling, storage, and disposal of chemicals/materials in accordance with local, state, and federal safety and environmental regulations.

ELECTRICAL/ELECTRONIC SYSTEMS (A6)

TASK	TEXTBOOK PAGE NO.	WORKTEXT PAGE NO.
A. GENERAL ELECTRICAL SYSTEM DIAGNOSIS		
1. Complete work order to include customer information, vehicle identifying information, customer concern, related service history, cause, and correction. (P-1)	2–4	4
2. Identify and interpret electrical/electronic system concern; determine necessary action. (P-1)	150–161	32
3. Research applicable vehicle and service information, such as electrical/electronic system operation, vehicle service history, service precautions, and technical service bulletins. (P-1)	2–4	5, 6, 7
4. Locate and interpret vehicle and major component identification numbers. (P-1)	2–4	8, 9
5. Diagnose electrical/electronic integrity of series, parallel, and series-parallel circuits using principles of electricity (Ohm's Law). (P-1)	65–92	16–24, 33
6. Use wiring diagrams during diagnosis of electrical circuit problems. (P-1)	144–160	34
7. Demonstrate the proper use of a digital multimeter (DMM) during diagnosis of electrical circuit problems, including: source voltage, voltage drop, current flow, and resistance. (P-1)	100–116	25
8. Check electrical circuits with a test light; determine necessary action. (P-2)	98–100	26
9. Check electrical/electronic circuit waveforms; interpret readings and determine needed repairs. (P-2)	119–124	28
10. Check electrical circuits using fused jumper wires; determine necessary action. (P-2)	98	27
11. Locate shorts, grounds, opens, and resistance problems in electrical/electronic circuits; determine necessary action. (P-1)	65–67	35
12. Measure and diagnose the cause(s) of excessive parasitic draw; determine necessary action. (P-1)	256–258	42
13. Inspect and test fusible links, circuit breakers, and fuses; determine necessary action. (P-1)	131–136	29
14. Inspect and test switches, connectors, relays, solenoid solid state devices, and wires of electrical/electronic circuits; determine necessary action. (P-1)	136–137, 176–177, 189–204	30, 37
15. Remove and replace terminal end from connector; replace connectors and terminal ends. (P-1)	136–137	31
16. Repair wiring harness (including CAN/BUS systems). (P-1)	136–137	31
17. Perform solder repair of electrical wiring. (P-1)	138–140	31
18. Identify location of hybrid vehicle high-voltage circuit disconnect (service plus) location and safety procedures. (P-2)	35–36	12

TASK	TEXTBOOK PAGE NO.	WORKTEXT PAGE NO.
B. BATTERY DIAGNOSIS AND SERVICE		
1. Perform battery state-of-charge test; determine necessary action. (P-1)	248–251	43
2. Perform battery capacity test; confirm proper battery capacity for vehicle application; determine necessary action. (P-1)	248–251	44
3. Maintain or restore electronic memory functions. (P-1)	257–258	45
4. Inspect, clean, fill, and/or replace battery, battery cables, connectors, clamps, and hold-downs. (P-1)	246–247	47
5. Perform battery charge. (P-1)	252–254	48
6. Start a vehicle using jumper cables or auxiliary power supply. (P-1)	255	49
7. Identify high voltage circuits of electric or hybrid electric vehicle and related safety precautions. (P-3)	35–36, 141	11
8. Identify electronic modules, security systems, radios, and other accessories that require reinitialization or code entry following battery disconnect. (P-1)	257–258	46
9. Identify hybrid vehicle auxiliary (12v) battery service, repair and test procedures. (P-3)	252–253	50
C. STARTING SYSTEM DIAGNOSIS AND REPAIR		
1. Perform starter current draw tests; determine necessary action. (P-1)	278–279	53
2. Perform starter circuit voltage drop tests; determine necessary action. (P-1)	276–277	54
3. Inspect and test starter relays and solenoids; determine necessary action. (P-2)	278–280	52
4. Remove and install starter in a vehicle. (P-1)	279, 282	55
5. Inspect and test switches, connectors, and wires of starter control circuits; perform necessary action. (P-2)	278–279	55
6. Differentiate between electrical and engine mechanical problems that cause a slow-crank or no-crank condition. (P-2)	279	53
D. CHARGING SYSTEM DIAGNOSIS AND REPAIR		
1. Perform charging system output test; determine necessary action. (P-1)	311	59
2. Diagnose charging system for the cause of undercharge, no-charge, and overcharge conditions. (P-1)	305–311	58, 60
3. Inspect, adjust, or replace generator (alternator) drive belts, pulleys, and tensioners; check pulley and belt alignment. (P-1)	306–308	62
4. Remove, inspect, and install generator (alternator). (P-1)	312, 317	62
5. Perform charging circuit voltage drop tests; determine necessary action. (P-1)	309–310	61
E. LIGHTING SYSTEMS DIAGNOSIS AND REPAIR		
1. Diagnose the cause of brighter than normal, intermittent, dim, or no light operation; determine necessary action. (P-1)	330–331	68
2. Inspect, replace, and aim headlights and bulbs. (P-2)	328–341	70
3. Inspect and diagnose incorrect turn signal or hazard light operation; perform necessary action. (P-2)	333–336	69
4. Identify system voltage and safety precautions associated with high intensity discharge headlights. (P-2)	338–340	71

TASK	TEXTBOOK PAGE NO.	WORKTEXT PAGE NO.
F. GAUGES, WARNING DEVICES, AND DRIVER INFORMATION SYSTEMS DIAGNOSIS AND REPAIR		
1. Inspect and test gauges and gauge sending units for cause of abnormal gauge readings; determine necessary action. (P-1)	357–360	72
2. Inspect and test connectors, wires, and printed circuit boards of gauge circuits; determine necessary action. (P-3)	357–360	73
3. Diagnose the cause of incorrect operation of warning devices and other driver information systems; determine necessary action. (P-1)	357–362	74
4. Inspect and test sensors, connectors, and wires of electronic (digital) instrument circuits; determine necessary action. (P-3)	366–369	75
G. HORN AND WIPER/WASHER DIAGNOSIS AND REPAIR		
1. Diagnose incorrect horn operation; perform necessary action. (P-1)	383–384	76
2. Diagnose incorrect wiper operation; diagnose wiper speed control and park problems; perform necessary action. (P-1)	385–390	77
3. Diagnose incorrect washer operation; perform necessary action. (P-2)	390–392	77
H. ACCESSORIES DIAGNOSIS AND REPAIR		
1. Diagnose incorrect operation of motor-driven accessory circuits; determine necessary action. (P-1)	406–411	79
2. Diagnose incorrect heated glass, mirror, or seat operation; determine necessary action. (P-3)	403–405, 412–413	80
3. Diagnose incorrect electric lock operation (including remote keyless entry); determine necessary action. (P-1)	415–423	81
4. Diagnose incorrect operation of cruise control systems; determine necessary action. (P-3)	398–403	82
5. Diagnose supplemental restraint system (SRS) concerns; determine necessary action. (P-1)	436–444	86
6. Disarm and enable the airbag system for vehicle service. (P-1)	442–444	10, 86
7. Diagnose radio static and weak, intermittent, or no radio reception; determine necessary action. (P-3)	454–455, 464–466	36, 87
8. Remove and reinstall door panel. (P-1)	430–431	83
9. Diagnose body electronic system circuits using a scan tool; determine necessary action. (P-2)	391, 401, 408, 415–423, 440, 443, 446	84
10. Check for module communication (including CAN/ BUS systems) errors using a scan tool. (P-2)	223–233	40
11. Diagnose the cause of false, intermittent, or no operation of anti-theft systems. (P-3)	416–428	85
12. Describe the operation of keyless entry/remote-start systems. (P-3)	415–423	85
13. Perform software transfers, software updates, or flash reprogramming on electronic modules. (P-3)	416–428	39

ENGLISH GLOSSARY

3-minute charge test A method used to test batteries. Not valid for all types of batteries.

Above ground storage tank A type of oil storage.

AC coupling A signal that passes the AC signal component to the meter, but blocks the DC component. Useful to observe an AC signal that is normally riding on a DC signal; for example, charging ripple.

AC/DC clamp-on DMM A type of meter that has a clamp that is placed around the wire to measure current.

Active crossover A type of crossover that uses electronic components to block certain frequencies.

Actuator An electromechanical device that performs mechanical movement as commanded by a controller.

Adhesive-lined heat shrink tubing A type of heat shrink tubing that shrinks to one-third of its original diameter and has glue inside.

AFS Active Front headlight System. A name for the system that causes the headlights to turn when cornering.

AGM Absorbed glass mat. AGM batteries are lead-acid batteries, but use an absorbent material between the plates to hold the electrolyte. AGM batteries are classified as valve-regulated lead-acid (VRLA) batteries.

AGST Above Ground Storage Tank used to store oil.

Airbag An inflatable fabric bag that deploys in the event of a collision that is severe enough to cause personal injury.

Alternator An electric generator that produces alternating current; also called an *AC generator.*

Alternator whine A noise made by an alternator with a defective diode(s).

AM Amplitude modulation.

American wire gauge (AWG) A method used to measure wire diameter.

Ammeter An electrical test instrument used to measure amperes (unit of the amount of current flow).

Ampere The unit of the amount of current flow. Named for André Ampère (1775–1836).

Ampere hours A method used to rate battery capacity.

Ampere-turns The unit of measurement for electrical magnetic field strength.

Analog A type of instrument that indicates values by use of the movement of a needle or similar device. An analog signal is continuous and variable.

Analog-to-digital (AD) converter An electronic circuit that converts analog signals into digital signals that can then be used by a computer.

Anode The positive electrode; the electrode toward which electrons flow.

Armature The rotating unit inside a DC generator or starter, consisting of a series of coils of insulating wire wound around a laminated iron core.

Arming sensor A sensor used in an air bag circuit that is most sensitive and completes the circuit first of two sensors that are needed to deploy an air bag.

Asbestosis A health condition where asbestos causes scar tissue to form in the lungs causing shortness of breath.

Auto link A type of automotive fuse.

Backlight Light that illuminates the test tool's display from the back of the LCD. Also the rear window of a vehicle.

Backup camera A camera that mounts on the rear of the vehicle that is used to display what is behind a vehicle when the gear selector is placed in reverse.

Base The name for the section of a transistor that controls the current flow through the transistor.

Battery cables Cables that attach to the positive and negative terminals of the battery.

Battery electrical drain test A test to determine if a component or circuit is draining the battery.

Baud rate The speed at which bits of computer information are transmitted on a serial data stream. Measured in bits per second (bps).

BCI Battery Council International. This organization establishes standards for batteries.

Bench testing A test of a component such as a starter before being installed in the vehicle.

Binary system A computer system that uses a series of zeros and ones represent to information.

Bipolar transistor A type of transistor that has a base, emitter, and collector.

Bluetooth A short range wireless communication standard named after a Danish king that had a bluetooth.

BNC connector Coaxial-type input connector. Named for its inventor, Neil Councilman.

Bolt A threaded fastener with a head at one end used for a wrench or socket to turn to install or remove.

Bound electrons Electrons that are close to the nucleus of the atom.

Braided ground straps Ground wires that are not insulated and braided to help increase flexibility and reduce RFI.

Brake Lights Lights at the rear of the vehicle which light whenever the brake pedal is depressed.

Branches Electrical parts of a parallel circuit.

Breaker bar A hand tool used to rotate a socket.

Break-out box (BOB) An electrical tester that connects to a connector or controller and allows access to each terminal so testing can be performed using a meter or scope.

Brush-end housing The end of a starter or generator (alternator) where the brushes are located.

Brushes Carbon or carbon-copper connections used to pass electrical current to a rotating assembly such as an armature in a starter motor or a rotor in a generator (alternator).

Bulb test A test to check the operation of certain circuits controlled by the ignition switch.

Bump cap A hat that is plastic and hard to protect the head from bumps.

Burn in A process of operating an electronic device for a period from several hours to several days.

Bus An electrical network which ties several modules together.

CA Cranking amperes. A battery rating.

CAA Clean Air Act. Federal legislation passed in 1970 and updated in 1990 that established national air quality standards.

Calibration codes Codes used on many powertrain control modules.

Campaign A recall where vehicle owners are contacted to return a vehicle to a dealer for corrective action.

CAN Controller Area Network, a type of serial data transmission.

Candlepower A rating of the amount of light produced by a light source such as a light bulb.

Capacitance Electrical capacitance is a term used to measure or describe how much charge can be stored in a capacitor (condenser) for a given voltage potential difference. Capacitance is measured in farads or smaller increments of farads such as microfarads.

Casting number An identification number cast into an engine block and other large castings.

Cathode The negative electrode.

CCA Cold Cranking Amps. A rating of a battery tested at zero degrees F.

Cell A group of negative and positive plates to form a cell capable of producing 2.1 V.

CEMF Counter electromotive force.

CFL Cathode fluorescent lighting.

CFR Code of Federal Regulations.

Charging voltage test An electrical test using a voltmeter and an ammeter to test the condition of the charging circuit.

Cheater bar A pipe or other device used to increase the amount of force applied to a wrench or ratchet. Not recommended to be used because it can cause the wrench or ratchet to break and causing possible personal injury.

Chisels A sharpened tool used with a hammer to separate two pieces of an assembly.

CHMSL Centrally High Mounted Stop Light; the third brake light.

Circuit A circuit is the path that electrons travel from a power source, through a resistance, and back to the power source.

Circuit breakers A mechanical unit that opens an electrical circuit in the event of excessive current flow.

Clamping diode A diode installed in a circuit with the cathode toward the positive. The diode becomes forwarded biased when the circuit is turned off thereby reducing the high voltage surge created by the current flowing through a coil.

Class 2 A type of BUS communication used in General Motors vehicles.

Claw poles The magnetic points of a generator (alternator) rotor.

Clock generator A crystal that determines the speed of computer circuits.

Clockspring A flat ribbon of wire used under the steering wire to transfer airbag electrical signals. May also carry horn and steering wheel control circuits depending on make and model of vehicle.

CMOS Complementary metal oxide semiconductor.

Cold solder joint A type of solder joint that was not heated to high enough temperature to create a good electrical connection. Often a dull gray appearance rather than shiny for a good solder connection.

Collector The name of one section of a transistor.

Color shift A term used to describe the change in the color of an HID arc tube assembly over time.

Combination circuit Another name for a series-parallel electrical circuit.

Combination valve A valve used in the brake system that performs more than one function, such as a pressure differential switch, metering valve, and/or proportioning valve.

Commutator segments The name for the copper segments of the armature of a starter or DC generator.

Commutator-end housing The end of a starter motor that contains the commutator and brushes. Also called the brush end housing.

Complete circuit A type of electrical circuit that has continuity and current would flow if connected to power and ground.

Composite headlight A type of headlights that uses a separate, replaceable bulb.

Compound circuit Another name for a series-parallel electrical circuit.

Compression spring A spring which is part of a starter drive that acts on the starter pinion gear.

Condenser Also called a capacitor; stores an electrical charge.

Conductor A material that conducts electricity and heat. A metal that contains fewer than four electrons in its atom's outer shell.

Continuity A test to check wiring, circuits, connectors, or switches for breaks (open circuit) or short circuits (closed circuit).

Continuity light A test light that has a battery and lights if there is continuity (electrical connection) between the two points that are connected to the tester.

Control wires The wires used in a power window circuit that are used to control the operation of the windows.

Conventional theory The theory that electricity flows from positive (+) to negative (−).

Core A part that is returned to a parts store and which will be turned over to a company to be repaired or remanufactured.

Coulomb A measurement of electrons. A coulomb is 6.28 × 101 (6.28 billion billion) electrons.

Counter electromotive force (cemf) A voltage produced by a rotating coil such as a starter motor where the armature is being moved through a magnetic field.

Courtesy lights General term used to describe all interior lights.

CPA Connector Position Assurance. A clip used to help hold the two parts of electrical connector together.

CPU Central Processor Unit.

Crimp and seal connectors A type of electrical connector that has glue inside which provides a weather-proof seal after it is heated.

Crossover An electronic circuit that separates frequencies in a sound (audio) system.

CRT Cathode Ray Tube. A type of display which is commonly used in TVs.

Cruise control A system that maintains the desired vehicle speed. Also called speed control.

Darlington pair Two transistors electrically connected to form an amplifier. This permits a very small current flow to control a large current flow. Named for Sidney Darlington, a physicist at Bell Laboratories from 1929 to 1971.

DC coupling A signal transmission that passes both AC and DC signal components to the meter.

Deceleration sensor A sensor mounted to the body of frame of a vehicle that detects and measures the deceleration of the vehicle. Used to control the activation of the air bags and vehicle stability systems.

Decibels (dB) A unit of the magnitude of sound.

Deep cycling The full discharge and then the full recharge of a battery.

Delta winding A type of stator winding where all three coils are connected in a triangle shape. Named for the triangle-shape Greek capital letter.

Despiking diode Another name of clamping diode.

Dielectric An insulator used between two conductors to form a capacitor.

Digital computer A computer that uses on and off signals only. Uses an A to D converter to change analog signals to digital before processing.

Diode An electrical device that allows current to flow in one direction only.

Direction wires The wires from the control switch to the lift motor on a power window circuit. The direction of current flow through these wires determines which direction the window moves.

Division A specific segment of a waveform, as defined by the grid on the display.

DMM Digital multimeter. A digital multimeter is capable of measuring electrical current, resistance, and voltage.

Doping The adding of impurities to pure silicon or germanium to form either P or N type material.

DOT Abbreviation for the Department of Transportation.

DPDT Double-pole, double-throw switch.

DPST Double pole, single throw switch.

Drive sizes The size in fractions of an inch of the square drive for sockets.

Drive-end (DE) housing The end of a starter motor that has the drive pinion gear.

DRL Daytime Running Lights. Lights that are located in the front of the vehicle and come on whenever the ignition is on. In some vehicles the vehicle has to be moving before they come on. Used as a safety device on many vehicles and required in many countries such as Canada since 1990.

DSO Digital Storage Oscilloscope.

Dual inline pins (DIP) A type of electronic chip that has two parallel lines of pins.

Dual-stage airbags Airbags that can deploy either with minimum force or full force or both together based on the information sent to the airbag controller regarding the forces involved in the collision.

Duty cycle The percentage of time a unit is turned on.

DVOM Digital volt-ohm-milliammeter or digital volt-ohm-meter.

Dynamic voltage Voltage measured with the circuit energized and current flowing through the circuit.

E & C Entertainment and comfort.

E²PROM Electronically erasable programmable read only memory. A type of memory that can be electronically erased and reprogrammed.

ECM Electronic Control Module. The name used by Ford to describe the computer used to control spark and fuel on older model vehicles.

ECU Electronic Control Unit. A generic term for a vehicle computer.

EDR Event data recorder. The hardware and software used to record vehicle information before, during, and after an airbag deployment.

EEPROM See E²PROM.

Electrical load Applying a load to a component such as a battery to measure its performance.

Electrical potential Another term to describe voltage.

Electricity The movement of free electrons from one atom to another.

Electrochemistry The term used to describe the chemical reaction that occurs inside a battery to produce electricity.

Electrolyte Any substance which, in solution, is separated into ions and is made capable of conducting an electric current. The acid solution of a lead-acid battery.

Electromagnetic The magnet field around an electromagnet which consists of a soft iron core surrounded by a coil of wire. Electrical current flowing through the coiled wire creates a magnetic field around the core.

Electromotive force (EMF) The force (pressure) that can move electrons through a conductor.

Electron theory The theory that electricity flows from negative (–) to positive (+).

EMF *See* Electromotive force.

Emitter The name of one section of a transistor. The arrow used on a symbol for a transistor is on the emitter and the arrow points toward the negative section of the transistor.

Engine mapping A computer program that uses engine test data to determine the best fuel–air ratio and spark advance to use at each speed of the engine for best performance.

EPA Environmental Protection Agency. A federal government agency that oversees the enforcement of laws related to the environment. Included in these laws are regulations on the amount and content of automotive emissions.

EPM Electrical Power Management. A General Motors term used to describes a charging system control sensor and the control of the generator (alternator) output based on the needs of the vehicle.

ESD Electrostatic discharge. Another term for ESD is static electricity.

ETC Electronic throttle control.

ETR Electronically tuned radio. A type of radio now used in all vehicles that use electronics to tune the frequencies instead of using a variable capacitor.

Extensions Steel bars with a male and female ends to extend the reach of a ratchet to rotate a socket wrench.

External trigger Outside source or signal that is used to trigger or start a trace.

Eye wash station A unit that looks similar to a drinking fountain but used to wash the eyes with a large amount of water at relatively low pressure. To be used in the event that a person gets some chemical in the eyes.

Farad A unit of capacitance named for Michael Faraday (1791–1867), an English physicist. A Farad is the capacity to store 1 coulomb of electrons at 1 volt of potential difference.

Feedback The reverse flow of electrical current through a circuit or electrical unit that should not normally be operating. This feedback current (reverse-bias current flow) is most often caused by a poor ground connection for the same normally operating circuit.

FET Field Effect Transistor. A type of transistor that is very sensitive and can be harmed by static electricity.

Fiber optics The transmission of light through special plastic that keeps the light rays parallel even if the plastic is tied in a knot.

Field coils Coils or wire wound around metal pole shoes to form the electromagnetic field inside an electric motor.

Field housing The part of a starter that supports the field coils.

Field poles The magnets used as field coils in a starter motor.

File A hand tool used to smooth metal.

Fire blanket A fire-proof wool blanket used to cover a person who is on fire to smother the fire.

Fire extinguisher classes The types of fires that a fire extinguisher is designed to handle is referred to as fire class.

Floating ground system An electrical system that uses a ground that is not connected to the chassis of the vehicle.

Flooded cell battery A type of secondary (rechargeable) battery that uses a liquid electrolyte.

Flux density The density of the magnetic lines of force around a magnet or other object.

Flux lines Individual magnetic lines of force.

FM Frequency modulation. A type of radio transmission.

Forward bias Current flow in normal direction. Used to describe when current is able to flow through a diode.

Free electrons The outer electrons in an atom that has fewer than four electrons in its outer orbit.

Frequency The number of times a waveform repeats in one second, measured in Hertz (Hz), frequency band.

Fuse link A safety device used on a solvent washer which would melt and cause the lid to close in the event of a fire. A type of fuse used to control the maximum current in a circuit.

Fuse An electrical safety unit constructed of a fine tin conductor that will melt and open the electrical circuit if excessive current flows through the fuse.

Fusible link A type of fuse that will melt and open the protected circuit in the event of a short circuit, which could cause excessive current flow through the fusible link. Most fusible links are actually wires that are four gauge sizes smaller than the wire of the circuits being protected.

Gassing The release of hydrogen and oxygen gas from the plates of a battery during charging or discharging.

Gauss gauge A gauge used to measure the unit of magnetic induction or magnetic intensity named for Karl Friedrich Gauss (1777–1855), a German mathematician.

GAWR Gross axle weight rating. A rating of the load capacity of a vehicle and included on placards on the vehicle and in the owner's manual.

Gel battery A lead-acid battery with silica added to the electrolyte to make it leak proof and spill proof. Also called a valve-regulated lead acid (VRLA) battery.

Generator A device that converts mechanical energy into electrical energy. Also called an alternator.

Generator output test A test used to determine the condition of a generator (alternator).

Germanium A semiconductor used in early diodes.

GMLAN General Motors Local Area Network. GM's term for CAN used in GM vehicles.

GMM Graphing Multimeter.

GPS Global Positioning System. A government program of 24 satellites which transmit signals and used by receivers to determine their location.

Grade The measure of the strength or quality of a bolt or fastener.

Graticule The series of squares on the face of a scope. Usually 8 by 10 on a screen.

Grid A part of a battery onto which the active material is pasted.

Ground The lowest possible voltage potential in a circuit. In electrical terms, a ground is the desirable return circuit path. Ground can also be undesirable and provide a shortcut path for a defective electrical circuit.

Ground (return) path The electrical return path that the current flows through in a complete circuit.

Ground brushes The brushes in a starter motor that carry current to the housing of the starter or ground.

Ground plane A part of antenna that is metal and usually the body of the vehicle.

Grounded An electrical fault where the current is going to ground rather than through the load and then to ground.

Growler Electrical tester designed to test starter and DC generator armatures.

GVWR Gross vehicle weight rating. The total weight of the vehicle including the maximum cargo.

Hacksaw A type of saw used to cut metal and uses a replaceable blade.

Hammer A hand tool used to deliver a force to a concentrated place.

Hazard warning A sticker or decal warning that a hazard is close.

Heat shrink tubing A type of rubber tubing that shrinks to about half of its original diameter when heated. Used over a splice during a wire repair.

Heat sink Usually, a metallic-finned unit used to keep electronic components cool.

HEPA vacuum High efficiency particulate air filter vacuum used to clean brake dust.

Hertz A unit of measurement of frequency. One Hertz is one cycle per second, abbreviated Hz. Named for Heinrich R. Hertz, a 19th century German physicist.

HID High Intensity Discharge. A type of headlight that uses high voltage to create an arc inside the arc tube assembly which then produces a blue-white light.

High energy ignition (HEI) The brand name for the electronic ignition used in General Motors vehicles.

High impedance meter A digital meter that has at least 10 million ohms of internal resistance as measured between the test leads with the meter set to read volts.

High-pass filter A filter in an audio system that blocks low frequencies and only allows high frequencies to pass through to the speakers.

Hold-in winding One of two electromagnetic windings inside a solenoid; used to hold the movable core into the solenoid.

Hole theory A theory which states that as an electron flows from negative (–) to positive (+), it leaves behind a hole. According to the hole theory, the hole would move from positive (+) to negative (–).

HomeLink A brand name of a system used and included in many new vehicles to operate the automatic garage door opener.

Horn An electromechanical device that creates a loud sound when activated.

HUD Head up display.

Hybrid flasher A type of flasher unit that can operate two or more bulbs at a constant rate.

Hydrometer An instrument used to measure the specific gravity of a liquid. A battery hydrometer is calibrated to read the expected specific gravity of battery electrolyte.

IEC International Electrotechnical Commission. Set the safety standards for meters such as CAT III.

Impedance The resistance of a coil of wire, measured in ohms.

Impurities Doping elements used in the construction of diodes and transistors.

Independent switches Switch located at each door and used to raise or lower the power window for that door only.

Inductive ammeter A type of ammeter that is uses a Hall Effect senor in a clamp that is used around a conductor carrying a current.

Input Information on data from sensors to an electronic controller is called input. Sensors and switches provide the input signals.

Input conditioning   What the computer does to the input signals to make them useful; usually includes an analog to digital converter and other electronic circuits that eliminate electrical noise.

Insulated brushes   Brushes used in a starter motor that connect to battery power through the solenoid.

Insulated path   The power side of an electrical circuit.

Insulator   A material that does not readily conduct electricity and heat. A nonmetal material that contains more than four electrons in its atom's outer shell.

Integral sensor   A term used to describe a crash sensor that is built into the airbag control module.

Integrated circuit (IC)   An electronic circuit that contains many circuits all in one chip.

IOD   Ignition off draw. A Chrysler term used to describe battery electrical drain or parasitic draw.

Ion   An atom with an excess or deficiency of electrons forming either a negative or a positive charged particle.

IP   Abbreviation for instrument panel.

ISO   International Standards Organization.

IVR   Instrument voltage regulator.

Jumper cables   Heavy-gauge (4 to 00) electrical cables with large clamps, used to connect a vehicle that has a discharged battery to a vehicle that has a good battery.

Junction   The point where two types of materials join.

KAM   Keep alive memory.

Kelvin (K)   A temperature scale where absolute zero is zero degrees. Nothing is colder than absolute zero.

Key fob   A decorative unit attached to keys. Often includes a remote control to unlock/lock vehicles.

Keyword   A type of network communications used in many General Motors vehicles.

Kilo (k)   Means 1000; abbreviated k or K.

Kirchhoff's current law   A law that states "The current flowing into any junction of an electrical circuit is equal to the current flowing out of that junction."

Kirchhoff's voltage law   A law about electrical circuits that states: "The voltage around any closed circuit is equal to the sum (total) of the resistances."

LCD   Liquid-crystal display.

LDWS   Lane departure warning system.

LED   Light-emitting diode. A high-efficiency light source that uses very little electricity and produces very little heat.

LED test light   A test light used by technicians to test for voltage that has high impedance and uses an LED with a 470 ohm resistor to control current through the tester.

Left-hand rule   A method of determining the direction of magnetic lines of force around a conductor. The left-hand rule is used with the electron flow theory (– flowing to +).

Legs   Another name for the branches of a parallel circuit.

Lenz's Law   The relative motion between a conductor and a magnetic field is opposed by the magnetic field of the current it has induced.

Leyden jar   A device first used to store an electrical charge. The first type of capacitor.

Load   A term used to describe a device when an electrical current is flowing through it.

Load test   A type of battery test where an electrical load is applied to the battery and the voltage is monitored to determine the condition of a battery.

Lock tang   A mechanical tab that is used to secure a terminal into a connector. This lock tang must be depressed to be able to remove the terminal from the connector.

Lockout switch   A lock placed on the circuit breaker box to insure that no one turns on the electrical circuit while repairs are being made.

Logic probe   A type of tester that can detect either power or ground. Most testers can detect voltage but most of the others cannot detect if a ground is present without further testing.

Low-pass filter   A device used in a audio system that block high frequencies and only allow low frequencies to pass to the speakers.

Low-water loss battery   A type of battery that uses little water in normal service. Most batteries used in cars and light trucks use this type of battery.

Lumbar   The lower section of the back.

Magnetic flux   The lines of force produced in a magnetic field.

Magnetic induction   The transfer of the magnetic lines of force to another nearby metal object or coil of wire.

Magnetism   A form of energy that is recognized by the attraction it exerts on other materials.

Maintenance-free battery   A type of battery that does not require routine adding of water to the cells. Most batteries used in cars and light truck are maintenance-free design.

Master control switch   The control switch for the power windows located near the driver who can operate all of the windows.

MCA   Marine cranking amps. A battery specification.

Mega (M) Million.   Used when writing larger numbers or measuring large amount of resistance.

Meniscus   The curve shape of a liquid when in a tube. Used to determine when a battery has been properly filled with distilled water.

Mercury   A heavy metal that is liquid at room temperature.

Mesh spring   A spring used behind the starter pinion on a starter drive to force the drive pinion into mesh with the ring gear on the engine.

Meter accuracy   The accuracy of a meter measured in percent.

Meter resolution   The specification of meter that indicates how small or fine a measurement the meter can detect and display.

Metric bolts   Bolts manufactured and sized in the metric system of measurement.

Metric wire gauge   The metric method for measuring wire size in the square millimeters. This is the measure of the core of the wire and does not include the insulation.

Micro (µ)   One-millionth of a volt or ampere.

Milli (m)   One-thousandth of a volt or ampere.

Modulation   A combination of a carrier wave frequency with an audio frequency.

Momentary switch   A type of switch that toggles between on and off.

MOSFET   Metal Oxide Semiconductor Field Effect Transistor. A type of transistor.

MOV   Metal oxide varistor. An electronic device that operates like two back-to-back zener diodes.

MSDS   Material Safety Data Sheets.

Multiplexing   A process of sending multiple signals of information at the same time over a signal wire.

N.C.   Normally Closed.

N.O.   Normally Open.

Network   A communications system used to link multiple computers or modules.

Neutral charge   An atom that has the same number electrons as protons.

Neutral safety switch   An electrical switch which allows the starter to be energized only if the gear selector is in neutral or park.

Node   A module and computer that is part of a communications network.

Nonvolatile RAM   Computer memory capability that is not lost when power is removed.

NPN transistor   A type of transistor that has the P-type material in the base and the N-type material is used for the emitter and collector.

NTC   Negative temperature coefficient. Usually used in reference to a temperature sensor (coolant or air temperature). As the temperature increases, the resistance of the sensor decreases.

N-type material   Silicon or germanium doped with phosphorus, arsenic, or antimony.

Nuts   A female threaded fastener to be used with a bolt or stud.

NVRAM   Nonvolatile random access memory.

OAD   Override alternator dampener.

OAP   Override alternator pulley.

Occupant detection systems   An airbag system that includes a sensor in the passenger seat used to detect whether or not a passenger is seated in the passenger side and the weight range of that passenger.

Ohm   The unit of electrical resistance. Named for Georg (spelled without an "e") Simon Ohm.

Ohm's Law   An electrical law that requires 1 volt to push 1 ampere through 1 ohm of resistance.

Ohmmeter   An electrical tester deigned to measure electrical resistance in ohms.

OL   Overload or over limit.

OP-amps   An abbreviation for operational amplifier. Used in circuits to control and simplify digital signals.

Open circuit   Any circuit that is not complete and in which no current flows.

Open circuit voltage   Voltage measured without the circuit in operation.

Oscilloscope (scope)   A tester that displays voltage levels on a screen.

OSHA   Occupational Safety and Health Administration. OSHA is the main federal agency responsible for enforcement of workplace safety and health legislation.

Overrunning alternator dampener   An alternator (generator) drive pulley that has a one-way clutch and a dampener spring used to smooth the operation of the alternator and reduce the stress on the drive belt.

Overrunning alternator pulley   An alternator (generator) drive pulley that has a one-way clutch used to smooth the operation of the alternator and reduce the stress on the drive belt.

Overrunning clutch   A part of a starter drive assembly that allows the engine to rotate faster than the starter motor to help protect the starter from harm in the event the ignition switch is held in the crank position after the engine starts.

Pacific fuse element   A type of automotive fuse.

Parallel circuit   An electrical circuit with more than one path from the power side to the ground side. Has more than one branch or leg.

Parasitic load test   An electrical test that measures how much current (amperes) is draining from the battery with the ignition off and all electrical loads off.

Partitions   Separations between the cells of a battery. Partitions are made of the same material as that of the outside case of the battery.

Passenger presence system (PPS)   An airbag system that includes a sensor in the passenger seat used to detect whether or not a passenger is seated in the passenger side and the weight range of that passenger.

Passkey I and II   A type of anti-theft system used in General Motors vehicles.

Passlock I and II   A type of anti-theft system used in General Motors vehicles.

PATS   Passive Anti-Theft System. A type of anti-theft system used in Ford, Lincoln, and Mercury vehicles.

PCM   Powertrain control module.

Peltier Effect   A French scientist Peltier found that electrons moving through a solid can carry heat from one side of the material to the other side. This effect is called the **Peltier effect.**

Permanent magnet electric motors   Electric motors that use permanent magnets for the field instead of electro-magnets.

Permeability   The measure of how well a material conducts magnetic lines of force.

Phosphor   A chemical-coated light-emitting element called a phosphor is hit with high-speed electrons which cause it to glow and creates light.

Photodiodes   A type of diode used as a sun-load sensor. Connected in reverse bias, the current flow is proportional to the sun load.

Photoelectricity   When certain metals are exposed to light, some of the light energy is transferred to the free electrons of the metal. This excess energy breaks the electrons loose from the surface of the metal. They can then be collected and made to flow in a conductor which is called photoelectricity.

Photons   Light is emitted from an LED by the release of energy in the form of photons.

Photoresistor   A semiconductor that changes in resistance with the presence or absence of light. Dark is high resistance and light is low resistance.

Phototransistor   An electronic device that can detect light and turn on or off. Used in some suspension height sensors.

Piezoelectricity   The principle by which certain crystals become electrically charged when pressure is applied.

Pinch weld seam   The area under a unit-body vehicle where two body panels join and are bent together and then welded. A typical location to place a jack if the vehicle needs to be hoisted.

Pitch   The number of threads per inch of a threaded fastener.

PIV   Peak Inverse Voltage. A rating for a diode.

Pliers   A hand tool with two movable jaws.

PM generator   A sensor that has a permanent magnet and a coil of wire and produces an analog voltage signal if a metal wheel with notches passes close to the sensor.

PNP transistor   A type of transistor that used N-type material for the base and P-type material for the emitter and collector.

Polarity   The condition of being positive or negative in relation to a magnetic pole.

Pole   The point where magnetic lines of force enter or leave a magnet.

Pole shoes   The metal part of the field coils in a starter motor.

Porous lead   Lead with many small holes to make a surface porous for use in battery negative plates; the chemical symbol for lead is Pb.

Positive temperature coefficient (PTC) Usually used in reference to a conductor or electronic circuit breaker. As the temperature increases, the electrical resistance also increases.

Potentiometer A 3-terminal variable resistor that varies the voltage drop in a circuit.

Power line capacitor A capacitor used to boost the output of a sound system to move the speakers especially when reproducing low frequencies.

Power source In electrical terms the battery or generator (alternator).

PPE Personal Protective Equipment which can include gloves, safety glasses, and other items.

Pressure differential switch Switch installed between the two separate braking circuits of a dual master to light the dash board "brake" light in the event of a brake system failure, causing a *difference* in brake pressure.

Pretensioners An explosive device used to remove the slack from a safety belt when an airbag is deployed.

Primary wire Wire used for low voltage automotive circuits, typically 12 volts.

Processing The act of a computer when input data is run through computer programs to determine what output is needed to be performed.

Programmable Controller Interface (PCI) A type of network communications protocol used in Chrysler brand vehicles.

PROM Programmable read-only memory.

PRV *See* peak inverse voltage.

PTC circuit protection Usually used in reference to a conductor or electronic circuit breaker. As the temperature increases, the electrical resistance also increases.

P-type material Silicon or germanium doped with boron or indium.

Pull-in winding One of two electromagnetic windings inside a solenoid used to move a movable core.

Pulse train A DC voltage that turns on and off in a series of pulses.

Pulse width The amount of "on" time of an electronic fuel injector.

Pulse wipers Windshield wipers that operate intermittently. Also called delay wipers.

Punches A hand tool used with a hammer to drive out pins and other small objects.

PWM Pulse width modulation; operation of a device by an on/off digital signal that is controlled by the time duration the device is turned on and off.

Radio choke A small coil of wire installed in the power lead, leading to a pulsing unit, such as an IVR to prevent radio interference.

Rain-sense wipers Windshield wiper that use an electronic sensor to detect the presence of rain on the windshield and start operating automatically if the wiper switch is in the Auto position.

RAM Random access memory. A nonpermanent type of computer memory used to store and retrieve information.

Ratchet A reversible hand tool used to rotate a socket.

RCRA Resource Conservation and Recovery Act.

Recall A notification to the owner of a vehicle that a safety issue needs to be corrected.

Recombinant battery A battery design that does not release gasses during normal operation. AGM batteries are known as recombinant batteries.

Rectifier bridge A group of six diodes, three positive (+) and three negative (–) commonly used in generators (alternators).

Relay An electromagnetic switch that uses a movable arm.

Reluctance The resistance to the movement of magnetic lines of force.

Reserve capacity The number of minutes a battery can produce 25 A and still maintain a battery voltage of 1.75 V per cell (10.5 V for a 12 V battery).

Residual magnetism Magnetism remaining after the magnetizing force is removed.

Resistance The opposition to current flow measured in ohms.

Reverse bias When the polarity of a battery is connected to a diode backwards and no current flows.

RF Radio frequency.

Rheostat A two-terminal variable resistor.

Right-to-know laws Laws that state that employees have a right to know when the materials they use at work are hazardous.

Ripple voltage Excessive AC voltage produced by a generator (alternator usually caused by a defective diode.

RMS Root Mean Square. A method of displaying variable voltage signals on a digital meter.

ROM Read-only memory.

Rosin-core solder A type of solder for use in electrical repairs. Inside the center of the solder is a rosin that acts as a flux to clean and help the solder flow.

Rotor The rotating part of a generator where the magnetic field is created.

RPA Rear Park Assist. The General Motors term to describe the system used to detect objects and warn the drive when backing.

Rubber coupling A flexible connection between the power seat motor and the drive cable.

RVS Remote Vehicle Start. A general Motor's term for the system that allows the driver to start the engine using a remote control.

SAE Society of Automotive Engineers.

SAR Supplemental Air Restraints. Another term used to describe an airbag system.

Saturation The point of maximum magnetic field strength of a coil.

SCR Silicon Controller Rectifier.

Screw jack assembly A screw jack that is used to raise or lower a power seat.

Screwdrivers A hand tool used to install or remove screws.

SDARS Satellite Digital Audio Radio Services. Another term used to describe satellite radio.

Sediment chamber A space below the cell plates of some batteries to permit the accumulation of sediment deposits flaking from the battery plates. A sediment chamber keeps the sediment from shorting the battery plates.

Semiconductor A material that is neither a conductor nor an insulator; has exactly four electrons in the atom's outer shell.

Serial Communication Interface (SCI) Serial Communication Interface, a type of serial data transmission used by Chrysler.

Serial data Data that is transmitted by a series of rapidly changing voltage signals.

Series circuit An electrical circuit that provides only one path for current to flow.

Series circuit laws   Laws that were developed by Kirchhoff which pertain to series circuits.

Series-parallel circuits   Any type of circuit containing resistances in both series and parallel in one circuit.

Series-wound field   A typical starter motor circuit where the current through the field windings is connected in series with the armature before going to ground. Also called a series-wound starter.

Shim   A thin metal spacer.

Short circuit   A circuit in which current flows, but bypasses some or all the resistance in the circuit. A connection that results in a "copper-to-copper" connection.

Shorted   A condition of being shorted such as a short circuit.

Short-to-ground   A short circuit in which the current bypasses some or all the resistance of the circuit and flows to ground. Because ground is usually steel in automotive electricity, a short to ground (grounded) is a "copper-to-steel" connection.

Short-to-voltage   A circuit in which current flows, but bypasses some or all the resistance in the circuit. A connection that results in a "copper-to-copper" connection.

Shunt field   A field coil used in a starter motor that is not connected to the armature in series but is grounded to the starter case.

Shunt   A device used to divert or bypass part of the current from the main circuit.

Silicon   A semiconductor material.

SIR   Supplemental inflatable restraints. Another term for air bags.

SKIS   Sentry Key Immobilizer System. A type of anti-theft system used in Chrysler vehicles.

SLA   Abbreviation for sealed lead acid battery.

SLI   The battery that is responsible for starting, lighting and ignition.

Slip-ring end (SRE)   The end of a generator (alternator) that has the brushes and the slip rings.

Snips   A hand tool designed to cut sheet metal.

Socket   A tool used to grasp the head of a bolt or nut and then rotated by a ratchet or breaker bar.

Socket adapter   A tool used to adapt one size of socket drive for use with another size drive unit such as a ratchet or breaker bar.

Solar cells   A device that creates electricity when sunlight hits a semiconductor material and electrons are released. About one kilowatt from a solar cell that is one square meter in size.

Solvent   Usually colorless liquids that are used to remove grease and oil.

SPDT   Single pole, double throw. A type of electrical switch.

Speakers   A device consisting of a magnet, coil of wire, and a cone which reproduces sounds from the electrical signals sent to the speakers from a radio or amplifier.

Specific gravity   The ratio of the weight of a given volume of a liquid divided by the weight of an equal volume of water.

Spike protection resistor   A resistor usually between 300 and 500 ohms that is connected in a circuit in parallel with the load to help reduce a voltage spike caused when a current following through a coil is turned off.

Splice pack   A term used by General Motors to describe the connection of modules in a network.

Sponge lead   Lead with many small holes used to make a surface porous or sponge-like for use in battery negative plates; the chemical symbol for lead is Pb.

Spontaneous combustion   A condition that can cause some materials, such as oily rags to catch fire without a source of ignition.

SPST   Single pole, single throw. A type of electrical switch.

Squib   The heating element of an inflator module which starts the chemical reaction to create the gas which inflates an air bag.

SRS   Supplemental Restraint System. Another term for an airbag system.

SST   Special Service Tools. Tools specified by a vehicle manufacturer needed to service a vehicle or a unit repair component of a vehicle.

Standard Corporate Protocol (SCP)   A network communications protocol used by Ford.

Starter drive   A term used to describe the starter motor drive pinion gear with overrunning clutch.

Starter solenoid   A type of starter motor that uses a solenoid to activate the starter drive.

State-of-health (SOH)   A signal sent by modules to all of the other modules in the network indicating that it is well and able to transmit.

Static electricity   An electrical charge that builds up in insulators and then discharges to conductors.

Stator   A name for three interconnected windings inside an alternator. A rotating rotor provides a moving magnetic field and induces a current in the windings of the stator.

Stepper motor   A motor that moves a specified amount of rotation.

Stiffening capacitor   See powerline capacitor.

Storage   The process inside of a computer where data is stored before and after calculations have been made.

Stud   A short rod with threads on both ends.

Subwoofer   A type of speaker that is used to reproduce low frequency sounds.

Suppression diode   A diode installed in the reverse bias direction and used to reduce the voltage spike that is created when a circuit that contains a coil is opened and the coil discharges.

SVR   Sealed Valve Regulated. A term used to describe a type of battery that is valve regulated lead acid or sealed lead acid.

SWCAN   An abbreviation for single wire CAN (Controller Area Network).

Telltale lamp   A dash warning light. Also called an idiot light.

Tensile strength   The strength of a bolt or fastener in the length-wise direction.

Terminal   The metal end of a wire which fits into a plastic connector and is the electrical connection part of a junction.

Terminating resistors   Resistors placed at the end of a high-speed serial data circuit to help reduce electromagnetic interference.

Test light   A light used to test for voltage. Contains a light bulb with a ground wire at one end and a pointed tip at the other end.

THD   Total Harmonic Distortion. A rating for an amplifier used in sound system.

Thermistor   A resistor that changes resistance with temperature. A positive-coefficient thermistor has increased resistance with an increase in temperature. A negative-coefficient thermistor has increased resistance with a decrease in temperature.

Thermocouple   Two dissimilar metal when connected and heated creates a voltage. Used for measuring temperature.

Thermoelectricity   The production of current flow created by heating the connection of two dissimilar metals.

Threshold voltage   Another name for barrier voltage or the voltage difference needed to forward bias a diode.

Through bolts   The bolts used to hold the parts of a starter motor together. The long bolts go though field housing and into the drive-end housing.

Throws   The term used to describe the number of output circuits there are in a switch.

Time base   The setting of the amount of time per division when adjusting a scope.

Tone generator tester   A type of tester used to find a shorted circuit that uses a tone generator. Headphones are used along with a probe to locate where the tone stops which indicates where in the circuit the fault is located.

Total circuit resistance (R_T)   The total resistance in a circuit.

Trade number   The number stamped on an automotive light bulb. All bulbs of the same trade number have the same candlepower and wattage, regardless of the manufacturer of the bulb.

Transistor   A semiconductor device that can operate as an amplifier or an electrical switch.

Trigger level   The voltage level that a waveform must reach to start display.

Trigger slope   The voltage direction that a waveform must have to start display. A positive slope requires the voltage to be increasing as it crosses the trigger level; a negative slope requires the voltage to be decreasing.

Troxler effect   The Troxler effect is a visual effect where an image remains on the retina of the eye for a short time after the image has been removed. The effect was discovered in 1804 by Igney Paul Vital Troxler (1780–1866), a Swiss physician. Because of the Troxler effect, headlight glare can remain on the retina of the eye and create a blind spot.

TSB   Technical service bulletin.

TTL   Transistor-Transistor Logic.

Turns ratio   The ratio between the number of turns used in the primary winding of the coil to the number of turns used in the secondary winding. In a typical ignition coil the ratio is 100:1.

Tweeter   A type of speaker used in an audio system that is designed to transmit high frequency sounds.

Twisted pair   A pair of wires that are twisted together from 9 to 16 turns per foot of length. Most are twisted once every inch (12 per foot) to help reduce electromagnetic inference from being induced in the wires as one wire would tend to cancel out any interference picked up by the other wire.

UART   Universal Asynchronous Receive/Transmit, a type of serial data transmission.

UBP   UART based protocol.

UNC   Unified national coarse.

Undercut   A process of cutting the insulation, usually mica, from between the segments of a starter commutator.

UNF   Unified national fine.

Universal joint   A joint in a steering or drive shaft that allows torque to be transmitted at an angle.

Used oil   Oil that has been used in an engine and has a chance to absorb metal particles and other contaminants.

UST   Underground storage tank.

Valence ring   The outermost ring or orbit of electrons around a nucleus of an atom.

Variable-delay wipers   Windshield wipers whose speed can be varied.

Varistors   Resistors whose resistance depends on the amount of voltage applied to them.

VATS   Vehicle Antitheft System. A system used on some General Motors vehicles.

VECI   Vehicle emission control information. This sticker is located under the hood on all vehicles and includes emission-related information that is important to the service technician.

VIN   Vehicle identification number.

Voice recognition   A system which uses a microphone and a speaker connected to an electronic module which can control the operation of electronic devices in a vehicle.

Voltage drop   Voltage loss across a wire, connector, or any other conductor. Voltage drop equals resistance in ohms times current in amperes (Ohm's law).

Voltmeter   An electrical test instrument used to measure volts (unit of electrical pressure). A voltmeter is connected in parallel with the unit or circuit being tested.

VRLA   Valve regulated lead-acid battery. A sealed battery that is both spill proof and leakproof. AGM and gelled electrolyte are both examples of VRLA batteries.

VTF   Vacuum Tube Florescence. A type of dash display.

Washers   Flat or shaped pieces of round metal with a hole in the center used between a nut and a part or casting.

Watt   An electrical unit of power; 1 watt equals current (amperes) × voltage (1/746 hp). Named after James Watt, a Scottish inventor.

Watt's Law   The formula for Watts is the voltage times the amperes in the circuit which represents the electrical power in the circuit.

WHMIS   Workplace Hazardous Materials Information Systems.

Window regulator   A mechanical device that transfers the rotating motion of the window hand crank or electric motor to a vertical motion to raise and lower a window in a vehicle.

Windshield wipers   The assembly of motor, motor control, operating linkage plus the wiper arms and blades which are used to remove rain water from the windshield.

Wiring schematic   A drawing showing the wires and the components in a circuit using symbols to represent the components.

WOW display   A dash display when it first comes on and lights all possible segments. Can be used to test the dash display for missing lighted segments.

Wrenches   Hand tools used to rotate bolts or nuts.

Xenon headlights   Headlights that use an arc tube assembly that has a xenon gas inside which produces a bright bluish light.

Zener diode   A specially constructed (heavily doped) diode designed to operate with a reverse-bias current after a certain voltage has been reached. Named for Clarence Melvin Zener.

SPANISH GLOSSARY

Prueba de carga de 3 minutos Un método usado para probar baterías. No es válido para todo tipo de batería.

Depósito de almacenamiento no subterráneo Un tipo de depósito para aceite.

Acoplamiento de corriente alterna Una señal que atraviesa el componente de la señal de corriente alterna en su trayecto al medidor, pero que bloquea el componente de corriente continua. Sirve para observar una señal de corriente alterna que típicamente viaja sobre una señal de corriente continua; por ejemplo, una ola cargante.

Multímetro digital de corriente alterna y continua con sujetador Un tipo de medidor que tiene una tenaza, o clip, que se sujeta al cable para medir la corriente.

Crossover activo Un tipo de circuito divisor de frecuencias que usa componentes electrónicos para bloquear ciertas frecuencias.

Actuador Un aparato electromecánico que realiza movimientos mecánicos dirigidos por un controlador.

Tubo aislante termocontraíble revestido con adhesivo Un tipo de tubo aislante termocontraíble que se contrae a un tercio de su diámetro original y cuyo interior está recubierto de pegamento.

Sistema activo de faros delanteros (*AFS por sus siglas en inglés*) Un nombre para el sistema que causa que los faros se enciendan cuando el vehículo dobla una esquina.

Baterías AGM Las baterías de diseño de lámina de vidrio absorbente, o *AGM* por sus siglas en inglés, son baterías de plomo-ácido, pero que usan un material absorbente entre sus placas para retener los electrolitos. Las baterías *AGM* se clasifican como baterías de plomo-ácido reguladas por válvula (Baterías *VRLA* por sus siglas en inglés). *Véase también* **VRLA.**

AGST Siglas en inglés para depósito de almacenamiento no subterráneo; usado para almacenar aceite.

Bolsa de aire Un saco de tela inflable que se activa y despliega por causa de un impacto lo suficientemente grave como para causar daño personal.

Alternador Un generador eléctrico que produce corriente alterna. También se lo conoce como un *generador de CA.*

Zumbido del alternador El ruido que hace un alternador que tiene un(os) diodo(s) defectuoso(s).

MA Modulación de amplitud.

Galga americana para alambres (*AWG por sus siglas en inglés*) Un método usado para determinar el diámetro de los cables y alambres eléctricos.

Amperímetro Un instrumento de medición eléctrica usado para medir amperios (la unidad de la cantidad de flujo de corriente).

Amperio La unidad de la cantidad de flujo de corriente. Nombrada así en honor a André Ampère (1775–1836).

Amperio-hora Un método usado para determinar la capacidad de una batería.

Amperio-vueltas La unidad de medida para la fuerza de un campo electromagnético.

Análogo Un tipo de instrumento en el tablero de instrumentos que indica valores por medio del movimiento de una aguja o de algún instrumento parecido. Una señal análoga es continua y variable.

Convertidor de análogo a digital (*ADC por sus siglas en inglés*) Un circuito electrónico que convierte señales análogas en señales digitales que pueden ser usadas por una computadora.

Ánodo El electrodo positivo hacia el cual fluyen los electrones.

Inducido, o rotor La unidad rotante dentro de un generador de corriente continua o un arrancador compuesta de una serie de bobinas de material aislante enrolladas alrededor de un núcleo de hierro laminado.

Sensor de seguridad Un sensor usado en un circuito de bolsas de aire que es muy sensible y que completa el circuito. Es el primero de dos sensores que se necesitan para activar y desplegar una bolsa de aire.

Asbestosis Una condición médica en la que el asbesto produce la formación de tejido cicatrizal en los pulmones, lo cual conduce a la falta de aliento.

Enlace automático Un tipo de fusible automotriz.

Luz trasera Luz que ilumina la pantalla de cristales líquidos de una herramienta de prueba por detrás. Este término también se refiere a la ventana trasera de un vehículo.

Cámara de marcha atrás Una cámara colocada en la parte posterior del vehículo que se usa para visualizar lo que está detrás del vehículo cuando este retrocede.

Base El nombre para la sección del transistor que controla el flujo de corriente a través del transistor.

Cables de batería Cables que se adjuntan a los terminales negativos y positivos de la batería.

Prueba de fuga eléctrica de la batería Una prueba para determinar si un componente o circuito está causando que la batería se agote.

Velocidad de línea en baudios La velocidad a la que se transmiten bits de información en un flujo de datos en serie. Se mide en bits por segundo (bps).

BCI Siglas en inglés del Concilio Internacional de la Batería. Esta organización se encarga de fijar estándares para baterías.

Prueba de banco Una prueba que se lleva a cabo sobre un componente, tal como un arrancador, antes que éste sea instalado en el vehículo.

Sistema binario Un sistema de computadora que usa una serie compuesta de ceros y unos para representar la información.

Transistor bipolar Un tipo de transistor que tiene una base, es decir, un emisor y un colector.

Bluetooth Un protocolo de comunicación inalámbrico con baja cobertura, así llamado en honor a un rey danés que tenía un diente azul.

Conector *BNC* Conector de entrada tipo coaxial. Nombrado por ser tipo bayoneta y por su inventores, Paul Neil y Carl Concelman.

Perno Un remache o fijador enroscado que tiene una cabeza en un extremo y que se usa en coordinación con una llave o herramienta de buje para que el buje gire para instalarse o retirarse.

Electrones ligados Electrones que están cerca del núcleo de un átomo.

Pulsera trenzada puesta a tierra Cables a tierra trenzados y sin aislamiento para ayudar a incrementar la flexibilidad y reducir la interferencia electromagnética.

Luces de freno Luces ubicadas en la parte trasera del vehículo que se prenden cuando se oprime el pedal de freno.

Derivación Partes eléctricas de un circuito eléctrico paralelo.

Barra rompedora Una herramienta de mano que se utiliza para girar un buje.

Caja de desconexión (BOB por sus siglas en inglés) Un probador eléctrico que se conecta a un conector o controlador y que permite el acceso a cada terminal para que se pueda probar con un medidor o un osciloscopio.

Caja del extremo de las escobillas El puntal de un arrancador o generador (alternador) donde se ubican las escobillas.

Escobillas Conexiones de carbono o carbono-cobre, utilizadas para pasar una corriente eléctrica a un ensamblaje rotante como un inducido en un motor de arranque o un rotor en un generador (alternador).

Prueba de bombilla Una prueba para verificar el funcionamiento de determinados circuitos controlados por el interruptor de encendido.

Casco Un gorro plástico y duro que protege la cabeza de golpes potenciales.

Rodaje, o envejecimiento El proceso mediante el cual se opera un aparato electrónico por un periodo prolongado que puede durar desde varias horas hasta varios días.

Bus de datos Una red eléctrica que vincula varios módulos.

CA Siglas en inglés para capacidad de arranque. Una medida de evaluación para una batería.

CAA Siglas en ingles para *Clean Air Act*. Legislación federal adoptada en 1970 y actualizada en 1990 que introdujo estándares de calidad de aire a nivel nacional.

Códigos de calibración Códigos usados en muchos de los módulos de control del tren de fuerza.

Campaña Una llamada efectuada cuando los dueños de un vehículo son contactados para devolver el vehículo a una concesionaria de venta de vehículos para que dicho vehículo se pueda reparar.

CAN Siglas en inglés de red de control de área. Un tipo de transmisión de datos en serie.

Potencia en candelas Una clasificación de la cantidad de luz producida por una fuente de luz tal como un foco.

Capacitancia La capacitancia eléctrica es un término usado para medir o describir la cantidad de carga que se puede almacenar en un capacitor (condensador) para una dada diferencia potencial de voltaje. La capacitancia se mide en faradios o en incrementos más pequeños de faradios como los microfaradios.

Número de fundición Un número de identificación fundido al bloque del motor y otros componentes metálicos fundidos de gran tamaño.

Cátodo El electrodo negativo.

CCA Siglas en inglés para capacidad de amperaje de arranque en frío. Una clasificación de batería probada a $-18°$ C ($0°$ F).

Célula Un grupo de placas negativas y positivas que forman una célula capaz de producir 2,1 V.

CEMF Siglas en inglés para fuerza contraelectromotriz.

CFL Siglas en inglés para iluminación catódica fluorescente.

CFR Siglas en inglés para el Código de Regulaciones Federales.

Prueba de carga voltaica Una prueba eléctrica que se lleva a cabo utilizando un voltímetro y un amperímetro para comprobar el estado del circuito de carga.

Barra alargadora Un tubo u otro instrumento utilizado para aumentar la cantidad de fuerza aplicada a una llave, matraca o maneral. No se recomienda su uso puesto que puede causar que la llave o matraca se rompa, infligiendo daño personal a aquel que lo intente.

Cincel Un instrumento afilado que se usa junto a un martillo para separar dos piezas de un ensamblaje.

CHMSL Siglas en inglés para luz montada al centro superior; la tercera luz de freno.

Circuito El trayecto por el que viajan los electrones desde una fuente de poder, a través de una resistencia, y de regreso a la fuente de poder.

Disyuntor Un dispositivo mecánico que abre un circuito eléctrico en caso de que ocurra un flujo excesivo de corriente.

Diodo protector Un diodo instalado en un circuito con el cátodo hacia el positivo. El diodo adquiere una polarización negativa frontal cuando el circuito se apaga, lo cual reduce el aumento de alto voltaje creado por la acción de una corriente que fluye a través de una bobina.

Clase 2 Un tipo de protocolo de comunicación BUS utilizado por los vehículos de *General Motors*.

Polos en forma de garras Los polos magnéticos del inductor, o rotor, de un generador (alternador).

Cristal oscilante Un cristal que determina la velocidad de los circuitos electrónicos.

Muelle de reloj Un resorte metalico plano utilizado bajo el cable de la dirección para transferir señales electricas de las bolsas de aire. Dependiendo del diseño y del modelo del vehículo, también podría incluir circuitos electrónicos de control de la bocina y del volante.

CMOS Siglas en inglés para óxido de metal complementario semiconductor.

Acoplación soldada fría Un tipo de acoplación soldada que no ha sido calentada a una temperatura lo suficientemente elevada como para formar una buena conexión eléctrica. A menudo presenta una apariencia gris opaca, al contrario de una buena conexión eléctrica, que suele exhibir una coloración brillante y dorada.

Colector El nombre para una sección del transistor.

Muda de color Un término utilizado para describir el cambio de coloración que sufre un tubo arqueado *HID* (de alta intensidad de descarga por sus siglas en inglés) con el transcurso del tiempo.

Circuito combinado Otro nombre para un circuito eléctrico en serie paralelo.

Válvula combinada Una válvula utilizada en el sistema de frenos que ejecuta más de una función, tal como el interruptor de la presión diferencial, la válvula de medición y / o la válvula de proporcionamiento.

Segmentos de conmutador El nombre que se le da a los segmentos de cobre del inducido de un arrancador o generador de corriente directa.

Caja final del colector El extremo o parte trasera de un motor de arranque que contiene el colector o conmutador y las escobillas. También se llama la caja del extremo de las escobillas.

Circuito completo Un tipo de circuito eléctrico que tiene continuidad y en el que la corriente fluiría si estuviese conectado a la corriente y puesto a tierra.

Faros delanteros compuestos Clase de faro que utiliza una lámpara distinta y reemplazable.

Circuito compuesto Otro nombre para un circuito eléctrico en serie paralelo.

Resorte de compresión   Un resorte que es parte de la transmisión de arrancador que actúa sobre el piñón satélite de la transmisión.

Condensador   También llamado un *capacitor;* almacena una carga eléctrica.

Conductor   Un material que conduce la electricidad y el calor. Un metal que tiene menos de cuatro electrones en el aro exterior de su átomo.

Probador de continuidad   Instalación de un instrumental para medir el cableado, los circuitos y los conectores o interruptores para verificar la existencia de brechas (circuitos abiertos) o cortocircuitos (circuitos cerrados).

Luz de prueba de continuidad   Una luz de prueba que contiene una batería y que se enciende si detecta la presencia de la continuidad (corriente eléctrica) entre los dos polos que están conectados al probador.

Cables de control   Los cables utilizados en los circuitos de ventanas eléctricas que, a su vez, se utilizan para controlar el funcionamiento de las ventanas del vehículo.

Teoría convencional   Aquella teoría que propugna que la electricidad fluye del positivo (+) al negativo (−).

Parte principal   Una parte que se devuelve a la tienda para ser posteriormente enviada a una empresa para su reparación o reciclaje industrial.

Coulomb o culombio   Una unidad de medida de los electrones. Un coulomb consta de 6.24 × 10^{18}, es decir, seis millones doscientos cuarenta mil (6,240,000) billones de electrones.

Fuerza contraelectromotriz (CEMF por sus siglas en inglés)   Un voltaje producido por un inducido tal como un motor de arranque donde el inducido se mueve a través de un campo magnético.

Luces interiores o de cortesía   Un término genérico para describir todas las luces al interior del vehículo.

CPA   Siglas en inglés para clip de conector de posición. Un clip utilizado para ayudar a mantener juntas los dos componentes de un conector eléctrico.

CPU   Siglas en inglés para unidad de procesamiento central.

Conector de presión y de sello   Un tipo de conector eléctrico que tiene pegamento en su cara interior lo cual constituye un sello a prueba de agua después de que ha sido calentado.

Filtro de cruce o circuito crossover   Un circuito electrónico divisor de frecuencias que separa las frecuencias en un sistema de sonido (audio).

CRT   Siglas en inglés para tubo de rayo catódico. Un tipo de pantalla de visualización comúnmente utilizado en televisores.

Control de crucero   Un sistema que mantiene la velocidad deseada del vehículo. También conocido como *control de velocidad.*

Par Darlington   Dos transistores eléctricamente conectados para formar un amplificador. Esto permite que una muy pequeña corriente controle el flujo de una corriente mucho mayor. Nombrada así en honor a Sidney Darlington, físico de los laboratorios Bell desde 1929 hasta 1971.

Acoplamiento de corriente directa   Una señal que transmite tanto el componente de corriente alterna como el componente de corriente directa al medidor.

Sensor de desaceleración   Un sensor montado al cuerpo o armazón de un vehículo que detecta y mide la desaceleración del vehículo. Utilizado para controlar la activación de las bolsas de aire y los sistemas de estabilidad del vehículo.

Decibelio (dB)   Una unidad de medida de la magnitud del sonido.

Ciclado / ciclaje completo   La descarga completa de una batería seguida de una recarga completa.

Enroscado delta   Una forma de enrollar o enroscar el reactor/stator en la cual las tres bobinas se conectan en forma triangular. Este tipo de enroscado toma su nombre de la forma triangular que tiene la letra mayúscula Delta en griego.

Diodo despuntador   Otro nombre para un *diodo de bloqueo.*

Dieléctrico   Un aislante usado entre dos conductores para formar un condensador.

Computadora digital   Una computadora que usa solo señales de encendido y apagado. Usa un convertidor de analógico a digital para transformar las señales analógicas antes de comenzar a procesarlas.

Diodo   Un aparato electrónico que permite que la corriente eléctrica fluya en una sola dirección y la bloquea en otra dirección.

Alambres de dirección   Los cables que van desde el interruptor de control al motor de elevación de un circuito de ventanas eléctricas. La dirección de flujo del corriente a través de estos alambres determina la dirección en que se mueve la ventana.

División   Un segmento específico de la configuración de la onda, tal cual está definido por la matriz en la visualización de la pantalla.

DMM   Siglas en inglés para multímetro digital. Un multímetro digital tiene la capacidad de medir simultáneamente la corriente eléctrica, la resistencia y el voltaje.

Dopar   Añadir impurezas al silicio o al germanio puro para crear materiales de tipo P o tipo N.

DOT   Siglas en inglés de Departamento o Ministerio de Transporte.

DPDT   Siglas en inglés para un interruptor de polo doble y tiro doble.

DPST   Siglas en inglés para un interruptor de polo doble y tiro sencillo.

Tamaño del propulsor   El tamaño en fracciones de pulgada del propulsor cuadrado para bujes.

Caja de extremo de arrancador   El puntal de un motor de arranque que contiene el piñón satélite de arrancador.

DRL   Siglas en inglés de faros diurnos. Luces ubicadas en la parte delantera del vehículo y que se encienden al mismo tiempo que el encendido del motor. En algunos vehículos, el vehículo en cuestión debe estar en movimiento antes de que estas luces se enciendan. Utilizadas como un dispositivo de seguridad en muchos vehículos y de uso obligado en muchos países tales como el Canadá desde 1990.

DSO   Siglas en inglés para osciloscopio de almacenamiento digital.

Chip de doble línea de pines (DIP por sus siglas en inglés)   Un tipo de chip electrónico que contiene dos líneas paralelas de pines.

Bolsas de aire de dos etapas   Bolsas de aire que se pueden activar ya sea con una fuerza mínima o con la fuerza máxima o ambas juntas dependiendo de la información recabada por el controlador de las bolsas de aire respecto a las fuerzas dinámicas presentes en la colisión.

Ciclo de duración   Porcentaje de tiempo en el que una señal se mantiene encendida.

DVOM   Siglas en inglés para un miliamperímetro de voltios ohmios digital.

Voltaje dinámico   El voltaje que se mide cuando el circuito está cargado y la corriente fluye a través del circuito.

E & C   Siglas en inglés para entretenimiento y confort.

E²PROM   Siglas en inglés para memoria de sólo lectura borrable y programable. Un tipo de memoria artificial que puede ser borrada y reprogramada por medios electrónicos.

ECM   Siglas en inglespara Módulo de Control Electrónico. El nombre utilizado por *Ford* para describir la computadora utilizada para controlar el abastecimiento de combustible y el encendido en los modelos de vehículos más antiguos.

ECU Siglas en inglés para unidad de control electrónico. Un término genérico para una computadora vehicular.

EDR Siglas en inglés para registro de información de sucesos. Los componentes electrónicos y los programas de computación utilizados para registrar la información vehicular antes, durante y después de la activación de las bolsas de aire.

EEPROM *Véase* **E²PROM.**

Carga eléctrica La acción de aplicar una carga a un componente tal como una batería a fin de medir su desempeño.

Potencial eléctrico Otro término para voltaje.

Electricidad Movimiento de electrones libres de un átomo a otro.

Electroquímica: El término utilizado para describir la reacción química que ocurre al interior de una batería para producir electricidad.

Electrolito Cualquier sustancia que al disolverse o diluirse se descompone en iones y de esta manera adquiere la capacidad de conducir una corriente eléctrica; la solución ácida de una batería de ácido-plomo.

Inducción electromagnética El campo magnético que rodea un electroimán que consiste en un núcleo de hierro suave envuelto por bobinas. La corriente eléctrica que fluye a través del embobinado genera un campo magnético alrededor del núcleo.

Fuerza electromotriz La fuerza (presión) que tiene la capacidad de mover electrones a través de un conductor.

Teoría de electrones Teoría que propugna que la electricidad fluye desde el negativo (−) al positivo (+).

EMF *Véase* **Fuerza electromotriz.**

Emisora Nombre de un componente de un transistor. La flecha que se usa en un símbolo para un transistor se encuentra en la emisora e indica la parte negativa del transistor.

Mapeo de motor Un programa de computadora que utiliza la información de las pruebas de motor para determinar la mejor relación aire-combustible y la velocidad apropiada de avance de chispa para el desempeño ideal del motor.

EPA Siglas en inglés de Agencia de Protección Ambiental. La EPA es la agencia gubernamental estadounidense encargada de la creación y cumplimiento de las normas medioambientales, incluyendo las regulaciones respecto a la cantidad y el contenido de las emisiones vehiculares.

EPM Siglas en inglés para manejo de la potencia eléctrica. Un término utilizado por *General Motors* para describir un sistema de carga de sensor de control y la salida del control del generador (alternador) basado en las necesidades del vehículo.

ESD Siglas en inglés para descarga electrostática. Otro nombre para el ESD es electricidad estática.

ETC Siglas en inglés para control electrónico de la mariposa.

ETR Siglas en inglés para radio electrónicamente sintonizada. Un tipo de radio que ahora se utiliza en todo tipo de vehículos, que en vez de usar un capacidor variable utiliza una serie de medios electrónicos para sincronizar las frecuencias.

Extensión Barras de acero con puntales hembra y macho que se utilizan para extender el campo de acción de una matraca o mango articulado a fin de rotar una llave de buje.

Selector de modo de disparo exterior Un selector de modo de disparo exterior se usa en un osciloscopio activando la señal de un circuito externo para iniciar o activar la forma de la onda.

Estación de lavado de ojos Una unidad dispensadora de agua que dirige chorros de gran cantidad de agua pero con una presión baja hacia los ojos. Se debe usar en caso de que una persona tenga un elemento contaminante en sus ojos.

Faradio Unidad de capacitancia. Llamado en honor del físico inglés Michael Faraday (1791–1867). Un faradio es la capacidad de almacenar 1 Coulomb de electrones a 1 voltio de diferencia de potencial.

Retroalimentación Flujo inverso de la corriente eléctrica por un circuito o unidad eléctrica que normalmente no debería estar funcionando. Esta corriente de retroalimentación (flujo de corriente de retorno) muchas veces se atribuye a un contacto a tierra defectuoso para el mismo circuito que normalmente funciona de forma regular.

FET Siglas en inglés para transistor de efecto de campo. Un tipo de transistor muy sensible que se puede dañar por la estática.

Transmisión por fibra óptica Transmisión de luz por medio de un plástico especial que mantiene los rayos paralelos aún cuando el plástico se anuda.

Bobinas de inducción Bobinas o alambre enroscado en superficies polares de metal para crear un campo magnético dentro de un motor eléctrico.

Carcasa o casco del arrancador El componente de un arrancador que sostiene las bobinas de campo.

Zapatas polares Los imanes utilizados en una bobina de campo de un arrancador.

Lima Un instrumento manual usado para desgastar o alisar (limar) el metal.

Frazada antiincendios Una frazada de lana a prueba de incendios que se utiliza para apagar el fuego al envolverla alrededor de una víctima.

Extintor, tipos de incendios Tipos de incendios que un extintor de fuego está diseñado para manejar.

Sistema no puesto en tierra Un sistema eléctrico que usa un puesto en tierra que no está conectado al chasis.

Batería de célula mojada Un tipo de batería secundaria (recargable) que utiliza un líquido electrolítico.

Densidad del flujo La densidad de las líneas de fuerza magnética que rodean un imán u otro objeto.

Líneas de flujo Las líneas de fuerza magnética individuales.

FM Siglas de Frecuencia Modulada. Un tipo de transmisión de radio.

Corriente de diseño Flujo de corriente en la dirección normal. Término utilizado para describir la corriente cuando esta fluye a través de un diodo.

Electrones libres Los electrones en la capa exterior de un átomo que contiene menos de cuatro electrones en su órbita exterior.

Frecuencia Número de veces o ciclos que una onda se repite en un segundo, lo cual se mide en hertzios (hercios) (Hz) en una banda de frequencia.

Alambre fusible (eslabón fusible) Un dispositivo de seguridad, que se derretirá y causará que la tapa se cierre en caso de incendio. Un tipo de fusible usado para controlar la corriente máxima al interior de un circuito.

Fusible Una unidad de seguridad eléctrica que se fabrica a partir de un conductor de estaño u hojalata fina que se derrite y abre el circuito en caso que un flujo de corriente sea excesivo.

Elemento fusible (fusible de cartucho) Fusible que se derrite y abre el circuito protegido en caso de que haya un corto circuito que puede resultar en un flujo de corriente excesivo a través del alambre fusible. La mayoría de los alambres fusibles en realidad son alambres cuyas entrevías tienen un diámetro menor en cuatro números que el alambre de los circuitos que protegen.

Proceso de gaseado El proceso de liberación de hidrógeno y oxígeno de las placas de una batería durante la carga o la descarga de dicha batería.

Medidor Gauss Un medidor utilizado para medir la unidad de inducción o intensidad magnética, así llamada en honor a Karl Friedrich Gauss (1777–1855), un matemático alemán.

GAWR Abreviación en inglés para peso bruto nominal por eje. Una valuación o medición de la capacidad de carga de un vehículo que figura en los afiches y planillas del vehículo y en el manual del conductor.

Batería de gel Una batería de plomo-ácido a la que se añade silicio o dióxido de silicio, el cual protege contra los derrames y también contra goteras. También llamada una batería de plomo-ácido sellada, regulada por válvula o batería VRLA por sus siglas in inglés. *Véase también* **VRLA.**

Generador Artefacto que convierte la energía mecánica en energía eléctrica. También llamado un *alternador.*

Prueba de salida de generador Una prueba utilizada para determinar la condición de un generador (alternador).

Germanio Un material semiconductor utilizado en diodos primitivos.

GMLAN Siglas en inglés para red de área local de *General Motors* (GM). Un término utilizado por GM para describir la red bus CAN usada en vehículos GM. *Véase también* **CAN.**

GMM Siglas en inglés para multímetro gráfico.

GPS Siglas en inglés para Global Position System. Un programa gubernamental que hace uso de una red de 24 satélites para retransmitir señales utilizadas por recibidores para determinar su ubicación.

Grado La medida de la fuerza o calidad de un perno de tuercas o de un sujetador.

Cuadrícula Conjunto de cuadrados en la cara de un osciloscopio. Usualmente de 8 por 10 en una pantalla.

Rejilla Parte de una batería donde se pega el material activo.

Tierra El potencial más bajo posible en un circuito. En términos eléctricos, una tierra es el camino deseable para el circuito de retorno. La puesta en tierra también puede resultar contraproducente y proporcionar un trayecto de corte para un circuito eléctrico defectuoso.

Camino (de retorno) a tierra El camino de retorno a través del cual fluye la corriente en un circuito cerrado.

Escobillas puestas a tierra Las escobillas en un motor de arranque que transportan la corriente al encendido o al puesto a tierra.

Plano puesto a tierra El componente metálico de una antena que usualmente consiste en el cuerpo del vehículo.

Puesto a tierra Una corriente de corto circuito que va directamente a tierra en vez de atravesar la carga antes de ir a tierra.

Probador de inducidos Un medidor o probador eléctrico diseñado para probar los inducidos del arrancador y de los generadores de corriente directa.

GVWR Siglas en inglés de nivel de peso total del vehículo. El peso total del vehículo incluyendo la carga máxima.

Sierra para metales Un tipo de sierra utilizada para cortar metales, que utiliza una cuchilla reemplazable.

Martillo Un instrumento manual de percusión utilizado para percutir en un mismo lugar.

Señal de peligro Una señal de peligro en una pegatina, adhesivo ("sticker") o calcomanía que indica la proximidad de un peligro.

Tubo aislante termocontraíble Un tipo de tubo de goma que se contrae y reduce su diámetro por la mitad cuando se calienta. Utilizado sobre un nodo durante la reparación de un cable o alambre eléctrico.

Absorbente de calor Un término que generalmente se refiere a una unidad de metal con planos de derive que se usa para mantener frescos los componentes electrónicos.

Aspiradora de filtro APEE Aspiradora con filtro de aire particulado de elevada eficiencia utilizado para limpiar el polvo de freno.

Hertzio, o hercio Unidad de medida de la frecuencia, abreviada Hz. Un Hertzio es un ciclo por segundo. Llamado en honor de Heinrich R. Hertz, físico alemán del siglo diecinueve.

Luces HID Luces de descarga de alta intensidad. Un tipo de faro, o luz delantero, que hace uso de un alto nivel de voltaje para generar un arco de luz al interior del ensamblaje de tubo arqueado, el cual produce una luz blanquecina azuleada.

HEI Siglas en inglés para la marca de encendido de alta energía utilizada en los vehículos de *General Motors Corporation.*

Medidor de alta impedancia Un medidor digital que tiene por lo menos 10 millones de ohmios de resistencia interna medida entre los conductores de pruebas cuando el medidor está programado para leer voltios.

Filtro de paso alto Un filtro en un sistema de audio que bloquea las frecuencias bajas y permite que solo las frecuencias altas lleguen a los altoparlantes.

Bobinado de sujeción Uno de dos embobinados electromagnéticos dentro de un solenoide; se usa para fijar el núcleo movible del solenoide.

Teoría convencional del flujo de corriente Una teoría que afirma que a medida que un electrón fluye de lo negativo (−) a lo positivo (+) deja a su paso un espacio o hueco. De acuerdo a esta teoría, dicho hueco viajaría de lo positivo (+) a lo negativo (−).

HomeLink® La marca registrada de un sistema utilizado e incluido en muchos vehículos nuevos para operar la puerta de garaje automática.

Bocina Un aparato electromecánico que produce un fuerte sonido al activarse.

HUD Abreviatura en inglés de la pantalla integrada.

Pulsador híbrido Un tipo de unidad emisora de destellos que puede operar dos o más bombillas eléctricas a un ritmo constante.

Aerómetro Un instrumento que se usa para medir la gravedad específica de un líquido. Un aerómetro de la batería se calibra para medir la gravedad específica esperada de electrolito de batería.

IEC Siglas en inglés para Comisión Electrotécnica Internacional. Este organismo fija los estándares de seguridad para medidores tales como los CAT III (categoria tres).

Impedancia La resistencia de una bobina o alambre, que se mide en ohmios.

Impurezas Elementos de dopaje utilizados en la fabricación de diodos y transistores.

Interruptores independientes Interruptores ubicados en cada puerta del vehículo y utilizados para bajar la ventana eléctrica solamente de aquella puerta a la cual están conectados.

Amperímetro inductivo Un tipo de amperímetro que utiliza un sensor de efecto Hall en una tenaza que se usa para envolver un conductor que transporta una corriente. Nombrado por Edwin Hall.

Entrada (de datos o información) A la información recolectada por los sensores enviada a un controlador electrónico que se le llama *datos de entrada.* Los sensores y los interruptores proporcionan las señales de entrada.

Procesamiento de datos o información Los cambios que una computadora u ordenador ejecuta sobre las señales de entrada a fin de convertirlas en información útil. Estos procesos usualmente requieren un convertidor de analógico a digital y otros circuitos electrónicos que eliminan la interferencia.

Escobillas aislantes Escobillas utilizadas en un motor de arranque que conectan a la fuente de poder de la batería a través del solenoide.

Trayecto eléctrico aislado El lado potenciado de un circuito eléctrico.

Aislante Un material que no conduce fácilmente ni la electricidad ni el calor. Un material no metálico que contiene más de cuatro electrones en la orbita exterior de su átomo.

Sensor integral Un término utilizado para describir a un sensor de impacto integrado al módulo de control de las bolsas de aire.

Circuito integrado (CI) Un circuito electrónico que a su vez contiene múltiples circuitos en un solo chip.

IOD Siglas en inglés para consumo de corriente en apagado.Un termino utlizado por la compañía *Chrysler* para describir el fenómeno dedescarga parasítica de la batería cuando el encedido está apagado.

Ión Un átomo con un exceso o deficiencia de electrones que forma una partícula cargada, ya sea de carga positiva o negativa.

IP Siglas en inglés para panel de instrumentos, o salpicadero.

ISO Abreviación de la Organización Internacional para la Estandarización.

IVR Siglas en inglés de regulador de voltaje para instrumentos.

Cables para paso de corriente Cables eléctricos pesados (4 a 00) con abrazaderas grandes que se usan para conectar un vehículo con una batería descargada a otro que tiene una batería cargada.

Junta, o unión El extremo donde dos tipos de materiales se unen.

KAM Siglas en inglés para memoria siempre activa.

Kelvin (K) Una escala de temperatura donde el cero absoluto equivale a cero grados. No existe nada más frió que el cero absoluto (−273.15° C; −459.67° F).

Llavero o dije de llave Un elemento decorativo adherido a las llaves. A menudo incluye un control remoto para abrir o cerrar un vehículo.

Palabra clave Un tipo de comunicación en red usada en muchos vehículos de *General Motors.*

Kilo Significa 1,000; se abrevia *k* o *K*.

Ley de corrientes de Kirchhoff Un principio científico-matemático que afirma que "La corriente que fluye a cualquier nodo de un circuito eléctrico equivale a la corriente que sale de dicho nodo." Nombrado por Gustav Robert Kirchhoff.

Ley de tensiones de Kirchhoff Un principio científico-matemático en relación con los circuitos eléctricos que afirma que "El voltaje que rodea cualquier circuito cerrado es igual a la suma total de las resistencias." Nombrado por Gustav Robert Kirchhoff.

LCD Siglas en inglés de pantalla de cristal líquido.

LDWS Siglas en inglés para sistema de aviso de cambio involuntario de carril.

LED Siglas en inglés para diodofotoemisor. Una fuente de luz de alta eficiencia que utiliza muy poca electricidad y produce muy poco calor.

Luz de prueba tipo LED Una luz de prueba usada por técnicos y electricistas para probar el voltaje que tiene una impedancia alta y que utiliza diodos fotoemisores con un resistor de 470 ohmios para controlar la corriente que fluye a través de un probador.

Regla de la mano izquierda Un método utilizado para determinar la dirección del movimiento de las líneas magnéticas de fuerza que rodean un conductor. La regla de la mano izquierda se usa en coordinación con la teoría del flujo de electrones (− fluye hacia el +).

Patas Otro nombre para las ramas de un circuito en paralelo.

Ley de Lenz La variación del flujo magnético entre un conductor y un campo magnético es contraria al sentido de la corriente inducida que ha producido, nombrado por Heinrich Lenz.

Botella de Leyden Un aparato utilizado para almacenar una carga eléctrica por primera vez. El primer tipo de condensador o capacidor. Nombrado por Leiden en los Países Bajos.

Carga Un término usado para describir un aparato cuando una corriente eléctrica fluye a través del mismo.

Prueba de capacidad de carga Un tipo de prueba de la batería donde una carga eléctrica se aplica a la batería y se monitorea el voltaje para determinar el estado de la batería.

Mecanismo de seguridad del conector eléctrico (tapa) Una lengüeta mecánica que se utiliza para afianzar el extremo de una terminal a un conector eléctrico. Este mecanismo debe deprimirse con la presión a fin de liberar la terminal del conector.

Interruptor de cierre eléctrico Un cierre eléctrico ubicado en la caja de interruptor de circuito para asegurarse de que nadie prenda el circuito eléctrico mientras se llevan a cabo las reparaciones del automóvil.

Sonda lógica Un tipo de medidor que puede detectar potencia eléctrica o corriente puesta a tierra. La mayoría de los medidores pueden determinar la presencia del voltaje, pero la mayoría de los otros no pueden detectar la presencia de una corriente puesta a tierra sin llevar a cabo pruebas adicionales.

Filtro de paso bajo Un aparato utilizado en un sistema de audio que bloquea la frecuencia alta y sólo permite que la frecuencia baja llegue a los altoparlantes.

Batería de baja pérdida de agua Un tipo de batería que normalmente utiliza poco agua para su funcionamiento regular. La mayoría de las baterías utilizadas en automóviles y camiones ligeros son de este tipo.

Lumbar Perteneciente a la sección baja de la espalda humana.

Flujo magnético Las líneas de fuerza producidas por un campo magnético.

Inducción magnética La transferencia de las fuerzas magnéticas a un objeto cercano, o bobina de alambre.

Magnetismo Un tipo de energía reconocida por la atracción que un objeto ejerce sobre otro.

Batería libre de mantenimiento Un tipo de batería que no requiere un aumento regular de agua a sus celdas. La mayoría de las baterías utilizadas en los automóviles y camionetas son de este tipo.

Interruptor de control maestro El interruptor de control para las ventanas eléctricas ubicado cerca del conductor del vehículo quien puede operar todas las ventanas.

MCA Siglas en inglés para amperios de arranque en aplicaciones marinas. Un indicador para batería.

Mega millón (M) Utilizado para describir números sumamente grandes o para medir una gran cantidad de resistencia.

Menisco / meniscal El fruncimiento, o la curvatura, de un líquido en un tubo. Usada para determinar cuándo una batería ha sido apropiadamente llenada con agua destilada.

Mercurio Un metal pesado que a temperatura ambiente se encuentra en estado líquido.

Resorte de acoplamiento Un resorte usado detrás del piñón del arrancador en un mecanismo del arrancador para engranar el piñón satélite con el engranaje anular en el motor.

Fidelidad de medidor El porcentaje de acierto, precisión o exactitud de un medidor.

Resolución del medidor Las especificaciones de un medidor que indican a qué grado de precisión puede llegar la detección y visualización de una medida por parte de un medidor.

Pernos métricos Pernos que se fabrican y diseñan según el sistema métrico.

Medida de cable métrica El método métrico para medir el tamaño de un alambre en milímetros cuadrados. Ésta es la medida del núcleo del cable sin incluir el material aislante.

Micro (μ) La millonésima parte de un voltio o amperio.

Mili (mm) La milésima parte de un voltio o amperio.

Modulación La combinación de frecuencias de onda larga y de onda corta comúnmente se conoce como *modulación*.

Interruptor oscilante Un tipo de interruptor que oscila entre prendido y apagado.

MOSFET Siglas en inglés para transistor de efecto de campo del semiconductor de óxido de metal. Un tipo de transistor.

MOV Siglas en inglés de varistor de oxido metálico. Un dispositivo electrónico que opera como dos diodos Zener conectados en serie.

MSDS Siglas en inglés de hoja de datos de seguridad física, que contienen una descripción de materiales peligrosos.

Multiplexación Un sistema en que se conectan varias computadoras de tal manera que puedan compartir información entre sí, utilizando solo un cable.

N.C. Siglas en inglés para normalmente cerrado.

N.O. Siglas en inglés para normalmente abierto.

Red Un sistema de comunicaciones utilizado para conectar múltiples computadoras o módulos entre si.

Carga neutral Un átomo que tiene el mismo número de electrones como protones.

Interruptor de seguridad neutral Un interruptor eléctrico que permite que el encendido se recargue solo si el selector de engranaje está en neutro o estacionado.

Nodo Un módulo y una computadora que forman parte de una red de comunicaciones.

Memoria permanente del acceso aleatorio (RAM por sus siglas en inglés.) Capacidad de memoria de computadora que no se pierde cuando se rompe la corriente.

Transistor NPN Un tipo de transistor bipolar que utiliza material del tipo P en su base y material del tipo N en su emisor y colector.

NTC Siglas en inglés para coeficiente de temperatura negativa. Usualmente utilizado en referencia a los sensores de temperatura (de refrigerante o de temperatura ambiente). A medida que la temperatura aumenta, la resistencia del sensor disminuye.

Material del tipo N Silicio o germanio dopado con fósforo, arsénico o antimonio.

Tuerca Un sujetador enroscado hembra que se usa con un perno (prisionero) o un espárrago.

NVRAM Siglas en inglés para memoria permanente del acceso aleatorio.

OAD *Véase* **Amortiguador del alternador de rotación libre.**

OAP Siglas en inglés para polea del alternador de rotación libre.

Sistema de detección de pasajeros Un sistema de bolsas de aire que incluye un sensor en el asiento de pasajeros que se utiliza para detectar si el pasajero está o no está sentado en el lado del pasajero así como el rango de peso de dicho pasajero.

Ohmio Unidad de la resistencia eléctrica; llamada así en honor de Georg Simon Ohm (1787–1854).

Ley de Ohm: Ley que propugna que se requiere un voltio de voltaje para mover un amperio de corriente a través de un ohmio de resistencia.

Ohmiómetro Un instrumento de prueba eléctrico diseñado para medir la resistencia eléctrica en ohmios.

OL Siglas en inglés para sobrecarga o sobre límite.

A.O. Una abreviación de amplificador operacional, u OP-amps por sus siglas en inglés. Usado en circuitos para controlar y simplificar las señales digitales.

Circuito abierto Cualquier circuito que no está cerrado y en el cual no fluye la corriente.

Voltaje de circuito abierto El nivel de voltaje que se mide cuando el circuito no está funcionando.

Osciloscopio (sonda) Un medidor que muestra una visualización de los niveles de voltaje en una pantalla.

OSHA Siglas en inglés de la Administración de la Seguridad y Salud Ocupacionales. OSHA es la principal agencia federal que se ocupa de la seguridad en el lugar de trabajo y de la legislación de salud ocupacional.

Amortiguador del alternador de rotación libre Una polea de propulsión del alternador (generador) que tiene un embrague unidireccional y un resorte o muelle de amortiguación que se usa para amortiguar el funcionamiento del alternador y reducir la tensión en la banda o correa.

Polea del alternador de rotación libre Una polea de propulsión del alternador (generador) que tiene un embrague unidireccional que se usa para amortiguar el funcionamiento del alternador y reducir el la tensión en la banda, o correa, de transmisión.

Embrague de sobremarcha Parte de un ensamblaje del piñón del motor de arranque que permite que el motor gire más rápido que el motor de arranque a fin de proteger el arrancador de daños que podría sufrir en caso de que el interruptor de encendido se mantenga en la posición de arranque después de que el motor se haya encendido.

Alambre-fusible de cartucho o fusible Pacific Un tipo de fusible automotriz.

Circuito en paralelo Un circuito eléctrico que sigue más de un trayecto desde la fuente de poder hasta el puesto a tierra. Tiene más de un brazo, o pata.

Prueba de descarga parásita de la batería Una prueba que mide el nivel de descarga de corriente (en amperios) de la batería con el encendido apagado y con todas las cargas eléctricas apagadas.

Divisiones Particiones entre las células de una batería. Las divisiones se hacen del mismo material que el casco o cuerpo exterior de la batería.

Sistema de presencia de pasajeros (PPS por sus siglas en inglés) Un sistema de bolsas de aire que incluye un sensor en el asiento de pasajeros utilizado para detectar si un pasajero está o no está sentado en el lado del pasajero y el rango de peso de dicho pasajero.

Passkey I y II Un tipo de sistema antirrobo utilizado en los vehículos de *General Motors.*

Passlock I y II Un tipo de sistema antirrobo utilizado en los vehículos de *General Motors.*

PATS Siglas en inglés de sistema antirobo pasivo. Un tipo de sistema antirobo usado en los modelos *Ford, Lincoln,* y *Mercury.*

PCM Siglas en ingles de módulo de control del tren de poder.

Efecto Peltier Jean Charles Peltier, un científico francés, descubrió que los electrones que fluyen a través de un material sólido pueden transportar el calor al otro lado del objeto. A este efecto se le denomina el Efecto Peltier.

Motor eléctrico de imanes permanentes Motores eléctricos que utilizan imanes permanentes en el campo magnético en vez de electroimanes.

Permeabilidad Una medida de la habilidad de una materia para conducir las líneas magnéticas de fuerza.

Fósforo Un elemento químico luminiscente que es impactado con electrones lanzados a altas velocidades lo cual lleva a que este objeto se ilumine y produzca luz.

Fotodiodo Un tipo de diodo utilizado como un sensor de carga de energía solar. Cuando se conecta con polarización inversa, el flujo de la corriente es proporcional a la intensidad de luz.

Fotoelectricidad Cuando algunos metales son expuestos a la luz, parte de la energía luminosa se transfiere a los electrones libres del metal. Esta energía excedente libera a los electrones de su adhesión a la superficie del metal. Como consecuencia, éstos pueden ser recolectados y alistados para fluir al interior de un conductor. A este fenómeno se le denomina fotoelectricidad.

Fotones La luz se emite desde los diodosfotoemisores por medio de la liberación de la energía en forma de fotones.

Fotorresistor Un semiconductor que cambia su resistencia ante la presencia o ausencia de la luz. En la oscuridad tiene mucha resistencia y poca resistencia ante la presencia de la luz.

Fototransistor Un dispositivo electrónico quepuede detectar la presenciade la luz y encenderse o apagarse como efecto de aquello. Se utiliza en algunos sensores de altura de la suspensión.

Piezoelectricidad Principio por lo cual ciertos cristales llegan a recargarse eléctricamente cuando se les aplica presión.

Ranura de soldadura de pinza Una sección en la parte inferior del vehículo donde dos paneles del cuerpo del automóvil se juntan y se enroscan para posteriormente soldarse. Este es uno de los lugares comunes donde se inserta una gata si el vehículo necesita elevarse.

Distancia entre roscas El número de roscas por pulgada de un sujetador enroscado.

PIV Siglas en inglés para pico de voltaje inverso. Un tipo de medición o valuación de un diodo.

Pinzas o alicates Un instrumento manual que tiene dos brazos movibles que se juntan.

Generador de imán permanente Un sensor que contiene un imán permanente y una bobina que produce una señal de voltaje análogo si una rueda de metal ranurada pasa cerca del sensor.

Transistor PNP Un tipo de transistor bipolar que utiliza material del tipo N en su base y material del tipo P en su emisor y colector.

Polaridad La condición positiva o negativa en relación con un polo magnético.

Polo El lugar donde las líneas de fuerza magnética ingresan o salen de un imán.

Superficies magnéticas La parte mecánica de una bobina de campo en un motor de arranque.

Plomo poroso Plomo con muchos poros diminutos utilizado para crear una superficie porosa para uso en platos negativos de la batería; el símbolo químico para el plomo es Pb.

Coeficiente de temperatura positiva (PTC por sus siglas en inglés) Término normalmente usado para referirse a un conductor o cortacircuitos electrónico. A medida que la temperatura aumenta, la resistencia eléctrica también se eleva.

Potenciómetro Un resistor variable de tres terminales que incide en la variación de la baja de voltaje en un circuito.

Condensador de alto voltaje Un condensador utilizado para reforzar la salida de un sistema de sonido que mueve los altoparlantes, especialmente cuando reproduce las frecuencias bajas.

Fuente de poder En términos eléctricos la batería o el generador (alternador).

Equipo de protección personal (PPE por sus siglas en inglés) Prendas que los trabajadores llevan o utilizan a fin de protegerse de peligros en el lugar de trabajo, incluyendo los anteojos de seguridad, los guantes y otros elementos de protección.

Interruptor de diferencial de presión Interruptor instalado entre los dos circuitos de frenos separados de un circuito maestro doble, para iluminar la luz de freno del tablero de instrumentos, en caso de una falla en el sistema de frenos, la cual causaría una *diferencia* en la presión de los frenos.

Pretensores Aparatos explosivos utilizados para disminuir la holgura derivada de un cinturón de seguridad cuando se activan y despliegan las bolsas de aire.

Alambre primario Alambre utilizado para circuitos de bajo voltaje, usualmente de 12 voltios.

Procesamiento El proceso que lleva a cabo una computadora cuando la información fluye a través de sus programas de computación a fin de determinar qué acción debe ser llevada a cabo.

Controlador de Interconexión Programable (PCI por sus siglas en inglés) Un tipo de protocolo de comunicación de red utilizado en vehículos marca *Chrysler*.

PROM Siglas en inglés de memoria de sólo lectura programable.

PRV *Véase* **PIV**.

Protección de circuito PTC Término usualmente reservado para referirse a un conductor o disyuntor electrónico. A medida que la temperatura se eleva, la resistencia eléctrica también se eleva.

Material del tipo P Silicio o germanio dopado con boro o indio.

Bobinado de atracción Una de dos bobinados electromagnéticas dentro de un solenoide que se usa para mover un núcleo movible.

Tren de pulso Voltaje de corriente directa que se conecta y se desconecta en una serie de pulsos.

Anchura de pulso Duración del tiempo de encendido/funcionamiento de un inyector de combustible electrónico.

Limpiaparabrisas de accionamiento intermitente Limpiaparabrisas que operan intermitentemente. También conocidos como limpiaparabrisas de acción demorada.

Botador Un instrumento manual que se utiliza con un martillo para arrancar, o botar, los clavos y otros objetos pequeños.

PWM Siglas en inglés de modulación de la anchura de pulso: El manejo de un artefacto por medio de una señal digital binaria que se controla variando la duración de tiempo que el artefacto está conectado y desconectado.

Limpiaparabrisas con sensor de lluvia Limpiaparabrisas que utilizan un sensor electrónico para detectar la presencia de la lluvia en el parabrisas y que se activan automáticamente al detectarla si el interruptor de los limpiaparabrisas está en la posición "auto."

Bobina de choque Una bobina de escaso tamaño instalada en la guía de poder que se conecta con una unidad pulsatoria, tal como un regulador de voltaje de instrumentos, para prevenir la interferencia de ondas radioeléctricas.

RAM Siglas en inglés para memoria de acceso aleatorio. Una memoria temporal de una computadora utilizada para propósitos de almacenamiento.

Matraca, o maneral Un instrumento manual utilizado para propulsar una llave de buje.

RCRA Siglas en inglés para Ley de Conservación y Recuperación de Recursos.

Campaña Una notificación efectuada al dueño de un vehículo que le informa que él debe atender y corregir algún asunto que está atentando contra la seguridad vehicular.

Batería recombinante   Un diseño de batería que no libera los gases durante la operación normal. Las baterías tipo AGM (por sus siglas en inglés: absorbed glass mat) son baterías recombinantes.

Puente rectificador   Grupo de seis diodos, tres positivos (+) y tres negativo (−) que a menudo se utiliza en los alternadores.

Relé   Un interruptor electromagnético que utiliza un brazo giratorio.

Reluctancia   Resistencia al movimiento de las líneas magnéticas de la fuerza.

Capacidad de reserva   El número de minutos que una batería puede producir 25 amperios y aún así mantener un voltaje de 1.75 voltios por celda (10.5 voltios para una batería de 12 voltios).

Magnetismo residual   Magnetismo remanente que queda después que la fuerza magnetizante ha sido retirada.

Resistencia   Oposición al flujo de la corriente.

Polarización inversa   Cuando la polarización de una batería se conecta a un diodo en la dirección opuesta y no fluye ninguna corriente.

RF   Siglas en inglés para radiofrecuencia.

Reóstato   Un resistor variable de dos terminales.

Leyes de divulgación de información sobre materiales peligrosos   Una serie de leyes que afirman que los empleados tienen el derecho de enterarse cuando los materiales que usan en el trabajo constituyen un peligro.

Voltaje de rizado   Voltaje de corriente alterna excesivo producido por un generador (alternador), usualmente como consecuencia de un diodo defectuoso.

RMS   Siglas en inglés de raíz cuadrada de la media de los cuadrados de los valores instantáneos. Un método para visualizar las señales de voltaje variable en la pantalla de un medidor digital.

ROM   Siglas en inglés de memoria de solo lectura.

Soldadura con núcleo de rosina   Un tipo de soldadura usada en las reparaciones eléctricas. Al interior de la soldadura hay una rosina que actúa como un flujo lubricante-limpiador para limpiar la soldadura y ayudarla a fluir.

Rotor   El elemento rotante de un generador donde se produce un campo magnético.

RPA   Siglas en inglés para asistente de retroceso seguro. El término que utiliza *General Motors* para referirse a su sistema de alarma en parachoques traseros utilizada para detectar y advertir al conductor sobre la cercanía de los objetos durante la maniobra del retroceso.

Acoplamiento de goma   Una conexión flexible entre el motor del asiento eléctrico y el cable de arranque.

RVS   Siglas en inglés para encendido remoto del vehículo. Un término de *General Motors* para un sistema que le permite al conductor encender el motor de su vehículo utilizando un control remoto.

SAE   Siglas en inglés para la Sociedad de Ingenieros Automotrices.

SAR   Siglas en inglés de sistema de bolsas de aire suplementarias. Otro nombre para un sistema de bolsas de aire.

Saturación   El punto de máxima fuerza del campo magnético de una bobina.

SCR   Siglas en inglés para rectificador de controlador de silicona.

Ensamblaje de gato de rosca   Un gato de rosca o husillo que se usa para levantar o bajar un asiento eléctrico.

Desentornillador   Un instrumento manual usado para sacar o retirar tornillos.

SDARS   Siglas en inglés para servicio de audio y radio digital satelital. Otro nombre para radio satelital.

Cámara del sedimento   Un espacio debajo de los platos de la célula de algunas baterías que se utiliza para recolectar la acumulación de sedimento que se desprende de los platos de la batería. El uso de una cámara de sedimento previene que el sedimento cause un cortocircuito en las placas de la batería.

Semiconductor   Un material que no es ni conductor ni aislador y que tiene exactamente cuatro electrones en el nivel exterior de átomo.

Interfaz de Comunicación Serial (SCI por sus siglas en inglés)   Un tipo de transmisión de datos en serie utilizado por la marca *Chrysler*.

Intercambio en serie de datos   Datos transmitidos en serie por medio de señales de voltaje altamente variable.

Circuito en serie   Un circuito eléctrico que proporciona sólo un camino para que fluya la corriente.

Leyes de circuito en serie de Kirchhoff   Leyes desarrollados por Kirchhoff en relación con los circuitos en serie.

Circuito en serie paralelo   Cualquier circuito que contenga resistencias tanto en serie como en paralelo en un solo circuito.

Campo de arrollado en serie   Un circuito típico de encendido de motor donde la corriente que atraviesa el campo embobinado está conectada en serie con el inducido antes de salir a tierra. También llamado un *encendido arrollado en serie*.

Lámina de ajuste   Espaciador de metal delgado.

Cortocircuito   Circuito en que la corriente fluye, pero evita un poco de o toda de la resistencia en el circuito; una conexión que tiene como resultado una conexión "cobre a cobre."

En cortocircuito   El estado en el cual un objeto está cortocircuitado tal como cuando ocurre un cortocircuito.

Corto a tierra   Circuito corto por lo cual la corriente fluye pero evita algo de o toda de la resistencia en el circuito y fluye a tierra. Porque el suelo es generalmente acero en la electricidad automotriz, un corto a tierra (puesto a tierra) es una conexión "cobre a acero."

Cortocircuito al voltaje   Circuito en que la corriente fluye pero evita un poco de o toda de la resistencia en el circuito; una conexión que tiene como resultado una conexión "cobre a cobre".

Derivación   Artefacto que se usa para desviar parte de la corriente del circuito principal.

Campo derivado   Una bobina de campo usada en un motor de arranque que no está conectada al inducido de forma serial y, al contrario, está puesta en tierra a través de la caja de encendido.

Silicona   Material semiconductor.

SIR   Siglas en inglés para elementos de seguridad inflables auxiliares. Otro nombre para bolsas de aire.

SKIS   Siglas en inglés para systema inmovilizador electronico de llave centinela. Un tipo de sistema antirrobo utilizado en los vehiculos marca *Chrysler*.

SLA   Siglas en inglés de suspensión de brazo corto y largo.

Batería de arranque o tipo SLI   La batería que se encarga del arranque el alumbrado y el encendido del sistema eléctrico de un automóvil.

Extremo del anillo de deslizamiento   El extremo de un generador (alternador) que contiene escobillas y anillos de deslizamiento.

Tijera de mano para chapa fina   Un instrumento manual diseñado para cortar metal.

Buje, casco o casquillo   Un instrumento utilizado con el objetivo de retener el cabezal de un perno o tuerca para luego girarlo por medio de un maneral o barra rompedora.

Adaptador de buje   Un instrumento utilizado para adaptar un tamaño de un propulsor de bujes para ser usado con otro propulsor de bujes de distinto tamaño tal como un maneral o barra rompedora.

Célula fotovoltáica   Un aparato que produce electricidad como resultado de la liberación de electrones cuando la luz solar choca contra un material semiconductor. Se produce aproximadamente un kilovatio de electricidad en una célula fotovoltáica de un metro cuadrado de tamaño.

Solvente   Líquido, usualmente incoloro, que se utiliza para quitar el aceite y la grasa.

SPDT   Siglas en inglés para interruptor de polo sencillo y tiro doble. Un tipo de interruptor eléctrico.

Altoparlante   Un aparato que consiste en un imán, una bobina de alambre y un cono que reproduce los sonidos generados por señales eléctricas que se envían a los altoparlantes desde una radio o un amplificador.

Peso específico   Ratio del peso del volumen de un líquido dividido por el peso de un volumen equivalente de agua.

Reóstato o resistor de protección de alza de potencia (sobretensión)   Un resistor, usualmente de entre 300 y 500 ohmios, que está conectado a un circuito en paralelo con una carga para ayudar a reducir los picos de tensión causados cuando se corta la corriente que fluye a través de un alambre.

Ensamblaje de empalme   Un término utilizado por *General Motors* para describir la interconexión de los módulos en una red.

Esponja de plomo   Plomo elaborado con un alto nivel de porosidad a fin de que su superficie tenga una consistencia o textura esponjosa para su uso en los platos negativos de batería; el símbolo químico para el plomo es Pb.

Combustión espontánea   Un fenómeno por el cual un incendio comienza espontáneamente en trapos llenos de aceite.

SPST   Siglas en inglés para un interruptor de polo sencillo y tiro sencillo. Un tipo de interruptor eléctrico.

Dispositivo de inflado   El elemento de calefacción de un módulo inflable, que comienza la reacción química que genera el gas que infla las bolsas de aire.

SRS   Siglas en inglés de sistema auxiliar de seguridad. Otro nombre para un sistema de bolsas de aire.

SST   Siglas en inglés de herramientas especiales de servicio. Herramientas especificadas por un fabricante de vehículos que se necesitan para reparar o mantener un vehículo o una componente defectuosa de un vehículo.

Protocolo SCP   Un protocolo de red utilizado por *Ford*.

Transmisión del motor de arranque   Término que se usa para describir el piñón satélite de propulsión del motor de arranque con acoplamiento libre.

Solenoide del arrancador   Un tipo de motor de arranque que utiliza un solenoide para activar la transmisión del motor de arranque.

Medida dinámica del estado de salud (SOH por sus siglas en inglés)   Una señal enviada por uno de los módulos a los demás módulos en la red, informándoles que está funcionando correctamente y que mantiene su habilidad de transmitir señales.

Electricidad estática   Una carga eléctrica que se sobrecarga en un cuerpo aislante y que se descarga en un material conductor.

Estator   Nombre utilizado para un conjunto de tres bobinados interconectados dentro de un alternador. Un inducido giratorio proporciona un campo magnético móvil e induce una corriente en los bobinados del estator.

Motor de etapas   Motor que se mueve una cantidad especificada de rotación.

Capacidor de refuerzo   Condensador para mejorar el factor de potencia.

Almacenamiento   El proceso al interior de una computadora a través del cual se almacena información antes y después de los cómputos.

Espárrago   Vara corta con roscas de tornillo a ambos extremos.

Subwoofer   Un tipo de altoparlante usado para reproducir sonidos de baja frecuencia.

Diodo de supresión de voltaje   Un diodo ubicado en dirección de la corriente de retorno y utilizado para reducir el pico de voltaje generado cuando un circuito que contiene una bobina se abre y dicha bobina se descarga.

SVR   Siglas en inglés de acumulador de plomo-ácido sellado, regulado por válvula. Un término utilizado para describir un tipo de batería de plomo-ácido o de tecnología de gel sellado que es regulada por válvula.

SWCAN   Siglas en inglés de alambre sencillo de protocolo de comunicaciones CAN o CAN bus (inglés controller area network).

Lámpara de aviso   Lámpara de advertencia del tablero (a veces se llama *idiot light* en inglés (luz de idiota).

Fuerza de tensión   La resistencia máxima de un perno o fijador en la dirección longitudinal.

Terminal   La punta metálica de un alambre o cable que encaja en un conector de plástico y que constituye el componente conector de una junta.

Resistor terminal   Un resistor colocado en el extremo de un circuito de transmisión de datos en serie de alta velocidad a fin de reducir la interferencia electromagnética.

Luz de prueba   Una luz utilizada para comprobar el nivel de voltaje. Contiene un foco conectado, en un extremo, a un cable puesto a tierra y a un puntal en el otro extremo.

THD   Siglas en inglés para distorsión armónica total. Una medida de evaluación utilizada con equipos y sistemas de sonido.

Termistor   Resistor que varía su resistencia según la temperatura. Un termistor de coeficiente positivo aumenta la resistencia ante el aumento de la temperatura. Un termistor de coeficiente negativo aumenta la resistencia ante la disminución de temperatura.

Termopar   Dos metales disímiles que al unirse y calentarse producen un voltaje. Utilizado para medir la temperatura.

Termoelectricidad   La creación de un flujo de corriente por medio del calentamiento de la conexión entre dos metales distintos.

Voltaje de entrada   Otro nombre para tensión umbral o la diferencia de voltaje necesaria para polarizar negativamente un diodo.

Perno pasante   El perno utilizado para mantener unidas las diversas partes del motor de arranque. Este perno largo atraviesa la caja de campo hasta ingresar al cuerpo del extremo de arranque.

Tiros   El término utilizado para describir el número de circuitos de salida (posiciones) que tiene un interruptor eléctrico.

Tiempo base / unidad de tiempo   La cantidad fija de tiempo por división cuando se regula un osciloscopio.

Comprobador de generador de audiofrecuencia   Un tipo de aparato de pruebas usado para encontrar un cortocircuito mediante el uso de un generador de audiofrecuencia. Se utilizan audífonos y una sonda para comprobar dónde termina la audiofrecuencia lo cual indica dónde se encuentra la falla en el circuito.

Resistencia total del circuito (R_t)   El valor de la resistencia total de un circuito.

Número de comercio   Número estampado en un bombillo automotriz. Cada bombillo del mismo número de comercio tiene la misma potencia lumínica y vataje, independiente del fabricante de la bombilla.

Transistor   Dispositivo semiconductor que puede funcionar como un relé o un amplificador.

Nivel de disparo   El nivel de voltaje al cual debe llegar una configuración de onda para activar la visualización en la pantalla.

Pendiente de disparo   Dirección de voltaje que una onda debe tener para comenzar visualización en la pantalla. Una pendiente positiva requiere que el voltaje se aumente mientras cruza el nivel del disparado; una pendiente negativa requiere que el voltaje se disminuya.

Efecto de atenuación de Troxler   El efecto de atenuación de Troxler, conocido como el efecto Troxler describe un efecto visual mediante el cual la retina del ojo retiene una imagen por un corto periodo después de que dicha imagen haya desparecido del campo visual. Este efecto visual fue descubierto por un médico suizo llamado Ignaz Paul Vital Troxler (1780–1866). Debido al efecto Troxler el brillo causado por los faros delanteros puede permanecer por unos momentos en la retina, lo que puede ocasionar un punto ciego.

TSB   Siglas en inglés de boletín de servicio técnico.

TTL   Siglas en inglés para lógica transistor-transistor.

Relación de vueltas   La ratio entre el número de vueltas que se dan en un bobinado primario y el número de vueltas en un bobinado secundario. Un típico bobinado de encendido tiene una ratio de 100:1.

Altoparlante de súperfrecuencias   Un tipo de altoparlante utilizado en un sistema de sonido que está específicamente diseñado para transmitir en alta frecuencia.

Conductor doble retorcido   Un par de cables trenzados en una ratio de 9 a 16 vueltas por pie longitudinal. La mayoría de estos cables se trenzan una vez cada pulgada (12 vueltas por cada pie longitudinal) para reducir la interferencia electromagnética que podría resultar al ser inducida en el alambrado, ya que un alambre tendería a cancelar la interferencia inducida en otro alambre.

UART   Siglas en inglés de receptor-transmisor asíncrono universal. Un tipo de transmisión de datos en serie.

UBP   Siglas en inglés de protocolo basado en UART.

UNC   Siglas en inglés de estándar nacional unificado de roscas.

Rebajado de micas   Un proceso de cortar el aislante, usualmente de mica, de entre el medio de los segmentos de un conmutador del arrancador.

UNF   Siglas en inglés de estándar de lámina fina (delgada) del tornillo.

Unión universal   Una unión o junta en un eje de propulsión o transmisión que permite que se transmita fuerza de torsión en un ángulo.

Aceite usado   Aceite que ya ha sido usado previamente en un motor y que ha tenido la oportunidad de absorber partículas de metal y otros contaminantes al interior de dicho motor.

UST   Siglas en inglés de depósito de almacenamiento subterráneo.

Banda de valencia: El intervalo u órbita de electrones más afuera del núcleo de un átomo.

Limpiaparabrisas intermitentes variables   Limpiaparabrisas cuya velocidad puede variar.

Varistores   Resistores cuya resistencia depende de la cantidad de voltaje que se les aplica.

VATS   Siglas en inglés para sistema antirrobos de vehículos utilizado en algunos vehículos de *General Motors.*

VECI   Siglas en inglés para información de control de emisiones de vehículos. Se escribe en una etiqueta o calcomanía que se encuentra debajo del capo de todos los vehículos y que incluye aquella información relativa al control de emisiones importante para el mecánico o técnico automotriz.

VIN   Siglas en inglés para número de identificación de vehículo.

Reconocimiento automático de voz   Un sistema que hace uso de un micrófono y un parlante, conectados a un módulo electrónico, con el objetivo de controlar el funcionamiento de los dispositivos electrónicos de un vehículo por medio de comandos de voz.

Caída de tensión   Pérdida de voltaje a través de un alambre, conector o cualquier otro conductor. La caída de voltaje equivale a la resistencia en ohmios por la corriente en amperios (la ley de Ohm).

Voltímetro   Instrumento eléctrico de prueba que se usa para medir voltios (la unidad de la presión eléctrica). El voltímetro se conecta en paralelo con la unidad o el circuito que se está probando.

VRLA   Siglas en inglés de baterías de plomo-ácido selladas, reguladas por válvula. Una batería sellada que protege contra los derrames y también contra goteras. Las baterías AGM y los acumuladores de electrolítico gel son ejemplos de este tipo de batería.

VTF   Siglas en inglés para tubo de vacío fluorescente. Un tipo de visualización de salpicadero o panel de instrumentos.

Arandela   Pieza fina y plana de metal o circular y perforada por el medio por un hueco, utilizado entre un perno o tuerca y una parte o plancha de metal.

Vatio   Unidad eléctrica de poder; un vatio equivale al voltaje de la corriente (amperios) $\times$ (1/746 hp). Llamado así en honor de James Watt, inventor escocés.

Ley de Watt   Fórmula que establece que un vatio equivale a un amperio multiplicado por un voltio en un circuito, lo cual representa la potencia eléctrica en dicho circuito.

WHMIS   Siglas en inglés para sistema de información sobre materiales peligrosos en el lugar de trabajo.

Control eléctrico de ventana   Un dispositivo mecánico que transforma el movimiento giratorio del manivela manual de la ventana o del motor eléctrico en un movimiento vertical para subir o bajar una ventana en un vehículo.

Limpiaparabrisas   El ensamblaje de motor, controlador de motor y varillaje, así como las escobillas y rasquetas que se utilizan para retirar la lluvia excesiva que se acumula en el parabrisas.

Diagrama de conexiones eléctricas   Un diagrama que consiste en una serie de símbolos y líneas que representan el alambrado y los componentes de un circuito eléctrico.

Visualización WOW   Visualización del tablero de instrumentos en que todos los elementos posibles se alumbran cuando se enciende por primera vez. Puede ser usado para probar el tablero de instrumentos, buscando segmentos que no se han alumbrado.

Llave   Instrumento manual usado para girar pernos o tuercas.

Faros delanteros de xenón   Luces delanteras que usan un ensamblaje de tubo arqueado lleno de gas xenón, el cual produce una iluminación intensa de color azuleado.

Diodo Zener   Diodo especialmente construido (muy dopado) y diseñado para operar con una corriente de retorno después de que se alcanza un cierto nivel de voltaje. Llamado así en honor a Clarence Melvin Zener.

INDEX